KU-070-348

Belgium
& Luxembourg

THE ROUGH GUIDE

There are more than one hundred Rough Guide titles
covering destinations from Amsterdam to Zimbabwe

Forthcoming titles include
Dominican Republic • Jerusalem • Laos • South India

Rough Guide Reference Series
Classical Music • European Football • The Internet • Jazz
Opera • Reggae • Rock Music • World Music

Rough Guide Phrasebooks
Czech • French • German • Greek • Hindi & Urdu • Hungarian • Indonesian
Italian • Japanese • Mandarin Chinese • Mexican Spanish • Polish
Portuguese • Russian • Spanish • Thai • Turkish • Vietnamese

Rough Guides on the Internet
www.roughguides.com

ROUGH GUIDE CREDITS

Text editor: Kieran Falconer
Series editor: Mark Ellingham
Editorial: Martin Dunford, Jonathan Buckley, Jo Mead, Kate Berens, Amanda Tomlin, Ann-Marie Shaw, Paul Gray, Chris Schüler, Helena Smith, Judith Bamber, Orla Duane, Olivia Eccleshall, Ruth Blackmore, Sophie Martin, Jennifer Dempsey, Geoff Howard, Claire Saunders, Anna Sutton, Gavin Thomas, Alexander Mark Rogers (UK); Andrew Rosenberg, Andrew Taber (US)
Production: Susanne Hillen, Andy Hilliard, Link Hall, Helen Ostick, James Morris, Julia Bovis, Michelle Draycott, Cathy McElhinney

Cartography: Melissa Flack, Maxine Burke, Nichola Goodliffe, Ed Wright
Picture research: Eleanor Hill, Louise Boulton
Online editors: Alan Spicer, Kate Hands (UK); Geronimo Madrid (US)
Finance: John Fisher, Neeta Mistry, Katy Miesiaczek
Marketing & Publicity: Richard Trillo, Simon Carloss, Niki Smith, David Wearn (UK); Jean-Marie Kelly, SoRelle Braun (US)
Administration: Tania Hummel, Charlotte Marriot

ACKNOWLEDGEMENTS

The authors would like to thank Pauline Owen and Kate Smith of Tourism Flanders-Brussels, and Serge Moes and Jean-Claude Conter of the Luxembourg National Tourist Office for their help in compiling this guide. Special thanks also to Cathy Giorgetti of the Luxembourg City Tourist Office for her helpful hints; Ruth Rigby for Internet steerage; Filip D'Huyvetter and Randi Roose of WegWijzer in Bruges; Medard Janssens for his advice on Antwerp; and Lucy Leveugle for help on Brussels. As usual, compliments to our brilliant editor, Kieran Falconer, and for Jack Holland his original contribution to the book. A special thanks goes to all those involved in producing this book especially Cathy McElhinney and Helen Ostick for excellent

typesetting, Michael Larby, Cartographic Services and Maxine Burke for some great maps, and Anne Hegerty for some eagle-eyed proofreading.

Thanks to all those who wrote in with comments on the first edition of Belgium & Luxembourg: Barbara Ellingham, Geoff Garvey, Gerald Holm, Christopher Bradshaw, Lucy Williams, John Francis, Lucy C. Porter, Philip Tetley-Jones, Drs D.R. & A.M. Tipping, Paul & Eve Booy, Johan Segars, David James, Taft Kiser, P.J. Cartwright, Emily Lewis, Kathleen & Roy Taylor, Nat Goodden, Steven Quentzel, Stephen Hayward, Kevin Heyes, Francis Wilkinson, Dr Del Howard, Terry Reddacliff and Chris Melia.

PUBLISHING INFORMATION

This second edition published April 1999 by Rough Guides Ltd, 62–70 Shorts Gardens, London, WC2H 9AB.
Distributed by the Penguin Group:
Penguin Books Ltd, 27 Wrights Lane, London W8 5TZ
Penguin Books USA Inc., 375 Hudson Street, New York 10014, USA
Penguin Books Australia Ltd, 487 Maroondah Highway, PO Box 257, Ringwood, Victoria 3134, Australia
Penguin Books Canada Ltd, 10 Alcorn Avenue, Toronto, Ontario, Canada M4V 1E4
Penguin Books (NZ) Ltd, 182–190 Wairau Road, Auckland 10, New Zealand
Typeset in Linotron Univers and Century Old Style to an original design by Andrew Oliver.
Printed in England by Clays Ltd, St Ives PLC
Illustrations in Part One and Part Three by Edward Briant.

Illustrations on p.1 & p.349 by Henry Iles
© Martin Dunford and Phil Lee 1997
No part of this book may be reproduced in any form without permission from the publisher except for the quotation of brief passages in reviews.
416pp – Includes index
A catalogue record for this book is available from the British Library
ISBN 1-85828-427-9

Belgium
& Luxembourg

THE ROUGH GUIDE

written and researched by

Martin Dunford and Phil Lee

with additional contributions by

Martin Battersby

THE ROUGH GUIDES

THE ROUGH GUIDES

TRAVEL GUIDES • PHRASEBOOKS • MUSIC AND REFERENCE GUIDES

 We set out to do something different when the first Rough Guide was published in 1982. Mark Ellingham, just out of university, was travelling in Greece. He brought along the popular guides of the day, but found they were all lacking in some way. They were either strong on ruins and museums but went on for pages without mentioning a beach or taverna. Or they were so conscious of the need to save money that they lost sight of Greece's cultural and historical significance. Also, none of the books told him anything about Greece's contemporary life – its politics, its culture, its people, and how they lived.

So with no job in prospect, Mark decided to write his own guidebook, one which aimed to provide practical information that was second to none, detailing the best beaches and the hottest clubs and restaurants, while also giving hard-hitting accounts of every sight, both famous and obscure, and providing up-to-the-minute information on contemporary culture. It was a guide that encouraged independent travellers to find the best of Greece, and was a great success, getting shortlisted for the Thomas Cook travel guide award,

and encouraging Mark, along with three friends, to expand the series.

The Rough Guide list grew rapidly and the letters flooded in, indicating a much broader readership than had been anticipated, but one which uniformly appreciated the Rough Guide mix of practical detail and humour, irreverence and enthusiasm. Things haven't changed. The same four friends who began the series are still the caretakers of the Rough Guide mission today: to provide the most reliable, up-to-date and entertaining information to independent-minded travellers of all ages, on all budgets.

We now publish more than 100 titles and have offices in London and New York. The travel guides are written and researched by a dedicated team of more than 100 authors, based in Britain, Europe, the USA and Australia. We have also created a unique series of phrasebooks to accompany the travel series, along with an acclaimed series of music guides, and a best-selling pocket guide to the Internet and World Wide Web. We also publish comprehensive travel information on our Web site:

www.roughguides.com

THE AUTHORS

Martin Dunford was born and raised in southeast London. After years of travelling and dead-end jobs, he took up travel guide writing, authoring several books and co-founding the Rough Guide series. He is now editorial director and spends his weekends watching his favourite team, Charlton Athletic FC.

Phil Lee has worked as a freelance for the Rough Guides for the last ten years. Previous books include the Rough Guides to Norway, Brussels, Mallorca and Menorca, Pacific Northwest, and Canada. He has also written extensively for British magazines and newspapers. He lives in Nottingham where he was born and raised.

HELP US UPDATE

We've gone to a lot of effort to ensure that the second edition of *The Rough Guide to Belgium & Luxembourg* is accurate and up-to-date. However, things change – places get "discovered", opening hours are notoriously fickle, restaurants and rooms raise prices or lower standards. If you feel we've got it wrong or left something out, we'd like to know, and if you can remember the address, the price, the time, the phone number, so much the better.

We'll credit all contributions, and send a copy of the next edition (or any other Rough Guide if you prefer) for the best letters. Please mark letters: "Rough Guide Belgium & Luxembourg Update" and send to:
Rough Guides, 62–70 Shorts Gardens, London WC2H 9AB, or
Rough Guides, 375 Hudson St, 9th floor, New York NY 10014.
Or send email to: mail@roughguides.co.uk
Online updates about this book can be found on Rough Guides' Web site at www.roughguides.com

CONTENTS

Introduction ix

PART THREE CONTEXTS   351

LIST OF MAPS

MAP SYMBOLS

- - - -	Chapter division boundary	◉	Hotel
▬ ▬ ▬	International boundary	—	Wall
·· ▬	Regional boundary	⌂	Abbey
═══	Road	ⓘ	Information office
⊞⊞⊞	Steps	⊠	Post office
▬▬	Railway	♟	Museum
▬▬▬	River	■	Building
— —	Ferry route	⊞	Church
- - - - -	Footpath	▨	Park
Ⓜ	Metro station	▨	National Park
✈	Airport	⁺⁺⁺	Cemetery
★	Bus/tram stop	▨	Beach

INTRODUCTION

There isn't a country on earth quite like **Belgium**. It's one of the smallest nations in Europe, yet it has a federal system, three official languages, and is intensely regionalized, to the extent that northerners frequently demand secession from the south. And its cuisine, manifest most famously in its marvellous array of different beers and a sumptuous reputation as a producer of fine chocolate, is startlingly diverse. For a small country with an identity problem, Belgium is anything but dull.

The country has its scenic highlights, too, most notably in the rolling hills of the Ardennes, which continue down into the connected but entirely independent Grand Duchy of Luxembourg. Though known as a tiny refuge of bankers and diplomats, this too has surprises in store: its capital, Luxembourg City, is one of the most striking capitals in Europe, and the rest of the country – small though it is – is a beautifully green and hilly landscape of castles, steep wooded valleys and slate-roofed villages.

Both Belgium and Luxembourg are underrated as a destination for holidaymakers: for the British at least, they are viewed as a perfect weekend break or home of the EU but not much else. This is a pity, as this is historically one of the most complex and intriguing parts of Europe. Squeezed in between France, Germany and Holland, Belgium and Luxembourg occupy a spot that has often decided the European balance of power. It was here that the Holy Roman Empire shared an important border with the Germanic tribes to the north; here that the Spanish Habsburgs finally met their match against the Protestant rebels of the Netherlands; here that Napoleon was finally defeated at the Battle of Waterloo; and here, too, that the British and Belgians slugged it out with the Germans in World War I. Indeed so many powers have had an interest in this region over the years that it was only in 1830 that Belgium and Luxembourg became separate, independent states, free from all colonial rule.

It's perhaps partly because of this messy history that Belgium and Luxembourg have never become homogenous nation-states, like most of the rest of Europe. Belgium divides between the Dutch- or Flemish-speaking north of the country, and French-speaking Wallonia in the south. There's a small German-speaking community in the east, and in the centre lies Brussels, which is officially bilingual. The tenacity of regional (and linguistic) feeling is such that Belgium is a federal state, with much power devolved to the regions. In Luxembourg there has been a slightly different outcome. The people here are at ease with the linguistic ebb and flow of their European neighbours, switching comfortably between French, German and their own language, Letzeburgesch, a dialect of German – all without so much as an intercommunal ripple.

Where to go

There's more to the Flemish–Walloon divide than just language: the north and south of Belgium are visually very different places. The **North**, made up of the provinces of West and East Flanders, Antwerp, Limburg and the top half of Brabant, is mainly flat, with a landscape and architecture not unlike Holland. **Antwerp** is the largest city, a big, sprawling, bustling old port with doses of sleaze and high art in roughly equal measure. Further south, in the Flemish heartland of **Flanders**, are the great Belgian historic cities, **Bruges** and **Ghent**, tourist attractions in themselves, with a stunning concentration of Flemish art and architecture. Bruges especially is the country's biggest tourist pull, and although this inevitably means it gets very crowded, you shouldn't miss it on any account. Beyond lies the **Belgian coast**, which makes valiant attempts to compete with the seaside resorts of the rest of Europe but is ultimately let down by

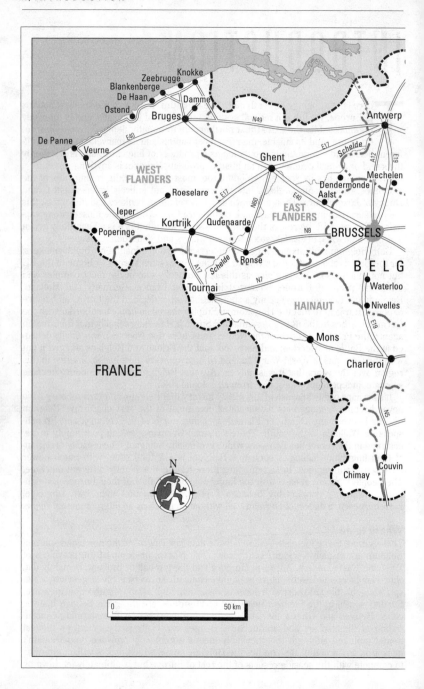

the crassness of its development and the coldness of the North Sea. There are a couple of appealing seaside spots, for example **De Haan**, and the beaches and duney interludes along the coast are delightful. But you might be better off spending time in some of the other inland Flanders towns, not least **Ieper**, formerly and better known as Ypres to the English-speaking world. Every year veterans and pilgrims come to visit the stark sights of the nearby World War I battlefields and the vast, sad acreages of cemeteries.

Marking the meeting of the Flemish and Walloon parts of Belgium, **Brussels**, the capital, is central enough to be pretty much unavoidable. It is more exciting and varied than its reputation as a bland Euro-capital would suggest and, because Belgium is not a large country, it is also useful as a base for day-trips. Bruges and Ghent are easily accessible from here, as is the old university city of **Leuven** to the east, or even the cathedral city of **Mechelen**, halfway to Antwerp.

Flemish Brabant encircles Brussels, but to the south of the capital it narrows into the slender corridor of Wallonian Brabant, which is distinguished by the splendid church at **Nivelles** and the elegaic abbey ruins at nearby **Villers-la-Ville**. West of here, the solely Walloon province of Hainaut is rich agricultural country, dotted with ancient cities like charming **Tournai** and industrial centres like **Charleroi** and the more appealing **Mons**. East of here lies Belgium's most scenically rewarding region, the **Ardennes**, spread across the three provinces of **Namur**, **Liège** and **Luxembourg**: an area of deep, wooded valleys, high elevations and heathy plateaux and caverns that, beyond the main tourist resorts, is very wild indeed. Use either Liège or Luxembourg as a jumping-off point, before heading into the heart of the region at **St-Hubert**, **Han-sur-Lesse** or **La Roche-en-Ardenne**.

The Ardennes reach across the Belgian border into the northern part of the **Grand Duchy of Luxembourg**, a green landscape of high hills topped with crumbling castles overlooking rushing rivers. **Vianden** and **Echternach** are perhaps the two best centres for touring the countryside – quiet, small towns with little life outside the tourist industry. However, the country's status as European nonentity is quite unjust; in fact it packs more scenic highlights into its tight borders than other more renowned holiday spots. And while its southern reaches are much more ordinary, **Luxembourg City** at least is worth a stop. Dramatically sited, it's about the closest the country gets to a proper urban environment, although its population of 75,000 people (around a fifth of the Grand Duchy's total) is still tiny by capital city standards.

Climate and when to go

Belgium enjoys a fairly standard temperate **climate**, with warm, if mild, summers and cold winters. Generally speaking, temperatures rise the further south you go, with

AVERAGE DAILY TEMPERATURES °C											
	Jan	Feb	Mar	April	May	June	July	Aug	Sept	Oct	Nov	Dec
Belgium	1	4	7	11	13	18	19	18	17	12	7	3
Luxembourg	0	1	7	11	13	17	19	16	15	9	4	2

AVERAGE MONTHLY RAINFALL (MM)											
	Jan	Feb	Mar	April	May	June	July	Aug	Sept	Oct	Nov	Dec
Belgium	66	61	53	60	55	76	95	80	63	83	75	88
Luxembourg	61	65	42	47	64	64	60	84	72	53	67	81

Wallonia a couple of degrees warmer than Flanders for most of the year, though in the east this is offset by the more severe climate of continental Europe, and emphasized by the increase in altitude of the Ardennes. Luxembourg, too, has more extreme temperatures and harsher winters, often accompanied by snow. In both countries rain is always a possibility, and you can expect a greater degree of precipitation in the Ardennes and upland regions than on the northern plains.

As regards **clothing**, you should take heavy coats and gloves in winter, and lighter clothes and warm sweaters for the evening in summer. Some sort of rainwear is advisable all year round.

PART ONE

THE

BASICS

GETTING THERE FROM BRITAIN AND IRELAND

There are several easy ways to reach Belgium or Luxembourg – you just have to decide between a swift but relatively expensive flight, a low-cost but more time-consuming ferry crossing, or a faster journey by train or car using the Channel Tunnel. Whichever alternative you opt for, you'll find a variety of competitive fares on these busy routes.

BY PLANE

The two major **airports** in Belgium and Luxembourg are, not surprisingly, Brussels and Luxembourg City, although Antwerp, which has its own small airport, is another possible gateway. Flying clearly represents a considerable time-saving as compared to the ferry and train with Brussels, for example, just 45 minutes' flying time from London. Of the three destination airports, Brussels is almost always the cheapest to get to.

With regard to **scheduled flights** – principally with Virgin Express, British Airways, British Midland, KLM UK, Sabena and Luxair – fierce competition means that there are frequently cheap deals on offer, which may not be available if you book through an agent. The best deal you'll get is usually an Apex or Saver ticket. These tickets – as well as other bargain returns – are likely to have restrictions, commonly requiring the booking to be made seven days in advance, and obliging you to spend one Saturday night abroad. Flying from London, Apex or Saver tickets average £100–150, but this can sink to as low as £65. To

gain more flexibility, you'll need to buy a standard return, which, flying from London, can cost anywhere up to £400 return – a few pounds more to Luxembourg.

If you don't live in London, bear in mind that there's a huge number of scheduled flights leaving from various **UK regional airports**, and that these can be good-value alternatives. From the regions, Apex fares to Brussels average £160–200 return, but bargains abound.

To find the **current bargains**, study the ads in the Sunday travel sections of the quality newspapers, Teletext or the Internet, where you can often book online. If you live in London, the back pages of the listings magazine *Time Out* and the *Evening Standard* are other sources of cheap flights. Alternatively, go to a **discount flight agent** such as STA Travel or Usit Campus (see box for details), who specialize in youth flights, and, if you're under 26 or a student, may offer savings on fares; they also offer ordinary discounted tickets. Finally, it may also be worth considering a **package deal** if you want to stay in one city and have your accommodation arrangements organized beforehand. These can be surprisingly good value (see below for more details).

BY TRAIN

Eurostar **trains** running through the Channel Tunnel put Belgium and especially Brussels within easy striking distance of London and considering the time checking in and out of the airport they compare very favourably time-wise with air travel. There are also train-and-ferry options, but inevitably these are much slower.

EUROSTAR SERVICES

There are normally nine **Eurostar** departures from London (Waterloo) to Brussels (Bruxelles-Midi) every day. The journey takes around 2 hours 50 minutes, usually stopping at Ashford (in Kent) and Lille (in France) on the way. It's a smooth ride, less hassle than flying, and, door to door from London, if not the UK's regions, no slower. Fares are set to compete with the airlines: full, unrestricted (and fully refundable) second-class returns go for around £170, although there's a youth fare (under 26) of around £92, and railcard (Eurailpass, Europass or Britrail Pass) holders pay about £96.

AIRLINE ADDRESSES AND ROUTES

British Airways, 156 Regent St, London W1R 5TA; other branches in Birmingham, Glasgow and Edinburgh (☎0345/222111).
www.british-airways.com/
Direct flights to Brussels from London Heathrow and Gatwick, Birmingham, Cardiff, Manchester and Southampton; one-stop flights from Aberdeen, Edinburgh, Glasgow, Jersey, Inverness, Newcastle, Newquay and Plymouth. Direct flights to Antwerp from London Gatwick and to Luxembourg from Gatwick and Heathrow.

British Midland Airways, Donington Hall, Castle Donington, Derby DE74 2SB (☎0345/554554 or 0845/607 1630).
www.iflybritishmidland.com/
To Brussels direct from London Heathrow, Birmingham, East Midlands; one-stop flights from Aberdeen, Edinburgh, Glasgow, Jersey, Leeds/Bradford, Manchester and Teesside.

Easyjet ☎0870/600 0000.
www.easyjet.com/
Flights from Luton to Amsterdam.

Luxair, Room 2004,Terminal 2, Heathrow Airport, Hounslow, Middx TW6 1HL (☎0181/745 4254, fax 759 7974).
www.luxair.lu/
London Heathrow, London Stansted and Manchester to Luxembourg.

Sabena, Gemini House, 2nd Flr, West Block, 10/18 Putney Hill, London SW15 6AA (☎0181/780 1444, fax 1502) and Room L5/10,Terminal 1, Manchester Airport (☎0161/489 2955, fax 437 5227).
www.sabena.com/
Direct flights to Brussels from London Heathrow, London City Airport, London Gatwick and London Stansted, Birmingham, Bristol, Edinburgh, Glasgow, Leeds/Bradford, Manchester and Newcastle. Also London City to Antwerp.

Virgin Express ☎ 0800/891199.
www.virgin-express.com/
Direct flights to Brussels from London Heathrow, Gatwick and Stansted.

VLM, London City Airport, Royal Docks Rd, London E16 2PX (☎0171/476 6677, fax 6427).
London City Airport to Antwerp.

DISCOUNT FLIGHT AGENTS

Cheapflights
www.cheapflights.co.uk/
This excellent UK website searches for the best fare bargains and provides links to the flight operators or agents.

Dial-a-Flight London ☎0171/334 0994, fax 7785; Croydon ☎0181/401 6670, Maidstone ☎ 01622/617200, Manchester ☎0161/962 9799.

STA Travel
86 Old Brompton Rd, London SW7 3LH (☎ 0171/581 4132); also with branches at Aberdeen, Brighton, Bristol, Cambridge, Glasgow, Manchester, Leeds, Newcastle, Oxford and at universities around the country.
www.statravel.co.uk/
Worldwide specialists in low-cost flights and tours for students and under-26s.

The Travel Bug
125 Gloucester Rd, London SW7 (☎0171/ 835 2222); 597 Cheetham Hill Rd, Manchester M8 5EJ (☎0161/740 8998).
www.travel-bug.co.uk/
Large range of discounted tickets for scheduled flights.

Usit Campus
52 Grosvenor Gardens, London SW1W 0AG (☎0171/730 3402); and branches at Aberdeen, Birmingham, Brighton, Bristol, Cambridge, Coventry, Edinburgh, Glasgow, Manchester, Oxford.
www.campustravel.co.uk/
Student/youth travel specialists, with branches also in YHA shops and on university campuses all over Britain.

Also, by accepting certain restrictions (no refunds, an enforced Saturday night stay), you can purchase the cheaper "Supersaver" ticket, which in conjunction with Eurostar's various special offers can drop the price to around £71 return.

OTHER RAIL SERVICES
The alternative method of reaching Belgium by train uses the Hoverspeed Seacat catamaran from Dover to Ostend. This makes the journey between London and **Brussels** considerably longer – about

RAIL ENQUIRIES
Rail Europe Information Line (☎0990/848848).
National Rail Enquiries (☎0345/484950) for UK rail travel only.
www.timetables.railtrack.co.uk/
Eurostar enquiries (☎0990/186186).
www.eurostar.com/

seven hours – but it's likely to be cheaper. A two-month return ticket from London to Brussels costs £65 return (£43 if you're under 26), and for a five-day return there's a flat rate of £49. The Seacat takes two hours to make the crossing (for more details see p.7). Tickets can be bought from most large train stations and travel agents. Ostend is linked to Brussels by high-speed Thalys trains. The Thalys network runs from Ostend in the west to Cologne in the east and from Amsterdam in the north to Paris in the south; Brussels is the centre of this network. Thalys trains run three times daily between Ostend and Brussels and Paris, taking just over an hour for the first, and two and a half hours for the second destination.

To Luxembourg, take either the Seacat or Eurostar options detailed above and change at Brussels Midi Station (Eurostar charges an extra £16 one-way). Journey time to Luxembourg City is around two and a half hours.

YOUTH FARES AND TRAIN PASSES

In almost every case, train fares are much reduced if you're **under 26**. "Youth" tickets are available from most student/youth travel agents, but remember the purchase of a "youth" ticket should be juggled with the benefits of holding a rail pass: for EU nationals (and one or two other countries) it's the InterRail pass (see below); for others it's the Eurailpass, the Eurail Youthpass, or the Eurail Flexipass (see p.28).

EU nationals (or people who've been resident in Europe for six months) can purchase an **InterRail pass**. There are two types, one for travellers under age 26, and another for people age 26 or over. Both passes entitle the holder to unlimited free travel within a specified area (with supplements payable on some high-speed trains). Both types of pass allow travel within between one and eight European zones. Prices increase depending on how many zones you wish to visit. Belgium and Luxembourg are part of Zone E, along with France and the Netherlands. An InterRail pass for just one zone for up to 22 days costs £159 if you're under

26 and £229 if you're over 26; monthly passes for two zones cost £209 (£279); and for three zones, £229 (£309). Access to all eight zones for up to one month costs £259 under age 26, and £349 if you're 26 or older. An under-26 InterRail pass also entitles you to a Young Person's Railcard, giving you discounts on rail journeys within the UK and on some cross-channel ferries. Passes can be bought from specialist youth travel agents or at major railway stations. (See also the Benelux Tourrail Card detailed on p.28.)

BY BUS

Travelling by long-distance **bus** is likely to be the cheapest but longest way of getting to Belgium or Luxembourg.

Eurolines, operated by National Express, offer two daily departures from London's Victoria coach station to Brussels-Nord, leaving at 10.30am and 10.30pm. Although the trip takes between eight and nine hours, cheap fares make this a useful option. Return fares are £49 for an adult and £45 for a young person (under 26). The return ticket is valid for up to six months. From Brussels, you can continue on to Luxembourg. Whilst not as keenly priced, it's still inexpensive with the total cost of your journey £82 if you're over 26, £77 if you're under. In total, the journey to Luxembourg takes around twelve hours, although this includes around an hour in Brussels, giving you time to stretch your legs. If you're not travelling from London, it's worth noting that the comparative cost of bus travel is considerably cheaper from other parts of the UK, than by air. For example, although an additional three hours journey, it's only around £10 more to travel from Birmingham to Luxembourg than from London Victoria.

If you are looking to travel around Europe by bus, it may be worth investing in a **Eurolines Pass**. The pass allows unlimited Eurolines bus travel (including any necessary sea crossings) between thirty European cities including Brussels, Amsterdam, Cologne, Copenhagen, Paris, London and Dublin,

BUS COMPANIES AND JOURNEY TIMES
National Express (☎0990 808080).
www.nationalexpress.co.uk/
Eurolines UK (☎0990/143219 or, for a Eurolines Pass, ☎01582/ 404 511, fax 400 694) plus agents nationwide.
www.eurolines.co.uk/

FERRY DETAILS – ROUTES AND PRICES

DESTINATION	OPERATOR	FREQUENCY	DURATION	ONE-WAY FARES Car, two adults, two kids	Foot passenger
Dover–Ostend	Hoverspeed	5–7 daily	2hr	£69–125	£25
Hull–Zeebrugge	P&O North Sea	1 daily	14hr	£148–182	£36–45
Hull–Rotterdam	P&O North Sea	1 daily	14hr	£148–182	£36–45
Dover–Calais	Hoverspeed	17 daily	35/50 mins	£79–109	£25
Dover–Calais	P&O Stena Line	30 daily	75 mins	£68–135	£24
Dover–Calais	SeaFrance	15 daily	90 mins	£78–123	£11

FERRY COMPANIES AND EUROTUNNEL

Eurotunnel, Cheriton Park, Cheriton High St, Folkstone, Kent CT19 4QS (☎0990/353535). *www.eurotunnel.com/*

Hoverspeed, Marine Parade, Dover, Kent CT17 9TG (☎0990/240241). *www.hoverspeed.co.uk/*

P&O North Sea Ferries, King George Dock, Hedon Rd, Hull HU9 5QA (☎01482/377177). *www.ponsf.com/*

P&O Stena Line, Channel House, Channel View Rd, Dover, Kent, CT17 9TJ (☎0990/980980). *www.posl.com/*

Scandinavian Seaways, Scandinavia House, Parkeston Quay, Harwich, Essex CO12 4QG (☎01255/243243, fax 245475). *www.scansea.com/*

SeaFrance, Eastern Docks, Dover, Kent CT16 1JA (☎0990/711711). *www.seafrance.com/*

Stena Line, *www.stenaline.co.uk/*

but not Luxembourg. The pass allows travel between the thirty cities *only*, and advises that seats should be booked in advance. There are thirty - or sixty- day passes available for travel at off-peak and peak times. Additionally, there is a separate rate if you are under 26 or 60+. A thirty-day off-peak pass is £199 for an adult and £159 for a youth/senior citizen. A sixty-day off-peak pass costs £249 and £199 respectively. Peak tickets cost an additional £30 for an adult and £40 for a youth/senior citizen. Passes can only be bought from Eurolines, direct. Details of the UK office are given above, the Belgian office is at the Eurolines coach station, part of the Bruxelles-Nord station complex in Brussels.

BY CAR: FERRIES AND EUROTUNNEL

Some people still prefer to go to Belgium **by sea**. They feel it's a more leisurely and enjoyable journey. It's also well worth considering if you're travelling with your own vehicle, even though the opening of the Channel Tunnel – and the operations of Eurotunnel – has provided a faster alternative to the ferry.

Eurotunnel operates through the **Channel Tunnel** and has gone some way to speeding up

journey times for those crossing the Channel by car. Trains run 24 hours a day (hourly at night), carrying cars, motorcycles, coaches, bicycles. It takes just 35 minutes to go from Folkestone to Calais, thus shaving a good couple of hours off the same journey by ferry. At peak times, services leave every fifteen minutes, and advance bookings are normally unnecessary, at least outside high season; at night, services are hourly. Summer fares, between mid-May and the end of August, range from £95–110 for a day return up to a fairly hefty £220 for a standard return, per vehicle (including passengers) at peak times. The five-day limit on most return tickets means you may be better off buying two singles – these are generally half the price of a return. There's also a flat rate charge of £15 for **bicycles** but these can only go on certain departures, with reservation by phone, at least 24 hours in advance. **Motorcycles** are charged as cars.

By **ferry**, there are a number of **routes** you might consider. If you're heading for Flanders, then Hoverspeed's two-hour catamaran service from Dover to Ostend is an attractive option. Alternatively, if you live in the north of England you may prefer P&O North Sea Ferries' Hull to

Zeebrugge ferry service – Zeebrugge is just a few kilometres from Bruges. The same company also runs a Hull to Rotterdam ferry service, which leaves you just an hour or so's drive from northern Belgium. Failing that, you might also want to consider the Stena Line service (2 daily) from Harwich to the Hook of Holland – itself no more than two hours drive from the Belgian border. Finally, there is the speedy (35min–1hr 30min) Dover–Calais route. Three companies run services here, Hoverspeed, P&O Stena Line and SeaFrance; Calais is 110km from Bruges and 200km from Brussels.

If you're going for a **weekend break**, check out the short-period excursion fares offered by all the companies; usually five-day returns can cost the same as the single fare. Look out also for cheap deals for **children**, and special-deal five-night returns. High street **travel agents** have fares and brochures and it's well worth shopping around. Prices vary with the month, day and even hour that you're travelling, how long you're staying, and the size of your car. The different ferry companies are always offering special fares to outdo their competitors – not to mention the Channel Tunnel. In particular, since the price structures are increasingly geared around one-way rather than return travel, you don't neces-

sarily have to cross over and back from the same port. **Booking ahead** is strongly recommended for motorists; indeed it's essential in high season. Foot passengers can normally just turn up and board, at any time of year.

FROM IRELAND

There are no direct **ferry links** from Ireland to the Dutch or Belgian coasts, although Irish Ferries have a "Landbridge" scheme which, in conjunction with P&O North Sea Ferries (see above), allows you to cross the Irish Sea from Dublin to Holyhead and then travel from Hull to either Zeebrugge or Rotterdam. This is, of course, a time-consuming process and most people opt for something a good deal quicker and more straightforward.

By **plane**, Aer Lingus flies directly to Brussels from Dublin three or four times a day, with connecting flights from Cork, Shannon, Galway, Sligo and Kerry. If you buy a Supersaver ticket, the return flight will cost you from IR£99 to 149 provided you stay a minimum of one Saturday and return within the month. The major competition to Aer Lingus is Ryanair, who have two or three flights a day to Brussels from Dublin and whose prices can go down to a bargain IR£60 return.

FERRY AND FLIGHT OPERATORS IN IRELAND

Aer Lingus
42 Grafton St, Dublin (☎01/705 6705). Other branches in Belfast, Cork and Limerick.
www.aerlingus.ie/

British Airways
c/o Aer Lingus, 13 St Stephen's Green, Dublin (☎1-800/626747);
1 Fountain Centre, College St, Belfast BT1 6ET (☎0345/222111).

British Midland
British Midland Buildings, Nutley, Merrion Rd, Dublin 2 (☎01/283 8833);
Suite 2, Fountain Centre, College St, Belfast BT1 6ET (☎0345/554554).

Irish Ferries
2/4 Merrion Row, Dublin 2 (☎01/661 0715);
St Patrick's Bridge, Cork (☎021/551 995).
www.irish-ferries.ie/

Ryanair
Phoenix House, Conyngham Rd, Dublin 8 (☎01/609 7800, flight information ☎1-550/200200 – 58p per min).
www.ryanair.ie

Sabena
Gemini House, 2nd Flr, West Block, 10/18 Putney Hill, London SW15 6AA (☎0181/780 1444, fax1502).
www.sabena.com/

FLIGHT AGENTS IN IRELAND

Tommy Tobin Travel, 10 Chatham Lane, Dublin 2 (☎01/679 4100).

Thomas Cook, 118 Grafton St, Dublin (☎01/677 1721); 11 Donegal Pl, Belfast BT1 5AJ (☎01232/554455).

USIT
O'Connell Bridge, 19/21 Aston Quay, Dublin 2 (☎01/602 1600). Other branches around the country.
www.usit.ie/

With regard to **other airlines**, Sabena operates three flights a day from Dublin and once daily from Belfast to **Brussels** direct; British Midland flies to Brussels from Dublin and Belfast, via Heathrow or East Midlands; and British Airways has one-stop flights to Brussels from both Belfast's City and International airports. The cheapest flights from Belfast to Brussels are likely to cost around £180–209. There are no direct flights to **Luxembourg** from Ireland, so it's best to fly to Brussels and continue on to Luxembourg by other means.

PACKAGE TOURS AND SHORT BREAKS

Don't be put off by the idea of going on a **package**: most comprise only travel and accommodation and can work out an easy way of cutting costs and hassle – especially if you live some distance from London, as many operators offer a range of regional (and Irish) flight departures. Depending on the type of hotel you opt for (anything from budget to five-star is available with most companies), city breaks in Antwerp, Brussels, Bruges, Ghent, Luxembourg and other cities can be very economical. For instance, travelling by car the price of a city break (inclusive of return ferry, hovercraft or Eurostar travel) starts at about £85 per person for two nights' accommodation in a one-star hotel; the cost rises to around £110 if you travel by bus or train, £200 if you fly. Travel agents can advise further on the best deals available, or you can contact one of the **operators** below.

PACKAGE HOLIDAY COMPANIES

Belgian Travel Service, Bridge House, 55–59 High Rd, Broxbourne, Herts EN10 7DT (☎01992/456156).
Inexpensive short breaks in various Belgian cities.

Hoverspeed, Marine Parade, Dover, Kent CT17 9TG (☎0990/240241).
Self-drive short breaks, by hovercraft or catamaran.

Simply Brief Encounters, Chiswick Gate, 598–608 Chiswick High Rd, London W4 5RT (☎0181/995 9323).
Short breaks in Brussels and Bruges.

Osprey City Holidays, Broughton Market, Edinburgh EH3 6NU (☎0990/605605).
Flight or Eurostar to Brussels.

Thomson Holidays, 1st Flr, Greater London House, Hampstead Rd, London NW1 7SD (☎0990/502555).
Short breaks in Brussels. Often the cheapest.

Travelscene, 11–15 St Ann's Rd, Harrow, Middlesex HA1 1AS (☎0181/427 8800).
Weekend breaks.

GETTING THERE FROM THE USA AND CANADA

Flying direct to Belgium from the United States and Canada should not be a problem, although getting to Luxembourg might take a bit more ingenuity – and money. Most of the major US and Canadian airlines service Brussels, and prices are about the same as travelling to Paris, although more expensive than going to London. Remember, too, that there are also plenty of flights with the Dutch carrier KLM to Amsterdam, which cost about the same; and in any case Amsterdam is no more than a couple of hours – by train or car – from the Belgian border.

FLIGHTS TO BELGIUM AND LUXEMBOURG

The cheapest flights to **Belgium** are to be found with the Belgian national carrier, Sabena, who offer three non-stop daily flights to Brussels from New York and two from Atlanta. They also fly to Brussels six times a week from Boston and Chicago. Low-season specials can drop as low as $420 return from all cities, and sometimes include a free one-way ticket to either Amsterdam, London or Paris (assuming you'd take the train back to Brussels for your return flight). Regular midweek fares for New York and Boston range from a low-season price of $418 to $745 in May and $839 in the summer. Atlanta and Chicago are $100 more. Flights with the Dutch carrier KLM require a change of planes in Amsterdam but

prices are generally the same as they are to fly to Amsterdam. Non-stop flights out of New York start at around $420 in low season, rising to $809 in May and peaking at around $1000 in July and August. From the West Coast, KLM fares start at around $735 in low season rising to $956 in May and $1250 in July and August.

Consolidators and **discount travel agents** offer flights to Brussels from a wide range of US cities. Some sample fares include Atlanta ($500–700); Boston ($450–688); Charlotte ($500–700); Cincinnati ($510–710); Dallas ($575–827); Los Angeles ($550–897); New York ($420–688); Seattle ($615–897); Washington DC ($475–688). Connections on to Antwerp are often available for the same price or for $15–20 more.

You can reach Brussels from **Canada** on scheduled services with Sabena, KLM, Air Canada and the small Dutch airline Martinair. Return tickets with KLM out of Toronto start at around $C960 in the low season, stepping up to $C1095 in May and $C1355 in the summer. Fares from Vancouver start at around $C1250 in the low season, climbing to $C1405 in May and $C1705 in the summer.

Icelandair flies direct to **Luxembourg** via Iceland from Boston (five times weekly), New York (daily), Baltimore (five times weekly), and Halifax, Nova Scotia (twice weekly). East Coast fares range from a low-season price of $298 to $956 for high-season travel. Canadian fares range from $C618 in the low season to $C838 in the high season.

ROUND-THE-WORLD COURIER FARES

If you're contemplating a longer trip, taking in a wider array of cities around the world, you might want to consider the following **round-the-world fare**: Los Angeles–Brussels–Kuala Lumpur–Hong Kong–Los Angeles ($1690). This is the best option for Brussels. Including Amsterdam in your itinerary instead of Brussels opens up many more options with fares starting from $1360–1510.

PACKAGE TOURS

There are any number of **packages or organized tours** to Belgium and Luxembourg, many

TOLL-FREE AIRLINE ENQUIRY NUMBERS

American Airlines
☎1-800/433 7300.
Daily non-stops from Chicago to Brussels.

Delta Airlines
☎1-800/241 4141 or 555 1212 (Canada).
Two daily non-stops to Brussels from Atlanta and one from New York.

Icelandair
☎1-800/223 5500.
Direct flights to Luxembourg via Iceland on various days from four US and Canadian cities.

KLM
☎1-800/374 7747 or ☎361 5073 (Canada).
Daily non-stops to Amsterdam with connections to Brussels from 12 US and Canadian cities.

Sabena
☎1-800/955 2000.
Non-stops to Brussels from New York, Chicago, Boston and Atlanta.

United Airlines
☎1-800/538 2929.
Daily non-stops to Brussels from Washington DC.

TRAIN OFFICES AND AGENCIES IN NORTH AMERICA

British Rail International, 230 Westchester Ave, White Plains, NY 10604 (☎1-800/677 8585 or 914/682 2999); 2087 Dundas East Suite 105, Mississauga, ON L4X 1M2 (☎416/929 3333).

CIE Tours International, 100 Hanover Ave, P.O. Box 501, Cedar Knolls, NJ 07927 (☎1-800/243 8687 or 973/292 3899).

Rail Europe, 226–230 Westchester Ave, White Plains, NY 10604 (☎1-800/848 7245 or 914/681 3232); and branches in Santa Monica, San Francisco, Fort Lauderdale, Chicago, Dallas, Vancouver and Montréal.

Rail Pass Express ☎1-800/722 7151.

DISCOUNT FLIGHT AGENTS

Air Brokers International, 150 Post St Suite 620, San Francisco, CA 94108 (☎1-800/883 3273).
www.airbrokers.com

Council Travel, 205 E 42nd St, New York, NY 10017 (☎1-800 226 8624, worldwide reservations and information). Branches in 50 US cities. Discount travel agent, student discounts.
www.ciee.org

Discount Airfares Worldwide On-Line A hub of consolidator and discount agent Web links.
www.etn.nl/discount.htm

Educational Travel Center, 438 N Frances St, Madison, WI 53703 (☎1-800/747 5551). Student/youth and consolidator fares.
www.edtrav.com

Flight Centre, S Granville St, Vancouver, BC (☎1-604/739 9539). Discount air fares from Canadian cities.

High Adventure Travel Inc, 442 Post St, 4th Flr, San Francisco, California 94102 (☎1-800/428 8735).
www.highadv.com

International Travel Network Online travel info and reservations site.
www.itn.net/airlines

Nouvelles Frontières, 12 E 33rd St, New York, NY 10016 (☎1-800/366 6387 or 212/779 0600).

With branches in Los Angeles, San Francisco, Montréal, Québec.

Overseas Tours, 199 California Dr, Suite 188, Millbrae, California 94030 (☎1-800/323 8777).
www.overseastours.com

Skylink, 265 Madison Ave, 5th Flr, New York, NY 10016 (☎1-800/AIR ONLY or 212/573 8980).

STA Travel ☎1-800/777 0112. Discount travel agent with branches all over the US, principally in New York, San Francisco, LA and Boston.

Travel Cuts ☎1-800/667 2887. Offices all over Canada, including Toronto, Montréal, Newfoundland, Calgary, Vancouver, Winnipeg, Halifax. The principal student/youth discount agency in Canada.
www.travelcuts.com

Travelocity Online consolidator.
www.travelocity.com

UniTravel, 11737 Administration Dr, Suite 120, St Louis, MO 63146 (☎1-800/325 2222). Consolidator.
www.unitravel.com

Voyages Cuts, 19 rue Ste-Ursule, Québec G1R4E1 (☎418/654 0224). With branches in Montréal and Saskatoon.

TOUR OPERATORS

Abercrombie & Kent ☎1-800/323 7308. Luxury seven-night river and canal cruising tours from Amsterdam to Bruges starting at $1600. *www.abercrombiekent.com*

Adventure Center ☎1-800/227 8747.

Adventures Abroad ☎1-800/665 3998.

AESU ☎1-800/638 7640. Tours, independent city stays, discount air fares. 31-day Classic Europe tour windsurfing, biking, canoeing in Holland and a stop in Brussels, $3100 including airfare. *www.aesu.com*

American Express Vacations ☎1-800/241 1700. *www.americanexpress.com/travel*

American Airlines Fly Away Vacations ☎1-800/433 7300. Package tours, fly-drive programmes.

Back Door Travel, Box 2009, Edmonds, WA 98020 (☎425/771 8303). Off-the-beaten-path, small-group travel with budget travel guru Rick Steves and his enthusiastic guides. Write or call for a free newsletter. *www.ricksteves.com*

CBT Bicycle Tours ☎1-800/736 BIKE. Affordable tours in Holland, Belgium and Luxembourg. 16-day Amsterdam to Luxembourg tour starts at $1570. Airfare extra. *www.cbttours.com*

Euro Bike Tours ☎1-800/321 6060. Upscale, 14-day cycling tours and "bicycling and barging" tours in Holland, Belgium and Luxembourg starting at $3095. *www.eurobike.com*

KLM/Northwest World Vacations ☎1-800/800 1504. Independent hotel and sightseeing packages, escorted tours. Five-day Holland–Belgium excursion, from $798. Contact travel agents. *www.nwa.com*

Roadrunner Worldwide Hosteling Treks 1-800/864 0335.

Saga International Holidays ☎1-800/343 0273. Nine-day Dutch waterways tours covering North Holland and South Holland and Belgium starting at $1899 including airfare. *www.sagaholidays.com*

United Vacations ☎1-800/328 6877. Amsterdam tours, 6 nights, starting at $295 including hotels and breakfast. Airfare extra.

including stops in Amsterdam and other parts of Holland. Some include the airfare from the United States, and some just cover accommodation, sightseeing, bicycling, hiking, canal cruising, etc around the country. Many airlines have fly-drive programmes which include transatlantic airfare, car rental and hotel for a week. Most European tours include Brussels and sometimes Bruges in their itineraries. KLM/Northwest World Vacations has a five-day Holland–Belgium excursion starting at $798 which includes hotels, some breakfasts and dinners, bus transportation and sightseeing in Amsterdam, Arnhem, Bruges and Brussels. Highly recommended are any of the Back Door Travel tours sponsored by Rick Steves, a specialist in independent, budget travel with an emphasis on simple accommodation and meeting the people wherever you go.

GETTING THERE FROM AUSTRALIA AND NEW ZEALAND

On average prices to Belgium are A$1750 in the low season and A$1900 in the peak period as offered by Olympic and Lufthansa. Ansett, Qantas and Alitalia combine to offer the cheapest flight to Belgium via Milan in the off season at around A$1400; return, however, conditions such as maximum length of stay apply. Scandinavian Airlines, and KLM via Amsterdam, are around A$1640 return respectively during the low season, A$1830 and A$2099 respectively in the peak period. British Airways in conjunction with Qantas offer the trip for A$1769 in the low period, A$2343 in the peak period. Ansett Australia and Lauda Air combine in the peak period to charge A$2391. From New Zealand prices are around NZ$2300 in the off season, NZ$2750 in the peak period.

Swissair/Singapore Airlines are the cheapest way of getting to **Luxembourg** from Australia. Their scheduled flight to Luxembourg costs A$1528 in the low season and A$2300 in the peak period. Qantas in conjunction with British

AIRLINES

Air New Zealand, 5 Elizabeth St, Sydney (☎02/9937 5111); 17th Flr, Quay Tower, Customs St, Auckland (☎09/366 2803). Several flights a week to Brussels from major New Zealand cities via LA and London.

Alitalia, 118 Alfred St (Sth), Milsons Point (☎1-300 653 747, or 9922 1555); 6th Flr, Trustbank Building, 229 Queen St, Auckland (☎09/379 4457). Three flights weekly to Brussels from Brisbane, Sydney, Melbourne and Auckland via Milan.

Ansett Australia, 19 Pitt St, Sydney (☎13 1414); 2/50 Grafton Rd, Auckland (☎09/796409). NZ office, 2/55 Oxford St, Darlinghurst, Sydney (☎02/9352 6820); 75 Queen St, Auckland (☎09/302 2146).

British Airways, Level 26, 201 Kent St, Sydney (☎02/9258 3300); 154 Queen St, Auckland (☎09/356 8690). Daily flights to Brussels from major Australian cities via Bangkok/Singapore and London.

KLM, 5 Elizabeth St, Sydney (☎02/9231 6333); toll-free 1-800 505 747). No NZ office. Three flights weekly to Brussels from Sydney via Singapore.

Lauda Air, 11/143 Macquarie St, Sydney (☎02/9241 4277), Trustbank Building, 229 Queen St, Auckland (☎09/379 4455).

Lufthansa, 12/143 Macquarie St, Sydney (☎02/9367 3888); 36 Kitchener St, Auckland (☎09/303 1529). Daily via Singapore or Bangkok then Frankfurt in conjunction with Singapore or Thai Airlines.

Olympic Airways, Flr 3, 37–49 Pitt St, Sydney (☎02/9251 2044). No NZ office. Twice-weekly service to Brussels from Sydney via a transfer or stopover in Athens.

Qantas, 70 Hunter St, Sydney (☎13 1211); 154 Queen St, Auckland (☎09/357 8900 or 0800/808767).

SAS Scandinavian Airlines, 350 Kent St, Sydney (☎02/9299 6688); NZ agent, Air New Zealand, 18/1 Queen St, Auckland (☎09/366 2400).

Singapore Airlines, 17–19 Bridge St, Sydney (local-call rate ☎13 1011); Lower Ground Floor, West Plaza Building, cnr Customs and Albert streets, Auckland (☎09/303 2129). Twice weekly to Brussels from major Australian, and New Zealand cities via either a transfer or stopover in Singapore.

Thai Airways, 75–77 Pitt St, Sydney (☎02/9844 0999; toll-free 1-300 651 960); Kensington Swan Building, 22 Fanshawe St, Auckland (☎09/377 3886).

DISCOUNT TRAVEL AGENTS

Anywhere Travel, 345 Anzac Parade, Kingsford, Sydney (☎02/9663 0411).

Northern Gateway, 22 Cavenagh St, Darwin (☎08/8941 1394).

Brisbane Flight Centre, 260 Queen St, Brisbane (☎07/3229 9211).

Budget Travel, 16 Fort St, Auckland; other branches around the city (☎09/366 0061 or 0800/808040).

Destinations Unlimited, 3 Milford Rd, Milford, Auckland (☎09/373 4033).

Flight Centres Australia, Level 11, 33 Berry St, North Sydney (☎13 1600, or 02/9460 0555); 19 Bourke St, Melbourne (☎03/9650 2899); plus other branches nationwide. New Zealand: National Bank Towers, 205–225 Queen St, Auckland (☎09/209 6171); Shop 1M, National Mutual Arcade, 152 Hereford St, Christchurch (☎03/379 7145); 50–52 Willis St, Wellington (☎04/472 8101).

Passport Travel, Kings Cross Plaza, Suite 11, 401 St Kilda Rd, Melbourne (☎03 /9867 3888).

STA Travel Australia, 855 George St, Sydney (☎02/9212 1255 or 1-300 360 960); 256 Flinders St, Melbourne (☎03/9654 7266); other offices in state capitals and major universities. New Zealand: Travellers' Centre, 10 High St, Auckland (☎09/309 0458); 233 Cuba St, Wellington (☎04/385 0561); 90 Cashel St, Christchurch (☎03/379 9098); other offices in Dunedin, Palmerston North, Hamilton and major universities.

Thomas Cook, Australia: 321 Kent St, Sydney (☎02/9248 6100); 257 Collins St, Melbourne (☎03/9282 0222); branches in other state capitals. New Zealand: Shop 250a, St Luke's Sq, Auckland (☎09/849 2071).

Topdeck Travel, 65 Glenfell St, Adelaide (☎08/8232 7222).

Tymtro Travel, 314 Victoria Ave, Chatswood, Sydney (☎02/9223 2211).

TOUR OPERATORS

All the following can arrange city sight seeing tours, car rental from A\$65 a day, and accommodation in Brussels from A\$70 twin share.

Adventure World, 73 Walker St, North Sydney (☎02/9956 7766, toll-free 1-800 221 931); Level 3, 33 Adelaide St, Brisbane (☎07/3229 0599); 8 Victoria Ave, Perth (☎08/9221 2300); 101 Great South Rd, Remuera, Auckland (☎09/524 5118).

CIT, 2/263 Clarence St, Sydney (☎02/9267 1255); offices in Melbourne, Brisbane, Adelaide and Perth. Also offers Eurailpasses.

Eurolynx, 3rd Flr, 20 Fort St, Auckland (☎09/379 9716).

European Travel Office, 122 Rosslyn St, West Melbourne (☎03/9329 8844); Level 20, 133

Castlereagh St, Sydney (☎02/9267 7727); 407 Great South Rd, Penrose, Auckland (☎09/525 3074). Also Eurobus passes.

KLM Vacations, Level 17, 456 Kent St, Sydney (☎02/9285 6844, toll-free 1-800 505 074); 326 Lambton Quay, Wellington (☎04/473 6427).

YHA Travel Centres

Sydney: 422 Kent St (☎02/9261 1111).

Melbourne: 205 King St (☎03/9670 9611).

Adelaide: 38 Stuart St (☎08/8231 5583).

Brisbane: 154 Roma St (☎07/3236 1680).

Perth: 236 William St, Northbridge (☎08/9227 5122).

Darwin: 69a Mitchell St (☎08/8981 2560).

Hobart: 28 Criterion St (☎03/6234 9617).

Airways is A\$1748 in the low period, A\$2369 in the peak period. Otherwise the best bet is to take the cheapest flight to either London, Brussels, Paris, or Amsterdam, and then travel on by air or land.

As for **round-the-world tickets**, these usually offer six free stopovers, limited backtracking and side trips with additional stopovers at around \$100 each in Australia/New Zealand. Fares start from A\$2200/NZ\$2600.

VISAS AND RED TAPE

Citizens of the UK and Ireland and other EU countries, Canada, the USA, Australia and New Zealand, need only a valid passport to stay ninety days in Belgium or Luxembourg.

On arrival, make sure you have enough money to convince officials you can support yourself.

For longer stays of over ninety days, **EU nationals** do not need to apply for a work permit, but they do need to apply for a **residence permit**. The local police grant these and will take details (and often fingerprints) before issuing a renewable, three-month residence card. After six months, EU nationals can then apply for an identity card, which is valid for five years.

Things are much more difficult for **non-EU nationals**. For visits of over ninety days, residence permits are compulsory and applicants must apply from their registered country of residence – an application from an Australian temporarily living in London would, for instance, not be processed. These residence permits are issued for various lengths of time – though a one-year permit is the most common – upon proof of

BELGIAN EMBASSIES AND CONSULATES ABROAD

Australia, 19 Arkana St, Yarralumla, Canberra, ACT 2600 (☎616/273 2501, fax 3392). Consulates in Adelaide, Brisbane, Darwin, Hobart, Melbourne, Perth.

Canada, 80 Elgin St, 4th Flr, Ottawa, Ontario, K1P 1B7 (☎613/236 7267, fax 613/236 7882). Consulates in Montreal, Toronto, Calgary, Edmonton, Halifax, Quebec, St John's, Saskatoon, Vancouver, Winnipeg.

Denmark, Øster Allé 7, 2100 Copenhagen Ø (☎35 25 02 00, fax 25 02 11). Consulates in Esberg, Haderslev, Odense.

Ireland, Shrewsbury House, 2 Shrewsbury Rd, Ballsbridge, Dublin 4 (☎01/269 2082, fax 283 8488). Consulates in Cork and Limerick.

Luxembourg, Résidence Champagne, rue des Girondins 4, 1626 Luxembourg (☎44 27 46, fax 45 42 82).

Netherlands, Lange Vijverberg 12, 2513 AC's Gravenhage (☎070/312 3456, fax 364 5579).

New Zealand, Willis Coroon House, 12th Flr, 1 Willeston St, Wellington (☎04/472 9558, fax 471 2764). Consulates in Auckland and Christchurch.

Sweden, 13A Villagatan, Stockholm (☎08/411 8958, fax 410 6443).

UK, 103 Eaton Sq, London SW1W 9AB (☎0171/470 3700, fax 259 6213). Consulates in Belfast, Birmingham, Cardiff, Dover, Edinburgh, Harwich, Kingston-upon-Hull, Manchester, Newcastle, Plymouth, Saint Helier, Southampton.

USA, 3330 Garfield St NW, Washington D C 20008 (☎202/333 6900, fax 652 7567). Consulates in Atlanta, Chicago, Los Angeles and New York.

LUXEMBOURG EMBASSIES AND CONSULATES ABROAD

Australia, c/o Mr Dunstan, Level 3, 345 George St, Sydney (☎02/932 0255; Mon–Fri 9am–2pm).

Belgium, 211 rue du Noyer, 1040 Brussels (☎02/733 9977, fax 736 2099).

Denmark, Fridtjof Nansens Plass 5, 2100 Copenhagen Ø (☎35 26 82 00, fax 26 82 08).

Netherlands, Nassaulaan 8, 2514 JS The Hague (☎070/360 7516, fax 356 3303).

UK, 27 Wilton Crescent, London SW1X 8SD (☎ 0171/235 6961, fax 9734).

USA, 2200 Massachusetts Ave NW, Washington DC 20008 (☎202/265 4171, fax 328 8270).

income from sources other than employment in the country receiving the application, and sometimes not even then.

Work permits for non-EU nationals are even harder to get: your prospective employer must apply locally (and prove that no other EU national can do the job) while you simultaneously apply at home; both parties must await its issuance (by no means automatic) before proceeding. Speak to the relevant embassy or consulate in your own country first.

DUTY-FREE RESTRICTIONS

All **EU citizens** are covered by the same **duty-free restrictions**, limiting purchases at duty-free shops to – among other regulations – a maximum of 200 cigarettes (or 250g of tobacco), two litres of table wine, and one litre of strong spirits or two litres of fortified wine (sherry etc) per person. However, duty-free shops are to be phased out in the next few years. Every EU citizen also has a **traveller's allowance**, whereby items bought in one EU coun-

try and brought back directly to another are deemed for personal use and do not attract taxes. The maximum levels per adult are generous: 800 cigarettes (or 1kg of tobacco), ten litres of strong spirit or twenty litres of fortified wine, ninety litres of table wine and 110 litres of beer. If you keep within these limits and are travelling direct from one EU state to another, you don't need to make a declaration to customs at your place of entry.

On arrival, **non-EU residents** have a tax- or duty-free import allowance of 200 cigarettes (or 250g of tobacco), and one litre of spirits or two litres of fortified wine and two litres of table wine and £145 worth of other goods. Returning home, the limits are generally the same, but check with the carrier if you're uncertain. There are also restrictions as to the value of goods you can take home without paying tax – again ask the carrier if you're unsure – and remember that the importing of fresh food, plants or animals back into Britain, Ireland, the USA, Canada, Australia or New Zealand is severely restricted.

HEALTH AND INSURANCE

As EU members, Belgium and Luxembourg have free reciprocal health agreements with other member states. To take advantage, British citizens will need form E111, which is available over the counter from most post offices; other EU nationalities need other, comparable documentation. Treatment within this scheme is, however, only provided by practitioners within the respective public health care systems.

Taking out your own medical insurance means you will cover the cost of items not within the EU's scheme, such as dental treatment and repatriation on medical grounds. Usually it will also cover your baggage and tickets in case of theft, as long as you get a crime report from the local police. Non-EU residents will need to insure themselves for all eventualities, including medical costs. The more worthwhile policies promise to sort matters out before you pay (rather than after) in the case of major expense; if you do, however, have to pay upfront, get and keep the receipts.

Note that some **bank** and **credit cards** have medical or other insurance included, and travel insurance is sometimes covered if you pay for your trip with a credit or charge card.

INSURANCE

In **Britain** and **Ireland**, travel insurance schemes (around £25–40 per person for a fortnight, £30–65 for a month) are sold by almost every travel agent and bank, and direct by several specialist insurance

TRAVEL INSURANCE COMPANIES

BRITAIN AND IRELAND

Columbus Travel Insurance ☎0171/375 0011.
www2.columbusdirect.com/
Endsleigh Insurance ☎0171/436 4451.
www.endsleigh.co.uk/
Frizzell Insurance ☎01202/292333.

Royal & Sun Alliance ☎01/677 1851.
Note: Good-value policies are also available through Usit Campus, and STA (see p.4 for addresses).

USA AND CANADA

Most travel agents will arrange travel insurance at no extra charge. The following insurance companies can be called directly.
Access America ☎1-800/284 8300.
www.accessamerica.com/
Carefree Travel Insurance ☎1-800/323 3149.
Desjardins Travel Insurance (Canada only) ☎1-800/463 7830.
www.desjardins.com/

International Student Insurance Service (**ISIS**) (sold by STA Travel) ☎1-800/777 0112.
www.sta-travel.com/
Travel Assistance International ☎1-800/821 2828.
www.worldwide-assistance.com/
Travel Guard ☎1-800/826 1300.
www.travel-guard.com/
Travel Insurance Services ☎1-800/937 1387.
www.travelinsurance.com/

AUSTRALIA AND NEW ZEALAND

AFTA ☎02/9264 3299.
Cover More ☎09/9202 8000 in Sydney, elsewhere toll-free ☎1-800/251881.

Ready Plan, toll-free ☎1-800/337462 (Australia) ☎09/379 3208 (New Zealand).
UTAG ☎02/9819 6855 in Sydney; elsewhere toll-free ☎1-800/809462.

firms. These policies are usually reasonable value, though as ever you should check the small print. If you feel the cover is inadequate, or you want to compare prices, any travel agent, insurance broker or bank should be able to help. If you have a good "all risks" home insurance policy it may well cover your possessions against loss or theft even when overseas, and many private medical schemes also cover you when abroad – make sure you know the procedure and the helpline number.

If you plan to participate in water sports, or do some climbing, you'll probably have to pay an extra premium; check carefully that any insurance policy you are considering will cover you in case of an accident. Note also that very few insurers will arrange on-the-spot payments in the event of a major expense or loss; you will usually be reimbursed only after going home. In all cases of loss or theft of goods, you will have to contact the local police to have a report made out so that your insurer can process the claim. Get the crime report number if at all possible.

US AND CANADIAN COVER

Before buying an insurance policy, check that you're not already covered. **Canadian provincial health plans** typically provide some overseas medical coverage, although they are unlikely to pick up the full tab in the event of a mishap. Holders of official **student/teacher/youth cards** are often entitled to accident coverage and hospital in-patient benefits – the annual membership is far less than the cost of comparable insurance. **Students** may also find that their student health coverage extends during the vacations and for one term beyond the date of last enrolment. Bank and credit cards (particularly American Express) often provide certain levels of medical or other insurance, and travel insurance may also be included if you use a major credit or charge card to pay for your trip. **Homeowners' or renters'** insurance often covers theft or loss of documents, money and valuables while overseas. After exhausting these possibilities, you might want to contact a specialist **travel insurance** company;

your travel agent can usually recommend one, or see the box for our recommendations.

Travel insurance **policies** vary: some are comprehensive while others cover only certain risks (accidents, illnesses, delayed or lost luggage, cancelled flights, etc). In particular, ask whether the policy pays medical costs upfront or reimburses you later, and whether it provides for medical evacuation to your home country. For policies that include lost or stolen luggage, check exactly what is and isn't covered, and make sure the per-article limit will cover your most valuable possession.

Remember that the policy may not cover all medical expenses, and that you'll need to keep receipts for any medicines you buy, or treatment you pay for, to claim from your insurance company once you're home. Similarly, if you have anything stolen, report the theft to the police (see "Trouble, the Police and Sexual Harrassment" p.50), and keep a copy of your statement.

The best **premiums** are usually to be had through student/youth travel agencies – ISIS policies, for example, cost $48–69 for fifteen days (depending on level of coverage), $80–115 for a month, $149–207 for two months, $510–700 for a year. If you're planning to do any "dangerous sports" (rockclimbing or suchlike), be sure to ask whether these activities are covered; some companies levy a surcharge. Most North American travel policies apply only to items lost, stolen or damaged while in the custody of an identifiable, responsible third party – hotel porter, airline, left-luggage, etc. Even in these cases you will have to contact the local police within a certain time limit to have a complete report made out so that your insurer can process the claim.

If you're currently a student, you may be covered on your college medical plan, and likewise a homeowners' policy may well cover vacations – though you should take a thorough look into the small print of both before setting off. Lastly, don't forget that flights paid for with a major credit or charge card offer an automatic degree of cover.

AUSTRALIAN AND NEW ZEALAND COVER

In **Australia** and **New Zealand**, travel insurance is put together by the airlines and travel agent groups (see boxes on pp.12–13) in conjunction with insurance companies. They're all broadly similar in terms of premium and coverage – a typical policy for Europe will cost A$190/NZ$220 for

a month, A$270/NZ$320 for two months and A$330/NZ$400 for three months. Most adventure sports are covered, but always check your policy carefully.

HEALTH

If you should fall ill, minor ailments can be remedied at **pharmacies** (French *pharmacie*, Flemish *apotheek*), which supply non-prescription drugs as well as toiletries, tampons, condoms and the like. Most are open Monday to Friday 9am to 6pm or 7pm, some on Saturdays too, and in the cities a rota system keeps at least one open 24 hours a day. The rota is displayed in the window of every pharmacy, and tourist offices also have details as do some of the better hotels. Outside the cities, you'll find a pharmacy in every town and most of the larger villages, but the smaller the place, the less likelihood there is of late-night opening.

In more serious cases you can get the address of an **English-speaking doctor** from your local pharmacy, tourist office, hotel or consulate. If you're seeking free treatment under EU health agreements, double-check that the doctor is working within (and seeing you as) a patient of the public health care system. Even within the EU agreement, you may still have to pay a significant portion of the **prescription** charges (senior citizens and children are exempt). Nor do most private insurance policies help cover prescription charges – their "excesses" are usually greater than the cost of the medicines, though it's worth keeping receipts just in case.

In medical **emergencies**, telephone ☎100 in Belgium and ☎112 in Luxembourg. If you're reliant on free treatment within the EU health scheme, try to remember to make this clear to the ambulance staff, and, if you're whisked off to hospital, to the medic you subsequently encounter. It's a good idea to hand over a photocopy of your E111 on arrival at hospital to ensure your non-private status is clearly understood. In terms of describing symptoms, you can anticipate that someone will speak English in Flemish Belgium and in Brussels and Luxembourg, though in parts of Wallonia you'll be struggling unless you have some rudimentary grasp of French.

Without an E111 you won't be turned away from a hospital, but you will have to pay for the treatment you receive and you should therefore get an official receipt. You will be reimbursed for at least part of the cost of your treatment and prescriptions if you present the receipts at the local sickness office, but it is unlikely to be the full cost. In Belgium, around three quarters of the cost should be reimbursed. If you can, contact the sickness office in advance of your treatment, ask them where to obtain the cheapest treatment, and to give you a certificate confirming they will

pay part of the cost. In Luxembourg, hospital treatment is usually free, but there is, in addition, a non-refundable daily charge.

Dental work is not within the scope of the EU's health agreements. To find an English-speaking dentist, ask at the local tourist office or, if you're staying in a good hotel, inquire at reception.

TRAVELLERS WITH DISABILITIES

Neither Belgium nor Luxembourg is particularly well equipped to accommodate travellers with disabilities. Lifts and ramps are few, steep steps and rough sidewalks are common – and even when an effort has been made, obstacles are frequent. That said, attitudes have changed: most new buildings are required to be fully accessible and the number of existing premises geared up for the disabled traveller has increased dramatically in the last few years. Today, all the big cities and some of the larger towns have at least one hotel with wheelchair access and other appropriate facilities, while around half of Belgium's youth hostels and 150 of its campsites are geared up (to some extent), as are some of Luxembourg's campsites and the youth hostel in Eisenborn.

The smoothest part of your journey may well be the trip across the North Sea; P&O have installed wheelchair-accessible toilets and cabins as well as lifts in their ferries, and the airlines flying into Belgium and Luxembourg also cater for (or will assist) travellers to some degree. Thereafter, **transport** in Belgium and Luxembourg is problematic, as buses, trains and train stations are not equipped for disabled travellers – instead you have the rigamarole of writing to the station master so that special arrangements can be made. On a more positive note, drivers will find that most motorway service stations are wheelchair-accessible, and that, if you're a UK resident, the orange disabled parking disc is honoured in both Belgium and Luxembourg.

CONTACTS FOR TRAVELLERS WITH DISABILITIES

The Belgian and Luxembourg tourist offices (see p.14 for addresses) will both provide useful information and contact addresses, as will the following:

BELGIUM AND LUXEMBOURG

Info-Handicap, rue de Contern 20, L-5955 ITZIG, Luxembourg (☎366466, fax 360885).
A general advice-giving agency for disabled people; also free tourist information.

Mobility International, rue de Manchester 25, 1080 Brussels (☎02/410 62 97, fax 410 68 74).

This large organization has a particular interest in tourism and travel throughout Europe. They have produced guides for disabled travellers in both

Belgium and Luxembourg, although they are not regularly updated.

Vlaams Commissariaat-Generaal voor Toerisme, Dienst Toerisme en Handicap, Heidi Straemans, Grasmarkt 61, 1000 Brussels (☎02/504 03 10).

Specialist advice and travel information from the tourist office.

continued opposite

BRITAIN AND IRELAND

British Airways (Minicom) ☎0141/242 1564.
British Midland (Textphone–CCIT) ☎01332/854015.
Disability Action Group, 2 Annadale Ave, Belfast BT7 3JH (☎01232/91011).
Eurostar ☎0345/881881.
Information regarding special rates for wheelchair users and companion.
Holiday Care Service, 2nd Flr, Imperial Building, Victoria Rd, Horley, Surrey RH6 9HW (☎01293/774535).
Hoverspeed ☎0990/240241 or 01304/865195 (Supertel).
Irish Wheelchair Association, Blackheath Drive, Clontarf, Dublin 3 (☎01/833 8241).

A national voluntary organization working for people with disabilities; related services for holiday makers.
RADAR, 12 City Forum, 250 City Rd, London EC1V 8AS (☎0171/250 3222, fax 0212; Minicom 4119). A good source of advice on holidays and travel abroad, RADAR produces a number of useful publications including *European Holidays* and *Travel Abroad* and *Access to Air Travel.*
Tripscope, The Courtyard, Evelyn Rd, London W4 5JL (☎0345/585641 (with Minicom), fax 0181/994 3618).
A national telephone information service offering free transport and travel advice.

THE NETHERLANDS

Travel and Tourism for All (TTFA), International Foundation, Heidestein 7, NL-3971 ND Dreibergen

(☎343/521751, fax 516776).
General travel advice and information.

USA AND CANADA

Directions Unlimited, 720 N Bedford Rd, Bedford Hills, NY 10507 (☎1-800/533 5343). Tour operator specializing in custom tours for people with disabilities.
Mobility International USA, PO Box 10767, Eugene, OR 97440 (Voice and TDD ☎541/343 1284; *www.miusa.org*). Information and referral services, access guides, exchange programmes. Annual membership $35 (includes quarterly newsletter).
Society for the Advancement of Travelers with Handicaps (SATH), 347 5th Ave, New York, NY 10016 (☎212/447 7284; *www.sath.org*). Non-profit travel-industry referral service that passes queries on to its members as appropriate; allow plenty of time for a response.

Travel Information Service, Moss Rehabilitation Hospital, 1200 West Tabor Rd, Philadelphia, PA 19141 (☎215/456 9600; *www.mossresourcenet.org*). Telephone information and referral service.
Twin Peaks Press, Box 129, Vancouver, WA 98666; ☎360/694 2462 or 1-800/637 2256; *www.pacifier.com/~twinpeak/disability/travel/*). Publisher of *the Directory of Travel Agencies for the Disabled* ($19.95), listing more than 370 agencies worldwide; *Travel for the Disabled* ($19.95); the *Directory of Accessible Van Rentals* ($12.95) and *Wheelchair Vagabond* ($19.95), loaded with personal tips.

AUSTRALIA AND NEW ZEALAND

ACROD (Australian Council for the Rehabilitation of the Disabled), PO Box 60, Curtin, ACT 2605 (☎06/682 4333); 55 Charles St, Ryde, NSW (☎02/9809 4488).

Disabled Persons Assembly, 173–175 Victoria St, Wellington (☎04/811 9100).

INFORMATION AND MAPS

Before you leave home, there's a wealth of information which you can pick up from each of the countries' national tourist offices (details below), while in both Belgium and Luxembourg all the major towns and most of the larger villages have well-equipped tourist information offices. The latter almost always issue maps of their town or city for free – or at minimal cost – and these maps mostly mark local hotels as well as tourist attractions. In addition, road and hiking maps are widely available in Belgian and Luxembourg bookshops, but buying one before you go helps in planning; if you're driving you will, of course, need a good road map as soon as you arrive.

TOURIST OFFICES

The **Belgian Tourist Office** offers a particularly efficient service, stocking a wide range of glossy, free booklets of both a general and specific nature. There are usually two versions of all the more general booklets – one for Wallonia, another for the Flemish-speaking regions. A couple of the most useful are the hotel and campsite guides, which provide comprehensive and classified listings. There are also brochures tailored to meet specific interests, though Flemish Belgium produces far more of these than Wallonia – the booklets on Flemish *Historic Cities* and *Events* are good examples. The Belgian Tourist Office also has a substantial collection of local material and is especially useful for material on the popular tourist destinations of Brussels, Antwerp, Bruges and Ghent. Furthermore, they issue a free map of the country, stock simplified train timetables and publicize a wide range of short-break holidays.

In Belgium itself, **tourist offices** are ten-a-penny. In the smaller towns and larger villages,

BELGIUM AND LUXEMBOURG ON THE INTERNET

Belgian Tourist Office for the Americas
www.visitbelgium.com/
This site provides standard tourist information with an American slant: on how to get there, visa information, as well as what to do and see.

Belgian Travel Network
www.trabel.com/
General advice and information plus useful links to the country's regional tourist offices.

Belgium artsite
www.artsite.be
A comprehensive list of the country's main art galleries with links to their often impressive websites. Also provides links to private galleries and antique dealers.

Confederation of Belgian Breweries
www.beerparadise.be/
One of a large number of sites extolling the virtues of Belgian beer, providing details of brewers, brewery tours and beer generally.

Hergé and Tintin
www.du.edu/tomills/tintin.htm
The most comprehensive catalogue of Hergé and Tintin sites on the net, albeit unofficial.

National Luxembourg Tourist Information
www.ont.lu/
A first-rate and comprehensive guide to the duchy's tourist attractions, with special interest links, as well as practical information.

Luxembourg City Tourist Information
www.luxembourgcity.lu/
A well-structured site which contains everything you want or need to know about the city.

BELGIAN TOURIST OFFICES

Canada, PO Box 760, Succursale NDG, Montréal, QC H4A 3S2 (☎514/484 3594, fax 489 8965).
Netherlands, Belgisch Verkeersbureau, Kennemerplein 3, 2011 MH Haarlem (☎023/534 4434, fax 2050).

UK, Belgian Tourist Office, 31 Pepper St, London E14 9RW (☎0891/887799 – calls cost 50p per minute daytime rate and 45p per minute at other times; fax 0171/629 0454).
USA Belgian Tourist Office, 780 3rd Ave, Suite 1501, New York, NY 10017 (☎212/758 8130, fax 355 7675, *info@visitbelgium.com*).

LUXEMBOURG TOURIST OFFICES

Belgium, av Louise 104,1050 Brussels (☎02/646 03 70, fax 648 6100).
Netherlands, 8 Nassau Laan, NL-2514 JS Den Haag (☎70/364 9041, fax 356 3303).
UK, 122 Regent St, London W1R 5FE (☎0171/434 2800, fax 734 1205,

tourism@luxembourg.co.uk).
www.luxembourg.co.uk/
USA, 17 Beekman Pl, New York, NY 10022 (☎212/9358888, fax 5896, *luxnto@aol.com*).

you can pretty much guarantee you'll get a free map and a list of local sights and hotels, as you can in the larger towns whose tourist offices frequently possess a small supply of accommodation in private houses too. Tourist offices will book hotel and private rooms on your behalf at no cost (though you'll usually need to stump up a refundable deposit) as part of their accommodation service – a practice repeated in the big cities where there's often a separate accommodation booking facility (see also under "Accommodation" on p.32). **Opening hours** of tourist offices vary considerably, but the larger offices are open all year, often every day of the week, while the smaller ones operate from April or May to September and October from Monday to Friday and sometimes on the weekend. We've specified individual opening hours in the *Guide*.

Branches of the **Luxembourg Tourist Office** abroad publish a free booklet of hotel and restaurant listings, with reliable prices and gradings, and issue a variety of first-class booklets, on camping, holiday apartments and short-break holidays, free maps and glossy guides to particular districts. Ask also for their annually updated *Tourist Info* booklet, detailing everything from the opening hours of the country's major tourist sights to where to go ballooning. In Luxembourg itself even the very smallest town will have a **tourist office** of some description, with maps of the immediate area and details of accommodation, which they can again sometimes book for you.

MAPS

The Belgian Tourist Office gives out a decent free **map** of the country that indicates the most important highways as well as provincial and international boundaries, though it doesn't mark in the railways. Otherwise, the best-value general road map is the clear and easy-to-use Baedeker & AA Belgium and Luxembourg (1:250,000) map. An alternative is the 1:300,000 Kummerly and Frey map of Belgium and Luxembourg, but this isn't as clear. Kummerly and Frey also produce a 1:500,000 map of Benelux and northeast France, and this is perfectly adequate if a little crowded. Several Michelin maps cover Belgium and Luxembourg or parts thereof – the 1:200,000 versions give all the detail you're likely to need. Widely available in better bookshops both in Belgium and Luxembourg and abroad, authoritative hiking maps (1:25,000) covering both countries are produced by the Institut Géographique National (Nationaal Geografisch Instituut), av Louise 306–310, 1050 Brussels (02/648 6480). Their maps cost around F230 each – about twice that abroad.

Specifically for Luxembourg, there is a guide to the country's so-called "Auto-Pedestre" tracks, which are laid out on the assumption that you drive to somewhere, leave the car and go for a walk of up to about 15km, in a circuit back to your vehicle. Some also take you between train stations, and you can often take the bus as well.

MAP OUTLETS

BRITAIN AND IRELAND

Daunt Books, 83 Marylebone High St, W1M 3DE (☎0171/224 2295).

John Smith and Sons, 57–61 St Vincent St, Glasgow, G2 5TB (☎0141/221 7472; *www.johnsmith.co.uk*). Specialist map department in long-established booksellers; full range of foreign maps; mail order service.

National Map Centre, 22–24 Caxton St, SW1H 0QU (☎0171/222 2466; *www.mapsworld.com*).

Stanfords, 12–14 Long Acre, WC2E 9LP (☎0171/836 1321, *sales@stanfords.co.uk*). Maps by mail or phone order are available on this number and via email.

The Travel Bookshop, 13–15 Blenheim Crescent, W11 2EE (☎0171/229 5260; *www.thetravelbookshop.co.uk*).

USA AND CANADA

Adventurous Traveler Bookstore, PO Box 64769, Burlington, VT 05406 (☎1-800/282 3963; *www.AdventurousTraveler.com/*).

Book Passage, 51 Tamal Vista Dr, Corte Madera, CA 94925 (☎1-800/999 7909 or 415/927 0960; *www.bookpassage.com*).

The Complete Traveler Bookstore, 199 Madison Ave, New York, NY 10016 (☎212/685 9007).

Elliot Bay Book Company, 101 S Main St, Seattle, WA 98104 (☎1-800/962 5311 or 206/624 6600; *www.elliottbaybook.com/ebbco*).

Map Link, 30 S La Petera Lane, Unit #5, Santa Barbara, CA 93117 (☎805/692 6777; *www.maplink.com*).

Open Air Books and Maps, 25 Toronto St, Toronto, ON M5R 2C1 (☎416/363 0719).

Phileas Fogg's Books & Maps, #87 Stanford Shopping Center, Palo Alto, CA 94304

(☎1-800/233 FOGG in California; ☎1-800/533 FOGG elsewhere in US).

Rand McNally. For locations, or for maps by mail order, call ☎1-800/333 0136 ext 2111.

Sierra Club Bookstore, 6014 College Ave, Oakland, CA 94618 (☎510/658 7470).

Travel Books & Language Center, 4437 Wisconsin Ave NW, Washington DC 20016 (☎1-800/220 2665).

Traveller's Bookstore, 22 W 52nd St, New York, NY 10019 (☎212/664 0995; *www.travellersbookstore.com*).

Ulysses Travel Bookshop, 4176 St Denis, Montréal (☎514/843 9447; *www.ulysses.ca*).

World Wide Books and Maps, 552 Seymour St, Vancouver, BC V6B 3J5 (☎604/687 3320).

AUSTRALIA AND NEW ZEALAND

Bowyangs, 372 Little Bourke St, Melbourne (☎03/9670 4383).

The Map Shop, 16a Peel St, Adelaide (☎08/8231 2033).

Perth Map Centre, 891 Hay St, Perth (☎08/9322 5733).

Specialty Maps, 58 Albert St, Auckland (☎09/307 2217).

Travel Bookshop, Shop 3, 175 Liverpool St, Sydney (☎02/9261 8200).

Worldwide Maps and Guides, 187 George St, Brisbane (☎07/3221 4330).

COSTS, MONEY AND BANKS

In terms of accommodation and food, Belgium and Luxembourg are by West European standards moderately expensive, though this is partly offset by low-priced public transport and, in Belgium at least, inexpensive beer. More precise costs for places to stay and eat are given in the *Guide*, and you should consult the box on p.33 for general guidelines on accommodation prices.

On average, if you're prepared to buy your own picnic lunch, stay in youth hostels, and stick to the less expensive bars and restaurants, you could get by on around £30/US$50 a day. Staying in two-star hotels, eating out in medium-range restaurants most nights and drinking in bars, you'll get through at least £65/$100 a day – in Luxembourg it might be more – with the main variable being the cost of your room. On £100/$160 a day and upwards, you'll be limited only by your energy reserves – though if you're planning to stay in a five-star hotel and to have a big night out, this still won't be enough. In both countries, but especially in Brussels and Wallonia, one of the real treats of a visit is the food. Restaurants don't come cheap, but costs remain manageable if you avoid the extras and concentrate on the main courses, for which around £10/$14 will normally suffice – twice that with a drink, starter and dessert. You can, of course, pay a lot more – a top restaurant in Brussels can be twice as expensive again, and then some. As always, if you're travelling alone you'll spend much more on accommodation than you would in a group of two or more: most hotels do have single rooms, but they're fixed at about 75 percent of the price of a double.

MONEY AND THE EXCHANGE RATE

Until the fully-fledged introduction of the EU's "euro" currency, both Belgium and Luxembourg will continue to use the franc, normally written as "F" or "BEF" and "LUF" and dividing into 100 centimes. The Belgian and Luxembourg franc are actually separate currencies, but they have the same rate of exchange against all other currencies. However, although Belgian francs are legal tender in Luxembourg, the reverse isn't true in Belgium. Also, it is advisable to change all spare Luxembourg francs into Belgian notes before you leave for home, since these are more easily exchangeable in foreign banks. Coins come in denominations of 50 centimes and 1, 5, 20 and 50 francs; notes in 100, 200, 500, 1000, 2000, 5000 and 10,000 francs.

At the time of writing the exchange rate for both currencies was around F50 to the pound sterling, F33 or so to the US dollar, and F21 to the Australian dollar.

TRAVELLERS' CHEQUES AND CREDIT CARDS

The safest way to carry your funds is in **travellers' cheques**; the usual fee for their purchase is one percent of face value. Make sure you keep the purchase agreement and a record of cheque serial numbers safe and separate from the cheques themselves. In the event that cheques are lost or stolen, the issuing company will expect you to report the loss immediately. Consequently, when you buy your travellers' cheques, ensure you have details of the company's emergency contact numbers or the addresses of their local offices. Most companies claim to replace lost or stolen cheques within 24 hours. American Express cheques are sold through most North American, Australasian and European banks, and they are the most widely accepted cheques in Belgium and Luxembourg. American Express also have offices in Brussels and Luxembourg City – see the relevant chapters for addresses. When you cash your cheques, you'll find that almost all banks make a percentage charge per transaction on top of a basic minimum charge. Note also that there is no charge for American Express cheques cashed at one of their offices.

THE EURO

Belgium and Luxembourg are two of eleven countries who have opted to join the European Monetary Union and, from January 1, 1999, are beginning to phase in the single European currency, the **euro**. Initially, however, it will only be possible to make paper transactions in the new currency (if you have, for example, a euro bank or credit-card account), and the franc will remain the normal unit of currency in Belgium and Luxembourg. Euro notes and coins are scheduled to be issued at the beginning of 2002, and to replace the franc entirely by the end of that year.

If you have an ordinary British/EU bank account you can use **Eurocheques** with a Eurocheque card in many banks and can write out cheques in francs in shops and hotels up to a value of around F7000. In terms of exchange rates, this works out slightly more expensive than travellers' cheques, but can be more convenient; bear in mind also that you nearly always need to have your passport with you as well as the Eurocheque card. Most Eurocheque cards, many Visa, Mastercard and British bank/cash cards, as well as US cards in the Cirrus or Plus systems, can also be used for withdrawing cash from **ATMs** in Belgium and Luxembourg; check with your bank to find out about these reciprocal arrangements. This can often be the quickest and easiest way of changing money – the system is highly sophisticated and can usually give instructions in a variety of languages. Make sure you have a personal identification number (PIN) that's designed to work overseas.

Credit cards are predictably useful for car rental, cash advances (though these attract a high rate of interest from the date of withdrawal), hotel bills, and of course shopping. American Express, Visa and Mastercard are all accepted all over Belgium and Luxembourg.

CHANGING MONEY

All but the tiniest of settlements in Belgium and Luxembourg has a **bank** or **savings bank**, and the vast majority will change foreign currency and travellers' cheques. Most of them will also handle Eurocheques, and many give cash advances on credit cards. **Banking hours** in Belgium are generally from Monday to Friday 9am to 4pm, sometimes with a one-hour lunch break between noon and 2pm. In Luxembourg normal banking hours are Monday to Friday 9am to 4.30pm, again with a one-hour lunch break between noon and 2pm; in cities some banks are open on Saturday mornings. For changing currency, almost every bank takes a

commission of around two percent with a minimum charge of about F250; if commission is waived, double-check the exchange rate to ensure that it hasn't been lowered to compensate the bank.

Outside banking hours, most major hotels, many travel agents and some hostels and campsites will change money at less generous rates and with variable commissions, as will the **exchange kiosks** to be found in the bigger cities: there's usually one in the train station concourse and/or near the Grand-Place (Grote Markt); see the relevant chapters for addresses and opening hours.

WIRING MONEY

Having **money wired** from home is never convenient or cheap, and should only be considered as a last resort. One option is to have your own bank send the money through, and for that you need to nominate a receiving bank in Belgium or Luxembourg. Any local branch will do, but those in the bigger cities will probably be more familiar with the process. Naturally, you need to confirm the co-operation of the local bank before you set the wheels in motion back home. The sending bank's fees are geared to the amount being transferred and the urgency of the service you require – the fastest transfers, taking two or three days, start at around £20/$32 for the first £300–400/$450–600.

Money can also be wired via American Express with the funds sent by one office and available for collection at the company's local offices, in Brussels and Luxembourg City, within minutes – see the relevant chapters for addresses. All transactions are done in US dollars and the service is only open to American Express card holders. Again, charges depend on the amount being sent, but as an example, wiring $400 from Britain to either Belgium or Luxembourg will cost $20, $5000 about $190. The maximum that can be sent in one go is $20,000.

GETTING AROUND

Travelling around Belgium is almost always easy. It's a small country which means that distances are short, and there's an extremely well-organized – and reasonably priced – public transport system in which an extensive train network is supplemented by (and tied in with) a plethora of local bus services. Luxembourg is, of course, even smaller, but here matters are not so straightforward: the train network is limited, and bus timetables often demand careful scrutiny if you're doing much independent travelling.

TRAINS

The best way of getting around **Belgium** is by **train**. Run by the Société Nationale des Chemins de Fer Belges/Belgische Spoorwegen (Belgian Railways), denoted by a simple "B" in an oval, the system is comprehensive and efficient, and fares are relatively low, with a standard, second-class **ticket** for a journey of 100km costing just F380, F565 for 150km, which, in Belgian terms, covers a lot of ground: Brussels to Ostend is a mere 120km. First-class tickets are about fifty percent more expensive. The price of standard tickets (*billets ordinaires/gewone biljetten*) is always calculated by distance, with a minimum charge of F40. Tickets are only valid for 24 hours. Children under the age of 6 travel free up to a maximum of four per adult, and 6-to 11-year-olds attract a fifty percent discount; you can buy a standard ticket a maximum of 31 days in advance providing you state the date of the journey. A variety of **special**

deals on specific routes at certain times can, however, cut costs by around forty percent: there are weekend tickets, special return tariffs and bargain deals on day returns, with a day-trip from Brussels and other inland towns to the seaside being one particularly popular option.

If you're going to be doing a lot of travelling, you should consider investing in a **rail pass**. The Belgian Tourrail pass (B-Tourrail) gives entitlement to five days' unlimited rail travel within a month-long period for F2100 (F3230 first class). There is also the so-called **fixed-price reduction card** (*Carte de réduction à prix fixe; Reductiekaart tegen vaste prijs*), which for F600 allows you to purchase first- and second-class tickets at half-price during the period of a month, and the Go Pass, for travellers aged between 6 and 25, which is valid for ten second-class journeys between two specified stations within six months – price F1420. Further general information on train travel is provided by the Belgian tourist office (for addresses see p.21), and Belgian Railways publish lots of information on their various offers and services, though the **national timetable** (*Indicateur/ Spoorboekje*; F150) contains all the data you're likely to need. The timetable is available within Belgium at any major station and in London from Belgian National Railways, Unit 200A, Blackfriars Foundry, 156 Blackfriars Rd, SE1 8EN (☎0171/593 2332, fax 2333).

In **Luxembourg** the railways are run by the Société Nationale des Chemins de Fer Luxembourgeois – CFL – and are not at all as wide-reaching as those in Belgium; a timetable is available from train stations and major bookshops at minimal cost and it can also be seen at *www.cfl.lu/*. The timetable is simplicity itself, with trains travelling to and from every station hourly at the same time past the hour between 8am and 8pm. There's one main north–south route down the middle of the country to Luxembourg City (from Belgium's Liège) and a couple of lines branching out from the capital, but overall the public transport system is mainly based around buses. Rail fares in Luxembourg are comparable with those in Belgium and there are also a number of **passes** available – giving unlimited travel for periods lasting an hour, a day or a month on the train network and that substantial part of the bus system run by the CFL-affiliate, RGTR.

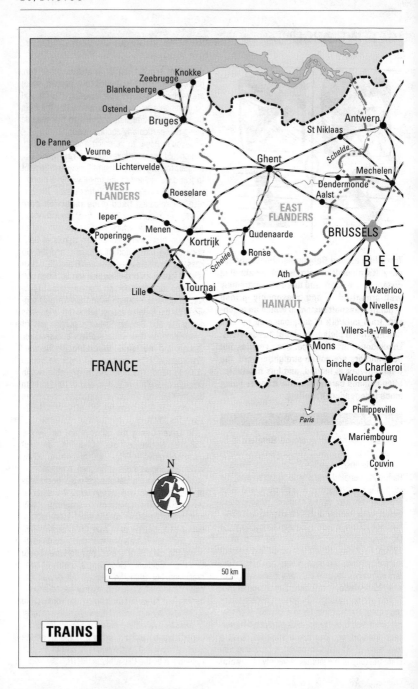

TRAINS

The price for a **one-day pass** (the *Oeko*) is F160, F640 for a pack of five. These are valid from the first time you use them (you must punch them in the machines provided to record the time) until 8am the following day, and as such are much the most flexible kind of pass you can get; there's also a short-distance ticket that's valid for just one hour and costs F40 (F320 for 10). Failing that, if you're going to be around for some time, **monthly passes**, valid for a full calendar month, cost F1400. Another option is the Luxembourg Card. Available between Easter and October, this card allows free travel on both buses and trains throughout the country and also provides free or discounted admission to many tourist attractions. A booklet giving details comes with the Card. It can be bought for one- two- or three-day periods, and costs F300, F500, F700 respectively per person or F700, F1100 or F1500 for a family card covering up to five people. The Card is widely available at rail and bus stations, youth hostels and tourist offices.

Another rail pass worth considering is the **Benelux Tourrail Card**. It's valid for any five days travel within a month on the Belgian, Dutch and Luxembourg national rail networks, as well as Luxembourg's CFL-affiliated RGTR buses; it also entitles bearers to discounts on Eurostar. It costs F4400 (first class F6600) or F3100 for under-26s. It's available in all three countries at major train stations and larger travel agents.

THE EURAILPASS AND EUROPASS

American, Canadian and other non-European travellers should consider investing in one or other of the following rail passes. (See p.5 for details on the InterRail pass.) The **Eurailpass** is valid for unlimited first-class travel throughout seventeen countries, including Belgium and Luxembourg. It's available for periods of fifteen days (US $538), 21 days ($698), one month ($864), two months ($1224) and three months ($1512). Travellers under 26 years of age are also eligible for the **Eurail Youthpass**, which offers unlimited second-class rail travel for fifteen days ($376), three weeks ($489), one month ($605), two months ($857) and three months ($1059). There's also the option of a **Eurail Flexipass**, which entitles travellers to a certain number of unlimited travel days in a two-month period. This also comes in two versions, under 26 and over 26. Periods are ten days ($444/634) and fifteen days ($585/836). All passes must be bought before you leave for

Europe from an authorized travel agent or from Rail Europe (see above for addresses).

The Europass is designed to offer cheap rail travel in the five most frequently visited European countries – France, Germany, Italy, Spain and Switzerland – but it also allows you to add other countries in specified zones. Belgium, Luxembourg and the Netherlands form the "Benelux zone". The cost of the basic pass plus the Benelux zone varies depending on the frequency with which you want to travel. For five days travel within a two-month period you would pay $386 for a single adult ($608 for two adults travelling together), under 26 $216 per person (no reductions for two). For fifteen days within a two-month period, the price increases to $866 ($1384, $599).

In terms of eligibility, these passes cannot be issued to EU residents and citizens of the CIS, Turkey, Morocco, Algeria and Tunisia.

BUSES

As so much of the country is covered by the rail network, **Belgian buses** are mainly of use for travelling short distances, and wherever there's a choice of transportation, the train is usually quicker and not much more expensive. That said, local buses are very useful for travelling around and into the environs of major towns and cities, and invaluable in some parts of rural Belgium, like the Botte de Hainaut and the Ardennes, where the train network is less comprehensive. Buses frequently link one rail route to another too. There are three major bus companies, De Lijn in the Flemish-speaking areas, STIB in Brussels, and TEC in Wallonia. Invariably, the main bus stop or terminal is next door to the train station.

In **Luxembourg** the reverse is true: because of the sparseness of the rail system, buses are much more essential – many of them run by CFL (Luxembourg Railways) – and in fact often replacements for former branch lines; timetables are available at nominal cost from bus and train stations and major newsagents. In all cases, the bus services are fully integrated with the trains, and fares are comparable. Furthermore, the various railway passes on offer (see under "Trains") also cover the country's buses. A one-day pass for Luxembourg's bus and train network costs just F160.

DRIVING AND CAR RENTAL

Getting around on public transport is easy enough, but you'll obviously have more freedom to nose around the quieter corners of Belgium and Luxembourg if you have your **own vehicle**. Both countries possess a first-rate road network, which includes toll-free motorways, though driving in Belgium is not without its difficulties: the country is so crowded – and the distances between places is often so small – that navigation often requires lightning reflexes and an intuitive sense of direction. Place names can also be very confusing. In Brussels and its environs, all the road signs are bilingual, but this is not the case in the rest of the country, which is straightforward enough until you cross the language divide. In most cases, the French and Flemish names are similar – or at least mutually recognizable – but this isn't always the case (see box for some of the trickier ones), and consequently the name you've been following on the road signs can simply disappear, with, for example, "Liège" suddenly transformed into "Luik". Finally, congestion and one-way systems can make big-city driving both time-consuming and difficult in equal measure, and drivers in Brussels are generally considered to be some of the most pugnacious in Europe. Whatever you do, make sure you've got a good map (see p.22). Petrol stations are plentiful and many accept major credit cards – but make sure you've got the cash just in case; fuel costs are broadly the same as the UK, and much higher than those of the US – reckon on about F36 per litre for

four-star fuel (96-octane). However, the distances are trivial.

Many foreign **driving licences** are honoured in Belgium and Luxembourg – including all EU, US, Australasian and Canadian ones – but an **International Driver's Licence** (available at minimum cost from your home motoring organization) is an easy way to set your mind at rest. A UK provisional licence is, however, not acceptable. If you're bringing your own car, you must have adequate insurance or a green card, a first-aid kit, and a warning triangle. Extra insurance coverage for unforeseen legal costs is also well worth having, as is an appropriate **breakdown policy** from a motoring organization. In Britain, for example, the RAC and AA charge members and non-members about £90 for a month's Europe-wide breakdown cover, with all the appropriate documentation, including green card, provided. Note, however, that rates vary depending on the age of the vehicle and increase if you're towing anything.

There are two major motoring organizations in Belgium: the Touring Club de Belgique (TCB), rue Joseph II 25, 1040 Brussels (☎02/223 2211), and the Royal Automobile Club de Belgique (RACB), rue d'Arlon 53, 1040 Brussels (☎02/287 0911; *www.racb.be/*). In Luxembourg there's the Automobile Club of Luxembourg (ACL), route de Longwy 54, L-8007 Bertrange (☎45 00 45; *www.acl.lu/*). All three organizations can be

FRENCH AND FLEMISH PLACE NAMES

The list below provides the French and Flemish names of some of the more important towns in Belgium where the difference may cause confusion. The official name comes first, the alternative afterwards, except in the case of Brussels where both languages are of equal standing.

FRENCH – FLEMISH

Bruxelles	Brussel	Namur	Namen
Ath	Aat	Nivelles	Nijvel
Liège	Luik	Soignies	Zinnik
Mons	Bergen	Tournai	Doornik

FLEMISH – FRENCH

Antwerpen	Anvers	Oostende	Ostende
Brugge	Bruges	Oudenaarde	Audenarde
De Haan	Le Coq	Ronse	Renaix
Gent	Gand	Sint Truiden	St Trond
Ieper	Ypres	Tienen	Tirlemont
Kortrijk	Courtrai	Tongeren	Tongres
Leuven	Louvain	Veurne	Furnes
Mechelen	Malines	Zoutleeuw	Léau

called upon in case of breakdown – and most major roads are dotted with phones – but only if your insurance grants you affiliated membership; check this out before departure. For emergency telephone numbers, see the box on p.51.

Throughout both countries **speed limits** are widely posted: in all built-up areas it's 50kph, 90kph on main roads and 120kph on motorways. If you're stopped for any violation, the police can (and usually will) levy a stiff fine of anything between F500 and F3000 before letting you go on your way. Most **driving rules** and regulations are pretty standard: seat belts are compulsory, penalties for drunken driving are severe – more than a glass of wine and you'll be pushing the limit – and you drive on the right. Remember also that trams

have right of way over any other vehicle, and that, unless indicated otherwise, motorists must give way to traffic merging from the right. Finally, drivers are supposed to stop at zebra crossings, but they rarely do – so if you intend to stop, try to make sure the vehicle on your tail has advance warning.

CAR RENTAL

All the major international **car rental** companies are represented in Belgium and Luxembourg, and useful addresses are given in the "Listings" section at the end of those parts of the *Guide* describing the larger cities. Many tourist offices have lists of local car rental companies too. To rent a car, you'll have to be 21 or over (and have

CAR RENTAL AGENCIES

BRITAIN

Avis ☎0990/900500
Budget ☎0800/181181
Europcar ☎0345/222525
National Car Rental ☎0990/365365

Hertz ☎0990/996699
Holiday Autos ☎0990/300400
Thrifty ☎0990/168238

IRELAND

Avis ☎01/874 5844
Budget Rent-A-Car ☎0800/973 159
Europcar Republic ☎01/874 5844

Hertz ☎01/676 7476
Holiday Autos ☎01/872 9366

USA AND CANADA

Alamo ☎1-800/522 9696
Avis ☎1-800/331 1084
Dollar ☎1-800/421 6868
Europe by Car ☎1-800/223 1516

Hertz ☎1-800/654 3001
Holiday Autos ☎1-800/422 7737
Thrifty ☎1-800/367 2277

AUSTRALIA

Avis ☎1-800/225533
Budget ☎1300/362848

Hertz ☎1-800/550067

NEW ZEALAND

Avis ☎09/526 2847
Budget ☎09/375 2222

Hertz ☎09/309 0989

WORLD WIDE WEB SITES

Alamo www.goalamo.com
Avis www.avis.com
Europe by Car www.europebycar.com

Hertz www.hertz.com
Holiday Autos www.kemwel.com
Thrifty www.thrifty.com

been driving for at least a year), and you'll need a credit card, though the occasional agency will accept a hefty cash deposit. Rental **charges** are high, beginning at around F14,000 per week for unlimited mileage in the smallest vehicle, but include collision damage waiver and vehicle (but not personal) insurance. To cut costs, watch for the special deals offered by the bigger companies (a Friday to Monday weekend rental might, for example, cost as little as F4000), or you could go to a smaller, local company, though you should, in this case, proceed with care. In particular, check the policy for the excess applied to claims and ensure that it includes collision damage waiver (applicable if an accident is your fault), and, in general, adequate levels of financial cover. Bear in mind also that it's almost always less expensive to rent your car before you leave home and pick it up at the airport on arrival.

CYCLING

Cycling is something of a national passion in **Belgium**, and it's also, given the short distances and largely flat terrain, a viable and fairly effortless way of getting around, though you have to be selective: cycling in most of the big cities and on the majority of trunk roads – where separate cycle lanes are a rarity – is precarious, verging on the suicidal. On the other hand, once you've reached the countryside, there are dozens of clearly signposted cycle routes to follow – and local tourist offices will invariably have maps and route descriptions, which you can supplement by the relevant IGN (NGI) map (see p.22). The logic of all this means that most Belgian cyclists – from Eddy Merckx lookalikes to families on an afternoon's pedal – carry their bikes to their chosen cycling location by another means of transport: either by car or train, but not by bus (it's not

allowed). Note that bicycles are transported for a flat rate of F150 per journey if you buy the ticket at the station; if you pay on the train, it costs F500.

If you haven't brought your own bike, you can **rent** seven-gear bikes from 35 train stations nationwide and 21-gear mountain bikes from four (most notably Spa). They have to be returned to the issuing station so you should check opening hours before you set off, though most are open daily from 7am to 8pm. For a full list of stations offering this service, consult the national timetable (*Indicateur/Spoorboekje*) or get hold of Belgian Railways' *Train & Vélo* (*Trein & Fiets*) leaflet, available from larger train stations in Belgium. Both the leaflet and the timetable also detail the special rates applied to day-trips by train and (one of their) cycles: a return ticket plus bike rental begins at F335 and rises to F615 depending on the length of the train journey. If you're not on one of these excursions, a charge of F325 per day is levied on the spot for bike rental, though note that during the summer it's wise to book. A refundable deposit of F500 is required from non-Belgians (F1500 for a mountain bike).

In **Luxembourg** you can rent bikes at an assortment of campsites, hostels, hotels and tourist offices for around F450 a day (F800 for a mountain bike), F400 in Luxembourg City; local tourist offices have details of locations where they're not mentioned in the *Guide*. Bear in mind also that you can take your bike on trains anywhere in Luxembourg for F40. The Grand Duchy is popular with cyclists and has over 300km of cycle tracks, many of them following old railway lines. The Luxembourg Tourist Office has all the information and helped produce the most detailed booklet on the subject, *40 Cycle Tours*, published by Guy Binsfeld and available at newsagents and bookshops in the Grand Duchy.

ACCOMMODATION

Inevitably, hotel accommodation is one of the major expenses you will incur on a trip to Belgium and Luxembourg – indeed, if you're after a degree of comfort, it's going to be the costliest item by far. There are, however, budget alternatives, principally the no-frills end of the hotel market, private rooms arranged via the local tourist office, student rooms – courtesy of a few of the larger universities – and unofficial and Hostelling International - registered youth hostels, though these are largely confined to the larger cities and more tourist-orientated locations.

HOTELS

A common **Benelux standard** is used to classify all **hotels, motels and guesthouses** that are recognized and licensed by the three governmental agencies concerned – one each for Luxembourg, French- and Flemish-speaking Belgium. This Benelux standard grades hotels within general categories which provide a guide to facilities, but not necessarily to cost. All licensed hotels carry a **blue permit shield** on which is indicated the number of stars allocated (up to a maximum of five); hotels which fail to obtain a licence are not allowed to offer accommodation. The classification system is, by necessity, measured against easily identifiable criteria – lifts, toilets, room service, etc – rather than aesthetics or specific location, and consequently can only provide a general guide to both quality and prices: a poky room in a three-star hotel in a

mediocre part of Bruges may, for instance, cost more than a comfortable room in a four-star hotel in the centre of a less popular town. In general terms, prices range from an absolute minimum of around F1500 for a double room in the least expensive, one-star establishment, through F3500 to F4500 for a double in a middle-range, three-star hotel, and on up to around F6500 and more in the big city luxury hotels. Nevertheless, watch out for summer discounts and weekend specials that can reduce costs by up to 35 percent. And don't necessarily be taken in by hotel foyers – some are tastefully decorated and comfortable, but beyond lie the dullest of rooms. Almost all hotels offer breakfast (included or extra), ranging from a roll and coffee at the less expensive places through to full-scale banquets at the top end of the market.

In summer you'd be well advised to **reserve** hotel rooms in advance, especially in the larger cities and Ardennes resorts. You can do this either by phoning or faxing direct – we've given phone and fax numbers throughout the *Guide* – or by using the free Belgian Tourist Reservations service (BTR), bd Anspach 111 B4, 1000 Brussels (☎02/513 7484, fax 513 9277), through which you can book rooms nationwide. Reservations can also be made through most tourist offices, again for free, though they'll almost always charge a deposit which will be deducted from your final bill.

For a full **list of approved hotels** throughout Belgium, with details of prices and facilities, pick up a copy of *Hotels in Flanders* (which covers the Flemish-speaking regions) and *Hôtels: Ardenne & Bruxelles* (for Wallonia and Brussels) before leaving, especially as it can be difficult to find copies once in Belgium. Note that in tourist material the designation "Flanders" often covers all Flemish areas, and "Ardennes" the French areas. The Luxembourg Tourist Office also has a booklet of approved hotels, with prices, which is well worth getting hold of either before you leave or on arrival.

HOSTELS, STUDENT AND PRIVATE ROOMS

Belgium has around thirty HI-registered **youth hostels** (*auberges de jeunesse/jeugherbergen*) run by two separate organizations, one for the Flemish regions and one for Wallonia. Each

OUR ACCOMMODATION PRICE CODES

All the **accommodation** we have listed in Belgium and Luxembourg has been graded according to the following categories. Our categories do not give an indication of the facilities you might expect other than the broad outlines we provide below – and as such they differ from the star-system applied by the tourist authorities; above all our categories are a guide to price.

Please note that the prices we give are for the least expensive double room – eg without private bath, etc – during high season. Many hotels in Belgium and Luxembourg have a wide range of rooms, and it's possible that in some places, on some occasions, the only rooms available will in fact be a grade higher than the one we have given.

① **Up to F1000 (per person)** Hostel accommodation, either a private establishment or an HI-registered youth hostel, where the charges for a bunk in a dormitory will normally be around F500 per person per night. Most hostels also have some form of private accommodation – single-, double- and triple-bedded rooms – and, in terms of price, these normally fall into the next category up. You may also find private rooms that fall into this category.

② **F1000–1500 (per room)** This category covers most private rooms and the family, triple-, double-, and single-bedded rooms provided at most hostels. They are normally without any kind of private facilities beyond a washbasin, or, sometimes, a shower. Expect decor, etc, to be fairly grim, particularly in big-city locations.

③ **F1500–2000 (per room)** Another category covering the bottom end of the market, consisting mainly of one-star or unstarred but licensed hotels, sporting a mixture of adequate, functional rooms with no private facilities and a selection of slightly more upscale choices with basic private facilities. Again, expect the decor to be dour.

④ **F2000–2500 (per room)** This grade comes up frequently in the *Guide*, basically one- merging into two-star hotels, a little more comfortable than the previous grouping, and with the emphasis on rooms with private facilities – though there may be a handful of less expensive (and more primitive) rooms on offer too.

⑤ **F2500–3000 (per room)** Standard two- and some three-star hotel accommodation, where facilities will almost always be private and you will often have the use of a phone and TV; at this price, you can expect the room to be small and the decor to be fairly uninspired.

⑥ **F3000–4000 (per room)** The majority of three and many four-star hotels, whose rooms are always en suite and mostly come equipped with phone, TV, perhaps a minibar, and occasionally room service. Many chain hotels (like *Ibis*) aim for this price range and you can expect rooms to be smart and neat, if hardly inspirational, though there are some notable (and delightful) exceptions.

⑦ **F4000–5000 (per room)** Three- and four-star hotels with all the attendant facilities you would expect – private bathroom, minibar, phone and TV, room service, and perhaps even a gym, swimming pool or sauna.

⑧ **F5000–6000 (per room)** Top quality, often attractively located three-, four- and occasionally five-star hotels with all amenities, and frequently a gym, swimming pool and sauna too. Some really superb places here.

⑨ **F6000 and over (per room)** This category takes in four-and five-star establishments with second-to-none service and facilities, along with really special places – notable either for their location, architecture, or perhaps their history.

operates a similar number of hostels, and both have hostels in Brussels. There's very little difference between the two groups, though the Flemish ones tend to be more geared up for school parties than those in Wallonia, which are perhaps a tad less regimented. In both regions, there are hostels in most of the major tourist towns, but many are situated in out-of-the-way places or less-visited towns.

Most Belgian hostels **charge** a flat rate per person of around F380 for a bed in a dormitory, more in major centres like Ostend and Ghent, where you can expect to pay around F450, and Brussels, where the rates are F395–660. Breakfast is included in the overnight rate, but where it isn't you can anticipate a charge of around F150; bed linen is usually included too but otherwise costs about F110. Many Belgian hostels also offer lunch and dinner, at around F200 for lunch, F300 or so for dinner.

If you're planning on staying at a lot of hostels, it's a good idea to join your home youth hostelling

YOUTH HOSTEL ASSOCIATIONS

Australia, Australian Youth Hostels Association, Level 3, 10 Mallett St, Camperdown, New South Wales 2050 (☎02/9565 1699, fax 1325).

Canada, Hostelling International – Canada, Room 400, 205 Catherine St, Ottawa, Ontario K2P 1C3 (☎1-800/444 6111, fax 613/237 7868).

England and Wales, Youth Hostel Association (YHA), Trevelyan House, 8 St Stephen's Hill, St Albans, Herts AL1 2DY (☎01727/855215, fax 844126). London shop and information centre: 14 Southampton St, London WC2E 7HY (☎0171/836 1036, fax 6372).

Ireland, An Óige, 61 Mountjoy St, Dublin 7 (☎01/830 4555, fax 5808).

New Zealand, Youth Hostels Association of New Zealand, PO Box 436, Christchurch 1 (☎03/379 9970, fax 365 4476).

Northern Ireland, Youth Hostel Association of Northern Ireland, 22 Donegall Rd, Belfast BT12 5JN (☎01232/315435, fax 439699).

Scotland, Scottish Youth Hostel Association, 7 Glebe Crescent, Stirling FK8 2JA (☎01786/891400, fax 891333).

USA, American Youth Hostels, 733 15th St NW, Suite 840, Washington DC 20005 (☎202/783 6161, fax 783-6171, *www.hiayh.org*).

organization before you leave (see the box for details) – the prices above will be higher by ten to fifteen percent if you're not a member, and annual membership fees are on the whole low. During the summer at least, you should also book in advance wherever possible, since many hostels, particularly those in more popular towns, are fully booked well ahead of time. We've detailed all the key hostels but for a complete list contact either your home hostelling organization before you leave or one of the Belgian ones direct. They are: the Vlaamse Jeugdherbergcentrale, Van Stralenstraat 40, 2060 Antwerp (☎03/232 7218, fax 231 8126); and Les Auberges de Jeunesse de Wallonie, rue Van Oost 52, 1030 Brussels (☎02/215 3100, fax 242 8356).

Some of the larger Belgian cities – Antwerp, Bruges and Brussels, for example – have a number of **unofficial youth hostels** (usually named as *logements pour jeunes/jeugdlogies*) in addition to the HI establishments. These normally cost about F500 for a dormitory bed and are often just as comfortable and a good deal more intimate – though the quality varies enormously and some are real dives. You'll also find some universities offering **student rooms** for rent during the summer holidays – Ghent being a good example. The rooms are frugal, but the rates are very reasonable – reckon on about F500 per person per night. Last of all, many Belgian towns have a limited supply of rooms in **private homes** (*chambres d'hôtes/gastenkamers*), which local tourist offices will book for you either at no charge or for a deposit which is subsequently subtracted from the final bill. On average, reckon on spending about F1200 a night for a double room – a good price, but the majority are inconveniently situated far from the respective town or city centre.

Luxembourg has fourteen **youth hostels**, all members of the Centrale des Auberges de Jeunesse Luxembourgeoises (AJL), 2 rue du Fort Olisy, L-2661 Luxembourg (☎22 55 88, fax 46 39 87). Average rates for HI members are in the vicinity of F350–650 per person for a dorm bed, but prices at the Luxembourg City and Larochette hostels rise to a maximum of F750 and F730 respectively. Breakfast is included in the overnight fee, but bed linen costs an extra F125 per stay. Some places also serve meals – reckon on about F200 for lunch, evening meals F100 more; advance reservations, especially in the high season, are pretty much essential. From December to February, most of the hostels are exclusively for use by groups of ten or more. If you're planning on staying at several hostels, then joining your home youth hostelling organization before you leave (see box for details) is a good way to cut costs. There are no unofficial youth hostels in Luxembourg and only a small number of **private rooms**, which average in the region of F1500 per double room per night.

CAMPSITES

Camping is a popular pastime in both Belgium and Luxembourg. In **Belgium**, there are literally hundreds of campsites to choose from, anything from a field with a few tent pitches through to extensive complexes with all mod cons. Of these, the Flemish tourist authorities recognize around 250 campsites, the Walloons some three hundred, classifying them on a one- to five-star grading (see box). Most sites are situated with the motorist (rather than the cyclist or walker) in mind and a good few occupy key locations beside the main roads. The vast majority are one-star establishments, for which a family of two adults, two children, a car and a tent can expect to pay between F500–700 per night; perhaps surprisingly most four-star sites don't cost much if any more – add about F100 – though the occasional five-star campsite is more like a recreation park and here the price can reach around F1500. The Belgian Tourist Office publishes two booklets detailing the country's campsites and their facilities – one for the Flemish-speaking regions and one for Brussels and Wallonia.

Luxembourg has a little over one hundred campsites, all detailed in the free booklet available from the national tourist board. They are classified into three broad bands with each category having minimum standards. The majority are in Category 1, the best-equipped and most expensive classification, where each site must have, for example, one hot shower per one hundred and one wash-stand per twenty guests, playgrounds, electric connections for camping installations, and 24-hour staffing. Simpler Category 3 sites must, among several requirements, have a washstand for every thirty guests and a camp leader on site or in the vicinity. Prices vary considerably even within each category, but are usually between F70 and F140 per person, plus F100–150 for a site.

During peak season it can, in both countries, be a good idea to **reserve ahead** if you have a car and large tent or trailer; phone numbers are listed in the free camping booklets, and in Luxembourg the national tourist board will gladly make a campsite reservation on your behalf – telephone ☎00352/42 82 82 1.

FARM AND RURAL HOLIDAYS

In both countries, the tourist authorities have developed an imaginative and extensive programme of short-break holidays – anything from cycling tours and gastronomic excursions through to beer and antique-buying weekends. They also co-ordinate farm and rural holidays, ranging from "*en famille*" accommodation in a **farmhouse**, to the renting of rural apartments and country dwellings (*gîtes ruraux/landelijke gîtes*). There are also **gîtes d'étapes** – dormitory-style lodgings situated in relatively remote parts of the country which can house anywhere between ten and one hundred people per establishment. You can often choose to rent just part of the gîte d'étape or stay on a bed and breakfast basis. Some of the larger gîtes d'étapes (or *gîtes de groupes*) cater for large groups only, accepting bookings for a minimum of 25 people. In all cases, advance booking is essential and prices, naturally enough, vary widely depending on the quality of accommodation, the length of stay and the season. As examples, a high season (mid-June to Aug), week-long booking of a pleasantly situated and comfortable farmhouse for four adults and three children might cost you in the region of F13,000, whereas a ten-person gîte d'étape might cost F10,000, F1000 less in winter. On the other hand, one night's bed and breakfast costs around F480 – sometimes less if you're under 26 – and about F250 for children under 6 years old. For further details, contact the Belgian or Luxembourg Tourist Office. In Belgium, you could also approach a specialist, youth agency, Les Gîtes d'Etapes du Centre Belge du Tourisme des Jeunes, rue van Orley 4, Brussels (☎02/209 0300, fax 223 0389).

BELGIAN CAMPSITE CLASSIFICATION

Belgian campsites are graded within the following general categories. They provide a guide as to facilities, but not necessarily to cost.

1-star. Must comply with minimum camping regulations by having drinking water facilities, cold water showers, flush toilets, washbasins and power points.

2-star. As for previous grade, but must have daytime supervision and more electrical facilities.

3-star. Must have warm water showers, sports facilities, and a shop.

4-star. As for previous grade, but must also possess a restaurant, children's playing area and electrical fixtures throughout the site.

5-star. As for previous grade, but more facilities per person and a high level of supervision.

EATING AND DRINKING

Belgian cuisine, particularly that of Brussels and Wallonia, is held in high regard worldwide, and in Europe at least is seen as second only to French in quality – indeed many feel it's of equal standing. The food of Luxembourg doesn't rise to quite such heights, but it's still of an excellent standard. As for drink, beer is one of the real delights of Belgium, and Luxembourg produces some very drinkable white wines along its bank of the Moselle.

FOOD

Wallonian cuisine is broadly similar to French, based upon a fondness for rich sauces and the freshest of ingredients. In **Flanders** the food is more akin to that of Holland, characteristically plainer and simpler, though there are many interesting traditional dishes. For such a small country there's a surprising amount of provincial diversity, but it's generally true to say that pork, beef, game, fish and seafood, especially mussels, are staple items, often cooked with butter, cream and herbs, or sometimes beer – which is, after all, the Belgian national drink. Soup is also common, hearty stew-like affairs offered in a huge tureen from which you can help yourself – a satisfying and reasonably priced meal in itself.

Belgian chefs are eclectic, dipping into many other cuisines, especially those of the Mediterranean, and also borrowing freely from across their own country's cultural/linguistic divide. Among the more traditional and commonplace **dishes** originating in the Flemish provinces

are *waterzooi*, a Flanders soup-cum-stew consisting of chicken or fish boiled with fresh vegetables; *konijn met pruimen*, an old Flemish standby of rabbit with prunes; *paling in 't groen*, eel braised in a green sauce with herbs; *karbonaden*, cubes of beef marinated in beer and cooked with herbs and onions; *stoemp*, mashed potato mixed with vegetable and/or meat purée; and *hutsepot*, literally hotchpotch, a mixed stew of mutton, beef and pork. From the French-speaking regions come *truite à l'Ardennaise*, trout cooked in a wine sauce; *chicorées gratinés au four*, chicory with ham and cheese; *fricassée Liègeois*, basically, fried eggs, bacon and sausage or blood pudding; *fricadelles à la bière*, or meatballs in beer; and *carbonnades de porc Bruxelloise*, pork with a tarragon and tomato sauce. The Ardennes, in particular, is well known for its cured ham (similar to Italian Parma ham) and, of course, its pâté, made from pork, beef, liver and kidney – though it often takes a particular name from an additional ingredient, for example *pâté de faisan* (pheasant) or *pâté de lièvre* (hare). As you might expect, game (*gibiers*) features heavily on most Ardennes menus. Among many salads you'll find are *salade de Liège*, made from beans and potatoes, and *salade wallonie*, a warm salad of lettuce, fried potatoes and bits of bacon.

Luxembourg cuisine is similar to that of Belgium, but, as you might expect, it has more Germanic influences, with sausages and sauerkraut featuring on menus, as well as pork, game and river fish. Favourite dishes include smoked pork with beans; liver dumplings with sauerkraut and potatoes; tripe – *tripe à la Luxembourgeoise*; *boudin* – black pudding served with apple sauce and mashed potatoes; *judd mat gardebœnen* – cooked ham served with sauté potatoes and broad beans in a cream sauce. On the Moselle many restaurants serve *friture de la Moselle* – small fried fish. At many annual celebrations and fairs restaurants serve *fesch* – whole fish fried in batter.

BREAKFAST, SNACKS AND DESSERTS

In most parts of Belgium and Luxembourg you'll **start the day** in routine fashion with a cup of coffee and a roll or croissant, though the more expensive hotels usually offer sumptuous banquet-like breakfasts with cereals, fruit, hams and cheeses. Everywhere, coffee is almost always first-rate – aromatic and strong, but rarely bitter; in Brussels and the south it's often accompanied by hot milk (*café au lait*), but throughout Belgium there's a tendency to serve it in the Dutch fashion, with a small tub of evaporated rather than fresh milk.

Later in the day, the most common **snack** is *frites* (chips) – served everywhere in Belgium from *friture* stands or parked vans, with salt or mayonnaise, or more exotic dressings. Mussels, cooked in a variety of ways, with chips, is something akin to Belgium's national dish, and makes a good fast lunch in cafeterias. Rather more wholesome are the filled baguettes (*broodjes*) that many bakeries and cafés prepare on the spot – nothing like the tired sandwiches often served across the Channel in the UK, but imaginative, tasty creations that make a meal in themselves. Many fish shops, especially on the coast, also do an appetizing line in seafood baguettes, while street vendors in the north sell various sorts of toxic-looking sausage (*worst*), especially black pudding (*bloedworst*). Everywhere there are stands selling waffles (*gaufres*), served up steaming hot with jam and honey. With this range of inexpensive foods on offer, it's depressing to report that multinational burger joints, mainly *McDonalds* and *Burger King* are popular too.

As for cakes and sweets, Belgium is known best for its **chocolate**. Each Belgian, apparently, eats 12.5kg of chocolate annually, and chocolates are the favoured gift when visiting friends. The big Belgian chocolatiers, Godiva and Leonidas, have stores in the main towns and cities, and their *pralines* – filled with cream, liqueurs or *ganache* (a fine dark chocolate) – and *truffles*, made of chocolate, butter, cream and sugar, are almost worth the trip alone. Of the two Leonidas is the cheaper outlet – reckon on spending around F300 for 500g of their chocolates – but you can pay much more (for what many feel is a far superior, less sugary chocolate) at one of the small and independent chocolate makers you'll find in all the bigger cities (one of the very best is *Neuhaus*). Regular chocolate by the bar (*Côte d'Or* is one of the major manufacturers) is also delicious. Apart from chocolate, look out for *speculaas*, a speciality of the northern part of the country – a rich and hard cinnamon-flavoured biscuit that was originally baked in the form of saints and religious figures but now comes in all shapes and sizes.

SIT-DOWN FOOD

At the inexpensive end of the **sit-down meal** scale, many **bars** serve food, at least at lunchtimes, and in all but the smallest of towns there's normally a good supply of **cafeterias** serving up basic dishes – omelettes, soups, chicken or steak with chips and suchlike. Nothing comes cheap, but the quality will regularly be excellent, even with the most humble dishes, and portions are usually substantial. In bars, basic restaurants and cafeterias, you can expect to pay about F250 on average for an omelette or something similar; a more substantial meat-and-chips affair might cost F350–450. Most bars and cafeterias that serve food normally have a *plat du jour* on offer too, usually for around F350, frequently including a starter and a dessert.

Though there's often a thin dividing line between them as regards the food, **restaurants** are mostly a little more formal and, not surprisingly, more expensive than bars and cafés. Even in the cheapest restaurant a main course will rarely cost under F400, with a more usual figure being between F450–600, especially in Luxembourg, where things are that much more expensive. Restaurants are usually open during the day, but the main focus is in the evening. Many restaurants close one day a week, often Monday or Tuesday, and note that in the smaller towns kitchens start to wind down around 9.30pm. Throughout the *Guide*, we've given phone numbers for restaurants where it's advisable to make reservations.

VEGETARIAN AND FOREIGN CUISINES

Traditional Belgian and Luxembourgeois food is fairly meat-based, which means vegetarians are in for a difficult time, especially if they want to sample the local specialities – though this is considerably easier if seafood is acceptable. Most of the larger towns have one or two **vegetarian** cafés or restaurants, but that's all – and even these are mostly part-time places, open for lunch and a couple of evenings only. The main exception is Brussels, where vegetarian menu options are fairly common and there's a reasonable selection of specifically vegetarian restaurants too.

The quality and diversity of Belgium's native cuisine means that the vast majority of restaurants stick to it, though many supplement their menus with **Italian** and **French** offerings. Indeed, among foreign cuisines, it's the Italian and French restaurants which dominate both in the major

FRENCH FOOD AND DRINK TERMS

Basics

Beurre	Butter	*Oeufs*	Eggs
Chaud	Hot	*Pain (complet)*	Bread
Dessert	Dessert	*Poisson*	Fish
Fromage	Cheese	*Poivre*	Pepper
Froid	Cold	*Salade*	Salad
Hors d'oeuvre	Starters	*Sel*	Salt
Legumes	Vegetables	*Sucre*	Sugar
		Viande	Meat

Typical Snacks

Un sandwich/une baguette . . .	A sandwich . . .	*brouillés*	scrambled eggs
		Omelette . . .	Omelette . . .
de jambon	with ham	*nature*	plain
de fromage	with cheese	*au fromage*	with cheese
de saucisson	with sausage	*Salade de . . .*	Salad of . . .
à l'ail	with garlic	*tomates*	tomatoes
au poivre	with pepper	*concombres*	cucumbers
Croque-monsieur	Grilled cheese and ham sandwich	*Crêpes . . .*	Pancakes . . .
Oeufs . . .	Eggs . . .	*au sucre*	with sugar
au plat	fried eggs	*au citron*	with lemon
à la coque	boiled eggs	*au miel*	with honey
durs	hard-boiled eggs	*à la confiture*	with jam

Soups and starters

Assiette anglaise	Plate of cold meats	*Bouillon*	Broth or stock
Bisque	Shellfish soup	*Consommé*	Clear soup
Bouillabaisse	Fish soup from Marseilles	*Crudités*	Raw vegetables with dressing
		Potage	Thick soup, usually vegetable

Meat and poultry

Agneau	Lamb	*Foie*	Liver
Bifteck	Steak	*Gigot*	Leg of venison
Boeuf	Beef	*Jambon*	Ham
Canard	Duck	*Lard*	Bacon
Cheval	Horsemeat	*Porc*	Pork
Cuisson	Leg of lamb	*Poulet*	Chicken
Côtelettes	Cutlets	*Saucisse*	Sausage
Dindon	Turkey	*Veau*	Veal

Fish

Anchois	Anchovies	*Cervettes roses*	Prawns
Anguilles	Eels	*Escargots*	Snails
Carrelet	Plaice	*Hareng*	Herring

Lotte de mer	Monkfish	*Moules*	Mussels
Maquereau	Mackerel	*Saumon*	Salmon
Morue	Cod	*Sole*	Sole
		Truite	Trout

Vegetables

Ail	Garlic	*Laitue*	Lettuce
Asperges	Asparagus	*Oignons*	Onions
Carottes	Carrots	*Petits pois*	Peas
Champignon	Mushrooms	*Poireau*	Leek
Choufleur	Cauliflower	*Pommes (de terre)*	Potatoes
Concombre	Cucumber	*Riz*	Rice
Genièvre	Juniper		

Sweets and desserts

Crème fraiche	Sour cream	*Glace*	Ice cream
Crêpes	Pancakes	*Madeleine*	Small, shell-shaped
Crêpes suzettes	Thin pancakes with		sponge cake
	orange juice and	*Parfait*	Frozen mousse, some-
	liqueur		times ice cream
Frappé	Iced	*Petits fours*	Bite-sized cakes or
			pastries

Fruit and nuts

Amandes	Almonds	*Noisette*	Hazelnut
Ananas	Pineapple	*Pamplemousse*	Grapefruit
Cacahouète	Peanut	*Poire*	Pear
Cérises	Cherries	*Pomme*	Apple
Citron	Lemon	*Prune*	Plum
Fraises	Strawberries	*Pruneau*	Prune
Framboises	Raspberries	*Raisins*	Grapes
Marrons	Chestnuts		

Drinks

Bière	Beer	*Thé*	Tea
Café	Coffee	*Vin . . .*	Wine . . .
Eaux de vie	Spirits distilled from	*rouge*	red
	various fruits	*blanc*	white
Jenever	Dutch/Flemish gin	*brut*	very dry
Lait	Milk	*sec*	dry
Orange/citron pressé	Fresh orange/lemon	*demi-sec*	sweet
	juice	*doux*	very sweet

Terms

A point	Medium	*Mijoté*	Stewed
Au four	Baked	*Pané*	Breaded
Bien cuit	Well done	*Rôti*	Roast
Bouilli	Boiled	*Saignant*	Rare
Frit/friture	Fried/deep fried	*Sauté*	Lightly cooked in butter
Fumé	Smoked	*Tourte*	Tart or pie
Grillé	Grilled	*Tranche*	Slice

FLEMISH FOOD AND DRINK TERMS

Basics

Boter	Butter	*Nagerechten*	Desserts
Brood	Bread	*Peper*	Pepper
Broodje	Sandwich/roll	*Pindakaas*	Peanut butter
Dranken	Drinks	*Sla/salade*	Salad
Eieren	Eggs	*Smeerkaas*	Cheese spread
Groenten	Vegetables	*Stokbrood*	French bread
Gerst	Semolina: the type of grain used in Algerian *couscous*, popular in vegetarian restaurants	*Suiker*	Sugar
		Vis	Fish
		Vlees	Meat
		Voorgerechten	Appetizers, hors d'oeuvres
Honing	Honey		
Hoofdgerechten	Entrées	*Vruchten*	Fruit
Kaas	Cheese	*Warm*	Hot
Koud	Cold	*Zout*	Salt

Appetizers and snacks

Erwtensoep/snert	Thick pea soup with bacon or sausage	*Uitsmijter*	Ham or cheese with eggs on bread
Huzarensalade	Egg salad	*Koffietafel*	A light midday meal of cold meats, cheese, bread and perhaps soup
Patats/Frites	French fries		
Soep	Soup		

Meat and poultry

Biefstuk (hollandse)	Steak	*Kalfsvlees*	Veal
Eend	Duck	*Karbonade*	Chop
Fricandeau	Roast pork	*Kip*	Chicken
Fricandel	A frankfurter-like sausage	*Kroket*	Spiced meat in breadcrumbs
Gehakt	Ground meat	*Lamsvlees*	Lamb
Ham	Ham	*Lever*	Liver
Hutsepot	Beef stew with vegetables	*Rookvlees*	Smoked beef
		Spek	Bacon
Kalkoen	Turkey	*Worst*	Sausages

Fish

Forel	Trout	*Mosselen*	Mussels
Garnalen	Shrimp	*Paling*	Eel
Haring	Herring	*Schol*	Flounder
Haringsalade	Herring salad	*Schelvis*	Shellfish
Kabeljauw	Cod	*Tong*	Sole
Makreel	Mackerel	*Zalm*	Salmon

Vegetables

Aardappelen	Potatoes	*Champignons*	Mushrooms	*Rijst*	Rice
Bloemkool	Cauliflower	*Erwten*	Peas	*Sla*	Salad, lettuce
Boerenkool	A kind of cabbage	*Knoflook*	Garlic	*Uien*	Onions
		Komkommer	Cucumber	*Wortelen*	Carrots
Bonen	Beans	*Prei*	Leek	*Zuurkool*	Sauerkraut

Indonesian, Chinese and Surinamese dishes and terms

Ajam	Chicken	*Nasi Rames*	*Rijsttafel* on a single plate
Bami	Fried noodles with meat/	*Pedis*	Hot and spicy
	chicken and vegetables	*Pisang*	Banana
Daging	Beef	*Rijsttafel*	Collection of different spicy
Gado gado	Vegetables in peanutsauce		dishes served with
Goreng	Fried		plain rice
Ikan	Fish	*Sambal*	Hot, chilli-based sauce
Katjang	Peanut	*Satesaus*	Peanut sauce to accompany
Kroepoek	Shrimp crackers		meat broiled on skewers
Loempia	Egg rolls	*Seroendeng*	Spicy fried, shredded
Nasi	Rice		coconut
Nasi Goreng	Fried rice with meat/	*Tauge*	Bean shoots
	chicken and vegetables		

Desserts

Appelgebak	Apple tart or cake	*Pannekoeken*	Pancakes
Drop	Dutch liquorice, available in	*Poffertjes*	Small pancakes, fritters
	zoet (sweet) or	*(Slag) room*	(Whipped) cream
	zout (salted) varieties	*Speculaas*	Spice- and honey-
Gebak	Pastry		flavoured biscuit
Ijs	Ice cream	*Stroopwafels*	Waffles
Koekjes	Cookies	*Vla*	Custard
Oliebollen	Doughnuts		

Fruit and nuts

Aardbei	Strawberry	*Druif*	Grape	*Peer*	Pear
Amandel	Almond	*Framboos*	Raspberry	*Perzik*	Peach
Appel	Apple	*Hazelnoot*	Hazelnut	*Pinda*	Peanut
Appelmoes	Apple purée	*Kers*	Cherry	*Pruim*	Plum/prune
Citroen	Lemon	*Kokosnoot*	Coconut		

Drinks

Anijsmelk	Aniseed-	*Karnemelk*	Buttermilk	*Pils*	Dutch beer
	flavoured	*Koffie*	Coffee	*Proost!*	Cheers!
	warm milk	*Koffie verkeerd*	Coffee with	*Sinaasappelsap*	Orange juice
Appelsap	Apple juice		warm milk	*Thee*	Tea
Bessenjenever	Blackcurrant	*Kopstoot*	Beer with a	*Tomatensap*	Tomato juice
	gin		*Jenever*	*Vieux*	Dutch brandy
Chocomel	Chocolate milk		chaser	*Vruchtensap*	Fruit juice
Citroenjenever	Lemon gin	*Melk*	Milk	*Wijn*	Wine
Droog	Dry	*Met ijs*	With ice	*(wit/rood/rose)*	(white/red/rosé)
Frisdranken	Sodas	*Met slagroom*	With whipped	*Zoet*	Sweet
Jenever	Dutch gin		cream		

Terms

Doorbakken	Well done	*Gerookt*	Smoked
Gebakken	Fried/baked	*Gestoofd*	Stewed
Gebraden	Roasted	*Half doorbakken*	Medium
Gekookt	Boiled	*Hollandse saus*	Hollandaise (butter and
Gegrild	Grilled		egg sauce)
Geraspt	Grated		

cities and the smaller towns, and the food they offer is almost invariably of good, if not excellent, quality. Other, less commonplace cuisines are to be found in Brussels in abundance, less so in the other conurbations, though Antwerp, in particular, is catching up. Among them, **Chinese** restaurants are fairly widespread and are nearly always decorated in a kitsch rendition of traditional motifs; **Turkish** and **Greek** restaurants are especially good in Brussels; **Balkan** restaurants appear here and there, but are generally overpriced; while Luxembourg's sizable Portuguese minority has spawned a higher than average quota of **Portuguese** places. In Brussels especially there are also a handful of **African** (Congolese) and a goodly selection of **North African** (Moroccan and Tunisian) restaurants – worth sampling, and often very good bargains.

DRINK

Apart from the quality, the price of food in both Belgium and Luxembourg is also offset by the cost of **drinking**, especially if you like beer, which is always good and comes in numerous varieties. There's a bar on almost every corner in both countries: most serve at least twenty types of beer, and in some beer lists run into the hundreds. Traditionally, they're cosy, unpretentious places, the walls stained brown by years of tobacco smoke, but in recent years many have been decorated in anything from a sort of potty medievalism (wooden beams etc) through to Art Nouveau and a frugal post-modernist style that is fashionable in the bigger cities. Many of them serve simple food, and an increasing number pride themselves on first-rate dishes from small, but well-conceived menus.

BEER

Beer has been a passion in Belgium since the Middle Ages, when monks did much of the brewing; later the brewers' guilds were founded and became among the most influential institutions in the region. Today there are up to five hundred different kinds of beer in Belgium, many brewed by small family breweries and some still produced by monasteries. Most of these are of the lager – or pilsener – type, but there are other tasty types too.

In both Belgium and Luxembourg, ask for a *bière/bier* in a **bar** and you'll be served a roughly cup-sized glass of whatever the bar has on tap. The most common beers you'll see in Belgium are the Leuven-based Stella Artois, Jupiler from Liège (the country's biggest-selling beer) and Maes. In Luxembourg the most widespread brands are Diekirch (the largest domestic brewer), Mousel and Bofferding. **Bar prices** don't vary much: in Belgium you'll pay around F60 for a glass of beer in all but the swankiest places; in Luxembourg count on F50 or so – about the only thing that is cheaper in Luxembourg than Belgium. For speciality bottled beers like Duvel and Chimay (see below) you'll pay around F110 – less in a supermarket.

For a detailed appreciation of **Belgium beer** turn to Michael Jackson's article "Belgium's Great Beers" in Contexts, p.372.

WINE AND SPIRITS

In Belgium, wine is very much overshadowed by beer, but it is widely available, at about F250 a bottle from the supermarket, F300 or so and upwards in a restaurant. French wines are the most commonly drunk, although Luxembourg is, in a small way, a wine producer, and its pleasant white wines, produced from vines grown along the west bank of the Moselle, are not unlike those of Germany, but drier and fruitier than those of France. They also produce some very palatable sparkling wines. As with beer, Luxembourgeois wines are relatively cheap to buy in shops: the sparkling, *méthode champenoise* varieties go for around F250–350 a bottle (try the St Martin brand, which is excellent and dry); ordinary white wine costs about F250; in restaurants, expect to pay F700–800 and F200–600 respectively.

There's no one national Belgian spirit, but the Flemings in particular have a penchant, like their Dutch neighbours, for *jenever* which is available in most ordinary as well as specialist bars, the latter selling as many as several hundred varieties. There is a domestic jenever industry, with the bigger producers to be found in the province of Limburg. In addition, all the usual kinds of spirit – gin, whisky etc – are widely available across the whole of the country. In Luxembourg, you'll also come across locally produced bottles of *eau de vie* – distilled from various fruits and around fifty percent alcohol by volume.

POST AND TELEPHONES

In Belgium and Luxembourg both the post and the telephones are very efficient. Telephone boxes are liberally distributed in cities and towns and call charges are reasonable.

POST

Post offices in Belgium and Luxembourg are plentiful: in Belgium they are usually open Monday to Friday 9am to noon and 2 to 4pm, and in Luxembourg Monday to Friday 9am to noon and 1.30 to 5pm. Some urban post offices open much longer hours (broadly 7am–7pm) and a handful open Saturday (or Saturday mornings) as well. Mail to the US takes seven days or so, within Europe two to three days. **Mail boxes** are painted red in Belgium and yellow in Luxembourg. You can receive letters at any main city post office by having them addressed "Poste Restante" followed by the surname of the addressee (preferably underlined and in capitals), and then the name of the town and country. To collect, take along your passport or identity card and – if you're expecting post and your initial enquiry produces nothing – ask the clerk to check under all of your names and initials as letters sometimes get misfiled. Alternatively, American Express, which has offices in Brussels and Luxembourg City (addresses are in the *Guide*), will hold incoming mail – but not parcels or registered mail – for a month on behalf of card and travellers' cheque holders.

TELEPHONES

Both countries have reliable telephone systems, and you can make domestic and international **telephone calls** with equal ease from public phones in either Belgium or Luxembourg. Phone booths are plentiful, but if you can't find one, many bars have pay phones you can use. All the more expensive hotel rooms have phones too, but note that there is always an exorbitant surcharge for their use.

Public telephones are of the usual European kind, where you deposit the money before you make your call. In both countries, they take F5, F20 and sometimes F50 coins, though coin-operated public phones are gradually being phased out in favour of those that only take **telecards**, which can be purchased at newsstands, post offices, major train stations and some supermarkets. In

---

INTERNATIONAL DIALLING CODES

From Belgium and Luxembourg to:

Australia	☎0061	New Zealand	☎0064	USA and Canada	☎001
Ireland	☎00353	UK	☎0044		

USEFUL NUMBERS

Within Belgium and Luxembourg:	Belgium	Luxembourg
Directory enquiries (domestic)	☎1307	☎017
Directory enquiries (international)	☎1304	☎016
Emergencies (fire and medical)	☎100	☎112
Emergencies (Police)	☎101	☎113
International operator assistance (inc. collect & reverse-charge calls)	☎1324	☎0010

Belgium, these will cost you F200 (for 20 units), F1000 (105 units); in Luxembourg F250 (50 units) and F550 (120 units). An increasing number of public phones also accept major credit cards.

Many phone booths have English instructions displayed inside. To make a direct **call to the UK**, dial the code listed in the box above, wait for the tone and then dial the number, omitting the initial 0. To make a direct **call to North America**, dial the code in the box above, wait for the tone and then dial 1 followed by the area code and number. Area **phone codes** for Belgium are given in the *Guide*; you'll notice, however, that Luxembourg is small enough not to need any kind of area coding system. To make a reverse-charge or collect call, phone the operator (they all speak English). Local telephone calls cost a minimum of F10, while F20 is enough to start an international telephone call, but not much more. Discount rates apply (of around 15–20 percent) from 7pm to 8am and on the weekend.

As an alternative, you should be aware that in the big cities there's usually a central **telephone exchange** where you can make your call and settle up afterward. Note also that various telephone companies, including British Telecom, issue phone cards to their subscribers for use abroad: you tap in an account and PIN number on any phone (or extension) and the subsequent call is automatically billed to your home telephone number; for further details, ask your phone company.

MEDIA

In the cities and on the Belgian coast, British newspapers and the more popular English-language magazines are widely available either on the day of publication, or the day after. In Brussels, Antwerp, Bruges, Ghent and Luxembourg City, internationally distributed American newspapers are easy to get hold of too.

The most widely available **American newspapers** in both Belgium and Luxembourg are the *Wall Street Journal, USA Today* and the trusty *International Herald Tribune*. Most **British newspapers** are easy to get hold of, from tabloid through to broadsheet, though often a day later than published, except in the cities, where you can generally get that day's paper. Train station bookstands in the large cities are always a good bet; many broadsheets list their foreign prices on the cover – expect to pay around F70.

As for the **domestic Belgian press**, the major newspapers in Wallonia are the influential, independent *Le Soir*; the right-wing, very Catholic *La Libre Belgique*; and *La Dernière Heure*, which is noted for its sports coverage. In Flanders you'll see the leftish *De Morgen*, traditionally the favourite of socialists and trade unionists; the right-leaning *De Standaard*; and the populist, vaguely liberal *Het Laatste Nieuws*. There's also an **English-language weekly magazine**, the Brussels-based *Bulletin*, catering for the sizable ex-pat community resident in the capital. Its news articles are pretty bland, but the listings section is excellent. It also carries a fair-sized classified section – useful if you've just arrived for an extended stay and are looking for an apartment or even work. In **Luxembourg**, the highest circulation newspaper is the *Luxemburger Wort*.

British radio stations can be picked up in Belgium and Luxembourg on the same frequencies. You'll find BBC Radio 4 on 198kHz long wave, and the World Service on 648kHz long wave, 463m medium wave. As far as **British TV** stations are concerned, BBC1 and BBC2 television channels are on most hotel room TVs in Belgium, and on some in Luxembourg. Many bars and some hotels are geared up for (at least a couple of) the big pan-European **cable and satellite** channels: MTV – 24-hour pop videos, news and (bland) reviews; CNN, which provides 24-hour news coverage and reportage; Sky, with films, news and current affairs; Superchannel, a dreadful mixture of videos, soaps and movies; and Eurosport, up-to-the-minute footage of contests like the European Handball League and roller skating extravaganzas. You can also, in most parts of both countries, pick up all the Dutch and German stations, and often those from France and Italy too.

OPENING HOURS AND PUBLIC HOLIDAYS

Although there's recently been some movement towards greater flexibility, opening hours for shops, businesses and tourist attractions – including museums, churches and castles – remain fairly restrictive. Travel plans can be disrupted on public holidays when most things close down (though not, of course, restaurants, bars and hotels) and public transport is reduced to a limited (Sunday) timetable.

SHOPS AND BUSINESSES

In both Belgium and Luxembourg, the weekend fades painlessly into the week with some shops staying closed till late on Monday morning, even in major cities. Nonetheless, normal **shopping hours** are Monday through Saturday 10am to 6pm or 7pm, with most supermarkets staying open on Fridays till 8pm or 9pm and many smaller places shutting down a little earlier on Saturday. In the big cities, a smattering of convenience stores (*magasins de nuit/avondwinkels*) stay open either all night or until around 1 or 2am every day including Sundays, but generally only die-hard money makers – including some souvenir shops – are open late or on Sunday. At the other extreme, some shops close for the half-day on Wednesday or Thursday afternoon, though this tradition has died out in all but the smaller towns and villages.

Business hours (ie office hours) normally run from Monday to Friday 8.30am or 9am to 5.30 or 6pm. Most towns have a market day, usually midweek (and sometimes Saturday morning), and this is often the liveliest time to visit, particularly when the stalls fill the central square (Grand-Place or Grote Markt).

MUSEUMS

Almost every Belgian town and most of the larger villages has a **museum** of some description, as do many places in Luxembourg. Most museums are open, with variations, Tuesday to Saturday from 9am to 4pm or 5pm, and frequently on Sunday; many of the smaller concerns close for lunch, sometime between noon and 2pm, and Monday is a common closing day. However, travelling outside the April–September period, expect

a lot of the less important and/or less popular museums to be closed – they often don't open until Easter and close down again at the end of September or October. Obviously enough, displays vary enormously, ranging from the extraordinary to the mundane, but you'll find the most interesting museums and art galleries concentrated in Brussels and the Flemish-speaking cities of Antwerp, Bruges and Ghent, which together possess easily the finest collection of early Flemish paintings in the world. All the major museums and galleries in both Belgium and Luxembourg are described in the *Guide*, but the sheer number of municipal and minor museums, many of which are only of specialist or local interest, means we have had to select: the rest you can miss with a clear conscience.

CHURCHES AND MONUMENTS

Exploring the magnificent medieval **churches** of Belgium and, to a lesser extent, Luxembourg is one of the highlights of a visit. Traditionally two of the more devout Catholic countries, both boast massive stone churches whose yawning interiors usually shelter a weight of gaudy decoration, from elaborate altars and chapels to fanciful pulpits, heavy-duty rood screens and intricately carved choir stalls. Many also contain fine treasuries and others have famous paintings on their walls, though the great churches of Flanders have little from before the sixteenth century on account of the vandalism endeavours of the Flemish Protestants. The most important and frequently visited of these churches are normally open Monday to Saturday from around 9am to 5pm, only closing for a couple of hours at lunchtime (often noon–2pm), and are usually open on Sunday too. Many of them have been deconsecrated and are owned by the state. There are, however, problems in getting into many less distinguished but still significant churches, particularly when they are rarely, if ever, opened for worship. In this second category, gaining access really is hit and miss – and even the local tourist office may be unaware of opening times – though, as a general rule of thumb, try around 5 or 6pm when the priest and the occasional worthy might drop by. This is less likely to happen in the winter than in the summer.

Wallonia and Luxembourg are also graced by an abundance of **castles**, ranging from stern medieval strongholds to dignified, stately chateaux, the catch being that most occupy remote – sometimes picturesque – locations that can be difficult to reach without a car. Luxembourg has an especially dense concentration, with some castles almost entirely ruined but worth visiting for the views, others sumptuously restored in period fashion. During the summer, those castles in public ownership are generally open all day every day, but those that remain in private hands characteristically open for just a couple of days (or afternoons) a week. Outside the April to September period you can expect all but the most important places – including those owned by the state – to be closed.

PUBLIC HOLIDAYS

National public holidays – as well as provincial and regional events and dozens of local festivals (see p.48) – are a major feature of the Benelux calendar and one that, sooner or later, you're almost bound to bump into even if it's just as an inconvenience to a well-laid travel plan. In **Belgium**, there are ten national public holidays per year, most of which are keenly observed, though the tourist industry carries on pretty

---

NATIONAL PUBLIC HOLIDAYS IN BELGIUM AND LUXEMBOURG*

New Year's Day
Easter Monday
Labour Day (May 1)
Ascension Day (mid-May)
Whit Monday
Luxembourg National Day (June 23)
Belgium National Day (July 21)
Assumption (mid-August)
All Saints' Day (November 1)
Armistice Day – Belgium only (November 11)
Christmas Day

*Note, that if any one of these falls on a Sunday, the next day becomes a holiday.

---

much regardless. Incidentally, all state-run and many provincial museums adopt Sunday hours on the public holidays listed below, except on Christmas Day and New Year's Day (and often December 26) when they close. Otherwise almost all businesses and shops close, and the public transport system operates a skeleton or Sunday service. With two exceptions, **Luxembourg** has the same national public holidays, and the same general cautions (as to businesses and transport etc) apply.

FESTIVALS

Both Belgium and Luxembourg are big on festivals and annual events – everything from religious processions to carnivals to more contemporary-based jazz binges and the like. These are spread right throughout the year, though, as you might expect, most tourist-orientated events take place in summer. As always, the national tourist offices at home, and tourist offices within Belgium and Luxembourg, can supply details of exact dates, which tend to change from year to year. For further information on some of the more important events themselves, see the appropriate entry in the *Guide*. Spectator sports are a big deal here too, the most popular being football and cycling.

FESTIVALS IN BELGIUM

Belgium's annual carnivals (*carnavals*), held in February and early March, are original, colourful and boisterous in equal measure. One of the most renowned is held in February at Binche, in Hainaut, when there's a procession involving some 1500 extravagantly dressed dancers – or *Gilles*. There are also **carnivals** in Ostend and Aalst, and in Eupen, where the action lasts over the weekend before Shrove Tuesday and culminates with *Rosenmontag* on the Monday – a pageant of costumed groups and floats parading through the town centre. And, most uniquely, there is Stavelot's carnival where the so-called *Blancs Moussis*, townsfolk clothed in white hooded costumes and equipped with long red noses, take to the streets.

Both countries have a number of **religion-inspired festivals**, which are among the most intriguing events you're likely to come across in the whole of the EU. The Brussels *Ommegang* is the best known, a largely secular event these days, held on the first Tuesday and Thursday of July, that nominally commemorates the arrival by boat of a miraculous statue of the Virgin Mary from Antwerp in the fourteenth century. If you want to see anything on the Grand-Place, however, where most of the action is, you have to reserve months in advance, and you might be better off visiting the town of Veurne in Flanders for its annual *Boetprocessie* (Processions of the Penitents), on the last Sunday in July, where cross-bearers dressed in the brown cowls of the Capuchins process through the town – a truly macabre sight. Other religious events include the *Heilig-Bloedprocessie* (Procession of the Holy Blood) held in Bruges on Ascension Day, when the shrine encasing the phial that supposedly contains the blood of Christ brought back from the Holy Land during the Crusades is carried solemnly through the streets.

More secular celebrations include Brussels' *Plantation du Meiboom*, in which a maypole is paraded round the streets before being planted at the corner of rue des Sables and rue du Marais on August 9; Ieper's *Kattestoet* (Festival of the Cats) held every three years on the second Sunday in May, with floats and costumes on a cat theme, and any number of folkloric events and fairs; and the *Gentse Feesten*, a big nine-day festival held in Ghent in late July, which has all sorts of events from music and theatre to fireworks and the circus.

FESTIVALS IN LUXEMBOURG

Carnival is a big thing in Luxembourg too, with most communities having some kind of knees-up. In the lead-up to carnival, all the patisseries sell small doughnut-like cakes, *knudd*, in the form of a knot. On Ash Wednesday, a great straw doll is set alight and then dropped off the Moselle bridge in Remich with much whooping-it-up, while on the first Sunday after carnival bonfires are lit on hilltops all over the country on *Buergsonndeg* (Bonfire Sunday). Mid-Lent Sunday is *Bretzelsonndeg* (Pretzel Sunday), when pretzels are sold in all the duchy's bakeries and there are all manner of processions. At **Easter**, no church bells are rung in the whole of the country between Maundy Thursday and Easter Saturday – folklore asserts that the bells fly off to Rome for confession. Their place is taken by children who walk the streets with rattles calling out the Masses from about 6am. On Easter Monday morning, with the bells "back", the children call on every house to collect their reward – brightly coloured Easter eggs. From the third to fifth Sunday after Easter, the Octave pilgrimage is held, when the duchy's devouter Catholics go on a pilgrimage to Luxembourg City's cathedral, a tradition since 1628.

Every village in Luxembourg has an annual *kermess* (local fair) which will vary in size and length according to the size of the village, ranging from a stand selling fries and hot dogs, to a full-scale funfair. The **Schueberfouer** in Luxembourg City – from the last week in August to the first week in September – is one of the biggest mobile fairs in Europe, held since 1340 and traditionally opened by the royal family. It started life as a sheep market and on the middle Sunday, in the Hammelsmarsch, shepherds bring their sheep to town, accompanied by a band, and work their way round the bars.

Luxembourg's **National Day** is on June 23, and on the previous evening, at 11 pm or so, there is an enormous fireworks display off the Pont Adolphe in the capital and all the bars and cafés are open through most of the night. On June 23 itself there are parades and celebrations across most of the country.

FESTIVAL CALENDAR

FEBRUARY
The five days before and on Shrove Tuesday Eupen *Carnaval*, climaxing with the *Rosenmontag* (Rose Monday) procession and festivities.

Saturday, Sunday, Monday & Shrove Tuesday Malmèdy *Carnaval*.

Sunday, Monday & Shrove Tuesday Binche *Carnaval*.

Sunday, Monday & Shrove Tuesday Aalst *Carnaval*.

MARCH
First Saturday Ostend's *Bal Rat Mort* (Dead Rat Ball) is a lavish, fancy dress carnival ball with a different theme each year.

Early March (first Sunday after Carnival) *Buergsonndeg* or "Bonfire Sunday" all over Luxembourg.

Refreshment Sunday (4th Sunday in Lent) Stavelot *Carnaval* with the famous parade of the "Blancs Moussis".

Mid-Lent Sunday *Bretzelsonndeg* (Pretzel Sunday) features – apart from pretzels – markets, processions and displays of folk art in the Luxembourg Moselle towns.

APRIL
April–September *Het Festival van Vlaanderen* (Flanders' Festival) offers an extensive programme of classical concerts and performances of ancient – mainly medieval – music in the major Flemish-speaking towns. Events often take place in fine medieval halls and churches.

Late April *Bloesemfeesten* (Blossom festival). Blessing of the blossoms in Sint Truiden, at the heart of the Haspengouw fruit-growing region.

MAY
From the third to fifth Sunday after Easter *Octave* pilgrimage in Luxembourg, culminating in a procession through the capital to the cathedral.

Second Sunday Every three years, Ieper holds a one-day *Kattestoet* (Festival of the Cats) with parades and parties celebrating all things feline.

Sunday before Ascension Day *Hanswijkprocessie* (Procession of our Lady of Hanswijck). Large and ancient religious procession held in the centre of Mechelen and focusing on the veneration of the Virgin Mary.

Mid-May *Heilig-Bloedprocessie* (Procession of the Holy Blood). Held in Bruges on Ascension Day. This is one of the oldest religious processions in Belgium, with hundreds of participants enacting the arrival of the Holy Blood in Bruges.

Whit Tuesday In Echternach, Luxembourg, the *Sprangprozessioun* is an ancient dancing procession commemorating the eighth-century English missionary St Willibrord.

Late May or early June Arlon's two-day *Maitrank* festival celebrates the eponymous drink, a traditional and punchy mixture of Moselle wine and a plant of the lily family.

Trinity Sunday (late May or early June) Ronse *Fiertel* pilgrimage. The reliquary of St Hermes is carried along a 32.6km route through the hills around Ronse.

JUNE
Second Saturday & Sunday *Les journées des quatre cortèges* (Days of the Four Processions) in Tournai. Two-day lively and popular carnival mixing modern and traditional themes and parades. Features include fifteen folkloric giants, representing historic figures with local connections, such as Louis XIV and the Merovingian king Childeric, flower-decked floats and military bands.

June 23 Luxembourg National Day. Fireworks in the capital and celebrations all over the Grand Duchy.

Late June to mid-Sept Knokke-Heist *Internationaal Cartoonfestival*. Established in the 1960s, the International Cartoon Festival showcases several hundred cartoons selected from a world-class and worldwide entry.

JULY
First Tuesday & Thursday Brussels *Ommegang* (literally "Doing the rounds"). Colourful spectacle-cum-parade celebrating the city and its history; focused on the Grand-Place.

Early July *Wereldfestival van Folklore*. Massive, week-long world folk music and dance festival in Schoten, in the province of Antwerp.

Early July *Rock Torhout-Werchter*. Four-day rock festival, two days each in Torhout (West Flanders) and Werchter (Brabant). One of the largest open-air festivals of its type in Europe. Lots of big names.

Early to mid-July The *Cactusfestival*, held in Bruges, is a three-day, open-air rock festival with music of many types – from bluegrass to blues, reggae to pop.

Late July *Gentse Feesten*, Ghent's main (and well-lubricated) shindig lasts for nine days and features everything from theatre, classical and rock music performances through to dances and fireworks.

continued opposite

FESTIVAL CALENDAR

Last Sunday in July *Boetprocessie* (Penitents' Procession). Morbid and fascinating in equal measure, the procession is made up of around 300 participants, dressed in the brown cowls of the Capuchins and dragging heavy crosses behind them.

AUGUST

Aug 9 Brussels *Plantation du Meiboom*, in which an uprooted tree is paraded round the streets and ceremoniously planted. Originally a celebration of a medieval victory over Leuven, it's now an excuse for a general knees-up.

Mid-Aug Leuven's lively *Marktrock* ("Market Square Rock") is a three-day event showcasing local rock groups with the occasional foreign artist thrown in too.

Late Aug Bruges' *Praalstoet van de Gouden Boom* (Pageant of the Golden Tree). Held every five years, this two-day festival with its parades and processions commemorates the fifteenth-century marriage of Charles the Bold to Margaret of York.

Fourth Sunday Ath's *Ducasse*, dating back to the thirteenth century, focuses on an exuberant parade in which giant figures – or goliaths – represent historical and folkloric characters.

Lat Thursday in the month Dendermonde's *Traditionele Reuzenommegang* has several hundred locals in fancy dress jigging away around three giants.

Last Sunday Blankenberge *Grote Bloemencorso*. Grand parade of floral floats wrapping up the resort's summer season.

End Aug Hasselt's one-day *Pukkelpop* is designed to showcase up-and-coming rock and pop talent of the indie kind.

End Aug to early Sept Luxembourg *Schoeberfouer*, a former shepherds' market that is now the capital's largest funfair.

Aug–Oct Wine festivals in Luxembourg's Moselle Valley.

SEPTEMBER

Second weekend Luxembourg, *Grevenmacher*, wine and grape festival, with processions, wine-tasting and fireworks.

Second Sunday Mechelen *Bloemen en Groentencorso*, horticultural and floral pageant, followed by a bell-throwing competition in the Grote Markt.

Second Sunday Tournai *Grande Procession Historique*. Part secular shindig in historic costume, part religious ceremony involving the carrying of the

reliquary of St Eleuthère through the streets, this one-day event dates back to the calling of the saint's assistance against a visitation of the plague in 1090.

OCTOBER

First Sunday in Oct Nivelles *Tour de Sainte Gertrude*. Beginning in the centre of town, this religious procession escorts the reliquary of Sainte Gertrude on a circular, 12km-long route out through the surrounding countryside. Townsfolk dressed in historic gear and several goliaths join the last leg of the procession when the jollity gets going. (Sometimes held at the end of September.)

Early to Mid-Oct Ghent *Internationaal Filmfestival*. Quality twelve-day international film festival.

Mid- to late-October Hasselt *Hasseltse Jeneverfeesten*, a two-day celebration of jenever, a gin-like spirit produced in this part of Belgium. It's all a bit silly, but good fun all the same from the "fastest-running waiter" competition to the *borrelmanneke* (little jenever man) who toddles round town dispensing free shots of the stuff.

NOVEMBER

Sunday after All Saints' Day The basilica at Scherpenheuvel, near Diest, is the site of Belgium's most important annual pilgrimage – the *Kaarskensprocessie* – in honour of the Virgin Mary. The main event is a candlelight procession which takes place in the afternoon and is accompanied by the offering of ex voto, etc.

Nov 10 Vianden Luxembourg *Miertchen* or "St Martin's Fire" – bonfires celebrating the end of the harvest and formerly the payment of the levy to the feudal lord.

Nov 11 Eupen *Procession de St Martin* (St Martin's Procession) through the town, with Roman legionaries and children bearing candles, finishing with a bonfire.

DECEMBER

First Sunday in Dec Bouillon *Fête de Saint Eloi* begins with an early morning procession in which stretcher-loads of cakes are carried round town. Mass is then celebrated and cakes are given out.

Dec 6 Arrival of St Nicholas, celebrated by processions and the giving of sweets to children right across Belgium and Luxembourg. In Luxembourg, he's accompanied by "Père Fouettard" (the bogey-man) dressed in black and carrying a whip to punish naughty children.

TROUBLE, THE POLICE AND SEXUAL HARASSMENT

There's little reason why you should ever come into contact with the police forces of either Belgium or Luxembourg – especially as this is an area of Europe that's relatively free of street crime. Even in Brussels and the larger cities you shouldn't have problems, though it's obviously advisable to be on your guard against petty theft. As far as personal safety goes, it's generally possible to walk around the larger cities without fear of harassment or assault, but Antwerp and Brussels do have their shady areas and everywhere it's better to err on the side of caution late at night, when – for instance – badly lit or empty streets should be avoided.

AVOIDING TROUBLE

Almost all the problems tourists encounter in Belgium and Luxembourg are to do with **petty crime** – pickpocketing and bag-snatching – rather than more serious physical confrontations, so it's as well to be on your guard and know where your possessions are at all times. Sensible **precautions** include: carrying bags slung across your neck and not over your shoulder; not carrying anything in pockets that are easy to dip into; having photocopies of your passport, airline ticket and driving licence; leaving passports and tickets in the hotel safe; and noting down travellers' cheque and credit-card numbers. When you're looking for a **hotel room**, never leave your bags unattended. If you have a car, don't leave anything in view when you park. Vehicle theft is still fairly uncommon, but luggage and valuables left in cars do make a tempting target. If you're on a **bicycle**, make sure it is well locked up – bike theft and resale is a big deal in most cities. At **night**, you'd be well advised to avoid walking round the tougher, rougher parts of any of the larger cities, particularly Antwerp (by the river to the north of the centre) and Brussels (round Gare du Midi). Also, as general precautions, avoid unlit streets, don't go out brimming with valuables, and try not to appear hopelessly lost – doubly so if you're travelling alone. Using public transport, even late at night, isn't usually a problem, but if in doubt – take a taxi.

Thieves often work in pairs and, although theft is far from rife, you should be aware of certain **ploys**, such as: the "helpful" person pointing out "birdshit" (actually shaving cream or similar) on your coat, while someone else relieves you of your money; the card or paper you're invited to read on the street to distract your attention; the move by someone in a café for your drink with one hand while the other is in your bag as you react to save your drink; and if you're in a crowd of tourists, watch out for people moving in unusually close.

WHAT TO DO IF YOU'RE ROBBED

If you're robbed, you need to go to the police to report it, not least because your insurance company will require a police report, so remember to make a note of the report number – or, better still, ask for a copy of the statement itself. Don't expect a great deal of concern if your loss is relatively small – and don't be surprised if the process of completing forms and formalities takes ages. In the unlikely event that you're **mugged** or otherwise threatened, never resist, and try to reduce your contact with the robber to a minimum. Either just hand over what's wanted, or throw money in one direction and take off in the other. Afterwards, go straight to the police, who will be much more sympathetic and helpful on these occasions – especially in tourist centres like Bruges. Many officers in Belgium's Flemish-speaking regions, Brussels and Luxembourg City speak English, but in Wallonia and rural Luxembourg you'll mostly be struggling to make yourself understood without at least a modicum of French.

THE POLICE

In Belgium, there are two basic types of police: the *Gendarmerie Nationale* (Flemish: *Rijkswacht*) and the *Police* (*Politie*). The former, who wear blue uniforms with red stripes on their trousers, patrol the motorways and deal with major crime; the latter, in their dark blue uniforms, cover everything else and many of them, especially in tourist centres like Bruges, speak English. Many members of Luxembourg's *Police* force speak English too. All the police are armed. If you do need to approach the police, you can expect a sympathetic hearing – especially if you're reporting a serious crime – but of course there are no guarantees.

MINOR OFFENCES

You ought to be aware of a couple of **offences** that you might commit unwittingly. In theory you're supposed to carry some kind of official identification and a minimum of F500 at all times, and the police can stop you in the streets and demand to see them. If you can't produce identification or otherwise prove your identity, you can be held at a police station even if this is your only "crime". Citizens of Luxembourg and Belgium carry identity cards (*carte d'identité*/*identiteitskaart*) as do most EU nationals, but for others – like the British – a passport will suffice. In practice, however, it's extremely unlikely that you'll be stopped unless there's a particular reason – for example involvement in a road accident.

In Belgium and Luxembourg the laws on the possession of illegal substances (ie **drugs**) are strict, though their use is often very visible in the big cities. Travellers arriving from Holland, where it is effectively legal to possess small amounts of cannabis for personal use, are sometimes blissfully unaware of the differences between the Benelux countries in this regard, which can mean a major hassle. If you're carrying dope, you'd be well advised to leave it at the Dutch border.

Should you be **arrested** on any charge, you have the right to contact your **consulate** – see "Listings" at the end of the big-city accounts in the *Guide* for local addresses. Unfortunately, consular

EMERGENCY TELEPHONE NUMBERS

BELGIUM
Ambulance/fire brigade ☎100
Police ☎101

LUXEMBOURG
Ambulance/fire brigade ☎112
Police ☎113

officials are notoriously reluctant to get involved, though most are required to assist you to some degree if you have your passport stolen or lose all your money. If you've been detained for a drugs offence, don't expect any sympathy or help.

SEXUAL HARASSMENT

In the normal course of events, women travellers are unlikely to feel threatened and intimidated or attract unwanted attention in almost any part of Belgium and Luxembourg. The main exception is in the seedier areas of the big cities, where the atmosphere may feel frightening especially late at night – but with common sense and circumspection you shouldn't have anything to worry about. In terms of nightclubs and bars, the men who hang around them pose no greater or lesser threat than similar operators at home, though the language barrier (where it exists) makes it harder to know who to trust.

GAY AND LESBIAN LIFE

Gay life in Belgium and Luxembourg isn't nearly so upfront as in nearby Holland. Brussels and Antwerp are the main centres, but both sit very firmly in Amsterdam's shadow – and most gay travellers overlook what is by and large a far less "international" scene.

That said, there are gay bars and clubs in almost every major town, gay switchboards and/or centres in some of the larger cities, and several periodicals catering for the gay community. The most informative of these is the monthly French-language magazine *Tels Quels*, which includes political reports and news of up-and-coming events – and whose premises, at rue du

Marché au Charbon 81, 1000 Brussels (☎ & fax 02/512 45 87), have a café-cum-meeting point with a bar open daily from 5pm to 2am. *Tels Quels* provides a base for many of the capital's lesbian and gay groups and houses a lesbian and gay library (Mon & Wed 6–8pm, Fri 6–9pm). You can also get your free map of gay Brussels here. If your main interest is in the bar and club scene, your best bet is to get a copy of *GayMag*, which gives details of what happens and where, with the focus on the male gay scene.

The gay scene is left largely unmolested by the rest of society, a pragmatic tolerance also reflected in the openly gay politicians in senior governmental posts. However, there remains a widespread perception in both countries that gayness is "abnormal". The legal age of consent for gay men is 16 in Belgium, 18 in Luxembourg.

By comparison, the **lesbian** scene is smaller, harder to find and more subdued than the gay one. It takes time for foreign visitors to find out what's happening, though at least in Brussels and Antwerp it's easy enough to locate those (very rare) café-bars specifically catering for lesbians.

WOMEN

By western European standards, Belgium has been slow off the mark when it comes to women's issues: abortion was only legalized in 1990 – and even then King Baudouin felt obliged to abdicate for the day while the law was ratified – and it wasn't until the mid-1990s that, for instance, sexual harassment and police treatment of raped women became serious items on the political agenda. On the other hand, Belgium's social legislation – from maternity leave arrangements to childcare facilities – has long conformed with best EU practice.

The tardiness of Belgian society (or its governing class) to address women's issues has been variously attributed to the country's innate conservatism, the influence of the Catholic Church and, perhaps most perceptively, to the intensity of the linguistic/cultural dispute (between the Walloons and the Flemish) which has consumed so much of the country's energy since the 1960s. But now at least (or at last) there are initiatives to remedy many specific areas of concern. Perhaps most encouraging of all, *Amazone*, rue du Méridien 10, 1210 Brussels (☎02/229 38 00, fax 229 38 01; *www.amazone/be*), was opened in 1995 as a womens' centre that houses under one roof the headquarters of many different women's groups from both the French- and Flemish-speaking communities. The *Amazone* centre is primarily a conference and meeting centre, and its restaurant, complete with it's original nineteenth-century décor, is open to all (men and women) for lunches.

DIRECTORY

ADDRESSES In the French-speaking areas of Belgium and in Luxembourg, addresses are usually written to a standard format with the first line beginning with the category of the street or thoroughfare (rue, boulevard etc), followed by the name and then the number; the second line gives the area – or zip – code, followed by the town or area. Common abbrevations include *bld* or *bd* for boulevard, *av* for avenue, *pl* for place (square) and *ch* for chaussée. An exception is the hyphenated *Grand-Place* (main square). In the Flemish-speaking areas, the first line gives the name of the street which is followed by (and joined to) its category – hence *Krakeelplein* is Krakeel square, *Krakeelstraat* is Krakeel street – and then comes the number; the second line gives the area – or zip – code followed by the town or area.

Consequently, Flemish abbreviations occur at the end of words: thus *Hofstr* for Hofstraat. An exception is *Grote Markt* (main square), which is not abbreviated. Common categories include *plein* for square, *plaats* for place, *laan* or *weg* for avenue, *kaai* for quay, and *straat* for street. In bilingual Brussels, all signs give both the French and Flemish versions. In many cases, this is fairly straightforward as they are either the same or similar, but sometimes it's extremely confusing, most notoriously in the name of one of the three principal train stations – in French, *Bruxelles-Midi*; in Flemish *Brussel-Zuid*.

CHILDREN Most hotels welcome children and many offer rooms with three or four beds – or will readily add an extra foldaway bed or cot. Certain hotels, particularly the better ones on the coast, offer a babysitting service, and some resorts organize a municipal service of registered babysitters too. Belgium has many attractions designed with children in mind – amusement parks and the like – and all the big cities have indoor swimming pools. Restaurants and cafés readily accept children, but they expect them to be well behaved – shouting and running around is definitely unacceptable. Disposable nappies and other basic supplies are widely available.

ELECTRICITY The current is 220 volts AC, with standard European-style two-pin plugs. Brits will need an adaptor to connect their appliances, North Americans both an adaptor and a transformer.

LEFT LUGGAGE Major train stations have luggage offices (normally open daily 6am–midnight) and many smaller stations have them too, though opening hours are more restricted (often Mon–Fri 9am–5pm). Most stations also have coin-operated lockers.

SMOKING Smoking is forbidden in many public places from theatres through to town halls. Most train compartments are no-smoking and so are the confined spaces of train stations, but you can light up on open-air platforms. No-smoking hotel rooms are a rarity (though they are catching on at the top end of the market) and remarkably few restaurants have no-smoking areas.

TIME One hour ahead of Britain; normally six hours ahead of Eastern Standard Time, nine hours ahead of Pacific Standard Time.

TIPPING There's no necessity to tip, but a ten to fifteen percent tip is expected by taxi drivers and anticipated by many restaurant waiters.

TOILETS Public toilets remain comparatively rare, but many cafés and bars run what amounts to an ablutionary side-line with (mostly middle-aged women) keeping the toilets scrupulously clean and charging users just F10–20. You'll spot the plate for the money as you enter.

PART TWO

THE

GUIDE

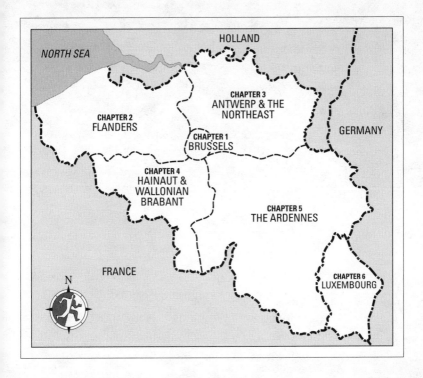

NORTH SEA

HOLLAND

CHAPTER 3
ANTWERP & THE
NORTHEAST

CHAPTER 2
FLANDERS

CHAPTER 1
BRUSSELS

GERMANY

CHAPTER 4
HAINAUT &
WALLONIAN
BRABANT

CHAPTER 5
THE ARDENNES

FRANCE

CHAPTER 6
LUXEMBOURG

N

CHAPTER ONE

BRUSSELS

Wherever else you go in Belgium, allow at least a little time for **BRUSSELS**, which is by any standard one of Europe's premier cities. Certainly, don't let Brussels' reputation as a dull, faceless centre of EU bureaucracy deter you: in postwar years, the city has become a thriving, cosmopolitan metropolis, a vibrant and fascinating place, with top-flight architecture and museums, not to mention a well-preserved late seventeenth-century centre, a superb restaurant scene and an energetic nightlife. Moreover, most of the key attractions are crowded into a centre that is small enough to be absorbed over a few long days, its boundaries largely defined by a ring of boulevards – the "**petit ring**".

First-time visitors to Brussels are often surprised by the raw vitality of this **city centre**. It's not neat and tidy, and many of the old tenement houses are shabby and ill-used, but there's a buzz about the place that's hard to resist. The city centre is itself divided into two main areas. The larger westerly portion comprises the **Lower Town**, fanning out from the marvellous **Grand-Place**, with its exquisite guildhouses and town hall, while up above to the east lies the much smaller **Upper Town**, home to the finest art collection in the country in the Musées Royaux des Beaux Arts. Broadly speaking, the boundary between the two zones follows the busy boulevard which swings through the centre under several names – Berlaimont, L'Impératrice and L'Empereur.

Since the eleventh century, monarchs, aristocrats and the well-heeled have lived in the Upper Town, keeping a beady eye on the workers and shopkeepers below – a state of affairs which is still in part true. This fundamental class division, so obvious in the layout of the centre, has in recent decades been further complicated by discord between Belgium's two main linguistic groups, the Walloons (the French-speakers) and the Flemish (basically Dutch-speakers). As a cumbersome compromise, the city is Belgium's only officially **bilingual region** and by law all road signs, street names and virtually all published information must be in both languages.

To add to these communal complexities, the Walloons and the Flemish now share their city with many other groups, with EU civil servants, diplomats, and immigrants from North and Central Africa, Turkey, and the Mediterranean currently constituting a quarter of the population. Each of these communities tends to live a very separate, distinct existence and there's a sharp contrast between, say, the internationalism of the centre and EU zone, to the east of the city centre – beyond the "petit ring" – and the sharp trendiness of the district round Ste Catherine or Turkish St Josse. The city's compact nature heightens the contrasts: in five minutes you can walk from a designer shopping mall into an African bazaar, or from a depressed slum quarter to a resplendent square of antique shops and exclusive cafés. This is something which only increases the city's allure, not least in the number and variety of affordable ethnic **restaurants**. But, even without these, Brussels would still be a

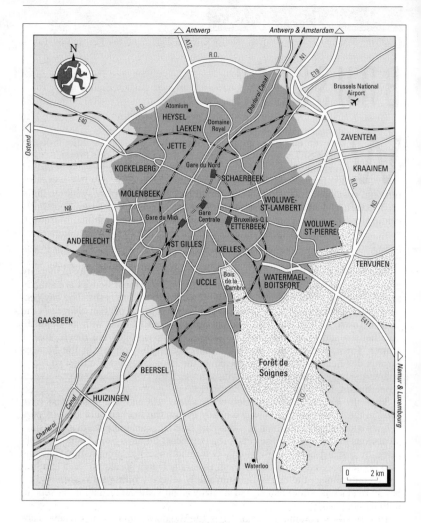

wonderful place to eat: its gastronomic reputation rivals that of Paris, and though traditional meals in homegrown restaurants are rarely cheap, there is great-value food to be had in many of the **bars**. The bars themselves can be sumptuous, basic, traditional or very fashionable – and one of the city's real delights.

The city's **specialist shops** are another pleasure. Everyone knows about Belgian chocolates, but here in the capital there are also huge, sprawling markets, contemporary art galleries, and establishments devoted to anything from comic books to costume jewellery and clubland fashion. Belgium is such a small country, and the rail network so fast and efficient, that Brussels also makes the perfect base for a wide range of day-trips. An obvious target is the battlefield of **Waterloo**, one of the region's most visited attractions.

LANGUAGE

In Brussels, the **languages** of the French- and Flemish-speaking communities have parity. This means that every instance of the written word, from road signs to the Yellow Pages, has to appear in both languages. For simplicity we've used the French version of street names, sights, etc throughout this chapter.

Some history

Brussels takes its name from Broekzele, or "village of the marsh", the community which grew up beside the wide and shallow River Senne in the sixth century allegedly around a chapel built here by St Géry. A tiny and insignificant part of Charlemagne's empire at the end of the eighth century, it was subsequently inherited by the dukes of **Lower Lorraine** (or Lotharingia – roughly Wallonia and northeast France), who constructed a fortress here in 979. Protected, the village benefited from its position on the trade route between Cologne and the burgeoning towns of Bruges and Ghent to become a significant trading centre in its own right. The surrounding marshes were drained to allow for further expansion, and in 1229 the city was granted its first charter by the dukes of Brabant, the new feudal overlords who controlled things here, on and off, for around two hundred years. In the early fifteenth century, marriage merged the interests of the Duchy of Brabant with that of Burgundy, whose territories passed to the **Habsburgs** in 1482, when Mary, the last of the Burgundian line, died to be succeeded by her husband, the Holy Roman Emperor Maximilian I.

The first Habsburg rulers had close ties with Brussels, and the **Emperor Charles V** (1519–1555) ran his vast kingdom from the city for over a decade, making it wealthy and politically important in equal measure. By contrast, his successor **Philip II** lived in Spain and ruled through a governor (for the whole of the Low Countries) resident in Brussels. It could have been a perfectly reasonable arrangement, but Philip's fanatical Catholicism soon unpicked the equlibrium of Charles's reign. He imposed a series of anti-Protestant edicts which provoked extensive rioting across the Low Countries, and in response he dispatched a hardline reactionary, the Duke of Alva, to Brussels with an army of 10,000 men. Alva quickly restored order and then, with the help of the Inquisition, set about the rioters with gusto, his Commission of Civil Unrest soon nicknamed the **"Council of Blood"** after its habit of executing those it examined. Goaded into rebellion by Alva's brutality, Brussels, along with much of the Low Countries, exploded in revolt, and, in 1577, the one-time protégé of the Habsburgs, William the Silent, made a triumphant entry into the city and installed a Calvinist government. Protestant control lasted for just eight years, before Philip's armies recaptured the city. The Protestants left in their hundreds and the economy slumped, though complete catastrophe was averted by the conspicuous consumption of the (Brussels-based) Habsburg elite, whose high spending kept hundreds of workers in employment. Brussels also benefited from the digging of the Willebroek Canal, which linked Brussels to the sea for the first time in its history.

By the 1580s, the Habsburgs had lost control of the northern part of the Low Countries (now the Netherlands) and Brussels was confirmed as the capital of the remainder, the **Spanish Netherlands** (broadly modern Belgium). Brussels prospered more than the rest of the country, but it was always prey to the dynastic squabbling between France and Spain. In 1695, **Louis XIV** bombarded Brussels for

The Brussels area telephone code is ☎02.

36 hours merely to teach his rivals a lesson, though the guilds rapidly rebuilt their devastated city – and it's this version of the Grand-Place that survives today. In 1700 Charles II, the last of the Spanish Habsburgs, died without issue. The ensuing **War of the Spanish Succession** dragged on for over a decade, but eventually the Spanish Netherlands were passed to the Austrian Habsburgs, who ruled – as had their predecessors – through a governor based in Brussels. It was during this period as capital of the **Austrian Netherlands** (1713–1794) that most of the monumental buildings of the Upper Town were constructed and the Neoclassical avenues and boulevards were laid out – grand extravagance in the context of an increasingly industrialized city crammed with a desperately poor working class.

The **French Revolutionary army** brushed the Austrians aside at the Battle of Fleurus in 1794 and the Austrian Netherlands became a *département* of France until, under the terms of the Congress of Vienna which followed the defeat of Napoleon, the great powers absorbed the country in the new **Kingdom of the Netherlands**, ruled by the Dutch King William I. Brussels took turns with The Hague as the capital, but the experiment was short-lived and in 1830 a Brussels-led rebellion removed the Dutch and led to the creation of an independent Belgian state with Brussels as the capital.

The nineteenth century was a period of modernization and expansion, during which the city achieved all the attributes of a modern European capital under the guidance of Burgomaster Anspach and **King Léopold II**. New boulevards were built; the free university was founded; the Senne – which by then had become an open sewer – was covered over in the city centre; many slum areas were cleared; and a series of grand buildings were erected. The whole enterprise culminated in the golden jubilee exhibition celebrating the founding of the Belgian state in the newly inaugurated Parc de Cinquantenaire.

Since the German occupation of Belgium in World War II, the modernization of Brussels has proceeded inexorably, with many major development projects – not least the new métro system – refashioning the city and reflecting its elevated status as the headquarters of both NATO and the EU.

Arrival

Brussels is the major air gateway for Belgium; it's on the main routes heading inland from the Channel ports via the Flemish towns; trains arrive here direct from London via the Channel Tunnel; and, in addition, it's a convenient stop on the railway line between France and Holland. Brussels itself has an excellent public transport system which puts the main **points of arrival** – its airport, train and bus stations – within easy reach of the city centre, where there are two **tourist offices**, one for the city, the other for the rest of the country.

By air

Arriving by air, you'll land at Brussels' **international airport** in Zaventem, 13km northeast of the city centre. There's a **tourist information** desk in the arrivals hall (daily 6.30am–9.30pm) and they have a reasonable range of information on

Brussels and its surroundings. They can also make hotel reservations, a service that is provided free – you just pay a percentage of the room rate as a deposit and this is then subtracted from your final hotel bill. There are several bureaux de change and ATMs in the arrivals hall too.

From the airport, trains run every twenty minutes to the city's main stations. The journey-time to Bruxelles-Centrale is about twenty minutes; the cost is F90 one-way, and tickets can be bought from the ticket office in the train station that is part of the airport complex. You can also pay the ticket inspector on the train, but there's a small surcharge. Trains run from around 5.30am until midnight, after that you'll need to take a **taxi** into the city centre – reckon on paying around F1400 for the trip. There's an hourly **bus** service from the airport complex through the city's northeastern suburbs to the Gare du Nord; the journey takes about 45 minutes – and much longer during rush hour.

By train

Brussels has three main **train stations** – Bruxelles-Centrale, Bruxelles-Nord and Bruxelles-Midi – each only a few minutes apart by public transport. Almost all **domestic** trains stop at all three but the majority of **international** services only stop at Bruxelles-Midi, including Eurostar trains from London and Thalys express trains from Amsterdam, Paris, Cologne and Aachen.

Bruxelles-Centrale is, as its name suggests, the most central of the stations, a five-minute walk from the Grand-Place; **Bruxelles-Nord** lies amongst the bristling tower blocks of the business area just north of the main ring road; and **Bruxelles-Midi** is located in a depressed area to the south of the city centre. Note that on bus timetables and on maps of the city transit system, Bruxelles-Nord appears as "Gare du Nord", Bruxelles-Centrale as "Gare Centrale" and Bruxelles-Midi as "Gare du Midi". The former name stands for the mainline train station while the latter usually signifies the métro stop.

Bruxelles-Midi and Bruxelles-Nord are linked by **métro** with several services (principally #23 and #55) shuttling underneath the city centre between the two stations. To reach the Grand-Place from either Bruxelles-Nord or Bruxelles-Midi, simply take the métro (#23 and #55) to the **Métro Bourse** station, and it's a couple of minutes' walk from there. Bruxelles-Centrale is on the **métro** line #1. It's easily reached from the other two train stations by simply jumping on the next available mainline train. If you arrive late at night, it's best to take a taxi to your hotel or hostel – and you should certainly avoid the streets around Bruxelles-Midi.

By bus

Most **international bus** services to Brussels, including those from Britain, are operated by Eurolines, whose terminal is in the Bruxelles-Nord station complex. Belgium's comprehensive rail network means that it's unlikely that you'll arrive in the city by long-distance domestic bus, but if you do, Bruxelles-Nord is the main terminal for these services too.

Information

Aside from the office at the airport, there are two **tourist information offices** in Brussels, both located right in the centre of town. The main one is the **TIB** (Office de Tourisme et d'Information de Bruxelles), in the Hôtel de Ville on the Grand-Place (Jan–April Mon–Sat 9am–6pm; May–Sept daily 9am–6pm; Oct–Dec Mon–Sat 9am–6pm, Sun 10am–2pm; ☎513 89 40, fax 514 45 38), which handles information on the city only. It has a wide range of handouts, including free public transport and city maps, and sells a variety of general- and specialist-interests guides, the most useful of which is the detailed *All Brussels Guide and Map* (F60). In addition, the TIB issues a list of all the city's hotels and makes hotel **reservations** for free – the deposit is subtracted from your final hotel bill. It can help with public transport too: the TIB sells the 24-hour *carte d'un jour* pass (see p.64) and the 24-hour Tourist Passport (F300), which entitles bearers to free use of the city's public transport network and provides substantial discounts at a variety of sights. The TIB also operates a theatre and concert booking service; you can make reservations in person or via a special hotline (☎0800/21 2 21).

If you need a large map buy the *Girault Gilbert* map (F200), which comes complete with an index. It's available at the TIB and most city centre paper and bookshops.

The **tourism centre** (Maison du Tourisme), nearby at rue Marché aux Herbes 63 (daily: April, May & Oct 9am–6pm; June–Sept 9am–7pm; Nov–March Mon–Sat 9am–6pm, Sun 1–5pm; ☎504 03 90, fax 02 70), provides information on the whole of Belgium. They do stock a few brochures on Brussels, but this is not their main concern – they leave the city largely to the TIB. They also operate a hotel room reservation service, but again it's for the rest of Belgium, not Brussels.

The weekly *Bulletin* (F90), the city's main English-language magazine, contains an excellent **entertainment listings** section, detailing what's on and where. The magazine is on sale at most downtown newsagents. The TIB also provides the *Bulletin*'s listings section – *What's On* – for free. *Le Soir*'s Wednesday supplement is useful as well.

City transport

The easiest way to get around the city centre, within the petit ring, is to **walk**. To get from one side of the centre to the other, or to reach some of the more widely dispersed attractions, you will, however, need to use **public transport**. Operated by STIB (information line ☎515 20 00), the urban system runs on an integrated mixture of bus, tram, underground tram (prémétro) and métro lines that covers the city comprehensively. It's a user-friendly network, with every métro station carrying métro system diagrams and with timetables posted at most bus and tram stops.

Métro and trams

The **métro** system consists of two underground train lines – lines #1 and #2. Line #1 runs west–east through the centre, and splits into two branches (#1A and #1B) at either end to serve the city's suburbs. Line #2 circles the centre, its route roughly following that of the petit ring up above. Brussels also has a substantial **tram** system serving the city centre and the suburbs. These trams are at their speediest when they go underground to form what is sometimes called the **prémétro**, that part of the system which runs underneath the heart of the city

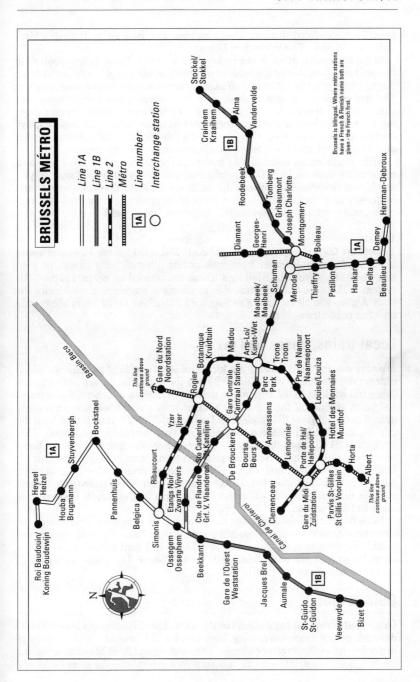

BRUSSELS MÉTRO

Line 1A
Line 1B
Line 2
Métro
1A Line number
○ Interchange station

Brussels is bilingual. Where metro stations have a French & Flemish name both are given – the French name first.

from Bruxelles-Nord, through de Brouckère and Bourse, to Bruxelles-Midi, Porte de Hal and on underneath St Gilles.

At the **beginning of each journey**, you're trusted to stamp tickets yourself in the machines provided on the concourse. After that, the ticket is valid for an hour, during which you can get on and off as many trams, métros and buses as you like. The system can seem open to abuse, as ticket controls at the métro stations are almost non-existent and you can get on at the back of any tram without ever showing a ticket. But bear in mind that there are roving inspectors who impose heavy on-the-spot fines for anyone caught without a valid ticket. Finally, remember that doors on métros, trams and buses mostly have to be opened manually.

STIB **route maps** are available free from the tourist office and from most major métro stations. The STIB has information kiosks at Porte de Namur, Rogier and Midi métro stations. Amongst the multitude of routes, times of operation and frequency vary considerably, but key parts of the system operate from 6am until midnight. Lone travellers should avoid the métro late at night.

Tickets
Tickets are fairly cheap. A single ticket costs F50, a strip of five F240, and a strip of ten F330, available either from tram or bus drivers, métro kiosks, or from newsagents displaying the STIB sign. These can be used on any part of the STIB system. Tickets can also be obtained from automatic machines at most métro stations. A go-as-you-please *carte d'un jour*, for F130, allows for 24 hours of city-wide travel on public transport.

Local trains, buses and taxis

In addition to the STIB network are **local trains**, run by Belgian Railways, which connect different parts of the inner city and the outskirts, though unless you're living and working in the city, you're unlikely to need to use them. These trains shuttle in and out of the city's four smaller train stations and are particularly geared to the needs of EU employees. De Lijn (☎526 28 28) runs **buses** from the city to the Flemish-speaking communities that surround the capital; TEC (☎010/230 53 53) does the same to the French-speaking areas. Most of these buses run from Gare du Nord complex and many from place Rouppe (just off boulevard Lemonnier). Both companies also run services to other Belgian cities, but they can take up to four times longer than the train. There is also a limited and sporadic **night bus** service – often just one bus operating on a route between midnight and around 3am.

Taxis don't cruise the streets but can be picked up at stands spread around the city – notably on Bourse, de Brouckère and Porte de Namur, at train stations and outside the smarter hotels. The minimum fare is F95 during the day and F170 at night. If you can't find one, phone Taxis Verts (☎349 49 49), Taxis Orange (☎513 62 00), or Autolux (☎411 12 21).

Guided tours

Organized tours are big business in Brussels. The TIB offers no fewer than 33 different guided tours, everything from a quick stroll round the city centre to themed visits – following, for example, in the footsteps of René Magritte or visiting the pick of the city's Art Nouveau buildings. As a general rule the more exotic and unusual tours need to be booked well ahead of time with the TIB normally requiring at least two weeks' advance notice. The TIB also arrange **walking tours** of the Grand-Place and its surroundings, which you can join without reserving (March–Sept 1 Mon–Sat; times vary; F350 per person).

In addition, Brussels has around a dozen companies offering guided tours, many of which are run in conjunction with the TIB. For a **bus tour**, book with De Boeck, rue de la Colline 8 (☎513 77 44), who operate a wide range of excursions including a three-hour breathless zip round the city and its major sights for F780 (students F600). Alternatively, Chatterbus, rue des Thuyas 12 (☎673 18 35), run well-regarded **walking and public transport tours** (mid-June to mid-Sept 1 daily; times vary). These city tours last about three hours and cost F300. Chatterbus supplements them with once- or twice-weekly (French-only) excursions devoted to a particular theme, for example Léopold II's Brussels or Belgian beers. Another recommendation is ARAU (Atelier de Recherche et d'Action Urbaines), boulevard Adolphe Max 55 (☎219 33 45), a heritage action group which provides tours exploring the city's architectural heritage with particular emphasis on Art Nouveau. Their three-hour bus tours are run once weekly at the weekend (times vary), from March through to December, and cost F600 each – double-check the tour you want has an English commentary.

Accommodation

Brussels has no shortage of **places to stay**, and there are around fifty hotels and several hostels dotted within its central ring of boulevards. Some of the most opulent – as well as some of the most basic – are scattered around the narrow lanes near the **Grand-Place**, and staying here is an attractive option which obviously puts you at the centre of the action. The fashionable neighbourhood of **Ste Catherine**, a five- to ten-minute walk northwest of the Grand-Place, is well worth considering too, its cobbled squares and sidestreets sprinkled with a reasonably good selection of both budget and moderately priced hotels. There's another cluster of hotels just beyond the southern edge of the centre in one of the older and more prosperous residential areas around **avenue Louise**, and another trailing north from the Bourse along dreary **boulevard Adolphe Max** to **place Rogier**.

Despite the number of hotels in Brussels, accommodation can still run short in the spring and summer, and to be sure of a bed it's prudent to **reserve** at least your first night. The simplest approach is to telephone or fax the hotel direct – language is rarely a problem as most hotel receptionists speak at least some English.

ACCOMMODATION PRICE CODES

All the **hotels and hostels** detailed in this chapter have been graded according to the following price categories. Apart from ①, which is a per-person price for a hostel bed, all the codes are based on the rate for the least expensive double room during high season. For more on accommodation, see p.33.

① Up to F1000 per person
② F1000–1500 per room
③ F1500–2000 per room

④ F2000–2500 per room
⑤ F2500–3000 per room
⑥ F3000–4000 per room

⑦ F4000–5000 per room
⑧ F5000–6000 per room
⑨ F6000 and over, per room

Alternatively, **BTR** (Belgian Tourist Reservation; ☎02/513 74 84; fax 513 92 77) will make an advance hotel reservation on your behalf at no charge. If you arrive in the city with nowhere to stay, note that the tourist office in the Grand-Place operates a free hotel booking service, taking a percentage of the room rate as a deposit that is subsequently deducted from your hotel bill. At the pricier hotels, **weekend discounts** are commonplace with the average discount being about fifteen percent, though some places (sometimes) knock down prices by up to fifty percent. Almost everywhere, breakfast is included in the overnight rate; where this isn't the case, reckon on paying an extra F200–300.

Expensive hotels (over F5000)

Amigo, rue de l'Amigo 1–3 (☎547 47 47, fax 513 52 77). Right in the middle of the old city centre, around the corner from the Grand-Place, this delightful hotel occupies an attractive 1950s building designed in the style of an eighteenth-century mansion. The hotel has bags of atmosphere, an amiable informality that's quintessentially Belgian, and the rooms are cosy and intimate with furnishings to match. Room rates range from F5100 per double per night to F9000. Métro Bourse. ⑧.

Le Dixseptième, rue de la Madeleine 25 (☎502 57 44, fax 502 64 24). Arguably the most charming small hotel in Brussels, located in a tastefully renovated seventeenth-century mansion a couple of minutes' walk from the Grand-Place. Parquet flooring, crystal chandeliers and pastel-painted woodwork all add to the flavour. Doubles cost F7100, but there's usually a hefty discount at the weekend. Métro Gare Centrale. ⑨.

Jolly Hotel Grand Sablon, rue Bodenbroek 2, place du Grand Sablon (☎512 88 00, fax 512 67 66). This plush chain hotel doesn't quite live up to its great location overlooking the place du Grand Sablon, but at least it's architecturally unobtrusive. Two hundred smart and well-equipped rooms. Métro Gare Centrale. ⑨.

Métropole, pl de Brouckère 31 (☎217 23 00, fax 218 02 20). Dating from 1895, this grand hotel boasts gorgeous Empire, Art Nouveau and Art Deco flourishes in its public areas, and although some of the rooms are comparatively routine, others retain their original fittings. The rack rate is F12,000 for a double, but there are usually large discounts at the weekend – down to about F45 00. Métro de Brouckère. ⑨.

Moderately priced hotels (F2500–5000)

Aris, rue du Marché aux Herbes 78–80 (☎514 43 00, fax 514 01 19). Spick-and-span hotel with smart, functional rooms to match. Despite the attractive late nineteenth-century stone facade, the place does lack character, but it's in a great location – near the Grand-Place. Significant discounts make the place a real snip on the weekend. Métro Bourse. Weekdays. ⑦.

Arlequin, rue de la Fourche 17–19 (☎514 16 15, fax 514 22 02). There's nothing homely about this straightforward, slightly unkempt hotel, but the rooms are adequate and it is right in the thick of the downtown action. Don't be too deterred by the grotty approach to the hotel. Métro Bourse. ⑤.

New Siru, pl Rogier 1 (☎203 35 80, fax 203 33 03). It may not look like much from the outside – just another skyrise overlooking place Rogier – but the interior of this hotel is the most original in town. Each room was individually decorated by an art student in a broadly modernistic style and all manner of figurines, mini-polystyrene effigies, murals and cartoon strips – everything from Tintin to Marilyn Monroe – pop up all over the place. It's delightful. Métro Rogier. ⑤.

Astrid, pl du Samedi 11 (☎219 31 19, fax 219 31 70). Crisp, modern hotel with smart, comfortable rooms in Ste Catherine. Weekend discounts of up to twenty percent. Métro Ste Catherine. ⑥.

Atlas, rue du Vieux Marché-aux-Grains 30–34 (☎502 60 06, fax 502 69 35). Comfortable if rather bland modern hotel in a refurbished townhouse in the fashionable Ste Catherine district, a five- to ten-minute walk northwest of the Grand-Place. Métro Ste Catherine. ⑦.

Auberge Saint-Michel, Grand-Place 15 (☎511 09 56, fax 511 46 00). One of the city's most distinctive hotels and the only one to look out over the Grand-Place. It occupies an old guildhouse on the east side of the square, but the grandness of the facade isn't universally matched by the rooms inside – which range from the basic and small at the back of the building (F3500) to more elegant period rooms at the front (F5400). For the latter, you'll almost certainly need to make an advance booking. Still, at these prices, and in this spot, the hotel represents a real bargain – though if you're a light sleeper, revellers on the Grand-Place may well disturb your slumbers. Métro Bourse. ⑥.

Du Congrès, rue du Congrès 42 (☎217 18 90, fax 217 18 97). Three-star hotel in a good-looking, turn-of-the-century mansion about five minutes' walk from the cathedral. A popular hotel with pleasant rooms, so advance booking is advised. F1000 discounts at the weekend. Métro Madou. ⑥.

La Madeleine, rue de la Montagne 22 (☎513 29 73, fax 502 13 50). Great location – just down the hill from Gare Centrale – but this is a mundane choice, a dowdy modern hotel with fifty functional and clean bedrooms. Métro Gare Centrale. ⑥.

Matignon, rue de la Bourse 10–12 (☎511 08 88, fax 513 69 27). Another central option, but a rather cramped modern hotel in an old, renovated building with twenty small but functional rooms above a brasserie. Métro Bourse. ⑥.

Orion, quai au Bois à Brûler 51 (☎221 14 11, fax 221 15 99). A somewhat characterless modern building, whose lack of charm is partly relieved by its neat (but compact) modern rooms. It's located in the lively Ste Catherine district, a ten-minute stroll northwest of the Grand-Place. Up to twenty percent discounts at the weekend. Métro Ste Catherine. ⑤.

Inexpensive hotels (under F2500)

Les Bluets, rue Berckmans 124, Saint Gilles (☎ & fax 534 39 83). Small, family-run hotel in a refurbished townhouse with garden and verandah. Well-maintained rooms one block south of the "petit ring". Métro Hôtel des Monnaies. ③.

Eperonniers, rue des Eperonniers 1 (☎513 53 66, fax 511 32 30). Basic, sometimes anarchic pension-style hotel in the heart of the city, a couple of minutes' walk east of the Grand-Place. Just over half the rooms are equipped with a shower and cost about F300 more than the others, but the communal washing facilities are hardly alluring. Breakfast an extra F150. Métro Gare Centrale. ③.

Georges V, rue 't Kint 23 (☎513 50 93, fax 513 44 93). A ramshackle period hotel in an atmospheric if slightly down-at-heel neighbourhood of big, old, balconied and grilled tenement blocks. A ten-minute walk west of the Grand-Place. Métro Bourse. ④.

La Légende, rue du Lombard 35 (☎512 82 90, fax 512 34 93). Pleasant if frugal accommodation in an old building set around a courtyard in the heart of the city, just metres from the Grand-Place. Half the rooms have sinks but not showers – en-suite rooms cost about F1000 extra. Métro Bourse. ③.

Résidence Rembrandt, rue de la Concorde 42, Ixelles (☎512 71 39, fax 511 71 36). Popular and pleasant small hotel with twee furnishings and fittings. Situated in a quiet residential area near place Stéphanie, off avenue Louise. Tram #93 or #94. ④.

Sabina, rue du Nord 78 (☎218 26 37, fax 219 32 39). Spruce, pretty rooms, in a turn-of-the-century house with a beamed and panelled breakfast room. Prices are low for what you get. In a quiet residential area that was once a favourite haunt of the city's nineteenth-century bourgeoisie. Métro Madou. ④.

Windsor, pl Rouppe 13 (☎511 20 14, fax 514 09 42). Clean and cheerful rooms in a decent if mundane location a good fifteen-minute walk southwest of the centre. Not to be confused with the much more expensive Royal Windsor. Métro Anneessens. ④.

Hostels

Bruegel, rue du Saint Esprit 2 (☎511 04 36, fax 512 07 11). This official HI hostel, housed in a smart and modern building, has 150 beds. A basic breakfast is included in the overnight fee – F660 per person for a double room, F560 in a room for four. It is also fairly central, located beside the church of Notre Dame de la Chapelle, close to the Upper Town and just 300m south of Gare Centrale. Reception closed 10am–2pm. Métro Gare Centrale. ①.

Le Centre Vincent van Gogh – CHAB (Centre de Hébergement de l'Agglomeration de Bruxelles), rue Traversière 8 (☎217 01 58, fax 219 79 95). A rambling, spacious hostel with a good reputation and slightly lower prices than the official youth hostels, though it can seem chaotic. Luggage lockers and laundry facilities. Sinks in all rooms, but shared showers and toilets. Sleep-in beds (own sleeping bag obligatory) cost F300, dorm beds F380, triples or quads F430, doubles F510, singles F620. All prices include breakfast. Sheet rental F100. Rooms closed 10am–3pm. Métro Botanique. ①.

Jacques Brel, rue de la Sablonnière 30 (☎218 01 87, fax 217 20 05). An official HI hostel – modern and comfortable, with a hotel-like atmosphere. Facilities include showers in every room, bar, restaurant and meeting room. Beds in 6- to 12-bed dorms F395, triples or quads F450, doubles F550, singles F660. No access to rooms between 10am and 3pm; no curfew. Prices include breakfast; sheets can be rented for F125. Métro Madou or Botanique. ①.

New Sleep Well, rue du Damier 23 (☎218 50 50, fax 218 13 13). Bright and breezy hostel in a recently refurbished building, a five-minute walk from Gare du Nord. Hotel-style facilities including a bar; bed linen rental. Doubles F650 per person, triples or quads F520. Métro Rogier. ①.

The City Centre

In terms of **layout**, the centre of Brussels sits neatly within the rough pentagon of boulevards that enclose it, a "petit ring" which follows the course of the four-teenth-century city walls, running from place Rogier in the north round to Porte de Hal in the south. The city centre divides into two, with the smaller easterly portion comprising the **Upper Town**, the traditional home of the Francophile upper classes, while below to the west lies the much larger **Lower Town**, built for the working and lower-middle classes and fanning out from the Grand-Place. The boundary between the two zones largely follows the boulevard which cuts through the centre under several names – Berlaimont, L'Impératrice and L'Empereur.

One of Europe's most beautiful squares, the **Grand-Place** is the unquestionable centre of Brussels, a focus for tourists and residents alike, who come to admire its magnificent guildhouses and Gothic town hall. It's also the focus of the **Lower Town**, whose cramped and populous quarters spread out in all directions bisected by one major north–south boulevard, variously named Adolphe Max, Anspach and Lemonnier. The Lower Town is at its most beguiling to the **northwest of the Grand-Place**, where the churches of Ste Catherine and St Jean Baptiste au Béguinage stand amidst a cobweb of quaint, narrow lanes and tiny squares. By comparison the streets to the **north of the Grand-Place** are of less immediate appeal with dreary rue Neuve, a pedestrianized main street that's home to the city's mainstream shops and department stores, leading up to the clumping skyscrapers that surround the place Rogier and the Gare du Nord. This is an uninviting part of the city, but relief is at hand in the precise if bedraggled Habsburg symmetries of the place des Martyrs and at the Belgian Comic Strip Centre, the Centre Belge de la Bande Dessinée. To the **south of the Grand-Place** lie the old working-class streets of the Marolles district and then the depressed and predominantly immigrant area in the vicinity of the Gare du Midi.

The **Upper Town** is quite different in feel from the rest of the city centre, a self-consciously planned, more monumental quarter, with statuesque buildings lining wide, classically imposed boulevards and squares. Appropriately, it's the home of the Belgian parliament and government departments, formal parks and the royal palace – the **Palais Royal**. More promisingly, it also accommodates the newly refurbished **cathedral**, a fine Gothic edifice with wonderful stained glass windows, and the superb **Musées Royaux des Beaux Arts**, Belgium's best collection of fine art. Here also are some of the city's swishest shops, clustered around the charming place du Grand Sablon, and the preposterous bulk of the Palais de Justice, which lords it over the rest of the city, commanding views that on clear days reach way across the suburbs.

The Lower Town

The **Lower Town** is the commercial centre of Brussels, a bustling quarter that's home to most of the city's best restaurants, shops and hotels. At its heart is the Grand-Place, which sits amongst a labyrinth of narrow, cobbled lanes and alleys whose names mostly reveal their original purpose – rue du Marché aux Fromages is an obvious example. This medieval street plan is interrupted by the boulevards that were inserted during the nineteenth century, but these have done little to disturb the crowded jostle and jangle that gives the Lower Town its character, with almost every street crimped by tall and angular town houses – and the whole lot dotted with superb buildings, everything from beautiful Baroque churches through to Art Nouveau department stores.

The Grand-Place

The obvious place to begin any tour of Brussels is the **Grand-Place**, where the Gothic extravagance of the Hôtel de Ville presides over the gilded facades of a full set of late seventeenth-century guildhouses, whose columns, scrolled gables and dainty sculptures encapsulate Baroque ideals of balance and harmony. Inevitably, such an outstanding attraction draws tourists and ex-pats in their droves, but the square is still stunning, and there's no better place to get a taste of Brussels' past and Eurocapital present – though the paltry flower market that occupies the square every day except Monday is a pale reflection of earlier markets.

Originally marshland, the Grand-Place was drained in the twelfth century, and by 1350 covered markets for bread, meat and cloth had been erected, born of an economic boom that was underpinned by a flourishing cloth industry. Later, the Grand-Place's role as the commercial hub of the emergent city was cemented when the city's guilds built their headquarters here, and, in the fifteenth century, it also assumed a civic and political function with the construction of the Hôtel de Ville (town hall). The ruling dukes visited the square to meet the people or show off in tournaments, official decrees and pronouncements were proclaimed here, and justice was meted out with public executions drawing large, excited crowds.

In 1482, Brussels, along with the rest of the Low Countries, became a fiefdom of the Habsburgs, whose zealously Catholic Philip II (1555–1598) transformed these executions into religious events as he stroved to crush the city's Protestants. His actions provoked widespread rioting and initiated a long period of bitter religious conflict, although when the Habsburgs finally recaptured the

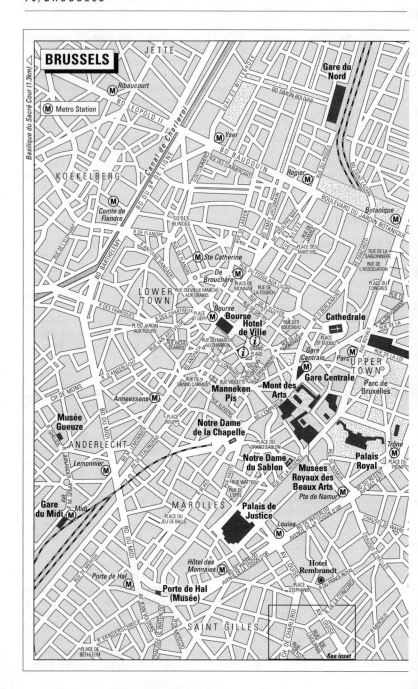

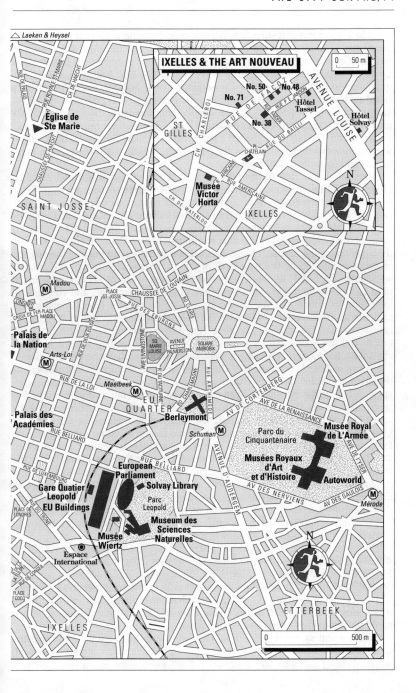

△ Laeken & Heysel

IXELLES & THE ART NOUVEAU

0   50 m

No. 50 No.48
No. 71
Hôtel
Tassel
No. 38
Hôtel
Solvay

Église de
Ste Marie

ST
GILLES

Musée
Victor
Horta

IXELLES

N

SAINT JOSSE

Madou

CHAUSSÉE DE LOUVAIN

PLACE
ST JOSSE

CONGRÈS

CROIX DE FER PLACE
MADOU

Palais de
la Nation

SQ
MARIE
LOUISE

SQUARE
AMBIORIX

Arts-Loi

RUE DE LA LOI

Maelbeek

EU
QUARTER

Berlaymont

DE CORTENBERG

AVE DE LA RENAISSANCE

Palais des
Académies

RUE BELLIARD

Schuman

Parc du
Cinquantenaire

Musée Royal
de L'Armée

RUE DE LUXEMBOURG

European
Parliament

RUE BELLIARD

Musées Royaux
d'Art
et d'Histoire

Autoworld

Gare Quatier
Leopold
EU Buildings

Solvay Library

Parc
Leopold

Mérode

PLACE DE
LONDRES

Museum des
Sciences
Naturelles

Musée
Wiertz

Espace
International

N

PLACE
F.COCQ

IXELLES

ETTERBEEK

0   500 m

town in 1585 they were surprisingly generous, granting a general amnesty and promising to honour ancient municipal privileges. The city's economy revived and the Grand-Place resumed its role as a commercial centre. Of the square's medieval buildings, however, only parts of the Hôtel de Ville and one or two guildhouses survive today, the consequence of a 36-hour **French artillery bombardment** which pretty much razed Brussels to the ground in 1695. An early example of the precepts of total war, the commander of the French artillery gloated, "I have never yet seen such a great fire nor so much desolation." Unperturbed, the city's guildsmen swiftly had their headquarters rebuilt, adopting a distinctive and flamboyant Baroque style, which made the square more ornate and more imposing than ever.

From the south side of the Grand-Place, the newly scrubbed and polished **Hôtel de Ville** dominates the proceedings, its 96m spire soaring above two long series of robust windows whose straight lines are mitigated by fancy tracery, intricate corbels, striking gargoyles and an arcaded gallery. The edifice dates from the beginning of the fifteenth century, when the town council decided to build itself a mansion that adequately reflected its wealth and power. Dating from the early fifteenth century, the first part to be completed was the **east wing** and the original entrance is marked by the twin lions of the Lion Staircase, though the animals were only added in 1770. Work started on the **west wing** in 1444 and continued until 1480. Despite the gap, the wings are of very similar style, and you have to look hard to notice that the later wing is slightly shorter than its neighbour, allegedly at the insistence of Charles the Bold who – for some unknown reason – refused to have the adjacent rue de la Tête d'Or narrowed. The niches were left empty and the statues you see now, which represent leading figures from the city's past, are modern, part of a heavy-handed nineteenth-century restoration.

By any standard, the **tower** of the Hôtel de Ville is quite extraordinary, its remarkably slender appearance the work of Jan van Ruysbroeck, the leading spire specialist of the day who also played a leading role in the building of the cathedral (see p.82) and Sts Pierre et Guido in Anderlecht (see p.99). Ruysbroeck had the lower section built square to support the weight above, choosing a design that blended seamlessly with the elaborately carved facade on either side – or almost: look carefully and you'll see that the main entrance is slightly out of kilter. Ruysbroeck used the old belfry porch as the base for the new tower, hence the misalignment, a deliberate decision rather than the miscalculation which, according to legend, prompted the architect's suicide. Above the cornice protrudes an octagonal extension where the basic design of narrow windows flanked by pencil-thin columns and pinnacles is repeated up as far as the pyramid-shaped spire, a delicate affair surmounted by a gilded figure of **St Michael**, protector of Christians in general and of soldiers in particular.

The tower is off-limits and **guided tours** in English (April–Sept Tues 11.30am & 3.15pm, Wed 3.15pm & Sun 12.15pm; Oct–March Tues 11.30am & 3.15pm only; F75) are confined to a string of lavish official rooms used for receptions and town council meetings. The most dazzling of these is the sixteenth-century **Council Chamber**, decorated with gilt moulding, faded tapestries and an oak floor inlaid with ebony. Tours begin at the reception desk off the interior quadrangle; be prepared for the guides' overly reverential script.

Flanking and facing the Hôtel de Ville are the **guildhouses** which give the Grand-Place its character, their slender, gilded facades swirling with exuberant, self-publicizing carvings and sculptures. Each guildhouse has a name, usually derived from one of the statues, symbols or architectural quirks decorating its facade – and the more interesting are described below.

On the west side of the square, at the end of the row, stands **no. 1: Roi d'Espagne**, a particularly fine building, which was once the headquarters of the guild of bakers and is named after the bust of Charles II (see above) on the upper storey. Charles is flanked by a Moorish and a Native American prisoner, symbolic trophies of war. Balanced on the balustrade are allegorical statues of Energy, Fire, Water, Wind, Wheat and Prudence, presumably meant to represent the elements necessary for baking the ideal loaf.

At **no. 4**, the **Maison du Sac** escaped the French bombardment of 1695. It was constructed for the carpenters and coopers, with the upper storeys being appropriately designed by a cabinet-maker, and featuring pilasters and caryatids which resemble the ornate legs of Baroque furniture.

Next door the **Maison de la Louve**, at **no. 5**, also survived the French artillery, and was originally home to the influential archers' guild. The pilastered facade is studded with sanctimonious representations of concepts like Peace and Discord, and the medallions just beneath the pediment carry the likenesses of four Roman emperors set above allegorical motifs indicating their particular attributes. Thus, Trajan is above the Sun, a symbol of Truth; Tiberius with a net and cage for Falsehood; Augustus and the globe of Peace; and Julius Caesar with a bleeding heart for Disunity. Above the door, there's a charming bas-relief of the Roman she-wolf suckling Romulus and Remus, while the pediment holds a relief of Apollo firing at a python; right on top the Phoenix rises from the ashes.

The **Maison du Cornet**, at **no. 6**, headquarters of the boatmen's guild, is a fanciful creation of 1697 sporting a top storey resembling the stern of a ship. Charles II makes another appearance here too – it's his head in the medallion, flanked by representations of the four winds and of a pair of sailors.

The house of the haberdashers' guild, **Maison du Renard** at **no. 7**, displays animated cherubs in bas-relief playing at haberdashery on the ground floor, while a scrawny, gilded fox – after which the house is named – squats above the door. Up on the third storey a statue of Justice, flanked by statues symbolizing the four continents, suggests the guild's designs on world markets – an aim to which St Nicholas, patron saint of merchants, glinting above, clearly gives his blessing.

On the south side of the square, this arcaded structure, **Maison de l'Étoile**, **no. 8**, is a nineteenth-century rebuilding of the medieval home of the city magistrate. In the passageway round the corner, on rue Charles Buls, the exploits of one Everard 't Serclaes are commemorated: in 1356 the Francophile Count of Flanders attempted to seize power from the Duke of Brabant, occupying the magistrate's house and flying his standard from the roof. 'T Serclaes scaled the building, replaced Flanders' standard with that of the Duke of Brabant, and went on to lead the recapturing of the city, events represented in bas-relief above a reclining statue of 't Serclaes. His effigy is polished smooth from the long-standing superstition that good luck will come to those who stroke it.

The mansion that takes its name from the ostentatious swan on the facade, **Maison du Cygne** at **no. 9**, once housed a bar where Karl Marx regularly met up with Engels during his exile in Belgium. It was in Brussels in February 1848 that they wrote the *Communist Manifesto*, only to be deported as political undesirables the following month. Appropriately enough, the Belgian Workers' Party was founded here in 1885, though nowadays the building shelters one of the city's more exclusive restaurants.

The adjacent **Maison de l'Arbre d'Or** at **no. 10** is the only house on the Grand-Place still to be owned by a guild – the brewers' – not that the equestrian figure stuck on top gives any clues: the original effigy (of one of the city's Habsburg governors) dropped off and the present statue, picturing the eighteenth-century aristocrat Charles of Lorraine, was moved here simply to fill the gap. Inside, the small and mundane **Musée de la Brasserie** (daily 10am–5pm; F100) has various bits of brewing paraphernalia; a beer is included in the price of admission.

The seven guildhouses (**nos. 13–19**) that fill out the east side of the Grand-Place have been subsumed within one grand facade, whose slender symmetries are set off by a curved pediment and narrow pilasters, sporting nineteen busts of the dukes of Brabant. Perhaps more than any other building on the Grand-Place, the **Maison des Ducs de Brabant** has the flavour of the aristocracy – as distinct from the bourgeoisie – and, needless to say, it was much admired by the city's Habsburg governors.

The guildhouses and private mansions (**nos. 20–39**) running along the north side of the Grand-Place are not as distinguished as their neighbours, though the **Maison du Pigeon** (**nos. 26–27**), the painters' guildhouse, is of interest as the house where Victor Hugo spent some time during his exile from France – he was expelled for his support of the French insurrection of 1848. The house also bears four unusual masks in the manner of the "green man" of Romano-Celtic folklore. The adjacent **Maison des Tailleurs** (**nos. 24–25**) is appealing too, the old headquarters of the tailors' guild adorned by a pious bust of St Barbara, their patron saint.

Much of the northern side of the Grand-Place is taken up by the late nineteenth-century **Maison du Roi**, a fairly faithful reconstruction of the palatial Gothic structure commissioned by Charles V in 1515. The emperor had a point to make: the Hôtel de Ville was an assertion of municipal independence and Charles wanted to emphasize imperial power by erecting his own building directly opposite. Despite its name, no sovereign ever lived here permanently, though this is where the Habsburgs installed their tax men and law courts, and held their more important prisoners – the counts of Egmont and Hoorn (see p.89) spent their last night in the Maison du Roi before being beheaded just outside.

The building now holds the **Musée de la Ville de Bruxelles** (Mon–Fri 10am–12.30pm & 1.30–5pm, Sat & Sun 10am–1pm; F80), a wide-ranging but patchy collection whose best sections feature medieval fine and applied art and include Pieter Bruegel the Elder's *Wedding Procession*. On a less artistic note it also houses the Manneken Pis' vast wardrobe, four hundred sickeningly saccharine costumes ranging from Mickey Mouse to a maharaja, all of them gifts from various visiting dignitaries.

Around the Grand-Place

Rue Charles Buls takes you to the corner of **rue des Brasseurs** (the first on the left), scene of a bizarre incident in 1873 when the French Symbolist poet Paul Verlaine shot his fellow poet and lover Arthur Rimbaud. This rash act earnt him a two-year prison sentence – and all because Rimbaud had dashed from Paris to dissuade him from joining the Spanish army. Even today, there's still a slightly offbeat feel to the area, totally at odds with the respectable tourism of the Grand-Place, with gutsy bars and cheap Greek eateries running up the slope to rue des Eperonniers.

Moving on, rue de la Violette is the second turn on the left, and here at no. 6 the **Musée de Costume et de la Dentelle** (April–Sept Mon–Fri 10am–12.30pm & 1.30–5pm; Oct–March Mon–Fri 10am–12.30pm & 1.30–4pm, Sat & Sun 2–4.30pm; F80) has many examples of antique and contemporary lace mixed in with various temporary displays on costume.

From the foot of rue de la Violette, rue de l'Etuve runs south to the **Manneken Pis**, a diminutive statue of a pissing urchin stuck high up in a shrine-like affair protected from the hoards of tourists by an iron fence. The Manneken is supposed to embody the "irreverent spirit" of the city, or at least that is reputed to have been the intention of Jerome Duquesnoy when he cast the original bronze statue in the 1600s to replace the medieval stone fountain that stood here before. It's likely that Duquesnoy invented the Manneken Pis and its popularity blossomed during the sombre, priest-dominated years following the Thirty Years' War, but it's possible his bronze replaced an earlier stone version of ancient provenance. There are all sorts of folkloric tales about its origins, from lost aristocratic children recovered when they were taking a pee, to peasant lads putting out dangerous fires and – least likely of the lot – boys slashing on the city's enemies from the trees and putting them to flight. As a talisman, it has certainly attracted the attention of thieves, notably in 1817 when a French ex-convict swiped it before breaking it into pieces. The thief and the smashed Manneken were apprehended, the former publicly branded on the Grand-Place and sentenced to a life of forced labour, while the fragments of the latter were used to create the mould in which the present-day Manneken was cast. It's long been the custom for visiting VIPs to donate a costume, and the little chap is regularly kitted out in different tackle – often military or folkloric gear.

Just to the north of the Grand-Place, the quarter hinging on the pedestrianized **rue des Bouchers** is the city centre's restaurant ghetto, the narrow cobblestone streets transformed at night into fairy-lit tunnels where restaurants vie for custom with elaborate displays of dull-eyed fish and glistening seafood. There's a feverish atmosphere here, of hard selling and high spending, and although there's no doubting the liveliness of the scene, this is Eurofun in the Eurocapital and you may well prefer something more obviously Belgian – indeed many of the restaurants are said to be Mafia-run and are not the best value for money. Things are certainly more subdued in the nearby **Galeries St Hubert**, whose trio of glass-vaulted galleries – du Roi, de la Reine and the smaller des Princes – cut across the top of rue des Bouchers. Opened by Léopold I in 1847, these galleries were one of Europe's first shopping arcades, and the pastel-painted walls, classical columns and cameo sculptures still retain an aura of dignified sophistication.

Northwest of the Grand-Place

Walking northwest out of the Grand-Place along rue au Beurre, the pint-sized church of **St Nicholas** (Mon–Sat 8am–6.30pm, Sun 8am–12.30pm & 4–7.30pm; free), on the right-hand side, dates from the twelfth century, though it's been heavily restored on several occasions, most recently in the 1950s when parts of the outer shell were reconstructed in a plain Gothic style. The church is dedicated to St Nicholas of Bari as the patron saint of sailors, or as he's better known, Santa Claus. The church is unusual in so far as the three aisles of the nave were built at an angle to the chancel, in order to avoid a stream. Otherwise, the gloomy church hardly sets the pulse racing, although – among a scattering of *objets d'art* – there's a handsome, gilded copper reliquary shrine near the entrance. The

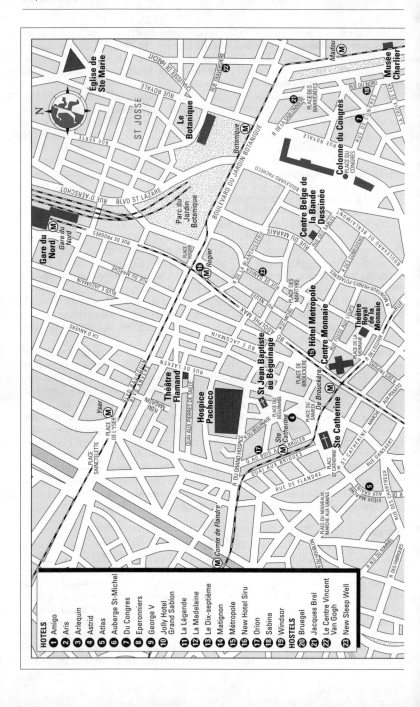

HOTELS
1 Amigo
2 Aris
3 Arlequin
4 Astrid
5 Atlas
6 Auberge St-Michel
7 Du Congres
8 Eperonniers
9 George V
10 Jolly Hotel Grand Sablon
11 La Légende
12 La Madeleine
13 Le Dix-septième
14 Matignon
15 Métropole
16 New Hotel Siru
17 Orion
18 Sabina
19 Windsor

HOSTELS
20 Bruegel
21 Jacques Brel
22 Le Centre Vincent Van Gogh
23 New Sleep Well

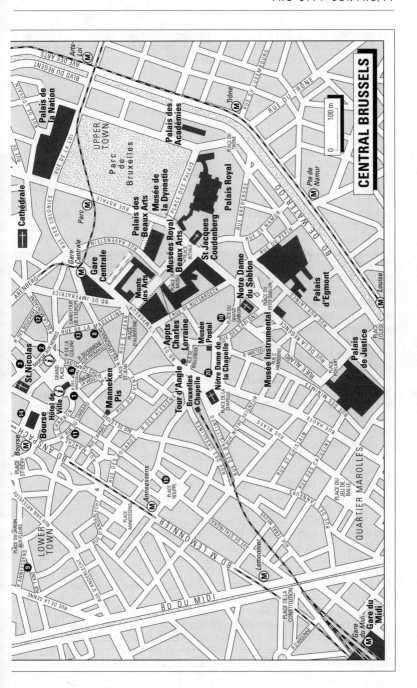

CENTRAL BRUSSELS

shrine was made in Germany in the nineteenth century to honour a group of Catholics martyred by Protestants in Gorinchem in the Netherlands in 1572. More cheerfully, **Maison Dandoy**, across the street at rue au Beurre 31, is a long-established confectioners whose tasty specialities are macaroons and *speculaas*, a sugary brown, cinnamon-flavoured biscuit that's prepared in a variety of traditional and intricate moulds.

Beyond rue au Beurre rises the **Bourse**, formerly the grandiose home of the city's stock exchange, a Neoclassical structure of 1873 caked with fruit, fronds, languishing nudes and frolicking putti. This breezily self-confident structure sports a host of allegorical figures (Industry, Navigation, Asia, Africa etc) which both reflect the preoccupations of the nineteenth-century Belgian bourgeoisie and, in their easy self-satisfaction, imply that wealth and pleasure are synonymous. The Bourse is in a bad state of repair, but the handsome town houses to either side are even worse – an unfortunate setting for two of the city's more famous cafés, the Art Nouveau *Falstaff*, on the south side at rue Henri Maus 17–23, and the fin-de-siècle *Le Cirio*, on the other side at rue de la Bourse 18.

The square in front of the Bourse – **place de la Bourse** – is little more than an unsightly, heavily trafficked pause along boulevard Anspach, but the streets on the other side of the boulevard have more appeal, with tiny **place St Géry** crowded by high-sided, somewhat run-down tenements, whose stone balconies and wrought-iron grilles speak of more prosperous days. The square is thought to occupy the site of the sixth-century chapel from which the medieval city grew, but this is a matter of conjecture – no archeological evidence has ever been unearthed and the only clue to the city's early history is in its name, literally "settlement in the marshes". Place St Géry has one specific attraction in the recently refurbished, late nineteenth-century covered market, the **Halles St Géry**, an airy glass and iron edifice.

Nearby, **place Ste Catherine** is, despite its dishevelled appearance, at the heart of one of the city's most fashionable districts, not least because of its excellent seafood restaurants. Presiding over the square – and the proceedings of a daily market – is the **church of Ste Catherine** (Mon–Sat 8.30am–5/6pm, Sun 9am–noon), a battered nineteenth-century replacement for the Baroque original, of which the creamy, curvy belfry is the solitary survivor. Venture inside the church and you'll see a fourteenth-century Black Madonna and Child, a sensually carved stone statuette that was chucked into the Senne by Protestants, but fished out while floating on a fortuitous clod of peat.

Just north of place Ste Catherine lies **place du Samedi**, a pretty little square from where rue du Cyprès squeezes in between high old buildings to reach place du Béguinage, dominated by **St Jean Baptiste au Béguinage** (July & Aug Tues–Sat 11am–5pm, Sun 10am–5pm; Sept–June Tues–Fri 10am–5pm plus occasional Sat and Sun morning; free), a supple, billowing structure dating from the second half of the seventeenth century. Recently restored, this beautiful church is the only building left from the Beguine convent founded here in the thirteenth century. The convent once crowded in on the church and only since its demolition – and the creation of the star-shaped place du Béguinage in 1855 – has it been possible to view the exterior with any degree of ease. There's a sense of movement in each and every feature, a dynamism of design culminating in three soaring gables where the upper portion of the central tower is decorated with pinnacles that echo those of the Hôtel de Ville. The church's light and spacious interior is lavishly decorated, the white stone columns and arches dripping with solemn-faced cherubs intent on reminding the congregation of their mortality. The nave and aisles are wide and open, offering unobstructed views of the high altar, but you can't fail to notice the enormous wooden pulpit featuring St Dominic preaching against heresy – and trampling a heretic under foot for good measure.

Around the back of the church, a short lane takes you through to a slender, tree-lined square framed by the austere Neoclassicism of the **Hospice Pacheco** (no access), built to house the destitute in the 1820s. It's a peaceful spot today, but the stern wall that surrounds the complex is a reminder of times when the hospice was more like a prison than a shelter, with draconian rules imposed with brutal severity.

The **Senne River** once flowed beside the hospice, but is no longer viewable here. By the nineteenth century it had become intolerably polluted – in the words of the Brussels writer Camille Lemonnier, "the dumping ground, not only of industry, but also of the houses lining the river: it was not unusual to see the ballooned stomach of a dog mixed pell mell with its own litter...". After an outbreak of cholera in 1866, which killed over 3500 townsfolk, the river was piped underground and paved over.

North of the Grand-Place

North of the Grand-Place, beyond rue des Bouchers, **place de la Monnaie** is a drab and dreary modern square that's overshadowed by the huge **centre Monnaie**, housing offices, shops and the main city post office. The only building of interest here is the **Théâtre Royal de la Monnaie**, Brussels' opera house, a Neoclassical structure built in 1819 and with an interior added in 1856 to a design by Poelaert, the architect of the Palais de Justice (see p.82). The theatre's real claim to fame, however, is as the starting-point of the revolution against the Dutch in 1830: a nationalistic libretto in Auber's *The Mute Girl of Portici* sent the audience wild, and they poured out into the streets to raise the flag of Brabant, signalling the start of the rebellion.

On the far side of the centre Monnaie is traffic-choked boulevard Anspach which forks and widens at **place de Brouckère**, a busy junction that accommodates the **Hôtel Métropole**, whose splendidly ornate public areas date from 1895 and were once the haunt of the likes of Sarah Bernhardt and Isadora Duncan.

From place de la Monnaie, **rue Neuve** forges north, a workaday pedestrianized shopping street lined with chain stores and the City 2 shopping mall. It leads up to the petit ring at **place Rogier**, whose big modern office blocks march north along rue du Progrès to the smart modernity of the revamped **Gare du Nord**. However, this is all rather uninspiring, so stop instead about halfway up rue Neuve and take rue St Michel east to the **place des Martyrs**, a cool, rational square imposed on the city by the Habsburgs in the 1770s. Long neglected, the square is very much the worse for wear – work has at last started on a thoroughgoing refurbishment – but there's still no mistaking the architectural elegance of the ensemble, completed in the last years of Austrian control. The only stylistic blip is the nineteenth-century centrepiece, a clumsy representation of the Fatherland Crowned rising from an arcaded gallery inscribed with the names of those 445 rebels who died in the Belgian revolution of 1830.

East of place des Martyrs, it's a dreary five-minute walk through run-down offices and warehouses to rue des Sables, where at no. 20 you come to the city's only surviving Horta-designed department store, the **Grand Magasin**

Waucquez. Recently restored after lying empty for many years, it's a wonderful-ly airy, summery construction, with light flooding through the stained glass that encloses the expansive entrance hall. It was completed in 1906, built for a textile tycoon, and exhibits all the classic features of Horta's work (see p.96) – from the soft lines of the ornamentation to the metal grills, exposed girders and balustrades.

Around the entrance hall is a first-rate café, the *Brasserie Horta* (see p.104), as well as the library, bookshop and ticket office of the **Centre Belge de la Bande Dessinée** (Tues–Sun 10am–6pm; F200; library Tues–Thurs noon–5pm, Fri noon–6pm, Sat 10am–6pm; F50). The centre's displays are devoted to the history of the Belgian comic strip with an especially interesting section on that national hero **Tintin**.

Moving east, it's another short walk up to the 47-metre-high **Colonne du Congrès** on place du Congrès. Erected in 1850 to commemorate the country's first national parliament, the column sports a statue of Léopold I on top and four allegorical female figures down below, representing the freedoms enshrined in the Constitution – the freedoms of worship, association, education and the press. The lions were added later, guarding the tomb of the unknown soldier in front of which burns the eternal flame honouring Belgium's dead of the two world wars. The col-umn dominates a bleak belvedere, flanked by the blank glass and concrete admin-istration buildings and offering a singularly unflattering view of the city.

Behind, beyond rue Royale and north of **rue du Congrès**, lies one of the most attractive parts of the city centre, a pocket-sized district where the grand man-sions of the nineteenth-century bourgeoisie, built with dignified balconies and wrought-iron grilles, overlook wide, straight streets and fetching little squares. Some of the earliest houses, dating to the 1820s, overlook the **place des Barricades**, named to commemorate the fighting that took place against the Dutch in 1830. Victor Hugo was living in exile here at no. 4 when he was thrown out of Belgium.

Running north from the Colonne du Congrès is **rue Royale**, a dead straight boulevard linking the place Royale with **Le Botanique**, an appealingly grandiose greenhouse dating from 1826. The building once housed the city's botanical gar-dens, but these were moved out long ago and the place has been turned into a Francophone cultural centre. The adjacent **park** slopes away to the west, its care-fully manicured woods, lawns and borders decorated by statues and a tiny lake. Despite the proximity of the traffic-congested boulevards of the petit ring, it's a pleasant spot, though be warned that dodgy characters haunt its precincts in the evening.

South of the Grand-Place: the Midi and Marolles

The labyrinth of cobbled lanes immediately to the southwest of the Grand-Place make for an enjoyable stroll, but inevitably you'll soon stumble on the two dead straight and uninteresting boulevards that run down from the Bourse to the **Gare du Midi**, which lies just beyond the petit ring. The area round the station is home to the city's many North African immigrants, a severely depressed and at times seedy quarter with an uneasy undertow by day and sometimes overtly threaten-ing at night. There's a closed, ghettoized feel to the streets and in many of the cheap cafés and bars.

If you'd rather avoid Midi, you could instead stroll south from the Grand-Place along rue de l'Etuve, passing the Manneken Pis (see p.75) before turning east down **rue des Alexiens**. This ends abruptly at boulevard de l'Empereur, a busy carriageway that disfigures this part of the centre. Across the boulevard, slightly to the north, you'll spy the crumbling brickwork of the **tour d'Angle**, a chunky remnant of the medieval city wall, while to the south gleams the recently restored **Notre Dame de la Chapelle** (June–Sept Mon–Fri 9am–5pm, Sat 1.30–5pm & Sun 1.30–3.30pm; Oct–May Mon–Fri 1–4pm; free), a sprawling, broadly Gothic structure with an attractive if somewhat incongruous Baroque belltower. The city's oldest church, founded in 1134, has a well-proportioned nave bathed in light from the huge clerestory windows and is supported by heavyweight columns with curly-kale capitals. The pulpit is an extraordinary affair, a flashy, intricately carved hunk featuring Eli in the desert beneath the palm trees. The prophet looks mightily fed up, but then he hasn't realized that there's an angel behind him with a loaf of bread (manna).

Round the corner from the tour d'Angle, **rue de Rollebeek** is a pleasant pedestrianized lane dotted with cafés and restaurants that will take you up into place du Grand Sablon (see p.89); or you can stroll down rue Blaes or the less appealing rue Haute, which together form the double spine of the **Quartier Marolles**, stacked on the slopes below the Palais de Justice. An earthy neighbourhood of run-down housing and cheap, basic restaurants, shops and bars, it's one of the few places in the city where you can still hear older people using the traditional dialect, "**Brusselse Sproek**" or "Marollien". A brand of Flemish which has, over the centuries, been influenced by the languages of the city's overlords, it is now in danger of dying out, and local people have set up an academy to preserve it.

The Marolles neighbourhood grew up in the seventeenth century as a centre for artisans working on the nearby mansions of Sablon. Industrialized in the eighteenth century, it remained a thriving working-class district until the 1870s, when the paving over of the Senne led to the riverside factories closing down and moving out to the suburbs. The workers and their families followed, abandoning Marolles to the old and poor. Today, gentrification is creeping into the district – along rue Blaes dilapidated houses are in the process of restoration and the occasional restaurant or antique shop has sprouted up among the bars and secondhand clothes shops. Yet **place du Jeu de Balle**, the heart of Marolles, is relatively unchanged, a shabby square surrounded by rough-edged bars and the scene of the city's best flea market (see "Markets", p.110). The market is a daily event, but it's at its most hectic on Sunday mornings, when the square and the surrounding streets are completely taken over by pile after pile of rusty junk alongside muddles of eccentric bric-a-brac – everything from a chipped buddha, a rococo angel or African idol, to horn-rimmed glasses, a top hat or a stuffed bear.

The Upper Town

The wide avenues and grand architecture of the **Upper Town**, the old aristocratic quarter, mostly date from the late eighteenth and nineteenth centuries. The district possesses a formal and dignified feel that's markedly different from the bustle of the Lower Town below.

The Lower Town ends and the Upper Town begins at the foot of the sharp slope which runs north to south from one end of the city centre to the other, its course marked – in general terms at least – by a traffic-choked boulevard that's variously named Berlaimont, L'Impératrice and L'Empereur. This slope is home to the city's **cathedral**, a splendid Gothic edifice that's recently been restored, but otherwise is little more than an obstacle to be climbed by a series of stairways. Among the latter, the most frequently used are the covered walkway running through the **Galerie Ravenstein** shopping arcade behind the **Gare Centrale**, and the open-air stairway that climbs up through the stodgy, modern buildings of the so-called **Mont des Arts**. Léopold II gave the area its name in anticipation of a fine art museum he intended to build, but the project was never completed, and the land was only properly built upon in the 1950s.

Above the rigorous layout of the Mont des Arts lie the exuberant **rue Royale** and **rue de la Régence**, which together make up the Upper Town's spine, a suitably smart location for the outstanding **Musées Royaux des Beaux Arts**, probably the best of Belgium's many fine art collections, and the surprisingly low-key **Palais Royal**. Further south, rue de la Régence soon leads to the well-heeled **Sablon** neighbourhood, whose antique shops and chic bars and cafés fan out from the medieval church of **Notre Dame du Sablon**. Beyond this is the monstrous **Palais de Justice**, traditionally one of the city's most disliked buildings.

The Cathedral and lower slopes

It only takes a couple of minutes' to walk from the Grand-Place to the east end of rue d'Arenberg, where a short, steep slope climbs up to the **Cathedral** (daily 8am–6pm; crypt F40), a fine Gothic building whose commanding position has been sorely compromised by a rash of modern office blocks. Begun in 1220, and three hundred years in the making, the cathedral is dedicated jointly to the patron and patroness of Brussels – St Michael the Archangel, and St Gudule, a vague, seventh-century figure whose reputation was based on gentleness.

The cathedral sports a striking, twin-towered, whitestone **facade**, with the central doorway trimmed by fanciful tracery and statues of the Three Wise Men and the Apostles. The facade was erected in the fifteenth century in High Gothic style, but the intensity of the decoration fades away inside with the airy triple-aisled **nave**, completed a century before. Other parts of the interior illustrate several phases of Gothic design – and an explanatory panel just inside the entrance explains what was built when; the chancel is the oldest part of the church, built in Early Gothic style around 1280.

The interior is short on furnishings and fittings, reflecting the combined efforts of the Protestants, who ransacked the church (and stole the shrine of St Gudule) in the seventeenth century, and the French Republican army, who wrecked the place a century later. One survivor is the massive oak **pulpit**, an extravagant chunk of frippery by the Antwerp sculptor Hendrik Verbruggen. Among several vignettes, the pulpit features Adam and Eve, dressed in rustic gear, being chased from the Garden of Eden, while up above the Virgin Mary stamps on the head of the serpent.

The cathedral also boasts some superb sixteenth-century stained windows, especially in the **transepts**, where the glass is distinguished by the extraordinary clarity of the blue backgrounds. These windows are eulogies to the Habsburgs – in the north transept, Charles V kneels alongside his wife beneath a vast triumphal arch as their patron saints present them to God the Father, and in the south transept Charles V's sister, Marie, and her husband, King Louis of Hungary, play out a similar scenario. Both windows were designed by Bernard van Orley (1490–1541), long-time favourite of the royal family and the leading Brussels artist of his day.

South of the cathedral, just up from the unenticing modernity of the carrefour de l'Europe roundabout, lies the **Gare Centrale**, a bleak Art Deco creation seemingly dug deep into the slope where Lower and Upper Town meet. From the station, a covered walkway leads up through the **Galerie Ravenstein** shopping arcade to rue Ravenstein, home to the **Palais des Beaux Arts**, a drab, low-lying edifice designed by Victor Horta during the 1920s in complete contrast with his flamboyant earlier works. It holds a theatre and concert hall and hosts numerous temporary exhibitions, mostly of modern and contemporary art. Round the corner, up the stairway, the adjoining **Musée du Cinéma** (daily 5.30–10.30pm) has displays on the pioneering days of cinema and shows old movies every evening. One projection room presents two silent films with piano accompaniment every night, the other shows three early "talkies". From the museum, it's another short haul up the steps to rue Royale (see below).

The wide stone stairway that cuts up through the **Mont des Arts** also climbs the slope marking the start of the Upper Town. The stairs begin on **place de l'Albertine** where the figure of Queen Elizabeth, bouquet in hand, stands opposite a statue honouring her husband, Albert I, who is depicted in military gear on his favourite horse. Easily the most popular king Belgium has ever had, Albert became a national hero for his determined resistance to the Germans in World War I. He died in a climbing accident near Namur, in southern Belgium, in 1934.

From here it is a short stroll up to place Royale.

Place Royale, the Palais Royal and the Parc de Bruxelles

Composed and self-assured, the **place Royale** forms a fitting climax to rue Royale, the dead straight backbone of the Upper Town which runs the 2km north, past the Colonne du Congrés (see p.80), to the suburb of St Josse. Precisely symmetrical, the square is framed by late eighteenth-century mansions, each an exercise in architectural restraint, though there's no mistaking their size nor the probable cost of their construction. Pushing into this understated opulence is the facade of the church of **St Jacques sur Coudenberg** (Tues–Sat 10am–6pm, Sun & Mon 3–6pm; free), a fanciful version of a Roman temple with a colourfully frescoed pediment representing Our Lady as Comforter of the Depressed – and a building so secular in appearance that the French Revolutionary army had no hesitation in renaming it a Temple of Reason. The French also destroyed the statue of a Habsburg governor that originally occupied the middle of the square, and its replacement – a dashing equestrian representation of Godfrey de Bouillon, one of the leaders of the first Crusade – dates from the 1840s.

Around the corner from place Royale, the long and low **Palais Royal** (late July–Sept Tues–Sun 10.30am–4.30pm; free) is something of an anticlimax, a sombre nineteenth-century conversion of some late eighteenth-century town houses, begun by King William I, the Dutch royal who ruled both Belgium and the Netherlands from 1815 to 1830. The Belgian rebellion of 1830 polished off the joint kingdom and since then the kings of independent Belgium haven't spent much money on the palace. Indeed, although it remains their official residence, the royals have lived elsewhere (in Laeken, see p.100) for decades and it's hardly surprising, therefore, that the **palace interior** is formal and unwelcoming. It consists of little more than a predictable sequence of opulent rooms – all gilt trimmings, parquet floors, and endless royal portraits, though the tapestries designed by Goya and the magnificent chandeliers of the Throne Room make a visit (just about) worthwhile. The same cannot be said for the displays in the palace annexe, the **Hôtel Bellevue**, on the corner of place des Palais and rue Royale, where the

Musée de la Dynastie (Tues–Sun 10am–4pm; free) charts the brief history of the Belgian royal family, and will thrill only ardent monarchists.

Opposite the Palais Royal, the **Parc de Bruxelles** is the most central of the city's larger parks, along whose tree-shaded footpaths civil servants and office workers stroll at lunchtime, or race to catch the métro in the evenings. They might well wish the greenery was a bit more interesting. Laid out in the formal French style in 1780, the park undoubtedly suited the courtly – and courting – rituals of the times, but today the straight footpaths and long lines of trees merely seem tedious. Furthermore, the classical statues that once cheered things up are in a dire state of repair.

Beside the park's southeast corner stands the **Palais des Académies**, a grand edifice that once served as a royal residence, but now accommodates the Francophone Academy of Language and Literature. Just beyond is the **place du Trône**, where the big and bold equestrian statue of Léopold II was the work of Thomas Vinçotte, whose skills were much used by the king – look out for Vinçotte's chariot on top of the Parc du Cinquantenaire's triumphal arch (see p.92).

From place du Trône, it's a few minutes' stroll east to the EU Parliament building.

The Musées Royaux des Beaux Arts

A few metres from place Royale, at the start of rue de la Régence, the **Musées Royaux des Beaux Arts** comprise two museums, one displaying modern art, the other older works. Together they make up Belgium's most satisfying all-round collection of fine art, with marvellous collections of work by – amongst many – Pieter Bruegel the Elder, Rubens and the surrealists Paul Delvaux and René Magritte.

Both museums are large, and to do them justice you should see them in separate visits. Finding your way around is made easy by the detailed English-language **museum plan** on sale at the entrance (F20). The older paintings – up to the beginning of the nineteenth century – are exhibited in the **Musée d'Art Ancien** (Tues–Sun 10am–noon & 1–5pm; F150 for both museums), where the blue area shows paintings of the fifteenth and sixteenth centuries, including the Bruegels, and the brown area concentrates on paintings of the seventeenth and eighteenth centuries, with the collection of Rubens (for which the museum is internationally famous) as the highlight. The orange area comprises the small and undistinguished Gallery of Sculptures. The **Musée d'Art Moderne** (Tues–Sun 10am–1pm & 2–5pm) has a yellow area devoted to nineteeth-century works, notably the canvases of Ostend-born James Ensor, and a green area whose eight subterranean levels cover the twentieth century.

The Musée d'Art Ancien also hosts, in the red area, a prestigious programme of temporary exhibitions for which a supplementary admission fee is usually required. For the most popular you'll need to buy a ticket ahead of time; the ticket may specify the time of admission. The larger exhibitions may cause some disruption to the permanent collection, so treat the room numbers we've given with a little caution. Inevitably, the account below just scratches the surface; the museum's **bookshop** sells a wide range of detailed texts including a well-illustrated guide to the collections for F525.

MUSÉE D'ART ANCIEN

Well presented, if not exactly well organized, the **Musée d'Art Ancien** is saved from confusion by its colour-coded zones – blue, brown, orange and red. It's a large collection and it's best to start a visit with the **Flemish primitives**.

Rooms 11 and 12 hold several paintings by Rogier van der Weyden, the official city painter to Brussels in the middle of the fifteenth century. When it came to portraiture his favourite technique was to highlight the features of his subject – and tokens of rank – against a black background. The *Portrait of the Grand Bâtard de Bourgogne* is a good example with Anthony, the illegitimate son of Philip the Good, casting a haughty, tight-lipped stare to his right while wearing the chain of the Order of the Golden Fleece and clasping an arrow, the emblem of the guild of archers.

In **Room 13**, the two cautionary panels of the *Justice of the Emperor Otto* are the work of Weyden's contemporary, the Leuven-based Dieric Bouts. The story was well known: in revenge for refusing her advances, the Empress accuses a nobleman of attempting to seduce her. He is executed, but the man's wife remains convinced of his innocence and subsequently proves her point by means of an ordeal by fire in which she holds a red-hot iron bar.

Room 14 has some plain, commonsense portraits by Hans Memling as well as his softly hued *Martyrdom of St Sebastian*. Legend has it that Sebastian was an officer in Diocletian's bodyguard until his Christian faith was discovered, at which point he was sentenced to be shot to death by the imperial archers. Left for dead by the bowmen, Sebastian recovered and Diocletian had to send a bunch of assassins to finish him off with cudgels. The tale made Sebastian popular with archers across Western Europe, and Memling's picture – showing the trussed-up saint serenely indifferent to the arrows of the firing squad – was commissioned by the guild of archers in Bruges around 1470.

In **Room 15**, there's more early Flemish art in the shape of the *Scenes from the Life of St Barbara*, one panel from an original pair by the Master of the Legend of St Barbara. One of the most popular of medieval saints, Barbara, so the story goes, was a woman of great beauty whose father locked her away in a tower to keep her away from her admirers. The imprisoned Barbara became a Christian, whereupon her father, Dioscurus, tried to kill her, only to be thwarted by a miracle that placed her out of his reach – a part of the tale that's ingeniously depicted in this painting. Naturally, no self-respecting saint could escape so easily, so later parts of the story have Barbara handed over to the local prince, who tortures her for her faith. Barbara resists and the prince orders Dioscurus to kill her himself, which he does only to be immediately incinerated by a bolt of lightning.

Moving on, **Room 17** boasts a copy of the Hieronymous Bosch *Temptations of St Anthony* that's in the national museum in Lisbon. No one is quite sure who painted this triptych – it may or may not have been one of Bosch's apprentices – but it was certainly produced in Holland in the late fifteenth or early sixteenth century. The painting refers to St Anthony, a third-century nobleman who withdrew into the desert, where he endured fifteen years of temptation before settling down into his long stint as a hermit. It was the temptations that interested Bosch – rather than the ascetic steeliness of Anthony – and the central panel has an inconspicuous saint sticking desperately to his prayers surrounded by all manner of fiendish phantoms. The side panels develop the theme – to the right Anthony is tempted by lust and greed, and on the left Anthony's companions help him back to his shelter after he's been transported through the skies by weird-looking demons.

Next door, **Room 18** holds works by Martin Luther's friend, the Bavarian artist Lucas Cranach, whose *Adam and Eve* presents a stylized, Renaissance view of the Garden of Eden with an earnest-looking Adam on the other side of the Tree of Knowledge from a coquettish Eve, painted with legs entwined and her teeth marks visible on the apple.

In **Room 22**, Quentin Matsys is well represented by the *Triptych of the Holy Kindred*. Matsys' work illustrates a turning point in the development of Flemish painting, and in this triptych, which was completed in 1509, Matsys abandons the realistic interiors and landscapes of his Flemish predecessors in favour of the grand columns and porticos of the Renaissance, with each scene rigorously structured, its characters – all relations of Jesus – assuming lofty, idealized poses.

The museum's collection of works by the **Bruegel** family, notably **Pieter the Elder** (1527–1569), is concentrated in **Room 31**. Often regarded as the finest Netherlandish painter of the sixteenth century, little is known of Pieter the Elder's life, though it's likely he was apprenticed in Antwerp and he certainly moved to Brussels in the early 1560s. He also made at least one long trip to Italy, but judging by his oeuvre, he was – unlike most of his "Belgian" contemporaries – decidedly unimpressed by Italian art. He preferred instead to paint in the Netherlandish tradition and his works often depict crowded Flemish scenes in which are embedded religious or mythical stories. This sympathetic portrayal of everyday life revelled in the seasons and was worked in muted browns, greys and bluey greens with red or yellow highlights. Typifying this approach, and on display here, are the *Adoration of the Magi* and the *Census at Bethlehem* – a scene that Pieter, his son, repeated on several occasions – two particularly absorbing works with the traditionally momentous events happening, almost incidentally, among the bustle of everyday life. The versatile Pieter also dabbled with the lurid imagery of Bosch, whose influence is seen most clearly in *The Fall of the Rebel Angels*, a frantic panel painting which had actually been attributed to Bosch until Bruegel's signature was discovered hidden under the frame. *The Fall of Icarus* is, however, his most haunting work, its mood perfectly captured by Auden in his poem "Musée des Beaux Arts":

> *In Bruegel's Icarus, for instance: how everything turns away*
> *Quite leisurely from the disaster; the ploughman may*
> *Have heard the splash, the forsaken cry,*
> *But for him it was not an important failure; the sun shone*
> *As it had to on the white legs disappearing into the green*
> *Water; and the expensive delicate ship that must have seen*
> *Something amazing, a boy falling out of the sky,*
> *Had somewhere to get to and sailed calmly on.*

Apprenticed in Antwerp, **Pieter Paul Rubens** (1577–1640) spent eight years in Italy studying the Renaissance masters before returning home, where he quickly completed a stunning series of paintings for Antwerp Cathedral. His fame spread far and wide and for the rest of his days Rubens was inundated with work, receiving commissions from all over Europe. In **Room 52**, the popular misconception that Rubens painted nothing but chubby nude women and muscular men is dispelled with a sequence of portraits, each aristocratic head drawn with great care and attention to detail – in particular note the exquisite, brilliant white ruffs adorning the Archduke Albert and Isabella. *Studies of a Negro's Head* is likewise wonderfully observed, a preparation for the black magus in the *Adoration of the Magi*, a luminous work that's one of several huge canvases next door in **Room 62**. Here you'll also find *The Ascent to Calvary*, an intensely physical painting, capturing the confusion, agony and strain as Christ struggles on hands and knees under the weight of the Cross. There's also the bloodcurdling *Martyrdom of St Lieven*, whose cruel torture – his tongue has just been ripped out and fed to a dog – are watched from on high by cherubs and angels.

Two of Rubens' pupils, Anthony van Dyck (1599–1641) and Jacob Jordaens (1593–1678), also feature in this part of the museum with the studied portraits of the former clustered in **Room 53** and the big and brassy canvases of Jordaens dominating **Room 57**. Like Rubens, Jordaens had a bulging order-book and for years he and his apprentices churned out paintings by the cart load. His best work is generally agreed to have been completed early on – between about 1620 and 1640 – and there's evidence here in the two versions of the *Satyr and the Peasant,* the earlier work clever and inventive, the second a hastily cobbled-together piece that verges on buffoonery.

Close by, in **Room 60**, is a modest sample of Dutch painting, including a couple of sombre and carefully composed Rembrandts (1606–1669). One of them – the self-assured *Portrait of Nicolaas van Bambeeck* – was completed in 1641, when the artist was finishing off his famous *Night Watch*, now exhibited in Amsterdam's Rijksmuseum. Rembrandt's pupils are displayed in the same room, principally Nicolaes Maes (1634–1693), who is well represented by the delicate *Dreaming Old Woman*.

MUSÉE D'ART MODERNE

To reach the **Musée d'Art Moderne** you'll need to use the underground passageway which leads from the main entrance to the yellow area whose nineteeth-century works are spread over five small floors – two underground and three above. You arrive on **Level –2**, where the obvious highlight is Jacques-Louis David's famous *Death of Marat*, an extravagantly romantic painting showing the French revolutionary hero dying in the bath (after being stabbed by Charlotte Corday). David (1748–1825) was a leading light of the Neoclassical movement and more importantly a Jacobin who voted for the execution of Louis XVI; he ended his days in exile in Brussels. On this floor also are examples of the work of Henri Leys, *The Spanish Fury in Antwerp*, and Louis Gallait, *Antioch taken by the Crusaders*. Historical romanticism was very much in vogue in Belgium during the later part of the nineteenth century, and these painters were two of its leading exponents.

Two floors up, **Level +1** features the work of the Social Realists, whose paintings and sculptures championed the working class. One of the early figures in this movement was Charles de Groux (1825–70), whose *Poor People's Pew* is typical of his work, but it's Constantin Meunier who is really worth seeking out and he's well represented by two particularly forceful bronzes, *Firedamp* and *The Iron Worker*. Their friend Eugene Laermans (1864–1940) shifted from the Realist style into more Expressionistic works as in the overtly political *Strike Night* and *The Corpse,* a sorrowful vision that is perhaps Laermans' most successful painting. The museum has little work by Vincent van Gogh, but it's here you'll find his fiery *Portrait of a Peasant*.

The Symbolists are clustered on **Level +2** and amongst them are the disconcerting paintings of Fernand Khnopff (1858–1921), a founding member of Les XX art movement. Khnopff painted his sister, Marguerite, again and again, using her refined, almost plastic, beauty to stir a vague sense of passion – for she's desirable and utterly unobtainable in equal measure. His haunting *Memories of*

Lawn Tennis is typical of his oeuvre, a work without narrative, a dream-like scene with each of the seven women bearing the likeness of Marguerite. In *Caresses* Marguerite pops up once more, this time with the body of a cheetah pawing sensually at an androgynous youth.

Pressing on, **Level +3** has a sprinkling of French Impressionists and Post-Impressionists – Monet, Seurat, Gaugin – and a superb sample of the work of **James Ensor** (1860–1949). Ensor, the son of an English father and Flemish mother, spent nearly all of his long life working in Ostend, his home town. His first paintings were rather sombre portraits and landscapes, but in the early 1880s he switched to a more Impressionistic style, delicately picking out his colours as in *The Lady in Blue*. It is, however, Ensor's use of masks which sets his work apart, ambiguous carnival masks with the sniff of death or perversity. His *Scandalized Masks* of 1883 was his first mask painting, a typically unnerving canvas that works on several levels, whilst his *Skeletons Quarrelling for a Kipper* (1891) is one of the most savage and macabre paintings you're ever likely to see.

A stairway leads down from Level –2 to the six subterranean half-floors which hold an extremely varied collection of modern art and sculpture. It's a challenging collection of international dimensions that starts as it means to continue – at the entrance to **Level –3/4** – with a lumpy, uncompromising Henry Moore and an eerie Francis Bacon, *The Pope with Owls*. Beyond lies an assortment of works by Picasso, Braque and Matisse, a Dufy *Port of Marseille*, and two fanciful paintings by Chagall, one of which is the endearingly eccentric *The Frog that Wanted to Make Itself as Big as a Bull*. Another highlight is Léon Spillaert's evocations of intense loneliness, from monochromatic beaches to empty rooms and train cars. Spillaert lived in Ostend, the setting for much of his work including the piercing *Woman on the Dyke*. Another noteworthy Belgian is Constant Permeke, whose grim and gritty Expressionism is best illustrated by *The Potato Eater* of 1935.

Level –5/6 is given over to the Surrealists. There's a fine Dali, *The Temptation of St Anthony*, a hallucinatory work in which spindly-legged elephants tempt the saint with fleshy women, and a couple of de Chirico's paintings of dressmakers' dummies. Of the Belgian Surrealists, **Paul Delvaux** is represented by his trademark themes of ice-cool nudes set against a disintegrating backdrop as well as trains and stations: see the *Evening Train*. Even more elusive is the gallery's collection of paintings by **René Magritte** (1898–1967), perplexing works, whose weird, almost photographically realized images and bizarre juxtapositions aim to disconcert. Magritte was the prime mover in Belgian surrealism, developing – by the time he was thirty – an individualistic style that remained fairly constant throughout his entire career. It was not, however, a style that brought him much initial success and, surprising as it may seem today, he remained relatively unknown until the 1950s. The museum has a substantial sample of his work amongst which two of the more intriguing pieces are the baffling *Secret Player* and the subtly discordant *Empire of Lights*.

Most of the work down on **Level –7/8** is by living artists and although displays are regularly rotated you'll usually spot – amongst mostly modern incomprehensible stuff – the swirling abstracts of Brussels-born and Paris-based Pierre Alechinsky.

The Sablon neighbourhood

From place Royale it's a short walk along rue de la Régence to the **place du Petit Sablon**, a small rectangular area which was laid out as a public garden in 1890 after previous use as a horse market. The garden is surrounded by a wrought-iron fence decorated with 48 statuettes representing the medieval guilds and inside, near the top of the slope, are ten more slightly larger statues honouring some of the country's leading sixteenth-century figures. The ten are hardly household names in Belgium never mind anywhere else, but one or two may ring a few bells – Mercator, the geographer and cartographer responsible for Mercator's projection of the earth's surface; William the Silent, the founder of the Netherlands; and the painter Bernard van Orley. Here also, on top of the fountain, are the figures of the counts Egmont and Hoorn, beheaded on the Grand-Place for their opposition to the Habsburgs in 1568 (see p.74).

Count Egmont is further remembered by the **Palais d'Egmont** (no entry) at the back of the square. This elegant structure was originally built in 1534 for Françoise of Luxembourg, mother of the executed count. It was remodelled on several subsequent occasions and in 1972 it was here that Britain signed the treaty admitting it to the EEC. Across from the foot of the park, the **place du Grand Sablon** is one of Brussels' most charming squares, a sloping wedge of cobblestones flanked by tall and slender townhouses plus the occasional Art Nouveau facade. The square serves as the centre of one of the city's wealthiest districts, and is busiest at weekends, when an antiques market clusters below the church. Many of the shops on Sablon and the surrounding streets are devoted to antiques and art, and you could easily spend an hour or so window-browsing from one to another – or you can soak up the atmosphere eating or drinking in one of Sablon's cafés.

From place du Grand Sablon follow rue de la Régence up the hill to place Poelaert, named after the architect who designed the immense **Palais de Justice**, a great Greco-Roman wedding cake of a building, dwarfing the square and everything around it. It's possible to wander into the main hall of the building, a sepulchral affair with tiny audience tables where lawyers huddle with their clients, but really it's the size alone that is impressive – not that it pleased the several thousand townsfolk who were forcibly evicted so that the place could be built. Poelaert became one of the most hated men in the capital, and, when he went insane and died in 1879, it was widely believed a *steekes* (witch) from the Marolles had been sticking pins into an effigy of him.

A stone's throw from the Palais de Justice, **place Louise**, part square, part traffic junction, heralds the start of the city's most exclusive shopping district. It's here and in the immediate vicinity that you'll find designer boutiques, jewellers and glossy shopping malls as well as the discreet emporia of the likes of Hermès, Gucci and Chanel. The glitz spreads east along boulevard de Waterloo and south down avenue Louise, which is described on p.97.

Outside the petit ring

Brussels by no means ends with the **petit ring**. Léopold II pushed the city limits out beyond the course of the old walls, grabbing land from the surrounding *communes* (or boroughs) to create the irregular boundaries that survive today. To the **east**, he sequestered a rough rectangle of land across which he ploughed two wide boulevards to link the city centre with **Le Cinquantenaire**, a self-glorifying and over-sized monument erected to celebrate Belgium's golden jubilee and now housing three sprawling museums. There's no disputing the grandness of

Léopold's design, but in recent decades it has been overlaid with the uncompromising office blocks of the EU. These high-rises coalesce hereabouts to form the loosely defined **EU quarter**, not a particularly enjoyable area to explore, though the brand new and strikingly flashy European Parliament building is of passing interest – and it's also just footsteps from the fascinating paintings of the Musée Antoine Wiertz. If, however, you've an insatiable appetite for the monuments of Léopold, then you should venture further east to **Tervuren**, where the king built the grandiose Musée Royal de L'Afrique Centrale on the edge of the Forêt de Soignes.

Léopold's hand doesn't lie so heavily on the *communes* to the **south** of the city centre. Here, **St Gilles** is an animated and cosmopolitan district, though the immigrant areas around the Gare du Midi are scarred by poverty, while neighbouring **Ixelles** has become the trendiest part of Brussels, its old, well-worn streets much favoured by artists, intellectuals and students. These two *communes* also boast the best of the city's **Art Nouveau** architecture, including the sinuous virtuosity of the one-time house and studio of Victor Horta. Ixelles is cut into two by **avenue Louise**, a prosperous corridor that is actually part of the city – a territorial anomaly inherited from Léopold II – and one which merits a visit for the Musée Constantin Meunier.

West of the city centre, the partly industrialized suburb of **Anderlecht** is famous for its soccer team, but it's an ancient *commune* that possesses the fascinating Maison d'Erasme, where the polyglot scholar and church reformer Desiderius Erasmus lodged in 1521, and the Musée Bruxellois de la Gueuze, a museum in an operational brewery. Finally, **north** of the city centre, beyond the tough districts of St Josse and Schaerbeek, is **Laeken**, city residence of the Belgian royal family, and **Heysel**, with its infamous soccer stadium and the Atomium, a clumsy leftover from the 1958 World's Fair.

East of the petit ring: the EU quarter, Parc Léopold and Le Cinquantenaire

To enjoy a visit to this part of the city, you'll need to follow a clear itinerary, one which avoids the worst of the EU area, where the streets groan with traffic and a vast building programme has turned whole blocks into dusty construction sites. Essentially, this means dodging – as far as possible – rues de la Loi and Belliard, the two wide boulevards that serve as the area's main thoroughfares. The best place to start is in the vicinity of **Parc Léopold**, where – just a few minutes stroll from the petit ring – you'll find the intriguing **Musée Wiertz**, exhibiting the huge and eccentric paintings of the eponymous artist, and the brand new **European Parliament building**. From here, it's a ten-minute walk to **Le Cinquantenaire**, one of Léopold's most excessive extravagances, a triumphal arch built to celebrate the golden jubilee of Belgian independence and containing three museums, the pick of which is the wide-ranging **Musées Royaux d'Art et d'Histoire**.

From place du Trône to the European Parliament building

Part of the petit ring and on the métro line, **place du Trône** is distinguished by its double lion gates and life-size statue of Léopold II, perched on his horse. From here, **rue du Luxembourg** heads east to bisect a small park whose northern half contains a modest memorial to Julien Dillens, a popular nineteenth-century sculptor responsible for the effigy of Everard 't Serclaes on the Grand-Place (see p.73). Just

THE EU IN BRUSSELS

The **European Union** is operated by three main institutions, each of which does most of its work in Brussels:

The **European Parliament** sits in Strasbourg, but meets in Brussels for around six two-day plenary sessions per year. It's the only EU institution to meet and debate in public. During sessions, MEPs sit in political blocs and not in national delegations; there are eight blocs at present. The Parliament has a President and 14 Vice-Presidents, each of whom is elected for two and a half years by Parliament itself. The President (or a Vice-President) meets with the leaders of the political groups to plan future parliamentary business. Supporting and advising this political edifice is a complex network of committees and these are mostly based in Brussels.

The **Council of Ministers** consists of the heads of government of each of the member states and the President of the European Commission (see below). They meet regularly in the much-publicized "European Summits". Most Council meetings are not, however, attended by the heads of government, but by a delegated minister. There are complex rules regarding decision-making: some subjects only require a simple majority, others need unanimous support. This political structure is underpinned by scores of committees and working parties made up of both civil servants and political appointees. These committees and working parties are based in Brussels.

The **European Commission** acts as the EU's executive arm and board of control, managing funds and monitoring all manner of agreements. The twenty Commissioners are political appointees, nominated by their home country, but once they're in office they are responsible to the European Parliament. The president of the Commission is elected for a three-year period of office. Over 10,000 civil servants work for the Commission, whose headquarters are in Brussels.

along the street, the **place du Luxembourg** has had varying fortunes, but now it's on the up, with fashionable cafés moving in as the three-storey, stone-trimmed houses are refurbished. The reason for this gentrification is near at hand: follow the signs (to rue Wiertz) through the tatty railway station (Gare du Quartier Léopold) on the far side of the square and you'll behold a gigantic new EU office block whose undulating lines sweep way down to rue Belliard. There's a breach in this edifice dead ahead, and just beyond it – through the passageway and down the steps – is the equally new **European Union Parliament building**, another glass and steel behemoth equipped with a curved glass roof that rises to a height of 70m. Completed in 1997, the building contains a large, semi-circular assembly room as well as the offices of the President of the Parliament and their General Secretariat. The building has its admirers but is known locally as the "caprice des dieux".

Parc Léopold and its museums

Behind the European Parliament building at rue Vautier 62, the **Musée Wiertz** (Tues–Fri 10am–noon & 1–5pm; alternate weekends 10am–noon & 1–5pm; free) is devoted to the works of one of the city's most unique, if disagreeable, nineteenth-century artists. Once immensely popular – so much so that Thomas Hardy in *Tess of the d'Urbervilles* could write of "the staring and ghastly attitudes of a Wiertz museum" – Antoine Wiertz painted vast religious and mythological cavases, featuring gory hells and strapping nudes, which were critically well received at the time. The core of the museum is housed in his studio, a large, airy space that was built for him by the Belgian state on the understanding that he bequeathed his oeuvre to the nation. Amongst the paintings, his *Burnt Child* and *The Thoughts and Visions of a Severed Head* are not for the squeamish, and neither are *Premature Burial* and *Hunger, Folly, Crime*, in which a madwoman is depicted shortly after hacking off her child's ear. Yet, there's some relief to all this gruesomeness in a series of smaller, quasi-erotic pieces featuring coy nudes – but not nearly enough to justify Wiertz's belief that he was a better artist than his mentors, Rubens and Michelangelo.

The **Musée des Sciences Naturelles** (Tues–Sat 9.30am–4.45pm & Sun 9.30am–6pm; F150), just along the street from the Musée Wiertz, at rue Vautier 29, holds the city's natural history collection. It's a large, sprawling museum divided into fifteen clearly signed areas, each of which focuses on a particular aspect of the natural world, and several of which try to be child-friendly – robotic dinosaurs and suchlike. The dinosaur section is, indeed, the most impressive, featuring **iguanodons** whose skeletons parade across the ground floor. Iguanodons were two-legged herbivores who grazed in herds and a whole group of them was discovered in the coal mines of Hainaut in the late nineteenth century. Other museum highlights include a first-rate collection of tropical shells, an insect room, a section comparing the Arctic and Antarctic, and a whale gallery featuring eighteen skeletons, including the enormous remains of a blue whale.

On rue Vautier, almost opposite the Musée Wiertz, a scruffy back entrance leads into the rear of **Parc Léopold**, a hilly, leafy enclave landscaped around a lake. The park is pleasant enough, but its open spaces were encroached upon years ago when the industrialist Ernest Solvay began constructing the educational and research facilities of a prototype science centre here. The end result is a string of big old buildings that spreads along the park's northern periphery. The most interesting is the first you'll come to, the newly refurbished **Solvay Library** (no set opening times), a splendid barrel-vaulted structure with magnificent mahogany panelling. Down below the library and the other buildings, at the bottom of the slope, is the main entrance to Parc Léopold, where a set of stumpy stone gates bear the legend "Jardin royal de zoologie". Léopold wanted the park to be a zoo, but for once his plans went awry.

From the front entrance to the park, it takes a little less than ten minutes to walk east along traffic-choked rue Belliard to Parc du Cinquantenaire.

Le Cinquantenaire

The wide and largely featureless lawns of the **Parc du Cinquantenaire** slope up towards a gargantuan **triumphal arch** surmounted by a huge and bombastic bronze entitled *Brabant Raising the National Flag*. The arch and the two heavyweight stone buildings it connects make up **Le Cinquantenaire**, which was placed here by Léopold II for an exhibition to mark the golden jubilee of the Belgian state in 1880. By all accounts the exhibition of all things made in Belgium and its colonies was a great success, and the park continues to host shows and trade fairs of various kinds, while the buildings themselves – which are a brief walk from the Métro Merode – contain extensive collections of art and applied art, weapons and cars, displayed in three separate museums.

The **Musée Royal d'Art et d'Histoire** (Tues–Fri 9.30am–5pm, Sat & Sun 10am–5pm; F150), on the south side of the south wing of the complex, is made up of a maddening (and badly labelled) maze of pottery, carvings, furniture, tapestries, glassware and lacework from all over the world. There is almost too much to absorb in even a couple of visits, and your best bet is to pick up the plan and index at reception (F20) and select the areas which interest you most. There are enormous galleries of mostly run-of-the-mill Greek, Egyptian and Roman artefacts complete with mummies of a jackal, crocodile and falcon. Elsewhere, another part of the collection has an assortment of Near and Far Eastern gods, porcelain, jewellery and textiles, and there are pre-Columbian Native American carvings and effigies too. The **European decorative arts** sections have the most immediacy and these are located on Level 1 (Rooms 45–75) and Level 2 (Rooms 89–105). They are divided into over twenty distinct collections, featuring everything from Delft ceramics, altarpieces, porcelain and silverware through to tapestries, Art Deco and Art Nouveau furnishings. It's all a little bewildering, with little to link one set of artefacts to another, but the sub-section entitled **The Middle Ages to Baroque** (Level 1, Rooms 53–70) is outstanding and comparatively easy to absorb.

Finally, don't leave without poking your nose round the **Art Nouveau** sections, especially **Room 50**, where the display cases were designed by Victor Horta for a firm of jewellers, and now accommodate the celebrated *Mysterious Sphinx*, a ceramic bust of archetypal Art Nouveau design, the work of Charles van der Stappen in 1897.

Housed in a vast hangar-like building on the other side of the south wing of Le Cinquantenaire, **Autoworld** (daily: April–Sept 10am–6pm, Oct–March 10am–5pm; F200) is a chronological stroll through the short history of the automobile, with a huge display of vintage vehicles, beginning with early turn-of-the-century motorized cycles and Model Ts. Perhaps inevitably, European varieties predominate: there are lots of vehicles from Peugeot, Renault and Benz, and homegrown examples too, including a Minerva from 1925 which once belonged to the Belgian royals. American makes include early Cadillacs, a Lincoln from 1965 that was also owned by the Belgian king, and some great gangster-style Oldsmobiles. The museum's major drawback is its lack of contemporary vehicles – few cars date from after the mid-1970s. That said, there's good English labelling, at least on the downstairs exhibits, and a decent museum shop, with lots of automobile-related matter, including a great selection of model cars.

In the north wing of Le Cinquantenaire, on the other side of the triumphal arch from the other two museums, the **Musée Royal de l'Armée et d'Histoire Militaire** (Tues–Sun 9am–noon & 1–4.30pm; free) displays collections tracing the history of the Belgian army from independence to the present day by means of weapons, uniforms and paintings. There are also modest sections dealing with "Belgian" regiments in the Austrian and Napoleonic armies, and, more interestingly, the volunteers who formed the nucleus of the 1830 revolution. Most spectacular are the galleries devoted to armoured cars, artillery and military aircraft, though it's far from required viewing. One surprise is that from the top floor you can get out onto the triumphal arch and enjoy extensive views over the city.

The office blocks of the EU are concentrated along and between the two wide boulevards – **rues de la Loi and Belliard** – which Léopold II built to connect his Parc du Cinquantenaire with the city centre. It's not an interesting area to visit as the EU remains committed to modernistic, state-of-the-art high-rises. This is surprising given the difficulties the EU has had with its best-known construction, the **Centre Berlaymont**, a huge office building on rue de la Loi beside Métro Schuman. When it was opened in 1967, the Berlaymont was widely praised for its ground-breaking design, but in 1991 it was abandoned for health and safety reasons – the building was riddled with asbestos and work still continues on its refurbishment.

Tervuren's Musée Royal de L'Afrique Centrale

East of Parc du Cinquantenaire, the ten-kilometre-long avenue de Tervuren leads out of Brussels toward the suburb of **Tervuren**, lined with embassies and mansions in its upper reaches, and then delving through the wooded peripheries of the Forêt de Soignes, a route most easily covered by tram #44 from place Montgomery. The only attraction of Tervuren, aside from the mere pleasure of the journey there, is the **Musée Royal de L'Afrique Centrale** (Tues–Fri 10am–5pm, Sat & Sun 10am–6pm; F80), a short walk along the main road from the tram terminal, and housed in a pompous custom-built pile constructed on the orders of King Léopold II early in the twentieth century.

Personally presented with the vast Congo River basin by a conference of the European Powers in 1885, Léopold became one of the country's richest men as a result. His initial attempts to secure control of the area were abetted by the explorer – and ex-Confederate soldier – Henry Stanley, who went to the Congo on a five-year fact-finding mission in 1879, just a few years after he had famously found the missionary David Livingstone. Even by the standards of the colonial powers, Léopold's regime was too chaotic and too extraordinarily cruel to stomach, and in 1908, one year before the museum opened, the Belgian government took over the territory, installing a marginally more liberal state bureaucracy. The country gained independence as Zaire in 1960, and its subsequent history has been one of the most bloodstained in Africa.

The museum was Léopold's own idea, a blatantly colonialist and racist enterprise which treats the Africans as a naive and primitive people, and the Belgians as their paternalistic benefactors. Nevertheless, the collection is undeniably rich if a little old-fashioned, and sometimes positively eccentric: one room is entirely devoted to examples of different sorts of timber. Surprisingly there is little about Léopold's administration or its savagery. The most interesting displays cover many aspects of Congolese life, from masks, idols and musical instruments to weapons and an impressive array of dope pipes, and there's a superb 22-metre dugout canoe. The museum's grounds are also worth a stroll, with the formal gardens set around a series of geometric lakes, flanked by wanderable woods.

South of the ring: St Gilles, avenue Louise and Ixelles

Full of tiny squares and twisting streets, home to a plethora of local bars and some of the capital's finest Art Nouveau houses, the neighbouring areas of **St Gilles** and **Ixelles**, just south of the petit ring, make a great escape from the hustle and bustle of the city centre. This is Brussels without the razzamatazz and tourists are few and far between, especially in **St Gilles**, the smaller of the two *communes*, which is often regarded as little more than an example of inner city decay. Frankly, this is true enough of its most westerly section, comprising the depressing immigrant quarters of **Gare du Midi** and the downtrodden streets of **Porte de Hal**, but St Gilles gets more beautiful the further east it spreads, its run-down streets left behind for refined avenues interspersed with dignified squares.

Ixelles, for its part, is one of the capital's most attractive and exciting outer areas, with a diverse street-life and elegant squares – like the lively **place St Boniface**. Historically something of a cultural crossroads, Ixelles has long drawn artists, writers and intellectuals – Karl Marx, Auguste Rodin, and Alexandre Dumas all lived here – and today it retains an arty, sometimes Bohemian feel. Ixelles is divided into two portions by **avenue Louise**, home to the haute bourgeoisie ever since Léopold II had the avenue laid out in the 1840s. It's here you'll find some of the city's most expensive shops and hotels, pricy jewellers, slick office blocks and the interesting **Musée Constantin Meunier**, sited in the sculptor's old house.

More than anything else, however, it's the dazzling array of **Art Nouveau** buildings clustering the streets of St Gilles and Ixelles which really grab the attention, and there's a concentration of some of the finest on and around the boundary between the two communes – in between chaussée de Charleroi and avenue Louise. In particular, there's Horta's own house, now the glorious **Musée Horta**, one of the few Art Nouveau buildings in the country fully open to the public, as well as examples of the work of Paul Hankar. Access to most of the city's Art Nouveau buildings is restricted, so you can either settle for the view from outside, or enrol on one of ARAU's specialist tours (see p.65).

A convenient place to begin a visit to **St Gilles** is the imposing **Porte de Hal**, at the southern tip of the petit ring. It's the only one of the city's seven medieval gates to have survived – the rest were knocked down by Napoleon, but this one was left untouched because it was a prison. The gate is a massive, heavily fortified affair, with towers and turrets, battlements and machicolations, and – although it was clumsily remodelled in the 1870s – it gives a good idea of the strength of the city's medieval defences. Heading south from the gateway, down the chaussée de Waterloo, you're soon in the impoverished heart of St Gilles, where there's a daily morning **market** (Tues–Sun 6am–noon) at the **parvis de St Gilles** intersection. From here, it's another brief stroll south to the **Barrière de St Gilles**, a seven-road junction that was, until the middle of the nineteenth century, the site of a toll gate where taxes were levied on merchandise passing into the city. Close by, south again up avenue Paul Dejaer, is the *commune*'s **Hôtel de Ville**, a neo-Renaissance edifice, and behind that, at the top end of avenue Jef Lambeaux, rises the ersatz medieval castle which holds the **prison**.

East from the prison, the desultory avenue Ducpétiaux leads to the chaussée de Charleroi, within easy striking distance of the Musée Victor Horta.

Musée Victor Horta and Art Nouveau buildings

The **Musée Victor Horta** (Tues–Sun 2–5.30pm; weekdays F150, weekends F200), just off the chaussée de Charleroi at rue Américaine 23 and 25, occupies the two houses Horta designed as his home and studio at the end of the nineteenth century, and was where he lived until 1919. From the outside the structure is quite modest, a dark, narrow terraced house with a fluid facade and almost casually knotted and twisted ironwork, but it is for his interiors that Horta is famous. Inside is a sunny, sensuous dwelling exhibiting all the architect's favourite flourishes – wrought iron, stained glass, ornate furniture and panelling made from several different types of timber. The main feature is the staircase, which runs through the centre of the house up to the skylight, ensuring the house gets as much light as possible. Decorated with painted motifs and surrounded by mirrors, it remains one of Horta's most magnificent and ingenious creations, giving access to a sequence of wide, bright rooms. Also of interest is the modest but enjoyable selection of paintings, many of which were given to Horta by friends and colleagues, including works by Félicien Rops and Joseph Heymans.

VICTOR HORTA

The son of a shoemaker, **Victor Horta** (1861–1947) was born in Ghent, where he failed in his first career, being unceremoniously expelled from the city's music conservatory for indiscipline. He promptly moved to Paris to study architecture, returning to Belgium in 1880 to complete his internship in Brussels with Alphonse Balat, the architect to King Léopold II. Balat was a traditionalist, responsible for the classical facades of the Palais Royal – amongst many other prestigious projects – and Horta looked elsewhere for inspiration. He found it in the work of William Morris, the leading figure of the English Arts and Crafts movement, whose designs were key to the development of **Art Nouveau**. Taking its name from the Maison de l'Art Nouveau, a Parisian shop which sold items of modern design, Art Nouveau rejected the imitative architectures which were popular at the time – Neoclassical and neo-Gothic – in favour of a innovatory style that was characterized by sinuous, flowing lines. In England, Morris and his colleagues had focused on book illustrations and furnishings, but in Belgium Horta extrapolated the new style into architecture, experimenting with new building materials – steel and concrete – as well as traditional stone, glass and wood.

In 1893, Horta completed the curvaceous **Hôtel Tassel** (see opposite), Brussels' first Art Nouveau building – "hôtel" meaning town house. Inevitably, there were howls of protest from the traditionalists, but no matter what his opponents said, Horta never lacked for work again. The following years – roughly 1893 to 1905 – were Horta's most inventive and prolific. He designed over forty buildings, including the **Hôtel Solvay** and his own beautifully decorated house and studio, now the **Musée Victor Horta**. The delight Horta took in his work is obvious, especially when employed on private houses, and his enthusiasm was all-encompassing – he almost always designed everything from the blueprints to the wallpaper and carpets. He never kept a straight line or sharp angle where he could deploy a curve, and his use of light was revolutionary, often filtering through from above, atriumlike, with skylights and as many windows as possible. Curiously, Horta also believed that originality was born of frustration, and so he deliberately created architectural difficulties, pushing himself to find harmonious solutions. Horta felt that the architect was as much an artist as the painter or sculptor, and so he insisted on complete stylistic freedom. It was part of a well-thought-out value system that allied him with both Les XX and the Left; as he wrote, "My friends and I were reds, without however having thought about Marx or his theories."

Completed in 1906, the **Grand Magasin Waucquez** department store was a transitional building signalling the end of Horta's Art Nouveau period. His later works were more Modernist constructions, whose understated lines were a far cry from the ornateness of his earlier work. In Brussels, the best example of his later work is the **Palais des Beaux-Arts** of 1928 (see p.107).

From the Musée Victor Horta, it's a five-minute walk north to **rue Defacqz**, the site of several charming Art Nouveau houses. Three were designed by **Paul Hankar** (1859–1901), a classically trained architect and contemporary of Horta, who developed a real penchant for sgraffiti – akin to frescoes – and multicoloured brickwork. Hankar was regarded as one of the most distinguished exponents of Art Nouveau and **no. 48** sports a fine, flowing facade, decorated with sgraffiti representing the Ages of Man. **No. 50** is a Hankar creation too, built for the painter René Janssens in 1898, whilst the architect's old home, at **no. 71**, features four sgraffiti beneath the cornice – one each for morning, afternoon, evening and night. Hankar designed his home in the early 1890s, making it one of the city's earliest Art Nouveau buildings.

There are more Art Nouveau treats in store on neighbouring **rue Faider** where **no. 83** boasts a splendidly flamboyant facade with ironwork foliage round the windows and faint frescoes of languishing pre-Raphaelite women, all to a design by Armand Van Waesberghe. Directly opposite is rue Paul Emile Janson at the bottom of which, at no. 6, is the celebrated **Hôtel Tassel**, the building that made Horta's reputation. The supple facade is appealing enough, with clawed columns, stained glass and spiralling ironwork, but it was with the interior that Horta really made his mark, an uncompromising fantasy featuring a fanciful wrought-iron staircase and walls covered with linear decoration.

At the end of rue Paul Emile Janson you hit avenue Louise, where a right turn will take you the couple of hundred metres to the **Hôtel Solvay**, at no. 224 – another Horta masterpiece, and, like the Musée Horta, containing most of the original furnishings and fittings. The 33-year-old Horta was given complete freedom and unlimited funds by the Solvay family (they made a fortune in soft drinks) to design this opulent town house, whose facade is graced by bow windows, delicate metalwork and contrasting types of stone. Also on avenue Louise, a few minutes further along at no. 346, is Horta's **Hôtel Max Hallet**, a comparatively plain structure of 1904 where the straight and slender facade is decorated with elegant mouldings. Just beyond, the modern sculpture stranded in the middle of the traffic island looks like a pair of animal tusks, but is in fact a representation of the "V" for Victory sign of World War II. Named *Phénix 44*, it's the work of Olivier Strebelle.

From the Max Hallet residence, it's a quick tram ride north to the smart commercialism of place Louise or a five- to ten-minute stroll south to the Musée Constantin Meunier (see below).

Avenue Louise

Named after the eldest daughter of its creator, Léopold II, **avenue Louise** slices southeast from the petit ring, its beginnings lined by some of the city's most expensive shops and boutiques. Trams #93 and #94 speed up and down its length, psssing by Victor Horta's Hôtel Max Hallet (see above) to reach – about 500m further on – the foot of the rue de l'Abbaye, where the **Musée Constantin Meunier** is at no. 59 (Tues–Fri & alternate weekends 10am–noon & 1–5pm; free; ☎648 44 49). The museum is housed in the unassuming home and studio of Brussels-born Constantin Meunier, who lived here from 1899 until his death at the age of 74 six years later. Meunier began as a painter, but it's as a sculptor that he's best remembered, and the museum has an extensive collection of his dark and brooding bronzes. The biggest and most important pieces are in the room at the back, where a series of muscular men with purposeful faces stand around looking heroic – *The Reaper* and *The Sower* are typical. There are oil paintings in this room too, gritty industrial scenes like the coalfield of *Black Country Borinage* and the gloomy dockside of *The Port*, one of Meunier's most forceful works.

Meunier was angered by the harsh living conditions of Belgium's workers, particularly (like Van Gogh before him) the harsh life of the coal miners of the Borinage. This anger fuelled his art, which asserted the dignity of the working class in a style that was to be copied by the Social Realists of his and later generations. According to Hobsbawm's *Age of Empire*, "Meunier invented the international stereotype of the sculptured proletarian".

In a lovely little wooded dell on the other side of avenue Louise from the museum, and approached via rue de l'Aurore, lies the **Abbaye de la Cambre**. Of medieval foundation, the abbey was suppressed by the French Revolutionary army and its attractive eighteenth-century brick buildings, which surround a pretty little courtyard, are now used by several government departments. On the courtyard is the main entrance to the lovely little abbey **church** (Mon–Fri 9am–noon & 3–6pm free); whose nave, with its barrel vaulting, is an exercise in simplicity. The church is an amalgamation of styles incorporating both Gothic and Classical features and it holds one marvellous painting, Albert Bouts' *The Mocking of Christ*, an early sixteenth-century work showing a mournful, blood-spattered Jesus. Behind the abbey's buildings are the walled and terraced **gardens**, an oasis of peace away from the hubbub of avenue Louise.

Beyond the abbey, at the end of avenue Louise, the **Bois de la Cambre** is Brussels' most popular park, bustling with joggers, dog-walkers, families and lovers at weekends, and is the northerly finger of the large **Forêt de Soignes**, whose once mighty forests bear a clutch of dual carriageways, and, more promisingly, scores of quiet footpaths.

The chaussée d'Ixelles and around

To the east of avenue Louise, the more fashionable part of **Ixelles** radiates out from the petit ring, its busy streets spined by the **chaussée d'Ixelles**, whose unpromising beginnings – beside the Porte de Namur – should not deter: things get interesting just five minutes' walk down the boulevard at the **Galerie d'Ixelles**, the shopping centre of Ixelles' Central and North African community. In sharp contrast to the chic boutiques of the **Galerie Toison d'Or** across the road, this is packed with tiny shops selling anything from batik cloths to bizarre wigs and cosmetics.

On the far side of the **Galerie d'Ixelles** is the **chaussée de Wavre**. Head south past the exotic fruit stores and turn right down rue de Longue Vie, the heart of **Matongé**, the social centre of the African quarter. The street is thronged with small cheerful bars and cafés playing African music and serving cheap beer and traditional food till the early hours of the morning. Near here too, just west along rue de la Paix, is **place St Boniface**, home to a number of laid-back café-bars including the immensely popular *l'Ultime Atome* (see p.106).

After these enticements, the chaussée d'Ixelles becomes a bit of a bore as it ploughs on south to **place Fernand Cocq**, a small rectangular square named after a one-time Ixelles burgomaster. The square's centrepiece is the **Maison communale**, an imposing Neoclassical building built for the opera singer Maria Malibran, née Garcia (1808–1836), and her live-in lover, the Belgian violinist Charles de Bériot. One of the great stars of her day, Malibran's contralto voice created a sensation when she first appeared on the stage in London in 1825. Her father, one Manuel Garcia, trained her and organized her tours, but pushed his daughter into a most unfortunate marriage in New York. Mr Malibran turned out to be a bankrupt and Maria pluckily left husband and father behind, returning to Europe to pick up her career. She was fantastically successful and had this Ixelles mansion built for herself and Bériot in 1833. After her death, the house lay uninhabited until it was bought by the Ixelles commune in 1849.

The excellent **Musée d'Ixelles** (Tues–Fri 1–7pm, Sat & Sun 10am–5pm; permanent collection free; admission charged for temporary exhibitions), rue Jean van Volsem 71, is located about ten minutes' walk southeast of place Fernand

Cocq – just off the chaussée d'Ixelles. The museum has an excellent reputation for the quality of its temporary exhibitions but its permanent collection is of great interest also, containing mainly nineteenth- and early twentieth-century French and Belgian material as well as a small sample of earlier paintings in the first wing including *Tobie and the Angel* by Rembrandt and a sketch, *The Stork*, by Albrecht Dürer. In the same wing, Jacques-Louis David, one-time revolutionary and the leading light among France's Neoclassical painters, is well represented by *The Man at the Gallows*. The museum's **two other wings** hold an enjoyable sample of the work of the country's leading modern artists, including Magritte, Paul Delvaux and Marcel Broodthaers.

West of the petit ring: Anderlecht and Koekelberg

It's small surprise that the gritty suburbs to the immediate west of the petit ring – principally Anderlecht and Koekelberg – are little visited by tourists. For the most part, the area is distinctly short on charm, though it is home to one of Europe's premier football teams – Anderlecht – as well as a smattering of sights. **Anderlecht** easily outshines its neighbours, containing the fascinating Maison d'Erasme, where Erasmus holed up for a few months in 1521, and the Musée Gueuze, devoted to the production of the eponymous brew, whereas **Koekelberg** can only compete with the enormous Basilique du Sacré Coeur.

No one could say **Anderlecht** was beautiful, but it has its attractive nooks and crannies, particularly in the vicinity of **Métro St Guidon** on line #1B. Come out of the station, turn left and it's a few metres down the slope to place de la Vaillance, a pleasant triangular plaza flanked by little cafés and the whitestone tower and facade of the church of **Sts Pierre et Guidon** (Mon–Fri 9am–noon & 2.30–6pm; free). The facade, which mostly dates from the fifteenth century, is unusually long and slender, its stonework graced by delicate flourishes and a fine set of gargoyles. Inside, the church has a surprisingly low and poorly lit nave in a corner of which is a vaulted chapel dedicated to **St Guido**, otherwise known as St Guy, a local eleventh-century figure. Of peasant origins, Guido entered the priesthood but he invested all of his church's money in an enterprise that went bust. He was sacked and spent the next seven years as a pilgrim, a sackcloth-and-ashes extravaganza that ultimately earnt him a sainthood – as the patron saint of peasants and horses. The chapel contains a breezy *Miracle of St Guido* by Gaspard de Crayer, a local, seventeenth-century artist who made a tidy income from religious paintings in the style of Rubens.

From Sts Pierre et Guidon, it's just a couple of minutes' walk to the **Maison d'Erasme**(Mon, Wed & Thurs, Sat & Sun 10am–noon & 2–5pm; F50), at rue du Chapitre 31 – walk east along the front of the church onto rue d'Aumale and it's on the right behind the distinctive red-brick wall. Dating from 1468, the house, with its pretty dormer windows and sturdy symmetrical lines, was built to accommodate important visitors to the church. Easily the most celebrated of these guests was **Desiderius Erasmus** (1466–1536), who lodged here in 1521. The house contains none of Erasmus' actual belongings, but a host of contemporary artefacts, all squeezed into half a dozen, clearly signed rooms. The Cabinet de travail (study) holds original portraits of Erasmus by Holbein, Dürer and others, as well as a mould of his skull, but the best paintings are concentrated in the Salle du Chapitre (chapterhouse), which boasts a charmingly inquisitive *Adoration of the Magi* by Hieronymous Bosch, a gentle *Nativity* from Gerard

David, and an hallucinatory *Temptation of St Anthony* by Pieter Huys. Moving on, the Salle Blanche (white room) contains a good sample of first editions of Erasmus's work alongside an intriguing cabinet of altered and amended texts: some show scrawled comments made by irate readers, others are the work of the Inquisition and assorted clerical censors.

The **Musée Bruxellois de la Gueuze**(Mon–Fri 8.30am–5pm, Sat & Sun 10am–5pm; F100), rue Gheude 56, is located ten minutes' walk north of the Métro Gare du Midi via avenue Paul Henri Spaak and rue Limnander; to get there direct from Maison d'Erasme, take tram #56 from Métro St Guidon to Gare du Midi. Well worth the effort, the museum is a mustily evocative working brewery, still brewing Gueuze according to the traditional methods – and there's an excellent English-language leaflet to help you decipher what you see. The beer, made only of wheat, malted barley, hops and water, is allowed to ferment naturally, reacting with natural yeasts peculiar to the Brussels air, and is bottled for two years before it is ready to drink. The result is unique, as you can find out at the tasting at the end of a visit.

From Métro Simonis – two short subway rides from Métro Gare du Midi – take tram #19 which rattles west round the edge of the lawns leading up to the ugliest church in the capital, **Koekelberg**'s the **Basilique du Sacré Coeur** (Church daily: Easter–Oct 8am–6pm; Nov – Easter 8am–5pm; free. Dome daily: Easter–Oct 9am–5pm; Nov–Easter 10am–4pm; F100), a huge structure – 140m long with a ninety-metre-tall dome – which dominates the commune of **Koekelberg**. Begun in 1905 on the orders of Léopold II and still unfinished, the basilica was conceived as a neo-Gothic extravagance in imitation of the basilica to the Sacré Coeur in Montmartre, Paris – a structure which had made the Belgian king green with envy. But the construction costs proved colossal and the plans had to be modified. The result is a vaguely ludicrous amalgamation of the original neo-Gothic design with Art Deco features added in the 1920s. While you're here, it's worth climbing up to the top of the **dome** for a panoramic view of the city.

North of the petit ring: Laeken and Heysel

Beyond the tough neighbourhoods of St Josse and Schaerbeek, **Laeken** is the royal suburb of Brussels, home of the Belgian royal family, who occupy a large out-of-bounds estate and have colonized the surrounding parkland with their memorials. From the south, Laeken is best approached on tram #52 or #92. Get off at the Araucaria tram stop, which is just behind the **Pavillon Chinois** and just off avenue des Croix. This elegant and attractive replica of a Chinese pavilion was built here by Léopold II after he had seen one at the World Fair in Paris in 1900. The king intended his creation to be a fancy restaurant, but this never materialized and the pavilion now houses a first-rate collection of Chinese porcelain (Tues–Sun 10am–4.30pm; F120; joint ticket with Tour Japonaise, F150). Across the road and reached by a tunnel from beside the pavilion is the matching **Tour Japonaise** (same times as Pavillon Chinois; F100), another of Léopold's follies, this time a copy of a Buddhist pagoda with parts made in Paris, Brussels and Yokohama, and now in use as a venue for temporary exhibitions of Japanese art (admission extra).

Around the corner behind the railings, along the congested avenue du Parc Royal, lie the **Serres Royales**, enormous greenhouses built for Léopold II and covering almost four acres. They shelter a mind-boggling variety of tropical and

Mediterranean flora but the only problem is the restricted opening hours – the greenhouses are only open to the public during April and May (times from the tourist office) and the queues to see them can be daunting. Just beyond the greenhouses is the sedate **Château Royal** (no entry), the main royal palace. Built in 1790, its most famous occupant was Napoleon, who stayed here on a number of occasions and signed the declaration of war on Russia here in 1812.

Opposite the front of the royal palace, a wide footpath leads up to the fanciful neo-Gothic monument erected in honour of Léopold I. It's the focal point of the pretty **Parc de Laeken**, whose lawns and wooded thickets extend west for a couple of kilometres to Heysel.

Poking its knobbly head into the sky near the end of boulevard du Centenaire, **Heysel**'s lofty **Atomium** (daily: Sept–March 10am–6pm; April–Aug 9am–8pm; F200) is a curious model of a molecule built for the 1958 World Fair in Brussels. The structure has become something of a symbol of the city, and features temporary displays of general interest – for example "The Atomium in Comic Strips" – within its metallic spheres, although the main sensation is the disorienting feeling of travelling from sphere to sphere by escalator.

The Atomium borders a large trade fair area, the King Baudouin Stadium (formerly the Heysel stadium), and a leisure complex, the **Bruparck**, which includes a water funpark, a huge cinema and a model of selected buildings of Europe. Fortunately, the proximity of the Heysel métro makes an early exit easy.

Eating and drinking

Brussels has an international reputation for the quality of its cuisine. It's richly deserved. Even at the dowdiest snack bar, you'll almost always find that the food is well prepared and generously seasoned – and then there are the city's **restaurants**, many of which equal anywhere in Paris. Traditional Bruxellois dishes feature on many restaurant menus, canny amalgamations of Walloon and Flemish ingredients and cooking styles – whether it be rabbit cooked in beer, steamed pigs' feet or *waterzooi* (see p.36 for more on Belgian specialities). The city is also among Europe's best for sampling a wide range of different cuisines – from ubiquitous Italian places and the Turkish restaurants of St Josse through to Spanish, Vietnamese, Japanese, and even Buddhist vegetarian restaurants. You can also eat magnificent fish and seafood, especially in and around the fashionable district of Ste Catherine.

For the most part, eating out is rarely inexpensive, but the **prices** are almost universally justified by the quality. As a general rule the less formal the restaurant, the less expensive the meal – and indeed it's hard to distinguish between the less expensive restaurants and the city's **cafés**, some of which provide some of the tastiest food in town. In addition, many **bars** serve food, often just spaghetti, sandwiches and croque-monsieurs, but many have wider-ranging menus, taking in traditional Brussels cuisine.

For **fast food**, aside from the multinational burger and pizza chains, there are plenty of *frites* stands and kebab places around the Grand-Place, notably on rue du Marché aux Fromages and near the beginning of rue des Bouchers. Pitta is also popular, stuffed with a wide range of fillings – though vegetarian ones are rare – along with the more substantial thin Turkish pizzas, or *pide*, topped with combinations of cheese, ground meat or even a fried egg, sold at any number of cafés along the chaussée de Haecht and rue du Méridien in St Josse.

Restaurants – inside the petit ring

L'Auberge des Chapeliers, rue des Chapeliers 1–3 (☎513 73 78). Sited just south of the Grand-Place, this well-established restaurant serves excellent Belgian cuisine such as salmon steak in white beer, *stoemp*, and *waterzooi*. It also specializes in mussels prepared in a variety of ways, *provençales*, *gratinées* and *marinières*. Set menus, of three courses, are from F700.

Aux Armes de Bruxelles, rue des Bouchers 13 (☎511 55 50). Right in the centre of the restaurant district near the Grand-Place, this polished and fairly expensive spot divides into two – a formal restaurant popular with the pearls-and-blue-rinse brigade, and a bistro with wooden benches. Both serve traditional Belgian cuisine to a very high standard.

La Belle Maraichère, pl Ste Catherine 11 (☎512 97 59). Smart restaurant where the waiters hover as you eat the superbly prepared Belgian cuisine. The seafood is a treat, but prices are high.

Bij den Boer, quai aux Briques 60. There's nothing pretentious here in this good old neighbourhood café-bar with its tiled floor and bygones on the wall. A great place for a drink or a meal, though the service can be slow. The seafood is delicious.

Bonsoir Clara, rue Antoine Dansaert 22 (☎502 09 90). One of the capital's trendiest restaurants on arguably the hippest street in Brussels. Moody, atmospheric lighting, 1970s geometrically mirrored walls and zinc-topped tables. The food on offer, though expensive, is excellent. Expect to find a menu full of Mediterranean, French, and Belgian classics and make sure you reserve. Daily noon–2.30pm & 7–11.30pm. Métro Bourse.

Brasserie de la Roue d'Or, rue des Chapeliers 26. Attractive brasserie with wood panelling, stained glass and brass fittings. Offers a good range of seafood.

Les Brigittines aux Marchés de la Chapelle, pl de la Chapelle 5 (☎512 68 91). Excellent bistro-style restaurant with Belle Epoque flourishes that manages to be smart and informal at the same time. The menu is fairly short, but the food is superb – the *cabillaud danois poché aux poireaux* (Danish cod poached with pears) is particularly exquisite. Closed Sun. Located behind the church of Notre Dame de la Chapelle, on the north edge of the Marolles.

Chez Léon, rue des Bouchers 18–22. Touristy but good-value bistro-style restaurant near the Grand-Place serving traditional Belgian fare. Most famous for its mussels. Daily noon–midnight.

Les Crustacés, quai aux Briques 8 (☎511 56 44). Long-established, smart seafood restaurant in the Ste Catherine district. Lobster – cooked in many different ways – is the house speciality.

La Grande Porte, rue Notre Seigneur 9 (☎512 89 98). Long, narrow, and cosy old restaurant, whose walls are plastered with ancient posters and photos. The food is good, hearty and traditional, and you're quite free to go just for a drink. Be warned, though, that it can get very crowded. On the northern edge of the Marolles near Notre Dame de la Chapelle. Closed Sun.

Iberica, rue de Flandre 8 (☎511 79 36). Agreeable Spanish restaurant in a pleasant seventeenth-century building at the place Ste Catherine end of rue de Flandre. Delicious paella, sardines, Parma ham etc. Closed Wed.

Jacques, quai aux Briques 44 (☎513 27 62). A long-established and extremely popular fish restaurant – the *cabillaud de poche* (poached cod) is highly recommended. Expect a sedate, middle-aged clientele at lunchtime, and a younger, international crowd in the evenings. Reservations a good idea.

Kasbah, rue Antoine Dansaert 20. Popular with a youthful, groovy crowd, this Moroccan eatery is famous for serving enormous portions of couscous and other North African specialities. It's run by the same people as *Bonsoir Clara* next door, and although equally hip, the lantern-lit decor makes it seem slightly less fashion-conscious and more welcoming. Vibrant atmosphere. Set menus from F700.

't Kelderke, Grand-Place 15. Busy cellar restaurant right on the Grand-Place specializing in traditional Bruxellois dishes. Serves an excellent *lapin à la gueuze* (rabbit cooked in gueuze) and a superb *carbonnades flamandes à la bière* (beef in beer). Bear in mind that you can't make reservations and you may have to stand in line for a table.

La Marée, rue du Flandre 99 (☎511 00 40). Outstanding, pocket-sized restaurant near Ste Catherine. The speciality is seafood, always fresh and always prepared in a simple, direct manner. A full meal (without wine) costs in the region of F1000. Closed Sun.

Le Paon Royale, rue du Vieux-Marché-aux-Grains 6 (☎513 08 68). Popular bar-restaurant in the place Ste Catherine locale that serves good, hearty Belgian grub at low prices – and supplements this with a fine array of Belgian speciality beers. A good choice for lunch, with plats du jour running at around F280. Open Tues–Sat 11.30am–2.30pm.

La Papaye Verte, rue Antoine Dansaert 53 (☎502 70 82). First-rate Vietnamese food at bargain basement prices.

Les Petits Oignons, rue Notre Seigneur 13 (☎512 47 38). First-rate and popular restaurant serving Belgian cuisine with flair – although at top prices. On the northern edge of the Marolles district. Closed Sun.

Le Pré Salé, rue de Flandre 16 (☎513 43 23). Friendly, old-fashioned neighbourhood restaurant just off place Ste Catherine, and providing a nice alternative to the swankier restaurants of the district. Very Bruxellois. Great mussels, fish dishes and Belgian specialities. Daily specials and a fixed-price menu for F995. Closed Mon.

In 't Spinnekopke, pl du Jardin aux Fleurs 1 (☎511 86 95). Ancient restaurant and bar that serves many traditional Bruxellois dishes cooked in beer – the owner has published a book of beer recipes. It's also one of the few places to serve beers from the Cantillon brewery in Anderlecht. Just west of place St Géry. Closed Sun.

Au Stekerlapatte, rue des Prêtres 4 (☎512 86 81). Situated on the far (southern) side of the Palais de Justice, this is a wonderful old brasserie, popular with a youngish crowd, that offers a wide-ranging menu featuring the best of traditional Bruxellois cuisine – everything from eel through to pigs' feet. The dish of the day will cost you just F450. Usually very crowded; great atmosphere. Closed Mon.

La Tortue du Zoute, rue de Rollebeek 31 (☎513 10 62). Swish little restaurant with an imaginative menu in the French style – set evening meal for F900, plat du jour a reasonable F400. Lobster is the speciality of the house. Closed Tues. Metres from the place du Grand Sablon.

Totem, rue des Grands Carmes 6 (☎513 11 52). Though hidden away behind the Grand-Place, this small but fashionable ground-floor restaurant is a hit with Brussels-based veggies, who come for the friendly atmosphere and wholesome food – organic soups, fresh salads, tofu, and a delicious selection of cakes and pastries. It's quite cheap too, a main course costing less than F350, and there's a good choice of organic wines. Open Wed–Sun 2–11pm.

Restaurants – outside the petit ring

L'Amadeus, rue Veydt 13, Ixelles (☎538 34 27). Restaurant and trendy wine bar in the one-time studio of Auguste Rodin. Top-drawer Belgian dishes and an all-you-can-eat Sunday breakfast – 10am–2pm – for F670. Off chaussée de Charleroi a couple of blocks south of the avenue Louise junction.

Le Fils de Jules, rue du Page 37, Ixelles (☎534 00 57). First-class Basque cuisine is the speciality of this pricy bistro-style restaurant. In the swankiest part of Ixelles, not far from the Musée Victor Horta. Open Mon–Fri noon–2.30pm & 7–11pm, Sat & Sun 7–11pm.

Le Jugurtha, rue de Moscou 34, St Gilles (☎538 23 67). Well-established Moroccan restaurant that serves a marvellous couscous for under F500.

La Meilleure Jeunesse, rue de l'Aurore 58, off avenue Louise (☎640 23 94). Smart restaurant with an uncomplicated French menu. The terrace at the back has a smashing view of the Abbaye de la Cambre. Set menu F700.

Le Paradoxe, ch d'Ixelles 329 (☎649 89 91). A Buddhist-run wholefood restaurant and tearoom, with an ascetic feel, and an eclectic programme of live folky/eastern music on most Friday and Saturday evenings. Set menus start at F500, plats du jour for F350; it's also a peaceful place to retreat during the day for a herbal tea and toast. Open Mon–Fri noon–2pm & 7–10pm, Sat noon–2pm.

La Quincaillerie, rue du Page 45, Ixelles (☎538 25 53). Mouth-watering Belgian and French cuisine in this delightful restaurant that occupies an old hardware shop. Specialities include fish and fowl, often cooked up in imaginative ways. There's normally a plat du jour at a very reasonable F980, but the à la carte is very pricy. Open Mon–Fri noon–2pm & 7pm–midnight, Sat & Sun 7pm–midnight.

Sahbaz, ch de Haecht 102, just beyond the northern boundary of St Josse in Schaerbeek (☎217 02 77). Reckoned to be among the city's best Turkish restaurants. The prices are low – with main courses from around F280 – and the atmosphere very friendly.

Trave Negra, rue Théodore Verhaegen 9, St Gilles (☎539 28 87). Excellent, quiet and simple Portuguese restaurant. Very welcoming, too. Just west of the Barrière de St Gilles.

La Tsampa, rue de Livourne 109, Ixelles (☎647 03 67). Congenial vegetarian restaurant one block west of avenue Louise, with set menus for around F600, plat du jour for F350. Mon–Sat noon–2pm & 7–8pm.

Bars and cafés

Drinking in Brussels, as in the rest of the country, is a joy. The city has an enormous variety of **bars and cafés** – sumptuous Art Nouveau cafés; traditional bars with ceilings stained brown by a century's smoke; bars whose walls are plastered with sepia photographs and ancient beer ads; speciality beer bars with literally hundreds of different varieties of ale; and, of course, more modern hangouts. Many of the centrally located places, especially those considered "typical", are frequented by tourists and ex-pats, but in areas like Ste Catherine and place St Géry, and even tucked away in the narrow sidestreets off the Grand-Place, there are places which remain refreshingly local. A number serve meals as well as snacks, and often offer better value than eating in a restaurant. Bars stay open till late – most until 2am or 3am, some until dawn.

Bars and cafés – inside the petit ring

Arcadi, rue de L'Ecuyer 99. At the north end of the Galeries St Hubert, this tiny café is a pleasant spot for lunch, with a great selection of homemade quiches – their speciality – as well as salads and cakes.

À la Bécasse, rue Tabora 11. This spartan, old-fashioned bar not far from the Grand-Place has long wooden benches, serves beer in earthenware jugs, and has heavy Moorish architecture. The beer menu is excellent, and the food on offer, though simple, is tasty and relatively inexpensive.

Au Bon Vieux Temps, rue du Marché aux Herbes 12. Cosy old place tucked down an alley and only a minute's walk from the Grand-Place, with tile-inlaid tables and a seventeenth-century chimney piece. The building dates back to 1695 and the stained glass window depicting the Virgin Mary and St Michael was originally in the local parish church. Popular with British servicemen just after the end of World War II, the bar still has comforting old-fashioned signs advertising Mackenzies' Port and Bass pale ale. A great place for a quiet drink.

Au Brasseur, rue des Chapeliers 9, just off Grand-Place. Unpretentious, spick and span little wood-panelled bar ideal for late-night drinks – it often stays open until first light. The beer is cheap, and you can usually find a table.

Brasserie Horta, rue des Sables 20. The café of the *Centre Belge de la Bande Dessinée* (see p.80). Tasty food, including smoked salmon, good salads and a generally inventive menu in a summery Art Nouveau building designed by Victor Horta. Reasonable prices. Open Tues–Sun noon–3pm.

Le Cercueil, rue des Harengs 10–12. Funereal concept bar just off the Grand-Place, where the tables are coffins, the only light UV, and the music alternates between Gregorian chant and Chopin's Funeral March. Expensive, though, and more than a little seedy. Daily 11am–3am, until dawn on Fri & Sat.

Le Cirio, rue de la Bourse 18. One of Brussels' oldest bars, sumptuously decorated in fin-de-siècle style, though now somewhat frayed round the edges. Once frequented, they say, by Jacques Brel.

Le Falstaff, rue Henri Maus 17–23. Art Nouveau café next to the Bourse, attracting a mixed bag of tourists, gays, Eurocrats and bourgeois Bruxellois. Full of atmosphere, and so crowded in the evenings that you're unlikely to find a seat. Inexpensive beer and sandwiches, plus great pastries. Daily 11.30am–2am.

La Fleur en Papier Doré, rue des Alexiens 53. Cluttered, cosy locals' bar, with walls covered with doodles and poems, that was once (one of) the chosen drinking places of René Magritte. The novelist Hugo Claus apparently held his second wedding reception here. Just south of the Grand-Place.

Le Greenwich, rue des Chartreux 7. Brussels' traditional chess café with a lovely old wood-panelled and mirrored interior. Laid-back atmosphere. Close to place St Géry.

À l'Imaige de Nostre-Dame, rue du Marché aux Herbes 6. A welcoming if extremely quiet bar at the end of a long alley, decorated like an old Dutch kitchen. Good range of speciality beers. Near the Grand-Place.

Café Métropole, pl de Brouckère 31. Sumptuously ritzy fin-de-siècle café, belonging to an equally opulent hotel. Astonishingly, many people prefer to sit outside, for a view of flashing ads and zipping traffic. If you've got cash to spare, indulge in a brunch of smoked salmon or caviare. Popular with tourists.

À la Mort Subite, rue Montagne aux Herbes Potagères 7. Twenties bar that loaned its name to a widely available bottled beer. A long, narrow room with nicotine-stained walls and mirrors, a dissolute-arty clientèle and an animated atmosphere. Snacks served, or just order a plate of cheese cubes to accompany your beer. Daily 11am–1am. Just northeast of the Grand-Place opposite the far end of the Galeries St Hubert.

Le Pain Quotidien, rue des Sablon 11. Not really a bar at all, but an excellent café (part of a small chain) decked out with long wooden tables selling wholesome salads, various types of brown bread, soup, cakes, pastries and snacks. Open Mon–Fri 7.30am–7pm, Sat & Sun 8am–7pm, and a good choice for a bite to eat at lunchtime. Also at rue Antoine Dansaert 22.

Le Perroquet, rue Watteau 31. Busy semi-circular café-bar occupying attractive Art Nouveau premises in the Sablon area, just down from the Palais de Justice. Imaginative range of stuffed pitta and salads and other tasty snacks – though you'll find it difficult to get a seat on a Friday or Saturday night.

Pi Pi, rue J. Van Praet 26. Dimly lit, fashionable (or at least very popular) café-bar metres from the Bourse. Great place to warm up; world music soundtrack.

Les Postiers, rue Fossé aux Loups 14. Old-established and unpretentious bar neatly placed close to place de la Monnaie and serving basic snacks and light meals.

Le Roi d'Espagne, Grand-Place 1. Supremely touristy bar in a seventeenth-century guild-house with a collection of marionettes and inflated animal bladders suspended from the ceiling and naff pikes in the boys' toilet. You get a fine view of the Grand-Place from the rooms upstairs, as well as from the pavement-terrace, and the drinks aren't too expensive. Daily 10am–midnight.

De Skieven Architek, pl du Jeu de Balle 50. The smartest café-bar on the square at the heart of the Marolles quarter. Serves a wide range of meals and snacks – omelettes from F150, croissants and coffee from F100 – and has newspapers to browse, but can't but seem a little tame compared to the rough and ready bars flanking the rest of the square.

Au Soleil, rue Marché au Charbon 86. Popular bar with a wide choice of beers, crowded every night until late with a young, self-consciously trendy crowd. Close to the Grand-Place.

Toone, Impasse Schuddeveld 6, off Petite rue des Bouchers. Largely undiscovered bar belonging to the Toone puppet theatre, just north of the Grand-Place. Two small rooms with old posters on rough plaster walls, a reasonably priced beer list, a modest selection of snacks, and a soundtrack of classical and jazz, make it one of the centre's more congenial watering-holes.

Bars and cafés – outside the petit ring

L'Amour Fou, ch d'Ixelles 185, Ixelles. Upbeat cybercafé off place Fernand Cocq, where you can drink a delicious selection of vodkas, mezcal and tequila while taking in the latest works of obscure modern artists decorating the walls. The food is pretty good as well, with a main meal (pasta, quiche) for F250–350, a large salad for F280, and bar snacks (mushrooms on toast, croque-monsieur) for under F200. Open late and often busy.

Chez Moeder Lambic, rue de Savoie 68, St Gilles. Small bar in a down-at-heel part of St Gilles, just behind the borough's Hôtel de Ville, that has over 1000 beers available, including 500 Belgian varieties. Not at all expensive either. Daily 4pm–3am.

Conway's, av de la Toison d'Or 10. Lively late-night Irish-American bar frequented by the young, free, and extremely desperate. If you want to get drunk and stand on a barstool playing air-guitar, this is the place to come. Needless to say, it's a meat market.

James Joyce, rue Archimède 34. Cliquey and sometimes boisterous hangout for the ex-pat Irish, within staggering distance of the Centre Berlaymont. Occasional Irish folk music.

Kitty O'Shea's, bd Charlemagne 42. Large ex-pat bar right opposite the Centre Berlaymont. Serves Irish food, draught Guinness and the like. An older clientèle than the *Joyce*.

Le Passiflore, rue du Bailli 97, Ixelles. Informal, arty café selling wholesome salads and snacks. A couple of minutes walk from the Musée Horta. Open Mon–Fri 8am–7pm, Sat & Sun 9am–7pm.

La Porteuse d'Eau, av Jean Volders 48a, St Gilles. Refurbished Art Nouveau café on the corner of rue Vanderschrick, near the Porte de Hal. One of the few signs of gentrification in this rundown section of St Gilles. The food is not good, but the ornate interior is better – well worth the price of a beer.

Rick's, av Louise 344. Situated in a smart part of the city towards the southern end of avenue Louise, this bar-restaurant has been a gathering-place of resident English-speakers for close on thirty years. The bar can get lively, and there's a full menu available, though it's most famous for its ribs.

SiSiSi, ch de Charleroi 174, St Gilles. Youthful, laid-back bar offering a splendid range of salads and stuffed pittas. Especially popular at lunchtimes. Very economical. Located in the eastern – and more prosperous – part of St Gilles, a five to ten-minute walk north of the Musée Victor Horta, close to place Paul Janson. Open daily 10am–2am, from noon at the weekend; food served noon–3pm & 6pm–midnight.

De Ultieme Hallucinatie, rue Royale 316. Well-known and fancifully ornate Art Nouveau bar done up like an old Twenties train car. A youngish crowd sinking a good choice of beers, reasonably priced drinks and food – omelettes, lasagne, etc. There's also a sumptuous restaurant in the front. Occasional live music too. Open Mon–Fri 11am–2am, Sat & Sun 5pm–3am. Near Métro Botanique, in an area that has a bad reputation for street crime.

L'Ultime Atome, rue St Boniface 14, Ixelles. Congenial café. Good range of beers, superb food and a youngish clientele. Food – at lunchtime & 7pm–12.30am – ranges from pasta and elaborate salads to more exotic fare, such as ravioli with artichokes and *osso bucco*. Near the Porte de Namur, in between the chaussées d'Ixelles and de Wavre.

Wild Geese, av Livingstone 2–4. This enormous Irish theme pub is the preferred watering hole of the EU crowd, especially Thursday nights when the Euro-youth strut their stuff en masse. It also serves good-value bar food including large baked potatoes with salads and fillings for under F200. Occasional live music.

Nightlife: music, clubs, film and theatre

As far as **nightlife** goes, it's likely you'll be happy to while away the evenings in one of the city's bars – there are plenty in which you can drink until sunrise. However, although it's not as lively a scene as in some European capitals, Brussels is also a reasonably good place to catch **live bands**. Along with

Antwerp, the city is a regular stop on the European tours of major artists – though admittedly the indigenous rock and indie scene is pretty thin. Rather better is the **jazz** with several bars playing host to local and international acts; jazz has been popular here since the 1920s.

After a slow start, **club** culture has made some headway in the city and, although it's hardly cutting edge stuff, the centre now boasts several really good places. As a general rule, clubs **open** Thursday to Saturday from 11pm to 5/6am and entry **prices** are low: you rarely have to pay more than F400 and many of the smaller clubs have no cover at all, though you do have to tip the bouncer a nominal fee (F20) on the way in.

The **classical musical scene** is also well established, though it has suffered from serious under-funding in recent years. The Orchestre National de Belgique continues to thrive under Yuri Simonov, and there are a number of excellent classical music festivals, notably the *Ars Musica* festival of contemporary music held annually in March, and the prestigious four-yearly Concours Musical Reine Elisabeth, a competition for piano, violin and voice which numbers among its prize-winners Vladimir Ashkenazy, David Oistrakh and Gidon Kremer.

In terms of the **cinema**, about half the **films** shown in Brussels are in English with French and Flemish subtitles (coded "VO", *version originale*). Most screens are devoted to the big US box-office hits, but there are several more adventurous cinemas showing an eclectic mix of foreign films. There's also the annual **International Brussels Film Festival** in January, the highlight of which is the "Tremplin" or "Springboard" section, which features international films favoured by critics but not yet taken on by Belgian distributors.

As for **theatre**, Brussels is home to a new generation of young and talented playwrights like Philippe Blasband and Jean-Marie Piemme. Obviously almost all productions are staged in French or Flemish, though the city is regularly visited by big-name touring troupes who perform in their own language. There's also the **Théâtre Royal de Toone**, which puts on puppet plays in the Bruxellois dialect and has become one of the city's major tourist pulls.

For **listings** of concerts and events, check the *What's On* section of the weekly *Bulletin* or the Wednesday supplement of *Le Soir*. **Tickets** for most things are available from both Fnac in the City 2 complex, rue Neuve (☎209 22 11) and the TIB on the Grand-Place (reservation hotline ☎0800/21 2 21).

Concert halls and large performance venues

AB, bd Anspach 110 (☎548 24 24). The AB (Ancienne Belgique) is one of the leading rock venues, and is paricularly good for international indie bands who perform in either the main auditorium or the smaller club on the first floor. Also showcases jazz and folk.

Cirque Royal, rue de l'Enseignement 81 (☎218 20 15). Some big names in international rock, dance and classical music have appeared here, in a venue that was formerly an indoor circus.

Forest National, av du Globe 36 (☎340 22 11). Brussels' main arena for big-name international concerts, holding around 11,000 people.

Palais des Beaux Arts, rue Ravenstein 23 (☎507 82 00). With a concert hall holding around 2000, as well as some smaller theatres, the Palais is primarily used for contemporary dance, ballet, theatre and classical music. It's the home of the Orchestre National de Belgique.

Théâtre royal de la Monnaie, pl de la Monnaie (☎229 12 11). This is Belgium's premier opera house. Renowned for its adventurous repertoire and production style, it has earned itself glowing reviews over the years. It has a policy of nurturing promising singers rather than casting the more established stars, so it's a good place to spot potential stars. Book in advance as tickets are often difficult to come by. Capacity is 1200.

Live music bars

L'Archiduc, rue Antoine Dansaert 6 (☎512 06 52). Small and tasteful bar with regular live jazz on the weekend. Near place St Géry.

Le Cercle, rue Ste Anne 20 (☎514 03 53). Small, unremarkable venue in itself, but the live music is a real attraction – everything from jazz and Latino through to *chanson française* three or four times a week. Just off place du Grand Sablon.

Magazin 4, rue du Magasin 4 (☎223 34 74). Favourite venue for up-and-coming Belgian indie bands. Only opens when there's a gig. In an old warehouse off the Petit Ring near Métro Yser.

Sounds, rue de la Tulipe 28, Ixelles (☎512 92 50). Seedy, smoky American-oriented bar, showcasing local and touring modern jazz artists. Off place Ferdinand Cocq. Closed Sun.

Travers, rue Traversière 11 (☎218 40 86). Informal jazz club with an impressive reputation for showcasing new Belgian musicians. Within easy walking distance of Métro Botanique. Closed Sunday.

Clubs

Le Bazaar, rue des Capucins 63. In the Marolles, off rue Haute. Split-level club with a dimly lit restaurant upstairs and a dancefloor below offering funk, soul, rock and indie.

Cartagena, rue du Marché au Charbon 70. Enjoyable downtown club offering arguably the best and certainly the widest range of South American and Latin sounds in town. Attracts the late-twenties age range, and gets going around midnight. Open Friday and Saturday nights only.

The Fuse, rue Blaes 208. Large, young, and vibrant techno, jungle and house club in the Marolles district. Big-name, international DJs are a regular feature. Chill-out rooms and visuals. Saturday nights only.

Pitt's Bar, rue des Minimes 53. Near the Palais de Justice, the music here is techno, garage, bhangra and house and it's popular with students. Open Tues–Sun.

Who's Who Land, rue du Poinçon 17. This trendy house club (with occasional foam parties) often sees enormous teenage crowds, even from abroad. Open Thurs–Sat (Thurs is rap and ragga night). In the Marolles.

Cinemas

Actors Studio, petite rue des Bouchers 16 (☎512 16 96). This small cinema is probably the best place in the city centre to catch arthouse or independent films. It's also one of the leading venues for the Brussels Film Festival.

Arenberg Galleries, Galerie de la Reine 26, Galeries St Hubert (☎0900 29 550). Best known for its "Sneak Previews", this cinema also screens an adventurous variety of world films.

Musée du Cinéma, in the Palais des Beaux Arts, rue Baron Horta 9 (☎507 83 70). This small museum-cum-cinema is popular with film buffs who come to watch an excellent selection of old silent movies with piano accompaniment. See p.83 for a review of the museum.

UGC de Brouckère, pl de Brouckère 38 (☎0900 29 930). A ten-screen cinema showing the usual Hollywood films. If you go on Sunday morning you get a coffee and croissant in the price of the ticket. Its sister cinema, the UGC Acropole at Galerie de la Toison d'Or 17, screens the same sort of stuff. Both cinemas usually screen in English.

Vendôme, ch de Wavre 18 (☎502 37 00). A trendy five-screen cinema well known for screening a wide selection of arty films – *The Ice Storm*, *Kundrun* – as well as more mainstream stuff like *Titanic* and *Scream*. They usually have at least two English-language films showing at the same time.

Theatres

Théâtre National, Centre Rogier, pl Rogier (☎203 53 03). This French-only theatre offers high-quality productions ranging from Molière to Brecht, and it's popular with a wide range of visiting theatre companies including the RSC, the Parisian Théâtre Odeon and the Berlin-based Berliner Scubuhne. Visting companies perform in their native language.

Théâtre Royal de Toone (Puppet Theatre), Impasse Schuddeveld 6, off Petite rue des Bouchers 21 (☎511 71 37). Excellent puppet plays in the Bruxellois dialect, though there are occasional English renditions. Performances at 8.30pm from Tuesday to Saturday. Tickets (at F400) are available at the box office half an hour before the performance, but advance booking is advised. A couple of minutes' walk from the Grand-Place.

Shopping

Like every other EU capital city, Brussels is swimming with **shops**. The main central shopping street is **rue Neuve**, which runs from place de la Monnaie to place Rogier, and this is home to most of the leading chains. At the top end of rue Neuve, **City 2** is the ultimate in sanitized shopping malls, with cinemas, restaurants, department stores, clothes shops and a large supermarket. More distinctive are the city's covered shopping "streets", or **galeries**, principally the cloistered elegance of the Galeries St Hubert near the Grand-Place; the African shops of the **Galerie d'Ixelles**; and the deluxe designer shops of the **Galerie de la Toison d'Or**. But visitors to Brussels mostly go hunting for two commodities – **chocolate** and **lace** – while others track down **comic strips** and the city's **markets**.

Generally speaking, shops and stores are **open** from 10am to 6pm or 7pm Monday through Saturday. On Fridays, most department stores stay open till 8pm or 9pm, and some tourist-oriented shops open on Sundays too.

Chocolates

Leonidas, bd Anspach 46. Leonidas remains one of the most popular and widespread outlets for Belgian chocolates and pralines. Like *Godiva* – another mainstream, if slightly pricier choc chain – the chocolates are straight off the production line. Léonidas chocs are rather sickly-sweet in comparison with other brands, but then they won't mind back home. Branches all over the city.

Mary's, rue Royale, 73. A very exclusive and pricey shop, with beautiful period decor, selling handmade chocolates. You can taste the difference between this and the chains'.

Neuhaus, Grand-Place 27. A chocoholic's paradise, this expensive shop stocks the best that Belgium has to offer in the chocolate department. Check out their specialities – the hand-made Caprices, which are pralines stuffed with crispy nougat, fresh cream and soft-centered chocolate. Also sample the delicious Manons, stuffed white chocolates, which come in fresh cream, vanilla, and coffee fillings. They have branches all over the town, but the other most central are at avenue de la Toison d'Or 27 and in the Galerie de la Reine.

Wittamer, pl du Grand Sablon 6. Brussels' most famous patisserie and chocolate shop, established in 1910 and still run by the Wittamer family, who sell gorgeous if expensive light pastries, cakes, mousses, and chocolates. They serve speciality teas and coffees in their tearoom along the street at no. 12.

Lace

Manufacture Belge de Dentelle, Galerie de la Reine 6–8, in the Galeries St Hubert. The city's largest lace merchant, in business since 1810. Sells a wide variety of modern and antique lace at fairly reasonable prices. The service is helpfully old-fashioned.

F. Rubbrecht, Grand-Place 23. Traditional lace shop specializing in hand-made Brussels lace. It's not as tacky as some of the tourist traps around the Manneken Pis and the items are authentic. They do wholesale and retail, and also valuing and buying. Open Mon–Sat 9am–7pm, Sunday 10am–6pm.

Comic strips

Le Bande des Six Nez, ch de Wavre 179. Stocks a variety of new comics, as well as original editions from the 1940s and 1950s. It also sells original drawings. Vintage comics cost anything from F60 to F6000. There's a modest, but interesting English-language section too.

La Boutique de Tintin, rue de la Colline 13. Set up, no doubt, by someone with an unhealthy obsession with Hergé's quiffed hero. Expect to find anything and everything to do with Tintin – comic books, postcards, stationery, figurines, T-shirts, and sweaters and all Hergé's other cartoon creations, such as Quick & Flupke. Just off the Grand-Place. Open Mon 11am–6pm, Tue–Sat 10am–6pm, Sun 11am–5pm.

Brüsel, bd Anspach 100. This well-known comic shop stocks more than 8000 new issues and specializes in French underground editions – *Association*, *Amok*, and *Bill* to name but three. You'll also find the complete works of the Belgian comic book artist Schuiten, most popularly known for his controversial comic *Brüsel* which depicts the architectural destruction of a city (guess which one) in the 1960s.

Centre Belge de la Bande Dessinée, rue des Sables 20. The museum bookstore is definitely worth a visit for its wide range of new comics.

Markets

Gare du Midi Brussels' largest and most colourful food market is held here every Sunday at a bazaar-like affair, with traders crammed under the railway bridge and spilling out into the surrounding streets. Stands sell pitta, olives, North African raï tapes, spices, herbs and pulses, among the vegetables and cheap clothes (Sun 7am–2pm).

Grand-Place A small flower market is held here (Tues–Sun 8am–6pm) and there's a bird market on Sundays (7am–2pm).

Place du Châtelain, Ixelles. A food and general market takes place in this pretty square every Wednesday. It's packed with stalls selling fresh vegetables, cheeses, cakes and pastries, as well as fine laces, plants and flowers, and home made wines (2–7pm)

Place du Grand Sablon The swankiest antiques and collectibles market in town. Pricey antique shops in the surrounding streets too (Sat 9am–6pm, Sun 9am–2pm).

Place du Jeu de Balle in the Marolles quarter. Vivid, sprawling flea market held every morning, but it's at its biggest on the weekend, when an eccentric muddle of colonial spoils, quirky odds and ends and domestic and ecclesiastical bric-a-brac give an impression of a century's fads and fashions (daily 7am–2pm).

Listings

Airlines Aer Lingus, rue du Trône 98 (☎548 98 48); British Airways, rue du Trône 98 (☎725 60 00); British Midland, av des Pléiades (☎772 94 00); KLM, at the airport (☎507 70 70); Sabena, at the airport (☎723 31 11).

Airport information 24-hour information line ☎723 23 45.

American Express pl Louise 2 (Mon–Fri 9am–5.30pm; ☎676 27 27).

Books and magazines There are two major English-language bookshops in the city centre – Waterstones, bd Adolphe Max 71–75, and Sterling Books, rue du Fossé aux Loups 38, off pl de la Monnaie. Alternatively, Standaard Boekhandel, pl de la Monnaie 4, has a good English-language book section, including a reasonable range of travel guides and hiking maps, as has Fnac, in the City 2 shopping centre. A wide selection of **English-language magazines** is also available from Waterstones and Sterling Books as well as from leading city newsagents, among which L'Agora, rue de la Madeleine 21, and Libraire de Rome, av Louise 50, are two of the best.

Bureaux de change Outside bank hours you can change money and travellers' cheques at bureaux de change in the Gare du Nord (daily 7am–10pm), Gare du Midi (daily 7am–10pm), and the Gare Centrale (daily 7am–9pm), though none of these places give cash advances on credit cards. Otherwise there's GWK Change, rue du Marché aux Herbes 88 (daily 9am–6pm), and Best Change, rue de la Colline 2 (daily 9am–7pm). There are also bureaux de change at the airport. There are ATMs dotted right across the city centre – check with your home bank for accessibility and access codes in regard to your own bank cashcard.

Buses Information: within the city, STIB (☎515 20 00); TEC for the Walloon communities south of the city (☎010/230 53 53); De Lijn for the Flemish communities north of the city (☎526 28 28).

Car rental Avis, rue Américaine 145 (☎537 12 80) and at the airport (☎720 09 44); Budget, at the airport (☎753 21 70); Europcar-Interrent, av Louise 235 (☎640 94 00) and at the airport (☎721 05 92); Hertz, at the airport (☎720 60 44).

Chemists Details of 24-hour chemists are available from the tourist office. Also, on Saturdays, Sundays & holidays, and outside normal working hours, details of duty pharmacies are (usually) posted on the front door of all other pharmacies.

Dentists Standby dentist ☎426 10 26 or ☎428 58 88.

Doctors Standby doctor ☎479 18 18.

Embassies Australia, rue Guimard 6–8 (☎286 05 00); Canada, av de Tervuren 2 (☎741 06 11); Ireland, rue Froissart 89 (☎230 53 37); New Zealand, bd du Régent 47–48 (☎512 10 40); UK, rue d'Arlon 85 (☎287 62 11); USA, bd du Régent 27 (☎508 21 11).

Emergencies Police ☎101; ambulance/fire brigade ☎100.

English-speaking Brussels If you've recently come to Brussels to live, a number of social groups advertise in *The Bulletin*.

Festivals Brussels has several first-rate festivals and annual events. The **Ommegang** (literally "Walkabout"), is the best known. It is a grand procession from Grand Sablon to the Grand-Place that began in the fourteenth century as a religious event, celebrating the arrival by boat of a statue of the Virgin from Antwerp (see p.46). The celebration became increasingly secular – an excuse for the nobility, guilds and civic bigwigs to parade their finery, reaching a peak in 1549, when it was witnessed by Charles V. Today's Ommegang, which finishes up with a dance on the Grand-Place, is so popular that it is now held twice annually on the first Tuesday and Thursday of July (or thereabouts); if you want a ticket for the finale, you'll need to reserve (at the TIB on the Grand-Place) at least six months ahead. Another fun annual event is the more modest planting of the **meiboom** (maypole) at the corner of rue des Sables and rue du Marais on August 9 – a procession involving much boozing, food and general partying. The story goes that in 1213 a wedding party was celebrating outside the city gates when it was attacked by a street gang from Leuven. They were beaten off (with the help of a group of archers, who just happened to be passing by), and in thanks, the local duke gave them permission to plant a maypole (*meiboom*) on the eve of their patron saints' feastday. Anther event to look out for is the biannual **Tapis des Fleur**, in mid-August on even-numbered years, when the entire Grand-Place is covered with an intricate design made entirely of begonias.

Football Brussels has several teams, of which Royal Sporting Club (RSC) Anderlecht are by far the best known and most consistent, regularly among the contenders for the Belgian league championship. Their stadium is the Stade Constant Vanden Stock, at av Théo

Verbeeck 2 (☎522 15 39), within easy walking distance of Métro St Guidon. The season lasts from August to April.

Gay and lesbian scene For the most up-to-date information on the Brussels gay scene, contact *Tels Quels*, rue du Marché au Charbon 81 (daily 5pm–2am; ☎512 45 87). This is something of a city institution, a social centre with a political slant that welcomes both lesbians and gay men. Over the years, it's had a great influence on the development of the city's gay and lesbian scene, one of the more obvious results being the concentration of gay bars nearby: *H₂O*, along the street at no. 27, is a small and pleasant café-bar and *Le Belgica*, at no. 32 (Thurs–Sat), is the most fashionable gay bar in town, despite its battered decor – though the smarter *Le Comptoir*, a café-bar near Gare Centrale at place de la Vieille Halle aux Blés 25, would dispute that. In terms of clubs, the biggest event for gay men is the once-monthly shindig (currently every third Sunday) *La Démence*, held at the *The Fuse* club (see p.108), in the Marolles district at rue Blaes 208 (☎511 97 89). The music is pretty down to earth – mainstream rave, house, and garage anthems – and the crowd very mixed. There is less of a lesbian scene, but there are two popular spots, *Sapho*, rue St Géry 1 (Fri–Sat 10pm–late), where the atmosphere is friendly, and members of the opposite sex are not made to feel unwelcome, and *Pussy Galore* (currently on the second Friday of the month), which also takes place at *The Fuse*, rue Blaes 208.

Hospital Medical emergencies and ambulances on ☎100.

Infor-Jeunes rue du Marché aux Herbes 27 (☎514 41 11). An information centre for young people new to the city, giving advice on accommodation, the law and other matters.

Laundry Quick Wash, rue de Flandre 129.

Lost property For the métro, buses and trams, the lost property office is at av de la Toison d'Or 15 (☎515 23 94); for items lost on the train, inquire at the terminus of the service you were using or on ☎555 25 25; on a plane, contact the airport on ☎723 60 11.

Police Brussels Central Police Station, rue du Marché au Charbon 30 (☎517 96 11).

Post office The main central post office is on the first floor of the Centre Monnaie, pl de la Monnaie (Mon–Fri 8am–7pm & Sat 9.30am–3pm).

Train enquiries Belgian Rail (☎555 25 25); British Rail International, rue de la Montagne 50 (☎548 00 40); Le Shuttle, bd de L'Impératrice 56 (☎512 79 99); Eurostar, Gare du Midi (☎224 88 56).

Women's contacts Artemys, Galerie Bortier 8–10, off rue St Jean, is Brussels' largest feminist bookstore, and stocks a large number of books in English; there's a bulletin board upstairs which is useful for contacts and information. Also Amazone, rue du Méridien 10 (☎229 38 00), brings together under one roof many different women's organizations, and has a café too.

AROUND BRUSSELS: WATERLOO

Confusingly, the bilingual city of Brussels constitutes one-third of the federation which these days makes up Belgium, and also lies at the centre of the province of Brabant, which is divided between the French- and Flemish-speaking communities to the south and north respectively. The Flemish claim the lion's share of Brabant and their portion of the province actually encircles the capital with a narrow corridor of land running round the southern limits of the city. The highlights of Brabant are covered in other chapters, but the **battlefield of Waterloo**, one of Belgium's most popular attractions, is best seen on a day-trip from the capital.

Waterloo

Waterloo, now a run-of-the-mill suburb about 18km south of the centre of Brussels, has a resonance far beyond its size. It was here on June 18, 1815, at this

THE BATTLE OF WATERLOO

Napoleon escaped from imprisonment on the island of Elba on February 26, 1815. He landed in Cannes three days later and moved swiftly north, entering Paris on March 20 just as his unpopular replacement – the slothful King Louis XVIII – high-tailed it to Ghent. Thousands of Frenchmen rushed to Napoleon's colours and, as soon as possible, Napoleon marched northeast to crush the two armies that threatened his future. Both were in Belgium. One, an assortment of British, Dutch and German soldiers, was commanded by the **Duke of Wellington**, the other was a Prussian army led by **Marshal Blücher**. At the start of the campaign, Napoleon's army was about 130,000 strong, larger than each of the opposing armies but not big enough to fight them both at the same time. Napoleon's strategy was, therefore, quite straightforward – he had to stop Wellington and Blücher from joining together – and to this end he crossed the Belgian frontier near Charleroi to launch a quick attack. On June 16, the French hit the Prussians hard, forcing them to retreat and giving Napoleon the opportunity he was looking for. Napoleon detached a force of 30,000 soldiers to harry the retreating Prussians, while he concentrated his main army against Wellington, hoping to deliver a knock-out blow. Meanwhile, Wellington had assembled his troops at **Waterloo**, on the main road to Brussels.

At dawn on **Sunday June 18**, the two armies faced each other. Wellington had some 68,000 men, about one third of whom were British, and Napoleon around 5,000 more. The armies were deployed just 1500 metres apart with Wellington on the ridge north of – and uphill from – the enemy. It had rained heavily during the night, so Napoleon delayed his first attack to give the ground a chance to dry. At **11.30am**, the battle began when the French assaulted the fortified farm of Hougoumont, which was crucial for the defence of Wellington's right. The assault failed and at approximately **1pm** there was more bad news for Napoleon when he heard that the Prussians had eluded their pursuers and were closing fast. To gain time he sent 14,000 troops off to impede their progress and at **2pm** he tried to regain the initiative by launching a large-scale infantry attack against Wellington's left. This second French attack also proved inconclusive and so at **4pm** Napoleon's cavalry charged Wellington's centre, where the British infantry formed into squares and just managed to keep the French at bay – a desparate engagement that cost hundreds of lives. By **5.30pm**, the Prussians had begun to reach the battlefield in numbers to the right of the French lines and, at **7.30pm**, with the odds getting longer and longer, Napoleon made a a final bid to break Wellington's centre, sending in his Imperial Guard. These were the best soldiers Napoleon had but, slowed down by the mud churned up by their own cavalry, the veterans proved easy targets for the British infantry, and they were beaten back with great loss. At **8.15pm**, Wellington, who knew victory was within his grasp, rode down the ranks to encourage his soldiers before ordering the large-scale counterattack that proved decisive. The French were vanquished and Napoleon subsequently abdicated, ending his days in exile on St Helena. He died there in 1821.

small crossroads town on what was once the main route into Brussels from France, that Wellington masterminded the battle which put an end to the imperial ambitions of Napoleon. Indeed, the battle actually had far more significance than even its generals realized, for not only was this the last throw of the dice for the formidable army born of the French Revolution, but it also marked the final end of France's prolonged attempts to dominate Europe militarily.

The historic importance of Waterloo has not, however, saved the **battlefield** from interference – a motorway cuts right across it – and if you do visit you'll need a lively imagination to picture what happened and where, unless, that is, you're around to see the large-scale re-enactment which takes place every five years in June; the next one is scheduled for 2000. Scattered round the battlefield are several monuments and memorials, the most satisfying of which is the **Butte de Lion**, a huge earth mound that's part viewpoint and part commemoration. The battlefield is 3km north of the centre of Waterloo, where the **Musée Wellington** is the pick of the district's museums.

Practicalities: Arrival and information

To get to Waterloo from Brussels, catch the train from any of Brussels' three main stations (Mon–Fri 2 hourly, Sat & Sun 1 hourly; 20min), or take orange bus #W from place Rouppe (every 30min). The disadvantage with the train is that the railway station is a dreary 1km walk west from the centre of Waterloo along rue de la Station, whereas bus #W goes through Waterloo and then continues on to the battlefield. In the centre of Waterloo, bus #W stops outside the **Syndicat d'Initiative et de Tourisme**, at chaussée de Bruxelles 149 (daily: April–Oct 9.30am–6.30pm; Nov–March 10.30am–5pm; ☎02/354 99 10). They provide free town maps and have several booklets recounting the story of the battle. The most competent of them is titled *The Battlefield of Waterloo Step by Step*. The tourist office also sells (at F385) a combined ticket for all the battle-related attractions, though if you're at all selective (and you should be) this won't work out as a saving at all.

The Musée Wellington

The best starting point for a visit to Waterloo is actually next door to the tourist office in the old inn where Wellington slept the night before the battle, and Alexander Gordon, Wellington's aide-de-camp, was brought to die. The inn has been turned into the **Musée Wellington** (daily: April–Sept 9.30am–6.30pm; Oct–March 10.30am–5pm; F100) detailing the events of the battle with plans and models, and displaying the assorted personal effects of Wellington, Gordon and Napoleon. There are also copies of the messages Wellington sent to his commanders during the course of the battle, curiously formal epistles laced with phrases like "Could you be so kind as..." and "We ought to...", as well as the artificial leg of Lord Uxbridge: "I say, I've lost my leg," Uxbridge is reported to have said during the battle, to which Wellington replied, "By God sir, so you have!" After the battle, Uxbridge's leg was buried here in Waterloo, but it was returned to London when he died to join the rest of his body; as a consolation his artificial leg was donated to the museum. Such insouciance was not uncommon among the British ruling class – Wellington's ADC, Lord Fitzroy, had his arm smashed by a musket ball and did not even murmur when it was amputated, only calling out when the surgeon tossed it away: "Hey, bring my arm back. There's a ring my wife gave me on the finger." And neither were the bits and pieces of dead soldiers considered sacrosanct: tooth dealers roamed the battlefields of the Napoleonic Wars pulling out teeth which were then stuck on two pieces of board with a spring at the back – primitive dentures known in England as "Waterloos".

After the museum, allow time also to drop at by the church of **Saint Joseph**, across the street, where the original Habsburg chapel, with its attractive Neoclassical facade and cupola, forms the frontispiece to a newer church, which shelters dozens of memorial plaques to the British soldiers who died at Waterloo.

The battlefield – the Butte de Lion

From outside the tourist office, pick up orange bus #W again and head on down to the **battlefield** – an undulating landscape of fields punctuated by the odd clump of trees and the whitewashed walls of the occasional farmstead. Avoid the **Centre du Visiteur**, on route du Lion (daily: April–Sept 9.30am–6.30pm; Oct–March 10.30am–4pm; F200), and instead walk up the adjacent hundred-metre-high **Butte de Lion** (daily: same hours; F50), built by local women with soil from the battlefield to mark the spot where Holland's Prince William of Orange – later King William II of the Netherlands – was wounded. It's a commanding monument, topped by a regal 28-ton lion atop a stout column, and one that provides a panoramic view over the battlefield.

There are two modest attractions at the base of the Butte – a dire wax museum, the **Musée de Ceres** (April–Oct daily 9.30am–6.30pm; Nov–March Sat & Sun 10am–5pm; F60), and the **Panorama de la Bataille** (daily: April–Oct 9.30am–6.30pm; Nov–March 10.30am–4pm; F110), where a circular naturalistic **painting** of the battle, a canvas no less than 110m in circumference, is displayed in a purpose-built, rotunda-like gallery. The painting is the work of the French artist Louis Demoulin; both the building and the painting are in need of a refit.

Napoleon spent the eve of the battle at **Le Caillou** (Tues–Sun: April–Oct 10.00am–6.30pm; Nov–March 1–5pm; F60), a two-storey brick farmhouse about 4km south from the Butte de Lion on the chaussée de Bruxelles, and you can visit this, too, though there are no public transport connections. The mementos here, including Napoleon's army cot and death mask, are a memorial to the emperor and his army, but it's hardly riveting stuff.

travel details

Trains

All trains stop at Midi, Centrale and Nord unless otherwise indicated.

Brussels to: Amsterdam (hourly; 3hr); Antwerp (3 hourly; 40min); Basle, from Brussels Midi & Nord (5 daily; 7hr 30min); Bruges (hourly; 1hr); Charleroi (hourly; 50min); Ghent (hourly; 40min); Liège (hourly; 1hr 20min); Leuven (every 30 min; 20min); Luxembourg (6 daily; 3hr 30min); Maastricht (hourly; 2hr); Metz, from Brussels Midi & Nord (5 daily; 3hr 45min); Mons (hourly; 55min); Ostende (hourly; 1hr 23min); Paris, from Brussels Midi & Nord (10 daily; 3hr); Rotterdam (hourly; 2hr); Strasbourg, from Brussels Midi & Nord (5 daily; 5hr).

CHAPTER TWO

FLANDERS

The Flemish-speaking provinces of Oost and West Vlaanderen (**East and West Flanders**) spread out from the North Sea coast south as far as Kortrijk and east to the peripheries of Antwerp. As early as the thirteenth century, Flanders was one of the most prosperous areas of Europe, with an advanced, integrated economy dependent on the cloth trade. By the sixteenth century, the region was in decline as trade slipped north toward Holland, and England's cloth manufacturers began to undermine Flanders' economic base. The speed of the collapse was accelerated by religious conflict, for the great Flemish towns were by inclination Protestant, their kings and queens Catholic, and once Habsburg domination was assured, thousands of weavers, merchants and skilled artisans poured north to escape religious persecution. The ultimate economic price was the closure of the Scheldt at the insistence of the Dutch in 1648. Thereafter, Flanders sank into poverty and decay, a static and traditional society where nearly every aspect of life was controlled by decree, and only three percent of the population could read or write. As Voltaire quipped:

> In this sad place wherein I stay,
> Ignorance, torpidity,
> And boredom hold their lasting sway,
> With unconcerned stupidity;
> A land where old obedience sits,
> Well filled with faith, devoid of wits.

The Flemish peasantry of the seventeenth and eighteenth centuries saw their lands crossed and recrossed by the armies of the Great Powers, a region where the relative fortunes of dynasties and nations were decided. Only with Belgian independence did the situation begin to change: the towns started to industrialize, tariffs protected the cloth industry, Zeebrugge was built and Ostend was modernized, all in a flurry of activity that shook the land from its centuries-old torpor. Today, despite the devastating dislocation of World War I and the occupation of World War II, Flanders has emerged prosperous, its citizens maintaining a distinctive cultural and linguistic identity that's become a powerful political force in opposition to their Walloon neighbours.

With the exception of the range of low hills around Ronse and the sea dunes along the coast, Flanders is unrelentingly flat, a somewhat dreary landscape at its best in its quieter recesses where poplar trees and whitewashed farmhouses still decorate sluggish canals. More remarkably, there are many reminders of the Flemings' medieval greatness and these are readily accessible by means of a comprehensive public transport network. The ancient and fascinating cloth cities of **Bruges** and less well-known **Ghent** both hold marvellous collections of early Flemish art; and, of the smaller towns, **Oudenaarde** has a delightful town hall

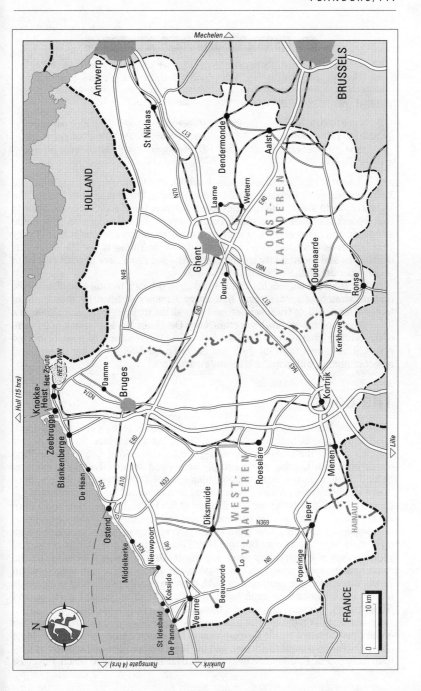

ACCOMMODATION PRICE CODES

All the **hotels and hostels** detailed in this chapter have been graded according to the following price categories. Apart from ①, which is a per-person price for a hostel bed, all the codes are based on the rate for the least expensive double room during high season. For more on accommodation, see p.33.

① Up to F1000 per person	④ F2000–2500 per room	⑦ F4000–5000 per room
② F1000–1500 per room	⑤ F2500–3000 per room	⑧ F5000–6000 per room
③ F1500–2000 per room	⑥ F3000–4000 per room	⑨ F6000 and over, per room

and is famed for its tapestries, whilst **Kortrijk** and **Veurne** sport some fine old buildings and have a classic small-town ambience. There is also, of course, the legacy of World War I. The trenches extended from the North Sea coast, close to Nieuwpoort, as far as Switzerland, cutting across West Flanders via Diksmuide and Ieper, and many of the key engagements of the war were fought here. Every year hundreds of visitors head for **Ieper** (formerly Ypres) to see the numerous cemeteries and monuments around the town – sad reminders of what proved to be a desperately futile conflict.

Not far from the battlefields, the Belgian coast is beach territory, an almost continuous stretch of golden sand that every summer is filled by thousands of tourists. An excellent **tram** service connects all the major resorts, and although a lot of the development has been crass, cosy **De Haan** has kept much of its turn-of-the-century charm, and **Knokke** has all the pretensions of a sophisticated resort. The largest town on the coast is **Ostend**, a lively, working seaport and resort crammed with popular bars and restaurants.

The coast

Much of the 70km or so of Belgian **coast** groans under an ugly covering of apartment blocks and bungalow settlements, obscuring a landscape that was largely untouched until the nineteenth century, the beach backing onto a line of sand dunes on which nothing grew except rushes and stunted Lombardy poplars. Behind them, a narrow strip of undulating ground ("Ter Streep"), seldom more than a kilometre or so in width and covered with moss and bushes, connected the barren sand hills with the cultivated farms of the Flemish plain. The dunes were always an inadequate protection against the sea, and the inhabitants here were building dykes as early as the tenth century, an arrangement formalized two hundred years later when Count Baldwin IX of Flanders appointed guardians charged with the duty of constructing defensive works. Despite these efforts, life on the coast remained precarious, and most people chose to live inland; indeed, when Belgium achieved independence in 1830, there were only two coastal settlements of any size – **Ostend**, a small fortified town with an antiquated harbour, and **Nieuwpoort**, in a state of what was thought to be terminal decay.

It was Leopold I, the first king of the Belgians, who began the transformation of the coast, assisted by the development of the country's rail system. In 1834 he chose Ostend as a royal residence, had the town modernized and connected it by train to Brussels. Fashionable by royal approval and now easy to reach, the coast was soon dotted with resorts, and the number of seaside visitors rose meteorically. The next king carried on the work of his father, building a light railway along the shore and completing the chain of massive sea walls that still punctuate the coastline from one end to the other. Barring anything extraordinary happening, the Belgian coast seemed safe at last.

Popular ever since as a holiday destination, the coast has long been thronged by dozens of hotels, though nowadays these rarely offer sea views as the prime sites are almost exclusively occupied by apartment blocks. Bear in mind also that, although there are scores of campsites, many are no more than a few caravans on a field – and surprisingly few are listed by the tourist authorities. Another distinctive feature is the long lines of tiny wooden huts that cut a dash across the more popular beaches. Owned by the local municipalities, each is rented out for the season and, if you're planning to glue yourself to the beach, some are available by the week at reasonable rates – check with the local tourist office.

Ostend

The 1900 *Baedeker* distinguished **OSTEND** as "One of the most fashionable and cosmopolitan watering places in Europe". The gloss may be long gone, and the town's aristocratic visitors have moved on to more exotic climes, but Ostend remains a likeable, liveable seaport with regular catamaran connections to Dover. Ostend is also the focal point of the region's public transport system, including the fast, frequent and efficient trams that run behind the beach to Knokke-Heist in the east and De Panne in the west.

The old fishing village of Ostend was given a town charter in the thirteenth century, in recognition of its growing importance as a port for trade across the Channel. Flanked by an empty expanse of sand dune, it remained the only important harbour along this stretch of the coast until the construction of Zeebrugge in the nineteenth century. Like so many other towns in the Spanish Netherlands, it was attacked and besieged time and again, winning the admiration of Protestant Europe in resisting the Spaniards during a desperate siege that lasted from 1601 to 1604. Later, convinced of the wholesome qualities of sea air and determined to impress other European rulers with their sophistication, Belgium's first kings, Leopold I and II, turned Ostend into a chi-chi resort, demolishing the town walls and dotting the outskirts with prestigious buildings and parks – some of which were destroyed during World War II, when the town was a prime bombing target. Curiously enough it was here that **Marvin Gaye** hunkered down with friends from 1981 until 1982 when family and musical ties pulled him back to the US.

Arrival, information – and transport along the coast
Ostend's **catamaran terminal** at Montgomery Dok is next to the **train station**, a couple of minutes' walk from the centre of town – you couldn't wish for a more convenient set-up if you're heading straight through. The station's **information office** (Mon–Sat 8am–6.30pm, Sun 9.30am–5.30pm) has comprehensive details of international train times and there's a 24-hour left luggage office as well as coin-operated luggage lockers. There is a small information **kiosk** inside the station (July & Aug daily 9am–1pm & 4–7.30pm) and a main **tourist office** a ten-minute walk away on Monacoplein (June–Aug Mon–Sat 9am–7pm, Sun 10am–7pm; Sept–May Mon–Sat 10am–6pm, Sun 10am–5pm; ☎059/70 11 99).

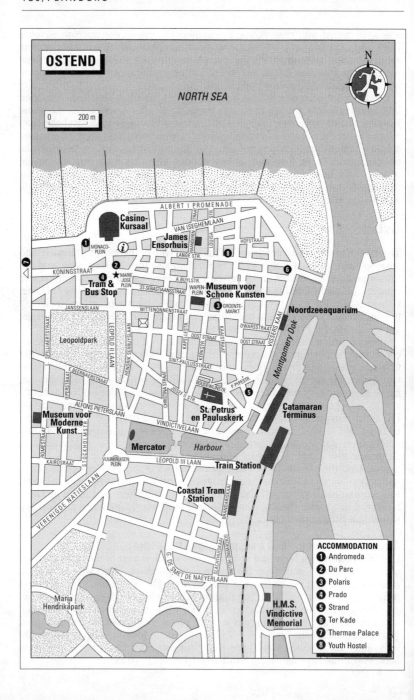

OSTEND

NORTH SEA

0   200 m

N

ALBERT I PROMENADE

Casino-Kursaal

James Ensorhuis

MONACO-PLEIN

KONINGSTRAAT

Tram & Bus Stop

MARIE JOSE PLEIN

ST-SEBASTIAANSSTRAAT

VAN ISEGHEMLAAN

LOUISA

HOFSTRAAT

LANGE STR.

A. BUYLSTR.

WAPEN-PLEIN

Museum voor Schone Kunsten

GROENTE-MARKT

Noordzeeaquarium

JANSSENSLAAN

WITTENONNENSTRAAT

SPILLIAERTSTRAAT

LEOPOLD II LAAN

HENDRIK SERRUYSLAAN

KAPELLESTR.

OOST STRAAT

KERKSTR.

OOST STRAAT

KAAISTRAAT

DWARSSTRAAT

VISSERS KAAI

Leopoldpark

E. BEERNAERTSTRAAT

SINT-PAULUSSTRAAT

CHRISTINA STRAAT

JOSEF II STR.

BOUDEWIJNSTR.

P. PYPESTR.

Montgomery Dok

IJFERSTRAAT

ALFONS PIETERSLAAN

ROMESTRAAT

STOCKHOLMSTR.

KAIROSRAAT

Museum voor Moderne Kunst

VINDICTIVELAAN

St. Petrus en Pauluskerk

Mercator

Harbour

Catamaran Terminus

LEOPOLD III LAAN

Train Station

VUURKRUISEN-PLEIN

VERENIGDE NATIESLAAN

Coastal Tram Station

BRANDARISKAAI

G. DE SMET DE NAEYERLAAN

SLACHTHUISKAAI

DOKSTRAAT

KONING

Maria Hendrikapark

H.M.S. Vindictive Memorial

ACCOMMODATION

1 Andromeda
2 Du Parc
3 Polaris
4 Prado
5 Strand
6 Ter Kade
7 Thermae Palace
8 Youth Hostel

For destinations along the coast, **trams** leave from beside the train station and head east to Knokke-Heist and west to De Panne, putting all the Belgian resorts within easy striking distance. Winter services in both directions depart every half-hour, in summer every twenty minutes (every 10min in the central section between Nieuwpoort and Blankenberge). Fares are relatively inexpensive – Ostend to either Knokke-Heist or De Panne, for instance, costs F170. You can also buy tickets for unlimited tram travel, valid for either one day (F330) or three days (F560). Tickets from the driver. The region's **buses** are operated by De Lijn; timetables are posted at most bus stops and there are information lines, one for West Flanders (☎059/56 53 53), the other for East Flanders (☎092/10 94 91). **Car rental** is available from Avis, Visserskaai 8 (☎059/70 07 89), and Europcar, Vindictivelaan 6 (☎059/70 01 01).

Accommodation

The tourist office (see above) will help you find accommodation in one of Ostend's many **hotels** and **guesthouses** at no extra charge. The best option is to head for a beachside hotel, but these are few and far between – most of the seashore is given over to apartment blocks. Alternatively, plump for the area round Leopoldpark on the west side of the centre – it's a pleasant district with a relaxed and easy air. For those on a budget, there's a good HI **hostel** in the centre of town and several bargain basement hotels.

HOTELS

Andromeda, Albert I Promenade 60 (☎059/80 66 11, fax 80 66 29). Smart modern high-rise next door to the Casino, and overlooking the town's best beach. Most rooms have balconies and sea views. ⑦.

Du Parc, Marie Joséplein 3 (☎059/70 16 80, fax 80 08 79). Located in a handsome Art Deco block just south of the Casino, this medium-sized hotel offers comfortable rooms at reasonable prices. The ground-floor café, with its Tiffany glass trimmings, is a favourite with locals. ④.

Polaris, Groentemarkt 19 (☎059/50 16 02, fax 51 40 01). A good-looking *belle époque* exterior hides modest but perfectly adequate rooms right in the centre of town. ③.

Prado, Leopold II-laan 22 (☎059/70 53 06; fax 80 87 35). Likeable three-star hotel with neatly furnished modern rooms. Just south of the Casino. Ask for a room on the front overlooking Marie Joséplein – and a few floors up from the traffic. ⑤.

Strand, Visserskaai 1 (☎059/70 33 83, fax 80 36 78). No-nonsense, three-star, modern hotel a stone's throw from the train station, but a tad over-priced. ⑥.

Ter Kade, Visserskaai 49 (☎059/50 09 15, fax 51 04 87). A high-rise near the corner of Visserskaai and Albert I Promenade, this three-star hotel has bright and cheerful rooms, most of which have views of the harbour and seashore. ⑤.

Thermae Palace, Koningin Astridlaan 7 (☎059/80 66 44, fax 80 52 74). Much hyped, this enjoys the reputation of being Ostend's best hotel. The building is certainly striking – an Art Deco extravagance with expansive public rooms and spacious bedrooms offering sea views – but the place has been neglected and seems a bit sorry for itself. A ten-minute walk west of the centre. ⑥.

HOSTEL

Youth hostel, De Ploate, Langestraat 82 (☎059/80 52 97, fax 80 92 74). Spick and span hostel with 100 beds, and some family rooms. The overnight fee of F465 per person includes breakfast. Reservations are strongly advised in summer. ①.

The Town

There's precious little left of medieval Ostend, and today's town centre fans out from beside the train station – a series of narrow, straight streets edged by the beach to the north, Leopold II-laan, the site of the old walls, to the west, and the marina, the former harbour, to the south. Across the Visserskaai from the station, the whopping **St Petrus en Pauluskerk** looks old but in fact dates from the early twentieth century. Behind the church, the last remnant of its predecessor is a massive sixteenth-century brick tower with a canopied, rather morbid shrine of the Crucifixion at its base. From near here, Kerkstraat, as well as neighbouring Kapellestraat, the principal, pedestrianized shopping street, lead to the main square, **Wapenplein**, where the **Museum voor Schone Kunsten** (Wed–Thurs 10am–noon & 2–5pm; F50) is located on the third floor of the Feest-en Kultuurpaleis (Festival and Culture Hall), a big bruiser of a building that looms over one whole side of the square. The museum has a lively programme of temporary art exhibitions and these supplement a small but enjoyable permanent collection. Highlights include the harsh surrealism of Paul Delvaux's *The Izjzer Time* and several piercing canvases by Leon Spilliaert (1881–1946), a native of Ostend whose works combine both Expressionist and Symbolist elements. Spilliaert was smitten by the land and seascapes of Ostend, using them in his work time and again – as in *The Gust of Wind*, with its dark, forbidding colours and screaming woman, and the comparable *Fit of Giddiness*. There's also an excellent sample of the work of James Ensor, who was born in Ostend in 1860, son of an English father and Flemish mother. Barely noticed until the 1920s, Ensor spent nearly all his 89 years working in his home town, and is nowadays considered a pioneer of Expressionism. His first paintings were rather sombre portraits and landscapes, but in the early 1880s he switched to brilliantly contrasting colours, most familiar in his *Self-portrait with Flowered Hat*, a deliberate variation on Rubens' famous self-portraits. Less well known is *The Artist's Mother in Death*, a fine, penetrating example of his preoccupation with the grim and macabre. Look out also for portraits of Ensor by his contemporaries, particularly those by the talented Henry de Groux, and – as a curiosity – Charles Louis Verboeckhoven's *The Visit of Queen Victoria to Ostend in 1843*: the painting is pretty dire, but it celebrates one of the royal events that put the resort firmly on the international map.

A couple of minutes' walk north of the Wapenplein, the **James Ensorhuis**, Vlaanderenstraat 27 (June–Sept Wed–Mon 10am–noon & 2–5pm; Nov–May Sat & Sun only 2–5pm; F50), was the artist's first home and has been restored to something like its former state. On the ground floor there's the old shop where his aunt and uncle sold shells and souvenirs, while up above are the painter's living room and studio, though the works on display aren't originals. From here, it's a brief stroll west to the **Casino-Kursaal** (gaming daily from 3pm), an unlovely structure built in 1953 as a successor to the first casino of 1852, and another short stretch to the little lakes, mini-bridges and artificial grottoes of **Leopoldpark**.

Just beyond the south side of the park, at Romestraat 11, is the **Museum voor Moderne Kunst** (Tues–Sun 10am–6pm; F100), where a wide selection of modern Belgian paintings, sculptures and ceramics is exhibited in rotation – everything from the Expressionists of the St Martens-Latem group (see p.184) through to Pop and Conceptual art. Artists represented in the permanent collection and whose works you can expect to see include Delvaux, Spilliaert, Edgard Tygat, Constant Permeke and the versatile Jean Brusselmans (1884–1953), who tried his hand at several different styles. The museum also puts on an imaginative range of temporary exhibitions (when the entry fee is usually increased).

To the west of the Casino is Ostend's main attraction, its sandy **beach** which extends west as far as De Panne. On summer days thousands drive into the town to soak up the sun, swim and amble along the seafront **promenade**, which runs along the top of the sea wall. Part sea defence and part royal ostentation, the promenade was once the main route from the town centre to the Wellington race-course 2km to the west, an intentionally grand walkway designed to pander to Leopold II, whose imperial statue, with fawning Belgians and Congolese at its base, still stands in the middle of a long line of stone columns that now adjoin the **Thermae Palace Hotel**. Built in the 1930s, this is similarly regal, although it spoils the lines of the original walkway.

Heading east from the casino, Albert I Promenade leads along the seashore into the Visserskaai, where the **Noordzeeaquarium** (April–Sept Mon–Fri 10am–noon & 2–5pm, plus Sat & Sun all year 10am–noon & 2–6pm; F75), housed in the former shrimp market on the east side of the street, holds a series of displays on North Sea fish, crustacea, flora and fauna. To the south, in the marina, the sailing ship **Mercator** (April–June & Sept daily 10am–1pm & 2–6pm; July & Aug daily 9am–6pm; Oct–March Sat & Sun 10am–1pm & 2–5pm; F100) is the old training vessel of the Belgian merchant navy, convert-ed into a marine museum holding a hotch-potch of items accumulated during her world voyages.

A five- to ten-minute walk south of the train station, in a sunken garden at the end of Westkaai, is the prow of the **HMS Vindictive**. On the night of May 9, 1918, the British made a desperate attempt to block Ostend's harbour. The sacrificial ships were crewed by volunteers, and the *Vindictive* was successfully sunk at the port entrance. After the war the bow was retrieved and kept as a memorial to the sailors who lost their lives. This was one of the most audacious operations of the war, but tragically it was based on false intelligence: German submarines hardly ever used the harbour.

Eating and drinking

The sheer variety of places to eat in Ostend is almost daunting. Along Visserskaai (where in summer there's also a long line of seafood stalls) and through the cen-tral city streets are innumerable **cafés**, **café-bars** and **restaurants**. Many of them serve some pretty mediocre stuff, but there are lots of good spots too, and everywhere there are plates of fresh North Sea mussels and french fries.

Brasserie Café Leffe, Wapenplein 110. Pleasant café-bar serving Leffe on draught.

Lobster, Van Iseghemlaan 64. Small restaurant close to the tourist office which specializes in (you guessed it) lobster. Closed Tues.

Lusitania, Visserskaai 35. Excellent and long-established restaurant serving great seafood, especially lobster.

Mosselbeurs, Dwarsstraat 10. One of the liveliest restaurants in town with cheerfully naff nautical fittings and top-notch fishy dishes, especially eels and mussels. Reasonable prices.

Café du Parc, Marie Joséplein 3. Sociable, old-fashioned café-bar with Art Deco bits and pieces close to the Casino.

Savarin, Albert I Promenade 75 (☎059/51 31 71). Arguably the best and certainly one of the priciest restaurants in town. Classic Franco-Belgian cuisine with the emphasis on seafood. On the seafront a five-minute walk west of the Casino. Reservations advised.

De Zeebries, Albert I Promenade 73. Straightforward, spick and span seashore restaurant with a good line in mussels. A couple of hundred metres west of the Casino. Closed Tues & Wed April–Sept.

East of Ostend

Trams leave from beside Ostend train station for the journey east to Knokke-Heist every twenty minutes in summer and every thirty minutes in winter. Clearing the town's suburbs, they shoot through a series of tourist developments on the way to **DE HAAN**, arguably the prettiest resort on the coast. Established at the end of the nineteenth century, De Haan was carefully conceived as an exclusive seaside village in a rustic Gothic Revival style, called *style Normand*. The building plots were irregularly dispersed between the tram station and the sea, around a pattern of winding streets reminiscent of – and influenced by – contemporaneous English suburbs such as Liverpool's Sefton Park. The only formality was provided by a central circus around a casino (demolished in 1929). The casino apart, De Haan has survived pretty much intact, a welcome relief from the surrounding high-rise development, and, flanked by empty sand dunes, it's now a popular family resort, with a good beach and pleasant seafront cafés.

The **tourist office** (April–Oct daily 9am–noon & 2–5/6pm; Nov–March Mon–Fri 10am–noon & 2–5pm; ☎059/24 21 35) is next to De Haan Aan Zee tram stop, five minutes' walk from the beach along Leopoldlaan, and has a small cache of private **rooms** to offer. There are no fewer than 25 **hotels** in or near the village centre, including a couple of reasonably priced places in Gothic Revival piles a few steps from the tram stop: the one-star *Des Brasseurs,* Koninklijk Plein 1 (☎059/23 52 94, fax 23 65 96; ③), which offers very frugal rooms, and the rather more agreeable, three-star *Belle Vue,* at Koninklijk Plein 5 (☎059/23 34 39, fax 23 75 22; ⑤). However, the pick of the hotels is the first-rate *Auberge des Rois*, Zeedijk 1 (☎059/23 30 18, fax 23 60 78; ⑥), a smart, medium-sized hotel overlooking the beach and adjacent to an undeveloped tract of sand dune – ask for a room with a sea view. Needless to say, it's popular – reservations are advised.

For **food**, there are **café-restaurants** all along the seafront, and, on the central circus at Leopoldlaan 18, *L'Auteuil* serves particularly good mussels.

Blankenberge

Nine kilometres east of De Haan, **BLANKENBERGE** is one of the busiest places on the coast, but there's precious little to recommend it. Hopelessly overcrowded during the summer, it's the archetypal seaside town, with a 1930s pier, a tiled Art Deco casino, dozens of cheap hotels – and fast-food bars pumping out high-energy singalongs. The **tourist office** (daily: April–June & Sept 9am–12.30pm & 2–6pm; July & Aug 9am–9pm; Oct–March Mon–Sat 9am–12.30pm & 2–6pm, Sun 10am–1pm; ☎050/41 22 27) is on Koning Leopold III plein, five minutes' walk from the beach along the main pedestrianized street, Kerkstraat; it's also next to the train station and the Blankenberge Station tram stop.

Zeebrugge

In 1895 work began on a brand new seaport and harbour next to the tiny village of **ZEEBRUGGE**, a few kilometres beyond Blankenberge. The key to the project was a crescent-shaped mole some 2.5km long and 100m wide that was built up from the shore, protecting incoming and outgoing shipping from the vagaries of the North Sea. Connected to the rail and canal systems, the harbour was an ambitious attempt to improve Belgium's coastal facilities and provide easy access to the sea from Bruges via the Leopoldkanaal. Completed in 1907, it was a great commercial success, although two world wars badly damaged its prospects. During

THE ZEEBRUGGE DISASTER

On Friday March 6, 1987, the 7pm ferry from Zeebrugge to Dover sank shortly after departure, still in sight of land. Townsend Thoresen's *Herald of Free Enterprise* was a drive-on, drive-off car ferry with an open car deck: as soon as the ship had left its moorings, the car deck began to fill with water because the bow doors had not been closed. Despite the crew's desperate efforts to secure the doors, the ship keeled over within minutes; 193 people were crushed or drowned in the icy waters of the harbour. The fundamental cause of the disaster was obvious enough, though the immediate reasons for it have been variously attributed to poor communications between bridge and deck, human error and crew fatigue as a result of the tight schedule of sailings. The biggest controversy has been around the underlying limitations of this sort of open-deck car ferry, and many have argued that if the ferries were fitted with bulkheads on the car decks then they would be far safer. However, the ferry companies remain unconvinced, not least because bulkheads decrease capacity and therefore profits. More than a decade later, bulkheads remain optional.

World War I, the Allies were convinced that Zeebrugge was a German submarine base, and, in conjunction with the assault on Ostend, attempted to obstruct the harbour in April 1918. Block ships, crewed by volunteers, were taken to strategic positions and sunk, resulting in heavy casualties and only partial success. There's a **monument** to the dead sailors and a map of the action at the base of the mole, restored after it was destroyed during the German occupation. World War II saw the same job done rather more proficiently, but it didn't stop further bombing raids and the demolition of the port by the retreating Germans in 1944. The last of the block ships (the *Thetis*) was finally cleared and the harbour reopened in 1957, since when business has boomed and the port has been greatly expanded.

Spreading out along the coast among the series of giant docks, present-day Zeebrugge divides into sections, each with its own tram stop. On the west side, a couple of minutes' walk from Zeebrugge Strandwijk tram stop, is the small **beach resort**. There's nothing much to see, but, pushed up against the base of the original mole to the east and edged by sand dunes to the west, it's a surprisingly pleasant place to stay particularly if you've got a ferry to catch. There's one good hotel here too, the *Maritime,* Zeedijk 6 (☎050/54 40 66, fax 54 66 08; ④), a well-kept modern high-rise whose rooms offer sea views; the seafront *'t Zandlopertje* café-bar has a wide range of beers. The **tourist office** (July & Aug daily 10am–1pm & 1.30–6pm; ☎050/54 50 42) is in a small kiosk on the seafront and can provide up-to-date details of the **bus** service to Bruges train station (#791, Mon–Sat 2 daily, increasing to 3–4 daily in July & Aug; 30min) and of **ferries** to England. P&O North Sea Ferries (☎050/54 22 11) has sailings to Hull from the terminal about 1km out along the mole; tickets are available direct from the office in the terminal building.

A twenty-minute walk east of the beach resort along the main road, or a couple of minutes from tram stop Zeebrugge Vaart, Zeebrugge **train station** (for Bruges, hourly; 15min) is surrounded by several blocks of terraced houses built for harbour workers at the start of this century. The ferry company usually runs a bus service from the station to coincide with sailings. A further 1km to the east, the oldest part of Zeebrugge fans out north from the tram line to the original fishing harbour, now part of the general dock complex.

Knokke-Heist

Generally regarded as Belgium's most sophisticated resort, **KNOKKE-HEIST** is the collective name for five villages whose individual identities have disappeared in a sprawling development which stretches for some 6km along the coast almost to the Dutch frontier. Jam-packed in summer, the sophistication is hidden by the confusion of high-rise apartment blocks that string along the beach, but reveals itself if you wander the leafy avenues of expensive holiday homes hidden away on the resort's eastern peripheries. To attract the crowds, a lot of effort goes into planning Knokke-Heist's varied special events programme, notably an annual sandcastle-building competition and the **International Cartoon Festival**, with eight hundred entries selected by an international panel and shown in the **Cultureel Centrum Scharpoord** exhibition centre, at Meerlaan 32 (☎050/63 04 30), during the second half of June and July. Up-to-date details of all events are available from Knokke tourist office (see below).

The most agreeable part of this elongated resort is at the east end around **KNOKKE**, a resolutely bourgeois holiday town with a splendid beach, an excellent range of sporting facilities and a clutch of private art galleries where many of the big names of contemporary Belgian and Dutch art come to exhibit and sell. A ten-minute walk west of Knokke along the seafront, in adjacent **ALBERT-STRAND**, and you discover the centre of all this conspicuous consumption, the sumptuous **Casino** (gambling daily from 3pm), which is decorated with canvases by Paul Delvaux in the lobby and René Magritte's *Le Domaine Enchanté* in the gaming room.

To the east of Knokke is the even ritzier **HET ZOUTE**, whose well-heeled villas stretch along the seashore for about 6km before finally fizzling out to be replaced by a 4km-wide slice of undeveloped coastline, whose polders and dykes, salt marshes and mud flats extend to the Dutch border. Strange as it seems today, this tranquil area was once one of the busiest waterways in the world, connecting Bruges with the North Sea until the River Zwin silted up in the sixteenth century. In 1340, it was also the site of one of the largest naval engagements of the century, when Edward III of England sailed up the estuary with his Flemish allies to destroy a French fleet gathered for a projected invasion of England. Nowadays it's a remote rural retreat, with some unusual flora and fauna nourished by a combination of the river and occasional sea flooding. The best way to see it is by bike – and these can be rented at Knokke train station for F335 per day. You'll also need a detailed map, available from the Knokke tourist office. Incidentally, part of the area has been incorporated into the 360-acre **Het Zwin Natuurreservat**, which is very popular with school parties.

Practicalities

Knokke is well connected to Ostend by **tram** and to Bruges by **train** (every 30min; 15min). Knokke's tram terminus, train and bus stations are grouped together at the south end of the long and featureless main street, Lippenslaan, an inconvenient 2km south of the seafront, where the Knokke **tourist office**, Zeedijk 660 (daily: May–Sept 9am–12.30pm & 1.30–6pm; Oct–April Mon–Fri 8.30am–noon & 1.30–5.30pm, Sat & Sun 9am–12.30pm & 1.30–6pm; ☎050/63 03 80), will phone around to make a booking in any local **hotel**. There are plenty to choose from, though in Knokke and Het Zoute there's only one right on the seafront, *Des Nations*, Zeedijk Het Zoute 704 (☎050/61 99 11, fax 61 99 99; ⑨), a swanky, modern high-rise a five-minute walk east of the tourist office. More affordably, Knokke's *The Prince's Hotel*, above the shops at Lippenslaan 171 (☎050/60 11 11, fax 62 46 24; ⑤), offers run-of-the mill but reasonably comfortable rooms, while the similar three-star *Prins Boudewijn*, along the street at no. 35 (☎050/60 10 16, fax 62 35 46; ④), provides a bit more space and comfort. The nearest listed **campsites**, *De Vuurtoren* (mid-March to mid-Oct; ☎050/51 17 82) and *De Zilvermeeuw* (March to mid-Nov; ☎050/51 27 26), are some 5km to the west in Heist, at Heistlaan 168 and 166.

West of Ostend

West of Ostend, the tram skirts the sand dunes of a long and almost entirely undeveloped stretch of coast, until it rattles into **MIDDELKERKE**, the first of a sequence of undistinguished seaside resorts whose apartments and villas crimp the western reaches of the Belgian coast.

Nieuwpoort

Further along, the tram line cuts inland to round the estuary of the River Ijzer (Yser) at the small town of **NIEUWPOORT** (tram stop Nieuwpoort Stad) – not to be confused with the unenticing high-rise development of **Nieuwpoort-aan-Zee** just up the road. Nieuwpoort hasn't had much luck. Founded in the twelfth century, it was besieged nine times in the following six hundred years, but this was nothing compared to its misfortune in World War I. In 1914, the first German campaign reached the Ijzer prompting the Belgians to open the sluices along the Noordvaart canal, just to the east of the town centre. The water stopped the invaders in their tracks and permanently separated the armies, but it also put Nieuwpoort on the front line, where it remained for the rest of the war. Every day volunteers had to abandon the safety of their bunkers to operate the ring of sluice gates, without which the water would either have drained away or risen to flood the Belgian trenches. Beside the bridge near the tram stop, you can still see – and walk round – the ring of sluice gates, dotted with memorials to the hundreds who died. The largest monument consists of a sombre rotunda with King Albert I at the centre.

Four years of shelling reduced the town to a ruin, and what you see now is the result of a meticulous restoration that lasted well into the 1920s. There's nothing remarkable here, and the town is only worth a brief visit, but the heavyweight **Onze Lieve Vrouwekerk** church, the neo-Renaissance **Stadhuis** and the **Halle**, all in a row beside the Marktplein, serve as reminders of more prosperous days.

In the unlikely event you decide to stay, the **tourist office** (Mon–Fri 8am–noon & 1.30–5.30pm; ☎058/22 44 44), in the Stadhuis at Marktplein 7, has a small stock of inexpensive private **rooms** (②). The nearest **campsite**, *IC-Camping*, Brugsesteenweg 49 (☎058/23 60 37; Easter to early Nov), is a big and well-equipped affair beside the River Ijzer about 2km southeast of town. For somewhere to **eat**, try the *Mondial*, Kaai 15, which specializes in fresh eels and mussels.

Some 7km west of Nieuwpoort, a few of the fishermen of **OOSTDUINKERKE** maintain the picturesque tradition of riding into the sea on horseback at low tide to sweep the ocean for shrimp. It's now mostly done to entertain the tourists – just as well as the resort has precious little else to recommend it.

St Idesbald

Heading west, Oostduinkerke merges seamlessly into **Koksijde** and then **ST IDESBALD**, which the Belgian artist Paul Delvaux (1897–1994) stumbled across at the end of World War II and where he remained for the rest of his life. His old home and studio have been turned into the **Paul Delvaux Museum**, Kabouterweg 42 (tram stop St Idesbald; April–June & Sept Tues–Sun 10.30am–5.30pm; July & Aug daily 10.30am–5.30pm; Oct–Dec Fri–Sun 10.30am–5.30pm; closed Jan–March; F250), with the addition of a large subterranean extension – to avoid disfiguring the house above. The museum holds a comprehensive collection of Delvaux's work, following his development from early Expressionist days through to the Surrealism which defined his oeuvre from the 1930s. Two of his pet motifs are train stations, in one guise or another, and nude or semi-nude women set against some sort of classical backdrop. The intention is to usher the viewer into the unconscious with dream-like images where every perspective is exact, but, despite the impeccable craftsmanship, there's something very cold about his vision. At their best, his paintings achieve an almost palpable sense of foreboding, good examples being *The Garden* of 1971 and *The Procession* dated to 1963, while *The Station in the Forest* of 1960 has the most wonderful trees. A full catalogue of the collection is available at reception.

Finding the museum is a bit tricky. From the St Idesbald tram stop, walk back towards Ostend for about 400m, turn right (away from the coast) just after the gas station and follow the signs. The walk takes fifteen to twenty minutes.

De Panne

A couple of kilometres further west, sitting close to the French frontier, **DE PANNE** is now one of the largest settlements on the Belgian coast, though as late as the 1880s it was a tiny fishing village of low white cottages, nestling in a slight wooded hollow (*panne*) from which it takes its name. Most of the villagers had their own fishing boats and a plot of land surrounded by trees and hedges. The peace and quiet ended with the arrival of surveyors and architects who reinforced the sea dyke, and laid out paths and roads in preparation for the rapid construction of lines of villas and holiday homes. However, with the exception of the buildings on the seafront, the contours of the land were respected and the houses of much of today's resort perch prettily among the dunes to the south of the beach.

The peripheries of De Panne may be appealing, but the town centre is unprepossessing, its humdrum modern buildings jostling a seafront that becomes decidedly overcrowded in the summer. That said, the beach is excellent and De Panne comes equipped with all the amenities of a seaside resort, including land sailing. There's one specific sight too, the rather grand **monument** at the west end of Zeedijk marking the spot where King Leopold I first set foot on Belgian soil in 1831. Otherwise, the town achieved ephemeral fame in World War I, when it was part of the tiny triangle of Belgian territory that the German army failed to occupy, becoming the home of King Albert's government from 1914 to 1918. A generation later, the retreating British army managed to reach the sand dunes between De Panne and Dunkirk, 15km to the west, just in time for their miraculous evacuation back to England. In eight days, an armada of vessels of all sizes and shapes rescued over 300,000 Allied soldiers, a deliverance that prompted Churchill to his most famous speech: ". . .we shall fight on the beaches, . . . we shall fight in the fields and in the streets, we shall fight in the hills; we shall never surrender".

On the western edge of De Panne, a small segment of these same sand dunes has been protected by the creation of the **De Westhoek Staatsnatuurreservaat** (state nature reserve), an open-access, 800-acre expanse of wild, unspoiled coastline criss-crossed by five marked footpaths ranging from 1.5km to 2.4km in length. It's a lovely area to wander and occasionally there are guided walks – ask at the tourist office for information. The main access point is about 2km west of the town centre: follow Duinkerkelaan to the island, turn right down Dynastielaan and keep going as far as the T-junction at the end where you make a left turn along Schuilhavenlaan. There are no buses, and the walk is a bore, but **bikes** can be rented in town at several central locations including Roger, Zeedijk 46 (☎058/41 21 46) and Marius, Zeedijk 40 (☎058/41 30 79).

PRACTICALITIES
Trams travel the length of De Panne's main street, Nieuwpoortlaan/ Duinkerkelaan, which cuts through the centre of the resort running parallel to, and one block south of, the beach. Beside De Panne Centrum tram stop, there's a combined De Lijn **bus** and **tourist information kiosk** on Koning Albertplein (mid-June to mid-Sept daily 10am–noon & 2–6pm), but the main tourist office is in the **Gemeentehuis** (Sept–June Mon–Fri 9am–noon & 1–5pm, plus July & Aug Mon–Sat 9am–noon & 1–6pm; ☎058/42 18 18), five to ten minutes' walk south from the kiosk at Zeelaan 21. Note that De Panne **train station** is a good thirty-minute walk south from the beach along Zeelaan – or hop on bus #781 which runs hourly between the kiosk on Koning Albertplein and the station.

Both tourist offices have lists of **private rooms** (③) and will phone around to find vacancies, providing they aren't too busy. Alternatively, about half of De Panne's thirty-odd **hotels** are clustered near where Zeelaan, the principal north–south axis, meets the main street, Nieuwpoortlaan/Duinkerkelaan. Options include the *Terlinck,* Zeelaan 175 (☎058/42 01 08, fax 42 05 86; ⑤), a pleasant three-star hotel right on the seafront, and the *Hostellerie L'Avenue,* Nieuwpoortlaan 56 (closed in Jan; ☎058/41 13 70, fax 42 12 21; ③), a well-tended pension-like hotel with just four small and cosy rooms. Nearby, the *Artevelde*, Sloepenlaan 24 (058/41 10 51, fax 42 14 44; ③), is an unassuming family two-star hotel in an attractive Art Deco building, while the *Seahorse*, at Toeristenlaan 7 (☎058/41 27 47, fax 41 27 48; ④), is a standard-issue, medium-range hotel with a sleek modern interior.

There are literally dozens of places to **eat**; the best bet is to walk along the seashore promenade until you find somewhere that takes your fancy.

Veurne and around

Founded in the ninth century, **VEURNE** was part of a chain of fortresses built to defend Flanders from the raids of the Vikings, but without much success. The town failed to flourish and two centuries later it was small, poor and insignificant. But all that changed when Robert II of Flanders returned from the Crusades in 1099 with a piece of the True Cross. His ship was caught in a gale, and in desperation he vowed to offer the relic to the first church he saw if he survived. The church was St Walburga at Veurne, and the annual procession that commemorated the gift made the town an important centre of medieval pilgrimage for some three hundred years. These days Veurne is one of the more popular day-trip destinations in West Flanders, a neat and dreamy backwater whose one real attraction is its Grote Markt, one of the best-preserved town squares in Belgium.

The Town

All the main town sights are on or around the **Grote Markt**. Beginning in the northwest corner, the modest **Stadhuis** is a mixture of Gothic and Renaissance styles built between 1596 and 1612, with a fine blue and gold decorated stone loggia projecting from the original brick facade. Inside, a **museum** (April–Sept guided tours 4 times daily, Oct–March 2 daily; F50) displays items of unexceptional interest, the best of which is a set of leather wall coverings made in Cordoba. The Stadhuis connects with the more austere classicism of the **Gerechtshof**, whose symmetrical pillars and long, rectangular windows once sheltered the offices of the Inquisition as it set about the Flemish peasantry with gusto. The attached tiered and balconied **Belfort** (no public access) was completed in 1628, its Gothic lines culminating in a dainty Baroque tower, from where **carillon concerts** (Wed 10.30–11.30am, plus July & Aug Sun 8–9pm) ring out over the town. The belfry is, however, dwarfed by the adjacent **St Walburga** (June–Sept daily 10am–noon & 3–6pm; free), the objective of the medieval pilgrimages, an enormous buttressed and gargoyled affair with weatherbeaten brick walls dating from the thirteenth century. It's actually the second church to be built on the spot; the original version – which in turn replaced a pagan temple dedicated to Wotan – was razed by the Vikings. The hangar-like interior has one virtue, the lavishly carved Flemish Renaissance choir stalls.

Moving on to the northeast corner of the Grote Markt, at the end of Ooststraat, the **Spaans Paviljoen** (Spanish Pavilion) was built as the town hall in the middle of the fifteenth century, but takes its name from its later adaptation as the officers' quarters of the Habsburg garrison. It's a self-confident building, the initial square brick tower, with its castellated parapet, extended by a facade of long, slender windows and flowing stone tracery in the true Gothic manner – an obvious contrast to the Flemish shutters and gables of the old **Vleeshuis** standing directly opposite. Crossing over to the southeast side of the square, the **Hoge Wacht**, which originally served as the quarters of the town watch, displays a fetching amalgam of styles, its brick gable cheered up by a small arcaded gallery. The east side of this building edges the Appelmarkt, home to the clumping medieval mass of **St Niklaaskerk**, whose detached **tower** (mid-June to mid-Sept 10am–noon & 2–5pm; F40) gives spectacular views of the countryside around.

THE PENITENTS' PROCESSION

In 1650 a young soldier named Mannaert was on garrison duty in Veurne when he was persuaded by his best friend to commit a mortal sin. After receiving the consecrated wafer during Communion, he took it out of his mouth, wrapped it in a cloth, and returned to his lodgings where he charred it over a fire, under the delusion that by reducing it to powder he would make himself invulnerable to injury. The news got out, and he was later arrested, tried and executed, his friend suffering the same fate a few weeks later. Fearful of the consequences of this sacrilege in their town, the people of Veurne resolved that something must be done, deciding on a procession to commemorate the Passion of Christ. This survives as the **Penitents' Procession** (*Boetprocessie*), held on the last Sunday in July – an odd and distinctly macabre reminder of a remote past. Trailing through the streets, the leading figures dress in the brown cowls of the Capuchins and carry wooden crosses that weigh anything up to 50kg.

Guildhouses, Grand Place, Brussels

BRUSSELS

Euro Mannekin Pis

Café Society, Brussels

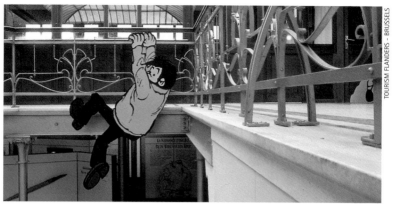

Captain Haddock, Centre Belge de la Bande Dessineé, Brussels

Windowshopping, Brussels

Van Eyck's *Adoration of the Mystic Lamb*

Place du Jeu de Balle, Brussels

The Tyne Cot cemetery, Paaschendaele

Art Nouveau house front

Bird's eye view of the Markt, Bruges

The Vismarkt, Bruges

A windmill near Bruges

Reflections of canalside buildings, Ghent

Practicalities

Hourly trains connect Veurne with the seaside resort of De Panne 6km to the west, as well as with Diksmuide and Ghent to the east. Regular buses also link the town with Ieper, some 30km to the south. **Buses** drop passengers outside the **train station**, a ten-minute stroll from the town centre – turn right out of the station building, first left along Statiestraat and over the canal straight down Ooststraat. **Accommodation** can be a bit of a problem. The **tourist office**, Grote Markt 29 (Easter–Sept daily 10am–noon & 1.30–5.30pm; Oct–Easter Mon–Sat 10am–noon & 2–4pm; ☎058/31 21 54), has details of a couple of private **rooms**, but they're often full. The only alternative is the town's two **hotels**, the three-star *Croonhof* (☎058/31 31 28, fax 31 56 81; ⑤), a trim, well-cared-for little place in an attractively converted old house with spotless rooms just off the Grote Markt at Noordstraat 9; and the two-star *Atrium*, a pretty little place amongst the quiet cobbled streets just to the west of St Walburga at Zwarte Nonnenstraat 19 (☎058/31 68 68, fax 31 68 70; ⑥). In both cases, call ahead in summer to make sure of a bed.

The Grote Markt is lined with **cafés** and **bars**. One of the more popular places is *'t Centrum,* Grote Markt 33 (closed Mon Sept–June), which offers reasonably priced snacks and meals from a straightforward Flemish menu. It's here you can also sample a Veurne delicacy, *potjesvlees* – boiled veal, chicken and rabbit pieces served cold in jellied brawn – and wash it down with the local Trappist ale, Westvleteren. Another option is the comparable *Flandria*, at Grote Markt 30 (closed Thurs). Moving up-market, both the *Croonhof* (closed Mon) and the *Atrium* (closed Mon) have excellent restaurants, featuring Flemish regional dishes.

Around Veurne: Beauvoorde, Lo and Diksmuide

Veurne is the capital of the **Veurne-Ambacht**, a pancake-flat agricultural region of quiet and unremarkable villages which stretches south of the town, encircled by the French border and the River Ijzer. The best way to see it is by bike – cycles can be rented at Veurne train station and maps of cycle routes are available from the tourist office. The region's prime attraction is the Renaissance chateau of **Beauvoorde** (June–Sept Tues–Sun, guided tours at 2, 3, 4 & 5pm; F80), about 8km south of Veurne in the drowsy hamlet of Wulveringem. Built in the early seventeenth century, the castle's crow-stepped gables and unadorned brick walls sit prettily behind a narrow moat, and the interior has displays of ceramics, silverware and glass. There are no buses from Veurne; by car, the quickest way to get there is to take the main Ieper road, the N8, for about 5km and then watch for the signed turning on the right, from where it's 2km to Beauvoorde.

Lo

The most pleasant village in the district is **LO**, 12km southeast of Veurne, on the bus route between Veurne and Ieper (Mon–Fri 7 daily, Sat 4 daily, Sun 2 daily; 30min). It was here, on his way across Gaul, that Julius Caesar is supposed to have tethered his horse to a yew by the Westpoort, an event recalled by a plaque and a battered old tree which adjoin two turrets and a gateway, the remains of the medieval ramparts. Less apocryphally, the village once prospered under the patronage of its Augustinian abbey, founded in the twelfth century and suppressed by the French at the time of the Revolution. Only the dovecote of the abbey survives, hidden away beside the *Hotel Oude Abidj*, which is itself tucked in behind the present church, a great big edifice graced by a crocketed spire. But it's the peace and quiet that appeal rather than the sights.

There's a choice of two **hotels**, the more expensive of which is the *Oude Abidj*, Noordstraat 3 (☎058/28 82 65, fax 28 94 07; ④), a three-star hotel with a garden and modern rooms. Its only rival is the one-star *Stadhuis*, Markt 1 (☎058/28 80 16, fax 28 89 05; ②), which has clean and simple rooms, and operates a pleasant restaurant-bar within part of the old Stadhuis, a much-modified sixteenth-century structure made appealing by a slender, arcaded tower. Lo's seasonal **tourist office**, by the main square, has maps of the district and does cycle hire.

Diksmuide

Dominating the western approaches to the small town of **DIKSMUIDE**, 11km northeast of Lo and 10km southeast of Veurne, is the Ijzertoren, a massive war memorial bearing the letters AVV-VVK – *Alles voor Vlaanderen* ("All for Flanders") and *Vlaanderen voor Kristus* ("Flanders for Christ"). At 84 metres high, this gloomy tower recalls the sufferings of Diksmuide during World War I when it was so extensively shelled that by 1918 its location could only be identified from a map, the obliteration a consequence of its position immediately east of the River Ijzer, which formed the front line from October 1914.

Rebuilt, the careful reconstruction of the town works best round the **Grote Markt**, a pleasant, spacious square flanked by brick gables in the traditional Flemish style. There's nothing spectacular to see, but it's an enjoyable spot to nurse a coffee and you could drop by the enormous church of St Niklaaskerk, built to the original Gothic design complete with a splendid spire. Otherwise, for a fine view across the Flanders plain, it's a fifteen-minute walk from the Grote Markt along Reuzemolenstraat and then Ijzerlaan to the looming **Ijzertoren** (April–May & Sept to mid-Nov Mon–Fri 9am–noon & 1–5pm, Sat & Sun from 10am; June–Aug Mon–Fri 9am–6pm, Sat & Sun 10am–6pm; F150). Built in the 1950s to replace an earlier tower, which was blown up in mysterious circumstances – probably by Fascist sympathizers in 1946 – the Ijzertoren also incorporates a small war museum. There's another reminder of World War I about 2km to the north along the west bank of the Ijzer in the **Dodengang** (Easter–Sept daily 9am–noon & 1.30–5pm; F60), an especially dangerous slice of trench which was held by the Belgians throughout the war. Around 300 metres of trench are viewable, but the preservation has been heavy-handed: twisting lines of concrete "sand bags" – and that's pretty much all there is – convey little, and the orientation table-cum-viewpoint needs an overhaul.

Diksmuide is easy to reach by **bus** from Lo and Ieper, and by **train** from Veurne. From the town's bus and train stations, it's a five- to ten-minute walk west along Stationsstraat to the Grote Markt where the **tourist office** (Mon–Fri 8.30am–noon & 1.30–5pm, plus mid-May to late Sept Sat & Sun 10am–noon & 2–5pm; ☎051/51 91 46) has all the usual material. There are two comfortable three-star **hotels** among the Flemish-style buildings on the Grote Markt – the *Polderbloem*, at no. 8 (☎051/50 29 05, fax 50 29 06; ④), and the larger and slightly more expensive *De Vrede*, at no. 35 (☎051/50 00 38, fax 51 06 21; ④).

Ieper

Readily accessible by train from Kortrijk, and by bus from Veurne and Diksmuide, **IEPER** (Ypres) was founded in the tenth century at the point where

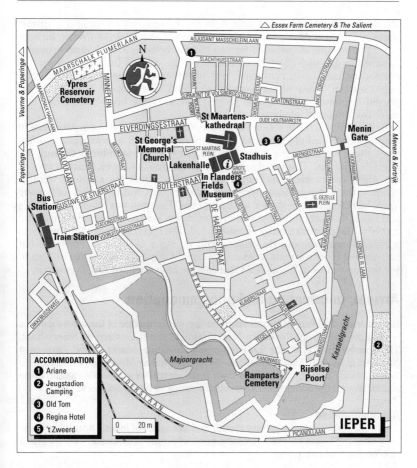

the Bruges to Paris trade route crossed the River Ieperlee. The town rapidly became a major player in the cloth trade, its thirteenth-century population of two hundred thousand sharing economic control of the region with rival Ghent and Bruges. The most precariously sited of the great Flemish cities, Ypres, as it was then known, was, however, too near the French frontier for comfort, and too strategically important to be ignored by any of the armies whose campaigns crisscrossed the town's environs with depressing frequency. The city governors kept disaster at bay by reinforcing their defences and switching alliances whenever necessary, fighting against the French at the Battle of the Golden Spurs in 1302, and with them forty years later at Roosebeke, where the popular Ghentish leader, Philip van Artevelde, was killed.

The first major misjudgement came in 1383 when Henry Spencer, bishop of Norwich, landed at Calais under the pretext of supporting the armies of Pope Urban VI, who occupied the Vatican, against his rival Clement VII, who was installed in Avignon. The burghers of Ghent and Bruges flocked to Spencer's standard, and the allies had little difficulty in agreeing on an attack against Ypres, which had decided to champion Clement and trust the French for support. The ensuing siege lasted for two months before a French army appeared to save the day, and all of Ypres celebrated the victory. In fact, the town was ruined, its trade never recovered, and, unable to challenge its two main competitors again, many of the weavers migrated. The process of depopulation proved irreversible, and by the sixteenth century the town had shrunk to a mere five thousand inhabitants.

In World War I, the first German thrust of 1914 left a bulge in the Allied line to the immediate east of Ypres, and for the next four years a series of futile offensives attempted to use the bulge – or **Salient** – as a base to break through the enemy's front line. This had disastrous consequences for Ypres, which served as the Allied communications centre. Comfortably within the range of German artillery, the whole population was evacuated in 1915, and by the end of the war Ypres had literally been shelled to smithereens. The town was rebuilt in the 1920s and 1930s, its most prominent medieval buildings, the Lakenhalle (cloth hall) and cathedral, being meticulously reconstructed. The end result can't help but seem a little antiseptic – old-style edifices with no signs of decay or erosion – but nonetheless Ieper warrants at least an overnight stay, especially if you're keen to see the mementos of World War I that speckle both the town and its environs.

Arrival, information and accommodation

Ieper's **train** and **bus stations** stand on the western edge of the town centre, a ten-minute walk from the Grote Markt, straight down Gustave de Stuersstraat. The **tourist office**, in the Lakenhalle on the Grote Markt (daily: April–Sept Mon–Sat 9.30am–5.30pm, Sun 10am–6pm; Oct–March Mon–Sat 9am–5pm, Sun 1–5pm; ☎057/20 07 24), has good town maps, details of suggested car and cycle routes around the Salient and a reasonable range of books on World War I.

Accommodation

There are no pensions or private rooms, and almost all of Ieper's **hotels** are on or very near the Grote Markt. Prices are generally quite reasonable. There's also a small municipal **campsite**.

HOTELS

Ariane, Slachthuisstraat 58 (☎057/21 82 18, fax 21 87 99). A prim and proper garden surrounds this ultra-modern four-star hotel about five minutes' walk north of the Grote Markt along Boezingepoort. Presumably it was built with the passing business trade in mind, but somehow it doesn't quite work – it looks marooned rather than secluded. ⑥.

Old Tom, Grote Markt 8 (☎057/20 15 41, fax 21 91 20). These plain but pleasant en-suite rooms above a café-bar are favoured by English visitors. Very reasonably priced near the bottom of the range for this price code. ④.

Regina, Grote Markt 45 (☎057/21 88 88, fax 21 90 20). This four-star establishment, housed in a 1920s copy of a grand turn-of-the-century edifice, is the most expensive hotel on the Grote Markt. Frankly, the bland, modern rooms aren't worth the extra – though it's perfectly adequate and often has vacancies when its competitors are full. ⑥.

't Zweerd, Grote Markt 2 (☎057/20 04 75, fax 21 78 96). A little less cheery than its main rival, *Old Tom*, this hotel is still a good deal. Its twelve mundanely modern rooms are located above a café-bar; nine are en-suite, the rest make do with just a washbasin. ③.

CAMPSITE

Jeugstadion Camping, Leopold III-laan 16 (☎21 72 82, fax 21 61 21). Merely eleven pitches are available on this municipal campsite just east of the old moat, behind the sports ground. Hook-ups, toilets and showers. Bike hire. Fifteen minutes' walk from the train station. Mid-March to Oct.

The Town

A monument to the power and wealth of the medieval guilds, the replica **Lakenhalle**, on the Grote Markt, is a copy of the thirteenth-century original which stood beside the River Ieperlee, which now flows underground. Too long to be pretty and too square to be elegant, it seems to have been built with practical considerations upper-most: no fewer than 58 doors once gave access from the street to the old selling halls, while boats sailed in and out of the jetty on the west wing, under the watchful eyes of its majestic belfry, flanked by four sharp turrets. During winter, wool was stored on the upper floor and cats were brought in to keep the mice down. The cats may have had a good time in winter, but they couldn't have relished the prospect of spring when they were thrown out of the windows to a hostile crowd below as part of the **Kattestoet** or Cats' Festival – the slaughter intended to symbolize the killing of evil spirits. The festival ran right up until 1817, and was revived in 1938, when the cats were replaced by cloth imitations. Since then it's developed into Ieper's principal shindig, held every three years on the second Sunday in May. The main event is the parade of cats, a large-scale celebration of all things feline, complete with proces-sions, dancers and bands, and some of the biggest models and puppets imaginable.

The interior of the Lakenhalle holds the ambitious **In Flanders Fields Museum** (April–Sept daily 10am–6pm; Oct–March Tues–Sun 10am–5pm; closed for three weeks after Xmas; F250), which focuses on the experiences of those caught up in the war rather than the ebb and flow of the military campaigns. In part this is very successful – the section simulating a gas attack is most effective – but the interactive clutter (touch screens and the like) tends to get in the way and there's not nearly enough about individuals – lots of personal artefacts but precious little about the men and women who owned them. That said, the muse-um is wide-ranging and thoughtful and the (multilingual) quotations are well-chosen. The photographs are particularly powerful: soldiers grimly digging trenches, the pathetic casualties of a gas attack, flyblown corpses in the mud and panoramas of a blasted landscape.

Back outside, the east end of the Lakenhalle is attached to the **Stadhuis**, whose fancy Renaissance facade rises above an elegant arcaded gallery, and round the back is **St Maartenskathedraal**, built in 1930 as a copy of the thirteenth-centu-ry Gothic original. The church's cavernous nave is a formal, rather stodgy affair, but the rose window above the south transept door is a fine tribute to King Albert I, its yellow, red and blue stained glass the gift of the British armed forces. Just to the northwest, near the end of Elverdingsestraat, stands **St George's Memorial Church** (daily 10am–5pm, often longer; free), a modest brick building finished in 1929. The interior is crowded with brass plaques honouring the dead of many British regiments and the chairs carry individual and regimental tributes. Again, it's hard not to be moved, for there's nothing vainglorious in this public space, so consumed as it is with private grief.

A few minutes' walk away, just beyond the far side of the Grote Markt, the **Menin Gate** war memorial was built on the site of the old Menenpoort that served as the main route for British soldiers heading for the front. It's a simple, brooding monument, towering over the edge of the town, its walls covered with the names of those fifty thousand British and Commonwealth troops who died in the Ypres Salient but have no grave. The simple inscription above the lists of the dead has none of the arrogance of the victor but rather a sense of great loss, though the waste of human life is no less striking. The self-justifying formality of the memorial did, however, offend many veterans and prompted a bitter verse from Siegfried Sassoon:

Was ever an immolation so belied
As these intolerably nameless names?
Well might the Dead who struggled in slime
Rise and deride this sepulchre of crime.

The Last Post is sounded beneath the gate every evening at 8pm. Oddly enough, the seventeenth-century brick and earthen **ramparts** on either side of the Menin Gate were well enough constructed to survive World War I intact – the vaults even served as some of the safest bunkers on the front. These massive ramparts and the protective moat still extend right round the east and south of the town centre and there's a pleasant footpath along the top. The stroll takes you past the **Ramparts Cemetery**, a British Commonwealth War Cemetery beside the old Lille Gate (the present Rijselsepoort); and there's another graveyard, the **Ypres Reservoir Cemetery**, on the far side of the town centre – from the cathedral, walk down Elverdingsestraat and turn right along Minneplein.

Eating and drinking

Like the hotels, most of Ieper's **cafés** and **restaurants** are dotted round the Grote Markt. With one exception, they're not a particularly distinguished bunch, but the meals they offer are substantial and reasonably priced. Almost all of Ieper's **bars** are on the main square too, and although the action could hardly be described as frenetic, there's enough to keep most visitors happy.

Hostellerie St Nicolas, Gustave de Stuersstraat 6. The best restaurant in town, this is a sedate and slightly formal establishment on the street linking the station with the Grote Markt. Tasty and well-presented Flemish and French main courses from around F500, though the full set menu will set you back much more.

In 't Klein Stadhuis Bar, adjacent to the Stadhuis on the Grote Markt. The nearest thing Ieper has to a hot spot, this lively bar stays open till late.

Old Tom, Grote Markt 8. Straightforward restaurant offering good-quality Flemish cuisine at affordable prices, and a promising selection of Belgian beers to wash it down.

Vivaldi, Grote Markt 21. Busy tea room-cum-restaurant that's particularly good for inexpensive snacks and light meals during the day.

Around Ieper: Poperinge

Some 12km west of Ieper, at the centre of a hop-growing area, **POPERINGE** was a posting station for soldiers heading in and out of the Ypres Salient. It was here that the Reverend Philip Clayton opened the Everyman's Club at Talbot House, Gasthuisstraat 43, where everyone, regardless of rank, was able to come and rest or seek spiritual help. Clayton went on to found **Toc H**, the worldwide Christian fellowship that took its name from the army signallers' code for Talbot House – after Gilbert Talbot, the son of the Bishop of Winchester, who was killed at Hooge. The original building is still run as a charity and offers simple hostel-style **accommodation** (☎057/33 32 28, fax 33 21 83; F500) – though little remains to remind you of its history.

The Ypres Salient

The **Ypres Salient** occupies a basin-shaped parcel of land about 25km long and never more than 15km deep immediately to the east of Ieper. For the generals of World War I, the area's key feature was the long and low sequence of ridges which sweep south from Langemark to the French border. These vantage points gave the occupants a clear view of Ieper and its surroundings, and consequently the British and Germans spent the war trying to capture and keep them. The dips and sloping ridges which were then so vitally important are still much in evidence, but today the tranquillity of the landscape makes it difficult to imagine what the war was actually like.

In fact it's surprisingly difficult to find anything which gives any real impression of the scale and nature of the conflict. The most resonant reminders of the blood

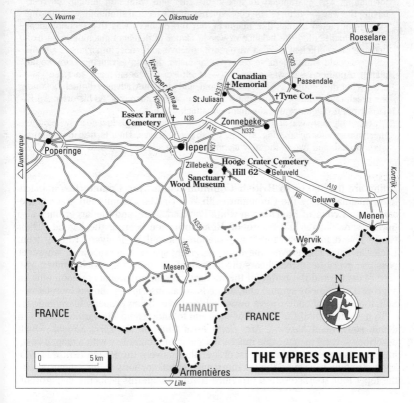

THE YPRES SALIENT

THE YPRES SALIENT

The battle site of Ieper was entirely accidental. When the German army launched the war in the west by invading Belgium, they were following the principles – if not the details – laid down by a chief of the German General Staff, Alfred von Schlieffen, who had died eight years earlier. The idea was simple: to avoid fighting a war on two fronts, the German army would outflank the French and capture Paris by attacking through Belgium, well before the Russians had assembled on the eastern frontier. It didn't work, with the result that as the initial German offensive ground to a halt, so two lines of opposing trenches were dug – and these soon stretched from the North Sea down to Switzerland. No one knew quite what to do next, but attention focused on the two main bulges – or salients – in the line, one at Ieper, the other at Verdun, on the Franco-German frontier just to the south of Luxembourg. To the Allied generals, the bulge at Ieper – the **Ypres Salient** – was a good place to break through the German lines and roll up their front; to the Germans it represented an ideal opportunity to break the deadlock by attacking key enemy positions from several sides at the same time. Contemporary **military doctrine** on both sides held that the way to win a war was to destroy the enemy's strongest forces first. In retrospect this may seem strange, but the generals of the day were schooled in cavalry tactics, where a charge that broke the enemy's key formations was guaranteed to spread disorder and confusion among the rest, paving the way for victory. The consequence of this tactical similitude was that the salients attracted armies like magnets, but the problem was that technological changes had shifted the balance of war in favour of defence: machine guns had become more efficient, barbed wire more effective, and, most important of all, the railways could shift defensive reserves far faster than an advancing army could march. Another issue was **supply**. Great efforts had been made to raise vast armies but they couldn't be fed off the land, and once they advanced much beyond the reach of the railways, the supply problems were enormous. As historian A.J.P. Taylor put it, "Defence was mechanized; attack was not".

Seemingly incapable of rethinking their strategy, the generals had no answer to the stalemate save for an amazing profligacy with people's lives. Their tactical innovations were limited, and two of the new techniques – gas attack and a heavy preliminary

---

letting are the 160 or so **British Commonwealth War Cemeteries**, immaculately maintained by the Commonwealth War Graves Commission. Each cemetery has a **Cross of Sacrifice** in white Portland stone, and the larger ones also have a sarcophagus-like **Stone of Remembrance** bearing the legend "Their Name Liveth for Ever More", a quotation selected by Rudyard Kipling from Ecclesiasticus. The graves line up at precisely spaced intervals and, wherever possible, every headstone bears the individual's name, rank, serial number, age, date of death, and the badge of the military unit, or a national emblem, plus an appropriate religious symbol and, at the base, an inscription chosen by relatives. Still, thousands of bodies were buried without ever being properly identified.

To navigate round the scores of sites and to understand the various battles in detail, you'll need *Major & Mrs Holt's Field Guide to the Ypres Salient*, which describes several manageable itineraries and comes complete with a map; it costs F825 and is on sale at Ieper tourist office. Alternatively, the **Peace Route** is a 45-kilometre bike trip round the northern and central portions of the Salient. Again, the Ieper tourist office sells a brochure (F40), though this lacks the background

bombardment – actually made matters worse. The **shells** forewarned the enemy of an offensive and churned the trenches into a muddy maelstrom where men, horses and machinery were simply engulfed; the **gas** was as dangerous to the advancing soldiers as it was to the retreating enemy. Tanks could have broken the impasse, but their development was never prioritized.

Naturally enough, the soldiers of all the armies involved lost confidence in their generals, and by 1917, despite court martials and firing squads, the sheer futility of the endless round of failed offensives made **desertion** commonplace and threatened to bring mass mutiny to the western front. However, although it is undeniably true that few of the military commanders of the day showed much understanding of how to break the **deadlock** – and they have been savagely criticized for their failures – some of the blame must be apportioned to the politicians. They demanded assault rather than defence, and continued to call for a general "victory" even after it had become obvious that this was beyond reach and that each ill-conceived attack cost thousands of lives. Every government concerned had believed that a clear victor would emerge by Christmas 1914, and none of them was able to adjust to the new situation. There were no moves toward a negotiated settlement, because no one was quite sure what they would settle for – a lack of clarity that contrasted starkly with the jingoistic sentiments stirred up to help sustain the conflict, which demanded victory or at least military success. In this context, how could a general recommend a defensive strategy or a politician propose a compromise? Those who did were dismissed.

This was the background to the four years of war that raged in and around the Ypres Salient. There were four **major battles**. The first, in October and November of 1914, settled the lines of the bulge as both armies tried to outflank each other; the second was a German attack in the following spring that moved the trenches a couple of miles west. The third, launched by British Empire soldiers in July 1917, was even more pointless, with thousands of men dying for an advance of only a few kilometres. It's frequently called the Battle of Passchendaele, but Lloyd George more accurately referred to it as the "battle of the mud", a disaster that cost 250,000 British lives. The fourth and final battle, in April 1918, was another German attack inspired by General Ludendorff's desire to break the British army. Instead it broke his own and led to the **Armistice** of November 11.

detail provided by the *Holt's* guide. The most illuminating guided tours are those offered by English-owned and -operated **Salient Tours** (Thurs–Tues; ☎051/50 57 88), who offer both four-hour (F950) and two-hour (F650) tours. At present, the shorter version begins beside the Menin Gate at 2.30pm and the longer one starts on the Grote Markt at 10am. Advance booking is required for the longer tour and recommended for the other.

A tour of the Salient

A detailed exploration of the Salient would take weeks; below we've outlined an abbreviated itinerary which can be completed comfortably by car in half a day. Beginning and ending in Ieper, the route focuses on the Salient's central – and most revealing – section.

Ieper's one-way system initially makes things confusing, but leave the town to the north along the N369, the road to Diksmuide. After about 3km, just beyond the flyover, watch for **Essex Farm Cemetery** on the right, where the dead from the battlefield across the adjacent canal were brought. In the bank behind (and to the left of) the cemetery's Cross of Sacrifice are the remains of several British bunkers, part of a combined forward position and first-aid post where the Canadian John McCrae wrote arguably the war's best-known poem, *In Flanders Fields*:

...We are the Dead. Short days ago
We lived, felt dawn, saw sunsets glow,
Loved and were loved, and now we lie
In Flanders fields...

Retracing your route briefly from Essex Farm, take the N38 east by turning right onto the flyover from its southern side (confusingly signed Brugge). The N38 leads into the N313 and after 6km you pass through the village of St Juliaan immediately beyond which is Vancouver Corner. Here, the **Canadian Memorial**, a ten-metre high granite statue topped by the bust of a Canadian soldier, was raised in honour of those who endured the first German chlorine gas attacks in April 1915. At the memorial, turn right and then first left at the little roadside shrine to follow the country lane leading 5km east to **Tyne Cot**. This is the largest British Commonwealth war cemetery in the world, containing 11,956 graves and the Memorial to the Missing, a semi-circular wall inscribed with the names of a further 35,000 men whose bodies were never recovered. The soldiers of a Northumbrian division gave the place its name, wryly observing, as they tried to fight their way up the ridge, that the German blockhouses on the horizon looked like Tyneside cottages. The largest of these concrete bunkers was, at the suggestion of George V, incorporated within the mound beneath the Cross of Sacrifice – you can still see a piece of it where a slab of stone has been deliberately omitted. The scattered graves behind the Cross were dug during the final months of the war and have remained in their original positions, adding a further poignancy to the seemingly endless lines of tombstones below. Strangely, the Memorial to the Missing at the back of the cemetery wasn't part of the original design: the intention was that these names be recorded on the Menin Gate, but there wasn't enough room.

Tyne Cot cemetery overlooks the valley which gently climbs up to Passendale, known then as **Passchendaele**. This village was the British objective in the Third Battle of Ypres, but torrential rain and intensive shelling turned the valley into a giant quagmire. Men, horses and guns simply sank into the mud and disappeared without trace. The whole affair came to symbolize the futility of the war and the incompetence of its generals: when Field Marshal Haig's Chief of Staff ventured out of his HQ to inspect progress, he allegedly said, "Good God, did we really send men to fight in that?"

Follow the road round the back of Tyne Cot to the right and after about 600m you reach a wider road – the N303 – which runs along the top of the Passendale ridge. Turn right onto it and shortly afterwards turn right again, down the N332 into **Zonnebeke**. Just beyond the village fork left onto the N37, keep straight over the motorway and you'll soon reach the N8, the Ieper–Menen road, which cuts across the back of the Salient – crowded with marching armies at night and peppered by German shrapnel during the day. Go round the island onto the N8 heading east and after about 1km turn right up Canadalaan for the 1.5km trip to Sanctuary Wood Cemetery, where Gilbert Talbot, who gave his name to Talbot

House in Poperinge (see pp.136–137), lies buried. Just beyond, the **Sanctuary Wood Museum** (daily 10am–7pm; F120) holds a ragbag of shells, rifles, bayonets, billycans, and incidental artefacts. Outside, things have been left much as they were the day the war ended, with some primitive zigzags of sand-bagged trench, shell craters and a few shattered trees that convey something of the desolateness of it all. The woods and the adjacent Hill 62 saw ferocious fighting – and there's a modest Canadian monument on the brow of the hill 300m up the road from the museum. From here, you can spy Ieper, 5km away, across the rolling ridges of the countryside. The N8 leads back to the Menin Gate.

Kortrijk

From Ieper, hourly trains slip south to Comines past a pair of spruce **war cemeteries** – Railway Dugouts and Larch Wood – just outside the village of **Zillebeke**, scene of some of the bloodiest fighting of World War I. Further along the tracks, **Comines** is a French-speaking town at the centre of a tiny enclave of the province of Hainaut, a sliver of land backing onto the River Leie, the frontier with France. From here, trains travel on to **Menen**, the terminus of the infamous "Menin" road from Ypres on which Allied troops were cruelly exposed to German guns positioned on the higher ground to the east.

Just 7km both from Menen and the French border, **KORTRIJK** (Courtrai) is the largest town and main rail junction in this part of West Flanders, tracing its

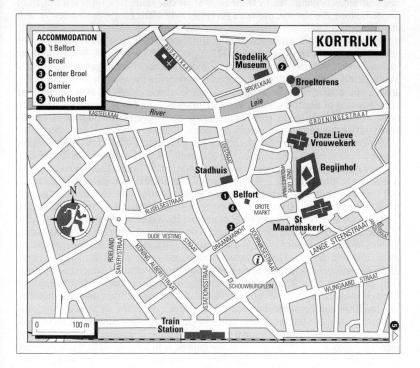

origins to a Roman settlement named *Cortracum*. In the Middle Ages, its fortunes paralleled those of Ypres, but although it became an important centre of the cloth trade, it was far too near France for comfort. Time and again Kortrijk was embroiled in the wars that swept across Flanders, right up to the two German occupations of this century. Yet, Kortrijk is quite different from its Flemish neighbours: it's very much a Francophile town, with a lively café scene and several ritzy hotels, which – together with its smattering of medieval buildings – makes for an enjoyable overnight stay.

The Town

Heavily bombed during World War II, the **Grote Markt**, at the centre of Kortrijk, is an architecturally incoherent mixture of bits of the old and a lot of the new, surrounding the forlorn, turreted **Belfort** – all that remains of the medieval cloth hall. The rather grand **war memorial** at its base is still tended with much care and attention. At the northwest corner of the Grote Markt, the **Stadhuis** (Mon–Fri 9am–noon & 2–5pm; free) is a sedate edifice with modern statues of the counts of Flanders on the facade, above and beside two lines of ugly windows. Inside, there are two fine sixteenth-century chimneypieces: one in the old Aldermen's Room (*Schepenzaal*) on the ground floor, a proud, intricate work decorated with municipal coats of arms and carvings of the Archdukes Albert and Isabella of Spain; the other, upstairs in the Council Chamber (*Raadzaal*), a more didactic affair, ornamented by three rows of precise statuettes, representing, from top to bottom, the virtues, the vices (to either side of the Emperor Charles V), and the torments of hell.

Opposite, by the southeast corner of the Grote Markt, the heavyweight tower of **St Maartenskerk** (Mon–Fri 8am–12.30pm & 2.30–5pm, Sat & Sun 10am–1pm & 5.30–7pm; free) dates from the fifteenth century, its gleaming white-stone exterior recently cleaned of decades of grime. Pop inside the church for a look at the gilded stone tabernacle (near the high altar), whose cluster of slender columns hide a series of figurines, including a grumpy-looking Jesus with his Cross, the work of Hendrik Maes in 1585. Immediately to the north, the **Begijnhof**, founded in 1238 by a certain Joanna of Constantinople, preserves the cosy informality of its seventeenth-century houses, and a small **museum** (Sat–Mon, Wed & Thurs 2–5pm; F30) sheds a little light on the simple life of the Beguines. On the far side of the Begijnhof, pushing into Groeningestraat, is the **Onze Lieve Vrouwekerk** (Mon–Fri 8.30am–noon & 2–6.30pm, Sat till 4pm, & Sun 9am–noon; free), a hulking grey structure that formerly doubled as part of the city's fortifications. In July 1302, the nave of the church was crammed with hundreds of spurs, ripped off the feet of dead and dying French knights at what has become known as the Battle of the Golden Spurs. These plundered spurs were the pathetic remains of the army Philip the Fair had sent to avenge the slaughter of the Bruges Matins earlier that year. The two armies, Philip's heavily armoured cavalry and the lightly armed Flemish weavers, had met outside Kortrijk on marshy ground, which the Flemish had disguised with brushwood. Despising their lowly-born adversaries, the French knights made no reconnaissance and fell into the trap, milling around in the mud like cumbersome dinosaurs. They were massacred, victims of their own arrogance, and the battle was a military landmark, the first time an amateur civilian army had defeated professional mail-clad knights. The spurs disappeared long ago and today much of the inside of the church is in a predictable Baroque style, though the gloomy and truncated north transept holds one splendid painting, van Dyck's *Raising of the Cross*, a muscular, sweeping work with a pale, almost vague-looking Christ completed by van Dyck just before he went to England. Across the church, the Counts' Chapel has an unusual series of somewhat crude, nineteenth-century portraits painted into the wall niches, but the highlight is a sensuous medieval alabaster statue of St Catherine, her left hand clutching a representation of the spiked wheel on which her enemies tried to break her, hence the "Catherine wheel" firework.

From beside the church, an alley cuts through to the River Leie, where the squat and sturdy twin towers, the **Broeltorens**, are all that remain of the old town walls. On the far side of the bridge, the **Stedelijk Museum**, Broelkaai 6 (Tues–Sun 10am–noon & 2–5pm; free), houses a fine sample of Flemish tiles and porcelain-ware, an interesting collection of locally made damask, and several paintings by the sixteenth-century Flemish artist Roelandt Savery. Trained in Amsterdam, Savery worked for the Habsburgs in Prague and Vienna before returning to the Netherlands. To suit the tastes of his German patrons, he infused many of his land-scapes with the romantic classicism that they preferred – the Garden of Eden and Orpheus were two favourite subjects – but the finely observed detail of his paint-ings was always in the true Flemish tradition. Among the works on display is the striking *Plundering of a Village*, where there's a palpable sense of outrage, in con-trast to *The Drinking-Place*, depicting a romanticized, arboreal idyll.

Practicalities

The town's **train station** is a five-minute walk from the Grote Markt: take the sec-ond road from the right out of Stationsplein. En route to the Grote Markt, the **tourist office**, at Schouwburgplein 14 (Mon–Fri 8.30am–5pm; mid-April to mid-Oct also Sat 10am–4pm; July & Aug only, Sun 10am–4pm; ☎056/23 93 71), has free town maps and an **accommodation** list, and will make bookings on your behalf at no extra charge. The list includes a couple of inexpensive private rooms (③). Otherwise, there are several convenient – and two particularly enticing – hotels. The plain exterior of the *Broel*, opposite the Broeltorens at Broelkaai 8 (☎056/21 83 51, fax 20 03 02; ⑥), is deceptive, for the inside of the building, which was once a tobacco factory, has a mock-monastic theme, its tunnels and stone-trimmed arches all entirely bogus but great fun. By comparison, there's no subtle modesty at the *Damier*, Grote Markt 41 (☎056/22 15 47, fax 22 86 31; ⑥), a plush and classy establishment with commodious rooms set behind an extravagant Neoclassical facade. Another good though less distinctive option is the *'t Belfort*, Grote Markt 53 (☎056/22 22 20, fax 20 13 06; ⑥), a smart and comfortable, medi-um-sized hotel across from the Stadhuis, while the *Center Broel*, Graanmarkt 6 (☎056/21 97 21, fax 20 03 66; ⑤), is a standard-issue, modern three-star hotel that's marginally less expensive than its rivals. There's also a **youth hostel**, an inconvenient twenty-minute walk east of the station at Passionistenlaan 1a (☎056/20 14 42, fax 20 46 63).

The best **restaurant** in town is *Evergreens*, opposite the church at Onze Lieve Vrouwestraat 48 (closed Thurs), a cosy, intimate and reasonably priced spot with an adventurous and wide-ranging menu featuring everything from reindeer to mussels. There's also *Den Engel*, Roelandt Saverystraat 6 (closed Mon & Tues), an attractive café kitted out in a sort of bright Baroque style and offering afford-able, homemade specials – lasagne, moussaka and the like; it's situated to the west of the Grote Markt – along Rijselsestraat and left at Louis Robbeplein. Alternatively, you'll find a long line of **cafés** and **bars on** the main square – just stroll along until somewhere takes your fancy. The *Arte*, at Grote Markt 3, has salads and pasta from around F350. One of the town's busiest bars is at the north end of Stationsstraat – the run-of-the-mill *Falstaff*, at no. 1.

Oudenaarde and around

Some 25km east across the Flanders plain from Kortrijk, the small town of **OUDE-NAARDE**, literally "old landing place", hugs the banks of the River Scheldt as it twists its way toward Ghent, 30km to the north. Granted a charter in 1193, the town concentrated on cloth manufacture until the early fifteenth century, when its weavers switched to tapestry-making, an industry that made its burghers rich and the town famous. The best tapestries became the prized possessions of the kings of France and Spain. Oudenaarde was also a key military objective during the religious and dynastic wars of the sixteenth to the eighteenth centuries; time and again it was attacked and besieged, perhaps most famously in July 1708 when the Duke of Marlborough came to the rescue and won a spectacular victory here against the French in the War of the Spanish Succession. With the demise of the tapestry industry in the late eighteenth century, the town became an insignificant backwater, a stagnant place in one of the poorest districts of Flanders. In the last few years, things have improved considerably due to its skilful use of regional development funds, and today's town makes an interesting and pleasant day out.

Arrival, information and accommodation

Oudenaarde's old neo-Gothic **train station**, with its chandelier in the hallway and coat of arms on the facade, stands in the shadow of the new fast line from Brussels, whose concrete bridges and raised track tower over the north side of town. From the train station, it's a fifteen-minute walk south to the town centre – along Stationsstraat and Nederstraat – where the **tourist office**, in the Stadhuis (April–Oct Mon–Fri 8.30am–5.30pm, Sat & Sun 10am–noon & 2–5pm; Nov–March Mon–Fri 8.30am–noon & 1.30–5.30pm; ☎055/31 72 51) issues free maps and has an **accommodation** list, though there are no private rooms and only three central **hotels**.

The pick of the bunch is *De Rantere*, Jan zonder Vreeslaan 8 (☎055/31 89 88, fax 33 01 11; ⑥), a spruce and comfortable modern hotel overlooking the Scheldt on the south side of the Markt: walk down Voorburg and veer right just beyond the entrance to the Begijnhof. The other tempting choice is *La Pomme d'Or*, Markt 62 (☎055/31 19 00, fax 30 08 44; ⑥), which occupies a big old house on the main square and offers plain, but perfectly adequate, high-ceilinged rooms. The nearest **campsite**, *IC-Camping*, is part of the holiday complex *Vlaamse Ardennen* (April to mid-Nov; ☎055/31 54 73, fax 30 08 65), some 2km west of the Markt along Minderbroedersstraat, at Kortrijkstraat 342.

The Town

Heading into Oudenaarde along Stationsstraat, the middle of the **Tacambaroplein** is taken up by a romantic war memorial that commemorates those who were daft

THE OUDENAARDE TAPESTRY INDUSTRY

Tapestry manufacture in Oudenaarde began in the middle of the fifteenth century, an embryonic industry that soon came to be based on a dual system of **workshop** and **outworker**, the one with paid employees, the other with workers paid on a piecework basis. From the beginning, the town authorities took a keen interest in the business, ensuring its success by a rigorous system of quality control which soon gave the town an international reputation for consistently well-made tapestries. The other side of this interventionist policy was less palatable: wages were kept down and the Guild of the Masters cunningly took over the running of the Guild of Weavers in 1501. To make matters worse, tapestries were by definition a luxury item, and workers were hardly ever able to accumulate enough capital to buy either their own looms or even raw materials.

The first great period of Oudenaarde tapestry-making lasted until the middle of the sixteenth century, when religious conflict overwhelmed the town and many of its Protestant-inclined weavers, who had come into direct conflict with their Catholic masters, migrated north to the rival workshops of Antwerp and Ghent. In 1582 Oudenaarde was finally incorporated into the Spanish Netherlands, precipitating a revival of tapestry production, fostered by the king and queen of Spain, who were keen to support the industry and passed draconian laws banning the movement of weavers. Later, however, French occupation and the shrinking of the Spanish market led to diminishing production, until the industry finally fizzled out in the late eighteenth century.

The **technique** applied to the production of tapestries was a cross between embroidery and ordinary weaving. It consisted of interlacing a wool weft above and below the strings of a vertical linen "chain", a process similar to weaving. However, the weaver had to stop to change colour, requiring as many shuttles for the weft as he had colours, as in embroidery. The appearance of a tapestry was entirely determined by the weft, the design being taken from a painting to which the weaver made constant reference. Standard-size Oudenaarde tapestries took six months to make and were produced exclusively for the very wealthy, the most important of whom would, on occasion, insist on the use of gold and silver thread and the employment of the most famous artists of the day for the preparatory painting – Pieter Paul Rubens, Jacob Jordaens and David Teniers all had tapestry commissions.

There were only two significant types of tapestry: **decorative**, principally *verdures*, showing scenes of foliage in an almost abstract way (the Oudenaarde speciality), and **pictorial** – usually variations on the same basic themes, particularly rural life, knights, hunting parties and religious scenes. Over the centuries, changes in style were strictly limited, though the early part of the seventeenth century saw an increased use of elaborate woven borders, an appreciation of perspective and the use of a far brighter, more varied range of colours. Oudenaarde tapestries are normally in yellow, brown, pale blue and shades of green, with an occasional splash of red.

or unscrupulous enough to volunteer to go to Mexico and fight for Maximilian, son-in-law of the Belgian king, Leopold I. Unwanted and unloved, Maximilian was imposed on the Mexicans by a French army provided by Napoleon III, who wished to take advantage of the American Civil War to develop a western empire. It was all too fanciful and the occupation rapidly turned into a fiasco. Maximilian paid for the adventure with his life in 1867, and few of his soldiers made the return trip.

The Markt: Stadhuis and Lakenhalle

Further south, the wide open space of the **Markt** is edged by the **Stadhuis**, one of the finest examples of Flamboyant Gothic in the country. An exquisite creation of around 1525, its elegantly symmetrical facade spreads out on either side of the extravagant tiers, balconies and parapets of a slender central tower, topped by the gilded figure of a knight, *Hanske de Krijger* ("Little John the Warrior"). Underneath the knight, the cupola is in the shape of a crown, a theme reinforced by the two groups of cherubs on the dormer windows below, who lovingly clutch at the royal insignia. To the rear of the Stadhuis, the dour and gloomy exterior of the adjoining Romanesque **Lakenhalle**, or cloth hall, dates from the thirteenth century.

Inside the Stadhuis (April–Oct Sat & Sun 2–5pm with guided tours on Sat at 2pm & 4pm; F100; group tours by prior arrangement April–Oct Mon–Thurs hourly 9–11am & 2–4pm – it's sometimes possible to tag along; call ☎055/31 72 51 for details) a magnificent oak **doorway** forms the entrance to the old *Schepenzaal* (Aldermen's Hall). A stylistically influential piece of 1531, the work of a certain Paulwel Vander Schelden, it consists of an intricate sequence of carvings, surmounted by miniature cherubs who frolic above three coats of arms and a 28-panel door, each rectangle a masterpiece of precise execution. Of the paintings, the most distinguished are those by Adriaen Brouwer, a native of Oudenaarde, whose representations of the five senses are typical of his ogre-like, caricaturist's style. Beyond, in the Lakenhalle, is a superb collection of **tapestries**, the first being the eighteenth-century *Nymphs in a Landscape*, a leafy romantic scene in which four nymphs pick and arrange flowers. The adjacent *Return from Market*, which also dates from the eighteenth century, features trees in shades of blue and green, edged by sky and bare earth – a composition reminiscent of Dutch landscape paintings. Glamorized pastoral scenes were perennially popular: the seventeenth-century *Landscape with Two Pheasants* frames a distant castle with an intricate design of trees and plants, while *La Main Chaude* depicts a game of blindman's buff. The classical proclivities of the sixteenth century are evident in both *Hercules and the Stymphalian Birds*, a scene set among what appear to be cabbage leaves, and *Scipio and Hannibal*, in which the border is decorated with medallions depicting the Seven Wonders of the World – though the Hanging Gardens of Babylon appear twice to create the symmetry.

South of the Markt

Immediately southwest of the Markt, a couple of minutes' walk from the Stadhuis, **St Walburgakerk** (July–Sept Tues & Sat 2.30–4.30pm, Thurs 10–11am) is a decaying mass of masonry badly in need of the restoration work which has just begun – the massive tower has started to crack and lean precariously. Inside there are several locally made tapestries and a monument to four Catholic priests who in 1572 were thrown into the Scheldt from the windows of Oudenaarde's castle (since demolished). Across the road opposite the church, a group of old and ruinous mansions follow the bend in what was once the line of the town wall, while, from the southern side of the Markt, Voorburg and subsequently Kasteelstraat lead down to the river past a trim seventeenth-century **portal**, the entrance to the old Begijnhof. Finally, if you're keen to discover more about tapestries, head for the municipal repair workshops sited in a grand old mansion, the **Huis de Lalaing** (Mon–Thurs 9am–noon & 1–5pm, Fri 9am–noon & 1–3pm; free), on the far side of the river at Bourgondiestraat 9 – cross over the bridge near the end of Kasteelstraat and veer left. The workshops don't make a big thing out of showing visitors around, but everyone seems quite friendly and you can poke around looking at the various restorative processes.

Eating and drinking

The Grote Markt is lined with **cafés** and bars, one good option being *De Cridts,* at no. 58, an old-fashioned café-restaurant serving standard-issue Flemish dishes at very reasonable prices. Close by, at no. 63, the *Harmonie Restaurant* is a tad more formal, but there's a slightly wider choice, with snacks from F300 and main courses for around F550. For a break from Flemish cuisine, the *Crêperie*, at no. 28, is a straightforward tearoom selling tasty crêpes from F150.

As for **drinking**, the local Roman brewery rules the roost, its most distinctive products being Tripel Ename, a strong blond beer, and Roman Dobbelen Bruinen, a snappy, filtered stout. These are usually available at the best bars in town: try *N'oni's*, a fashionable, pastel-decorated bar off the east side of the Grote Markt at Einestraat 3, and the *Fox*, a similarly lively and youthful spot directly opposite. A third option is *De Carillon*, a quieter place in the old brick-gabled building in the shadow of St Walburgakerk.

Around Oudenaarde: Ronse

To the south of Oudenaarde, the flattened fields of the Flanders plain give way to a ridge of low hills that make up the southwest corner of the province of East Flanders. It's a pretty area, though the sobriquet **Vlaamse Ardennen** (Flemish Ardennes), used by local tourist offices, is desperately optimistic. The best scenery is actually beside the N36, the road from Kortrijk, which crosses the ridge from the west, passing near the hilltop vantage point of **Kluisberg** (Mont de l'Enclus).

In the middle of these hills, 12km south of Oudenaarde on the N60 (or by hourly train; 10min), lies the tiny textile town of **RONSE**, whose main claim to fame is **St Hermeskerk**, an imposing late Gothic edifice situated in the town centre, a ten-minute walk from the train station straight down Stationsstraat. The church takes its name from a Roman martyr, Hermes, who was recognized for his skills as an exorcist. His relics were presented to Ronse during the ninth century and became the object of pilgrimages, the "possessed" dragged here from all over the Low Countries in the hope of a miraculous cure. The chapel on the south side of the choir is dedicated to St Hermes: above the chapel altar, a kitsch marble statue portrays St Hermes on horseback, dragging a devil behind him, while the three rusted iron rings opposite recall the time when those considered insane were chained up waiting for exorcism. The church's other interesting feature is its capacious Romanesque **crypt** (Tues–Fri 10am–noon & 1.30–5pm, Sat & Sun 10am–12.30pm & 2–6pm; F40), dating from 1089.

Known as the **Bruul**, the parcel of land immediately to the east of the church has been tidied and landscaped to house Ronse's other tourist attractions – primarily a textile museum – but these are of only limited interest, as is the adjacent Grote Markt, an ugly square whose obelisk was originally surmounted by a "W" in honour of William I, though this soon disappeared after the Revolution of 1830. In the unlikely event you decide to stay the night, the Ronse **tourist office** (Mon–Fri 9am–noon & 12.30–4.30pm, mid-May to Sept also Sat & Sun

10am–noon & 2–5pm; ☎055/23 28 16), on the Bruul, has accommodation details as well as town maps.

Bruges

"Somewhere within the dingy casing lay the ancient city", wrote Graham Greene of **BRUGES**, "like a notorious jewel, too stared at, talked of, trafficked over". And it's true that Bruges's (justified) reputation as one of the most perfectly preserved medieval cities in western Europe has made it the most popular tourist destination in Belgium, packed with visitors throughout the summer season. Inevitably, the crowds tend to overwhelm the town, but you'd be mad to come to Flanders and miss the place: its museums hold some of the country's finest collections of Flemish art; and its intimate, winding streets, woven around a skein of narrow canals and lined with gorgeous ancient buildings, live up to even the most inflated tourist hype. See it out of season, or in the early morning before the hordes have descended, and it can be memorable.

Some history

Bruges originated from a ninth-century fortress built by the warlike first count of Flanders, Baldwin Iron Arm, who was intent on defending the Flemish coast from Viking attack. The settlement prospered, and by the fourteenth century it shared effective control of the cloth trade with its two great rivals, Ghent and Ypres, turning high-quality English wool into clothing that was exported all over the known world. It was an immensely profitable business which made the city a focus of international trade: at its height, the town was a key member of – and showcase for the products of – the Hanseatic League, the most powerful economic alliance in medieval Europe. Through the harbours and docks of Bruges, Flemish cloth and Hansa goods were exchanged for hogs from Denmark, spices from Venice, hides from Ireland, wax from Russia, gold and silver from Poland and furs from Bulgaria. The business of these foreign traders was protected by no fewer than 21 consulates, and the city developed a wide range of support services, including banking, money-changing, maritime insurance and an elementary shipping code, known as the *Roles de Damme*.

Despite (or perhaps because of) this lucrative state of affairs, Bruges was dogged by war. Its weavers and merchants were dependent on the goodwill of the kings of England for the proper functioning of the wool trade, but their feudal overlords, the counts of Flanders and their successors the dukes of Burgundy, were vassals of the rival king of France. Although some of the dukes and counts were strong enough to defy their king, most felt obliged to obey his orders and thus take his side against the English when the two countries were at war. This conflict of interests was compounded by the designs the French monarchy had on the independence of Bruges itself. Time and again, the French sought to assert control over the towns of West Flanders, but more often than not they encountered armed rebellion. In Bruges, the most famous insurrection was precipitated by Philip the Fair at the beginning of the fourteenth century. Philip and his wife, Joanna of Navarre, had held a grand reception in Bruges, but it had only served to feed their envy. In the face of the city's splendour, Joanna moaned "I thought that I alone was Queen; but here in this place I have six hundred rivals."

The Bruges area **telephone code** is ☎050.

The opportunity to flex royal muscles came shortly afterwards when the town's guildsmen flatly refused to pay a new round of taxes. Enraged, Philip dispatched an army to restore order and garrison the town, but at dawn on Friday, May 18, 1302, a rebellious force of Flemings crept into the city and massacred Philip's sleepy army – an occasion later known as the **Bruges Matins**. Anyone who couldn't correctly pronounce the Flemish shibboleth *schild en vriend* ("shield and friend") was put to the sword.

By the end of the fifteenth century, however, Bruges was in decline, partly because of a general recession in the cloth trade, but principally because of the silting of the River Zwin – the city's trading lifeline to the North Sea. By the 1490s, the stretch of water between Sluis and Damme was only navigable by smaller ships, and by the 1530s the town's sea trade had collapsed completely. Bruges simply withered away, its houses deserted, its canals empty and its money spirited north with the merchants.

Georges Rodenbach's novel *Bruges-la-Morte* alerted wealthy nineteenth-century Europeans to the town's aged, quiet charms, and Bruges – frozen in time – escaped damage in both world wars to emerge the perfect tourist attraction.

Arrival, information and city transport

Bruges **train station** adjoins the **bus station** about 2km southwest of the town centre. Beside the station, there's an **information desk** and **hotel booking** service (April–Sept Mon–Sat 9.30am–6.30pm; Oct–March Mon–Sat 9.30am–1.15pm & 1.45–5.30pm; ☎44 86 86, fax 44 86 00), which will make reservations on your behalf at no charge, though they do require a deposit which is deducted from your final bill. If the twenty-minute walk into town doesn't appeal, most of the local buses that leave from outside the station building head off to either the Biekorf or the neighbouring Markt, bang in the centre – check with the driver before you get on. The taxi fare from the station to the centre is about F250.

Just footsteps away from the Markt, at Burg 11, the **tourist office** (April–Sept Mon–Fri 9.30am–6.30pm, Sat & Sun 10am–noon & 2–6.30pm; Oct–March Mon–Fri 9.30am–5pm, Sat & Sun 9.30am–1pm & 2–5.30pm; same phone & fax; *www.brugge.be/brugge*), provides a similar accommodation-booking service, and also has currency exchange, city maps for F25, suggestions for cycle trips in the surrounding countryside, plus a useful, complimentary, multilingual *Agenda Brugge*, which contains details of all current events and performances (usually you can buy tickets here as well). Local bus timetables are displayed on the walls near the entrance.

City transport

The best way to see Bruges is on foot, and the centre is certainly compact enough to make this an easy proposition. But the city does have an excellent network of local **bus** services, shuttling round the centre and out into the suburbs from the main bus station. Most of these services are routed through the city centre, calling at the **Biekorf bus stops**, at the foot of Kuipersstraat a few metres northwest of the Markt. The standard single fare is F40, or a booklet of ten tickets costs

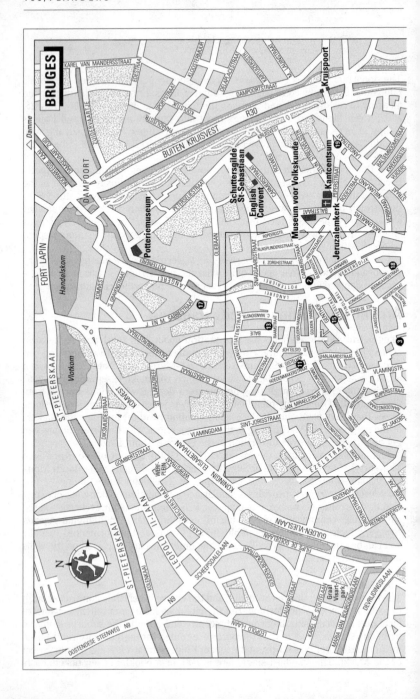

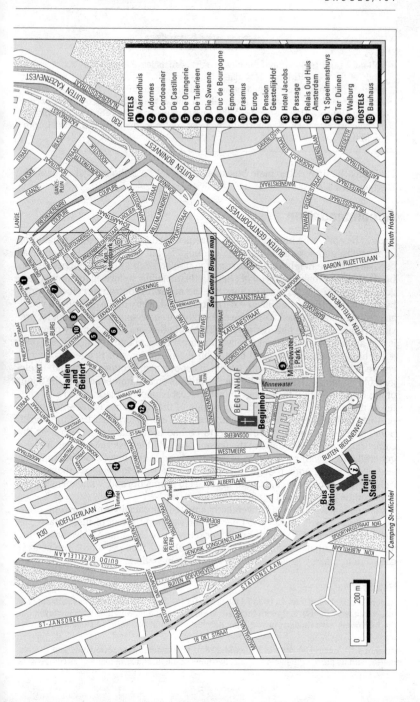

HOTELS
1 Aarendhuis
2 Adornes
3 Cordoeanier
4 De Castillon
5 De Orangerie
6 De Tuilerieen
7 Die Swaene
8 Duc de Bourgogne
9 Egmond
10 Erasmus
11 Europ
12 Pension Geestelijkhof
13 Hotel Jacobs
14 Passage
15 Relais Oud Huis Amsterdam
16 't Speelmanshuys
17 Ter Duinen
18 Walburg

HOSTELS
19 Bauhaus

BOAT TRIPS

Half-hour **boat trips** around the city's central canals leave from a number of jetties south of the Burg (March–Nov daily 10am–6pm; F170). Boats depart every few minutes, but long queues build up in the high season. In wintertime (Dec–Feb), there's a spasmodic service on the weekend only. As for **trips out of town**, excursions to **Damme** (Easter–Sept 5 daily; 40min; one-way F170, return F230) start at the Noorweegse Kaai, 2km north of the town centre (connecting with bus #4 from the Markt).

F290; pay the driver. The main bus station also sells a 24-hour city bus pass, the Dagpas, for F110.

Accommodation

Bruges has over one hundred hotels, dozens of bed-and-breakfasts, a smattering of pensions, and several unofficial youth hostels, but still can't accommodate all its visitors at the height of the season. If you're arriving in July or August, either **book ahead** or make sure you get here in the morning, before all the rooms have gone. Given the crush, most visitors use the **accommodation service** provided by the tourist office (see above) – it's efficient, and pretty much essential if you're after a bed-and-breakfast. Otherwise, the city's free accommodation booklet provides comprehensive **listings** along with hotel photographs and a city map; this is also available by post direct from your nearest Belgian tourist office (see p.149).

Fortunately, there's no need to stay on the peripheries of Bruges as the city centre is liberally sprinkled with **hotels**, most of which occupy quaint and/or elegant old buildings. The greatest concentration is on and immediately to the south of the Burg, although these tend to be the most expensive places. There's a cluster of more affordable hotels in the vicinity of the Spiegelrei canal – one of the prettiest and quieter parts of the centre, and just a brief stroll north of the Markt. Some of the best deals, however, are to be had in the narrow streets near the cathedral, which retain some of the flavour of an old Flemish town. Standards are generally high, with room tariffs primarily related to the hotel's facilities and the size of the room; note, though, that hoteliers are wont to deck out their foyers rather grandly, often in contrast to the spartan rooms beyond, while many places offer rooms of widely divergent size and comfort.

Bruges has a handful of conveniently situated unofficial **youth hostels**, offering dormitory beds at F350–450 per person per night. Most of these places, as well as the **official** (HI) **youth hostel** tucked away in the suburbs, also have a limited supply of smaller rooms with doubles at about F1000 per night. The nearest campsite to the city is 3km southwest of the train station.

Hotels

Aarendshuis, Hoogstraat 18 (☎33 78 89, fax 33 08 16). Spacious doubles in a handsome old mansion east of the Burg, though the place is slightly unkempt. Antiques litter the foyer, but the bedrooms have modern furnishings. Ask for a room at the back, as Hoogstraat can be noisy. ⑤.

Adornes, St Annarei 26 (☎34 13 36, fax 34 20 85). This tastefully converted old Flemish town house, with its plain, high-gabled facade, has none of the fussiness of many of its competitors

– both the public areas and the comfortable bedrooms are decorated in bright whites and creams, which emphasize the antique charm of the place. Great location, too, at the junction of two canals near the east end of Spiegelrei. ⑤.

De Castillion, Heilige-Geeststraat 1 (☎34 30 01, fax 33 94 75). Two old Flemish houses, with high crow-stepped gables, have been transformed into this neat hotel across from the cathedral. Just twenty small but comfortable bedrooms with spruce and modern furnishings. The public areas are done out in a repro style that can be a little overpowering. ⑧.

Cordoeanier, Cordoeaniersstraat 18 (☎33 90 51, fax 34 61 11). Medium-sized, family-run hotel handily located in the narrow sidestreets a couple of minutes north of the Burg. Mosquitoes can be a problem here, but the small rooms are clean and pleasant. ④.

Duc de Bourgogne, Huidenvettersplein 12 (☎33 20 38, fax 34 40 37). The hotel's pride and joy is its restaurant-cum-breakfast room overlooking a particularly picturesque slice of canal close to the Burg. The public rooms are in a heavy-duty neo-baronial style somewhere between kitsch and imposing. Just ten rooms – ask for one with a canal view. One to be avoided in summer, though, when herds of tourists cramp the surrounding streets. ⑥.

Egmond, Minnewater 15 (☎34 14 45, fax 34 29 40). There are only eight bedrooms in this rambling old house which stands in its own gardens just metres from the Minnewater on the southern edge of the city centre. The interior has wooden beamed ceilings and fine eighteenth-century chimneypieces, harking back to the days when it was a manor house. Attractive rooms in a quiet location at surprisingly affordable prices. ⑥.

Erasmus, Wollestraat 35 (☎33 57 81, fax 33 47 27). Simple, frugal rooms above a restaurant in the centre of town, just south of the Markt. ⑤.

Europ, Augustijnenrei 18 (☎33 79 75, fax 34 52 66). This dignified early nineteenth-century townhouse overlooks a canal about five minutes' walk north of the Burg. The public areas are somewhat frumpy and the modern bedrooms are a little too spartan, but it's a pleasant place to stay all the same. ⑤.

Jacobs, Baliestraat 1 (☎33 98 31, fax 33 56 94). A family-run hotel just a few minutes from the Markt in a quiet location. Doubles without the frills can be as cheap as F1750 and they serve up a good breakfast. ⑤.

De Orangerie, Kartuizerinnenstraat 10 (☎34 16 49, fax 33 30 16). Excellent four-star hotel in a surprisingly quiet location a couple of minutes' south of the Burg. The original eighteenth-century mansion has been remodelled and extended to house twenty elegant bedrooms – several of which are quite small – and there's a charming terrace bar at the back overlooking the canal. ⑨.

Passage Hotel, Dweersstraat 28 (☎34 02 32, fax 34 01 40). Simple but well-maintained rooms a ten-minute stroll west of the Markt. A real steal, with en-suite doubles at just F1400, other rooms at F1200. The hotel also has its own bar. Next door to the *Passage Hostel* (see below). ②.

Relais Oud Huis Amsterdam, Spiegelrei 3 (☎34 18 10, fax 33 88 91). Smooth, tastefully furnished hotel in an eighteenth-century mansion overlooking the Spiegelrei canal. Most of the rooms are done out in a rich repro style. ⑧.

't Speelmanshuys, 't Zand 3 (☎33 95 52). Frugal rooms popular with budget travellers – and mosquitoes from the adjacent canal. Ten minutes' walk west of the Markt. ②.

Die Swaene, Steenhouwersdijk 1 (☎34 27 98, fax 33 66 74). The unassuming brick exterior of this long-established hotel is deceptive as the rooms beyond are luxuriously furnished in antique style. The location is perfect too, beside a particularly pretty section of canal a short walk from the Burg. ⑧.

Ter Duinen, Langerei 52 (☎33 04 37, fax 34 42 16). This handsome, three-storey canalside hotel is situated in one of the most charming parts of Bruges, a little less than ten minutes' walk northeast of the Markt. There are just twenty rooms, each furnished in crisp modern style, and the breakfasts are tremendous. ⑥.

De Tuilerieen, Dijver 7 (☎34 36 91, fax 34 04 00). Occupying an old and tastefully refurbished mansion close to the Burg, this delightful hotel is one of the best in town. Some rooms overlook the Dijver canal. Breakfast is taken in a lovely neo-Baroque salon. ⑨.

Walburg, Boomgaardstraat 13 (☎34 94 14, fax 33 68 84). Attractive, family-run hotel in an elegant nineteenth-century mansion – with splendidly large wooden doors – a short walk east of the Burg along Hoogstraat. The rooms are smart and comfortable, and there are also capacious suites. ⑨.

Hostels, pensions and campsites

Bauhaus International Youth Hotel, Langestraat 135 (☎34 10 93, fax 33 41 80). Laid-back hostel with four dormitories, sleeping eight apiece, and a mish-mash of double and triple rooms. The lively downstairs bar serves filling portions of food. It's situated about fifteen minutes' walk east of the Burg. ①.

International Youth Hostel Europa, Baron Ruzettelaan 143 (☎35 26 79, fax 35 37 32). Big, modern HI-affiliated hostel situated 2km south of the centre in the suburb of Assebroek. Breakfast is included in the overnight fee. Bus #2, from either the train station or Biekorf, goes within 100 metres (stop: Wantestraat). ①.

Passage, Dweersstraat 26 (☎34 02 32, fax 34 01 40). The most agreeable hostel in Bruges. Accommodates fifty people in ten comparatively comfortable dormitories. Located in an old and quiet part of town, about ten minutes' walk west of the Markt. The *Passage Hôtel* next door is also a bargain – see above. ①.

Pension Geestelijk Hof, Heilige-Geeststraat 2 (☎34 25 94, fax 33 94 75). Rudimentary but satisfactory pension occupying an old gabled house in the shadow of the St Salvators-kathedraal. There are seven doubles, five of which are en suite but it remains one of the cheaper deals in town with two-, three- and four-bedded rooms. ③.

St Michiel, Tillegemstraat 55 (☎38 08 19, fax 80 68 24). This is Bruge's nearest campsite, situated near the N31 motorway, 3km out of the city: take bus #7 and get off at the junction of St Michielslaan and Rijselstraat; head west from here along Jagersstraat and take the left turn under the motorway, which brings you onto Tillegemstraat. Open all year.

The City

In 1896 Arnold Bennett complained, "The difference between Bruges and other cities is that in the latter you look about for the picturesque, while in Bruges, assailed on every side by the picturesque, you look curiously for the unpicturesque, and don't find it easily." Perhaps so, but a fair slice of Bruges is not quite what it seems: the pretty little bridge beside the Onze Lieve Vrouwekerk is nineteenth century; the carved wood facades behind the Halle are from the 1950s; and the "beguines" are, in fact, Benedictine nuns. Bruges has spent time and money preserving its image, and although the bulk of the buildings are genuine enough, occasionally it can resemble nothing so much as a medieval theme park.

The Markt

A twenty-minute walk northeast of the main train and bus stations, the older sections of Bruges fan out from two interlocking central squares, the Markt and the Burg. The **Markt**, edged on three sides by rows of gabled buildings, is the larger of the two, an impressive open space with horse-drawn buggies clattering over the cobbles. On the south side, the **belfry** (daily: April–Sept 9.30am–5pm; Oct–March 9.30am–12.30pm & 1.30–5pm; F100), built in the thirteenth century when the town was at its richest and most extravagant, is a potent symbol of civic pride and municipal independence, its distinctive octagonal lantern visible for miles across the surrounding polders. Inside, the belfry staircase passes the room where the town charters were locked for safe keeping, and an eighteenth-century carillon, before emerging onto the roof. It's well worth the haul up for the view, especially

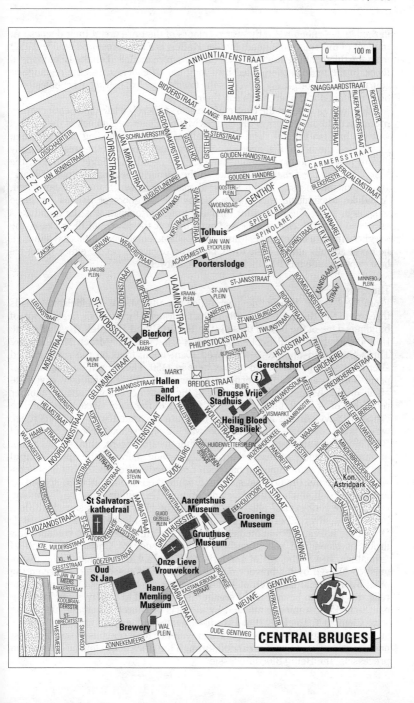

CENTRAL BRUGES

in the late afternoon when the warm colours of the town are at their deepest. At the foot of the belfry, the quadrangular **Hallen** is a much-restored edifice dating from the thirteenth century, its style and structure modelled on the Lakenhalle at Ieper. In the middle, overlooked by a long line of galleries, lies the rectangular courtyard which originally served as the town's principal market, its cobblestones once crammed with merchants and their wares.

A few metres away, at the centre of the Markt, there's a late nineteenth-century **monument** to the leaders of the Bruges Matins, Pieter de Coninck of the guild of weavers and Jan Breidel, dean of the guild of butchers. Standing close together, they clutch the hilt of the same sword, their faces turned to the west in slightly absurd poses of heroic determination. There's no other building of note on the Markt, though the *Craenenburg* café, on the corner of St Amandsstraat at Markt 16, is built on the site of the medieval mansion in which the Habsburg heir, Archduke Maximilian, was imprisoned by the burghers of Bruges for three months in 1488. The reason for their difference of opinion was the archduke's efforts to limit the city's privileges, but whatever the justice of their cause, the burghers made a big mistake. Maximilian became emperor in 1493, and although he never actually attacked the town, he never forgave its people either, doing his best to push trade north to their great rival, Antwerp.

The Burg

From beside the neo-Gothic post office on the Markt, Breidelstraat leads through to the **Burg**, whose southern half is fringed by the city's finest group of buildings. One of the best of these is the **Heilig Bloed Basiliek** (Basilica of the Holy Blood; daily: April–Sept 9.30am–noon & 2–6pm; Oct–March Mon–Tues & Thurs–Sun 10am–noon & 2–4pm, Wed 10am–noon; free) on the right, named after the holy relic that found its way here in 1150. The church divides into two parts. Tucked away in the corner, the **lower chapel** is a shadowy, crypt-like affair, originally built at the beginning of the twelfth century to shelter another relic, that of St Basil, one of the great figures of the early Greek Church. The chapel's heavy, simple Romanesque lines are decorated with just one relief, which is carved above an interior doorway – a representation of the baptism of Basil in which a strange giant bird, depicting the Holy Spirit, plunges into a pool of water. Next door, approached up a wide, curving staircase, the **upper chapel** was built at the same time but has been renovated so frequently that it's impossible to make out the original structure, while the interior has been spoiled by excessively rich nineteenth-century decoration. The building may be disappointing, but the rock-crystal phial that contains the Holy Blood is stored within a magnificent silver **tabernacle**, the gift of Albert and Isabella of Spain in 1611. One of the holiest relics in medieval Europe, the phial purports to contain a few drops of blood and water washed from the body of Christ by Joseph of Arimathea. It was the gift of Diederik d'Alsace, a Flemish knight who distinguished himself by his bravery during the Second Crusade and was given the phial by a grateful patriarch of Jerusalem. After several weeks in Bruges, the relic was found to be dry, but thereafter it proceeded to liquefy every Friday at 6pm until 1325, a miracle attested by all sorts of church dignitaries, including Pope Clement V. The Holy Blood is still venerated in the upper chapel on Fridays at 6pm, and despite modern scepticism, reverence for it remains strong, not least on Ascension Day when it is carried through the town in a colourful but solemn procession, the Heilig-Bloedprocessie.

The extravagant gold and silver jewel-encrusted reliquary that holds the phial when it's moved from the basilica during the procession is displayed in the tiny **treasury** (same times as basilica; F40), next to the upper chapel. Here also, just inside and above the door, the faded strands of a locally woven seventeenth-century tapestry depict St Augustine's funeral, the sea of helmeted heads and pikes that surround the monks and abbots very much a Catholic view of a muscular State supporting a holy Church.

Immediately to the left of the basilica, the **Stadhuis** has a beautiful, turreted sandstone facade, a much-copied exterior that dates from 1376 – though its sequence of statues (of the counts and countesses of Flanders) is a 1960s replacement of those destroyed by the occupying French army in 1792. Inside on the second floor, the **Gothic Hall** (daily: April–Sept 9.30am–5pm; Oct–March 9.30am–12.30pm & 2–5pm; F100), dating from 1400, was the magnificent setting for the first meeting of the States General (parliamentary assembly) in 1464. The ceiling has been restored in a vibrant mixture of maroon, dark brown, black and gold, dripping pendant arches like decorated stalactites. The ribs of the arches converge in twelve circular vault-keys, picturing scenes from the New Testament, while below they're supported by sixteen gilded corbels, representing the months and elements. The paintings around the walls were commissioned in 1895 to illustrate the history of the town, and an adjoining room has a modest display of incidental artefacts, including navigational aids and heaps of old maps.

Next door to the Stadhuis, the **Oude Griffie** (no admission) was built to house the municipal records office in 1537, its elegant facade decorated with Renaissance columns and friezes superimposed on the Gothic lines of the gables below. The **Renaissancezaal 't Brugse Vrije**, a room inside the adjacent building (daily: April–Sept 9.30am–12.30pm & 1.15–5pm; Oct–March 9.30am–12.30pm & 2–5pm; free with admission to the Gothic Hall), has just one exhibit, an enormous marble and oak **chimneypiece** located in the province's old *Schepenkamer* (Aldermen's Room). This is the only room to have survived from the original fifteenth-century mansion, sited within the municipal archives office. A fine example of Renaissance carving, the chimneypiece was completed in 1531 under the direction of Lancelot Blondeel, to celebrate the defeat of the French at Pavia in 1525 and the advantageous Treaty of Cambrai that followed. A paean of praise to the Habsburgs, the work is dominated by figures of the Emperor Charles V and his Austrian and Spanish relatives, each person identified by the free leaflet provided, although it's the trio of bulbous codpieces that really catch the eye. Adjoining the Bruges Vrije, the plodding courtyard complex of the **Gerechtshof** (Law Courts) dates from 1722 and houses the tourist office, while close by, the *Holiday Inn Crowne Plaza* stands on the site of the Cathedral of St Donatian, destroyed by the French at the end of the eighteenth century.

Along the Dijver

From the arch beside the Oude Griffie, Blinde Ezelstraat ("Blind Donkey Street") leads south across the canal to the eighteenth-century Doric colonnades of the **Vismarkt**. Just to the right is a huddle of picturesque houses crimping the **Huidenvettersplein**, the old tanners' quarter that now accommodates some of the most popular drinking and eating places in town. Nearby, the **Dijver** begins by the bridge at the bottom of Wollestraat, which is overseen by a statue of the patron saint of bridges, **St John Nepomuk**, who is reputed to have been thrown into a Bohemian river for refusing to reveal the confessional secrets of the consort of King Wenceslas IV. From here, the Dijver – scene of a busy weekend flea market from March to October – tracks along the canal as far as Nieuwstraat, passing opposite the path to the first of the city's main museums, the Groeninge.

A combination ticket for Bruges' central **museums**, the Groeninge, Arentshuis, Gruuthuse and Memling, is available from any of the four and costs F400.

The Groeninge Museum

The **Groeninge Museum** at Dijver 12 (April–Sept daily 9.30am–5pm; Oct–March Wed–Mon 9.30am–12.30pm & 2–5pm; F200) houses the city's art collection, a superb sample of Flemish paintings from the fourteenth to the twentieth centuries. A clear plan of the place is laid out by the entrance, and the exhibits are well displayed in a series of small, connecting rooms. Most of the paintings carry a multilingual label and some have an information board providing useful background. The Groeninge doesn't have enough room to display all its paintings at one time, so lesser works are rotated, though the kernel of the collection, the early paintings in rooms 1–6, remains fairly constant.

The museum's best section is without doubt the one holding **early Flemish paintings**, among which there are several by Jan van Eyck, who lived and worked in Bruges from 1430 until his death eleven years later. Arguably the greatest of the early Flemish masters, he was a key figure in the development of oil painting, modulating its tones to create paintings of extraordinary clarity and realism. Room 1 showcases two gorgeous examples in the miniature *Portrait of Margareta van Eyck* and the *Madonna with Canon George van der Paele*, a glowing and richly analytical work with three figures surrounding the Madonna: the kneeling canon, St George (his patron saint), and St Donatian, to whom he is being presented.

Next door, Room 2 boasts two fine, fifteeenth-century copies of paintings by Rogier van der Weyden. There's a tiny *Portrait of Philip the Good*, in which the pallor of the duke's aquiline features, along with the brightness of his hatpin and chain of office, are skilfully balanced by the sombre cloak and hat, while *St Luke Drawing the Portrait of Our Lady* is notable for the detail of its Flemish background and the cheeky-chappie smile of the baby Christ. Moving on to Room 3, the two matching panels of *The Legend of St Ursula* also date from the fifteenth century, the work of an unknown artist known as the "Master of the Ursula Legend". The panels were probably inspired by the discovery of the bones of St Ursula and the nuns who were massacred with her in Cologne, a couple of centuries earlier – a sensational story in medieval times that would certainly have been common knowledge in Bruges. In Room 4, highlights include the riotous violence of the unattributed *Scenes of the Legend of St George*, and the *Moreel Triptych* by Hans Memling, in which the formality of the scene contrasts with the gentleness of such vignettes as the priest stroking the fawn, or the knight's hand on a neighbour's shoulder.

There's also work by Hieronymus Bosch: his *Last Judgement*, in Room 5, is a trio of oak panels crammed with mysterious beasts, microscopic mutants and scenes of awful cruelty – men boiled in a pit or cut in half by a giant knife. It looks like unbridled fantasy, but in fact the scenes were read as symbols, a sort of strip cartoon of legend, proverb and tradition. Indeed Bosch's religious orthodoxy is confirmed by the appeal his work had for that most Catholic of Spanish kings, Philip II. Usually displayed in the same room is the *Judgement of Cambyses*, a painting by

Gerard David on two oak panels. Based on a story of the Persian court told by Herodotus, the first panel has the corrupt judge Sisamnes being sentenced to be flayed alive; in the gruesome second panel the judgement is carried out by the king's servants, who apply themselves to the task with clinical detachment. The painting was hung in the town hall by the city burghers as a sort of public apology for the imprisonment of Archduke Maximilian here in 1488. Opposite, the *Baptism of Christ* is a later work by the same artist, depicting a boyish, lightly bearded Christ as part of the Holy Trinity. David (c1460–1523) was the city's leading artistic light, and was honoured with many official commissions – although he was born near Gouda, moving to Bruges in his early twenties to be speedily admitted into the local painters' guild in 1484.

In Room 6, there's more grim symbolism in Jan Provoost's striking *The Miser and Death*, which portrays the merchant with his money in one panel, trying desperately to pass a promissory note to the grinning skeleton in the next. Provoost's career (1465–1529) was typical of many of the Flemish artists of the early sixteenth century. Initially he worked in the Flemish manner, his style greatly influenced by Gerard David, but from about 1521 his work was reinvigorated by contact with the German painter and engraver Albrecht Dürer, who had himself been inspired by the artists of the early Italian Renaissance.

The museum's selection of **late sixteenth- and seventeenth-century paintings** is far more modest, though there's a delightfully naturalistic *Peasant Lawyer* by Pieter Bruegel the Younger in Room 7, while Pieter Pourbus is well represented in Room 9 by a series of austere and often surprisingly unflattering portraits of the movers and shakers of his day. A larger canvas, the *Last Judgement*, is an atypical work of his, crammed with muscular men and fleshy women; completed in 1551, its inspiration came from Michelangelo's Sistine Chapel. Room 10 is largely given over to Jacob van Oost the Elder (1603–1671), the city's most prominent artist during the Baroque period, but his canvases aren't a patch on what's gone before – the *Portrait of a Theologian*, for example, is a stultifyingly formal and didactic affair only partly redeemed by the fine draughtsmanship, while his *Portrait of a Bruges Family* drips with bourgeois sentimentality.

The **modern paintings**, too, are less than riveting, but look out for Jean Delville's enormous and weird *De Godmens*, a repulsive, yet compelling picture of writhing bodies yearning for salvation; it's displayed upstairs in the converted chapel (Room 11). Also of note, in Room 13, is the charcoal drawing *Het Angelus* by Constant Permeke – a typically dark and earthy representation of Belgian peasant life dated 1934 – while Room 14 accommodates both the spookily stark surrealism of Paul Delvaux's *Serenity* and Magritte's characteristically unnerving *The Assault*.

The Arentshuis

A footpath leads from the west side of the Groeninge into a tiny park, where the tiniest of humpbacked bridges is framed against a tumble of antique brick houses as it spans the canal behind the Gruuthuse – altogether one of Bruge's most picturesque (and photographed) spots. On this side of the bridge, in the mansion at the far corner of the park, is the **Arentshuis Museum**, at Dijver 16 (April–Sept daily 9.30am–5pm; Oct–March Wed–Mon 9.30am–12.30pm & 2–5pm; F80), which contains two separate collections. The ground-floor **Kant Museum** boasts an excellent sample of Belgian lace and upstairs is the **Brangwyn Museum**, which displays the paintings of the artist Sir Frank Brangwyn.

Beautifully presented and clearly labelled, the **lace collection** occupies four rooms, its glass cabinets arranged by type and chronology. Room I features **needlepoint lace**, the earliest examples of which date from the sixteenth century, although it's display case #7 which grabs the attention, its exquisite and extraordinarily detailed nineteenth-century *Point de Gaze* representing the apotheosis of this type of Belgian lacework. Moving into Room II, the **bobbin lace** includes two magnificent seventeenth-century collars (case #10A & B) and an exquisite benediction veil of 1725 (case #15A). There's also a large portrait of the empress Maria Theresa, who is decked out in the amazing lace dress she had made for her in Flanders in 1744: she obviously felt it suited her – witness the haughty pose and the dainty foot poking out from under the hem. Room III is devoted to bobbin lace too, but this time arranged according to its places of origin, with the French Valenciennes lace notable for the constancy of design right from the seventeenth century until now. Finally, Room IV has an enjoyable selection of Chantilly lace as well as examples of Bruges floral or Duchesse lace, the result of the rediscovery of old lace-making techniques in the middle of the nineteenth century.

Upstairs are the moody etchings, studies and paintings of Frank Brangwyn (1867–1956), who was born in Bruges, of Welsh parents, and donated this sample of his work to his native town in 1936. Look out for the sequence of paintings exploring industrial themes – powerful, almost melodramatic scenes of shipbuilding, construction and the like. Brangwyn's liking for strong colours and bold design bore little relationship to the British artistic trends of his day, but did give him an international reputation as a painter of giant murals, the best of which, on the theme of the British Empire, resides in Swansea's Guildhall.

The Gruuthuse Museum

Just along the street, the Gruuthuse Museum, at Dijver 17 (same times as the Groeninge; F130), occupies a rambling fifteenth-century mansion, a fine example of civil Gothic architecture which takes its name from the owners' historical right to tax the *gruit*, the herb and flower mixture added to the barley in the beer-brewing process. The mansion's ancient beams and chimneypieces frame a varied collection of fine and applied art, well laid out in a series of 22 numbered rooms. The exhibits are labelled but hardly any background information is provided, so you might consider buying the detailed English guidebook available at the reception desk for F595.

Antique furniture is spread throughout the museum, along with a smattering of pictorial tapestries dating from the sixteenth and seventeenth centuries. Particular highlights include – in Room 1 – the acclaimed polychromatic terracotta bust of Charles V, a German carving of 1520 which reveals a young and disconcertingly thin-faced emperor. There's also a gruesomely graphic mini-section on medieval remedies for the relief of haemorrhoids in Room 2 and an eclectic collection of old wood carvings and alabasters in Rooms 5, 6 and 7. Most intriguing of all, however, is the 1472 oak-panelled chapel (Room 17), which juts out from the second floor of the museum to overlook the high altar of the cathedral next door. A curiously intimate room, its low, hooped ceiling is decorated with simple floral tracery, and its corbels are cut in the form of tiny angels.

The Onze Lieve Vrouwekerk

Also on the Dijver, next door to the Gruuthuse, the **Onze Lieve Vrouwekerk** (April–Sept Mon–Fri 10–11.30am & 2.30–5pm, Sat 10–11.30am & 2.30–4pm, Sun

2.30–5pm; Oct–March Mon–Sat 10–11.30am & 2.30–4.30pm, Sun 2.30–4.30pm; free) is a massive shambles of a building, a clamour of different dates and different styles, whose bleak spire is the tallest in Belgium. Of the accumulated treasures inside, the most famous is a delicate marble *Madonna and Child* by Michelangelo, an early work which seems sadly out of place at the centre of an eighteenth-century altar, beneath the cold stone walls of the south aisle. Brought from Tuscany by a Flemish merchant living in Bruges, it was the only work to leave Italy during the artist's lifetime and had a significant influence on the painters working here at the beginning of the sixteenth century.

There's a small charge (F60) to enter the choir and ambulatory, where the **mausoleums** of Charles the Bold and his daughter Mary of Burgundy are fine examples of Renaissance carving, the panels decorated with coats of arms connected by the most intricate of floral designs. The royal figures are enhanced in the detail, from the helmet and gloves placed gracefully by Charles' side to the pair of dogs nestled at Mary's feet. The earth beneath the mausoleums has been excavated, and mirrors now reveal the coffins placed here over the centuries, as well as the original frescoes, which were painted on the tomb walls at the start of the sixteenth century. Both Mary and Charles died in unfortunate circumstances, she after a riding accident in 1482, when she was only 25, and Charles came to grief during the siege of Nancy in 1477. However, there is some argument as to whether this is the body of Charles at all, since identification was, apparently, difficult; the body was buried in Nancy, but eighty years later Charles V had it exhumed for a more suitable burial in Bruges.

St Janshospitaal: the Hans Memling Museum

Opposite the entrance to Onze Lieve Vrouwekerk, a passageway leads from Mariastraat into **St Janshospitaal**, a six-hundred-year-old complex used as an infirmary until the nineteenth century. At the back, the main body of the hospital has been turned into the sleek exhibition and visitors' centre of **Oud St-Jan** (daily 10am–6pm; free); to the front, housed within the old chapel, is the small but important **Hans Memling Museum** (April–Sept daily 9.30am–5pm; Oct–March Thurs–Tues 9.30am–12.30pm & 2–5pm; F160), which also includes the well-preserved seventeenth-century **Apotheek** (dispensary) in the cloister next door.

Born near Frankfurt in 1433, Hans Memling spent most of his working life in Bruges, where he was taught by Rogier van der Weyden – whose themes he elaborated upon. Of the six works on display, the *Mystical Marriage of St Catherine* forms the middle panel of a triptych painted for the altar of the hospital church between 1475 and 1479. Its symbolism was easily understood by the sisters of the hospital who were well versed in the stories of the saints: St Catherine, representing contemplation, receives a ring from the baby Jesus to seal their spiritual union, while the figure to the right is St Barbara, symbol of good deeds. Behind stand the patron saints of the hospital, St John with his customary chalice and St John the Baptist accompanied by a fragile-looking Lamb of God. The complementary side panels depict the beheading of St John the Baptist and a visionary St John writing the book of *Revelation* on the bare and rocky island of Patmos. Graceful and warmly coloured, Memling's figures here (and elsewhere) bear grave and pious faces, and have a velvet-like quality that greatly appealed to the city's burghers. Indeed, their enthusiasm made Memling a rich man – in 1480 he was listed among the town's major moneylenders. Close by, the *Reliquary of St Ursula* is an unusual and lovely piece of work, a miniature wooden Gothic church painted with the story of St Ursula and the ten thousand martyred virgins. Memling subscribed to the rather unpopular theory that the number of virgins had been erroneously multiplied by a thousand somewhere along the line, and his six panels show Ursula and ten companions on their way to Rome, only to be massacred by Huns as they passed through Germany. It's the mass of incidental detail that makes the reliquary so enchanting – the tiny ships, figures and churches in the background effortlessly evoking the late medieval world.

St Salvators-kathedraal

From St Jans hospitaal it's a couple of minutes' walk north along Mariastraat and Heilige-Geeststraat to **St Salvators-kathedraal** (Mon 2–5.45pm, Tues–Fri 8.30–11.45am & 2–5.45pm, Sat 8.30–11.45am & 2–5pm, Sun 9am–noon & 3–5.45pm; free), which became the city's cathedral after the French burnt down the earlier one at the end of the eighteenth century. Nearing the end of a long-term refurbishment, the cathedral's nave has recently emerged from centuries of accumulated grime, but it's a cheerless, cavernous affair supported by over-mighty pillars. Most of the nave dates from the late fourteenth century, but the oldest part of the building is the thirteenth-century choir, a more appealing section that's equipped with a finely carved set of stalls, whose misericords are decorated with folksy scenes of everyday life. Here too are eight splendid tapestries, produced in Brussels in the eighteenth century, each a fluent composition featuring a familiar Biblical story – from the Nativity and the Resurrection, complete with muscular Roman soldiers in the style of Rubens, through to a Palm Sunday, with a remarkably determined-looking donkey.

Some of the earlier cathedral's treasures were moved here following its destruction, and these form the heart of today's **museum** which is ranged around the old cloisters (Mon–Sat 2–5pm, Sun 3–5pm; F60). There's not much to get excited about – this small collection is mainly a miscellany of ecclesiastical knick-knacks, with vestments, croziers, reliquaries and so forth – but there is a striking triptych, *The Presentation in the Temple*, by Adriaen Isenbrant (Room 3), who worked in Bruges in the first half of the sixteenth century.

South of the city centre

Strolling south from St Jans hospitaal along Mariastraat, take any of the signposted turns to the **Begijnhof** (daily 9am–6pm; free), a rough circle of old and infinitely pretty whitewashed houses surrounding a green. The best time to visit is in spring, when a carpet of daffodils grow up between the wispy elms, creating another of the most photographed sights in Bruges. The houses are occupied by Benedictine nuns, but one is open to the public – the **Begijnenhuisje** (March–Nov daily 10.30am–noon & 1.45–5pm; Dec–Feb Mon, Wed, Fri 11am–noon, Wed & Thurs 2–4pm; F60), a pint-sized celebration of the simple life of the Beguines. The prime exhibit here is the *Schapraai*, a traditional Beguine's cupboard, which was a frugal combination of dining table, cutlery cabinet and larder.

The streets to the east of the Begijnhof have kept their seventeenth-century design, but the simple terraced houses now contain dozens of restaurants and bars. Among them, the **Huisbrouwerij Straffe Hendrik**, a brewery at Walplein 26, offers guided visits for F140 per person, including a glass of beer (April–Sept 10am–5pm; Oct–March 11am & 3pm), but note that tours only begin when there are at least 15 people waiting. Immediately to the south of the Begijnhof, the picturesque **Minnewater** is another popular spot, edged by a fifteenth-century lock gate, which serves as a reminder of the lake's earlier use as a town harbour.

North and east of the city centre

A five-minute walk northeast of the belfry, **Jan van Eyckplein** stands at the western edge of a canal that once ran as far as the Markt. In medieval times, this was Bruge's busiest harbour, with its frenetic quays overlooked by the trade missions of many of its trading partners. Nowadays, the uncrowded streets surrounding the canal in the vicinity of Spiegelrei and St Annarei are some of the most charming in Bruges – classically picturesque terraces dating from the town's golden age, enriched by grand eighteenth-century mansions. Jan van Eyckplein itself is edged on its north side by the slim fifteenth-century **Tolhuis**, decorated with the coat of arms of the dukes of Luxembourg, who levied tolls here, while poking up above the rooftops on the west side is the tower of the **Poortersloge**, all that remains of the fourteenth-century edifice where the most powerful of the town's merchants once met.

Further afield, to the east, the complex of buildings that originally belonged to the wealthy Adornes family, who migrated here from Genoa in the thirteenth century, is located at the foot of Balstraat in the middle of an old working-class district of low, brick cottages. Inside the complex, the **Kantcentrum** (Lace Centre; Mon–Fri 10am–noon & 2–6pm, Sat 10am–noon & 2–5pm; F60), on the right-hand side of the entrance, has a couple of busy workshops and offers demonstrations of traditional lace-making in the afternoon. Across the passageway, to the left of the entrance, is one of the city's real oddities, the **Jeruzalemkerk** (same times and ticket). It was built by the Adornes family in the fifteenth century as a copy of the church of the Holy Sepulchre in Jerusalem after one of their number, Pieter, had returned from a pilgrimage to the Holy Land. The interior is on two levels: the lower level is dominated by a large and ghoulish altarpiece, decorated with skulls and ladders, in front of which is the black marble tomb of Anselm Adornes, the son of the church's founder, and his wife Margaretha. The pilgrimage didn't bring the Adornes family much luck: Anselm was murdered in gruesome circumstances in Scotland in 1483 while serving as Bruges' consul. There's more grisliness at the back of the church where the small vaulted chapel holds a replica of Christ's tomb – you can glimpse the imitation body down the tunnel behind the iron grating. From beside the main altar, steps ascend to the choir which is situated right below the eccentric, onion-domed lantern tower. Finally, the tiny **Lace Museum** (same times and ticket) behind the church is of passing interest for its samples of antique lace.

A couple of minutes' walk away, at the north end of Balstraat, the **Museum voor Volkskunde**, Rolweg 40 (April–Sept daily 9.30am–5pm; Oct–March Wed–Mon 9.30am–12.30pm & 2–5pm; F80), occupies a long line of low-ceilinged almshouses set beside a trim courtyard. The setting is, in fact, rather more interesting than the ensuing predictable plod through period rooms and workshops focused on everyday life in nineteenth-century Flanders. More diverting by far is the **English Convent**, further east at Carmersstraat 85 (daily except the first Sun in the month 2–3.40pm & 4.15–5.15pm; free), where the nuns provide an enthusiastic twenty-minute guided tour of the lavishly decorated Baroque church. Founded in 1629, the convent was long a haven for English Catholic exiles, as well as Charles II. The church, which comes complete with a handsome cupola, has an extraordinary altar made of 23 different types of marble, the gift of that persistently Catholic family, the Nithsdales, in the eighteenth century.

Just along the street, at Carmersstraat 174, the **Schuttersgilde St Sebastiaan** (archers' guildhouse; April–Sept Mon, Wed, Fri & Sat 10am–noon & 2–5pm; F40) dates from the middle of the sixteenth century and has records of the guild alongside a mundane collection of gold and silverwork. It's situated near the east end of Carmersstraat, where the earthen banks mark the path of the old town walls. Perched on top today are a pair of relocated windmills and a stroll past them takes you south to the **Kruispoort**, a much modified and strongly fortified city gate dating from 1402. In the opposite direction, a fifteen-minute walk north along the old ramparts brings you to the Dampoort, from where it's another five minutes southwest to the canalside **Museum Onze-Lieve-Vrouw van de Potterie**, at Potterierei 79 (April–Sept daily 9.30am–noon & 12.45–5pm; Oct–March Thurs–Tues 9.30am–12.30pm & 2–5pm; F60). Originally a hospital, the museum consists of a handful of the old sick rooms and the hospital church. The rooms are sprinkled with old religious paintings of no particular distinction, though there are several spectacularly unflattering portraits of Habsburg officials, and the church is distinguished by its splendid Baroque altarpieces. From here, you can continue along the canal back to Jan van Eyckplein.

Eating and drinking

Inevitably, most of the **cafés** and **restaurants** in Bruges are geared to the tourist industry, with the majority working from a fairly uniform Flemish menu, usually translated into several languages. By and large, standards are high, portions substantial and prices quite reasonable, the only problem being the crowds that make many city-centre places unbearable in the peak season. Note that kitchens start to wind down at about 9pm, and most establishments close for one day a week. If funds are very limited, bear in mind that several of the youth hostels offer **inexpensive meals**, the best of which are those served up by the hostel *Passage*, Dweersstraat 26, and the *Bauhaus International Youth Hotel*, Langestraat 135. For fresh seafood **snacks**, the fish shops along the Vismarkt are a good bet, with delicious specialities for around F200.

The distinction between Bruges's restaurants, cafés, and bars is blurred: good beer bars often sell excellent food and cafés frequently boast a good beer list. The only important rule of thumb is that restaurants are usually more expensive and slightly more formal than their café competitors. Most visitors to Bruges **drink** where they eat, though there is a smattering of decent specialist **bars** in and around the town centre – and several of them offer a mind-boggling variety of Belgian beers. Generally speaking, tourists congregate in the café-bars of the Markt and the Burg, leaving locals to gather in the more distinctively Flemish places tucked among the quieter streets nearby.

Cafés and restaurants

Beethoven, St Amandsstraat 6, off the Markt. Intimate, pocket-sized restaurant serving first-rate regional Belgian dishes prepared by up-and-coming chefs.

Craenenburg, Markt 16. Most of the café-restaurants lining the Markt are preoccupied with the tourist trade, but this old-fashioned place, with its wood panelling and stained glass, has avoided the trend. Serves Flemish snacks and full meals at affordable prices. Has a good range of beers too, including the locally produced, tangy brown ale Brugse Tripel.

Taverne Curiosa, Vlamingstraat 22 (☎34 23 34). Lively bar-restaurant in an old vaulted cellar a couple of minutes' walk north of the Markt. Specialities are grilled meats, smoked fish and regional dishes, with a wide-ranging beer menu to wash it down. Closed Mon and two weeks in July. Booking advised.

Het Dagelijks Brood, Philipstockstraat 21. Excellent bread shop which doubles as a wholefood café with one long wooden table. Mouth-watering homemade soup and bread makes a meal in itself for just F150; other filling snacks and cakes are also on offer. Central location, close to the Burg. Open 7am to 6pm but closed Tues.

La Dentellière, Wijngaardstraat 33 (☎33 18 98). The most agreeable of the somewhat overpriced restaurants around the Minnewater. Regional dishes and steaks dominate the menu. Closed Tues.

Den Dyver, Dijver 5 (☎33 60 69). First-rate restaurant specializing in traditional Flemish dishes cooked in beer – the quail and rabbit are magnificent. Expensive; reservations advised. Closed Wed, also Tues in winter.

Erasmus, Wollestraat 35 (part of the *Hotel Erasmus*). Straightforward, brightly lit café with reasonably priced, mostly Flemish dishes – cod with leeks, for example, costs F550 – plus a wide range of Belgian brews. A couple of hundred metres south of the Markt. Closed Mon except July & Aug.

Brasserie Georges, Vlamingstraat 59. Attractively open and informal restaurant just north of the Markt. One of the more popular places in town, serving Flemish favourites: excellent *waterzooi* goes for F800, mussels for F700.

Taverne Groeninge, Dijver 13. Next to the Groeninge Museum, this café-restaurant occupies the ground floor of an attractively restored mansion. Most customers are here for the cakes and coffee, but there's also a main meal menu, principally steaks and salads from around F450.

L'Intermède, Wulfhagestraat 3 (☎33 16 74). Tastefully decorated, very chic little restaurant serving exquisite French cuisine with a Flemish twist. Reasonable prices and away from the tourist zone – Wulfhagestraat is a couple of minutes' walk northwest of the cathedral. Closed Sun & Mon.

Patrick Devos, Zilverstraat 41 (☎33 55 66). One of Bruge's premier restaurants, serving themed meals, such as Art Nouveau lunches and Belle Époque dinners. A full meal including wine will set you back about F3500, but you'll need to book a table. Closed Sun & Mon.

Poules-Moules, Simon Stevinplein 9 (☎34 61 19). Smart and agreeable restaurant specializing in mussels and chicken west of the Markt along Steenstraat.

Toermajiljn, Coupure 29a (junction with Schaarstraat) (☎34 01 94). Bruges's only purely vegetarian restaurant, with a pleasant ambience best enjoyed in summer. Half-hour walk from the town centre. Closed Sun–Tues.

De Visscherie, Vismarkt 8 (☎33 02 12). Pricey seafood restaurant, serving well-presented and imaginative dishes. Closed Tues.

Bars

Brouwerij Taverne, Walplein 26. The big and breezy bar of the Huisbrouwerij Straffe Hendrik brewery is a popular tourist spot. The sharp, pale (and only) ale they sell – Straffe Hendrik (Strong Henry) – is an enjoyable tipple. Open daily 10am–6pm.

't Brugs Beertje, Kemelstraat 5. Small and friendly speciality beer bar that claims a stock of two hundred ales, which aficionados reckon is one of the best beer selections in Belgium. Five minutes' walk southwest of the Markt, off Steenstraat. Closed Wed.

't Dreupelhuisje, Kemelstraat 9. Tiny bar specializing in jenevers and advocaats, of which it has an excellent range. Closed Tues.

De Garre, De Garre 1. Down an alley off Breidelstraat betwen the Markt and the Burg, this cramped but charming bar has a great range of Belgian beers and tasty snacks. Classical music and magazines add to the relaxed air. Closed Wed.

De Hobbit, Kemelstraat 8. Laid-back, student-style café-bar that's busy till late, and sometimes has live music; filling meals at affordable prices too. Closed Mon & Tues.

Oude Vlissinghe, Blekerstraat 2. With its wood panelling, old paintings and long wooden tables, this is one of the oldest and most distinctive bars in Bruges. Relaxed and easy-going atmosphere. Situated a couple of minutes' walk from Jan van Eyckplein: follow Spinolarei and it's a turning on the right.

Listings

Bike rental Available at standard rates (F335 per day) from the train station or, more cheaply, for F250 a day and F850 a week from either Popelier, Hallestraat 14 (☎34 32 62), or 't Koffieboontje, Hallestraat 4 (☎33 80 27).

Bike tours The Back Road Bike Company (☎37 04 70, fax 37 49 60) runs mountain bike tours of the villages around Bruges and Damme. Well organized, reasonably priced and justifiably popular, these are relaxing excursions that stick to the back roads. There's a 3hr, 30km trip costing F550 (March–Oct daily; 1pm from the Burg); and a 2hr, 18km trip for F500 (June–Sept Sat & Sun; 10am from the Burg). Reservations are essential.

Books A reasonable range of English titles and a good selection of Belgian walking maps are available at Brugse Boekhandel, Dijver 2, beside the bridge at the bottom of Wollestraat. Standaard Boekhandel, Steenstraat 88, has a competent selection of English titles too.

Bureaux de change Outside banking hours you can change money at the exchange desk in the tourist office (April–Sept Mon–Fri 9.30am–6.30pm, Sat & Sun 10am–6.30pm; October daily 9.30am–5pm; Nov–March Sat & Sun only 9.30am–5.30pm).

Buses City and regional bus information can be had from the kiosk outside the train station (Mon–Fri 7.30am–6pm, Sat 9am–6pm & Sun 10am–6pm). Information line ☎56 53 53; timetables also on display at the tourist office.

Car rental Avis, St Pieterskaai 48 (☎31 45 44); Hertz, Baron Ruzettelaan 6 (☎37 36 71).

Cinema Weekly cinema programmes are displayed at the tourist office. Among several central cinemas showing latest releases is Chaplin, at Zilverstraat 45.

Doctors List of doctors from the tourist office; weekend doctors (Fri 8pm–Mon 8am) ☎81 38 99.

Emergencies Fire/ambulance ☎100; police ☎101.

Football Club Bruges are Flanders' premier football club and regular recent winners of the Belgian league and cup. They play on the outskirts of town, a ten-minute drive from the centre, but on match days there are special buses to the ground from the train station. The season runs from early August to May and getting a ticket is rarely a problem. The cheapest seats cost around F500. Fixture details from the tourist office.

Hospital St Franciscus-Xavieriuskliniek, Spaanse Loskaai (☎33 98 01).

Left luggage Lockers at the tourist office and the train station.

Markets General markets on the Markt (Wed 7am–1pm) and on 't Zand (Sat 7am–1pm). Flea markets along Dijver (Sat & Sun afternoons from March to Oct).

Performing Arts Details of concerts and performances in *Agenda Brugge*, free from the tourist office. The Cactusclub, in the city centre at St Jakobsstraat 33 (☎34 86 43), hosts quality bands – everything from rock and R&B through to jazz and touring DJs.

Pharmacies Details of 24-hour pharmacies are available from the tourist office; duty rotas are also displayed in pharmacists' windows.

Police The main police station is at Hauwerstraat 7 (☎44 88 44).

Post office Markt 5 (Mon–Fri 9am–7pm, Sat 9am–noon).

Taxis Ranks at the Markt (☎33 44 44) and Stationsplein (☎38 46 60).

Train enquiries Bruges train station (daily 6.30am–10.30pm; ☎38 23 82). Timetables are also on display at the tourist office.

Tours Excellent, day-long minibus tours of the World War I battlefields outside Ieper (see p.132) by Quasimodo Tours, Leenhofweg 7 (☎37 04 70). Departures from mid-March to mid-November three times weekly. F1400 per person, F1100 under 26; all inclusive (includes picnic lunch). Reservations essential; hotel pick-up. Some winter battlefield tours too – ring for details.

Damme

Now a popular day-trippers' destination, the quaint village of **DAMME**, 7km northeast of Bruges, was originally the town's main port and fortified outer harbour. It stood on the banks of the River Zwin, which gave direct access to the sea until it silted up in the late fifteenth century, and at its height boasted a population of ten thousand. Damme also hosted the grand wedding of Charles the Bold and Margaret of York, and was the scene of a famous naval engagement on June 24, 1340. In the summer of that year, a French fleet assembled in the estuary of the Zwin to prepare for an invasion of England. To combat the threat, the English king, Edward III, sailed across the Channel and attacked at dawn. Although they were outnumbered three to one, Edward's fleet won an extraordinary victory, his bowmen causing chaos by showering the French ships with arrows at what was (for them) a safe distance. A foretaste of the Battle of Crecy, there was so little left of the French force that no one dared tell King Philip of France, until finally the court jester took matters into his own hands: "Oh! The English cowards! They had not the courage to jump into the sea as our noble Frenchmen did." Philip's reply is not recorded.

Today Damme sits beside the canal linking Bruges with tiny Sluis, over the border in Holland, though more importantly, 2km to the northeast of Damme, the waterway also intersects with the modern Leopoldkanaal which cuts down to Zeebrugge (see p.124). At right angles to the Sluis canal, Damme's one main street, Kerkstraat, is edged by what remains of the medieval town. Funded by a special tax on barrels of herrings, the fifteenth-century **Stadhuis** is easily the best-looking building, its elegant, symmetrical facade balanced by the graceful lines of its exterior stairway. In one of the niches you'll spy Charles the Bold offering a wedding ring to Margaret in the next niche along. Just down the street, **St Janshospitaal** (April–Sept Mon & Fri 2–6pm, Tues–Thurs 10am–noon & 2–6pm, Sun 11am–noon & 2–6pm; Oct–March Sat & Sun only 2–5.30pm; F40) accommodates a small museum of five rooms and a dainty little chapel. In Room 1 are a couple of curiously crude parchment-and-straw peasants' pictures of St Peter and St Paul and in Rooms 2 and 3 there's some fine old furniture. Room 4, the main room, displays an enjoyable sample of Delftware and pewter, but it's the chimneypiece which grabs the attention, a Baroque extravagance with a cast-iron backplate representing the penance of King David for the murder of Bathsheba's husband. Otherwise, the museum holds a mildly diverting assortment of liturgical objects, incidental ceramicware and folksy votive offerings.

From here, it's a couple of minutes' walk further down Kerkstraat to the **Onze Lieve Vrouwekerk** (May–Sept daily 10am–noon & 2.30–5.30pm), a sturdy brick structure whose partly ruined nave speaks volumes about Damme's decline: the church was built in the thirteenth century, but when the population shrank it was too big and so the inhabitants abandoned part of the nave – the remnants are now stuck between the present church and its massive **tower** (same times; F20), from the top of which there are fine views over the surrounding polders.

Getting there and around

A good way to get to Damme from Bruges is by **boat** (Easter–Sept 5 times daily each way; 40min; one-way F170, return F230), along the poplar-lined canal which begins at Noorweegse Kaai, about 2km northeast of the centre of Bruges – take connecting bus #4 from the Markt. An alternative is to take **bus** #799, though a day trip is only easy in July and August (6 daily each way; 30min); during the rest of the year, the bus runs less frequently and only on Saturdays is it possible to make the round trip, and even then you'll have an over-long stay of six hours. Instead, consider what is a pleasant and gentle **cycle ride**: bikes can be hired in Bruges (see p.166) and in Damme at Tijl en Nele, round the corner from the Stadhuis at Jacob van Maerlantstraat 2 (reservations advised; ☎050/35 71 92; closed Wed; F350 per day).

Damme also lies at the start of a pretty little parcel of land, a rural backwater criss-crossed by drowsy canals and causeways, each of which is framed by long lines of trees and sprinkled with comely farmhouses. This is perfect cycling country and it extends as far as the E34/N49 motorway, about 6km from Damme. There are lots of possible routes and if you want to explore the area in detail you should buy the appropriate Nationaal geografisch instituut map (1:25000) in Bruges before you set out. One delightful itinerary is to leave Damme to the northeast along the Kanaal Brugge–Sluis, cross over the Leopoldkanaal and proceed on to the hamlet of **Hoeke**. Here, a narrow causeway – the **Krinkeldijk** – wanders straight back in the direction of Damme, running to the north of the Kanaal Brugge–Sluis and drifting across a beguiling landscape before it reaches an intersection where you turn right for tiny **Oostkerke** and left to regain the Sluis waterway.

Accommodation and eating

If you decide to **stay** in Damme, some half-dozen private houses offer double **rooms** (③); just follow the signs on Kerkstraat. Otherwise, Damme has one pleasant, two-star **hotel**, *Gasthof De Gulden Kogge*, right by the canal at the top of Kerkstraat at Damse Vaart Zuid 12 (☎ & fax 050/35 42 17; ③). This cosy little place has just eight small rooms, half of which are en suite, and advance reservations are necessary throughout the summer. Damme's **tourist office**, across from the Stadhuis (mid-April to mid-Oct Mon–Fri 9am–noon & 2–6pm, Sat & Sun 10am–noon & 2–6pm; mid-Oct to mid-April Mon–Fri 9am–noon & 2–5pm, Sat & Sun 2–5pm ☎050/35 33 19), will help you find a bed if you're in difficulties. As for **food**, Kerkstraat is lined with **restaurants**, mainly aimed at day-trippers. One of the best is *Bij Lamme Goedzak*, Kerkstraat 13, which serves mouth-watering traditional Flemish dishes. If your budget won't stretch to its prices, head for *'t Uylenspieghel*, Kerkstraat 44 (closed Thurs), which has good bar snacks and fifty types of beer.

Ghent

The seat of the counts of Flanders and the largest town in western Europe during the thirteenth and fourteenth centuries, **GHENT** was at the heart of the Flemish cloth trade. By 1350, the city boasted a population of fifty thousand, of whom no fewer than five thousand were directly involved in the industry, a prodigious concentration of labour in a predominantly rural Europe. Like Bruges, Ghent prospered throughout the Middle Ages, but it also suffered from endemic disputes between the count and his nobles (who supported France) and the cloth-reliant citizens (to whom friendship with England was vital).

The relative decline of the cloth trade in the early sixteenth century did little to ease the underlying tension, the people of Ghent still resentful of their ruling class, from whom they were now separated by language – French against Flemish – and religion – Catholic against Protestant. Adapting to the new economic situation, the town's merchants switched from industry to trade, exporting surplus grain from France, only to find their efforts frustrated by an interminable series of wars. The catalyst for conflict was taxation: long before the Revolt of the Netherlands, Ghent's artisans found it hard to stomach the financial dictates of their rulers – the Habsburgs after 1482 – and time and again they rose in revolt and were punished. In 1540 the Holy Roman Emperor Charles V lost patience and stormed the town, abolishing its privileges, filling in the moat and building a new secure castle at the city's expense. Later, with the Netherlands well on the way to independence from Spain, Ghent was captured by Philip II's armies in 1584. It was a crucial engagement. Subsequently, Ghent proved to be too far south to be included in the United Provinces and was reluctantly pressed into the Spanish Netherlands. Many of its citizens fled north, and those who didn't may well have regretted their decision when the Dutch forced the Habsburgs to close the River Scheldt as the price of peace in 1648.

In the centuries that followed, Ghent slipped into a slow decline from which it emerged during the industrial boom of the nineteenth century. In optimistic mood, the medieval merchants had built the city's walls a fair distance from the town centre to allow Ghent to expand. But the expected growth never took place, and the empty districts ended up choked with factories whose belching chimneys encrusted the old city with soot and grime, a disagreeable measure of the city's economic revival. Indeed, its entrepreneurial mayor, Emille Braun, even managed to get the Great Exhibition, showing the best in design and goods, staged here in 1913. More recently, Ghent has struggled to maintain its economic success, mounting a concerted campaign to attract new business into the area.

Ghent is a larger, more sprawling and less immediately picturesque city than Bruges, which is, in many ways, to its advantage; it has also benefited from an extensive programme of restoration and refurbishment. Certainly if you're put off by the tourists or tweeness of Bruges, or you simply can't find a room, it's a good alternative base.

Arrival, information and city transport

Ghent has three **train stations**, but the one you're most likely to use is **St Pieters**, which adjoins the **bus station**, some 2km south of the city centre. From outside the train station, **trams** #1, #10, #11, #12 and #13 connect with the centre every few minutes, passing along Kortrijksesteenweg and Nederkouter before continuing through to the central square, Korenmarkt. A couple of minutes' walk east of the Korenmarkt, the **tourist office**, in the crypt of the belfry (daily: April–Oct 9.30am–6.30pm; Nov–March 9.30am–12.30pm & 1.15–4.30pm; ☎226 52 32), has a comprehensive range of information, including a full list of **accommodation**, which it will book on your behalf for a deposit that is deducted from your final hotel bill.

The Ghent area **telephone code** is ☎09.

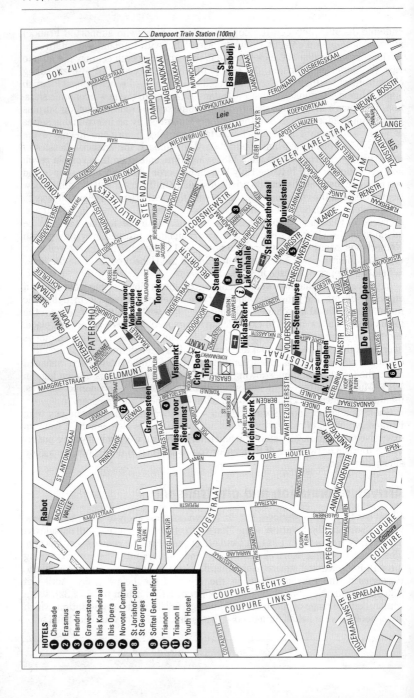

HOTELS
1 Chamade
2 Erasmus
3 Flandria
4 Gravensteen
5 Ibis Kathedraal
6 Ibis Opera
7 Novotel Centrum
8 St Jorishof-cour St Georges
9 Sofitel Gent Belfort
10 Trianon I
11 Trianon II
12 Youth Hostel

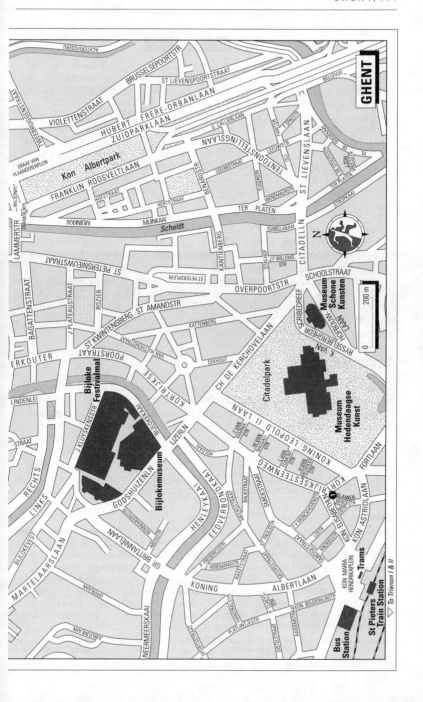

BOAT TRIPS

Between April and early November **boat trips** around Ghent's inner waterways depart from the Korenlei and Graslei quays daily between 10am and 7pm. Trips last 40 minutes, cost F160, and leave roughly once every 15 minutes, though the wait can be longer as boats often only leave when reasonably full.

Other excursions leave from the Ketelbrug, beside the Recollettenlei (Law Courts), at the west end of Zonnestraat. They include trips along the River Leie to Sint-Martens Latem (June–Sept 1–4 times weekly 1.30–6.30pm; F300) and day-trips to Bruges (July–Aug 4 times monthly, 9am–8pm; F450) – though the latter aren't quite as good as they sound: food and drink are expensive, and long sections of the canal are too deep to see over the banks. Further details from the tourist office or from Benelux Rederij, the boat operators, at Recollettenlei 32 (☎225 15 05).

The best way of seeing the sights is on foot, but Ghent is a large city and you may find you have to use a **tram** or **bus** at some point. This is easy enough: standard one-way fares cost F40, and a ten-journey Rittenkaart F290. One-way tickets and Rittenkaarts can be bought direct from the driver, who will give change if required; they are also sold at shops and newsstands all over town and at the **kiosks** by the tram stops on the Korenmarkt (Mon–Fri 7am–7pm, Sat 9.30am–4.30pm) and St Pieters (Mon–Fri 7am–7pm); these kiosks also sell a 24-hour city transport pass, the Dagpas, which represents good value at just F110, and maps of the transport system (the Netplan – F50).

Accommodation

Ghent has a good supply of inexpensive accommodation. The city possesses a bright, cheerful and centrally located **youth hostel**; several hundred student rooms are available for visitors during the summer recess; and there's a large **campsite** in the suburbs. Ghent also has a cluster of inexpensive **hotels** around the train station, but you really miss the atmosphere of the town around here, and you would do better to head for the youth hostel. If this is not your style, consider splashing out on a city centre hotel, several of which are stylish and enjoyable in equal measure. Note, however, that you'll be lucky to get anything at all during the city's main festival – the Gentse Feesten – a boozy, nine-day affair held in mid- to late July.

Hotels

Chamade, Blankenbergestraat 2 (☎220 15 15, fax 221 97 66). A chain hotel situated about five minutes' walk north of the train station. Standard 3-star accommodation in bright, modern bedrooms, though the building itself – a 6-storey block – is a bit of an eyesore. Prices are in the lower range of this price code and there are weekend discounts of 20 percent. ⑥.

Erasmus, Poel 25 (☎224 21 95, fax 233 42 41). Ghent's most distinctive hotel, located in an old and commodious town house a few yards away from the Korenlei. A small family-run affair with each room thoughtfully decorated – though it's a touch twee in places – and furnished with antiques. The breakfast is excellent and the family friendly. Reservations advised in summer. Room rates are at the lower end of this price range. ⑤.

Flandria, Barrestraat 3 (☎223 06 26, fax 233 77 89). Somewhat tatty hotel located in the narrow sidestreets off the Reep, a five-minute walk northeast of the cathedral. Apart from the youth hostel, these are the least expensive rooms in the city centre. ③.

Gravensteen, Jan Breydelstraat 35 (☎225 11 50, fax 225 18 50). Small, conducive hotel in an attractively restored nineteenth-century mansion adorned with Second Empire trimmings. Some of the rooms are on the small side, but they're snug enough and several overlook the castle. ⑥.

Ibis Kathedraal, Limburgstraat 2 (☎233 00 00, fax 233 10 00). Handily situated opposite the cathedral, this large hotel – one of the *Ibis* chain – offers comfortable modern rooms, though the noise from the square in front of the hotel can be irritating late at night. ⑤.

Ibis Opera, Nederkouter 24–26 (☎225 07 07, fax 223 59 07). Spick and span, modern five-storey block a five-minute walk south of the Korenmarkt. The rooms lack character, but they're perfectly functional. Slightly less expensive than most of its rivals, but still near the top of this price code. ⑤.

Novotel Centrum, Goudenleeuwplein 5 (☎224 22 30, fax 224 32 95). First-class modern hotel bang in the middle of the town centre – and with an outdoor swimming pool. ⑥.

St Jorishof-Cour St Georges, Botermarkt 2 (☎224 24 24, fax 224 26 40). Facing the Stadhuis, the main building dates from the thirteenth century and is notable for its Romanesque facade. However, the rooms are in a nearby annexe and are best described as adequate but plain. ④.

Sofitel Gent Belfort, Hoogpoort 63 (☎233 33 31, fax 233 11 02). The plushest hotel in town, daintily shoehorned behind an ancient facade by the Stadhuis. Spacious, pastel-shaded rooms and all mod cons. ⑦.

Trianon I, Sint Denijslaan 203 (☎221 39 44, fax 220 49 50). Motel-style accommodation on a quiet residential street about 2km south of the centre, beyond the station. The rooms are comfortable and spotless, but for "stylish and intimate" in their advertising, read kitsch. ③.

Trianon II, Voskenslaan 34 (☎220 48 40, fax 220 49 50). Similar to *Trianon I*, a couple of minutes' walk away, but here you're beside a busy main road. At the bottom end of this price code. ④.

Hostels, student rooms and campsites

Camping Blaarmeersen, Zuiderlaan 12 (☎221 53 99, fax 222 41 84). Among the woods beside the water sports centre to the west of town (bus #38 from Korenmarkt; 10mins), this site is well equipped with laundry, shop, cafeteria and various sports facilities. Open March to mid-Oct.

Jeugdherberg De Draecke, St Widostraat 11 (☎233 70 50, fax 233 80 01). Excellent, well-equipped and smart youth hostel in the city centre, a five-minute walk north of the Korenmarkt. Over a hundred beds, but advance reservations are advised in the height of the season. Family rooms and dormitory beds. Breakfast is included, and the restaurant offers lunch and dinner too. ①.

Universitaire Homes, Stalhof 6 (☎264 71 00, fax 264 72 96). Between mid-July and late September, over a thousand student rooms are let to visitors for F500 per person per night including breakfast. The rooms are dotted around the south of town in a number of complexes; ask at the tourist office for further details or enquire direct at Home Vermeylen, Stalhof 6. ①.

The City

The shape and structure of today's **city centre** reflects Ghent's ancient class and linguistic divide. The streets to the south of the Korenmarkt tend to be straight and wide, lined with elegant old mansions, the former habitations of the wealthier, French-speaking classes, while, to the north, Flemish Ghent is all narrow alleys and low brick houses. They meet at the somewhat confusing sequence of large squares that surrounds the town's principal buildings, spreading out to the immediate east of Korenmarkt.

St Baafskathedraal

The best place to start an exploration of the city centre is the mainly Gothic **St Baafskathedraal**, squeezed into the eastern corner of St Baafsplein (daily 8.30am–6pm; free). St Baaf's mighty nave, begun in the fifteenth century, is supported by tall, slender columns that give the whole interior a cheerful sense of lightness, though the seventeenth-century marble screens spoil the effect by darkening the choir. In a small side **chapel** (April–Oct Mon–Sat 9.30am–noon & 2–6pm, Sun 1–6pm; Nov–March Mon–Sat 10.30am–noon & 2.30–4pm, Sun 2–5pm; F60 including crypt) to the left of the entrance is the cathedral's – and Ghent's – greatest treasure, an **altarpiece** known as the *Adoration of the Mystic Lamb* by Jan van Eyck. Painted around 1432, it is one of the earliest oil paintings to exist by a painter who was reputed to have invented the technique.

The cover screens display a beautiful Annunciation scene with the archangel Gabriel's wings reaching up to the timbered ceiling of a Flemish house, the streets of a town visible through the windows. In a brilliant coup of lighting, the darkened recesses around the shadows of the angel – on the panel opposite – of Mary dapple the room, emphasizing the reality of the apparition. Below, the donor and his wife kneel piously alongside statues of the saints. The restrained exterior painting is, however, but a foretaste of what's within – a striking, visionary work of art that was only revealed when the shutters were opened on Sundays and feast days. On the upper level sit God the Father, the Virgin and John the Baptist in gleaming clarity; to the right are musician-angels and a nude, pregnant Eve; and on the left is Adam plus a group of singing angels who strain to read their music. In the lower panel the Lamb, the symbol of Christ's sacrifice, is approached by bishops, saintly virgins and Old and New Testament figures in a heavenly paradise – "the first evolved landscape in European painting", suggested Kenneth Clarke – seen as a sort of idealized Low Countries. Look closely and you can see the cathedrals of Bruges, Utrecht and Maastricht.

It's actually remarkable that the altarpiece has survived at all. Unsurprisingly, the Calvinists wanted to destroy it; Philip II of Spain tried to acquire it; the Emperor Joseph II disapproved of the painting so violently that he replaced the nude Adam and Eve with a clothed version of 1784 (exhibited today on a column just inside the church entrance); and during World War II the Germans stole the painting and hid it in an Austrian salt mine where it remained until American soldiers arrived in 1945.

Compared to the altarpiece, the rest of the cathedral is a bit of an anticlimax. The rococo **pulpit**, a whopping oak and marble affair stranded in the nave, is not much more than an enjoyable frippery, while in the ambulatory, on the left-hand side just beyond the steps, is one of Rubens' less impressive paintings, *St Bavo's Entrance into the Monastery of Ghent*. In fact, the cathedral's other principal attraction is its **crypt** (same hours as the *Adoration* chapel). Dating from the twelfth century, this preserves features of the earlier Romanesque church of St John, along with murals painted between 1480 and 1540 but only rediscovered in 1936. Full of religious bric-a-brac, one or two of the reliquaries are well worth a second look, though the prime exhibit is Justus van Gent's superb fifteenth-century **triptych**, *The Crucifixion of Christ* – with the crucified Christ flanked on the right by Moses and the bronze serpent that cured poisoned Israelites on sight, and to the left by Moses purifying the waters of Mara with wood.

Around the cathedral

Just west of St Baaf's, beyond the cheerily restored nineteenth-century theatre and a statue in honour of Jan Frans Willems, an early champion of Flemish culture, stands the sturdy **Lakenhalle**. Work began on the hall in the early fifteenth century, but the cloth trade slumped before it was completed and the northern facade was only added in 1903. Indeed, the building has never quite sorted itself out, and today it's little more than an empty shell with the city's tourist office tucked away in the basement. Its first-floor entrance remains, however, the only way to reach the adjoining **belfry**, a much-amended medieval edifice whose soaring spire is topped by a gilded copper and surprisingly corpulent dragon. Once a watchtower-cum-storehouse of civic documents, the interior is now a disappointment – a bare and dusty ruin displaying a few old bells and statues and equipped with a glass-sided lift that climbs up to the roof, where consolation is provided in the form of excellent views over the city centre (mid-March to mid-Nov 10am–12.30pm & 2–5.30pm; F100; free guided tours May–Sept daily 2.30pm, 3.30pm & 4.30pm).

Access to the **Stadhuis** across the street is limited (May–Oct Mon–Thurs guided tours only at 2pm; F100), and of the series of halls open to the public, the most interesting is the old Court of Justice or *Pacificatiezaal* (Pacification Hall), the site of the signing of the Pacification of Ghent in 1576. A plaque commemorates this agreement which momentarily bound north and south Flanders together against the Habsburgs, spurred on by the promise of religious freedom. The room's dark blue and white tiled floor is curiously designed in the form of a maze. No one's quite certain why, but it's supposed that more privileged felons or sinners had to struggle round the maze on their knees as a substitute punishment for a pilgrimage to Jerusalem – a good deal if ever there was one. Outside, the main stairway is framed by a section of facade whose severity is a good example of post-Reformation architecture, in stark contrast to the wild, curling patterns of the section to the immediate north, carved in the Flamboyant Gothic style and designed by Rombout Keldermans at the turn of the sixteenth century. Each of Keldermans' ornate niches was intended to hold a statuette, but the money ran out when the wool trade collapsed, and the city couldn't afford to finish the work off. The present carvings, representing important historical figures in characteristic poses, were substituted at the end of the last century. Look out for Keldermans, shown rubbing his chin and holding his plans for the Stadhuis.

The last of this central cluster of buildings is **St Niklaaskerk** (daily 10am–5pm; free), an architectural hybrid dating from the thirteenth century. Once again it's the shape and structure that please the eye most, especially the pencil-thin turrets which, in a classic example of the early Scheldt Gothic style, elegantly attenuate the lines of the nave. Inside, the giant-sized Baroque high altar is no mean piece, with its mammoth representation of God glowering down its back surrounded by a flock of cherubic angels.

West to the guildhouses

Dodging the trams of the Korenmarkt and heading west, you pass the main **post office building**, whose combination of Gothic Revival and neo-Renaissance themes illustrates the eclecticism popular in Belgium at the beginning of this century. The carved heads encircling the building represent the rulers who came to the city for the Great Exhibition of 1913 and among them, bizarrely, is a bust of Florence Nightingale. A few metres away, the **St Michielsbrug** bridge offers fine views of the towers and turrets that pierce the skyline. The bridge also overlooks the city's oldest harbour, the **Tussen Bruggen** (Between the Bridges), from whose quays **boats** leave for trips around the neighbouring canals from April to early November (see box on p.172). The **Korenlei**, the western side of the harbour, is home to a series of expansive, high-gabled Neoclassical merchants' houses mostly dating from the eighteenth century, while the **Graslei**, opposite, accommodates the late medieval, gabled guildhouses of the town's boatmen and grainweighers. Some of these are of particularly fine design, beginning with no. 14, the Gildehuis van de Vrije Schippers (Guildhouse of Free Boatmen), where the badly weathered sandstone is decorated with scenes of boatmen weighing anchor – and by a delicate carving of a caravel, the type of Mediterranean sailing ship used by Columbus, above the door. The adjacent, late seventeenth-century *Coorenmeters-huis* (Corn Measurers' House"), at nos. 12–13, was where city officials weighed and graded corn behind a facade graced by cartouches and bunches of fruit; next door, at no. 11, is the quaint Tolhuisje, another delightful example of Flemish Renaissance architecture, constructed to house the customs officers in 1698. Of contrasting appearance, the limestone Spijker (Staple House), at no. 10, boasts a Romanesque facade and a heavy crow-stepped gable dating to around 1200. It was here that the city stored its grain supply for over five hundred years until a fire gutted the interior. Finally, the splendid Den Enghel, three doors further along, takes its name from the angel bearing a banner that decorates the facade; the building was originally the stonemasons' guildhouse, as evidenced by the effigies of the four Roman martyrs who were the guild's patron saints.

Het Gravensteen and the Museum of Decorative Arts

A couple of minutes' walk north of Graslei, **Het Gravensteen** (daily: April–Sept 9am–6pm; Oct–March 9am–5pm; F200), the Castle of the Counts of Flanders, looks sinister enough to have been lifted from a Bosch painting. Cold and cruel, its dark walls and unyielding turrets were first raised in 1180 as much to intimidate the town's unruly citizens as to protect them. Considering the castle has been used for all sorts of purposes since then (it was even a cotton mill in the nineteenth century), it's survived remarkably intact, its gateway a deep-arched tunnel leading to the courtyard, which is framed by protective battlements complete with wooden flaps, ancient arrow slits and holes for boiling oil and water. Beside the courtyard stand the castle's two main buildings, the keep on the right and to the left the count's residence, riddled with narrow, interconnected staircases set within the thickness of the walls. A self-guided tour takes you through this labyrinth, and highlights include the cavernous state rooms of the count, a gruesome collection of instruments of torture, and a particularly dank dungeon.

On the opposite side of the square from the castle entrance, at the junction of the two main canals, is the extravagant facade of the old **Vismarkt**, dominated by a grand relief of Neptune, who lords it over two allegorical figures representing the Leie and the Scheldt. Beyond, the market itself is in a terrible state, scheduled for restoration – or possibly demolition. Crossing the bridge immediately to the west, turn first left for the **Museum voor Sierkunst**, Jan Breydelstraat 5 (Tues–Sun 9.30am–5pm; F100), one of the city's more enjoyable museums, focused on Belgian decorative and applied arts. The wide-ranging collection divides into two distinct sections. At the front, squeezed into what was once an eighteenth-century patrician's mansion, lies an attractive sequence of period rooms, culminating in the original dining room, complete with painted ceiling, wood panelling and Chinese porcelains. Linked to the back of the house is the other section, a gleamingly modern display area used both for temporary exhibitions and to showcase the museum's eclectic collection of applied arts dating from 1880 to 1940. There are examples of the work of many leading designers, but pride of place goes to the Art Nouveau material, especially the work of the Belgian Henry van der Velde, whose oeuvre is represented by a furnished room he decorated in 1899.

Back at the top of Jan Breydelstraat, cross over and follow Gewad, turning right down Braderijstraat for the **Lievekaai**, Ghent's second-oldest harbour, by the side of the canal to Bruges. Closed and partly filled in during the nineteenth century, the canal originally extended right up to the front of the old merchants' houses that now flank what remains of the waterway from behind a cobbled pavement. From here there's a choice of routes: you can follow Lievestraat east and turn right down Geldmunt for the Museum voor Volkskunde and the Patershol (see below); or head northwest where a mixture of tumbledown and renovated seventeenth- and eighteenth-century properties line the sides of the canal until it ends abruptly at the **Rabot**, a fortified medieval sluice which was crucial to the defence of old Ghent: the water level behind the sluice was higher than the water level outside, and in emergencies the gates could be opened and the surrounding fields flooded, keeping the enemy at a safe distance.

Museum voor Volkskunde

Retracing your steps to Het Gravensteen and continuing east across St Veerleplein onto the Kraanlei, you'll come to another major museum, the **Museum voor Volkskunde**, Kraanlei 65 (Tues–Sun: April–Oct 9am–12.30pm & 1.30–5.30pm; Nov–March 10am–noon & 1.30–5pm; F80). Housed in a series of restored almshouses surrounding a central courtyard, an array of period rooms depict local life and work in the eighteenth and nineteenth centuries; the reconstructed pipe-maker's, cobbler's and cooper's workshops are particularly interesting. The most curious exhibits are the two wooden "goliaths" in the church: of obscure origin, goliaths are a common feature of Belgian street processions and festivals.

The Patershol and around the Vrijdagmarkt

Behind the Kraanlei are the lanes and alleys of the **Patershol**, a web of terraced houses dating from the seventeenth century. Once the heart of the Flemish working-class city, this thriving residential quarter had, by the 1970s, become a slum threatened with demolition. The area was preserved and a process of gentrification began that has now crowded the streets with good bars and expensive bistros. The process is still under way – one of the stragglers being the ongoing refurbishment of the grand old Carmelite Monastery on Vrouwebroersstraat – and the fringes of the Patershol remain a ragbag of decay and restoration.

Back on the Kraanlei, a modern canal walkway opposite the Museum voor Volkskunde has replaced part of the original towpath and heads off northeast past gabled facades and nineteenth-century textile factories to re-emerge at the eastern end of the Patershol. Otherwise, the bridge adjacent to the start of the walkway leads to the **Vrijdagmarkt**, the old political centre of Ghent and the site of public meetings and executions. En route, by the bridge, there's a fifteenth-century cannon that proved more dangerous to the gunners than the enemy: supposed to be the most powerful siege gun ever manufactured, the cannon, named

Dulle Griet (Mad Meg), cracked its barrel the first time it was fired. In the middle of the Vrijdagmarkt stands a statue of the fourteenth-century guild leader Jacob van Artevelde, by all accounts one of the most abrasive men of his time, while the slim turret at the far end, the **Toreken**, was once the tanners' guildhouse. Adjoining the Vrijdagmarkt is the busy **Bij St Jacobs**, a sprawling square surrounding a hulking medieval church and sprinkled with antique shops.

From Bij St Jacobs, it's a couple of minutes' walk up Belfortstraat back to the Stadhuis. Across the street, lining up along the Hoogpoort, beyond the mullion windows of the *St Jorishof* restaurant, are some of the oldest **facades** in Ghent, heavyweight Gothic structures dating from the fifteenth century. The third house along is now the home of a music school, but the blackened remains of an antique torch-snuffer remain fixed to the wall.

East to St Baafsabdij

Hoogpoort leads into Nederpolder and a right turn at the end brings you to the forbidding **Geraard de Duivelsteen** (no admission), a fortified mansion of splendid Romanesque design dating from the thirteenth century. The stronghold, bordered by what remains of its moat, takes its name from Geraard Vilain, who earnt the soubriquet "duivel" (devil) for his acts of cruelty or, according to some sources, because of his swarthy features and black hair. In between the Duivelsteen and the nearby St Baafskathedraal is a monument to the Eyck brothers, a somewhat stodgy affair knocked up for the Great Exhibition of 1913.

East of the Duivelsteen, Ghent's eighteenth- and nineteenth-century industrial suburbs stretch out toward the Dampoort train station. A mish-mash of terrace, factory and canal, these suburbs were spawned by the sea canals that were dug to replace the obsolete, narrow waterways of the city centre. Right next to the station, the large water-filled hole on **Oktrooiplein** is the link between the old and the new systems. Visitors to Ghent rarely venture into this part of the city, but there is one enjoyable diversion, the ruins of **St Baafsabdij** (St Bavo's Abbey), which occupy a slice of land beside Gandastraat, about ten minutes' walk from the Duivelsteen (April–Oct Tues–Sun 9.30am–5pm; F80 – but check times with the tourist office as the abbey has recently been closed for restoration). Set at the confluence of the Leie and the Scheldt, the abbey was founded in 630 by the French missionary St Amand, whose evangelizing efforts were poorly received by the local townsfolk – they drowned him in the Scheldt. Nonetheless, the abbey survived to become a famous place of pilgrimage, on account of its guardianship of the remains of the seventh-century St Bavo. A wealthy and dissolute landowner, Bavo repented of his ways after the sudden death of his wife, giving his possessions to the poor and ending his days as a hermit outside Ghent. The abbey's heyday was during the fourteenth century, and it was here that Edward III's wife gave birth to John of "Gaunt" (an English corruption of Ghent) at the start of the Hundred Years' War. In 1540, however, Charles V demolished much of the abbey and the monks decamped to St Baafskathedraal. Today's ruins include the battered remnants of a Gothic cloister, bits and pieces of the old wash house, and a monumental Romanesque refectory, with a splendid timber ceiling, that now accommodates a modest lapidary museum. The grounds are a pleasant spot for gentle exploration and a picnic.

South to Bijlokemuseum

Ghent's main shopping street, **Veldstraat**, leads south from the city centre, running parallel to the course of the River Leie. The elegant mansion at no. 82, now the **Museum Arnold Vander Haeghen** was where the the Duke of Wellington stayed in 1815 after the Battle of Waterloo, popping across the street to the **Hotel d'Hane-Steenhuyse**, at no. 55, where Louis XVIII was in residence. Abandoning his throne, Louis had fled Paris for Ghent as soon as Napoleon landed in France after escaping Elba. While others did his fighting for him, Louis waited around in Ghent gorging himself – his daily dinner lasted all of seven hours and the bloated exile was known to polish off 100 oysters at a sitting. His fellow exile, François Chateaubriand, the writer and politician, ignored the gluttony and cowardice, writing meekly, "The French alone know how to dine with method". Today, the grand facade of the hotel, with its fanciful pediment, has survived in good condition, but at present there's no access to the rooms beyond.

Continuing south along Veldstraat, it's an easy ten-minute stroll to one of the city's most diverting museums, the **Bijlokemuseum** (presently Thurs 10am–1pm & 2–6pm & Sun 2–6pm; normally Tues–Sun 9.30am–5pm; F100), whose rambling collection of Ghent-produced applied and decorative art has been shoehorned into the old Cistercian abbey at Godhuizenlaan 2. Founded in the thirteenth century, the abbey was savaged by Calvinists on several occasions, but much of the medieval structure has survived, tidy brown-brick buildings which now provide a charming setting for all sorts of bygones, from collections of guild pennants and processional banners to Masonic tackle, porcelain, pottery, keys and costumes. Pending a promised reorganization, the labelling of the exhibits is woefully inadequate and Sellotaped arrows direct you round the complex. The main portal, an ornate seventeenth-century edifice, was brought to the museum from a local *beguinage* and across the garden is the entrance to the cloister. The first port-of-call here is the upper-level refectory, a massive affair with a high, vaulted ceiling and a striking, early fourteenth-century fresco of the Last Supper. Then, it's up the stairs again to the old **dormitory**, home to a motley collection of guild mementos including, in the centre of the room, a splendid model galleon that was carried in processions by the city's boatmen. Back in the cloister, the upper level is used to display cameo collections, notably an assortment of military hardware featuring the halberds and pikes favoured by the weaver-armies of Flanders. If you can pick it out, there's a rare example of a *goedenday*, literally "good-day": this primitive fourteenth-century weapon, no more than a long pole with a short spike at one end, was designed to stab the Adam's apple, a part of the body poorly protected by armour. In response, the French bobbed their heads down to protect their necks, a nodding motion which the Flemish wryly referred to as a greeting, hence the name of the weapon. Moving on, the cloister's lower level is given over to a series of period rooms, among which the Louis XV drawing room is the most distinguished. From the cloister, a connecting corridor leads through to the **house of the abbess**, where a further sequence of period rooms accommodates several magnificent carved fireplaces moved here from the Stadhuis.

Museum voor Schone Kunsten

Ten minutes' walk away to the southeast, the **Museum voor Schone Kunsten** (Tues–Sun 9.30am–5pm; F100) occupies an imposing Neoclassical edifice on the edge of Citadelpark at Nicolaas de Liemaeckereplein 3. Inside, the central atrium and conecting rotunda are flanked by a sequence of rooms, with the older paintings exhibited to the right, the nineteenth-century works on the left. There's not enough space to display all the works, so some are rotated, but you can expect to see those mentioned below and although the layout of the collection does not seem to follow much of a plan, it's small enough to be easily manageable.

The rotunda itself houses a fine head by Rodin and the atrium a series of eighteenth-century tapestries, flowing classical scenes depicting the *Glorification of the Gods*. Highlights amongst the older works to the right of the atrium include Rogier van der Weyden's *Madonna with Carnation*, a charming work where the proffered flower, in all its exquisite detail, serves as a symbol of Christ's passion, and Hieronymus Bosch's *Bearing of the Cross*, showing Christ mocked by some of the most grotesque and deformed characters Bosch ever painted. Look carefully and you'll see that Christ's head is at the centre of two diagonals, one representing evil, the other good – the latter linking the repentant thief with St Veronica, whose cloak carries the imprint of Christ's face. This same struggle between good and evil is the subject of an earlier canvas by Bosch, *St Jerome at Prayer,* in the foreground of which the saint prays, surrounded by a menacing landscape, while in the background a peaceful rural scene offers relief. Here also is Adriaen Isenbrandt's *Mary and Child*, a gentle painting showing Mary suckling Jesus on the flight into Egypt, with the artist choosing a rural Flemish landscape as the backdrop rather than the Holy Land.

Amongst the **seventeenth-century Flemish and Dutch paintings**, also to the right of the atrium, are several canvases by Jacob Jordaens. His *Studies of the Head of Abraham Grapheus* is an example of the high-quality preparatory paintings destined to be recycled within larger compositions, while his *Judgement of Midas* mimics the robust romanticism of his friend Rubens – who is well represented by *St Francis*, a powerful work showing the sick-looking saint bearing the marks of the stigmata. Van Dyck wins the bad taste award for his *Jupiter and Antiope*, showing the lecherous god, with his tongue hanging out, in anticipation of sex with Antiope. There's also work by Pieter Bruegel the Younger, who inherited his father's interest in the landscape and those who worked and lived on it, as evidenced by his *Wedding Feast* and *Peasant Wedding,* plus several striking canvases by Joachim Beuckelaer, who specialized in allegorical market and kitchen scenes. The collection of nineteenth-century works, to the left of the atrium, is rather skimpy, a quick runaround of Belgian peasant scenes, landscapes and seascapes by the likes of Emile Claus, plus several paintings by more original artists such as James Ensor, Meunier and Constant Permeke.

To view more contemporary Belgian artists, walk over to the **Museum van Hedendaagse Kunst** (Tues–Sun 9.30am–5pm; F100), housed in the old casino opposite the entrance to the Museum voor Schone Kunsten – if, that is, this new museum has finally been opened. Hopefully it will be, as they possess a wide-ranging collection of modern art with examples of all the major artistic movements since World War II – everything from surrealism, the Dutch CoBrA group and pop art through to minimalism, hyper realism and conceptual art – as well as their forerunners, most notably Rene Magritte and Paul Delvaux.

After visiting the museums, rather than heading straight back to the city centre, consider taking a stroll through **Citadelpark**, whose assorted fountains, ponds and artificial grottoes were laid out in the 1870s on top of what had once been a Habsburg castle.

Eating and drinking

Ghent's numerous **cafés** and **restaurants** offer the very best of Flemish and French cuisines with a sprinkling of Italian, Chinese and Arab places for variety. The more deluxe restaurants are concentrated in and around the narrow lanes of

GHENT SPECIALITIES

In Ghent there are several local dishes worth seeking out, tasty additions to the regional cuisine of Flanders as a whole.

Gentse waterzooi, a delicious and filling soup-cum-stew, is served either with chicken (*van kip*) or with fish (*van riviervis*).

Gentse stoverij consists of stewed beef and offal – especially liver and kidneys – slowly tenderized in dark beer and served with a slice of bread covered in mustard.

Gentse hutsepot is a winter-warmer dish: various bits of beef and pork (including pigs' trotters and ears) are casseroled with turnips, celery, leeks and parsnips.

the Patershol, while less expensive spots, including a rash of fast-food joints, cluster around the Korenmarkt. The less formal restaurants and most cafés welcome customers dropping by just for drinks, but the city also boasts dozens of **bars** – though the distinction between these categories is often hazy. Several of the more original bars, complete with a beer list long enough to strain any liver, are within a couple of minutes' walk of Het Gravensteen.

Cafés and restaurants

Amadeus, Plotersgracht 8 (☎225 13 85). In the heart of the Patershol, this busy, well-established restaurant specializes in spare ribs. Long tables, low ceilings and a sprinkling of bygones make the place relaxed and convivial; booking advised.

Auberge de Fonteyne, Gouden Leeuwplein 7 (☎225 48 71). Large café-restaurant serving Flemish food at very reasonable prices. The portions are huge and the kitsch Art Nouveau decor pulls in the tourists. Right in the centre of town, across the square from the Lakenhalle. Closed Sat & Sun.

Het Blauwe Huis, Drabstraat 17 (☎233 10 05). The outside of this restaurant is painted blue – hence its name. The interior is calm and subdued, all candles and varnished woods plus some of the finest seafood in the city at affordable prices – main courses from around F500–600. A real treat.

Patisserie Bloch, Veldstraat 60, on the corner with Volderstraat. One of the best and busiest tearooms in town, where shoppers pause for a break. Cakes, coffee and snacks are served in these delightfully old-fashioned premises until 5pm, Mon–Sat.

Brooderie, Jan Breydelstraat 8. Pleasant and informal café with a health-food slant. Wholesome breakfasts, lunches, sandwiches and salads from around F300. Open Tues–Sat 7.30am–6pm & Sun 9am–6pm.

De Hel, Kraanlei 81 (☎224 32 40). This tiny restaurant in the Patershol, enhanced by candle-lit tables and classical music, offers delicious Franco-Belgian fare at affordable prices – main courses around F700; booking advised. The building itself, dating from 1669, is adorned by terracotta reliefs of flying deer and the five senses. Closed Mon & Tues.

't Klokhuis, Corduwaniersstraat 65. Fashionable brasserie in the Patershol serving tasty and affordable snacks and meals. Flemish and French cuisine.

Koningshuis, St Michielsplein 31. A student favourite, this laid-back café-restaurant sells inexpensive pizzas and pastas as well as tasty vegetarian dishes albeit from a limited menu. Open late.

Malatesta, Hooiaard 2. Fashionable, sharply decorated café-restaurant offering tasty pizza and pasta dishes at affordable prices. It is at the bottom of Hooiaard, a sidestreet linking Korenmarkt with Poel – and there's an entrance on the Korenmarkt too.

't Marmietje, Drabstraat 30. Cosy restaurant just off Korenlei. Superb traditional Flemish cuisine – one of *the* places to try *Gentse waterzooi van kip* and *Gentse stoverij*. Prices are very reasonable – less than its rivals in the Patershol. Closed Sun & Mon evening.

Oudburg, Oudburg 2 (☎233 34 00). Smooth and classy, pint-sized restaurant (reservations recommended) in the Patershol. French and Flemish dishes. Full meals, excluding wine, from around F1200. Closed Tues & Wed.

Pascalino, Botermarkt 11. Straightforward, inexpensive café offering snacks and filling meals of average quality until 9.30pm every night. There's an old-fashioned, endearingly 1960s look to the place; great location too, opposite the Stadhuis. Closed mid-Aug to mid-Sept for annual holidays.

Rambler, Koningin Maria Hendrikaplein 3. This café-restaurant has competent Flemish dishes at inexpensive prices, and is convenient if you're staying near St Pieters train station.

Rococo, Corduwaniersstraat 57. Urbane and informal café on the ground floor of a grand eighteenth-century house in the Patershol.

St Jorishof, Botermarkt 2 (☎224 24 24). Across the street from the Stadhuis, this long-established restaurant has a well-deserved reputation for the quality of its traditional Flemish cuisine; booking advised. It is a fairly formal place and the meals are expensive – beginning at around F1400. Closed Sun and for a fortnight in the summer.

Sobrie, Mageleinstraat 43. Popular and smart little café providing Ghent's shoppers with snacks and light meals – but it's the cakes and pastries that will make your mouth water. Situated a couple of minutes' walk south of the Lakenhalle. Open Mon–Sat, 9am–5pm.

Theatercafé de Foyer, St Baafsplein. In the theatre (Schouwburg) on St Baafsplein, this smart and popular first-floor café has a lovely balcony with enjoyable views of the cathedral.

Vondel, Vrijdagmarkt 26. Large but laid-back café-restaurant which serves tasty and affordable food from a varied menu – and is a real treat for ice cream enthusiasts. Closed Tues and Wed.

Bars

't Dreupelkot, Groentenmarkt 10. Cosy bar specializing in jenever, of which it stocks over 100 brands, all kept at icy temperatures. Down a little alley, next door to the famous *Het Waterhuis* – see below.

Dulle Griet, Vrijdagmarkt 50. A long, dark and atmospheric bar with ceiling rugs, all manner of incidental objets d'art – and an especially wide range of beers. Bar snacks too – though these are missable.

't Galgenhuisje, Groentenmarkt 5. Lilliputian bar often frantic with the young and tipsy. If you can actually get in, the place offers something like 80 different beers. Closed Mon.

De Tap en de Tepel, Gewad 7. Dark bar with an open fireplace – whose name translates as "the tap and nipple" – with an open fire and a clutter of antique furnishings. Wine is the main deal here, served with a good selection of cheeses. Closed Sun–Tues & most of Aug.

De Tempelier, Meersenierstraat 9, near the Mad Meg cannon off Vrijdagmarkt. Few tourists venture into this small, dark and intriguing bar which offers a vast range of beers at lower than usual prices. Closed Sun.

Tolhuisje Tavern, Graslei 11. Tiny, sparsely furnished bar in the old tollhouse. The place heaves on the weekend.

De Trollekelder, Bij St Jacobs 17. Huge selection of beers in an ancient merchants' house, with trolls of all descriptions stuffed in the window. Closed 2–3 weeks in the summer.

Den Turk, Botermarkt 4. Opposite the Stadhuis, this long and thin little bar claims to have been serving drinkers since 1228. Great atmosphere in a highbrow-conversation sort of way and regular jazz. The beer menu is particularly good on Trappist brews.

Het Waterhuis aan de Bierkant, Groentenmarkt 9. Over 100 types of beer in a most attractive bar near the castle. Be sure to try Stropken (literally "noose"), a delicious local brew, named after the time in 1453 when Philip the Good compelled the rebellious city burghers to parade outside the town gate with ropes around their necks.

Listings

Banks and bureaux de change The two most central banks are Generale, Belfortstraat 41 (Mon–Fri 9am–12.30pm & 1.30–4.30pm), and Driege, St Baafsplein 12 (Mon–Fri 9am–4pm). Best bureaux de change are in the city centre at Mageleinstraat 36 (Mon–Sat 9am–6pm, Sun 10am–4pm).

Bikes Can be rented for F335 per day at St Pieters station.

Books Fnac, Veldstraat 88 (Mon–Sat 10am–6.30pm), close to the junction with Zonnestraat, has a reasonable selection of English titles as well as Belgian walking maps. Atlas & Zanzibar, Kortrijksesteenweg 100 (Mon–Fri 10am–1pm & 2–7pm, Sat 10am–1pm & 2–6pm), is a specialist travel bookshop with a comprehensive collection of Belgian walking maps and many English guidebooks; it's about ten minutes' walk south of the centre on the way to the train station, at the junction with Meersstraat. An English edition of *Snoeck's Guide to Ghent*, which delves into the city's every architectural feature, is available at both these bookshops for F400.

Buses and trams City and regional transport enquiries at the kiosks on the Korenmarkt (Mon–Fri 7am–7pm & Sat 9.30am–4pm) and beside St Pieters station (Mon–Fri 7am–7pm).

Car rental Avis, Kortrijksesteenweg 676 (☎222 00 53); Europcar, Savaanstraat 13 (☎226 81 26); Hertz, Coupure Links 707 (☎224 04 06).

Chocolates The excellent *Neuhaus* have an outlet in front of the cathedral at St Baafsplein 20.

Cinema New releases, with most English-language films subtitled (rather than dubbed), at the *Sphinx*, off the Korenmarkt at St Michielshelling 3 (☎225 60 86).

Emergencies Police ☎101. Fire/ambulance ☎100.

Festivals Ghent's main festivals are the Lentebeurs van Vlaanderen, the Flanders Spring Fair, in early March; the Gentse Feesten or town fair, held for 10 days in mid- to late July (always including July 21); the Patersholfeesten, the Patershol knees-up in mid-Aug; and the Festival van Vlaanderen, the Flanders Music Festival, in September and early October.

Gay scene Ghent's gay scene is pretty low-key. Contacts and details from FWH, Vlaanderenstraat 22 (Mon–Fri 9am–4.30pm; ☎223 69 29).

Left luggage Office at Ghent St Pieters station (6am–midnight), plus lockers in the station concourse.

Markets On Saturdays and Sundays, there's a flower market on the Vrijdagmarkt (7am–1pm). There's also a daily fruit and veg market on Groentenmarkt (Mon–Fri & Sun 7am–1pm, Sat 7am–5pm); a flea market (*prondelmarkt*) on Beverhoutplein/Bij St Jacobs (Fri–Sun 8am–1pm); an antique and art market (*kunstmarkt*) on Groentenmarkt (March–Nov Mon-Thurs 10am–5pm); and a bird market on Vrijdagmarkt (Sun 7am–1pm).

Mustard Superb mustard can be bought from Tierenteyn-Verlent, an old-fashioned store at Groentenmarkt 3; the smallest pot will set you back about F200.

Performing arts The Kunstencentrum Vooruit, St Pietersnieuwstraat 23 (☎267 28 20), is the main performance hall for **rock, pop** and **jazz** concerts. De Vlaamse Opera (Flemish Opera) perform at the opera house, near the Kouter at Schouwburgstraat 3 (reservations & information on ☎225 24 25). Visiting **orchestras** often appear at the Bijloke Festivalhal, at Jozef Kluyskensstraat (☎233 68 78). Ghent has half a dozen good **theatre** troupes performing at locations across the city. The best-known is Nederlands Toneel Gent (NTG), the regional repertory company, based in the theatre house at St Baafsplein 17 (☎225 32 08). Most shows are in Flemish, but it's worth asking at the tourist office for details of performances in English.

Pharmacies Details of 24-hour chemists are available from the tourist office, and are also displayed in pharmacists' windows.

Post office The main post office is at Korenmarkt 16 (Mon–Fri 8am–6pm, Sat 9am–noon).

Tapestries Tapestries are still produced in Flanders and 't Vlaams Wandtapijt, footsteps from the Cathedral at St Baafsplein 6, showcases the province's best products.

Taxi V-Tax, Overpoortstraat 38 (☎222 22 22).

Train enquiries ☎222 44 44 (daily 7am–9pm).
Travel agents Divantoura, Bagattenstraat 176 (☎223 00 69); Nouvelles Frontières, Nederkouter 77 (☎224 01 06).

Around Ghent

Rivers and canals radiate out from Ghent in all directions, slicing across the flatness of the Flemish plain. By and large there's little here of much interest in what is primarily an industrial area, although – if you have your own transport – you might consider a day-trip southwest to the art museums of **Deurle**, or travel east to the moated castle of **Laarne**.

Deurle

A leafy, prosperous village which spreads out among the woods beside the winding course of the River Leie, **DEURLE** lies about 10km southwest of the city. To get there, take Kortrijksesteenweg out of Ghent, cross over the E40 motorway (at junction #14), proceed along the N43, and take the signed turning to Nevele (and Deurle) on the right. Take another right down P de Denterghemlaan, and then either turn right again along Dorpstraat, which leads to the old brick cottages that make up the centre of Deurle, or – a little further on – take the first left to a trio of (signposted) art museums. Deurle was a favourite with two successive schools of early twentieth-century artists who took up residence here and in the adjoining hamlet of **Sint Martens-Latem**, from which both groups took their name. The first school were Symbolists and their leading light was the sculptor Georges Minne; the second group were Expressionists, and counted among their number Constant Permeke and Gustave de Smet.

In Deurle, this first left turn off P de Denterghemlaan leads to the **Museum Dhondt-Dhaenens**, Museumlaan 14 (mid-Feb to Nov Wed–Fri 2–6pm, Sat–Sun 10am–noon & 2–6pm; F70), which provides an overview of the period and its key players. The adjacent **Museum Leon de Smet**, Museumlaan 18 (Easter–Oct Sat & Sun 2–6pm, Nov–Dec & Feb–Easter Sat & Sun 2–5pm; F50), features the work of the eponymous artist, whose striking blocks of colour and bold lines were clearly influenced by the Fauves. By comparison, Leon's brother Gustave (1877–1943) was much inspired by the Cubists, and some of his canvases and drawings are on display in the nearby **Museum Gustaaf de Smet**, at Gustaaf de Smetlaan 1 (Easter–Sept Wed–Sat 2–6pm, Sun 10am–noon & 2–6pm; Oct–Easter Wed–Sun 2–5pm; F50), the second left turn off P de Denterghemlaan. There are several other art museums in the vicinity of Deurle, the pick of them being the **Museum Gevaert-Minne**, where a few works by Georges Minne are displayed at Kapitteldreef 45, a big old house down a forested track in Sint Martens-Latem (Easter–Sept Wed–Sat 2–6pm, Sun 10am–noon & 2–6pm; Oct–Easter Wed–Sun 2–5pm; F50). To get there, carry on down P de Denterghemlaan; take a right along Rode Beukendreef; turn first left onto Warandedreef; and left onto Kapitteldreef at the third crossroads.

Around Deurle: Kasteel Ooidonk

In wooded parkland about 4km from Deurle, the onion domes and crow-stepped gables of the handsome **Kasteel Ooidonk** (Easter to mid-Sept Sun 2–5.30pm, plus July–Aug Sat 2–5.30pm; F180) mostly date from the 1590s and occupy a scenic spot beside the Leie. The chateau's interior is, however, disappointing, with heavy-handed nineteenth-century fittings providing an unexciting setting for a large but rather undistinguished collection of antique tapestries, porcelain, silver and furniture. To get here from Deurle, head north toward Nevele from the T–junction at the start of P de Denterghemlaan and then follow the signs. From the chateau, it's around 13km back to Ghent along the north side of the Leie.

Laarne

On the opposite side of Ghent, 15km east of the city, is the moated and turreted chateau of **Laarne** (Easter–Oct Sun 2–5.30pm, July & Aug also Tues–Thurs & Sat 2–5.30pm; F200). Most of the present building dates from medieval times, though successive restorations transformed the original castle into a spacious country mansion long ago, enhancing its stately rooms with the addition of a Renaissance entrance hall. Abandoned in the nineteenth century, Laarne was given to the state in 1964, since when there has been a thorough refurbishment which has graced the chateau with antique furnishings, including several fine Brussels tapestries. An extensive collection of old silver is exhibited here too. The easiest way to reach Laarne by public transport is to take the train from Ghent to Wettern (every 20min; 10min), from where bus #688 leaves every hour for the ten-minute trip to Laarne.

The Waasland

To the northeast of Ghent lies the agricultural region of the **Waasland**, its sand and clay soils sandwiched between the Dutch border to the north, the Ghent–Terneuzen canal to the west, and the River Scheldt to the east. Once an isolated area of swamp and undrained forest, the lands of the Waasland were first cultivated by pioneering religious communities who cleared the trees and built the dykes. The soil was poor and conditions were hard until Ghent's demand for wool encouraged local landowners to introduce the sheep that produced the district's first cash crop and provided some degree of prosperity. Today, the area is popular with day-trippers seeking the quiet of the countryside.

St Niklaas, the district's only sizeable settlement, will not detain you long, while further south, directly east of Ghent, a desultory landscape encases two small towns, workaday **Dendermonde** and enjoyable **Aalst**, the latter distinguished by its splendid belfry and the late medieval St Martinuskerk.

St Niklaas

Some 35km northeast of Ghent and 25km west of Antwerp, **ST NIKLAAS** is an unremarkable town whose principal feature is its Grote Markt, the largest in Belgium. It's edged by a motley combination of old and new buildings, including an attractive, bright-white, towered and turreted **Stadhuis** dating from the nineteenth century. Behind lurks the hulking mass of **St Niklaaskerk**, a jumble of architectural styles dominated by a huge tower surmounted by a gilded statue of the Madonna and Child. Subtle it certainly isn't – and neither is the gaudily painted church interior. The only real surprise is the tiny old castle, **Kasteel Walburg**, a couple of minutes' walk from the Grote Markt: take Apostelstraat from beside the tourist office and continue along Walburgstraat and it's on the right. Built of reddish brick in the middle of the sixteenth century, the castle is in the Flemish Renaissance style and was clearly built for comfort rather than defence. Part of an attractively wooded city park and encircled by a slender moat, it's classically picturesque – and nowadays it accommodates a bar and restaurant.

The **Stedelijk**, Sint Niklaas' municipal museum, consists of several collections displayed at different sites around the city centre. The only one of note is the **Mercator Museum** (Tues–Sat 2–5pm, Sun 10am–5pm; F100) at Zamanstraat 49, about five minutes' walk from the Grote Markt: leave the square via its northeast corner, along Houtbriel, and take the first turning on the left. This museum has an interesting collection of maps, atlases and globes made by the Flemish cartographer **Mercator**, who was born in the neighbouring village of Rupelmonde in 1512. Mercator's projection of the spherical earth onto a two-dimensional map is now accepted as the usual view of the world's surface, and it was originally an invaluable aid to navigation. However, his projection distorts the relative size of the continents at the expense of the southern hemisphere; the other deception is in the layout, which vaingloriously places the colonizing nations of Europe at the centre.

Practicalities

St Niklaas **train station** is situated on the northern edge of the centre, some ten minutes' walk from the Grote Markt – turn right outside the station building, then left down Stationsstraat. There's nowhere very enticing to stay in the centre of town, so that's not much of an option, but the **tourist office**, Grote Markt 45 (Mon–Fri 8am–5pm, mid-May to mid-Sept also Sat & Sun 10am–4pm; ☎03/777 26 81), will provide a list of **campsites** and **hotels** in the vicinity. They also have a comprehensive selection of cycling brochures detailing routes that explore every nook and cranny of the Waasland. One popular option is to make for the quiet villages west of town, such as Sinaai and Eksaarde. You can **rent bikes** at the train station (Mon–Fri 8.30am–noon & 1–4.45pm; F335 per day), and leave luggage there too.

Dendermonde

East of Ghent, the River Scheldt twists its way across the industrial heartland of eastern Flanders, its towns home to the host of factories that sprang up in the nineteenth century as Belgium was transformed from a predominantly agricultural society to – briefly – the fourth-greatest industrial power in the world. Some 25km from Ghent, **DENDERMONDE**, at the confluence of the rivers Scheldt and Dender, shared in the industrial boom, just as previously its strategic location had seen it suffer its share of siege and assault. Badly damaged by the Germans in 1914, today's town centre is rather drab, but the Grote Markt remains a pleasant spot, its narrow confines flanked by a trim **Stadhuis**, originally the Lakenhalle, whose fourteenth-century structure was restored in the 1920s. Opposite, across the Grote Markt from the Stadhuis, the turreted **Vleeshuis**, with its petite dormer windows, dates from 1460, its cramped interior now home to a modest historical museum (April–Oct Tues–Sun 9am–12.30pm & 1.30–6pm). From behind the Vleeshuis, Kerkstraat leads west to the newly restored **Onze Lieve Vrouwekerk** (Easter–Sept Sat & Sun 2–4.30pm, plus July & Aug Tues–Fri

2–4.30pm), a stolid Gothic edifice sheltering a splendid blue-marble Romanesque font and two early canvases by van Dyck – *Crucifixion* and *Adoration of the Shepherds* – both typical of the painter's Rubens-like style.

Dendermonde is, however, best known for its **carnival**, an extraordinary attempt to re-enact the medieval story of the Steed Bayard – a medieval tale of knights and honour, loyalty and friendship, dynastic quarrels and disputes. Picaresque in form, the story doesn't seem to make much sense: the whole thing revolves around the trials and tribulations of a horse, represented by a giant fabricated model, and its masters, the four brothers who perch on top. The clearest part of the story is the end, where the redoubtable steed repeatedly breaks free from the millstones tied around its neck and refuses to drown. The third time he comes to the surface, one of his masters walks away, no longer able to watch the agonies of his horse; assuming he's been abandoned, the forlorn horse cries out and promptly drowns. The carnival is currently held every ten years at the end of May, but there are plans to make it an annual event; check with the tourist office for the latest.

Practicalities

Dendermonde's **train** and **bus stations** are on the southern edge of town, a ten-minute walk from the centre via Stationsstraat (ahead but slightly to the right of the train station), Brusselsestraat and Vlasmarkt, beyond which you cross the bridge into the Grote Markt. The **tourist office**, in the Stadhuis (Mon–Fri & Sun 10am–noon & 2–4pm, plus Easter–Sept Sat 10am–noon & 2–4pm; ☎052/21 39 56), supplies free town maps and local information. For a drink or a meal, try the cafés on the Grote Markt.

Aalst

About 15km south of Dendermonde and 25km east of Ghent, the ancient town of **AALST** was first fortified in the eleventh century and became a settlement of some importance as a seat of the counts of Flanders, at the point where the Bruges to Cologne trade route crossed the River Dender. Later on, Aalst became a key industrial centre, producing beer and textiles, as well as some of the worst slum and factory conditions in the country. Cleaned up in the 1950s, the town has one outstanding building, the fifteenth-century **belfry**. A slender, balconied turret that rises elegantly from the Grote Markt, the belfry is adorned by the statues of a knight and an armed citizen, symbols of municipal power and individual freedom, and inscribed with the town motto, *Nec spe nec metu* ("Neither by hope nor by fear"). The belfry is attached to the **Schepenhuis** (Aldermen's House), a somewhat incoherent jangle of odds and ends shoved together over the centuries, with a flamboyant Gothic **gallery** protruding into the square from the main body of the building. Elsewhere on the Grote Markt, there are two more buildings of interest: to the left of the belfry is the ornately gabled and arcaded **Borse van Amsterdam**, which started life as the city meat market but now holds one of the best restaurants in town (see "Practicalities" below), while along the square to the belfry's right stands the colonnaded, nineteenth-century facade of the **Stadhuis**.

Just to the east of the Grote Markt is the towering sandstone mass of **St Martinuskerk** (daily 8am–noon & 2–7pm), a fine example of late Gothic, though work on the church was interrupted by the Thirty Years' War and only the transept, apse and ambulatory were completed – the brick in-fills mark the interruption. The church interior boasts a fine vaulted ceiling, rounded pillars with delicately carved capitals, and Aalst's only famous painting, the clumsily named *St Roch Receiving from Christ the Gift of Healing Victims of the Plague* by Rubens. Commissioned by the guild of beer brewers and hop growers in 1623, the painting is displayed to the right of the entrance in the transept, still in its original carved wooden frame. The composition flaunts the artist's fluent, exuberant lines, with the pallid arms of the sick reaching up to the saint, who shudders at the appearance of a windswept Christ wrapped in a flowing red cloak. Typically, Rubens broke with convention in his chosen arrangement: the saint's dog had always been shown licking a plague blemish on his master's leg, but Rubens' animal simply looks agog at Christ. Nearby, beside the high altar, a wedding-cake **tabernacle** fills out the space between two of the church's pillars, its extravagant mixture of columns and statuettes in several different sorts of marble the work of Jerome du Quesnoy in 1604.

At the back of the church, down the hill, the old hospital has been turned into a **museum** (Tues–Fri 10am–noon & 2–5pm, Sat & Sun 2–5pm; free), whose rambling collection has everything from religious paintings through to ceramic tiles. Although the labelling is only in Flemish, it's worth having a look at the two small display areas near the entrance, one dedicated to the local writer and anarchist Paul Boon (1912–1979), the other commemorating the work of a nineteenth-century radical Catholic priest, Adolf Daens, who campaigned to improve the pay and conditions of local workers. It's a modest section, but an engaging one, with sepia photographs illustrating the work of the priest, the organization of a local Catholic-led trade union, and the harsh poverty of the period.

The best time to be in Aalst is during its boisterous **carnival**, known as the **Vastelauved**, held over the four days preceding Ash Wednesday. This is the town's principal festival and, among all sorts of municipal high jinks, there are parades with floats satirizing local and national bigwigs, Broom Dancing by the fancifully dressed Gilles of Aalst, and a (rather dubious) parade of the *Voil Jeannetten* – men in drag – on Shrove Tuesday. The whole thing is rounded off by the burning of the Mardi Gras puppet in front of the Stadhuis on the final night of revelry.

Practicalities

Aalst **train station** is five minutes' walk from the town centre: take Albert Lienartstraat from the square in front of the station building and keep going straight. The **tourist office**, in the Schepenhuis (Mon–Fri 9am–noon & 1.30–5pm; June–Sept also Sat–Sun 10–noon & 2–5pm; ☎053/73 21 21), has maps of the town and can help with accommodation. Aalst has seven centrally situated **hotels** and easily the most charming is the *Hostellerie Mirage*, a family-run affair in a comfortably furnished old townhouse near the station at Stationsstraat 21 (☎ 053/77 41 60, fax 77 40 94; ⑤). The three-star *Hotel de la Gare*, Stationsplein 11 (☎053/21 39 11, fax 78 14 69; ④), with twenty comfortable rooms, is a good if fairly run-of-the-mill second choice. The *Mirage* also has a first-rate **restaurant**, serving both French and Flemish dishes, and the equally smart *Borse van Amsterdam*, on the Grote Markt, specializes in Flemish cuisine – try the eels. For something lighter and less expensive, try the *Graaf van Egmont* café, next to the belfry.

travel details

Trains

Bruges to: Brussels (every 20min; 65min); Ghent (every 20min; 25min); Knokke (every 15min; 15min); Ostend (every 20min; 15min); Zeebrugge (hourly; 15min).

Ghent to: Aalst (every 20min; 25min); Antwerp Centraal (every 30min; 45min); De Panne (hourly; 80min); Dendermonde (every 30min; 30min); Kortrijk (every 30min; 30min); Mechelen (every 30min; 65min); Oudenaarde (hourly; 35min); St Niklaas (every 30min; 25min); Veurne (hourly; 70min).

Ieper to: Kortrijk (hourly; 30min).

Kortrijk to: Ghent (every 30min; 25min); Ieper (hourly; 30min); Lille, France (hourly; 30min); Oudenaarde (hourly; 20min).

Ostend to: Bruges (every 20min; 15min); Brussels (every 15min; 80min); Ghent (every 20min; 40min).

Veurne to: De Panne (hourly; 10min); Diksmuide (hourly; 10min); Ghent (hourly; 70min).

Buses

Ieper to: Diksmuide (7 daily; 25min); Lo (7 daily; 35min); Veurne (7 daily; 60min).

Ostend to: Nieuwpoort (Mon–Sat 8 daily, Sun 3 daily; 35min); Veurne (Mon–Sat 8 daily, Sun 3 daily; 75min).

Veurne to: Ieper (7 daily; 1hr); Nieuwpoort (Mon–Sat 8 daily, Sun 3 daily; 40min); Ostend (Mon–Sat 8 daily, Sun 3 daily; 75min).

Trams

Ostend to: De Panne (every 10min in summer, 30min in winter; 1hr 5min); Knokke (same frequency; 1hr).

CHAPTER THREE

ANTWERP AND THE NORTHEAST

The **provinces** of Antwerp and Limburg together with a chunk of Brabant constitute the Flemish-speaking northeastern rim of Belgium, stretching from the city of Antwerp in the west to the River Maas, which forms the border with Holland in the east. It's dull, flat countryside on the whole, and the main attraction of the region is undoubtedly **Antwerp**, a large and ancient port that is definitely worth a stopover of several days. It's a sprawling and intriguing place, the international centre of the diamond trade and in part still a hard-edged dock city. It also has many reminders of its sixteenth-century golden age – before it was upstaged by Amsterdam as the prime commercial centre of the Low Countries – from splendid medieval churches and guildhouses to as fine a set of museums as you'll find anywhere in Belgium (Rubens spent most of his career in the city and produced many of his finest works here). Outside of the city, Antwerp province has two other ancient towns deserving of a day-trip – **Lier**, with its quaint and diverting centre, and the dignified ecclesiastical capital of Belgium, **Mechelen**, complete with its magnificent cathedral. Southeast from here, just beyond the reaches of Brussels' sprawling suburbs, lies the lively university town of **Leuven**, which, boasting its own clutch of fine medieval buildings, is the principal attraction of this corner of Flemish Brabant, although **Diest**, most noteworthy for its well-preserved Begijnhof, comes a reasonable second.

The province of **Limburg** further to the east is, unlike Antwerp, seldom visited by tourists, its low-key mixture of small towns and tranquil farmland having limited appeal. Nevertheless, the workaday capital, **Hasselt**, does have a bustling centre, and the nearby **Bokrijk** estate holds one of the best open-air museums in the country, primarily dedicated to the rural traditions of Flemish Belgium. Of

ACCOMMODATION PRICE CODES

All the **hotels and hostels** detailed in this chapter have been graded according to the following price categories. Apart from ①, which is a per-person price for a hostel bed, all the codes are based on the rate for the least expensive double room during high season. For more on accommodation, see p.33.

① Up to F1000 per person	④ F2000–2500 per room	⑦ F4000–5000 per room
② F1000–1500 per room	⑤ F2500–3000 per room	⑧ F5000–6000 per room
③ F1500–2000 per room	⑥ F3000–4000 per room	⑨ F6000 and over, per room

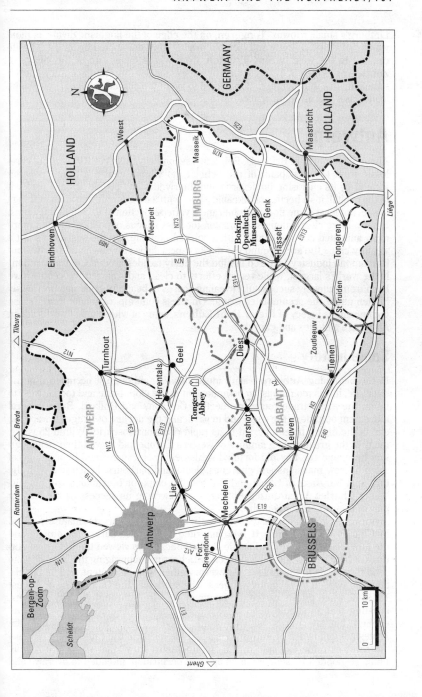

Limburg's smaller towns, **Tongeren**, on the edge of the linguistic divide, is most worthy of a visit, a pretty and likeable market town dominated by its giant basilica. Just to the west is **Sint Truiden**, from where buses run to the village of **Zoutleeuw**, which is distinguished by its spectacular fourteenth-century church – the only one in Belgium that managed to avoid the depredations of Protestants, iconoclasts and invading armies.

Antwerp

About 50km north of Brussels, Belgium's second city, **ANTWERP**, fans out carelessly from the east bank of the Scheldt, its vibrant centre a rough polygon formed by its enclosing boulevards and the river. Many people actually prefer it to the capital: it's a hectic and likeable place, with a denser concentration of things to see, not least some fine churches and a varied selection of excellent museums. It has a more clearly defined character, too, less a focus of political life and more of an animated cultural centre with a spirited nightlife. On the surface it's not a wealthy city – the area around the docks especially is run down and seedy – but its diamond industry (centred behind the dusty facades around Centraal Station) is the world's largest, while recent efforts to clean and smarten the centre have been tremendously successful, revealing scores of beautiful buildings previously hidden under the accumulated grime. On a less contemporary note there is also the enormous legacy of **Pieter Paul Rubens**, some of whose finest works adorn Antwerp's galleries and churches.

Some history

In the beginning **Antwerp** wasn't much desired: although it occupied a prime river site, it was too far east to be important in the cloth trade and too far west to be on the major trade routes connecting Germany and Holland. But a general movement of trade to the west, and in particular the decline of Bruges toward the end of the fifteenth century, led to its rapid rise from obscurity. Within 25 years, many of the great trading families of western Europe had moved their headquarters here, and the tiny old fortified settlement was transformed by a deluge of splendid new mansions and churches, docks and harbours. Frustrated with the turbulent burghers of Ghent and Bruges, the emperor Maximilian and his successor **Charles V** patronized Antwerp, underwriting its success as the leading port of their expanding empire.

Antwerp's golden age lasted for less than a hundred years, prematurely stifled by Charles V's son **Philip II**, who inherited the Spanish part of the empire and the Low Countries in 1555. Fanatically Catholic, Philip viewed the Reformist stirrings of his Flemish-speaking subjects with horror, encouraging the Inquisition to send thousands to the gallows. Antwerp seethed with discontent, and its population was swollen by religious refugees. The spark was the Ommegang of August 18, 1566, when priests carted the image of the Virgin through the city's streets, insisting that all should bend the knee as it passed. The parade was peaceful enough, but afterwards, with the battle cry of "Long live the beggars", the Protestant guildsmen of Antwerp smashed the inside of the cathedral to pieces – the most extreme example of the **"iconoclastic fury"** that swept the region. Philip responded by sending in an army of occupation, intended to overawe and intimidate from a brand new citadel on the south side of town. Nine years later, it was this same garrison that sat unpaid and underfed in its fortress, surrounded by the wealth of the "heretical" city. Philip's mercenaries mutinied, and at dawn on November 4 1576, they stormed Antwerp, running riot for three long days, plundering Antwerp's public buildings and private mansions, and slaughtering some eight thousand of its citizens in the "**Spanish fury**". It was a catastrophe that finished the city's commercial supremacy, and more disasters were to follow. Philip's soldiers were driven out after the massacre, but they were back in 1585 laying siege outside the city walls for seven months, their success leading to Antwerp's ultimate incorporation within the **Spanish Netherlands**. Under the terms of the capitulation, Protestants had two years to leave town, and a flood of skilled workers poured north to the relative safety of Holland, further weakening the city's economy.

In the early seventeenth century there was a modest recovery, but the Dutch, who were now free of Spain, controlled the seaways of the Scheldt and were determined that no neighbouring Catholic port would threaten their trade. In 1648, under the **Peace of Westphalia** which finally wrapped up the Thirty Years' War, they closed the river to all non-Dutch shipping. Antwerp was ruined, and remained so until the French arrived in 1797 – **Napoleon** declaring it to be "little better than a heap of ruins...scarcely like a European city". The French rebuilt the docks and revived the city, and Antwerp later became independent Belgium's largest port, a role that made it a prime target during both World Wars. In 1914, the invading German army overran the city's outer defences with surprising ease, forcing the Belgian government – which had moved here from Brussels a few weeks before – into a second hasty evacuation along with Winston Churchill and the Royal Marines, who had only just arrived. During **World War II** Antwerp was bombed by both sides, but the worst damage was inflicted after the Liberation when the city was hit by hundreds of Hitler's V1 and V2 rockets. After the war, Antwerp quickly picked up the pieces, becoming one of Europe's major seaports and – more recently – a focus for those Flemish looking for greater independence within (or without) a federal Belgium: the right-wing, nationalist Vlaams Blok (Flemish block) is now a major force in municipal politics. More positively, Antwerp has produced a string of innovative fashion designers, beginning with Olivier Strelli through to the so-called "Antwerp Six", graduates of Antwerp's Kunstakademie in the 1980s and including such figures as Martin Margiela and Dries van Noten. Look out for their clothes at branches of Stijl.

Arrival, information and city transport

Antwerp has two main **train stations**, Berchem and Centraal. A few domestic and international trains pause at Berchem, 4km southeast of downtown, before bypassing Centraal, but the vast majority call at both. Centraal is much the more convenient for the centre, lying about 2km east of the main square, the Grote Markt. If you do have to change, connections between the two stations are frequent and fast (10 hourly; 4min). Inside the **Centraal Station** complex, a Belgian Railways **information office** (daily Mon–Sat 8am–8pm, Sun 9am–5pm) has international and domestic timetables, along with details of special bargains and fares. Most long-distance **buses** arrive at the bus station on Franklin Rooseveltplaats, a five-minute walk northwest of Centraal Station. The **information kiosk** here deals with bus services throughout the province of Antwerp.

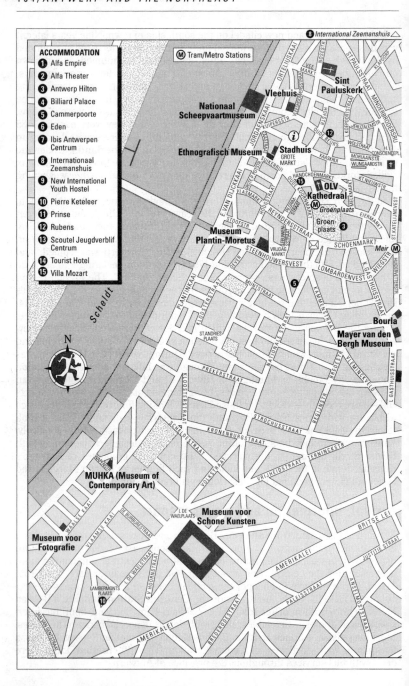

ACCOMMODATION
1. Alfa Empire
2. Alfa Theater
3. Antwerp Hilton
4. Billiard Palace
5. Cammerpoorte
6. Eden
7. Ibis Antwerpen Centrum
8. Internationaal Zeemanshuis
9. New International Youth Hostel
10. Pierre Keteleer
11. Prinse
12. Rubens
13. Scoutel Jeugdverblijf Centrum
14. Tourist Hotel
15. Villa Mozart

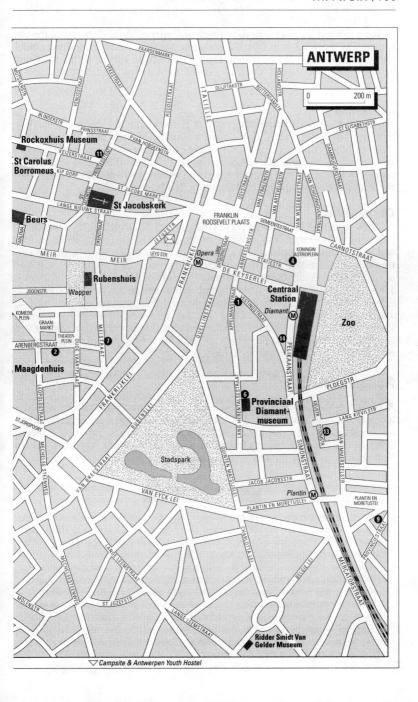

ANTWERP

0   200 m

Rockoxhuis Museum
St Carolus Borromeus
St Jacobskerk
Beurs
Rubenshuis
Wapper
Maagdenhuis
Opera
Centraal Station
Diamant
Zoo
Provinciaal Diamant-museum
Stadspark
Plantin
Ridder Smidt Van Gelder Museum

▽ Campsite & Antwerpen Youth Hostel

Antwerp's tiny **airport** is in the suburb of **Deurne**, about 6km east of the city centre. City bus #16 leaves from the main road straight ahead of the airport building (every 20–30min Mon–Fri 7am–11pm plus a limited service on the weekend) for Pelikaanstraat, beside Centraal Station in Antwerp. Failing that, taxis to Antwerp Centraal cost about F600.

Information

The **tourist office** is in the city centre at Grote Markt 15 (Mon–Sat 9am–6pm, Sun 9am–5pm; ☎03/232 01 03; Web site: *www.dma.be*), and has a comprehensive range of information on the city and its sights, including maps, an accommodation booklet, a transit map, and a number of specialist leaflets (F30 each) – principally a suggested driving route round the port and walking tours detailing where to see the works of Rubens and his contemporary, Jacob Jordaens.

City transport

A useful **tram** and **bus** system serves the city and its suburbs from a number of points around Centraal Station, with bus stops concentrated along Pelikaanstraat and in Koningin Astridplein. Tram services from Centraal Station to the city centre (#2 or #15 direction Linkeroever) go underground: for the city centre, get off at Groenplaats. A city transport **information office** (Mon–Fri 8am–12.30pm & 1.30–4pm), in the Diamant underground station beside Antwerp Centraal, sells tickets and has both simplified (free) and detailed (F60) maps of the city transport system (the *Netplan*). A standard one-way fare costs F40 and a ten-strip Rittenkaart F290, while a 24-hour unlimited city-wide travel card, a Dagpas, will cost you F110. Single tickets – which are valid for one hour – and the Dagpas are also available from tram and bus drivers.

Accommodation

Antwerp has the range of **hotels** you'd expect of Belgium's second city, as well as a number of both unofficial and official youth **hostels** and a small cache of bed-and-breakfasts. Consequently, finding accommodation is rarely a difficulty although there are surprisingly few places to stay in the centre, which is by far the best spot to soak up the city's atmosphere. Many medium-priced and budget

---

BOAT TRIPS

A variety of **boat trips** explore the Antwerp area. Cruises down the **Scheldt** leave from the landing at the end of Suikerrui (May–Sept 1–5 a day, Tues, Thurs–Sun; 90min; F300). There are also tours of the **port** (May–Aug Tues, Thurs–Sun at 2.30pm; April & Sept Sun only at 2.30pm; 180min; F450), leaving from Kaai (quay) 13 by Londenbrug, which is situated about 2km north of the city centre close to the end of Italielei boulevard – where you should turn left. Between May and September, a special bus runs from the west end of Suikerrui to connect with Kaai 13 sailings.

Further information, including details of extra (but very occasional) summer-season, day-long cruises to other parts of Flanders – for instance Ostend and Zeebrugge – can be had from the tourist office or the operators themselves, *Flandria*, whose offices are located at the west end of Suikerrui (May–Sept Tues, Thurs–Sun 9am–5pm; ☎03/231 31 00).

places are clustered in the scruffy area around Centraal Station, where you should exercise caution at night, particularly if travelling alone.

The tourist office has a comprehensive accommodation list and will make bookings on your behalf at no cost, charging only a modest deposit that is subtracted from your final bill. Their list covers all grades of accommodation, from dormitory-style beds to executive suites, but excludes the dodgier establishments. It's not that they're particularly dangerous – just sometimes unpleasantly seedy.

Hotels and B&Bs

Alfa Empire, Appelmansstraat 31 (☎03/231 47 55, fax 233 40 60). Enormous, sumptuous and well-equipped rooms in this four-star hotel close to Centraal Station. Weekend discounts bring the cost of a double down by about F1000. ⑦.

Alfa Theater, Arenbergstraat 30 (☎03/231 17 20, fax 233 88 58). Luxurious, four-star hotel in a wealthy part of town, just five minutes' walk south of the Rubenshuis. Commodious, appealing rooms. ⑨.

Antwerp Hilton, Groenplaats (☎03/204 12 12, fax 204 12 13). Big and tastelessly flashy hotel right in the city centre. Every facility, from a sauna and gym through to a hairdressers and piano bar. ⑨.

Billiard Palace, Koningin Astridplein 40 (☎03/233 44 55, fax 226 14 26). Grim, seedy but inexpensive hotel in the station area with doubles, triples and quadruple rooms. ③.

Cammerpoorte, Nationalestraat 38 (☎03/231 97 36, fax 226 29 68). Modern, one-star hotel with 39 frugal rooms in a building that looks a bit like a car park. The hotel has a forlorn air, but it is reasonably priced and has a handy location, just five minutes' walk south of Groenplaats. ⑥.

Eden, Lange Herentalsestraat 25 (☎03/233 06 08, fax 233 12 28). Standard-issue, medium-sized, three-star hotel in the diamond district near the station. The modern rooms are perfectly adequate but quite plain – and in the mosquito season stand by for attack. The breakfasts are very good. ⑥.

Ibis Antwerpen Centrum, Meistraat 39 (☎03/231 88 30, fax 234 29 21). Relatively inexpensive chain hotel with routine modern rooms hidden away behind a particularly ghastly concrete exterior but compensated by a decent location, close to the Rubenshuis. ⑤.

Pierre Keteleer, Edward Pecherstraat 37 (☎03/238 39 88). Among a handful of reasonably central B&Bs, this is the most distinctive – just three bedrooms in a delightful Art Nouveau town house near the Museum voor Schone Kunsten, about twenty minutes' walk south from the Groenplaats, or tram #8. ②.

Prinse, Keizerstraat 63 (☎03/226 40 50, fax 225 11 48). Smart if slightly characterless hotel whose modern furnishings and fittings occupy a big old house with its own courtyard. Good, quiet central location – only five minutes' walk north of the Rubenshuis. ⑦.

Rubens, Oude Beurs 29 (☎03/222 48 48, fax 225 19 40). Probably the best hotel in town, the *Rubens* occupies a handy downtown location just a couple of minutes' walk north of the Grote Markt. It's a small hotel (36 rooms) with a relaxing air, and the modern rooms are both comfortable and attractively furnished. ⑦.

Tourist Hotel, Pelikaanstraat 20 (☎03/232 58 70, fax 231 67 07). An inexpensive if rather uninspiring option near Centraal Station – OK for a night or two, though Pelikaanstraat can be noisy. Straightforward, modern rooms. ④.

Villa Mozart, Handschoenmarkt 3 (☎03/231 30 31, fax 231 56 85). Plush hotel with a great if noisy location opposite the cathedral. Each of the hotel's 25 rooms is pleasantly decorated. The rate is F6400 for a double including breakfast, but there are reductions of up to 30 percent at the weekend. Owned by the *Best Western* hotel group. ⑨.

Hostels

Antwerpen Youth Hostel, Eric Sasselaan 2 (☎03/238 02 73, fax 248 19 32). HI-affiliated hostel close to the ring road about 5km south of the centre, with around 130 beds in four-, six- and eight-bedded rooms. Breakfast is included in the overnight fee of F385 per person.

There's a canteen serving lunch and dinner, and there are also self-catering facilities and a laundry room. Tram #2 from Centraal Station, direction Hoboken. ①.

Internationaal Zeemanshuis (Seamen's House), Falconrui 21 (☎03/227 54 33, fax 234 26 03). Accommodation in spartan doubles mostly with shared toilets a ten-minute walk north of the Grote Markt. Despite the name, it's open to landlubbers and women as well as mariners. ③.

New International Youth Hotel, Provinciestraat 256 (☎03/230 05 22, fax 281 09 33). Inexpensive beds in dorms accommodating up to eight people, and bargain doubles, some en suite, just a ten-minute walk from Centraal Station. To get here head south down Pelikaanstraat, turn left along Plantin en Moretuslei, and take the third right. Breakfast is included. Dorms ①, rooms ②.

Scoutel Jeugdverblifcentrum, Stoomstraat 3 (☎03/226 46 06, fax 232 63 92). Spick and span hostel-cum-hotel offering frugal but perfectly adequate doubles and triples with breakfast. It's situated about five minutes' walk from Centraal Station: head south down Pelikaanstraat, turn left along Lange Kievitstraat, go through the tunnel and it's the first road on the right. There's no curfew (guests have their own keys), but be sure to check in before 6pm when reception closes. Reservations are advised in the summer. ② for under-25s, ③ for over-25s.

Campsite

Vogelzang, on Vogelzanglaan behind the Bouwcentrum (☎03/238 57 17, fax 216 91 17). Antwerp's closest campsite is situated about 6km south of the city centre, near the R1 motorway (Exit 5). It's also reachable by way of tram #2 from Centraal Station, direction Hoboken. Open April–Sept.

The city centre

The centre of Antwerp is the **Grote Markt**, at the heart of which stands the **Brabo Fountain**, a haphazard pile of roughly sculpted rocks surmounted by a bronze of Silvius Brabo, depicted flinging the hand of the prostrate giant Antigonus into the Scheldt. Legend asserts that Antigonus extracted tolls from all passing ships, cutting off the hands of those who refused to pay. He was eventually beaten by the valiant Brabo, who tore off his hand and threw it into the river, giving the city its name, which literally means "hand-throw". There are more realistic explanations of the city's name, but this is the most colourful, and it certainly reflects Antwerp's early success at freeing the river from the innumerable taxes levied on shipping by local landowners.

The north side of the Grote Markt is lined with daintily restored **guildhouses**, their sixteenth-century facades decorated with appropriate reliefs and topped by finely cast gilded figures basking in the afterglow of the city's Renaissance lustre. No. 7, the House of the Crossbowmen, with its figures of St George and the dragon, is the tallest and most distinctive, and it stands next to the Coopers' House, with its barrel motifs and statue of St Matthew. They are, however, overshadowed by the **Stadhuis**, completed in 1566 to an innovative design by Cornelis Floris (guided tours on Mon, Tues, Wed & Fri at 11am, 2pm & 3pm, Sat

If you're intending to visit several museums and churches, you can save money with a **combination ticket**, which gives entry to three sights for F200, and is available from all municipal museums; it's valid for a week. For longer stays, it may be worth investing in an **annual ticket**, which covers entry to the majority of sights and lasts for one year; this costs F500. Note that the Museum voor Schone Kunsten (see p.207) is not part of the scheme.

2pm & 3pm; F30) – though there have been several subsequent modifications. The building's pagoda-like roof gives it a faintly Oriental appearance, but apart from the central gable it's quite plain, with a long pilastered facade of short and rather shallow Doric and Ionic columns. These, along with the windows, lend a simple elegance, in contrast to the purely decorative gable (there's no roof behind it). The niches at the top contribute to the self-congratulatory aspect of the building, with statues of *Justice* and *Wisdom* proclaiming virtues the city burghers reckoned they had in plenty.

The **main entrance** is on the Suikerrui. Inside, the staircase of the lofty main hall used to be an open courtyard and was only covered in the late nineteenth century, accounting for the monumental gallery on all four sides. The paintings that have taken the place of the windows represent aspects of commerce and the arts – a balance of which Antwerp has long been aware, and is now anxious to preserve. Among the other rooms you can see are the Leys Room, named after Baron Hendrik Leys, who painted the frescoes in the 1860s, and the Wedding Room, which has a chimneypiece from the original interior, decorated with two splendid alabaster caryatids by Floris himself, who doubled as a master sculptor.

The Onze Lieve Vrouwekathedraal

Leaving the Grote Markt by its southeast corner, the triangular **Handschoenmarkt** (the old glove market) is framed by an attractive ensemble of antique gables, while its tiny stone well, adorned by a graceful iron canopy, bears the legend "It was love connubial taught the smith to paint" – a reference to the fifteenth-century painter Quentin Matsys, who learned his craft in order to successfully woo the daughter of a local artist: at the time marriage was strongly discouraged between families of different guilds. The Handschoenmarkt is the most westerly of a sequence of somewhat confusing pedestrianized squares that occupy the area around the **Onze Lieve Vrouwekathedraal** (Mon–Fri 10am–5pm, Sat 10am–3pm, Sun 1–4pm; F70 including diagrammatic leaflet), one of the finest Gothic churches in Belgium, mostly the work of Jan and Pieter Appelmans in the middle of the fifteenth century. A forceful and self-confident structure, the cathedral dominated the skyline of medieval Antwerp with a graceful spire that was finally completed in 1518. Long a source of fascination to travellers, William Beckford, fresh from spending millions on his own house Fonthill Abbey in Wiltshire at the start of the nineteenth century, was still impressed enough to write that he "longed to ascend it that instant, to stretch myself out upon its summit and calculate, from so sublime an elevation, the influence of the planets". What's more, the building is in better shape than it's been for centuries after a sensitive 25-year restoration.

The seven-aisled **nave** is breathtaking, if only because of its sense of space, an impression that's reinforced by the bright, light stonework revealed by the refurbishment. A fire of 1533, the Iconoclastic Fury of 1566, and the fact that the church briefly became Protestant later that century, have ensured that no Gothic decoration remains, so what you see today are a number of subsequent Baroque embellishments, notably four early paintings by **Rubens**. Of these, the *Descent from the Cross*, just to the right of the central crossing, is without doubt the most beautiful, a triptych painted after the artist's return from Italy in 1612 that displays an uncharacteristically moving realism, derived from Caravaggio. Christ languishes in the centre in glowing white, surrounded by mourners or figures tenderly struggling to lower him. As was normal practice at the time, students in

Rubens' studio worked on the painting, among them the young van Dyck, who completed the face of the Virgin and the arm of Mary Magdalen. His work was so masterful that Rubens is supposed to have declared it an improvement on his own, though this story appears to originate from van Dyck himself. Oddly enough, the painting was commissioned by the guild of arquebusiers, who asked for a picture of St Christopher, their patron saint; Rubens' painting was not at all what they had in mind, and they promptly threatened him with legal action unless he added a picture of the saint to the wings. Rubens obliged, painting in the muscular giant who now dominates the outside of the left panel.

A second Rubens painting, the *Assumption*, hangs over the high altar, a swirling Baroque scene, full of cherubs and luxuriant drapery, painted in 1625, while, on the left-hand side of the central crossing, *The Raising of the Cross* is a grandiloquent canvas full of muscular soldiers and saints; this triptych was painted in 1610, which makes it the earliest of the four. On the right-hand side of the ambulatory in the second chapel along, there's the cathedral's fourth and final Rubens, the *Resurrection*, painted in 1612 for the tomb of his friend, the printer Jan Moretus, showing a strident, militaristic Christ carrying a red, furled banner. Among the cathedral's many other paintings, the only highlight is Maarten de Vos's *Marriage at Cana*, hung opposite the *Descent from the Cross*, a typically mannered work completed towards the end of the artist's long life in 1597.

Groenplaats, Vrijdagmarkt and the Museum Plantin-Moretus

Behind the cathedral is the **Groenplaats**, an expansive open square that was once the town graveyard and now holds an uninspired statue of Rubens, as well as the overblown *Hilton Hotel*. From here, it takes a couple of minutes to thread your way west to **Vrijdagmarkt**, an appealing little square in the middle of an old working-class district. It's also the site of the **Museum Plantin-Moretus** (Tues–Sun 10am–4.45pm; F100), housed in the old mansion of the printer Christopher Plantin, who rose to fame and fortune in the second half of the sixteenth century. Born in Tours in 1514, Plantin moved to Antwerp when he was 34 to set up a small bookbinding business, but in 1555 he was forced to give up all heavy work when, in a case of mistaken identity, he was wounded by revellers returning from carnival. Paid to keep quiet about his injuries, Plantin used the money to start a printing business. He was phenomenally successful, his fortune assured when Philip II granted him the monopoly of printing missals and breviaries for the whole of the Spanish Empire. On Plantin's death, the business passed to his talented son-in-law, Jan Moerentorf, a close friend of Rubens, who Latinized his name, in accordance with the fashion of the day, to Moretus. The family donated their mansion to the city in 1876.

From the **entrance**, a clearly labelled route takes visitors through most of the rooms of the house, which is set around a compact central courtyard. The mansion is worth seeing in itself, and the museum as a whole provides a marvellous insight into how Plantin and his offspring conducted their business; a detailed guidebook is on sale at reception. Museum highlights include several well-preserved pictorial tapestries in Rooms 1 and 6, while in Room 4 there's a delightful seventeenth-century bookshop, equipped with a list of prohibited books, the Librorum Prohibitorum, along with a money-balance to help identify clipped and debased coins. Moving on, Room 11 has a fine portrait of *Seneca* by Rubens and Room 14 houses the old print workshop, with seven ancient presses. In Room 16, among several examples of the work of Christopher Plantin, look out for the *Biblia Polyglotta*, an annotated, five-language text produced on vellum for King Philip II in 1572. Throughout the museum there are scores of intriguing, precise woodcuts and copper plates, representing the best of an enormous number used by several centuries of print workers. In particular, look out for the superbly crafted sample prepared for the publication of a seventeenth-century naturalist book in Room 18. Concentrated in Room 19 are sketches by Rubens, who occasionally worked for the family as an illustrator, while Room 24 boasts a rare copy of the Gutenberg Bible.

Down to the waterfront and the National Maritime Museum

Heading east across Vrijdagmarkt from the museum, turn left down Leeuwenstraat and left again, and the first turn on the right is **Pelgrimstraat**, which provides one of the best views of the Onze Lieve Vrouwekathedraal, with a sliver of sloping, uneven roofs set against the majestic lines of the spire behind. At no. 15, a restored sixteenth-century merchant's house, **De Pelgrom**, has been converted into a tavern and upstairs is a tiny, privately-owned museum decked out with period bric-a-brac (Sat & Sun noon–7pm; F100). On the same street, by no. 6, an ancient alley called **Vlaaikensgang** (Pie Lane) twists its way down to **Oude Koornmarkt**, a surviving fragment of the honeycomb of narrow streets that made up medieval Antwerp. From the end of the alley, Oude Koornmarkt and subsequently Suikerrui lead west to the banks of the Scheldt, clearly separated from the town since Napoleon razed the riverside slums and constructed proper wharves in the early 1800s. Jutting out into the river at the end of Suikerrui is a big and formal **belvedere**, where the Belgian middle classes once took the air, looking out over the river, its barges and boats before taking the ferry from the jetty next door. The river ferry is long gone – several roads now run under the Scheldt – and there's precious little to gaze at today except the belvedere itself, which can't help but seem a little dejected.

A few metres north along the riverfront, the scant remains of the Steen fortress are approached past a statue of the giant **Lange Wapper**, a somewhat dubious local folklore figure – part practical joker, part Peeping Tom – who, as well as being fond of children, exploited his height by spying into people's bedrooms. The **Steen** marks the site of the ninth-century castle from which the rest of the town spread, later the location of an impressive medieval stronghold, successively reinforced and remodelled to keep the turbulent guildsmen of Antwerp in check. The gatehouse and front section are all that have survived, and today they house the **Nationaal Scheepvaartmuseum** (National Maritime Museum; Tues–Sun 10am–4.45pm; F100), whose cramped rooms hold exhibits illustrating a whole range of shipping activity from inland navigation to life on the waterfront and shipbuilding. Clearly laid out and labelled, with multilingual details on all the major displays, the museum is a delight, an appealing mixture of the personal and the public. The high points include a charming British scrimshaw engraved on a whale bone in Room 1, a fascinating fifth-century nautical totem in the form of a snake's head in Room 3, and several fine model ships in Rooms 6 and 9. You should also look out for a model of the Italianate barge that was built for Napoleon's second visit to Antwerp, and peek into the old council chamber, decorated by two large paintings of the city's harbour in the seventeenth century. Behind the Steen, the museum has an open-air section with a long line of tugs and barges parked under a rickety corrugated roof.

The Vleeshuis

Opposite the Steen across Jordaenskaai, filling out the end of narrow Vleeshuisstraat, are the tall, turreted gables of the **Vleeshuis** (Tues–Sun 10am–4.45pm; F100), built for the guild of butchers in 1503. This strikingly attractive building, with its alternating layers of red brick and stonework resembling rashers of bacon, was once the suitably grand headquarters of one of the most powerful of the medieval guilds. It was here in 1585, with the Spanish army approaching, that the butchers made the fateful decision to oppose the opening of the dykes along the Scheldt – a defensive ploy strongly recommended by William the Silent because it would have made it impossible for the Spaniards to mount a blockade of the river from its banks. However, the butchers were more worried about the safety of their sheep which grazed the threatened meadows, and so sent a deputation to the city magistrates to object. The magistrates yielded, and the consequences were disastrous – the Spaniards were able to close the Scheldt and force the town to surrender, a defeat that placed Antwerp firmly within the Spanish Netherlands.

Today, the enormous brick halls of the **interior** are used to display a mildly diverting but somewhat incoherent collection of applied arts. The exhibits are labelled exclusively in Flemish, but it's worth asking at reception to see if they've produced an English guide. On the ground floor, pride of place goes to the musical instruments, especially the primly decorated clavichords, which come in all sorts of unwieldy shapes and sizes, and the harpischords, some of which were produced locally in the Ruckers workshop in the seventeenth century. Amongst a smattering of medieval woodcarving, the pick is a retable from Averbode Abbey, near Diest, that's stuck right at the back of the hall. This charming triptych features a magnificent high-relief tableau of the "Descent from the Cross" which escapes religious cliché in the fineness of its detail – one onlooker wipes her eyes, another holds Christ's wrist tenderly in her hand.

Pressing on, it's down to the vaulted basement for temporary exhibitions or up a steep, spiralling staircase to the second floor, where there's a selection of military gear, coins, clocks and tapestries, and several period rooms, including the relocated *Raadzaal* (meeting room) of the council of the guild of butchers. Next to the coins is a contemporaneous – and anonymous – painting of the *Spanish Fury* of November 1576. It's a gruesome picture of a gruesome event, with bodies piled high in the streets and the city burning in the background as the Spanish mutineers continue to rob, rape and kill. The massacre was a disaster for Antwerp, but although the savagery of the attack was unusual, mutinies in the Spanish army were not. The Habsburgs often failed to pay their soldiers for years on end and this failure, combined with harsh conditions and seemingly interminable warfare, provoked at least a couple of mutinies every year. Indeed, the practice became so commonplace that it began to develop its own custom and practice, with the *tercio* (army unit) concerned refusing orders but keeping military discipline and electing representatives to haggle a financial deal with the army authorities. A deal was usually reached and punishments were unusual.

Sint Pauluskerk and the Falconplein

The streets around the Vleeshuis – and Sint Pauluskerk (see below) – were badly damaged by wartime bombing, leaving a string of bare, open spaces edged by some of the worst of the city's slums. The whole area is gradually being rebuilt, but progress is slow. Many of the crumbling rows of houses have yet to be restored, though most of the gaps have now been filled by solid modern houses whose pinkish stone facades imitate the style of what went before. Cosy and respectable, these new buildings are in stark contrast to the remaining areas of dilapidation – seedy little streets with sporadic tattoo parlours and bored faces at the windows signifying the start of the **red-light area**, whose centre of gravity is further north on **St Paulusplaats**.

From the Vleeshuis, it's a couple of minutes' walk north along Vleeshouwersstraat to the Veemarkt where an extravagant Baroque portal leads through to **Sint Pauluskerk** (May–Sept daily 2–5pm; free), one of the city's most delightful churches, a dignified late Gothic structure dating from 1517. Built for the Dominicans, the original church was looted by the Calvinists when they expelled the monks in 1578. Restored to their property after the siege of 1585, the Dominicans refashioned Sint Pauluskerk to illustrate the Catholic Church as the only means of salvation – with the choir symbolizing the Church Glorious, and the nave, aisles and transepts the Church Militant. Abiding by their theme, the Dominicans commissioned a series of paintings to line the wall of the north aisle depicting the "Fifteen Mysteries of the Rosary". Dating from 1617, the series has survived intact, a remarkable snapshot of Antwerp's artistic talent with works by the likes of Cornelis De Vos (*Nativity; Presentation at the Temple*), David Teniers the Elder (*Gethsemane*), van Dyck (*The Bearing of the Cross*) and Jordaens (*Crucifixion*). But it is Rubens' contribution – the *Scourging at the Pillar* – which stands out, a brilliant, brutal canvas showing Jesus clad in a blood-spattered loin cloth.

There's more Rubens nearby in the truncated north transept, where the *Adoration of the Shepherds*, an early work of 1609, has a jaunty secular air with a smartly dressed Mary imperiously lifting the Christ's bedsheet to the wonder of the shepherds, while, in the south transept, the same artist's *Disputation on the Nature of the Holy Sacrament*, again completed in 1609, forms part of a grand marble altarpiece sprinkled with frolicking cherubs. The marble was crafted by Pieter Verbruggen the Elder, who was also responsible for the extraordinary woodcarving of the confessionals and stalls on either side of the nave, flashy work of arabesque intricacy decorated with fruit, cherubs, eagles and pious saints. Verbruggen takes some responsibility for the huge and ugly high altar too: he didn't fashion the black and white marble – that was the work of a certain Frans Sterbeeck – but he erected it.

Look out also for *Our Lady of the Rosary*, a polychromed wood, early sixteenth-century figure stuck to the pillar next to the south transept. It's a charming statuette with the Virgin robed in the Spanish manner – it was the Spaniards who introduced dressed figurines to Flemish churches. The two unusual bas-relief medallions to the side of *Our Lady* are just as folksy, telling a Faustian story of a rich woman who is gulled by the devil, shown here as a sort of lion with an extremely long tail. The first panel sees the woman entrapped by the devil's letter, the second shows the good old Dominicans coming to the rescue and the devil being carted off by an angel.

Back outside, in between the gate and the church, lurks another curiosity in the form of the **Calvarieberg**, an artificial grotto of 1697–1747. The grotto clings to the buttresses of the south transept, eerily adorned with statues of Christ and other figures of angels, prophets and saints in a tawdry representation of the Crucifixion and Entombment. Writing in the nineteenth century, the traveller Charles Tennant described it as "exhibiting a more striking instance of religious fanaticism than good taste".

After St Pauluskerk, there's a choice of routes. Heading east then north, it's five minutes' walk along Zwartzustersstraat and Klapdorp to **Falconplein** and **Paardenmarkt**, at the heart of a solid working-class district bordering the docks. A far cry from the tourist trimmings of the Grote Markt, it's here that Slav and Jewish minorities have set up their textile and domestic appliance shops, advertising their goods in Cyrillic script for the benefit of those Russian sailors whose ships are in port. Alternatively, it's a short walk southeast down Zwartzustersstraat and subsequently Minderbroedersrui to the Rockoxhuis Museum, on Keizerstraat.

The Rockoxhuis Museum and Hendrik Conscienceplein

The **Rockoxhuis Museum**, at Keizerstraat 10 (Tues–Sun 10am–5pm; free; English guidebook F20), is housed in the attractively restored seventeenth-century townhouse of Nicolaas Rockox, friend and patron of Rubens. Inside, a sequence of rooms has been crammed with period furnishings and art work, based on an inventory taken after the owner's death in 1640. Nevertheless, it's far from a recreation of Rockox's old home, but rather a museum with a small but highly prized collection. Particular highlights include, in Room 1, a gentle *Holy Virgin and Child* by Quentin Matsys, as well as a *Calvary* by one of his sons, Corneliss, and a *St Christopher Bearing the Christ Child*, a typical work by Quentin's collaborator Joachim Patenier. Born in Dinant in around 1485, Patenier moved to Antwerp where he became the first Flemish painter to emphasize the landscape of his religious scenes at the expense of its figures, which he reduced to compositional elements within wide, sweeping vistas. Room 2 displays two pictures by Rubens: the small and romantic *Virgin in Adoration Before the Sleeping Christ Child*, which depicts the Virgin with the features of Rubens' first wife and has Jesus modelled on his son; and his *Christ on the Cross,* a fascinating oil sketch made in preparation for an altarpiece he never had time to paint. Look out also for *Two Studies of a Man's Head* by van Dyck, striking portraits which the artist recycled in several later and larger commissions.

Room 3 is distinguished by a flashy and fleshy genre painting, *Woman Selling Vegetables* by Joachim Beuckelaer, the sixteenth-century Antwerp artist whose work is seen again in Room 4, this time in the more restrained *Flight into Egypt*, revealing a bustling river bank where – in true Mannerist style – the Holy Family are hard to spot. There's another good illustration of genre painting in Room 5, this time the *Antwerp Fish Market* by Frans Snyders, who sometimes painted in the flowers and fruit on the canvases of his chum Rubens. Finally, in Room 6, Pieter Bruegel the Younger's *Proverbs* is an intriguing folksy work, one of several he did in direct imitation of his father (whose version is in the Staatliche Museum, Berlin), a frenetic mixture of the observed and imagined set in a Flemish village. The meaning of many of the pictured proverbs has been the subject of long debate; unfortunately the museum doesn't provide a caption – see the box opposite for some pointers – but there's little doubt about the meaning of the central image depicting an old man dressed in the blue, hooded cape of the cuckold at the behest of his young wife.

Footsteps away from the western end of Keizerstraat, **Hendrik Conscienceplein** takes its name from a local nineteenth-century novelist, who wrote prolifically on all things Flemish. One of the most agreeable places in central Antwerp, the square is flanked by the church of **St Carolus Borromeus** (Mon & Tues 2–4pm, Wed, Thurs & Fri 10am–noon & 2–4pm, Sat 10am–noon &

BRUEGEL'S PROVERBS

Pieter Bruegel the Younger's *Proverbs* illustrates over a hundred folk sayings. Some of the more diverting are explained below – to help pick them out we've divided the canvas into four squares.

UPPER LEFT
The cakes on the roof represent prosperity.
To fire one arrow after another is to throw good after bad.
The Cross hangs below the orb, which is crapped upon by the fool – it's an upside-down world.
The fool gets the trump card – luck favours the foolish.
The man with toothache behind his ear symbolizes the malingerer.

LOWER LEFT
He bangs his head against the wall – stupidity.
She carries water in one hand, fire in the other – a woman of contradictory opinions.
The pig opens the tap of the barrel – gluttony.
The knight, literally armed to the teeth, ties a bell to the cat – cowardice.
One woman holds the distaff, while the other spins – it takes two to gossip.
The hat on the post, as in to keep a secret "under your hat".
The pig shearer is a symbol of foolishness.

UPPER RIGHT
The opportunist on the tower hangs his cloak according to the wind.
To fall from the ox to the ass is to go from good to bad.
He opens the door with his arse – doesn't know if he is coming or going.
The man with the fan is so miserly he even resents the sun shining on the water.
To have the devil as a confessor – distorted values.

LOWER RIGHT
The imprudent man fills in the well after the cow has drowned.
The poor man cannot reach from one loaf to another.
The dogs fight over a bone – hence bone of contention.
The monk giving Jesus a false beard symbolizes blasphemy.
The man trapped within the globe suggests you have to stoop low to get through life.

3–6.30pm, Sun 9.30am–12.45pm; F20), whose finely contrived facade is claimed to have been based on designs by Rubens. Much of the interior was destroyed by fire at the beginning of the eighteenth century, but to the right of the entrance, the ornate Onze Lieve Vrouwekapel (Chapel of Our Lady) has survived, its streaky, coloured marble, which was a key feature of the original church, serving as a background for a series of tiny pictures on either side of the high altar.

From Hendrik Conscienceplein, walk west to the end of Wijngaardstraat, where a left and then a right turn takes you into the series of tiny squares that front the northern side of the cathedral. Here, the **Het Elfde Gebod** (The Eleventh Commandment) is one of the most unusual bars in the city, jam-packed with a bizarre assortment of kitsch religious statues – see "Bars", p.214.

South of the city centre

South of Groenplaats spread Antwerp's older residential areas, bounded by the Amerikalei and Britselei boulevards, which mark part of the course of a circle of city fortifications finished in the early years of this century. Enormously expensive and supposedly impregnable, the design was a disaster, depending on a series of raised gun emplacements that were sitting targets for the German artillery in September 1914. The Allies had expected Antwerp to hold out for months, but in the event the city surrendered after a two-week siege, forcing Churchill and his party of marines into a hurried evacuation just two days after their arrival.

The Mayer van den Bergh Museum and the Bourla

Five minutes' walk southeast of Groenplaats, the appealing **Mayer van den Bergh Museum**, at Lange Gasthuisstraat 19 (Tues–Sun 10am–4.45pm; F100; English guide F50), comprises the art collection of the Berghs, a wealthy merchant family who gave it to the city in 1920. Very much a connoisseur's collection, there are fine examples of many different branches of applied arts, from tapestries to ceramics, silver, illuminated manuscripts and furniture, all crowded into a reconstruction of a sixteenth-century townhouse. There are also a number of outstanding paintings, including a *Crucifixion* triptych by Quentin Matsys in Room 4, with the unidentified donors painted on the wings alongside a picture of one of the family's patron saints, Mary of Egypt – a repentant prostitute who spent her final years in the desert miraculously sustained by three little loaves.

Room 6 holds an early fourteenth-century carving of *St John Resting on the Breast of Jesus*, and two tiny panels from a fifteenth-century polyptych that once adorned a travelling altar; the panels are beautifully decorated with informal scenes – St Christopher, the patron saint of travellers, crosses a stream full of fish, and Joseph cuts up his socks to use as swaddling clothes for the infant Jesus. The next room holds another picture of *St Christopher*, the work of Jan Mostaert, its bold tones influenced by his long stay in Italy.

Moving on, Room 9 is home to the museum's best-known work, **Pieter Bruegel the Elder**'s *Dulle Griet* or "Mad Meg", one of his most Bosch-like paintings, a misogynistic allegory in which a woman, weighed down with possessions, stalks the gates of hell, a surrealist landscape of monsters and pervasive horror. The title refers to the archetypal shrewish woman, who, according to Flemish proverb, "could plunder in front of hell and remain unscathed". Hanging next to it, the same artist's *Twelve Proverbs* is a less intense vision of the world, a sequence of miniatures illustrating popular Flemish aphorisms.

From the museum, you can either proceed direct to the Maagdenhuis, just down the street (see below), or make a brief detour east along Arenbergstraat to the pleasant pedestrianized streets and squares which flank the **Bourlaschouwburg (Bourla Theatre)**, an elegant nineteenth-century rotunda with a handsomely restored interior. Just beyond, at the end of Arenbergstraat, lurks its modern concrete and steel equivalent, the huge and monstrous **Stadsschouwberg** (municipal theatre).

The Maagdenhuis

The **Maagdenhuis**, at Lange Gasthuisstraat 33 (Mon & Wed–Fri 10am–5pm, Sat & Sun 1–5pm; F100; including English catalogue), was formerly a foundling hospital for children of the poor but is now occupied by the city's social security offices and a small museum. Created in the middle of the sixteenth century, the refuge was strictly run, its complex rules enforced by draconian punishments. At the same time, those children who were left here were fed and taught a skill, and desperate parents felt that they could at least retrieve their children if their circumstances improved. To make sure their offspring could be identified, they were given tokens, usually irregularly cut playing cards or images of saints – one part was left with the child, the other kept by the parent – and there are examples here in the museum. If the city fathers didn't actually encourage this practice, they certainly accepted it, and several municipal buildings even had specially carved alcoves on their facades where foundlings could be left under shelter, certain to be discovered in the morning.

Entrance to the museum is through an ornamental archway decorated with figures representing some of the first girls to be admitted to the hospital depicted inside a tidy classroom, so finely chiselled that you can make out the tiny bookshelves. **Inside**, five ground-floor rooms and a chapel display a varied but modest collection of art. To the right of the entrance, particular highlights in the chapel include a cabinet of foundling tokens (labelled C, D, E), an assembly of some fifty colourful, late medieval porridge bowls (no. 46) – the largest collection of its sort in Belgium – and a sealed certificate confirming the election of Charles V as Holy Roman Emperor in 1519 (no. 49). There's also Jan van Scorel's tiny *Adoration of the Shepherds* (no. 36), in which the finely observed detail so typical of Flemish painting is suffused by Italianate influences, notably the romantic ruin in the background. Scorel, a one-time Vatican employee, was the first Dutch artist of importance to live in Italy and, returning to the Netherlands in 1524, he was largely responsible for introducing the Italian High Renaissance to his fellow artists back home. In the five rooms to the left of the entrance, three paintings are also worth seeking out: at the end of the corridor is *Orphan Girl at Work* by Cornelius de Vos (no. 1), a touching composition with the young woman cheered by the offer of a red carnation, a symbol of fidelity; and in the end room on the right are both van Dyck's mournful *St Jerome* (no. 16) and Jordaens' profound study of Christ in his *Descent from the Cross* (no. 12).

The Museum voor Schone Kunsten

Fifteen minutes' walk southwest of the Maagdenhuis (or tram #8 from Groenplaats), the **Museum voor Schone Kunsten** (Fine Art Museum, Tues–Sun 10am–5pm; F150) occupies an immense Neoclassical edifice built at the end of the last century. Inside, the permanent collection divides into two, with the **upper level** devoted to older pieces, from Flemish Primitives to seventeenth-century masters, while the **lower level** shows relatively modern works. Free plans of the museum are available at reception, and are extremely useful as everything is a little mixed up. The numbered rooms of the lower level mostly display the work of just one or two artists, but the paintings are not really in chronological order, and the same applies in the lettered rooms of the upper level. Here the Primitives are clustered round the entrance in rooms N, Q, S, and T; the larger rooms in the middle concentrate on Rubens and his cronies; and the remainder pick through the sixteenth and seventeenth centuries in haphazard fashion. Note also that arrangements are occasionally disturbed by temporary exhibitions.

On the upper level, the early Flemish section isn't as comprehensive as you might expect from a major museum, but the collection does include two fine, tiny works by Jan van Eyck in Room Q, a florid *Madonna at the Fountain* and a *St Barbara*, where the usual symbol of the saint's imprisonment, a miniature tower held in the palm of her hand, has been replaced by a palm and prayer book, to represent her faith and self-sacrifice. Behind, a full-scale Gothic tower looms over her, a more powerful indication of her confinement. Next door, in Room S, Rogier van der Weyden's *Portrait of Philippe de Croy* blends a dark background into the lines of his subject's cloak, a simple technique to emphasize the shape of the nobleman's angular face and his slender hands, while in Room T the same artist's *Triptych of the Seven Sacraments*, painted for the Bishop of Tournai in 1445, is graced by an inventive frame which merges with the lines of the Gothic architecture inside. Hans Memling's *Portrait of Giovanni de Candida* (Room S) and his *Angels Singing and Playing Instruments* (Room T) are not among his most distinguished works, but they have the finely textured quality for which he is famous. Room N features non-Belgian medieval painters, including Lucas Cranach, the German Protestant and friend of Luther, who is well represented by a sensuous picture of *Eve*. Jean Fouquet, the most influential French painter of the fifteenth century, has one canvas on display here too, a *Madonna and Child* in which remarkable, orange-red latex-like angels surround a chubby Jesus who looks away from a pale, bared breast.

From the early sixteenth century, look out for Quentin Matsys' triptych of the *Lamentation* in **Room R**. Commissioned for the carpenter's chapel in Antwerp's Onze Lieve Vrouwekathedraal, it's a profound and moving work, portraying the Christ, his forehead flecked with blood, surrounded by grieving followers including Mary Magdalen, who tenderly wipes his feet with her hair as tears roll down her face. The panel on the left shows Salome presenting the head of St John the Baptist to Herod, and on the right is the martyrdom of St John the Evangelist, in which the gargoyle-like faces of the men stoking the fire beneath the cauldron are fine illustrations of one of Matsys' favourite ways of representing evil.

In **Room M**, Flemish artists of the late sixteenth and early seventeenth century are represented by Pieter Aertsen and his nephew Joachim Beuckelaer, natives of Amsterdam who specialised in genre paintings – one of the better ones here is the latter's *Vegetable Market*. There's also a modest sample of work by the Bruegel family, notably several characteristic works by Pieter Bruegel the Younger (1564–1638) in which biblical stories are moved to the Flemish countryside – the *Census at Bethlehem* is the most appealing. From the same period, in **Room B**, are several earthy, sometimes raucous scenes of peasant life by Adriaen Brouwer and David Teniers. Born in Flanders, apprenticed to Frans Hals in Haarlem, and very much influenced by Bruegel the Elder, Brouwer bridges the gap between Flemish and Dutch art. When he was imprisoned in 1633, the prison baker, Joos van Craesbeeck, became his pupil, and his pictures are in this room too, often outdoing even Brouwer in their violence.

Works by **Rubens** are grouped together in two rooms, with smaller, preparatory sketches and paintings in **Room C** and a sequence of enormous canvases next door in **Room I**. Among the latter is an inventive *Last Communion of St Francis* (1619), showing a very sick-looking saint equipped with the marks of the stigmata, a faint halo and a half-smile: despite the sorrowful ministrations of his fellow monks, Francis can't wait for salvation. Also from 1619 is *Christ Crucified Between the Two Thieves*, which, with its muscular thieves and belligerent Romans, possesses all the high drama you might expect, but is almost overwhelmed by its central image – you can virtually hear the tearing of Christ's flesh as the soldier's lance sinks into him. From 1624 comes the outstanding *Adoration of the Magi*, a beautifully free and very human work apparently finished by Rubens in a fortnight. No doubt he was helped by his studio, the major figures of which – van Dyck and Jordaens – are represented in several rooms, but especially in **Room H** where you'll spot **Jordaens'** striking *Martydom of St Apollonia*. The painting relates the saint's story: during an anti-Christian riot in third-century Alexandria, Apollonia was seized by the mob, who pulled out her teeth in a vain attempt to make her renounce her faith. Frustrated by her steadfastness, the crowd then built a bonfire and threatened to burn her alive, but Apollonia walked into the flames voluntarily – all in all, a grisly martyrdom for which she is honoured as the patron saint of toothache.

On the lower level, the museum has an extensive collection of **modern Belgian art**, supplemented by a smattering of works by well-known foreign artists. For reasons of space the paintings are regularly rotated, making it difficult to give precise directions. Nonetheless, you should be able to see the work of James Ensor, whose subdued, conservative beginnings, such as *Afternoon at Ostend* (1881), contrast with his piercing later works – like *Intrigue* and *Skeletons Fighting for the Body of a Hanged Man*. Also likely to be on show is the work of Paul Delvaux, his *Red Bow* showing a classical city in the process of disintegration, and of Rik Wouters, whose impressionistic *Woman Ironing* is a sensitive picture of his wife completed in 1914. René Magritte, the Belgian surrealist, is represented by several works, including the macabre *Madame Recamier* and *Storm Cape*. Look out too for Constant Permeke (1886–1952), a leading member of the artistic coterie who first congregated at the village of Sint Martens-Latem near Ghent just before World War I. Dark and broody, Permeke's works are mostly Expressionistic studies of rural Flemish life, his style typified by *The Coffee Drinkers*, *Man with the Vest*, and *The Farmer.*

East of the city centre

From the northeast corner of Groenplaats, Eiermarkt curves round to **Meir**, Antwerp's broad and pedestrianized main shopping street, which connects the centre of town with Centraal Station, some fifteen minutes' walk to the east. At the start of Meir, just beyond its junction with St Katelijnevest, the short Twaalfmaandenstraat ends in the **Beurs**, the recently restored late nineteenth-century stock exchange, built as a rough copy of the medieval original which was burned to the ground in 1868. Used for special events but otherwise dusty and deserted, it's still a splendid extravagance, a high, glass-paned roof supported by spindly iron beams above the coats of arms of the maritime nations, with walls portraying a giant map of the world.

The Rubenshuis

Back on the Meir, it's a five-minute walk east to Wapper, a mundane little square, where the **Rubenshuis** at no. 9 (Tues–Sun 10am–4.45pm; F100) attracts tourists in droves. Rubens lived here for most of his adult life, but the house was only acquired by the town in 1937, by which time it was little more than a shell. Skilfully restored, it opened as a museum in 1946. It's not so much a house as a mansion, splitting into two parts – on the right the classical studio, where Rubens worked and taught, and on the left the traditional, gabled Flemish house; attached to the latter is the art gallery, an Italianate chamber where Rubens entertained the artistic and cultural elite of Europe. He had an enviably successful career, spending the first eight years of the seventeenth century studying the Renaissance masters in Italy, before settling in this house in 1608. Soon after, he painted the Antwerp Onze Lieve Vrouwekathedraal series and his fame spread, both as a painter and diplomat, working for Charles I in England, and receiving commissions from all over Europe.

Unfortunately, there are only a handful of his less distinguished paintings here, and very little to represent the works of those other artists he collected so avidly throughout his life. The restoration of the rooms is convincing, though, and a clearly arrowed tour begins by twisting its way through the neatly panelled and attractively furnished **domestic interiors** of the Flemish half of the house. Beyond, and in contrast to the cramped living quarters, is the elegant **art gallery** which, with its pint-sized sculpture gallery, was where Rubens displayed his favourite pieces to a chosen few, in a scene comparable to that portrayed in Willem van Haecht's *The Gallery of Cornelis van der Geest*, which is on show here. The arrows then direct you on into the classical studio, where a narrow gallery overlooks the **great studio**, equipped with a special high door to allow the largest canvases to be brought in and out with ease. Behind the house, the garden is laid out in the formal style of Rubens' day, as it appears in his *Amid Honeysuckle*, now in Munich. The Baroque portico might also be familiar from the artist's Medici series, on display in the Louvre.

St Jacobskerk

Rubens died in 1640 and was buried in **St Jacobskerk**, just to the north of the Wapper – take Eikenstraat off the Meir and it's at the end on Lange Nieuwstraat (April–Oct Mon–Sat 2–5pm, Nov–March Mon–Sat 9am–noon; F50). Very much the church of the Antwerp nobility, who were interred in its vaults and chapels, the church is a Gothic structure begun in 1491 but not completely finished until 1659. This delay means that much of its Gothic splendour is hidden by an over-decorous Baroque interior, the soaring heights of the nave flattened by heavy marble altars and a huge rood screen. Seven chapels radiate out from the ambulatory, including the **Rubens chapel**, directly behind the high altar, where the artist and his immediate family are buried beneath a tombstone in the floor whose lengthy Latin inscription gives details of his life. The chapel's altar was the gift of Helene Fourment, Rubens' second wife, and shows one of his last works, *Our Lady Surrounded by Saints*, in which he painted himself as St George, his wives as Martha and Mary, and his father as St Jerome. It's as if he knew this was to be his epitaph; indeed, he is said to have asked for his burial chapel to be adorned with nothing more than a painting of the Virgin Mary with Jesus in her arms, encircled by various saints.

The rest of the church is crammed with the chapels and tombs of the rich and powerful, who kept the city's artists busy with a string of commissions destined to hang above their earthly remains. Most are only of moderate interest, but the chapel next to the tomb of Rubens is worth a peek for its clumsily titled *St Charles Borromeo Pleading with the Virgin on Behalf of those Stricken by the Plague*, completed by Jacob Jordaens in 1655. A dark, gaudy canvas, it's not without its ironies: Borromeo, the Archbishop of Milan, was an ardent leader of the Counter Reformation, while the artist was a committed Protestant. In the north aisle of the nave – on the opposite side from the entrance – the third chapel down from the transept holds the remains of members of the Rockox family (see p.204). They are pictured on the side panels of a Jan Sanders' triptych, their demure modesty in stark contrast to the breezy Neoclassicism of a centrepiece which oozes bare flesh (nudity was permitted in the portrayal of classical figures). In the chapel at the far end of the south aisle, look out also for a flamboyant *St George and the Dragon* by van Dyck.

East to Centraal Station

Meir heads east from the Rubenshuis to its junction with Jezusstraat, where the carved figure on the building on the corner honours **Lodewyk van Bercken**, who introduced the skill of diamond-cutting to the city in 1476. From here, Leysstraat, a continuation of Meir, is lined by a sweeping facade ending in a pair of high, turreted gables, whose gilt figures and cupolas formed the impressive main entrance to the nineteenth-century town. Straight ahead, the magnificent neo-Baroque **Centraal Station** was finished in 1905, a medley of spires and balconies, glass domes and classical pillars designed by Louis Delacenserie, who had made his reputation as a restorer of Gothic buildings in Bruges. It's an extraordinary edifice, a well-considered blend of earlier architectural styles and fashions – particularly the Gothic lines of the main body of the building and the ticket hall, which has all the

ANTWERP'S SPECIALIST MUSEUMS

Antwerp has a number of specialist **museums** that are either shrines of arcane interest or good places to shelter on rainy afternoons, depending on your viewpoint. The following is a more or less comprehensive round-up.

Etnografisch Museum, Suikerrui 19 (Tues–Sun 10am–5pm; F75). Ethnographic collections from every part of the globe, with Africa and Melanesia especially well represented.

Middelheim Open-Air Statuary Museum (*Openluchtmuseum voor Beeldhouwkunst Middelheim*), Middelheim Park, Middelheimlaan 61 (Tues–Sun: April & Sept 10am–7pm, May & August 10am–8pm, June & July 10am–9pm; free). A substantial park whose manicured lawns and trees accommodate over 300 sculptures representing all the major schools, particularly Realism, Cubism and Surrealism. There are pieces by notable Belgians, such as Rik Wouters, as well as leading foreign practitioners like Henry Moore, Louise Nevelson and Auguste Rodin. The park is situated 5km south of the centre; take bus #17 from the Franklin Rooseveltplaats station to the stop on Beukenlaan.

Museum voor Hedendaagse Kunst (MUHKA), Leuvenstraat 16–30 (Tues–Sun 10am–5pm; F150). Museum of contemporary art featuring large-scale, ambitious, avant-garde exhibitions: *Anti-art*, *Metalanguage* and the like.

Provinciaal Museum voor Fotografie, Waalse Kaai 47 (Tues–Sun 10am–5pm; free). Mixes displays of all sorts of old photographic equipment with modern exhibitions of different photographic techniques. Labelling and guidebook in Flemish only.

Provinciaal Museum Sterckshof, Hooftvunderlei 160, Deurne (Tues–Sun 10am–5pm; free). Built in 1931 and surrounded by parkland, Sterckshof Castle houses an exhibition on silver, covering everything from mining the ore to the making of jewellery. There's also a substantial collection of antique silver and you can sometimes watch silversmiths at work. Tram #10 makes the 6km trip east from Koningin Astridplein to the top of Hooftvunderlei, about 1.5km from the entrance.

darkened mystery of a medieval church – yet displaying all the self-confidence of the new age of industrial progress. Sadly, the station was also the victim of one of the greatest cock-ups in Belgium: the construction of the underground tram tunnels alongside disturbed the water table, causing the oak pillars that support the station to dry out, and threatening it with collapse. The repairs took years and cost millions of francs, but the building has finally been restored to its full glory.

Immediately behind the station, just off Koningin Astridplein, Antwerp's **zoo** (daily summer 9am–5.30pm, winter 9am–4.30pm; F450) accommodates around four thousand animals, incorporating an aviary and an aquarium.

The diamond district

The discreetly shabby streets just to the southwest of Centraal Station are home to the largest **diamond** market in the world. Behind these indifferent facades precious stones pour in from every continent to be cut or re-cut, polished and sold. There's no show of wealth, no grand bazaar – though a rash of little diamond and gold shops does fringe Pelikaanstraat – and no tax collector could ever keep track of the myriad deals that make the business hum. The diamond trade is largely controlled by Orthodox Jews, many of whom arrived here from Eastern Europe towards the end of the nineteenth century, and whose presence is often the only outward indication that the business exists at all. They make most of their money by acting as middlemen in a chain that starts in South Africa, where eighty percent of the world's diamonds are mined. In what is effectively a form of price-fixing, the rate of production and the speed of distribution are strictly controlled by an all-powerful South African cartel led by the De Beers company, which organizes ten "showings" in London every year. Guests are there by invitation only, and although the quality of the assortment of diamonds in each lot is controlled by the producers, if potential purchasers fail to buy on three consecutive occasions they aren't usually invited again.

In the heart of the diamond district, the bright, modern **Provinciaal Diamantmuseum** at Lange Herentalsestraat 31–33 (daily 10am–5pm; free) – not to be confused with the nearby "Diamond Land" shop at Appelmansstraat 33 – deals with the geology, history, mining and cutting of diamonds in a series of clearly labelled, well-organized displays spread over four floors. The photographs of early prospectors and samples of most of the major types of diamond are of particular interest, but it's all a bit of a public relations job – glossing over, for example, the lucrative trade in stolen gems, mine conditions in South Africa under apartheid, as well as the various dubious price-fixing arrangements that are symptomatic of the trade. Every Saturday (1.30–4.30pm) there are diamond-cutting demonstrations.

Eating and drinking

Antwerp is an enjoyable and inexpensive place to **eat**, full of informal café-restaurants, which excel at combining traditional Flemish techniques and dishes with Mediterranean, French and vegetarian cuisines. There are places serving delicious food all over the city centre, and you don't even pay much of a premium on or around Grote Markt, though this is, of course, the prime tourist area. Several of the best café-restaurants are clustered on Suikerrui and Grote Pieter Potstraat, and there's another concentration in the vicinity of Hendrik Conscienceplein. For **food on the run**, try the kebab and falafel takeaways on Oude Koornmark.

Most **cafés** open earlyish in the morning – by about 9am – till late at night, but those geared up for shoppers and office workers mostly close at 5 or 6pm. Café-restaurants and restaurants are usually open every day of the week from 11am or noon to about 11pm, though some close for a few hours in the afternoon and the smarter establishments sometimes only open in the evening; others have a regular weekly closing day – usually Sunday, Monday or Tuesday. It's not necessary to book at most places, but where it's a good idea we've given the phone number.

Antwerp is also a fine place to **drink**. There are plenty of bars in the city centre, mostly dark and tiny affairs exuding a cheerful vitality. Some of them regularly feature live music, and on sunny evenings the pavement café-bars on Groenplaats and Handschoenmarkt make delightful places to watch the world go by. Opening hours are elastic, with many places only closing when the last customers leave – say 2 or 3am – and, unless otherwise stated in our listings below, all are open daily. The favourite local tipple, incidentally, is De Koninck, drunk in a *bolleke*, or small, stemmed glass. Its only real rival is *jenever*, a type of gin, served in many a city bar.

Cafés and restaurants

Het Dagelijks Brood, Steenhouwersvest 48. Enjoyable and distinctive café where the variety of breads is the main event, served with delicious, wholesome soups and light meals at one long wooden table. No smoking. Daily 7am–7pm.

Did's Bistro, St Jacobstraat 21. This student favourite is an unpretentious bistro-café offering tasty and inexpensive light meals and snacks, including vegetarian choices. A few minutes' walk east of the centre, near St Jacobskerk.

L'Entrepôt du Congo, De Burburestraat 2. Well-known and justifiably popular café-restaurant serving up fresh salads and pastas at inexpensive prices. In the most fashionable part of town – on the corner of Vlaamse Kaai, across from the Museum voor Schone Kunsten.

Facade, Hendrik Conscienceplein 18. Laid-back, funky café with good music and inexpensive vegetarian, meat and fish dishes. Popular with students.

Finjan, Graaf Van Hoornstraat 1. Excellent, and inexpensive, falafel and pitta till 4am in the morning. A short walk southwest of the Museum voor Schone Kunsten along Léopold de Waelstraat.

Hippodroom, Leopold de Waelplaats 10 (☎03/238 89 36), opposite Museum voor Schone Kunsten. Smooth and polished restaurant offering a wide range of Flemish dishes from around F700 per main course. You can eat outside in the garden in summer. Closed Sun.

Hoffy's, Lange Kievitstraat 52 (☎03/234 35 35). Outstanding, traditional Jewish restaurant and takeaway, off Pelikaanstraat, near Centraal Station. Very reasonable prices. Try the *gefillte fisch*.

Hoorn des Overloed, Melkmarkt 1 (☎03/232 83 99). Excellent, unpretentious fish restaurant, good for lunch and dinner; look out for the daily specials. Just east of the cathedral.

Koffiehuis Gulden Swaene, Hendrik Conscienceplein 14. Tiny, inexpensive, student-orientated café with especially tasty and filling soups.

De Matelote, Haarstraat 9. Modish, pastel-painted fish restaurant off Grote Pieter Potstraat, near the Grote Markt. Serving expensive but delicious food.

Metalurgie, Grote Pieter Potstraat 1, off Suikerrui (☎03/232 54 10). Popular café-restaurant with good food and a lively crowd. The decor has post-modernist touches in line with the menus, which are on pieces of steel.

De Peerdestal, Wijngaardstraat 8, just west of Hendrik Conscienceplein (☎03/231 95 03). Medium-range restaurant with an uninspiring menu, but *the* place to try horsemeat.

Pizzeria Da Toni, Grote Markt 6 on the corner of Suikerrui. Tasty and swiftly served pasta and pizza. Very popular and reasonably priced.

Popoff, Oude Koornmarkt 18. The best pies, desserts and gateaux in town served fron noon till 10pm. Closed Mon & Tues.

Quinten Matsys, Oude Koornmarkt 21. Family-run, pastel-painted café serving mouthwatering crêpes. Opposite the south side of the cathedral. Closes at about 6pm and most Sundays.

Satsuma, Wisselstraat 5 (☎03/226 24 43). For something completely different, try this Japanese restaurant located just off the north side of the Grote Markt. Set dinners from around F1200.

De Stoemppot, Vlasmarkt 12 (☎03/231 36 86). *Stoemp* is a traditional Flemish dish consisting of puréed meat and vegetables – and this is the best place to eat it. Closed Wed.

La Terrazza, Wisselstraat 2. High quality, bright and cheerful, moderately priced Italian restaurant down a narrow sidestreet off the north side of Grote Markt.

Bars

Babblebox, Grote Pieter Potstraat 18. Handily situated off Suikerrui, this small and darkly lit bar is an enjoyable place for a drink.

Den Billekletser, Hoogstraat 22. Dog-eared bar with diverse sounds and an off-beat clientele.

De Duifkens, Graanmarkt 5. Located on a pedestrianized square close to the Rubenshuis, this old-style Antwerp café-bar is a favourite haunt of the city's actors.

Het Elfde Gebod, Torfbrug 10. On one of the tiny squares fronting the north side of the cathedral, this long-established bar has become something of a tourist trap, but it's still worth visiting for the kitsch, nineteenth-century religious statues which cram the interior; don't bother with the food.

Den Engel, Grote Markt 3. Handily located, traditional bar with an easy-going atmosphere in a guildhouse on the northwest corner of the main square; attracts a mixture of businesspeople and those seeking respite from the red-light area.

De Faam, Grote Pieter Potstraat 12. Cool, thirtysomething bar in small, sparingly lit premises near the Grote Markt. An eclectic soundtrack – from *chanson* to jazz.

Gaz, Arme Duivelstraat 11. Just behind the Bourla, this fashionable, tiny, downbeat bar – with Kerouac-style habitués – is one of the most fashionable places in town.

De Groote Witte Arend, Reyndersstraat 18. Attractive café-bar in an old mansion set around a courtyard; the mood is made with classical music and softly spoken banter. Closed Tues.

Den Hopsack, Grote Pieter Potstraat 22. Frugal bar with spartan fittings and highbrow conversation but amenable atmosphere.

Kulminator, Vleminckveld 32–34. One of the best beer bars in Antwerp, serving over 500 varieties with a helpful beer menu. It's situated a 5min walk south of the centre – from the foot of Oude Koornmarkt, follow Kammenstraat which leads into Vleminckveld. Closed Sun and 2 weeks in July or Aug.

Café de Muze, Melkmarkt 15. With its bare brick walls and retro film posters, this chic and central little place is lively and popular. It regularly puts on live bands. Close to the cathedral.

Café Pelikaan, on the north side of the cathedral at Melkmarkt 14. There's nothing touristy about the *Pelikaan*, a packed and smoky bar where locals get down to some serious drinking.

't Stamineeke, Vlasmarkt 23. Vibrant downtown bar, in an old, high-gabled building, playing blues with occasional live bands. Sells over 100 different sorts of beer, some of them at high prices. Closed Mon & Tues Oct–March.

De Vagant, Reyndersstraat 21. Specialist gin bar serving an extravagant range of Belgian and Dutch jenevers in comfortable, laid-back surroundings.

De Volle Maan, Oude Koornmarkt 7. Lively, extremely likeable and off-beat bar close to the Stadhuis.

Entertainment and nightlife

Your first stop should be at the tourist office, who produce a useful bi-monthly **Cultural Bulletin**, a free newssheet listing all the major events, exhibitions and concerts alongside practical details of all the venues. They also issue a less detailed, bi-monthly *Antwerp Calendar* as well as an annual *Calendar of Events*. For special club nights, however, and other more off-beat events, keep your eyes peeled for fly posters. The city has several excellent **clubs**, which start to get going near midnight, and is also good for **live music**, especially jazz and blues. The city is on the international circuit for big-name rock/pop artists, who often appear at the the modern performance hall of deSingel, Desguinlei 25 (☎03/248 28 28; Web site *www.dma.be/cultuur*). The major ticket agency is *Ticket Antwerpen*, in the Fnac stores at both Groenplaats 31 and Meir 82.

Antwerp also boasts **orchestra** and **opera** companies with international reputations. De Vlaamse Opera (Flemish Opera) perform at the opera house, Frankrijklei 3 (reservations & information on ☎03/233 66 85), while the Filharmonisch Orkest van Vlaanderen (Flemish Philharmonic Orchestra) is based at the Koningin Elisabethzaal, Koningin Astridplein 26 (☎03/233 84 44). There's no shortage of **theatre** and **cinema** to view.

Live music and clubs

Bar Tabac, Waalse Kaai 43. This stylish, trendy bar-cum-club only gets going about 11pm often with the help of visiting DJs.

Café d'Anvers, Verversrui 15. Youthful, energetic club, billed as a "temple to house music", but perhaps a little too well established to be cutting edge. North of the centre in the red-light district.

Café Hopper, Leopold De Waelstraat 2. Smart and fairly pricey place but providing an excellent and varied programme of live jazz, showcasing some big international names.

De Muze, Melkmarkt 15. Pub-cum-club in the heart of the old town that specializes in jazz.

Kaaiman, Wapenstraat 12. This club is located on the ground floor of a converted warehouse. The DJs focus on techno, free jazz and hip hop. There are also club concert nights with a theme. Jam-packed at the weekend; free admission except on concert nights.

Sloppy Store, Jan van Gentstraat 7. A big, new club with ultra-cool credentials in terms of owners and premises. Almost bound to be trendy – at least for a year or two – and have occasional live sounds. Near the south end of Vlaamse Kaai. Thurs–Sat.

Swingcafé, off the Grote Markt at Suikerrui 13. Long-established bar offering a wide range of sounds – anything from swing to fusion – as well as live acts, mostly jazz and blues, some of which are very good indeed. It's an animated, popular place offering a wide range of beers. Open till midnight.

Zillion, Jan Van Gentstraat 2. Giant disco with moving dance floors in a former sports hall near the south end of Vlaamse Kaai. House and more, plus three smaller areas for musical alternatives and a chill-out room. Open Thurs–Sat and for specials.

Theatre and film

Antwerp has over a dozen first-rate **theatre** troupes performing at locations across the city. Most performances are, of course, in Flemish, but it's worth consulting the *Cultural Bulletin* for English renditions. At the **cinema**, some English-language films are dubbed in Flemish, but most are subtitled. The best downtown cinema is Cartoons, at Kaastraat 4–6, off Suikerrui (☎03/232 96 32), which shows both mainstream and arthouse films. There's also a vast new Gaumont just off De Keyserlei – west of Centraal Station – at Van Ertbornstraat 17 (☎03/206 70 00).

Listings

Airlines KLM, Deurne Airport (☎03/230 86 29); Sabena, Appelmansstraat 12 (☎03/231 68 21).

Airport enquiries ☎03/218 12 11.

Banks and bureaux de change There are plenty of banks in and around the city centre, and there's no problem cashing travellers' cheques at any of them. KB Kredietbank are at Eiermarkt 20, De Keyserlei 1, and Pelikaanstraat 30; BBL are at Lange Gasthuisstraat 14 and De Keyserlei 11. Usual opening hours are Mon–Fri 9am–4pm; outside these, head for the bureaux de change at Centraal Station (daily 9am–9pm) or Grote Markt (daily 9am–8pm).

Bike rental Cyclorent, St Katelijnevest 19 (☎03/226 95 59), hires out bikes. Closed Sun.

Books English books are available from Standaard, Huidevetterstraat 57, and Fnac, Groenplaats 31.

Buses and trams City transport enquiries at the Groenplaats (Mon–Fri 8am–6pm & Sat 9am–noon) and Centraal Station's Diamant (Mon–Fri 8am–12.30pm & 1.30–4pm) underground tram stations. Details of bus services in the province of Antwerp from De Lijn (☎03/218 14 06), or the kiosk on Franklin Rooseveltplaats.

Car rental Avis, Plantin en Moretuslei 62 (☎03/218 94 96); Budget, Ankerrui 20 (☎03/232 35 00) and at the airport (☎03/218 12 82); Europcar, Lombardenvest 24 (☎03/236 29 50).

Consulates and embassies Ireland, Rudolfstraat 40 (☎03/237 69 94); Netherlands, De Keyserlei 55 (☎03/233 20 33); New Zealand, Grote Markt 9 (☎03/233 16 08); Norway, Kilpperstraat 15 (☎03/545 39 51); Sweden, Oude Leeuwenrui 8 (☎03/224 18 30); UK, Korte Klarenstraat 7 (☎03/232 69 40).

Doctors List of 24-hour doctors' surgeries from the tourist office. Also on Saturdays, Sundays & holidays, details of duty doctors are posted on the front door of most pharmacies. Hotel receptions will help too.

Festivals The Festival van Vlaanderen, the Flanders Music Festival, runs from August to October; Jazz Middleheim is a prestigious biennial jazz event on years ending with odd numbers; and Sfinks is an open-air celebration of ethnic music lasting most of July.

Gay scene Antwerp's gay bars are concentrated in the seedy area just to the north of Centraal Station along Van Schoonhovenstraat and Dambruggestraat. Two of the more popular on Van Schoonhovenstraat are *Den Bazaar*, at no. 22, and *Borsalino*, no. 48. Further information from the Gay Switchboard (☎09/223 69 29).

Gin The De Vagant off-licence, opposite the bar of the same name at Reyndersstraat 21, sells a wide range of Dutch and Belgian gins. Mon–Sat 11am–6pm.

Hospital Algemeen Ziekenhuis Sint Elisabeth (St Elizabeth Hospital), Leopoldstraat 26 (☎03/234 4111).

Left luggage Office (daily 4am–midnight) and coin-operated lockers at Centraal Station.

Markets Second-hand goods: Friday mornings on Vrijdagmarkt. General and bric-a-brac, along with flowers, plants and birds: Sat & Sun mornings on Theaterplein. During the summer there are Sat antique and jumble markets on Lijnwaadmarkt, near Onze Lieve Vrouwekathedraal.

Pharmacies Details of 24-hour pharmacies are available from the tourist office. Also, on Sat, Sun & holidays, a duty rota should be posted on the door of all pharmacies. Downtown pharmacies include W. Lotry, Grote Markt 56, and Coppens, Groenplaats 42.

Post office Main office at Groenplaats 43 (Mon–Fri 9am–6pm, Sat 9am–noon).

Taxis There are taxi ranks outside Centraal Station and at the top of Suikerrui, on the edge of the Grote Markt. Antwerp Taxi are on ☎03/238 38 38.

Train enquiries Centraal Station (Mon–Sat 8am–10pm, Sun 9am–5pm; ☎03/204 20 40; nationwide ☎02/555 25 55).

North and east of Antwerp: the Kempen

Filling out the northeast corner of Belgium, just beyond Antwerp, are the flat, sandy moorlands of the **Kempen**. Once a barren wasteland dotted with the poorest of agricultural communities, and punctuated by tracts of acid heath, bog and deciduous woodland, its more hospitable parts were first cultivated and planted with pine by pioneering Cistercian monks in the twelfth century. The monks helped develop and sustain a strong regional identity and dialect, though today the area's towns and villages are drab and suburban, formless modern settlements with little to attract the visitor. The principal exception is **Geel**, with a couple of interesting medieval relics and a strong sense of its own long and unusual history.

Herentals and Geel

Some 20km east of Antwerp, dreary **HERENTALS** became the principal town of the Kempen in the fourteenth century and made a living by transporting fresh water by barge along the River Nete to supply Antwerp's brewers. Like many of the area's towns it was partly industrialized in the late nineteenth century, creating the careless, untidy sprawl that fans out into the surrounding countryside today. The only buildings of any real interest are the towered and turreted **Stadhuis**, a handsome, much-modified medieval structure marooned in the middle of the long and narrow Grote Markt, and the nearby Gothic **St Waldetrudiskerk**, on Kerkstraat, home to an intricate altarpiece carved by Pasquier Borremans in the sixteenth century.

Fourteen kilometres to the east of Herentals, **GEEL** has an international reputation for its treatment of the mentally ill, who have been cared for within the community here for hundreds of years, though the system finally came under orthodox medical control in the middle of the nineteenth century. The system has its origins in the tragedy of Saint Dimpna, a thirteenth-century Irish princess who fled her home and went into hiding near Geel as a result of her father's incestuous advances. The king managed to track her down and beheaded her, an act that could only have been committed, it was felt at the time, by a lunatic, and Dimpna's tomb became a centre of pilgrimage for those seeking a cure for madness. The **St Dimpnakerk** (usually Mon–Fri 9am–4pm, but check with the tourist office – see below), ten minutes' walk east of the Markt along Nieuwstraat, supposedly marks the spot where she was interred, its striped fourteenth-century brickwork home to several fine examples of medieval craftsmanship. These include a typically intricate alabaster and marble mausoleum by Cornelis Floris (the architect of Antwerp's town hall) and several fine retables, one illustrating the Passion, another the story of St Dimpna, carved with extraordinary attention to detail in the sixteenth century.

A ten-minute walk south from the train station along Stationsstraat, Geel **tourist office** (Mon–Fri 9am–noon & 1–3.30pm, Sat 9am–1pm; ☎014/58 29 09), in the town centre at Markt 1, will advise of any changes to the normal opening hours of St Dimpnakerk and, in the unlikely event you decide to stay, has a small cache of private **rooms** (③), which they'll book for you at no charge. As far as **eating** goes, there are several perfectly adequate cafés on the Markt – the *Taverne Toerist*, at no. 93, is as good as any.

Tongerlo Abbey

From Geel bus station, it takes just fifteen minutes for a local bus (every 30min) to make the 5km trip south to a bus stop that's a short walk from the low brown buildings of **Tongerlo Abbey**, a large complex on the edge of the village which took its name. Founded in 1130, the abbey played a key role in the district's agricultural development until it was forcibly dissolved by the French in 1796. Reestablished in 1840, it has become a flourishing farmstead once again, a hive of activity where the **Da Vincimuseum** (May–Sept Mon–Thurs & Sat–Sun 2–5pm; F50) houses a copy of the great man's *Last Supper* by his pupil Andrea del Solario.

South of Antwerp

Southwest of the city of Antwerp, the meandering course of the Scheldt defines the western boundary of the province of Antwerp, whereas its southern border with Brabant follows no geographical feature – it's just a line on the map. Crisscrossed by rivers and canals, this portion of Antwerp province is a densely populated area whose inhabitants occupy a string of industrial settlements dotted around two ancient and intriguing towns – **Mechelen** and **Lier**, each of which has several outstanding medieval buildings. Both are ideal for a day-trip.

Lier

Just 17km southeast of Antwerp, likeable **LIER** has a comfortable, small-town air. The town was founded in the eighth century and has always lived in the shadow of its larger neighbour Antwerp, though Felix Timmermans, one of Belgium's best-known Flemish writers, did add a certain sparkle when he lived here from 1886 to 1947. The sparkle may have been needed – other Belgians once referred to Lier's citizens as "sheepheads", a reference to their reputation for stubbornness and stupidity.

The Town

Central Lier spreads out from a large, rectangular **Grote Markt**, encircled and bisected by waterways that mark the course of its old harbours and moats. At the centre of the Grote Markt is the turreted fourteenth-century **Belfort**, an attractively spikey affair incongruously attached to the classically elegant **Stadhuis**, which was built to replace the medieval cloth hall in 1740. Otherwise, the square is without much architectural distinction, though it's a pleasant enough spot and close by, just off its northwest corner, is an enjoyable art gallery, the **Stedelijk Museum Wuyts**, at Florent Van Cauwenberghstraat 14 (April–Oct Tues–Thurs & Sat–Sun 10am–noon & 1.30–5.30pm; F40, combined ticket with Timmermans-Opsomerhuis – see below – F60). For a small town, the collection of paintings is surprisingly varied and includes several works by David Teniers the Younger, who made a small fortune from his realistically earthy peasant scenes, as represented by *The Jealous Wife* and *The Village of Perk*. There's also a cruelly drawn *Brawling Peasants* by Jan Steen and a pious portrait of *St Theresa* by Rubens, as well as several works by two of the Bruegels – Jan and Pieter the Younger. The most distinguished Bruegel is Pieter's *Flemish Proverbs* (*Vlaamse Spreekworden*), illustrating over eighty proverbs satirizing every vice and foolery imaginable. There are explanations below each picture in Flemish, but many – like the man pissing against the moon – speak for themselves. There's also a laughable, pseudo-religious painting by local artist Isidore Opsomer (see below) entitled *Christ Preaches to Lier*.

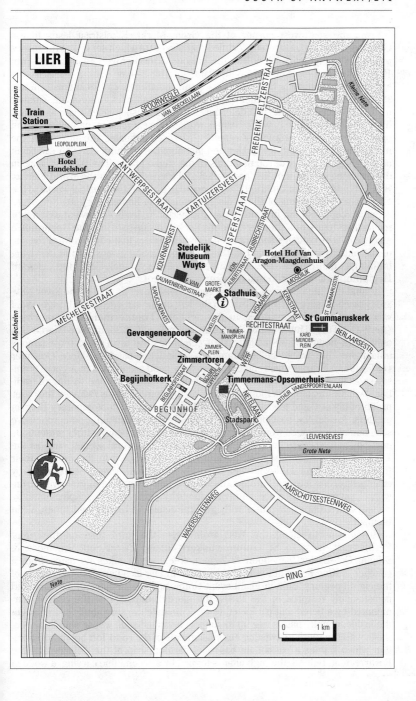

From the southwest corner of the Grote Markt, Eikelstraat leads to the **Gevangenenpoort**, a strongly fortified medieval gate which served as the town's prison for many years. Opposite, the curious **Zimmertoren** (daily: April–Sept 10am–noon & 1–6pm; Oct–March 10am–noon & 2–4 or 5pm; F60) is an old section of the ramparts that now houses the remarkable clocks and astronomic studio of one Lodewijk Zimmer (1888–1970). A wealthy city merchant, Zimmer made his clocks and dials in a determined effort to dispel superstition and show his fellow townspeople how the cosmos worked. An exercise in mathematical and pictorial precision, Zimmer's *Centenary Clock* co-ordinates the phases of the moon, the zodiac, the tides of Lier and just about everything else you can think of, with a similar bevy of rotating dials in the studio above. The *Wonder Clock*, in the adjoining **pavilion**, is just as detailed and was exhibited at the World Fairs of Brussels and New York in the 1930s. A guide explaining the internal works of the clocks and the meaning of all the dials is available in English for F50.

Schapekoppenstraat, in front of the Zimmertoren, leads southwest past a wry modern sculpture of a shepherd and his flock to a side-gate into the **Begijnhof**, a mixture of cosy cottages and cramped terraced houses that edges toward the site of the old city walls. Founded in the thirteenth century, most of the surviving buildings date from the seventeenth century, including the elegant **Begijnhofkerk** (Easter to mid-Oct Sun 2–5pm; free).

Behind the Zimmertoren, a narrow road crosses over an arm of the River Nete as it gracefully slices Lier into two. To the left, on the far side of the bridge, **Werf** was once the main city dock; to the right the **Timmermans-Opsomerhuis** (April–Oct Tues–Thurs, Sat & Sun 10am–noon & 1.30–5.30pm; Nov–March Sun only 10am–noon & 1.30–4.30pm; F40) celebrates the town's two most famous inhabitants, the writer Felix Timmermans and the painter Isidore Opsomer (1878–1967). Timmermans and Opsomer were good friends and thought of themselves as leading artistic custodians of Flemish culture: the one writing of traditional village life, most memorably in the earthy humour of his *Pallieter*; the other proud of his sea- and townscapes and of his influence on contemporary Belgian painters. Inside, the spacious rooms of the first floor contain a comprehensive selection of Opsomer's work, including a whole batch of heavy, rather pretentious portraits and, of more immediate appeal, a number of rural scenes, such as the Expressionistic *Middelburg*. An adjoining room is devoted to the work of their friend, the sculptor Lodewijk van Boeckel, whose old forge is surrounded by examples of his intricate, profoundly black – and somewhat aggressive – ironwork. Upstairs, there's a collection of writings by Timmermans, supplemented by several first editions, together with general details of his life and times, all in Flemish.

Heading north along the Werf from here, the third turn on the right, Rechtestraat, leads to **St Gummaruskerk** (daily: Easter–Sept 9am–noon & 2–5pm; Oct–Easter 9am–noon & 2–4pm; free), which takes its name from a courtier of King Pepin of France, who settled in Lier as a hermit in the middle of the eighth century. Built in Flamboyant Gothic style in the fifteenth century, and painstakingly restored in the 1980s, the sturdy buttresses of the church, surmounted by a tiered and parapeted tower, dominate the surrounding streets. On the inside, chunky pillars rise up to support a vaulted roof, whose simplicity contrasts with the swirling, twisting embellishments of the **rood loft** below, a decoration which frames a passionate bas-relief cartoon strip of the Calvary and the Resurrection. Behind, the high altar is topped by a second fine carving, a wooden altarpiece of the fourteenth century whose inside panels are alive with a mass of finely observed detail, from the folds of the bed linen to the pile of kindling underneath Abraham's son. The church's **stained glass windows** are reckoned to be some of the finest in Belgium. The five elongated windows above the high altar were presented to the town by the Emperor Maximilian in 1516. They are formal stately compositions in contrast to the more intimate themes and finely balanced yellows, reds, and blues of the windows overlooking the first section of the left-hand side of the choir, which were the work of Rombout Keldermans in 1475.

Practicalities

Departing every half hour, it takes just fifteen minutes for the train from Antwerp Centraal to reach Lier **train station**, which adjoins the **bus station**, on the north side of the town centre. It's a ten-minute walk from the Grote Markt: veer left out of the train station building, turn right at the main road, Antwerpsestraat, and carry straight on. The **tourist office**, in the basement of the Stadhuis in the Grote Markt (April–Oct daily 9am–12.30pm & 1.30–5pm; Nov–March Mon–Fri 9am– 12.30pm & 1.30–5pm; ☎03/488 38 88), can provide a glossy town brochure with a map (F10) and make **accommodation** bookings for free, although the options are limited. There are just two hotels and a couple of **private rooms** (③), with the latter inconveniently sited on the outskirts of town. Of the **hotels**, the better option is the *Hof van Aragon-Maagdenhuis*, Mosdijk 5 (☎03/491 08 00; ③), a small and unpretentious place occupying a pleasantly renovated old building in the town centre: take Kerkstraat from beside St Gummaruskerk and it's the first turn on the right, just beyond the canal. The other possibility is the *Handelshof*, a run-of-the-mill, modern hotel in front of the train station at Leopoldplein 39 (☎03/480 03 10; ④).

For **food**, most day-trippers head for the row of terraced cafés edging the Grote Markt and the Zimmerplein, in front of the Zimmertoren. Prices are generally reasonable, with the *Delfin*, Zimmerplein 6, and the popular *Den Engel,* on the west side of the Grote Markt, serving snacks and light meals as good as any of their rivals. But it's all pretty routine, and there's a much better option in the laid-back *Oude Komeet*, Florent van Cauwenberghstraat 18, an attractive café-restaurant offering wholesome food with the emphasis on vegetarian dishes. For something a little more formal, the pricey but first-rate restaurant *De Werf,* Werf 17 (closed Wed & Thurs), specializes in traditional Flemish cuisine. The liveliest **bars** in town are on tiny Felix Timmermansplein, beside the river just off Rechtestraat – between the Grote Markt and St Gummaruskerk. Here you'll find *De Fortuin*, a charming bar with a riverside terrace and a wide range of ales, and the fashionable *St Gummarus.*

Mechelen

Home of the Primate of Belgium and the country's ecclesiastical capital, **MECHELEN** was converted to Christianity by the itinerant eighth-century evangelist St Rombout. By the thirteenth century it had become one of the more powerful cities of medieval Flanders and entered a brief golden age when the Burgundian prince, Charles the Bold, decided to base his administration here in 1473. Impetuous and intemperate, Charles used the wealth of the Flemish towns to fund a series of campaigns that ended with his death on the battlefield in 1477. His widow, Margaret of York, and his daughter's regent, the remarkable

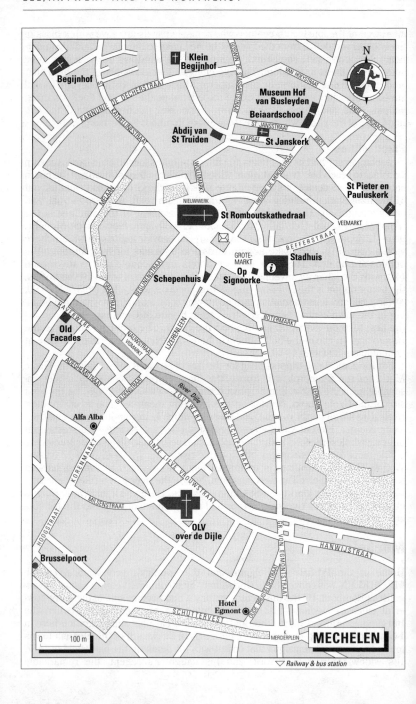

MECHELEN

Railway & bus station

Margaret of Austria, stayed in Mechelen and formed one of the most famous courts of the day. Artists and scholars were drawn here from all over Flanders, attracted by the Renaissance pomp and ceremony, with enormous feasts in fancy clothes in fancy buildings – a glamorous facade that camouflaged a serious political motive. Surrounded by wealthy, independent merchants and powerful, well-organized guilds, the dukes and duchesses of Burgundy realized that they had to impress and overawe as a condition of their survival.

Margaret of Austria died in 1530, the capital moved to Brussels and Mechelen was never quite the same. The *Baedeker* of 1900 described the town as a "dull place...totally destitute of the brisk traffic which enlivens most of the principal Belgian towns". Things aren't so bad today, but considering Mechelen's proximity to Antwerp and Brussels, it has a surprisingly provincial atmosphere – though its cache of medieval buildings, especially its splendid cathedral, make for an enjoyable day out from either of its neighbours.

The Town

The centre of town is, as ever, **Grote Markt**, a handsome expansive affair marked by a mundane statue of Margaret of Austria and flanked on the eastern side by the **Stadhuis**, whose bizarre and incoherent appearance was partly her responsibility. In 1526, she had the left-hand side of the original building demolished and replaced by what you see today, an ornate arcaded loggia fronting a fluted, angular edifice, to a design by Rombout Keldermans. The plan was to demolish and rebuild the rest of the building in stages, but after her death in 1530 the work was simply abandoned, leaving Keldermans' extravagance firmly glued to the plain stonework and the simple gables of the fourteenth-century section on the right. The interior of the later section (occasional opening; ask at the tourist office) is just as garbled as the exterior, though there are a couple of interesting paintings – principally Coussaert's *A Sitting of the Parliament of Charles the Bold* – and a fine sixteenth-century tapestry of the *Battle of Tunis*, glorifying an attack on that city by Emperor Charles V in 1535.

In front of the Stadhuis, just outside the tourist office, is a modern sculpture of **Op Signoorke**, the town's mascot, being tossed in a blanket. Once a generalized symbol of male irresponsibility, the doll and its forebears enjoyed a variety of names – *vuilen bras* (unfaithful drunkard), *sotscop* (fool) and *vuilen bruidegom* (disloyal bridegroom) – until the events of 1775 redefined its identity. Every year it was customary for the dummy to be paraded through the streets and tossed up and down in a sheet. In 1775, however, a young man from Antwerp attempted to steal it and was badly beaten for his pains: the people of Mechelen were convinced he was part of an Antwerp plot to rob them of their cherished mascot. The two cities were already fierce commercial rivals, and the incident soured relations even further. Indeed, when news of the beating reached Antwerp, there was sporadic rioting and calls for the city burghers to take some sort of revenge. Refusing to be intimidated, the people of Mechelen derisively renamed the doll after their old nickname for the people of Antwerp – "Op Signoorke", from "Signor", a reference to that city's favoured status under earlier Spanish kings. It was sweet revenge for an incident of 1687 which had made Mechelen a laughing stock: staggering home, a drunk had roused the town when he thought he saw a fire in the cathedral. In fact, the "fire" was moonlight, earning the Mecheleners the insulting soubriquet "Maneblussers" (Moondousers). Today, although the doll and the citizenry have kept their nicknames, the intense rivalry between the two cities has disappeared, and the Op Signoorke **festival**, held every year on the second Sunday in September, is just a good excuse for a prolonged drinking session.

THE CATHEDRAL

A little way west of the Grote Markt, St Romboutskathedraal (Mon–Sat 8.30am–5.30pm, Sun 2–5.30pm; free) dominates the centre of Mechelen just as it was originally supposed to. A gigantic, buttressed church attached to a great square tower, work began with the draining of the marshes on which it was to be constructed in 1217, but the money ran out before the tower was built, and the initial design had to be put on hold for over two hundred years. In 1451, the Pope obligingly provided the extra funds when he put St Rombout on a list of specified churches where pilgrims could seek absolution for their sins without visiting Rome. Pilgrims and money rolled into Mechelen, and the present tower was completed by 1546. The problem today is that the structure is literally breaking up as it sinks unevenly into its foundations. A long-term effort to hold the church together, begun in 1963, is still far from finished – hence the scaffolding.

The main **entrance** to the cathedral is just off Grote Markt. Inside, the thirteenth-century nave has all the cloistered elegance of the Brabantine Gothic style, although the original lines are spoiled by an unfortunate series of seventeenth-century statues of the apostles. Between the arches lurks an extraordinary Baroque **pulpit**, a playful mass of twisted and curled oak dotted with carefully camouflaged animal carvings – squirrels, frogs and snails, a salamander and a pelican. The main scene shows St Norbert being thrown from his horse, a narrow escape which convinced this twelfth-century German prince to give his possessions to the poor and dedicate his life to the church.

Moving on, the chapel next to the north transept contains the tomb of **Cardinal Mercier** of Mechelen and a plaque, presented by the Church of England, commemorating his part in co-ordinating the Mechelen Conversations. These ran from 1921 up to the time of Mercier's death in 1926 and investigated the possibility of reuniting the two churches – although in Belgium Mercier is more often remembered for his staunch opposition to the German occupation of World War I. His pastoral letters, notably "Patriotism and Endurance", proclaimed loyalty to the Belgian king, paid tribute to the soldiers at the front and condemned the invasion as illegal and un-Christian.

The most distinguished **painting** in the church is in the south transept, where van Dyck's dramatic *Crucifixion* portrays the writhing, muscular bodies of the two thieves in the shadows to either side of the Christ, who is bathed in a white light of wonderful clarity. The painting now forms part of a heavy, marble Baroque altarpiece carved for the Guild of Masons, but it was only installed here after the French revolutionary army flattened the church where it was originally displayed. Close by, twenty-five medieval panels telling the legend of St Rombout have been plonked in the **ambulatory**, which did need cheering up: its nine chapels are really rather dreary, with the exception of the Chapel of the Relics (on the right), dedicated to a group of monks and priests who were slaughtered by Protestants near Dordrecht in 1572. Their supposed remains are stored in a gilt reliquary that shares the chapel with the coats of arms of the Knights of the Golden Fleece, a Burgundian order established by Philip the Good in 1430. Take a look also at the elaborate doors of the high altar, which hide the gilt casket containing the remains of St Rombout. They are only opened on major religious festivals, when the reliquary is paraded through the town centre. Incidentally, many of the columns in and around the ambulatory are made of wood painted as marble, a trompe l'oeil technique for which Mechelen was famous.

Attached to the church, the cathedral tower contains Belgium's finest **carillon**, a fifteenth-century affair of 49 bells which resounds over the town on high days and holidays. There are also regular, hour-long performances on Saturdays (11.30am), Sundays (3pm), and from June through to mid-September on Monday evenings (8.30pm).

THE REST OF TOWN

From the side of the cathedral, Wollemarkt leads north into Goswin de Stassartstraat, where the refuge of the **Abdij van St Truiden** (not open to the public) sits prettily by an old weed-choked canal, its picturesque gables once home to the destitute. Almost opposite, an alley called Klapgat leads to the decaying sandstone of **St Janskerk** (visits by prior arrangement only – ask at the tourist office), worth a peek for the suitably Baroque setting it provides for an altar triptych by Rubens, painted in 1619. A fine example of the artist's use of variegated lighting, the central panel depicts the *Adoration of the Magi,* with Rubens' first wife portrayed as the Virgin.

A few metres further east, at the end of St Jansstraat, Mechelen's **Beiaardschool** (Carillon School; no public admission) has become one of the most prestigious institutions of its sort in the world, attracting students from as far away as Japan, and helping the town to sustain its international reputation for carillon playing. Next door, the **Museum Hof van Busleyden** (Tues–Fri 10am–noon & 2–5pm, Sat–Sun 2–6pm; F75) occupies a splendid early sixteenth-century mansion, built in high Gothic style with Renaissance touches for Hieronymus Busleyden, a prominent member of Margaret's court. Highlights of the rambling collection include an interesting assortment of mostly unattributed paintings, notably a seventeenth-century picture of Mechelen's Groot Begijnhof supplemented by 46 miniatures of the *beguines* at work, along with a graphic series of sixteen panels portraying the multiple sufferings of St Victor, painted for a local convent in around 1510. There's also a display of miscellaneous bells, a variety of guild knick-knacks and a collection of Gallo-Roman artefacts – hardly enough to set the pulse racing, but an agreeable way to spend an hour or so.

From opposite the Carillon School, Biest leads southeast to the Veemarkt where **St Pieter en Pauluskerk** (May–Sept Mon–Fri 9am–noon & 2.30–7pm, Sat & Sun 9am–noon & 2.30–5pm; Oct–April daily 9am–noon; free) was built for the Jesuits in the seventeenth century. The interior has a huge oak pulpit which honours the order's missionary work with a globe attached to representations of the four continents that were known when it was carved by Hendrik Verbruggen in 1701.

It's a short walk from the Veemarkt back to the Grote Markt, where you can extend your tour by strolling south, past the Gothic **Schepenhuis** (Aldermen's House) and onto the **Ijzerenleen**, site of one of the region's best Saturday food markets. At the far end of the Ijzerenleen, just before the bridge, turn right down Nauwstraat and you'll soon spy a quaint little pontoon bridge spanning the River Dilje over to the Haverwerf (Oats Wharf), which is graced by three old and contrasting **facades**. Each has been meticulously restored. On the right is *Het Paradijske* (The Little Paradise), a slender structure with fancy tracery and mullion windows that takes its name from the Garden of Eden reliefs above the first-floor windows. Next door, the all-timber *De Duiveltjes* (The Little Devils), a rare survivor from the sixteenth century, is also named after its decoration, this time for the carved satyrs above the entrance. Finally, on the left and dating to 1669, is *Sint-Jozef*, a graceful example of the Baroque merchant's house, whose fluent scrollwork swirls over the top of the gable and camouflages the utilitarian, upper-storey door: trade goods were once pulled up the front of the house by pulley and shoved in here for safe-keeping.

From Haverwerf, it's a five-minute walk southeast to the church of **Onze Lieve Vrouw over de Dijle**, on Onze Lieve Vrouwstraat (May–Sept Wed & Sat 2–5pm), begun in the fifteenth century, but only completed two hundred years later. Inside, Rubens' *Miraculous Draught of Fishes* was a triptych painted for the Fishmongers' Guild in 1618. Five minutes' walk away, on the southern edge of the centre, the **Brusselpoort** is the only survivor of Mechelen's twelve fourteenth-century gates.

Practicalities

From Mechelen's **train** and adjoining **bus stations**, it's a fifteen-minute walk north to the town centre, straight ahead down Hendrik Consciencestraat. The **tourist office**, in the Stadhuis on the east side of the Grote Markt (March–Oct Mon–Fri 8am–6pm, Nov–Feb Mon–Fri 8am–5pm; March–Sept also Sat & Sun 8.30am–12.30pm & 1.30–5pm, Oct–Feb Sat & Sun 10am–noon & 2–4.30pm; ☎29 76 55), has a handful of **private rooms** (③), which they will book on your behalf at no extra charge. Alternatively, the town has just two recommendable, centrally located **hotels**, the four-star *Alfa Alba*, Korenmarkt 22 (☎015/42 03 03, fax 42 37 88; ⑨), a smart, modern but rather characterless place a brief walk south of the Grote Markt via the Ijzerenleen; and the plain, three-star *Hotel Egmont*, a five-minute walk from the train station, near Kardinal Mercierplein at Oude Brusselsestraat 50 (☎015/42 13 99, fax 41 34 98; ⑥).

There are plenty of **cafés** and **restaurants** dotted round the town centre. Next to the tourist office is the *Mytilus*, a popular and unpretentious restaurant serving all the Flemish basics, or you could try bistro-style *Dali's*, in the shadow of the cathedral at Nieuwwerk 1, where the speciality is mussels. Different again is the moderately priced *Madrid*, a Spanish restaurant overlooking the Dilje off Ijzerenleen at Lange Schipstraat 4 (closed Tues) and specializing in tripe. Another good option is *De Gulden Rabat*, off the Ijzerenleen at Vismarkt 16 (closed Mon & Tues), which offers a wide-ranging menu including delicious seafood.

For a drink, the liveliest of Mechelen's **bars** are concentrated down Nauwstraat, a narrow sidestreet off Ijzerenleen – just opposite the *Madrid* restaurant. Here you'll find the laid-back *De Gouden Vis* as well as *De Cirque*, an amiable place with New Age decor. If you can't be bothered to stagger this far south, there's another group of bars beside the cathedral on Wollemarkt, including the *Lord Nelson* and the *Arms of York*. Mechelen is well known for its beers, especially *Gouden Carolus* (Golden Charles), a delicious dark-brown brew – as recommended by the Emperor Charles V.

Around Mechelen: Fort Breendonk

About 12km west of Mechelen, **Fort Breendonk** (April–Sept daily 9am–5pm; Oct–March daily 10am–4pm; F75) was a Gestapo headquarters during World War II. Built as part of the circle of fortifications that ringed early twentieth-century Antwerp, the fort's low concrete buildings were originally encased in a thick layer of sand until the Germans had this removed in 1940. After the war,

Breendonk was preserved as a national memorial in honour of the four thousand men and women who suffered or perished in its dark, dank tunnels and cells. As you might expect, it's a powerful, disturbing place to visit, with a clearly marked tour taking you through the SS tribunal room, poignantly graffitied cells, the prisoners' barrack room and the bunker, which was used as a torture chamber. There's also a museum dealing with the German occupation of Belgium, prison life and the post-war trial of Breendonk SS criminals and their collaborators. Other displays explore the origins of Fascism and the development of the Nazi concentration camps.

By car, Fort Breendonk is a stone's throw from the A12 highway linking Antwerp and Brussels – just follow the signs. By public transport, take the train from Mechelen to **WILLEBROEK** (hourly; 10min) and it's on the edge of town, a 1.5km walk west from the station along Dermondesestenweg. The smart and modern *Breendonck Taverne*, next door to the fort, serves snacks and meals at reasonable prices.

Leuven

Over the border in the province of Brabant, **LEUVEN** is less than half an hour by train from both Mechelen and Brussels, offering an equally easy and enjoyable day trip from either. The town is home to Belgium's oldest university, whose students give the place a lively, informal air – and sustain lots of inexpensive bars and cafés. There is also a couple of notable medieval buildings here, the splendid Stadhuis and St Pieterskerk, home to three wonderful early Flemish paintings. Otherwise, the centre is not much more than an undistinguished tangle of streets with a lot of the new and few remnants of the old. Then again, it's something of a miracle that any of Leuven's ancient buildings have survived, since the town suffered badly in both World Wars – some 1500 houses were destroyed in World War I, and the university library and main church were gutted, only to suffer further damage in World War II. If you stay a while, you may also pick up on the division between town and gown; some of the students see themselves as champions of the Flemish cause, but the locals seem largely unconvinced.

The history of the **university**, founded in 1425, isn't a particularly happy one. By the early sixteenth century it rated among Europe's most prestigious educational establishments: the cartographer Mercator was a student at Leuven, and Erasmus worked here, founding the *Collegium Trilingue* for the study of Hebrew, Latin and Greek, as the basis of a liberal (rather than Catholic) education. However, in response to the rise of Lutheranism, the authorities insisted on strict Catholic orthodoxy, and drove Erasmus into exile. In 1797 the French suppressed the university, and then, after the defeat of Napoleon, when Belgium fell under Dutch rule, William I replaced it with a Philosophical College – one of many blatantly anti-Catholic measures which fuelled the Belgian revolution. Re-established after independence as a bilingual Catholic institution, the university became a hotbed of Flemish Catholicism, and for much of this century French and Flemish speakers here were locked in a bitter nationalist dispute. In 1970 a separate, French-speaking university was founded at Louvain-la-Neuve, just south of Brussels – a decision that propelled Leuven into its present role as a bastion of Flemish thinking, wielding considerable influence over the region's political and economic elite.

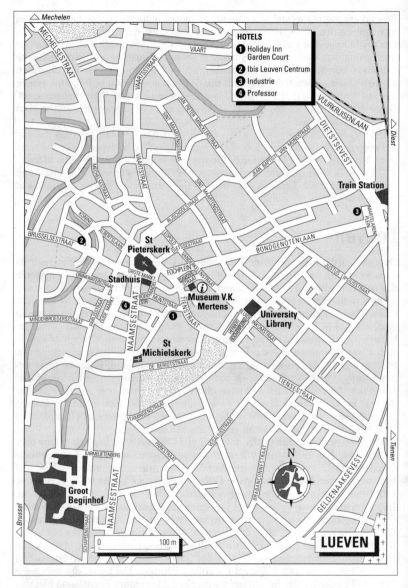

Arrival, information and accommodation

It's a gentle ten- to fifteen-minute walk west along Bondgenotenlaan from the **train** and adjacent **bus station** to the Fochplein, a tiny square that preludes the Grote Markt. Leuven's **tourist office** is just south of the Fochplein at Léopold

Vanderkelenstraat 30 (Mon–Fri 9am–5pm & Sat 10am–1pm & 1.30–5pm; March–Oct also Sun 10am–1pm & 1.30–5pm; ☎016/21 15 39). They sell a comprehensive town brochure and map (F25), detailing the town's hotels, sights and museums, and also have a limited supply of **private rooms** (②–③), though most of these are on the outskirts.

Leuven possesses a handful of central **hotels**, the least expensive of which are the three on Martelarenplein, the square in front of the train station. None of these is particularly enticing, but the recently renovated *Industrie*, a one-star hotel at no. 7 (☎016/22 13 49, fax 20 82 85; ③), has plain and perfectly adequate rooms. Other options, this time right in the centre, include the basic *Professor*, Naamsestraat 20 (☎016/20 14 14, fax 29 14 16; ⑤), a small, one-star hotel above a bar; the standard-issue, two-star *Ibis Leuven Centrum*, Brusselsestraat 52 (☎016/29 31 11, fax 23 87 92; ⑤); and the modern *Holiday Inn Garden Court*, a better than average three-star hotel off Tiensestraat at Alfons Smetplein 7 (☎016/29 07 70, fax 29 12 29; ⑧) – don't pay too much attention to the ugly entrance.

The Town

The centre of town is marked by two adjacent squares, the more easterly of which is the **Fochplein**, basically just a road junction whose one noteworthy feature is the modern **Font Sapienza**, a wittily cynical fountain of a student literally being brainwashed by the book he is reading. Next door, the wedge-shaped **Grote Markt** is Leuven's architectural high spot, dominated by two notable late Gothic buildings – St Pieterskerk and the Stadhuis. The **Stadhuis** is the more flamboyant of the two, an extraordinarily light and lacy confection, crowned by soaring pinnacles and a dainty, high-pitched roof studded with dormer windows. It's a beautiful building, but it is slightly spoiled by the clumsiness of its statues, representing everything from important citizens, artists and nobles, to virtues, vices and municipal institutions, and inserted in the nineteenth century. Until then, the lavishly carved niches stood empty for lack of money. In contrast, the niche bases are exuberantly medieval, depicting biblical subjects in a free, colloquial style and adorned by a panopoly of grotesques. After the slender beauty of the exterior, the **inside** of the Stadhuis is something of an anticlimax, with guided tours (Mon–Fri 11am & 3pm, Sat & Sun 3pm; F20) taking you through just four rooms, including overblown salons in high French style and the neo-Gothic council chamber.

Across the square, **St Pieterskerk** (Tues–Sat 10am–noon & 2–5pm, Sun 2–5pm; mid-March to mid-Oct also Mon 10am–noon & 2–5pm; free) is a rambling, heavily buttressed late Gothic pile whose stumpy western facade defeated its architects. Work began on the present church in the 1420s and continued until the start of the sixteenth century when the Romanesque towers of the west facade, the last remaining part of the earlier church, were pulled down to make way for a grand design by Joos Matsys, the brother of Quentin. It didn't work out – the foundations proved too weak – and finally, another hundred years on, the unfinished second-attempt towers were capped, creating the truncated versions that rise above the entrance today. Inside, the church is distinguished by its soaring nave whose enormous pillars frame a fabulous **rood screen**, an intricately carved piece of stonework surmounted by a wooden Christ. The nave's Baroque **pulpit** is also striking – a weighty wooden extravagance which shows St Norbert being thrown off his horse by lightning, a dramatic scene set beneath spiky palm trees. It was this brush with death that persuaded Norbert, a twelfth-century German noble, to abandon his worldly ways and dedicate himself to the church on whose behalf he founded a devout religious order, the Premonstratensian Canons, in 1120.

The **ambulatory** accommodates the **Museum voor Religieuze Kunst** (same times as church; F50), whose three key paintings date from the fifteenth century. There's a copy of Rogier van der Weyden's marvellous triptych, the *Descent from the Cross*, the original of which is now at the Prado in Madrid, and two of the few surviving paintings by Weyden's apprentice **Dieric Bouts** (c1415–75), who worked for most of his life in Leuven, ultimately becoming the city's official painter. An influential artist in his own right, Bouts' carefully contrived paintings are inhabited by stiff and slender figures in religious scenes that are almost totally devoid of action – a frozen narrative designed to stir contemplation rather than strong emotion. His use of colour and attention to detail are quite superb, especially in the exquisite landscapes which act as a backdrop to much of his work. Of the two triptychs on display here, the gruesome *Martyrdom of St Erasmus*, which has the executioner extracting the saint's entrails with a winch, is less interesting than the *Last Supper*, showing Christ and his disciples in a Flemish dining room, with the (half-built) Stadhuis just visible through the left-hand window; the two men standing up and the couple peeping through the service hatch are the rectors of the fraternity who commissioned the work. Dressed in a purple robe, the colour reserved for royalty, Jesus is depicted as taller than his disciples. It was customary for Judas to be portrayed in a yellow robe, the colour of hate and cowardice, but Bouts broke with tradition and made him almost indistinguishable from the others – he's the one with his face in shadow and his hand on his left hip. The change of emphasis, away from the betrayal to the mystery of the Eucharist, is continued on the side panels: to the left Abraham is offered bread and wine above a Jewish Passover; to the right the Israelites gather manna and below, the Prophet Elijah receives angelic succour.

Also in the ambulatory is the shrine of St Margaret of Leuven, otherwise known as **Proud Margaret**, patron saint of serving girls. A thirteenth-century servant, she witnessed the murder of her employers, was abducted by the murderers, and then killed for refusing to marry one of them. Working round the ambulatory from the right, her shrine is in the eighth chapel, where her story is illustrated in grim detail by the paintings of the eighteenth-century artist Pieter Verhagen.

There are more paintings in the underrated **Museum Vander Kelen-Mertens**, which occupies an old mansion at Savoyestraat 6 (Tues–Sat 10am–5pm, Sun 2–5pm; F50) – in the same complex as the tourist office. The labelling is poor, so pick up the free English leaflet at reception. In keeping with the taste of their day, the nineteenth-century owners had a sequence of rooms kitted out in pseudo-historical style, and the ground-floor Baroque, Renaissance, Rococo and Neoclassical salons survive today. In them is an appealing assortment of stained glass, ceramics, Oriental porcelain and medieval sculpture. There's modern sculpture too – notably a couple of pieces by Constantin Meunier (see p.97) – and a modest sample of nineteenth-century Belgian land- and seascapes. The highlight of the museum is, however, on the floor above, where a small collection of medieval religious sculptures and paintings includes an exquisite *Holy Trinity* by Rogier van der Weyden. At some point, the painting has actually been altered: if you look closely at Christ's shoulder, you'll spot a pair of bird's feet. Originally, these were the feet of the dove that represented the Holy Spirit, but someone decided God the Father and his Son would suffice. South of the Grote Markt is the boisterous core of Leuven's student scene, the **Oude Markt**, a large cobblestone rectangle surrounded by cafés and bars in good-looking gabled houses. To the immediate east of Oude Markt, Naamsestraat leads south past the supple Baroque facade of the Jesuit **St Michielskerk**, restored after wartime damage, towards the **Groot Begijnhof**, a sixteenth-century enclave of mellow red-brick houses tucked away beside the River Dijle: from Naamsestraat, turn right down the little lane called Karmelietenberg and then take the first left, Schapenstraat. Once home to around three hundred *begijns* – women living as nuns but without taking vows – the Begijnhof was bought by the university in 1962 since when it has been painstakingly restored as student residences. Even now during the day, when the students are out, a tranquil atmosphere pervades.

Eating and drinking

As a university town, Leuven is chock-a-block with inexpensive restaurants and cafés, not to mention any number of lively bars where drinking is a pleasure. In particular, there are several good and reasonably priced **restaurants** on Muntstraat, just south of the Grote Markt. Options here include the *Ascoli*, at no. 17 (closed Wed), which serves up tasty Italian and Flemish food – try the Brabantine rabbit – and the *Oesterbar*, at no. 23 (closed Sun & Mon), probably the best seafood place in town. Close by, another good choice is *De Troubadour*, Tiensestraat 32, a smart little place that's good for seafood, pasta and pizza, while *Universum*, a popular **café-bar** on the corner of Tiensestraat and Hooverplein, is a big and busy barn-like place stuffed with students and townies who shovel down platefuls of spaghetti and omelettes. Further south, *Lukemieke*, off Naamsestraat at Vlamingenstraat 55, is a good vegetarian restaurant (Mon–Fri noon–2pm & 6–8.30pm).

If you just want a **drink**, head for the informal, student bars of Oude Markt. The best tactic is to wander along until somewhere takes your fancy – and sometimes you'll catch a good live band too. *Gecko's* at no. 2, *Heaven's Door*, at no. 16, and *Eclips*, at no. 50, are currently three of the most fashionable – but the scene changes rapidly.

Diest

In a quiet corner of Brabant about 30km northeast of Leuven, the small and ancient town of **DIEST** lies just south of the River Demer, its cramped but leafy centre still partly surrounded by the remnants of the town's once-mighty fortifications, built to guard the eastern approaches to Brussels. Militarily obsolete for many decades, Diest has seen more prosperous days, but it's still worth a brief visit.

The obvious place to start is the **Grote Markt**, a wide-open, irregularly shaped area, edged by trim seventeenth- and eighteenth-century facades and the hulking Gothic stonework of **St Sulpitiuskerk** (June to Aug daily 2–5pm), whose interior is remarkable only for the wry, folksy carving of the choir stalls. Footsteps from the church, the stately Stadhuis accommodates the **Stedelijk Museum** (Jan–Oct daily 10am–noon & 1–5pm; Nov & Dec Sun 10am–noon & 1–5pm; F50) hidden away in the old vaulted cellars, where the prime exhibits are some seventeenth-century suits of armour and a fearful, anonymous *Last Judgement* from about 1430. More interesting is the **Begijnhof**, a five-minute walk northeast along

Koning Albertstraat, and one of the best preserved in this part of Belgium, founded in the thirteenth century and retaining much of its medieval shape and atmosphere. The main entrance at the far end of Begijnenstraat – a continuation of Koning Albertstraat – is marked by an extravagant Baroque portal with a niche framing a statue of the Virgin above a text that reads "Come into my garden, my sister and bride". Beyond the gateway, the weathered fourteenth-century **Begijnhofkerk** (Easter–Oct Sun 2–5pm), with its attractive Rococo interior, nestles among several rows of whitewashed cottages that once housed the beguines. On Kerkstraat, one of them now harbours **Gasthof 1618**, a restaurant adorned with all sorts of bric-a-brac ranging from pikes and swords to holy statues, though the main event is the excellent, traditional Flemish food, which you can wash down with the locally brewed *Gildenbier.*

For devotees of nineteenth-century municipal fortifications, the **Schaffensepoort**, a ten-minute stroll northwest from the Begijnhof – back to the beginning of Begijnenstraat and turn right down Schaffensestraat – is a dramatic passage through concentric lines of ramparts and across the River Demer. Heavy, studded oak gates indicate an enthusiasm for defence that was superseded by the development of more effective artillery.

Practicalities

It's a fifteen-minute walk south from Diest **train station** to the Grote Markt: veer left out of the station building, take the first right over the river and keep going down Statiestraat and subsequently Demerstraat. On the Grote Markt, in the basement of the Stadhuis adjoining the museum, is the **tourist office** (Jan–Oct daily 10am–noon & 1–5pm; Nov & Dec Mon–Fri 1–5pm, Sun 10am–noon & 1–5pm; closed Sat; ☎013/35 32 71), which has free town maps and – although it's unlikely you'll want to stay – a list of local accommodation. Easily the best and most convenient **hotel** is the three-star *De Fransche Croon*, a sprightly modern establishment with just a dozen rooms at Leuvensestraat 26 (☎013/31 45 40, fax 33 31 59; ⑥), a five-minute walk south of the Grote Markt: take Berchmansstraat from the square and then the first right turn. Alternatively head for the comfortable and slightly cheaper *Moderne*, which is in the same direction, though around 1km away on Leuvensesteenweg 93 (☎013/31 10 66, fax 31 32 72; ⑤). There's also a **youth hostel** at St Jansstraat 2 (☎ & fax 013/31 37 21; ①), in a pleasant old house overlooking the city park, ten minutes' walk east of the Grote Markt: again take Berchmansstraat, but this time continue onto Botermarkt and take the first left along Wolvenstraat; keep dead ahead as far as the T-junction in front of the fancy park gateway, and then turn right. In terms of restaurants, *Pergolesi*, Grote Markt 28, has a good range of **snacks** and **meals**, whereas both *Breugel*, nearby at no. 23, and *Casino* next door, serve well-priced, and tasty local cuisine. Moving upmarket, *De Zoete Inval*, at Grote Markt 6, beside the start of Koning Albertstraat, offers good fresh seafood in antique premises, and there's first-rate Flemish food at *Gasthof 1618* in the Begijnhof (see above). As for **nightlife**, *Café Leffe*, a convivial but sedate bar at Grote Markt 24, is about as lively as it gets.

Hasselt and around

The capital of the province of Limburg, **HASSELT** is a busy, modern town that acts as the administrative centre for the surrounding industrial region. A pleasant but unremarkable place, the roughly circular city centre fans out from a series of small interlocking squares, with surprisingly few buildings as evidence of its medieval foundation. To compensate for this lack of appeal and to attract foreign investment, the local authority has spent millions of francs on lavish and imaginative prestige projects, from an excellent range of indoor and outdoor sports facilities to a massive cultural complex that aims to attract some of the world's finest performers. But perhaps more than anything else, Hasselt is associated with the open-air museum of Bokrijk which lies some 8km northeast of town – an extraordinarily comprehensive evocation of traditional village life with buildings brought here from every corner of Flemish Belgium.

The Town

In Hasselt itself, there's nothing special to look at, although the **Gerechtshof** (Court of Justice) on Havermarkt, just off Grote Markt, is housed in the town's one surprise – a handsome Art Deco building, whose elegant interior of brown tiles, statuettes and lamps is in pristine condition. In addition, there are no fewer than seven modest **museums** in town, charging up to F90 for entry, or you can buy a combined ticket from the tourist office for F150, though the attached conditions (the museums are divided into two groups, and the ticket takes you into any two of one group and one of the other) seem unduly complicated. The pick of the bunch is the **Nationaal Jenevermuseum**, at Witte Nonnenstraat 19 (Tues–Fri 10am–5pm, Sat & Sun 2–6pm; closed Jan; F90); head north from the Grote Markt down Hoogstraat/Demerstraat and watch for the turning on the right. Sited in a restored nineteenth-century distillery, this shows how the stuff is made and details the history of local jenever production, with a free drink thrown in. Of the remaining museums, the best are: the **Stedelijk Modemuseum**, Gasthuisstraat 11 (April–Oct Tues–Sun 11am–5pm, Nov–March Tues–Sun 10am–5pm, Sat & Sun 2–6pm; F90) – take a left turn off Demerstraat opposite Witte Nonnenstraat – with its displays on the history of fashion from 1830 to the present; and the **Museum Stellingwerff-Waerdenhof**, five minutes' walk east of the Grote Markt at Maastrichterstraat 85 (same opening times; F90), where there are some lovely Art Nouveau ceramics and the oldest surviving monstrance in the world. Dating from the end of the thirteenth century, this ornamental receptacle held the much-venerated *Miraculous Host of Herkenrode*, which was reputed to bleed if subjected to sacrilege. Lastly, the **Stedelijk Beiaardmuseum** (June & Sept Sat & Sun 2–6pm, July & Aug Tues–Fri 10am–5pm, Sat & Sun 2–6pm; F60), in the tower of St Quintinuskathedraal on Vismarkt, deals with the development and workings of carillons. Around 1km out of town the lovely **Jardin Japonais** (April–Oct Tues–Fri 10am–5pm, Sat & Sun 2–6pm; F100) at Kapermolenpark is a joint venture between Hasselt and the Japanese town of Itami, the centrepiece of which is an impressive Japanese-style wooden structure known as the "house of ceremonies". To get there take the free bus, #H3, which runs every half an hour from the Hasselt train station.

Practicalities

A ten-minute walk east of the adjoining **train** and **bus stations** – along Stationsplein and keep straight ahead – Hasselt's **tourist office** is about 150m north of the Grote Markt, located down an alley off Hoogstraat at Lombaardstraat 3 (Mon–Fri 9am–5pm, Sat 10am–1pm & 2–5pm; May–Oct also Sun 11am–3pm;

☎011/23 95 40 or 23 95 41). They have free maps, information on Hasselt and its surroundings, and sell the combined museum ticket (see above). There are no private rooms in town, and the cheapest **hotel** is the *De Nieuwe Schoofs*, by the train station at Stationsplein 7 (☎011/22 31 88, fax 22 31 66; ②), but this is very basic and there are several more agreeble choices. Among them, the *Hotel Pax*, Grote Markt 16 (☎011/22 38 75, fax 24 21 37;④), occupies a prime location and has reasonably comfortable rooms, while the *Hassotel*, Sint Jozefsstraat 10 (☎011/23 06 55, fax 22 94 77; ⑦), is a well-equipped modern hotel with Art Deco flourishes about five minutes' walk south from the Grote Markt – take Maastrichterstraat and turn first right. A few minutes from the Grote Markt, *Century*, at Konig Leopoldplein 1 (☎011/22 47 99, fax 23 18 24; ⑤), is somewhat cheaper, and has a reasonable restaurant as well as a good bar.

Finding somewhere to eat in Hasselt is easy: there are numerous inexpensive **bars** and **restaurants** on the Grote Markt with yet more on Botermarkt – off Hoogstraat opposite the tourist office – and adjoining Zuivelmarkt. The popular *Majestic*, Grote Markt 2, is a good place for snacks; the *Martenshuys*, Zuivelmarkt 18, serves both light meals and more substantial dishes; and the cosy *De Karakol*, Zuivelmarkt 16 (closed Mon), offers a varied, more upmarket menu including vegetarian dishes. The *De Levensboom*, a five-minute walk south of the Grote Markt, via Havermarkt and left along Cellebroedersstraat at Leopoldplein 44 (Tues–Sat noon–2.30pm & 6.30–9pm, Sun noon–3pm), is exclusively vegetarian.

The Bokrijk Museum and estate

The **Bokrijk Openluchtmuseum** (April–Sept daily 10am–6pm; F200, Sundays F250) is one of the best of its type in the country, a series of reconstructed buildings and villages from various parts of Flemish Belgium spread out within a substantial chunk of rolling fields and forest. Each village has been meticulously recreated, each building thoroughly researched, and although the emphasis is still largely on rural life, it's a bias partly addressed by the reconstruction of a small medieval cityscape in its southwest corner. Perhaps inevitably, it gives a rather idealized picture, and certainly the assembled artefacts sometimes feel out of context and rather antiseptic, but the museum is tremendously popular and some of the individual displays are outstanding. An excellent English guidebook (F300) provides a wealth of detail about every exhibit, and the whole museum is clearly labelled and directions well marked.

The museum's collection is divided into five sections, each representing a particular geographical area and assigned its own colour code. The most extensive range of buildings is in the **yellow** sector, *The Poor Heathlands*, where there are a number of Kempen farmhouses, from the long gables of a building from Helchteren to a series of compound farms that come from every quarter of the provinces of Antwerp and Limburg. Other highlights include a lovely half-timbered blacksmith's workshop from the village of Neeroeteren, a bakehouse from Oostmalle, a fully operational oil-press from Ellikom, an entire eleventh-century church from Erpekom and a peat-storage barn from Kalmthout. In the same section – inside the wagon shed from Bergeyk – one particular curiosity is the skittle-alley and pall-mall. Throughout the Middle Ages, skittles was a popular pastime among all social classes, played in tavern and monastery alike. The original game had nine targets arranged in a diamond pattern, but this version was banned in the sixteenth century because of the association of the diamond shape with gambling, and replaced by the more familiar ten-skittle game. Pall-mall, where heavy balls are driven through an iron ring with a mallet, was popular throughout Europe in the seventeenth and eighteenth centuries, but is now confined to some of the more remote villages of Limburg.

The open-air museum occupies most of the western half of the 1440-acre **Bokrijk estate**, whose eastern portion comprises parkland, woods and lakes as well as several marked attractions, principally a fine arboretum, with over three thousand shrubs and trees, and a marshland nature reserve (Het Wiek Natuurreservat). Criss-crossed by footpaths, this part of the parkland is open daily during daylight hours throughout the year and entrance is free.

Practicalities

There are two easy ways of reaching Bokrijk from Hasselt: **bus** #46 (F80) leaves from the bus station every thirty minutes and halts beside the museum entrance (F50); **trains** (F70), which leave hourly, take ten minutes, and cost much the same, but drop you a five-minute walk away to the south. Right by the museum entrance are the nineteenth-century Kasteel Bokrijk – home to the estate's administration and an **information centre** – and the starting point for the toy-town autotrein that shuttles round the estate (but not the museum).

The museum's popular *St Gummarus* **restaurant**, straight ahead of the entrance, serves reasonable meals at affordable prices. There's nowhere to **stay** actually on the estate, and camping is not allowed, but accommodation is fairly near at hand in the Bokrijk **youth hostel**, Boekrakelaan 30 (☎089/35 62 20, fax 30 39 80; closed Nov–Feb; ①), reachable through the park and some 6km north of the train station – pick up a map at the information centre.

South of Hasselt

South of Hasselt, the Kempen opens out into the **Haspengouw**, a fertile expanse of gently undulating land that fills out the southern part of the province of Limburg, its soils especially suited to fruit growing. Frankly, the scenery is rather dreary, though cherry blossom time shows it at its best, and the area's tiny towns and villages spread carelessly alongside the roads are without much charm or style. Even so, **St Truiden** and more particularly **Tongeren** are well worth a visit for their small-town flavour and enjoyable range of historic monuments, while St Leonarduskerk, in the village of **Zoutleeuw**, possesses a splendid interior decked out with furnishings and fittings that survived the Reformation almost untouched.

Tongeren

Twenty kilometres southeast of Hasselt, **TONGEREN** is the oldest town in Belgium, built on the site of a Roman camp that guarded the important road to Cologne. Destroyed by the Franks and razed by the Vikings, its early history was plagued by misfortune, though it prospered during the Middle Ages as a dependency of the bishops of Liège. Nowadays, it's a small and amiable market town on the border of Belgium's language divide.

Five minutes' walk west of the train station, the haughty statue of Ambiorix, in the Grote Markt, is supposed to commemorate a local chieftain who defeated the Romans here in 54 BC, but this "noble savage" owes more to mid-nineteenth-century

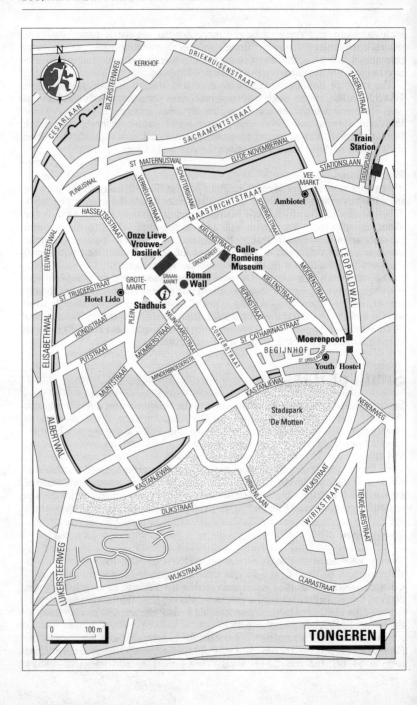

TONGEREN

Belgian nationalism than historical accuracy. Directly opposite, the mainly Gothic **Onze Lieve Vrouwebasiliek** (daily 8am–noon & 1.30–6pm) towers over the city centre, with an impressive, symmetrical elegance that belies its piecemeal construction: it's the eleventh- to sixteenth-century outcome of an original fourth-century foundation that was the first church north of the Alps to be dedicated to the Virgin. Still very much in use, the dark tomb-like interior, with its cavernous, vaulted nave, has preserved an element of Catholic mystery, its holiest object a bedecked, medieval, walnut statue of Our Lady of Tongeren – "Mariabeeld" – which stands surrounded by candles and overhung by a gaudy canopy in the north transept. Nearby, in the choir, an intricately carved retable depicts scenes from the life of the Virgin, and just outside are the well-preserved columns of the medieval cloister. The church's **schatkamer** (April–Sept daily 10am–noon & 1.30–5pm; F80) is full of reliquaries, monstrances and reliquary shrines from as early as the tenth century. Bones and bits of body poke out at you from every corner, but best are a beautiful sixth-century Merovingian buckle, a pious and passive *Head of Christ* and an eleventh-century *Reliquary Shrine of the Martyrs of Trier.*

A short distance away on the southern side of the Grote Markt, the graceful lines of the eighteenth-century **Stadhuis** are nicely balanced by an external staircase, the whole caboodle imitative of the town hall in Liège. Also close by, in the middle of Graanmarkt on the right-hand side of the church, a small section of the second **Roman city wall** has been carefully excavated. Dating from the fourth century AD, the masonry you can see actually covers the remains of a luxurious third-century villa, evidence that the city was shrinking – and its inhabitants becoming fearful – as the Roman Empire declined. From here, it's a couple of minutes' walk east round the Onze Lieve Vrouwebasiliek and along Groendreef to the **Gallo-Romeins Museum** (Mon noon–5pm, Tues & Fri 9am–5pm, Sat–Sun 10am–6pm; F200), at Kielenstraat 15, a flashy affair which makes the most of the town's ancient history in its extensive and well-labelled collection of Roman, Gallo-Roman and Merovingian archeological finds. Finally, you could also take a peek at the angular **Moerenpoort**, one of Tongeren's six medieval gates, which dominates the southern end of Kielenstraat and doubles as the eastern entrance to the pretty little **Begijnhof**.

Practicalities

From Tongeren's **train** and adjoining **bus stations**, it's a five-minute walk west to the Grote Markt, along Stationslaan and Maastrichterstraat. The town's **tourist office**, in the Stadhuis (Mon–Fri 8am–noon & 1–4.30pm; also Sat & Sun May–Sept 10am–5pm, Oct–April 10am–4pm; ☎012/39 02 55 or 39 02 27, fax 39 11 43), has details of a handful of private **rooms** in the ④ range, and will call ahead to make a booking. Another budget option is the **youth hostel**, *Jeugdherberg Begeinhof*, St Ursulastraat 1 (☎012/39 13 70, fax 39 13 48; ①), a smart, modern place charging just F385 for bed and breakfast, with family, four- and six-bedded rooms as well as a dormitory; it's centrally situated in the Begijnhof near the Moerenpoort, has a coffee bar and offers bike rental; reservations are advised. There are also a couple of central **hotels**, the two-star *Lido*, a basic affair with eight rooms above its café-bar at Grote Markt 19 (☎012/23 19 48, fax 39 27 27; ④); and the rather more comfortable *Ambiotel*, beside the east end of Maastrichterstraat at Veemarkt 2 (☎012/26 29 50, fax 26 15 42; ⑤), a straightforward modern hotel with spacious rooms. There's also a **camping** complex, *De Pliniusbron*, in the municipal park at Fonteindreef 3 (☎012/23 16 07), a twenty-minute walk away: take St Truiderstraat west from the Grote Markt, turn right down Beukenbergweg, the third road along, and head straight down past the eighteenth-century castle of Betho.

Places to **eat** in town include *'t Vrijthof*, by the Onze Lieve Vrouwekerk at Graanmarkt 5, which serves excellent and reasonably priced fish dishes; and the popular, pleasantly decorated (with classical furnishings), *Giardini Romano*, Maastrichterstraat 17 (closed Thurs), which offers first-rate and inexpensive Italian dishes made with the freshest of pastas. Just off Grote Markt at Hassletsestraat 23, *Biessenhüs* serves excellent French cuisine, whereas the old-fashioned, wood-panelled café *Du Phare*, Grote Markt 21, is good for simple snacks.

Sint Truiden

Around 20km west of Tongeren, the small market town of **SINT TRUIDEN** grew up around an abbey founded by St Trudo in the seventh century and is today surrounded by the orchards of the Haspengouw. Known for the variety, if not the excellence, of its ancient churches, St Truiden is a pleasant, easy-going sort of town, with a good-looking centre. It's also the best place to catch a bus to the spectacular church in the village of Zoutleeuw.

The town's spacious Grote Markt is edged by an elegant eighteenth-century **Stadhuis**, whose flowing lines have remained discordantly attached to an older **Belfry** – the middle of three imposing towers that puncture the skyline on the east side of the square. On the right, the spire of the **Onze Lieve Vrouwekerk** has had a particularly chequered history: built in the eleventh century, it's been dogged by misfortune and ravaged by fire on several occasions. In 1668 the spire gave everyone a shock when it simply dropped off; it wasn't replaced for two hundred years. On the left, the untidy, truncated **Abdijtoren** also dates from the eleventh century, a massive remnant of the original religious complex that once dominated the medieval town. The abbey has been replaced by a dull and forbidding seminary that spreads out from the tower, though the grimy, ornate **gateway** does break the monotony – a carved relief showing the misogynistic legend attached to the abbey's foundation. The story goes that every time St Trudo tried to build a church, it was pulled down by an interfering woman. Not to be thwarted so easily, Trudo prayed fervently and the woman was stricken with paralysis.

The pick of Sint Truiden's many other churches are **St Gangulfus**, northwest of the Grote Markt down Diesterstraat (daily 9am–5pm), and **St Pieters** (same times), south along Naamsesteenweg. Extensively built and renovated in the eleventh and twelfth centuries respectively, both these churches are classically Romanesque mixtures of cubic and square forms. For its period, the ribless cross-vaulting of St Pieters was experimental; the architect balanced the risk by deciding not to put windows in the upper walls.

Practicalities

St Truiden's **train** and adjacent **bus station** are on the south side of the centre, a five-minute walk along Stationsstraat/Tiensestraat from the Grote Markt, where the **tourist office**, in the Stadhuis (April–Oct daily 9am–6pm; Nov–March Mon–Fri 9am–4pm, Sat 9am–1pm; ☎011/68 62 55, fax 69 11 78), has free town maps and brochures with details of cycle routes in the surrounding countryside. There's just one central **hotel**, the spick and span, ultra-modern *Cicindria*, part of a shopping mall at Abdijstraat 6 (☎011/68 13 44, fax 67 41 38; ⑤) – take

Diesterstraat northwest from the Grote Markt and it's the first turn on the right. For a **drink** or a **snack**, the *Bistroke* café-bar, on an alley behind the Stadhuis, is a lively and enjoyable spot, or there's the *Théâtre*, a more formal bistro-type affair on the south side of the Grote Markt.

Buses for **Zoutleeuw** (see below) leave from the bus station (Mon–Fri every 30min 8am–6pm; Sat & Sun once every 2hr).

Zoutleeuw

In a sleepy corner of Brabant, just inside the provincial boundary, the tiny village of **ZOUTLEEUW**, well connected by bus to both St Truiden, 7km to the east, and Tienen, 15km west, was a busy and prosperous cloth town from the thirteenth to the fifteenth centuries. Thereafter its economy slipped into a long and slow decline whose final act came three hundred years later when it was bypassed by the main Brussels to Liège road. The village's rambling, irregularly turreted and towered **St Leonarduskerk** (Easter–Sept Tues–Sun 2–5pm; Oct Sat & Sun 2–5pm; F40) has a magnificently intact pre-Reformation interior that's among the most impressive in the country. Clearly labelled in English, it's crammed with the accumulated treasures of several hundred years, its dark and mysterious nave and chapels redolent of medieval superstition. There's a wrought-iron, sixteenth-century double-sided image of the Virgin suspended high in the nave, a whopping fifteenth-century wooden cross hanging in the choir arch, and an intricate altar and retable of St Anna to the right of the entrance in the second chapel of the south side aisle. The south transept is devoted to St Leonard with the chapel at its far end containing a fine collection of late medieval and Renaissance statues as well as gold and silver work. The adjacent altarpiece, beside the central crossing, dates from the late fifteenth century, a gorgeous, naive work by Arnould de Maeler which recounts the life of St Leonard, though, in fact, nothing certain is known about him. Traditionally described as a French hermit who founded a monastery near Limoges, Leonard's medieval popularity was based upon the enthusiasm of returning Crusaders, who regarded him as the patron saint of prisoners. Moving on to the north transept, pride of place goes to the huge stone tabernacle carved in almost miraculous perspective by Cornelis Floris, architect of Antwerp's town hall, between 1550 and 1552.

Opposite the church, the attractive sixteenth-century **Stadhuis** was designed by Rombout Keldermans and adjoins the Lakenhalle, home to the **tourist office** (April–Oct Mon–Fri 10am–noon & 1–4pm, Sat–Sun till 5pm; Nov–March Mon–Fri 10am–noon & 2–4pm; ☎011/78 12 88, fax 78 84 84).

Tienen

The undistinguished Brabantine town of **TIENEN** – sugar beet centre of Belgium – spirals out from a pleasant, open main square that's fringed by a tidy nineteenth-century **Stadhuis** and the solemn late medieval bulk of **Onze Lieve Vrouw ten Poelkerk** (Mon–Fri 9am–7pm). The interior of the church is predictably Gothic with Baroque furnishings, but it's unusual in that it has no nave, because the money ran out. Directly behind the Stadhuis and up on the hill, the church of **St Germanus** (daily 9am–4pm) is a ninth-century foundation that's been repeatedly rebuilt and reshaped. A church of mammoth proportions, it's in a poor state of repair, but worth a peek for its Gothic interior, whose highlight is the pelican lectern in the chancel.

The **tourist office** is at Grote Markt 4 (Mon–Fri 8.30am–12.30pm & 1.30–5pm; April–Sept also Sat & Sun 10am–6pm; ☎016/80 56 86, fax 81 04 79). Tienen has two central **hotels**, the no-frills, two-star *Le Nouveau Monde*, opposite the train station – a five-minute walk from the Grote Markt – at Lancierslaan 75 (☎016/81 23 21, fax 81 58 55; ⑤), and the equally basic *Alpha* in between the marketplace and the train station at Leuvensestraat 95 (016/82 28 00, fax 82 24 54; ④). There's also a **youth hostel**, 1km northeast of the train station at Kabbeekvest 93 (mid-June to mid-Sept; ☎016/82 14 60, fax 82 27 96; ①).

travel details

Trains

Antwerp to: Amsterdam (hourly; 2hr 15min); Bruges (hourly; 1hr 10min); Brussels (every 20 min; 40min) for Brussels–Paris (7 daily; 3hr); Diest (every 30 min; 50min); Geel (hourly; 40min); Hasselt (every 30 min; 70min); Lier (every 30 min; 15min); Mechelen (every 20 min; 20min).

Diest to: Leuven (hourly; 45min).

Hasselt to: Bokrijk (hourly; 15min); Diest (every 30 min; 15min); Liège (hourly; 55min); St Truiden (1 or 2 hourly; 15min); Tongeren (hourly; 20min).

Leuven to: Brussels (every 30min; 20min).

Mechelen to: Leuven (every 30min; 20min).

Tienen to: Brussels (hourly; 40min).

Tongeren to: Hasselt (hourly; 20min); Liège (hourly; 30min).

Turnhout to: Herentals (hourly; 15min).

Buses

Geel to: Turnhout (every 30 min; 40min).

St Truiden to: Zoutleeuw (Mon–Fri every 30 min, Sat & Sun every 2hr; 10min).

Tienen to: Zoutleeuw (Mon–Fri every 30 min, Sat & Sun every 2hr; 20min).

CHAPTER FOUR

HAINAUT AND WALLONIAN BRABANT

South of Brussels, the western reaches of Wallonia comprise the province of **Hainaut** and the French-speaking portion of **Brabant**, Brabant Wallon. By and large, it's an uninspiring landscape with rolling farmland interspersed by pockets of industrialization, which coalesce between Mons and Charleroi to form one of Belgium's most concentrated belts of industry, but tucked away here and there are a clutch of fascinating old towns, the beautiful ruins of a medieval abbey and a smattering of country houses. The highlight of Hainaut is **Tournai** in the western part of the province, close to the French border. Once part of France, it's a vibrant, unpretentious town, with a number of decent museums and a fine cathedral. East of Tournai, the agreeable if rather less impressive town of **Mons** perches on a hill just to the east of the coal-mining area of the Borinage, and is home to a fine Gothic church and a couple of interesting museums covering the town's role in both World Wars. Mons is also a useful base for seeing some of the region's more scattered attractions, especially if you're travelling by public transport. Within easy striking distance are several castles – of which **Beloeil** is the grandest and **Attre** the most elegant – and **Soignies**, a workaday town with an imposing Romanesque church. East of here, **Nivelles**, the principal town of Wallonian (ie French-speaking) Brabant, boasts an even more impressive example of religious Romanesque architecture in its church of Ste Gertrude, while the elegaic ruins of the abbey of **Villers-la-Ville** lie in a wooded valley just a few kilometres further east again.

Moving south, the industrial and engineering city of **Charleroi** is the capital of Hainaut, but it's an unappetizing sprawl with little to recommend it. Beyond Charleroi the **Botte du Hainaut** is actually an extension of the Ardennes and is named for its position jutting into France from the province's southeastern corner; the "boot" incorporates a narrow slice of Namur province, which for touring purposes we've also included in this chapter. Largely bypassed by the industrial revolution, the area became a quiet and insignificant backwater whose undulating farmland and forests are dotted with the smallest of country towns. Amongst them, Namur's **Walcourt** is the most diverting, a quaint old place that culminates in an imposing medieval church, with **Chimay**, which merits a visit for its castle and pretty old centre, running a close second. Just to the east, **Couvin** is also quite picturesque, and is well endowed with facilities for holidaymakers, since vacationing Belgians hunker down in cottages in the surrounding countryside. Outside of these three towns, each of which has a meagre supply of hotels and is readily reached by public transport, you'll definitely need a car – and more often than not a tent.

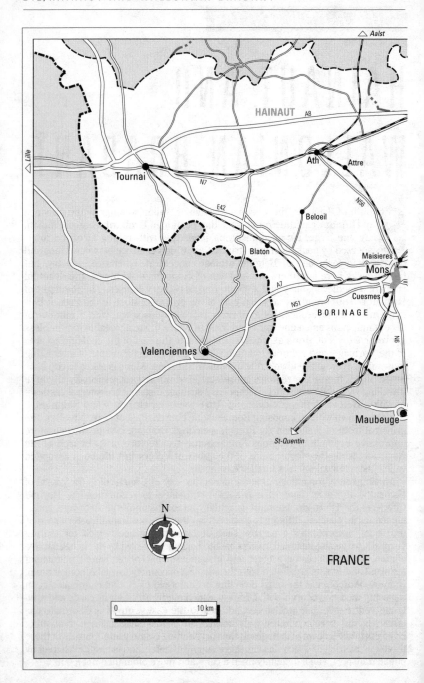

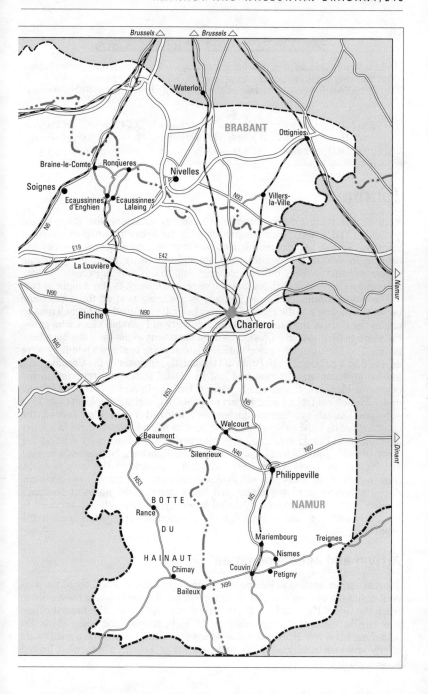

ACCOMMODATION PRICE CODES

All the **hotels and hostels** detailed in this chapter have been graded according to the following price categories. Apart from ①, which is a per-person price for a hostel bed, all the codes are based on the rate for the least expensive double room during high season. For more on accommodation, see p.33.

① Up to F1000 per person ④ F2000–2500 per room ⑦ F4000–5000 per room
② F1000–1500 per room ⑤ F2500–3000 per room ⑧ F5000–6000 per room
③ F1500–2000 per room ⑥ F3000–4000 per room ⑨ F6000 and over, per room

Tournai

With its absorbing cluster of medieval buildings straddling the River Escaut (Scheldt), **TOURNAI** bears comparison with the better-known cloth towns of Flanders, though here tourism is far lower-key. As a consequence the city has never quite managed to spruce itself up, and the centre has a gritty, lived-in appearance that is really rather endearing. Add to this several excellent restaurants and a clutch of lively bars, and you've reason enough to stay a night or two.

The city was founded by the Romans as a staging post on the trade route between Cologne and the coast of France. Later, it produced the French monarchy in the form of the **Merovingians**, a dynasty of Frankish kings who chose the place as their capital – Clovis, the most illustrious of the line, was born here in 465. The Merovingians ruled until the late seventh century when they were deposed by a palace official, Pepin of Heristal, the ancestor of the Carolingians, but in the meantime Tournai had lost its capital status and reverted to the counts of Flanders. It was finally handed back to France in 1187, remaining under French control for a large part of its history, and staying loyal to its king – despite English overtures – during the **Hundred Years War**. Indeed, the constancy of its citizens was legendary: Joan of Arc addressed them in a letter as "kind, loyal Frenchmen", and they returned the compliment by sending her a bag of gold. Tournai was incorporated in the Habsburg Netherlands in 1521 and retaken by Louis XIV in 1667, who left his mark on the town with the heavyweight stone walls that still flank the river and in a number of handsome riverside buildings, mostly along quai Notre-Dame. Sadly much of Tournai's ancient centre was damaged by Allied bombing, but enough has survived to reward exploration, and its cathedral is renowned as perhaps the finest in the country.

Arrival and accommodation

Tournai's **train station** is located on the northern edge of town, about ten minutes' walk from the centre: head straight down rue Royale, crossing the Escaut to reach the Grand-Place and the major sites on the south bank. The **tourist office** is at rue du Vieux Marché-aux-Poteries 14, right opposite the belfry (Mon–Fri 9am–7pm, Sat & Sun 10am–noon & 2–6pm; ☎069/22 20 45), and has a good range of city and provincial leaflets, as well as a list of Tournai's somewhat limited accommodation options.

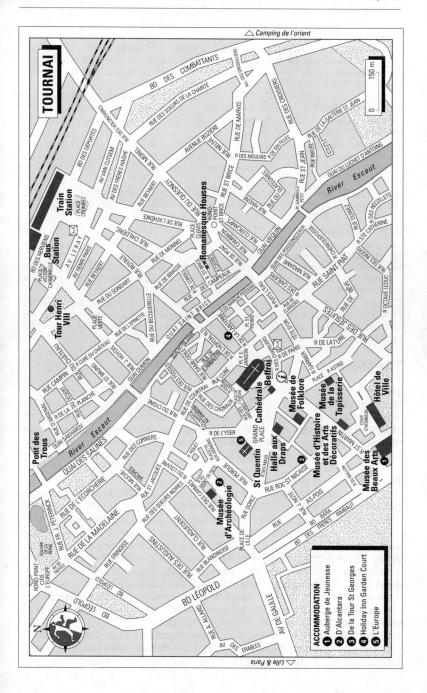

TOURNAI

△ Camping de l'orient

△ Lille & Paris

ACCOMMODATION
1. Auberge de Jeunesse
2. D'Alcantara
3. De la Tour St Georges
4. Holiday Inn Garden Court
5. L'Europe

Hotels

D'Alcantara, rue des Bouchers St Jacques 2 (☎069/21 26 48, fax 21 28 24). Delightful and chic modern hotel slotted in behind an old brick and stone facade about 400m northwest of the Grand-Place. The best place in town with fifteen smart bedrooms, some of which have pleasant courtyard views. ⑥.

L'Europe, Grand-Place 36 (☎069/22 40 67, fax 23 52 38). Just eight plain, high-ceilinged bedrooms in this slightly down-at-heel hotel at the northwest corner of the main square. The building is modern, though it's in a traditional high-gabled style, and the rooms are above the bar-cum-restaurant. ③.

Holiday Inn Garden Court, pl St Pierre 2 (☎069/21 50 77, fax 21 50 78). Spick and span modern hotel with an attractive facade featuring three long rows of windows. Right in the centre of town, close by the cathedral. Comfortable and enjoyable rooms with all conveniences. ⑤.

De la Tour St Georges, pl de Nédonchel 2 (☎069/22 50 35). Dowdy, frugal rooms in an unprepossessing modern brick building just behind the Halle aux Draps. ③.

Hostel and campsite

Auberge de Jeunesse, rue St Martin 64 (☎069/21 61 36, fax 21 61 40). Occupying an attractive old mansion a couple of minutes' walk south of the Grand-Place, the youth hostel is a well-cared-for and friendly place. It has around 100 beds, the majority in dormitories of 5 or 6, though there are also a handful of 2- and 4-bunk rooms. The restaurant serves breakfast, lunch and dinner, and self-catering facilities are available too. Open March–Sept. ①.

Camping de l'Orient, rue Vieux Chemin de Mons 8 (☎069/22 26 35, fax 21 62 21). Campground situated in a leisure and water sports complex about 4km east of the town centre off the chaussée de Bruxelles, the N7: turn south down rue de L'Orient before you reach the E42 motorway. Open all year.

The Town

Tournai's town centre is bisected by the River Escaut (Scheldt) and girdled by a ring road that follows the course of the old city ramparts. The best way to see Tournai is on foot – the town centre is only a few minutes' walk from end to end. Most things of interest are on the southwest side of the river, grouped around or within easy reach of the sprawling, roughly triangular **Grand-Place**. The principal sight, the **Cathédrale**, is just east of here.

The Cathédrale Notre-Dame

Dominating the skyline with its distinctive five towers is Tournai's Romanesque **Cathédrale Notre-Dame** (daily: April–Oct 9am–noon & 2–6pm; Nov–March 9am–noon & 2–4pm; free), built with the wealth of the flourishing wool and stone trades. The mammoth proportions of the cathedral in conjunction with the local slate-coloured marble were much admired by contemporaries and the design was imitated all along the Scheldt valley. The cathedral is the third church on this site, most of it completed in the latter half of the twelfth century, though the choir was reconstructed in the middle of the thirteenth. The full magnificence of the edifice is, however, difficult to appreciate through the jumble of humble, sometimes ancient buildings that crowd its precincts, the only half-reasonable vantage point being on the north side – from place Paul Emile Janson.

On this side too is the fascinating **Porte Mantile**, a Romanesque doorway adorned with badly weathered carvings of the Virtues and Vices. The scenes are hard to make out, but the animated, elemental force of the carvings is unmistakable – and you can spot Avarice, the man impeded by the money-bag round his neck, being carried off by a centaur-like Satan, while two knights are engaged in brutal conflict with one soldier sticking his spear in the face of the other below. The **west facade**, on place de l'Evêché, also has some interesting carvings, with three tiers of sculptures filling out the back of the medieval portico. Dating from the fourteenth to the seventeenth centuries, the oldest effigies, along the bottom, are mainly drawn from the Old Testament and include Moses with the Sinai tablets and scenes from the story of Adam and Eve. The next tier up has reliefs illustrating the history of the local church and finally come figures representing various apostles and saints. Adam and Eve appear again on the column between the double doors, this time almost life-size and separated by the Tree of Knowledge.

Today's main entrance is on the south side, the **choir** and **nave** unexpectedly almost the same length with the communication galleries running along the inside. The nave is part of the original cathedral structure, erected in 1171, as are the intricately carved capitals that distinguish the lowest set of columns, but the vaulted roof is eighteenth-century. The capitals were originally painted in bright colours, their fanciful designs inspired by illuminated manuscripts, imported tapestries and popular images of fearsome, mythological animals. The choir was the first manifestation of the Gothic style in Belgium, and its too-slender pillars had to be reinforced later at the base: the whole choir still leans slightly to one side due to the unstable soil beneath. In front of the choir the Renaissance **rood screen** is a flamboyant marble extravaganza by Cornelis Floris embellished by Biblical events, such as Jonah being swallowed by the whale.

The ample and majestic late twelfth-century **transepts** are the most impressive – and most beautiful – feature of the cathedral. Apsed and aisled to a very unusual plan, they impart a lovely diffuse light through their many windows, some of which (in the south transept) hold superb sixteenth-century **stained glass** by Arnoult de Nimegue, depicting semi-mythical scenes from far back in Tournai's history. Opposite, in the north transept, is an intriguing twelfth-century mural, a pock-marked cartoon strip relating the story of St Margaret, a shepherdess martyred on the orders of the Emperor Diocletian, its characters set against an exquisite blue background which shows a clear Byzantine influence in both style and form. Take a look, too, at Rubens' characteristically bold *The Deliverance of Souls from Purgatory*, which hangs, newly restored, beside the adjacent chapel.

Be sure to see the **trésor** (daily: April–Oct Mon–Sat 10.15–11.45am & 2–5.30pm, Sun 2–4.30pm; Nov–March Mon–Sat 10.15–11.45am & 2–3.45pm, Sun 2–3.45pm; F30) before you leave, its three rooms including a splendid wood-panelled, eighteenth-century meeting room, and a chapel hung with a rare example of a fourteenth-century Arras tapestry, made up of fourteen panels depicting the lives of St Piat and St Eleuthère, the first bishop of Tournai. The third room is crammed with religious bric-a-brac – reliquaries, liturgical vestments and so forth. Among this assorted ecclesiastical tackle are two especially fine reliquary shrines. The earlier piece is the silver and gilded copper *châsse de Notre-Dame*. Completed in 1205 by Nicolas de Verdun, it's festooned with relief figures clothed in fluidly carved robes, and the medallions depict scenes from the life of Christ. The second shrine, the *châsse de St Eleuthère*, is slightly later and more ostentatious, but it doesn't quite have the elegant craftsmanship of its neighbour. There is also an early sixteenth century *Ecce Homo* by Quentin Matsys, showing Christ surrounded by monstrous faces, and a wonderful Byzantine Cross, a classic example of seventh-century Constantinople artistry, its squat arms studded with precious stones. You can see a selection of the cathedral's treasures carried around the town each year in the Procession de Notre-Dame – held on the second Sunday in September.

Around the Grand-Place

A short stroll from the cathedral's main entrance, virtually on the corner of the Grand-Place, the ungainly **beffroi** (belfry) is the oldest such structure in Belgium, its lower portion dating from 1200. The bottom level once held a prison cell and the minuscule balcony immediately above was where public proclamations were announced. On top, the carillon tower has been subjected to all sorts of architectural tinkering from the sixteenth through to the nineteenth century.

A few steps west of the belfry, on the Grand-Place itself, the fine seventeenth-century **Halle aux Draps** maintains its original grey facade, a sombre affair graced by slender Renaissance pilasters, though the inside has been completely rebuilt after the wartime bombing. A few metres away, back towards the belfry, an alley leads through to the amiably old-fashioned **Musée de Folklore** (Wed–Mon 10am–noon & 2–5.30pm; F100), housed in an antique high-gabled brick mansion known as the Maison Tournaisienne. Here, several floors detail old Tournai trades and daily life in the nineteenth century, but the reconstructions of various workshops and domestic rooms that form the bulk of the collection are not terribly spectacular. The highlight is the replica cloister on the second floor, where one of the cells exhibits the pathetic tokens left by those impoverished parents forced to leave their children with the nuns. Particularly affecting are the letters and playing cards torn in half in the vain hope that they could be rejoined (and the child reclaimed) at a later date – something which rarely happened.

On the northwest side of the Grand-Place, the rock-solid, fortress-like church of **St Quentin** has an imposing facade, but it conceals a disappointingly humdrum interior. From here, it's a five-minute walk northwest to the **Musée d'Archéologie**, at rue des Carmes 8 (same times; F80), a rambling, rather forlorn museum housed in an old brick building that was once a pawnshop. On display is a hotch-potch of local archeological finds, the best of which are exhibited on the ground floor – a heavy-duty, Gallo-Roman lead sarcophagus and a smattering of rare Merovingian artefacts, from weapons and the skeleton of a horse through to brooches and bee-shaped jewellery thought to have come from the tomb of the Merovingian king Childeric.

In the opposite direction, just southeast of the Grand-Place on place Reine Astrid, the **Musée de la Tapisserie** (same times; F80) features a small selection of old tapestries alongside modern work and temporary exhibitions. Tournai was among the most important pictorial tapestry centres in Belgium in the fifteenth and sixteenth centuries, producing characteristically huge works, juxtaposing many characters and several episodes of history, and leaving no empty space – a stylized design without borders. Major themes included history, heraldry and mythology, and although several of the best surviving Tournai tapestries are in Brussels, there are a handful of good examples here, not least the three tapestries of **Hercules** and his chums in medieval attire – excellent and still richly coloured instances of the tendency to cram the picture with life and wry observation. The trio recount Homer's tale of Hercules and his dealings with Laomedon, the shifty king of Troy. Hercules saved the king's daughter from a sea-monster, but then the Trojan refused to pay Hercules the promised reward. Hercules had to sail away empty-handed, but swore vengeance, returning ten years later to capture Troy and slaughter the king.

Just along the street, cut up through the gardens to the eighteenth-century **Hôtel de Ville**, the grandest of several municipal buildings that share the same compound. Behind the town hall, the **Musée des Beaux Arts** (same times; F120) occupies an elegant, Art Nouveau edifice surmounted by a rather overblown bronze entitled *Truth, Empress of the Arts*. The building was designed by Victor Horta (see p.96) and on the inside its pillars, grilles and low, soft angles provide a suitably attractive setting for a small but enjoyable collection of mainly Belgian painting, from the Flemish primitives to the twentieth century. The paintings are displayed in a series of interconnected rooms which radiate out from a central hall. The exhibits are sometimes rotated, but in general the earlier works are concentrated on the left-hand side and you should work round the museum in a clockwise direction. The first room on the left is usually devoted to the work of the nineteenth-century medievalist Louis Gallait, two of whose vast and graphic historical canvases – of the *Plague of 1092* and the *Abdication of Charles V* – cover virtually a whole wall each. Subsequent rooms accommodate an exquisite *St Donatius* by Jan Gossaert; *The Fowlers*, by Pieter Bruegel the Younger; and a couple of big, fleshy pieces by Jordaens. There's also a *Holy Family* and a *Virgin and Child* by Rogier van der Weyden, a native of Tournai known around here as Roger de la Pasture. Weyden's artistic output is further celebrated by a separate section containing photographs of all the paintings attributed to him and now exhibited round the world. Among the more modern paintings are a number of works by French Impressionists. Manet's romantic *Argenteuil* and the swirling colours of Monet's *The Headland* stand out but there are also a couple of early, slightly tentative canvases by James Ensor, including *The Marsh*.

The rest of the town centre

Of Tournai's medieval ramparts, the only remaining chunk is the thirteenth-century **Pont des Trous**, spanning the Escaut on the northwestern edge of the centre. Also of some interest is the **quai Notre-Dame**, where many of the buildings show a clear French influence, especially those left from the time of Louis XIV. Curiously enough the town was also English for five years from 1513 to 1518. It was seized by Henry VIII during a war against France. All that's left of the citadel he built is a tower, located in a tiny park near the train station and known, logically enough, as the **Tour Henri VIII** – basically a cylindrical keep, with walls over six metres thick and a conical brick-vaulted roof. Nowadays it's home to Tournai's tiny **Musée d'Armes** (Wed–Mon 10am–noon and 2–5.30pm; F50), which has a dreary assortment of military hardware. Also on the north side of the river are two restored **Romanesque houses** (1172–1200), on rue Barre St Brice – said to be the oldest examples of bourgeois dwellings in western Europe. You can't go inside, but their precarious, leaning appearance is convincing enough.

Eating and drinking

Tournai's **cafés** and **restaurants** throng the town centre, offering plenty of choices for an affordable snack or meal. The more predictable places tend to be on the Grand-Place, while the more interesting congregate down by the river, in the vicinity of rue de l'Hôpital Notre-Dame and quai du Marché Poisson. As you would expect in Wallonia, the general standard is extremely high and the best restaurants offer truly superb food. The city's liveliest **bars** are down by the river, too.

Cafés and restaurants

La Bonne Planque, pl St Pierre 15. Fashionable restaurant serving Franco-Belgian cuisine in the enjoyable surroundings of a tastefully converted apothecary's – all porcelain drug jars and wooden shelving. Very reasonably priced set menus as well as à la carte. Close to the cathedral. Closed Sat & Sun lunchtimes and all day Monday.

Bistro de la Cathédrale, rue Vieux Marché aux Poteries 15. Next to the tourist office. Staid decor, but excellent daily specials for around F400. Meals are served until 11pm, and this is *the* place to try the local speciality *lapin à la Tournaisienne* (rabbit cooked in beer).

Chez Pietro, rue de l'Hôpital Notre-Dame 15. Extremely popular Italian place, just northeast of the cathedral, serving an excellent range of tasty pasta and pizza dishes at inexpensive prices. One of the best deals in town. Closed Tues.

L'Eau à la Bouche, quai du Marché Poissons 8. Trim little restaurant serving mouth-watering seafood, salmon and cheese dishes as well as vegetarian options. Set menus from F850. Closed Mon all day & Thurs eve.

Le Giverny, quai du Marché Poisson 6 (☎069/22 44 64). Small, intimate and tastefully furnished restaurant serving exquisite French cuisine. Set menus from F750–1700.

Petit Bedon, rue des Maux 6. Affordable, unassuming restaurant on the west side of the Grand-Place, near the St Quentin church. A good place to try horsemeat. Closed Wed.

Bars

Aux Amis Reunis, rue St Martin 89. This traditional Belgian bar has a good range of domestic beers and is, with its wood-panelled walls and cosy atmosphere, one of the nicest places to have a drink in town.

Le Café des Arts, quai du Marché Poisson 23. Café-bar with an animated crowd till early in the morning.

La Fabrique, quai du Marché Poisson 13b. Busy, boisterous bar with an off-beat clientèle.

Hangar, rue de l'Arbalète. Post-modernistic decor and thumping sounds at one of Tournai's liveliest spots. Down a narrow sidestreet halfway along rue de l'Hôpital Notre-Dame.

Quai des Brumes, pl St Pierre. Small and faded bar with a touch of cool. On one of the town's oldest squares, close to the cathedral.

Mons

About half an hour by train from Tournai, the name of **MONS** may be familiar for its military associations. It was the site of battles that for Britain marked the beginning and end of World War I, and in 1944 it was the location of the first big American victory on Belgian soil in the liberation campaign. It has also been a key military base since the last war: SHAPE (Supreme Headquarters Allied Powers in Europe) has its headquarters on the outskirts at Maisières, providing employment for thousands of Americans and other NATO nationals – something which gives the town a bustling, cosmopolitan feel for somewhere so small. It's a pleasant town, too, with a smattering of attractions spread over the hill which gave it its name, and makes a useful base for exploring the surrounding countryside – despite the limited number of hotels.

Arrival, information and accommodation

Mons **train station** is on the western edge of the town centre, on place Léopold. From here, it's a ten-minute walk up the hill to the Grand-Place: take rue de la Houssière and then rue du Châpitre, which skirts the massive church of Ste

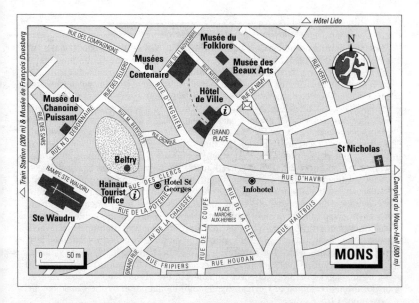

Waudru from where you continue along rue des Clercs. The **tourist office**, at Grand-Place 22 (daily: summer 9am–6.30pm; winter 9am–5.30pm; ☎065/33 55 80, fax 35 63 36), has information on the town, as well as on the battlefield sites on its outskirts. There's also a Hainaut regional tourist office at rue des Clercs 31 (Mon–Fri 10am–6pm; ☎065/36 04 64, fax 33 57 32).

Mons is short of decent **hotels**. Of the five dotted round the centre, two are exceedingly grim, leaving the choice between either the basic and rather unappetizing *Hôtel St Georges*, rue des Clercs 15 (☎065/31 16 29, fax 31 86 71; ③), or the oddly named but very friendly *Infohôtel*, at rue d'Havré 32 (☎065/40 18 30, fax 35 62 24; ⑤), whose pleasant and modern, if somewhat functional, doubles come equipped with TV and telephone. Alternatively head for the newly established *Hôtel Lido*, rue de Arbalestriers 112 (☎32 78 00, fax 84 37 22; ⑦), at the top of rue de Nimy, a ten-minute walk from the Grand-Place – it's the most comfortable of the lot, though considerably more expensive. The tourist office also has details of a handful of **private rooms** and studios for rent, though these tend to be available only during July and August (②). The nearest **campsite** is *Camping du Waux-Hall*, a twenty-minute walk east of the Grand-Place at avenue St Pierre 17 (☎065/33 79 23, fax 35 63 36): take rue d'Havré and then avenue Reine Astrid in the direction of Binche/Charleroi, then do a right.

The Town

The expansive **Grand-Place** is the centre of most Mons life and activity, its terrace cafés a fine place for an early evening drink. Presiding over the square is the fifteenth-century **Hôtel de Ville**, a considerably altered building whose tower dates from the early eighteenth century. The tiny cast-iron monkey on the front wall is reputed to bring good luck to all who stroke him, hence his bald, polished

MONS IN THE WARS

Mons has figured prominently in both World Wars. During **World War I**, in the latter part of August 1914, the British forces here found themselves outnumbered by the advancing Germans to the tune of about twenty to one. The subsequent Battle of Mons began on August 26, and the British – in spite of great heroics (the first two Victoria Crosses of the war were awarded at Mons) – were inevitably forced to retreat. The casualties might have been greater, had the troops not been experienced veterans of war. Meanwhile, back in England, the horror-story writer Arthur Machen wrote an avowedly fictional tale for the *Evening News* in which the retreating troops were assisted by a host of bowmen, the ghosts of Agincourt. Within weeks, rumour had transmogrified Machen's bowmen into the **Angels of Mons**, who had supposedly hovered overhead just at the point when the Germans were about to launch their final attack, causing them to fall back in fear and amazement. Machen himself was amazed at this turn of events, but the angel story was unstoppable, taking on the status of legend, and those soldiers lucky enough to return home reported similar tales of supernatural happenings on the battlefield. This was, in fact, the first of many myths that were to take root among World War I troops: the sheer terror of their situation prompted all sorts of superstitions, legends and rumours, which had a morale-boosting effect, giving brief respite at home from the horrible casualty figures being reported from the front. There's a painting of the angelic event, by one Marcel Gillis, in the Mons Hôtel de Ville. Angels or not, Mons remained in German hands until its liberation by the Canadians in November 1918.

Mons was also at the centre of the fighting during **World War II**: it was occupied by the French on May 10, 1940, but, after a vicious nine-day bombardment, they were forced to withdraw. By the time the Germans entered the town, it had been almost entirely abandoned. Four years later, on September 2, 1944, the Allies recaptured Mons after more fierce fighting.

crown. Inside, some of the rooms are open for guided tours in July and August (1 daily; F100), though the odd fancy chimneypiece, tapestries and paintings are hardly essential viewing.

Walk through to the back of the Hôtel de Ville, via the tunnel and courtyard to the Jardin du Mayeur beyond, and you'll come to the **Musées du Centenaire** (Tues–Sun noon–6pm; F100). This is a complex of four museums under one roof, with displays ranging from ceramics and coins to archeological finds, although the emphasis is on the town's involvement in the two World Wars. On the ground floor there's an extensive display on World War I featuring incidental battlefield relics, plans and photos outlining the course of the war near Mons, and the arms and uniforms of the various nationalities involved. Tucked away on the top floor is the section devoted to World War II, which examines Nazi persecution of the Jews, the American liberation of 1944 and 1945 and life under the German occupation – Mons itself was virtually abandoned after the French withdrawal in 1940, with just 2000 remaining out of a population of 28,000. Again, there are uniforms, weapons and battlefield mementos. In between these two sections, Floor 2 holds the Ceramics Museum, which has a fine collection of Delftware, over four hundred pieces in all, while Floor 3 houses both the Numismatic Museum, with some 18,000 coins, seals and medals, as well as a dreary Prehistoric Museum.

Around the corner from the Hôtel de Ville, on rue Neuve, the **Musée des Beaux Arts** (Tues–Sun noon–6pm; F100) has a collection of mainly Belgian paintings that ranges from the sixteenth century to the present day. It's not as heavyweight a museum as the one in Tournai, and its permanent collection is in any case only shown in rotation, much of the museum's space being given over to (often excellent) temporary exhibitions. However, among the works you can expect to see – on the ground floor – are a striking *Ecce Homo* by the fifteenth-century artist Dieric Bouts; a mischievous *The Soup Eater* by Frans Hals; and a ghoulish *The Entombment* by Paul Delvaux. There's also a rotating sample of modern sculpture. Next door, down an alleyway, is another museum, though of rather more limited appeal, the **Musée du Folklore** (same times; F100), which is housed in the infirmary of an old convent – the Maison Jean Lescarts – and has tidy displays on the development of Mons as a fortress town, local folklore, carnivals and customs.

To the southwest of the Grand-Place, along and around rue des Clercs, are the town's best-preserved medieval streets, a gaggle of twisting lanes and alleys that climb up to the Baroque **belfry** (May–Sept Tues–Sun 10am–5pm, extended until 8pm during July & Aug; free) and its gardens, from where there are fine views over the town and its surroundings. Close by, the **Collégiale Ste Waudru** (May–Sept Tues–Sun 10am–5pm; free) is a good example of the late Gothic style, a massive and majestic church which displays an unusual uniformity in its architecture. There is much to see inside, most importantly the works of the local sculptor Jacques du Broeucq, whose alabaster rood loft (1535–39) was broken up by French Revolutionary soldiers in 1797, and is now spread around different parts of the church. There are hyper realistic reliefs in the transepts, choir and on the high altar, though the most distinguished piece is arguably the swirling *Last Supper* in one of the ambulatory chapels. The **trésor** (same times; F25), too, is of interest, with local goldsmiths' work from the thirteenth to the nineteenth centuries.

Opposite the church, and housed in an impressive nineteenth-century building once home to the National Bank of Belgium, is the **Musée de François Duesberg** (Tues, Thurs, Sat & Sun 2–7pm; F150) which has a wide collection of decorative arts made in between 1775 and 1825 – porcelain, engravings, French gilded bronzes, bindings – as well as a strange and wonderful collection of exotic clocks from around the world.

Behind the church at the foot of rue Notre-Dame Debonnaire, the **Musée Chanoine Puissant** (Tues–Sun noon–6pm; F100) occupies a sixteenth-century house known as the Vieux Logis, and also overflows into the adjacent Ste Marguerite's chapel on rue des Sars. The museum holds the private collection of an eponymous canon, who died in 1934 bequeathing an eclectic mix of chimney-pieces, furniture, wrought-iron wares, and drawings from different periods, though mostly sixteenth- and seventeenth-century. The most impressive item is in the first room of the Vieux Logis – a 1531 wooden ceiling (upright against the back wall) beautifully carved in Renaissance style, taken from a pavilion in town.

Eating and drinking

For a town of Mons' size there are not a huge number of **restaurants**, and many of the most obvious ones, on and around the Grand-Place, aren't especially excit-ing. Despite its name, the *Copenhague Tavern*, Grand-Place 11, is a reliable old standard serving a decent array of mid-priced Flemish dishes. The *No Maison*, opposite at no. 21, is much the same sort of place, with reasonably priced daily specials, while *La Trattoria*, Grand-Place 31, is the best of a large number of Italian restaurants around here, with tasty pizzas baked in a wood-fired oven. *La Marchal*, Rampe Ste Waudru 4, right by the church, is the place to make for if you're willing to spend a little more – wonderful Wallonian cuisine and, considering the quality of the cooking, moderate prices (closed Sun evening, and all day Mon & Tues); the comparable *La Coquille St Jacques*, in between the main square and Ste Waudru at rue de la Poterie 27, is a very good second choice (closed Sun evening & all day Mon). Just south of the Grand-Place, *Devos*, on rue de la Coupe 7, serves excellent French cuisine, and is reasonably priced.

For **drinking**, *L'Excelsior*, Grand-Place 29, is an amiable spot with an extensive beer menu and filling snacks, while the cosy *Atelier*, south of the Grand-Place at the junction of rue de la Coupe and rue des Fripiers, has a wide choice of beers too; nearby, *La Podo*, rue de la Coupe 43, and *Quartier Latin*, place Marché-Aux-Herbes 27, are both lively, more youthful hangouts with, again, an extensive range of beers.

Around Mons

Railways and roads radiate from Mons in all directions, putting central Hainaut's key attractions within easy reach and making for enjoyable day-trips; what's more, using Mons as a base avoids the difficulty of finding somewhere to stay – accommodation is thin on the ground around here. The nearest and most obvious of these sights is the **Vincent van Gogh house**, southwest of the city in the suburb of Cuesmes, but this is disappointing and there are other much more worthwhile destinations. To the northwest lie the castles of **Attre** and (less appealing) **Beloeil**; to the east is the quaint little town of **Binche**, which boasts one of Belgium's most famous carnivals; while the northeast hides **Soignies**, with its splendid Romanesque church.

Vincent van Gogh and the Borinage

The region immediately west of Mons is known as the **Borinage**, a poor, densely populated industrial area that in the latter half of the nineteenth century was one of Belgium's three main coalfields, an ugly jigsaw of slag heaps and mining villages which spread toward the French frontier until decline set in early this century. In 1878, after a period in a Protestant school in Brussels, **Vincent van Gogh** was sent to the area as a missionary, living in acute poverty and helping the villagers in their fight for social justice – behaviour which so appalled the Church authorities that he was forced to leave. He came back the following year and lived in **CUESMES**, on the southern outskirts of Mons, until his return to the Netherlands in 1881. It was in the Borinage that van Gogh first started drawing seriously, taking his inspiration from the hard life of the miners: "I dearly love this sad countryside of the Borinage and it will always live with me." Although the connection was instrumental in the development of the painter's career, there's actually very little to see. In Cuesmes itself, the two-storey brick **house** (Tues–Sun 10am–6pm; F100) where van Gogh lodged has been tidily restored, but inside there's merely a couple of rooms containing no original work and not even a reconstruction of how he lived. If you're determined to make a thankless pilgrimage, take bus #1 or #2 from outside Mons train station (every 30min); it's a ten-minute walk to the van Gogh house from the bus stop.

Attre and Ath

From Mons, it takes 25 minutes for the train (en route to Ath) to reach **ATTRE** station (hourly Mon–Fri, but no service Sat & Sun), just over a kilometre from the elegant, Neoclassical **Château d'Attre** (April–June & Sept–Oct Sat & Sun 10am–noon & 2–6pm; July & Aug Thurs–Tues 10am–noon & 2–6pm; park and castle F150; park only F80) – just follow the road downhill from beside the station. Completed in 1752, the castle was built on the site of a distinctly less comfortable medieval fortress for the count of Gomegnies, chamberlain to the emperor Joseph II, and soon became a favourite haunt of the ruling Habsburg elite – especially the Archduchess Marie-Christine of Saxony, the governor of the Southern Netherlands. The original, carefully selected furnishings and decoration have survived pretty much intact, providing an insight into the tastes of the time – from the sphinxes framing the doorway and the silk wrappings of the Chinese room through to the extravagant parquet floors, the ornate moulded plasterwork and the archducal room hung with the first handpainted wallpaper ever to be imported into the country, in about 1760. There are also first-rate silver, ivory and porcelain pieces, as well as paintings by Frans Snyders, a friend of Rubens, and the Frenchman Jean-Antoine Watteau, whose romantic, idealized canvases epitomized early eighteenth-century aristocratic culture. Neither is the castle simply a display case: it's well cared for and has a lived-in, human feel, in part created by the arrangements of freshly picked flowers chosen to enhance the character of each room.

The surrounding **park** straddles the River Dender and holds several curiosities, notably a 25m-high artificial rock with subterranean corridors and a chalet-cum-hunting lodge on top – all to tickle the fancy of the archduchess. The ruins of a tenth-century tower, also in the park, must have pleased her risqué sensibilities too; it was reputed to have been the hideaway of a local villain, a certain Vignon, who, disguised as a monk, robbed and ravished passing travellers.

From Attre, it takes the train just five minutes to pull into **ATH**, a run-of-the-mill industrial town whose main claim to fame is its festival, the **Ducasse**, held on the fourth weekend in August and featuring the "Parade of the Giants", in which massive models, representing both folkloric and biblical figures, waggle their way round the town. If you're in the area around this time, don't miss it; otherwise, you'll probably want to make straight for the **bus** to Beloeil, 13km away. Bus #81a leaves from beside the train station (Mon–Fri hourly, Sat & Sun every 3hr; 20mins) – ask the driver to put you off at the bus stop about 150m from the castle. Incidentally, if you're **heading on** from here, the same bus continues south from Beloeil to Blaton train station (15min), on the Mons–Tournai line.

Beloeil

The castle of **BELOEIL** (June to Sept daily 10am–6pm; F280) broods over the village that bears its name, with its long brick and stone facades redolent of the enormous wealth and power of the Ligne family, the regional bigwigs since the fourteenth century. This aristocratic clan began by strengthening the medieval fortress built here by their predecessors, subsequently turning it into a commodious castle that was later remodelled and refined on several occasions. The wings of the present structure date from the late seventeenth century, while the main body, though broadly compatible, was in fact rebuilt after a fire in 1900. Without question a stately building, it has a gloomy, rather despondent air – in marked contrast to the Château d'Attre. The interior, though lavish enough, oozing with tapestries, paintings and furniture, is simply the collected indulgences – and endless portraits – of various generations of Lignes. Despite all this grandeur, only one member of the family cuts much historical ice, Charles Joseph (1735–1814), a diplomat, author and field marshal in the Austrian army, whose pithy comments were much admired by his fellow aristocrats: most famously, he suggested that the Congress of Vienna of 1814 "danse mais ne marche pas". Several of Beloeil's rooms contain paintings of Charles' life and times and there's also a small selection of his personal effects, including the malachite clock given to him by the Tsar of Russia. Otherwise, the best parts are the library, which contains twenty thousand volumes, many ancient and beautifully bound, and the eighteenth-century formal **gardens**, the largest in the country, whose lakes and flower beds stretch away from the house to a symmetrical design by Parisian architect and decorator Jean-Michel Chevotet – though even these are unkempt around the edges and dotted with stagnant ponds.

Binche

Halfway between Mons and Charleroi, **BINCHE**, a sleepy little town at the southern end of Hainaut's most decayed industrial region, comes to life in February with one of the best, and most renowned, of the country's **carnivals**.

The Town

Pretty much everything of any interest in Binche is clustered round the **Grand-Place** – a spacious square edged by the onion-domed **Hôtel de Ville**, built in 1555 by Jacques du Broeucq to replace a version destroyed by the French the previous year. At the far end of the Grand-Place stands a statue of a "Gille", one of the figures that dance through the city streets during carnival, sandwiched between the big but dilapidated **Collégiale St Ursmer** and the modern **Musée International du Carnaval et du Masque** (April–Oct Mon–Thurs 9.30am–12.30pm & 1.30–6pm, Sat 1.30–6pm, Sun 10am–noon & 1.30–6pm; Nov–March same times except closed Sun mornings; F180), which claims to have the largest collection of carnival artefacts in the world. Whether or not this is an exaggeration, its collection of masks and fancy dress from carnivals throughout Europe, Africa, Asia and Latin America is certainly impressive, and is complemented by an audiovisual presentation on the Binche carnival and temporary exhibitions on the same theme. Behind the church, a small **park** marks the site of the town's medieval citadel and contains what little remains of the former palace of Mary of Hungary. The park is buttressed by the original **ramparts**, which date from the twelfth to the fourteenth centuries and curve around most of the town centre, complete with 27 towers.

Carnival

Carnival has been celebrated in Binche since the fourteenth century. The festivities last for several weeks, getting started in earnest on the Sunday before Shrove Tuesday, when thousands turn out in costume, and leading up to the main events on **Shrove Tuesday** itself, when the traditional *Gilles* (males born and raised in Binche) appear in clogs and embroidered costumes from dawn onwards. In the morning they wear "green-eyed" masks, dancing in the Grand-Place carrying bunches of sticks to ward off bad spirits. In the afternoon they don their plumes – a mammoth piece of headgear made of ostrich feathers – and throw oranges to the crowd as they pass through town in procession.

The rituals of the carnival date back to pagan times, but the *Gilles* were probably inspired by the fancy dress worn by Mary of Hungary's court at a banquet held in honour of Charles V in 1549; Peru had recently been added to the Habsburg Empire, and the courtiers celebrated the conquest by dressing up in (their version of) Inca gear.

Practicalities

To get to Binche, take the hourly **train** from Mons to Charleroi and change at La Louvière-Centre – allow about an hour and a half for the whole journey; alternatively, **bus** #22 makes the forty-minute trip every half-hour, leaving from outside Mons train station. Binche **tourist office** is located in the Hôtel de Ville on the Grand-Place (Mon–Fri 9am–noon & 12.30–6pm, Sat & Sun 2–6pm; ☎064/33 67 27), a ten-minute walk from the train station: take rue Gilles Binchois from the square in front of the station building and keep straight ahead until you reach the end of rue de la Gaieté, where you turn left.

Accommodation is a problem: Binche has no hotels or private rooms, and the nearest **campsite**, *Aux Gloriettes*, rue de la Résistance 92 (☎064/33 26 11; mid-April to Oct), is in neighbouring Waudrez. If you're just after **food**, things look rosier: the *Restaurant Industrie*, tucked away in a corner of Binche at Grand-Place 4, serves hearty meals at very reasonable prices – mussels and chips for a mere F370 – or you could try the smart café, *La Parapluie National*, a few strides away serving up French and Belgian cuisine.

Soignies and around

About 15km northeast of Mons and on the Mons–Brussels train line, **SOIGNIES** is easy to reach, although there's nothing much to bring you here apart from the town's Romanesque church, the **Collégiale St Vincent** – bang in the centre on Grand-Place, a ten-minute walk from the train station via rue de la Station. The church is dedicated to one St Vincent Madelgar, a seventh-century noble who was both the husband of St Waudru of Mons and the founder of an abbey here in 650; work began on the church in 965 and continued over the ensuing three centuries. The end result is a squat and severe edifice with two heavy towers. Inside, the church's pastel-painted, twelfth-century nave, with its chunky Lombardic arches and plain arcades, is similar to that of Tournai, while the transepts are eleventh-century, their present vaulting added six centuries later. The oldest section is the huge choir, dating from 960 and containing one of the church's most outstanding features, a set of Renaissance choir stalls from 1576. Look out also for the finely crafted fifteenth-century terracotta entombment on the south side of the choir, and the fourteenth-century polychrome Virgin beneath the rood screen.

If all this has given you a thirst, wet your whistle at *Les Armoiries*, an old-fashioned brown bar near the church at Grand-Place 7.

Ronquières and Ecaussinnes

To the east of Soignies lies one of the quietest corners of Hainaut, a pocket-sized district where drowsy little villages and antique, whitewashed farmhouses scatter over a bumpy landscape patterned by a maze of narrow country lanes. If you're travelling by car – and especially if you're heading for Nivelles (see below) – the district makes for a pleasant detour, but is ill-served by public transport.

The most convenient starting point is **RONQUIÈRES**, about 15km northeast of Soignies: just outside the village is a massive sloping lock on the Charleroi–Brussels canal – just follow the signs. When it was built in 1963, this curious "lift" device cut the journey time between Charleroi and Brussels by around seven hours, a saving of around 25 percent. The lock consists of two huge water tanks, each 91m long, which shift barges up or down 70m over a distance of 1500m. The main **tower** (March–Nov daily 10am–7pm; F280) houses the winch room, and runs a video explaining how the whole thing works and, best of all, gives a bird's-eye view of proceedings. There are also boat trips through the lock (May–Sept Tues & Thurs–Sun 3–4 daily; 1hr; F100, combined ticket with tower F330), but the tower should be quite sufficient for all but the most enthusiastic.

Heading south from the lock, it's just 5km to the twin villages of **Ecaussinnes** –d'Enghien and Lalaing – though be warned that the signposted route, along a baffling series of lanes, is easy to lose and hard to rediscover, but there again the scenery around here is delightful for Sunday driving. There's just one specific sight, Ecaussinnes Lalaing's frumpy **castle** (April–June & Sept–Oct Sat & Sun 10am–noon & 2–6pm; July & Aug Thurs–Mon 10am–noon & 2–6pm; F150), an imposing towered and turreted edifice stuck on a rocky knoll. The earliest parts of the structure date from the twelfth century, though most is the result of much later modifications. Inside, the big and sparsely furnished rooms are hardly essential viewing, but highlights include two fine early sixteenth-century chimneypieces in the hall and armoury, an extremely well-preserved fifteenth-century kitchen and small but high quality examples of glassware and Tournai porcelain.

Into Brabant: Nivelles and Villers-la-Ville

Travel any distance north or east of Soignies and you cross the border into **Brabant**, whose southern French-speaking districts – known as Brabant Wallon – form a final band of countryside before you enter the sprawl of Brussels, beginning with the splurge of Waterloo (see p.112). **Nivelles** is the obvious distraction en route, an amiable, workaday town worth a visit for its interesting church as well as its proximity to the beguiling ruins of the Cistercian abbey at **Villers-la-Ville**, a short car ride away – though train travellers have to make the trip via Charleroi.

Nivelles

NIVELLES grew up around its abbey, which was founded in the seventh century and became one of the most powerful religious houses in Brabant until its suppression by the French Revolutionary Army in 1798. Nowadays, the abbey is recalled by the town's one and only significant sight, the **Collégiale Ste Gertrude** (Mon–Fri 9am–5pm, Sat & Sun 2–6pm; free), a sprawling affair built as the abbey church in the tenth century and distinguished by a huge and strikingly handsome chancel. The church is named after its first abbess – the daughter of its founder, Itta, who was the wife of Pepin the Elder. It has fared badly over the centuries, suffering fire damage on no less than nineteen occasions, most recently during World War II, and inevitably has become something of an architectural

The cathedral spire, Antwerp

Evening drinking, Antwerp

Flemish tapestry

Brabo Fountain, Antwerp

Watching Anderlecht, Brussels

Tournai by night

Ardennes specialities

The bridge and riverfront, Dinant

Church of St-Jean, Luxembourg

Kayaking, in the Ardennes

Vineyards near Remich, Luxembourg

hybrid as a result of repairs and alterations. Nonetheless, in better shape now than it has been for years following a long-winded restoration, it's a most unusual building, the design a rare example of an Ottonian abbey church – after the tenth-century Holy Roman Emperor Otto the Great. During the reign of Otto and his successors, Byzantine, early Christian and Carolingian influences were brought together to create an architectural style, **Ottonian**, which was the forerunner of Romanesque.

In terms of the Collégiale Ste Gertrude, Ottonian precepts are reflected by the presence of a transept and a chancel at each end of the nave, where the west chancel represents imperial and the east papal authority. The interior is extremely simple, its long and lofty nave equipped with a flat concrete roof painted in imitation of the wooden original. Between the pillars of the nave is a flashy oak and marble **pulpit** by the eighteenth-century Belgian artist Laurent Delvaux, while the heavily restored, fifteenth-century wooden **wagon**, in the west chancel to the left of the entrance, was used to carry the shrine of St Gertrude in procession through the fields once a year. Unfortunately, the original thirteenth-century shrine was destroyed in 1940, but a modern replacement has been made and the traditional autumn procession has been recently revived.

The **guided tours** are worth considering even if you don't understand French, as these take you around parts of the church that are otherwise out of bounds; note also that the tourist office sometimes arranges English-speaking tours (see "Practicalities" below). French tours leave at 2pm on weekdays and on Saturdays and Sundays at 2pm and 3.30pm, cost F150, and last about an hour and a half. They begin by heading upstairs to the large Salle Impériale over the west choir. The function of the room is unknown, but today it's used to house a few ecclesiastical bits and pieces, including the copy of Ste Gertrude's shrine alongside the remains of the original. The tour continues to the large Romanesque crypt and the excavations, where the foundations of a Merovingian chapel and church (seventh-century) and three Carolingian churches (ninth- and tenth-century) have been discovered, as well as the tombs of Ste Gertrude and some of her relations.

If you've time to spare after visiting the church, the **Musée Communal d'Archéologie**, in the old ivy-clad house a couple of minutes' walk north off the main square at rue de Bruxelles 27 (Wed–Mon 9.30am–noon & 2–5pm; F40), has assorted displays of fine and applied art on the ground floor – everything from locks, keys and weapons through to tapestries, sculptures and paintings. Much of the material on display has actually come from the church, notably four Brabantine Gothic statues of the Apostles from the former rood screen and the splendid terracotta sculptures by Delvaux. Upstairs is a ragbag of local archeological finds, beginning with prehistoric times and ploughing on through the Gallo-Roman period to the Merovingians.

Practicalities

It's a ten-minute walk west from Nivelles' **train station** via rue de Namur to the Grand-Place, where the **tourist office** (Mon–Fri 9am–noon & 1.30–5pm, plus Easter–Sept Sat 10am–noon & 2–4pm, Sun 2–5pm; ☎067/21 54 13), tucked away in a corner, has information on French-speaking Brabant and sells town maps. It's also worth asking if any English-language guided tours of Ste Gertrude have been scheduled.

There's only one central **hotel**, the no-frills, one-star *Commerce*, at Grand-Place 7 (☎067/21 12 41; ③), although with Brussels so near (30km – 20min by train) it's not really worth staying. For **food**, *Le Prévert* bistro, just off the main square on rue de Bruxelles, is a good and reasonably priced spot for lunch, with an enjoyably varied menu of pasta dishes, *tartines* (sandwiches) and imaginative salads.

Villers-la-Ville

Just off the N93 some 16km east of Nivelles, and accessible by train from Charleroi, the ruined Cistercian abbey of **VILLERS-LA-VILLE** (April–Oct Mon & Tues noon–6pm, Wed–Sun 10am–6pm; Nov–March Wed–Fri 1–5pm, Sat & Sun 11am–5pm; F150) nestles in a lovely wooded dell and is altogether one of the most haunting and evocative sights in these parts. The first monastic community settled here in 1146, consisting of just one abbot and twelve monks. Subsequently the abbey became a wealthy local landowner, managing a domain of several thousand acres, with numbers rising to about a hundred monks and three hundred lay brothers. A healthy annual income funded the construction of an extensive monastic complex, most of which was erected in the thirteenth century, though the less austere structures, like the Abbot's Palace, went up in a second spurt of activity some four hundred years later. In 1794 the monastery was ransacked by French revolutionaries, and later a railway was ploughed through the grounds.

The remains of the abbey comprise the monks' living quarters, including dormitories, refectory, parlour, chapter house and warming room, beside which lies the church and cloister. Away from the central area, the workshops and brewery are on one side, the mill and farm on the other. The site is wild and overgrown and the buildings are all in varying states of decay, but easily enough survives to pick out Romanesque, Gothic and Renaissance features and to make some kind of mental reconstruction possible. Most of the complex has multilingual labels and an English-language leaflet is available at reception.

From the entrance a path crosses the courtyard in front of the Abbot's Palace to reach the **warming room**, the only place in the monastery where a fire was kept going all winter, and which still has its original chimney. The fire provided (at least a little) heat to the adjacent rooms: on one side the monks' workroom, used for reading and studying; on the other the large Romanesque–Gothic **refectory**, lit by ribbed twin windows topped with a rose window. It was formerly divided into two naves by vaults, of which you can see the remains of the pillars. Next door is the **kitchen**, which contained the main drainage system to the river and a chimney for airing the room, and behind this lies the **pantry**, where a slice of the original vaulting has survived on top of a single column. Across the court, on the northwestern edge of the complex, is the **brewery**, one of the biggest and oldest buildings in the abbey.

The most spectacular building, however, is the **church**, which, filling out the northeastern corner of the complex, has the dimensions of a cathedral (90m long and 40m wide), with pure lines and elegant proportions, and displays the change from Romanesque to Gothic; indeed, the transept and choir are the first known examples of Gothic in the Brabantine area. An uncommon feature is the series of bull's-eye windows which light the transepts. Of the original twelfth-century **cloister** adjoining the church, only a pair of twin windows remain (rebuilt in Gothic style from the fourteenth to the sixteenth centuries). Around its edges are tombstones and the solitary sarcophagus of the Crusader Gobert d'Aspremont.

Practicalities

There is no public transport direct from Nivelles to Villers-la-Ville, but you can still make the trip by **train**. Every half-hour (hourly at the weekend), a service links Nivelles with Charleroi, where an hourly train (every 2hrs at the weekend) goes to Villers-la-Ville; allow about an hour and a half for the whole journey. To get here from Brussels, catch a Namur train and change at Ottignies. The abbey is 1.6km from the train station and there aren't any signs: from beside the Ottignies platform, follow the sign pointing to Monticelli up the cobbled street and, after 100m, you'll reach a T-junction; turn right and follow the road round.

Villers-la-Ville **tourist office** (Tues–Fri 1–5pm, Sat 2–6pm, Sun 10am–6pm; ☎071/87 98 98) is situated in a little building that was once the main gateway into the abbey – it's to the right of the present entrance – and from the bridge beside it there are good views over the whole complex. The tourist office sells an in-depth English guide to the abbey and another detailing sixteen local **walks** with maps, though this is in French only. In summer the cloister is sometimes used for amateur theatre productions.

Charleroi

The approaches to **CHARLEROI** are hardly inviting. Belching chimneys dot the horizon, beside which rise grass-covered slag heaps. Glass works, coal mines and iron foundries have made the town the centre of one of Belgium's main industrial areas, and, although you can reach it from just about anywhere in Belgium, there's little reason to do so. It has a couple of decent museums, but these can just as easily be seen using Mons (35km), or even Brussels (50km), as a base. You might, however, find yourself here in the course of travelling down to the Botte du Hainaut beyond the city to the south.

The town

Charleroi divides into two distinct parts: the lower town, where you will probably arrive, and the upper town, whose circular **place Charles II** marks the city centre. The **Hôtel de Ville**, on the western side, is home to Charleroi's best museum, the **Musée des Beaux Arts** (Tues–Sat 10am–6pm; F50), whose excellent works by Hainaut artists and others who lived or worked in the province can be found at the top of a magnificent Art Deco staircase. There are the naturalistic works of Constantin Meunier depicting life in the mines and factories, romantic paintings by the Charleroi artist François Navez and a number of canvases by Pierre Paulus, whose work combines an earnest attempt to depict the grimy Charleroi industrial landscape with a rather paternalistic view of factory workers in general. There are also paintings by Magritte, notably the whimsical *La Liberté de l'Esprit*, and an indifferent *Annunciation* by Delvaux, as well as an upstairs display devoted to the life and times of one Jules Destrée, a local poet and socialist politician who campaigned hard for improvements in working conditions hereabouts.

Charleroi's other main museum, the **Musée du Verre** (Tue–Sat 9am–5pm; F50), is housed in the *Institut National du Verre* at boulevard Defontaine 10, about 200m east of place Charles II. A fascinating survey of all things glassy, the museum displays many beautiful glass items from different periods: Egyptian jewellery

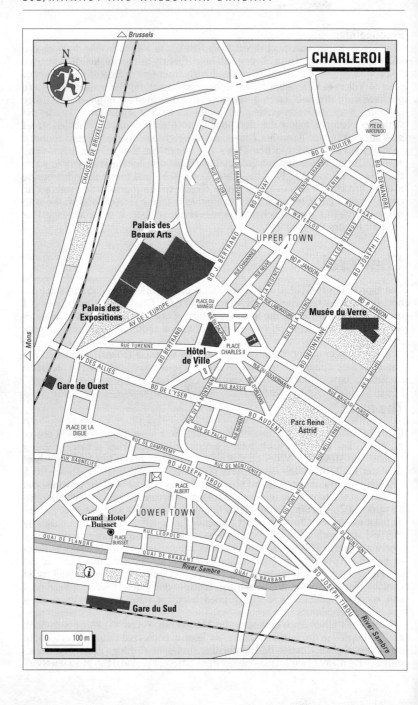

and vases, Roman and Venetian glass, and contemporary glass works. There's also a small archeology museum in the basement.

Out of town, a twenty-minute walk southwest of the tourist office along avenue Paul Pastur, you'll find the **Musée de la Photographie** (Tue–Sun 10am–6pm; F150), housed in the recently renovated neo-Gothic Carmelite monastery of Mont-sur-Marchienne. Though inconveniently located, a good 6km out of town, it's worth the effort, as the museum boasts a thought-provoking collection of nearly 60,000 creative and documentary-style photographs which are displayed in rotation. There's also a well-organized and interesting permanent exhibition over ten rooms around the cloister, which takes you through the history of photography to the present day. Temporary exhibitions are held regularly in the chapels.

Practicalities

Charleroi has two **train stations**, the Gare du Sud, where you're likely to arrive, and the Gare de Ouest, in the city centre. The **tourist office** occupies a kiosk in front of Gare du Sud (Mon–Fri 9am–5.30pm; ☎071/31 82 18) and hands out free city maps and leaflets. From beside Gare du Sud, buses run up to place du Manège, the main area for entertainment in the town, every few minutes throughout the day, and metro trains run to the same square every ten minutes. Failing that, it's only a ten-minute walk. In the unlikely event you want to **stay overnight**, the Hôtel Socatel Diplomat, boulevard Tirou 96 (☎071/31 98 11, fax 30 15 96; ⑤), just north of Gare du Sud, is competent and convenient.

There are plenty of **cafés** and **restaurants** around place du Manège and in the adjacent streets. Ethnic restaurants predominate: try *Athenes*, place du Manège 19, for excellent, well-priced Greek food, or the *Imperial* next door, which does a good line in home made Italian dishes – a neat option for a light lunch or big dinner. At the other end of the square, *La Bonne Fourchette*, boulevard Bertrand 55, serves couscous and kebabs, or, if all you want is straight Belgian grub, there's the moderately priced *Le Napoléon*, on place Charles II. Just off place du Manège, *Castel Naedery*, avenue de l'Europe 62, is the best place in town for traditional French and Belgian cooking, though it's a little pricey. Finally, for **entertainment**, it's worth checking out what's happening at the Palais des Beaux Arts, behind the Hôtel de Ville, on place du Manège. It's Charleroi's – and the region's – cultural and entertainment centre, attracting some of the big names in rock music.

South of Charleroi: the Botte de Hainaut

A tongue of land reaching south into France, the **Botte de Hainaut** (Boot of Hainaut) is shared between the provinces of Hainaut and Namur. A natural extension of the Ardennes range further east, if a little flatter and less wooded, it's mostly visited for its gentle scenery, though there are a few tangible attractions such as the basilica at Walcourt and the studied prettiness of Chimay. The tiny towns of the eastern – and more appealing – side of the Botte are readily accessible by public transport, with a regular train service leaving Charleroi to weave through the benign hills announcing Walcourt before continuing on to Philippeville and ultimately Couvin; there are no trains on the western side, but Chimay is easy to reach by bus from both Charleroi and Couvin. To tour beyond these main centres, you'll need a car; the other complication is that, apart from campsites, accommodation is extremely thin on the ground. Walcourt, with just one pleasant hotel, and Couvin, with a couple (though these are rather basic), are probably your best bases if you intend to overnight here.

Walcourt to Mariembourg

The straggling hillside settlement of **WALCOURT**, about 20km – and half an hour by train – from Charleroi, is a pleasant old town whose pride and joy is its thirteenth- to fifteenth-century, onion-domed **Basilique St Materne** (daily 10am–5pm; F100 or F120 combination ticket with the treasury), which dominates the town from its hilltop location at the top of the Grand-Place. Inside, the rood screen is a marvellous piece of work in which the Gothic structure is adorned by a flurry of Renaissance decoration. It was presented to the church by Charles V on the occasion of a pilgrimage he made to the Virgin of Walcourt, a silver-plated wooden statue that now stands in the north transept. An object of considerable veneration even today, the statue is believed to have been crafted in the tenth century, making it one of the oldest such figures in Belgium. The **treasury** (F100) has, among other items, a thirteenth-century reliquary cross in the style of Hugo d'Oignies (see p.274), a native of Walcourt. That's it as far as sights are concerned, but the town has an easy-going, old-fashioned charm and you may decide to hang around one of the bars on the square – the *Aigle Noir* is pleasant enough.

The **tourist office** (daily 10am–noon & 1–5pm; ☎071/61 25 26) is down from the church at the bottom of the wedge-shaped Grand-Place. From the **train station** it's a steep 1.2km walk to the church – turn right out of the station car park and follow the road as it curves upwards. There's only one recommendable **hotel**, the *Hôstellerie Dispa,* a tidy, well-cared-for place with modern furnishings down a narrow sidestreet near the station at rue du Jardinet 7 (☎071/61 14 23, fax 61 11 04; closed for 2 weeks during Sept; ④). The hotel also has the best **restaurant** in town, offering delicious seafood, not that there's much competition except for *Chez Martine* near the Basilique at Grand-Place 37, which serves tasty and good-value French cuisine.

Some 12km south of Philippeville, unexciting **MARIEMBOURG** started life, like its neighbour, as a Charles V fortress, though this time the emperor named the place after his sister, Mary of Hungary. Nothing survives of the stronghold today, but the town is the terminus of the **Chemin de fer à vapeur des Trois Vallées**, a refurbished steam engine that chugs its way east across the surrounding countryside to Treignes, near the French border (April–Oct; ring for times ☎060/31 24 40; F250). The steam train terminus is adjacent to Mariembourg train station, which is on the Charleroi Sud–Couvin line. Be warned that matters are further confused by an uninspiring *autorail* which plies the same route and is run by the same company.

Couvin and around

Just 5km south from Mariembourg and close to France, **COUVIN** was one of the first settlements in Hainaut to be industrialized, and its narrow streets were choked by forges and smelting works as early as the eighteenth century. In the event, Couvin was soon marginalized by the big cities further north, struggling on as a pint-sized manufacturing centre, a description that still applies. Tourism has also had an impact as the town lies at the heart of an increasingly popular holiday area, a quiet rural district whose forests and farmland are liberally sprinkled with country cottages. The prettiest scenery is to be found east of town along the valley of the River Viroin, which extends to Treignes and beyond across the French frontier.

Couvin itself, long and slim, and bisected by the Eau Noire River, is short on specific sights, but it does possess a good-looking ancient quarter, set on top of a rocky hill high above the river and the modern main square, place Général Piron. The other noteworthy feature is the **Cavernes de l'Abîme**, on rue de la Falaise, by the river on the east side of the town centre (April–June Sat & Sun only 10am–noon & 1.30–6pm; July to Sept daily 10am–noon & 1.30–6pm; Oct Sun only 10am–noon & 1.30–6pm; F140 or F320 including admission to Grottes de Neptune – see below). This series of caves is now home to an exhibition and audiovisual display on prehistoric times. Easy to reach by car or bike, but lacking in public transport, there's a rather more impressive limestone cave complex, the **Grottes de Neptune** (April–Sept daily 10am–noon & 1.30–6pm; Oct Sat & Sun only same hours; F230), about 5km northeast of Couvin on the road between the hamlets of Petigny and Frasnes. A well-developed stop on tourist itineraries, the guided tour includes a twenty-minute boat ride on a subterranean river, and an impressive sound and light show.

Back in Couvin, it's a ten-minute walk east from the **bus** and **train station** to the main square along rue de la Gare and its continuation Faubourg St Germain. The **tourist office** is on the way to the Cavernes de l'Abîme, at rue de la Falaise 3 (daily 9am–5pm; ☎060/34 74 63, fax 34 01 43). Neither of the two inexpensive central **hotels** exactly set the pulse racing – the *Hôtel de la Gare*, near the station at avenue de la Libération 3 (☎060/34 41 03; ②), is slightly smarter and probably the better bet. For **food**, there are a number of lively restaurants on and around the main square: try the busy *La Terrasse*, with simple, reasonably priced pasta dishes as well as more substantial choices.

As an alternative to Couvin, consider staying in **NISMES**, off the N99 about 4km east of town and easy to reach by bus. Neatly tucked in between the river and a cluster of wooded hills, this is the most picturesque of the Viroin valley villages, complete with the ruins of a seventeenth-century church and a rather cutesy tourist train (May–Sept 2–6pm; 50min; F120) that chugs through the surrounding countryside, where the limestone plateau is scarred by sharp ravines cut by the River Viroin.

Nismes has a **tourist kiosk** on the riverfront (Mon–Fri 9am–noon & 2–5pm; ☎060/31 11 28), and there are several **campsites** in the vicinity – try *Camping Le Sabot* at rue de la Station 52 (☎060/34 44 38, fax 34 70 56; year-round) or *Camping Baudets* rue de la Champagne 1(☎060/39 01 08), around 5km away in the tiny village of Olloy and accessible by bus #60 from Nismes. There's also a **hotel**, the small, smart and comfortable *Le Melrose*, on the southern edge of the village just off the N99 at rue Albert Grégoire 33 (☎060/31 23 39, fax 31 10 13; ④).

Beaumont to Rance

Accessible direct by bus from Charleroi, **BEAUMONT** is an old and somewhat dilapidated town crouched on a hill close to the French border. An important regional stronghold from as early as the eleventh century, parts of its fortifications are still intact, most notably the **Tour Salamandre** (May, June & Sept Mon–Fri 9am–5pm; July & Aug daily 10am–6pm; F50), a thick-walled rectangular structure that overlooks the river valley from its vantage point a brief, signposted walk away from the main square. Inside, there's a small museum of regional history, but really you climb the 136 steps for the view.

Twelve kilometres south of Beaumont, **RANCE** straggles along the main road, an uninviting town famous for its red marble quarries, which have spawned buildings worldwide, from Versailles to St Peter's in Rome. You can explore the subject in detail at the **Musée national du marbre** (National Marble Museum; April–Oct Tues–Sat 9.30am–6pm, Sun 2–6pm; Nov–March Tues–Sat 8.30am–5pm; F100), housed in the old town hall on the main street.

Chimay

Best known for the beer brewed by local Trappists, the small and ancient town of **CHIMAY** is a charming old place, governed for several centuries by the de Croy family, a clan of local bigwigs enlivened by a certain Madame Tallien. Born Jeanne Cabarrus, the daughter of a Spanish banker, her credentials were impeccably aristocratic until the French Revolution when, imprisoned and awaiting the guillotine, she wooed a revolutionary leader, Jean Tallien. He saved her, they got married, and she became an important figure in revolutionary circles, playing a role in the overthrow of Robespierre that earnt her the soubriquet Notre-Dame de Thermidor. Later, seeing which way the political wind was blowing, she divorced Tallien and hung about for another aristocrat – this time getting a de Croy. She married him in 1805 and lived the rest of her life in the tranquil environment of Chimay. She died in 1835 and her tomb is inside the **Collégiale des Sts Pierre et Paul** (Mon–Fri 9am–noon & 2–4.30pm, Sat 9am–5pm, Sun 11am–5pm; free), a mostly sixteenth-century limestone pile crammed with the graves of her adoptive family – among them the splendid mausoleum of Charles de Croy, a recumbent figure in alabaster dating from 1525. The church is bang in the middle of town and its walls crimp the slender **Grand-Place**, an eminently bourgeois square surrounding the rusting **Monument des Princes**, a water fountain of 1852, erected in honour of the de Croys.

From the Grand-Place, an elegant sandstone arch leads through to the **Château des Princes de Chimay** (March–Dec guided visits at 10.30am, 11.30am, 2.30pm, 3.30pm & 4.30pm; F200), the old home of the de Croy family. A considerably altered structure, it was originally built in the fifteenth century, but was reconstructed in the seventeenth century, then badly damaged by fire and partly rebuilt to earlier plans in the 1930s. Today the main body of the building is fronted by a long series of rectangular windows, edged by a squat turreted tower. Inside there are mainly old family portraits and a hotch-potch of period furniture, although the carefully restored theatre (modelled on the Louis XV theatre at Fortainebleau) is worth a look, and there are good views over the river valley and encompassing woods from the gardens.

Practicalities

With regular connections from Charleroi and Couvin, Chimay's **bus station** sits on the edge of the town centre, a five-minute walk from the Grand-Place. The **tourist office**, at rue de Noailles 4 (Mon–Fri 9am–noon & 1–5pm, Sat & Sun 10am–noon & 1.30–5pm; ☎060/21 18 46), a few paces east of the Grand-Place, has free maps and details of various tours. Some of the most popular incorporate beer tastings at the Chimay monastery's **brewery** (Mon–Fri 9am–2pm; free), 5km east of town, near the village of Baileux. (The monastery is actually situated 10km south of Chimay at Scourmont, but it's not open to the public.)

There are no **hotels** in the town centre – the nearest is the two-star *Motel Les Fagnes* (☎060/21 27 89, fax 21 45 38; ③), a good thirty-minute walk southeast of the Grand-Place at Chaussée de Couvin 77, on the road to Couvin. **Campers** should head for the *Camping Communal,* just west of the centre on the allée des Princes (April–Oct; ☎060/21 18 43), near a sports complex with swimming pool, shops and its own cafeteria. For a **snack** or light meal, *Aux Armes de Chimay*, on the Grand-Place, serves competent food at reasonable prices.

travel details

Trains

Charleroi to: Brussels (hourly; 50min); Couvin (1–2 hourly; 65min); Ligny (hourly; 20min); Mariembourg (1–2 hourly; 60min); Namur (every 30min; 30min); Nivelles (hourly; 20min); Ottignies (hourly; 45min); Villers-la-Ville (hourly; 30min); Walcourt (1–2 hourly; 30min).

La Louvière to: Binche (hourly; 10min); Charleroi (every 30min; 45min).

Mons to: Ath (hourly; 30min); Charleroi (hourly; 1hr 10min); La Louvière (hourly; 20min).

Tournai to: Ath (3 hourly; 20min); Brussels (3 hourly; 1hr).

Buses

Ath to: Beloeil (Mon–Fri hourly, Sat & Sun every 3hrs; 20min).

Charleroi to: Beaumont (hourly; 30min); Binche (hourly; 40min); Chimay (hourly; 80min); Rance (hourly; 60min).

Couvin to: Chimay (every 2hr; 35min); Namur (hourly; 1hr 15min); Nismes (hourly; 10min); Petigny (hourly; 10min).

Mons to: Binche (every 30min; 40min).

CHAPTER FIVE

THE ARDENNES

B elgium's southern reaches are in striking contrast to the crowded, industrial north, for it's here that the cities give way to the rugged, wilderness landscapes of the **Ardennes**. The Ardennes begins in France and stretches east across Luxembourg and Belgium before continuing on into Germany. Within Belgium, the Ardennes covers three **provinces**, those of Namur in the west, Luxembourg in the south and Liège in the east. The highest part is the **Hautes Fagnes** (aka Hohes Venn – the High Fens), in the German-speaking far east of the country, an expanse of windswept heathland that extends from Eupen to Malmédy. But this is not the Ardennes' most attractive or popular corner, which lies farther west, its limits roughly marked by Dinant, La Roche-en-Ardenne, and Bouillon. This region is given character and variety by its **river valleys**: deep, wooded, winding canyons reaching up to high green peaks, they are at times sublimely and inspiringly beautiful. The Ardennes' **cave systems** are also a major attraction, especially those in the Meuse, Ourthe and Lesse valleys, carved out by underground rivers that over the centuries have cut through and dissolved the limestone of the hills, leaving stalagmites and stalactites in their wake.

The obvious gateway to the most scenic portion of the Ardennes is **Namur**, strategically sited at the junction of the Sambre and Meuse rivers, and well worth a visit in its own right. The town's pride and joy is its massive, mostly nineteenth-century citadel – once one of the mightiest fortresses in Europe – but it also musters a handful of decent museums, great restaurants and (for the Ardennes) a lively night scene. From Namur you can follow the Meuse by train down to **Dinant**, a pleasant – and very popular – journey, going on to explore the **Meuse Valley** south of Dinant by boat or taking a canoe up the narrower and wilder **River Lesse**. From Dinant, routes lead east into the heart of the Ardennes – to **Han-sur-Lesse**, surrounded by undulating hills riddled with caves, **Rochefort**, and **St Hubert**, with its splendid Italianate basilica. Further east still is the unofficial capital of the Ardennes, **La Roche-en-Ardenne**, a rustic, hardy kind of town, pushed in tight against the river beneath wooded hills, and renowned for its smoked ham and game. The prettiest of all the towns hereabouts, however, is **Bouillon**, a delightfully picturesque little place whose narrow streets trail alongside the River Semois beneath an ancient castle; it's situated close to the French frontier, on the southern periphery of the Belgian Ardennes.

If you're visiting the eastern Ardennes the handiest starting point is big and grimy **Liège**, an industrial sprawl from where it's a short hop south to the long-established resort of **Spa**, which has little to offer except for its casino, and the much prettier town of **Stavelot**, with its marvellous carnival. You can use Stavelot as a base for hiking or canoeing into the surrounding

ACCOMMODATION PRICE CODES

All the **hotels and hostels** detailed in this chapter have been graded according to the following price categories. Apart from ①, which is a per-person price for a hostel bed, all the codes are based on the rate for the least expensive double room during high season. For more on accommodation, see p.000.

① Up to F1000 per person   ④ F2000–2500 per room   ⑦ F4000–5000 per room
② F1000–1500 per room   ⑤ F2500–3000 per room   ⑧ F5000–6000 per room
③ F1500–2000 per room   ⑥ F3000–4000 per room   ⑨ F6000 and over, per room

countryside, but to venture into the **Hautes Fagnes** your best bet is to stay in **Robertville**.

Getting around the Ardennes is difficult without your own transport. Only a handful of train services link the region's major towns and bus connections often involve long waits; a route that looks short and easy on the map may involve several time-consuming changes. Information about bus services can also be difficult to come by – though local tourist offices usually have a good set of timetables. With regard to **accommodation**, most of the major centres have been well developed, but rooms are often in short supply in high season (late July–August). Given all this, it's perhaps best to find a place you like and stay put, which gives you a chance to get stuck into the outdoor pursuits which attract so many visitors. Wherever you are, **walking** is the obvious pastime – rarely strenuous but often getting you out into some genuinely wild areas; the dedicated can follow the GR Namurois, which runs from Brussels through the three valleys of the Meuse, Lesse and Semois. **Canoes** can be rented at most river settlements, and **mountain bikes** are often available. Cross-country and – in some places – on-piste **skiing** are also popular in winter.

Namur

Just 60km southeast of Brussels, **NAMUR** is a logical first stop if you're heading into the Ardennes from the north or west, and is refreshingly clear of the industrial belts of Hainaut and Brabant. Many of Belgium's cities have suffered at the hands of invading armies and the same is certainly true of Namur: from the sixteenth century up until 1978, when the Belgian army finally moved out, Namur was the quintessential military town, its sole purpose being the control of the strategically important junction of the rivers Sambre and Meuse. Generations of military engineers have pondered how to make Namur's hilltop **citadel** impregnable – no one more so than Louis XIV's Vauban – and the substantial remains of these past efforts are now the town's main tourist attraction. Down below, the **town centre** crowds the north bank of the River Sambre, its cramped squares and streets lined by big old mansions in the French style and sprinkled with several fine old churches and a handful of decent museums. There are top-flight **restaurants** here too and a vibrant nightlife, lent vigour by the presence of the city's university. Finally, in an area of sparse public transport links, Namur is well connected to some far-flung parts of the Ardennes.

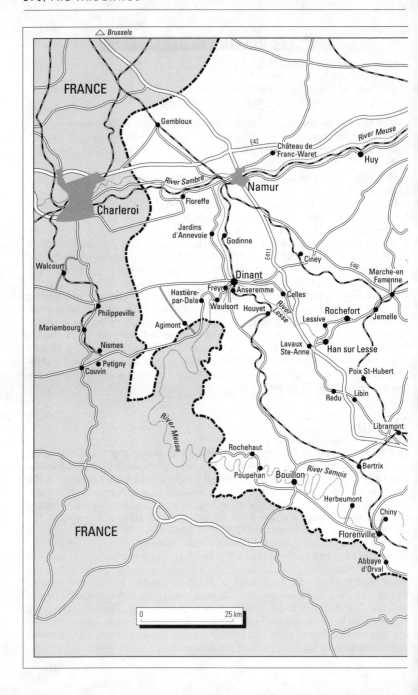

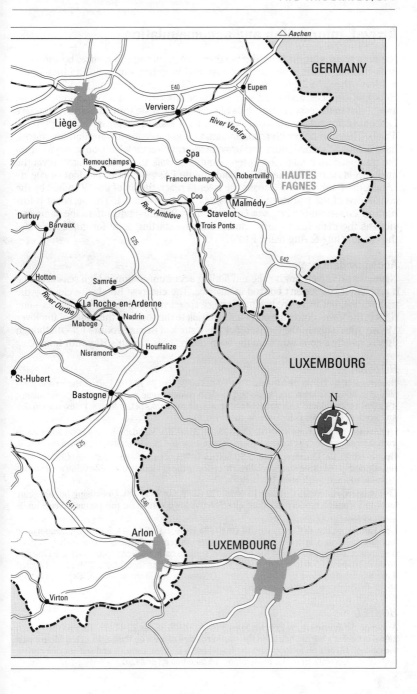

Arrival, information and accommodation

Namur's **train station** is on the northern fringe of the city centre, beside place de la Station, which is where you'll also find local bus stops and the **bus information office**, *La Maison du Tec*, at no. 28 (daily 7am–7pm; ☎081/25 35 55). Tec runs bus services across all of French-speaking Belgium. Two minutes' walk away – just to the east of place de la Station – is the main **tourist office**, on square Léopold (daily: summer 9.30am–6pm; winter 9.30am–12.30pm & 1–4pm; ☎081/24 64 49). They can help with accommodation, issue free town maps and brochures, have details of guided tours and provide information on what's on in town. From the train station, it takes about ten minutes to walk to the River Sambre via the main street, variously rue de Fer and rue de l'Ange. East of the foot of rue de l'Ange, the Pont de France spans the river to reach the tip of the "V" made by the confluence of the two rivers (the *grognon* or "pig's snout"). The seasonal **information chalet** on the *grognon* (summer daily 9.30am–6pm) offers the same services as the main tourist office and is also the starting point for guided tours of the citadel (July & Aug daily; F140).

Accommodation

Namur has relatively few hotels, and finding **accommodation** in high season can be a problem if you haven't booked in advance. The cheapest **hotels** are close by the train station, but there are two much more appetizing (and expensive) places – one right in the town centre, the other a short walk to the south on the banks of the River Meuse. Alternatively, the tourist office has a stock of **private rooms** (②–③), though they're mostly a good way from the town centre, as is Namur's HI **youth hostel**.

HOTELS

Beauregard, av Baron de Moreau 1 (☎081/23 00 28, fax 24 12 09). Part of the casino complex, this hotel has attractive, large and modern rooms, some with a river-view and balcony. It's a five- to ten-minute walk south of the centre, on the banks of the Meuse below the citadel. An excellent breakfast is included in the price. ⑥.

L'Excelsior, av de la Gare 4 (☎081/23 18 13, fax 23 09 29). Mundane budget hotel a few paces from the train station. Just fourteen rooms, above a bar and beside a traffic-congested avenue. ③.

Grand Hôtel de Flandre, pl de la Station 14 (☎081/23 18 68, fax 22 80 60). Competent if slightly dog-eared three-star hotel directly opposite the station. Reasonable value at F2500 for a double room, though breakfast is extra. ⑤.

Le Parisien, rue Emile Cuvelier 16 (☎081/22 63 79, fax 23 27 18). Unenticing but adequate hotel in a routine modern building close to the town centre on the corner of rue Emile Cuvelier and rue Pépin. ③.

Les Tanneurs, rue des Tanneries 13 (☎081/23 19 99, fax 26 14 32). Extremely comfortable four-star hotel in a lavishly renovated seventeenth-century brick building with two good restaurants, lots of marble and the occasional sunken bath. Sixteen rooms start at F1750 and go up in jumps of F500 to around F8500 for the palatial suites (breakfast F300 extra). Located down a quiet alley close to the town centre. Off-season and at the weekend, it's worth asking about discounts on the more expensive rooms. ③.

HOSTEL

Auberge de Jeunesse, av Félicien Rops 8 (☎081/22 36 88, fax 22 44 12). This 100-bed youth hostel occupies a big old house on the southern edge of town on the banks of the Meuse past the casino. There's no lock-out and the hostel has a kitchen, laundry and self-service restaurant. It's a 3km walk from the train station, or take bus #3 or #4. ①.

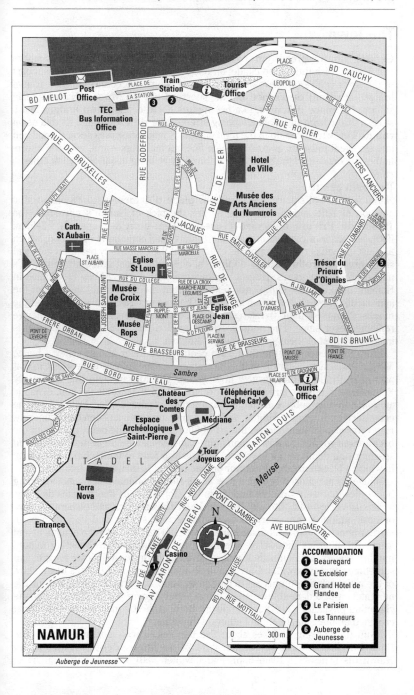

NAMUR

ACCOMMODATION
1 Beauregard
2 L'Excelsior
3 Grand Hôtel de Flandee
4 Le Parisien
5 Les Tanneurs
6 Auberge de Jeunesse

Auberge de Jeunesse ▽

The Town

Central Namur spreads out from around the confluence of the rivers Sambre and Meuse, with the hilltop citadel on one side of the Sambre and the main part of the town centre on the other. Citadel and centre are connected by a pair of bridges, the **Pont de France** and the shorter **Pont du Musée**. Namur's main square, the **place d'Armes**, is a few metres north of these two bridges and a stone's throw from the main shopping streets, **rue de l'Ange** and its extension **rue de Fer**, which run up to the train station. Namur possesses several good and one excellent museum as well as some fine old buildings – and, with the exception of the citadel, all the sights are within easy walking distance of each other.

The town centre

Namur's principal square, the shambolic **place d'Armes**, is now a busy traffic junction of little appeal, but close by lies the pick of Namur's museums, the **Trésor du Prieuré d'Oignies** (Tues–Sat 10am–noon & 2–5pm, Sun 2–5pm; F50), housed in a convent at rue Julie Billiart 17. This unique collection, which fills just one small room, comprises examples of the exquisitely beautiful gold and silver work of **Brother Hugo d'Oignies**, one of the most gifted of the region's medieval metal workers. Hugo's works were kept at the Abbey of Oignies in Hainaut until the late eighteenth century, when the monks hid them from the approaching French revolutionary army. The soldiers trashed the abbey and the monks smuggled their treasures to Namur for safekeeping – where they've remained ever since. The nuns provide a guided tour and their enthusiasm is infectious; most of them speak excellent English.

From the eleventh to the thirteenth century, the River Meuse valley – hence **Mosan** – was famous for the skill of its craftsmen, especially those working in that part of the valley which is now in Belgium. The Mosan style was essentially Romanesque, but its practitioners evolved a more naturalistic and dynamic approach to their subject matter, a characteristic of early Gothic. Dating from the early thirteenth century, Hugo's work demonstrates this transition quite superbly. Hugo was also an innovator in the art of filigree, raising the decoration from the background so that the tiny human figures and animals seem to be suspended in space, giving depth to the narrative. He was also fond of the technique of *niello*, in which a black mixture of sulphur or lead is used to incise lines into the gold.

Whatever his chosen style, they're wonderful devotional pieces, most holding holy relics that were brought back from the Holy Land by one Jacques de Vitry, a Parisian ecclesiastic who met Hugo in 1208. They are rich and elaborate pieces of work, studded with precious and semiprecious stones, and they display an extraordinary level of craftsmanship, an exquisite balance between ornament and form. The filigrees themselves are lively and realistic, often depicting minute hunting scenes, with animals leaping convincingly through delicate foliage, and sometimes engraved with a Christian dedication, or embossed with a tiny picture of the artist offering up his art to God in worship. In particular, look out for the intricately worked double-crosses, the reliquary cover for St Peter's rib, the charming phylacteries and a magnificent Book of the Gospels cover with Christ crucified on one side, God the Father on the other.

From the convent, it takes about five minutes to walk northwest along rue Emile Cuvelier to rue de Fer, where, at no. 24, the **Musée des Arts Anciens du Namurois** (Tues–Sun 10am–6pm, 5pm in winter; F50) occupies one of the finest of Namur's eighteenth-century mansions, an elegant structure set back from the street behind a formal gateway and courtyard. The collection begins with an enjoyable sample of Mosan metalwork, religious pieces amongst which the dinky geometrics of the brass enamels (*cuivre émaillé*) stand out. The craftsmanship is not, perhaps, as fine as that of Hugo d'Oignies, but it's still excellent metalwork and it's put into artistic context by the museum's (modest) collection of medieval sculptures and painted wooden panels. Of the museum's many paintings, the most distinguished are by Henri met de Bles, an early sixteenth-century, Antwerp-based artist who favoured panoramic landscapes populated by tiny figures. Look out also for the temporary exhibitions, most of which are displayed in the gatehouse.

Leaving the museum, it's a short stroll southwest to the finest of Namur's churches, the **Église Saint Loup**, a Baroque extravagance that overshadows a narrow pedestrianized street, the rue du Collège. Built for the Jesuits between 1621 and 1645, the church boasts a fluently carved facade and a sumptuous interior of marble walls and sandstone vaulting. The high altar is actually wood painted to look like marble – the ship carrying the last instalment of Italian marble sank and the Jesuits were obliged to finish the church off with this imitation. At the west end of rue du Collège, **on place St Aubain,** the **Cathédrale St Aubain** might well be the ugliest church in Belgium, a monstrous Neoclassical pile remarkably devoid of any charm. The interior isn't much better, with acres of creamy white paint and a choir decorated with melodramatic paintings by Jacques Nicolai, one of Rubens' less talented pupils. The attached **Musée Diocésain et Trésor de la Cathédrale** (Easter–Oct Tues–Sat 10am–noon & 2.30–6pm, Sun 2.30–6pm; Nov–Easter Tues–Sun 2.30–4.30pm; F50) displays objects gathered from diocesan churches across Namur and Luxembourg provinces. Highlights include a golden crown reliquary with thorns supposedly from Christ's crown of thorns, a twelfth-century portable altar with eleventh-century ivory carvings, and a silver statuette of St Blaise.

Heading south from the cathedral towards the river, turn left along rue des Brasseurs and then first left for the **Musée Felicien Rops**, rue Fumal 12 (Tues–Sun 10am–5pm, daily during July & Aug; F100), devoted to the life and work of the eponymous painter, graphic artist and illustrator. Born in Namur, **Felicien Rops** (1833–98) settled in Paris in the 1870s, acquiring a reputation for his dabblings in the occult and his debauched lifestyle. He also dabbled in art as well and illustrated the works of Mallarmé and Baudelaire. He was, apparently, greatly admired by the latter, but he is better known for his erotic drawings, which reveal an obsession with the macabre and perverse – skeletons and nuns and priests are depicted in oddly compromising poses, and old men are serviced by young, partly-clad women. He also drew many satirical cartoons, savagely criticizing the art establishment with which he never had much of a rapport, partly because his Impressionistic paintings were (justifiably) considered dull and derivative. The museum possesses a large collection of his works and is currently being extended to provide enough space to display it all.

The citadel

On the south side of the River Sambre, Namur's **citadel** (June–Sept & Easter daily 11am–5pm; April–May except Easter, Sat & Sun only 11am–5pm; F210) is an immense complex that takes at least a couple of hours to explore. The entrance fee includes an audiovisual display on the citadel's history, a miniature train ride around the grounds to see the various structures, a guided visit of the deepest underground passages, and access to the fortress's museums.

Namur was first fortified by a Gallic tribe, the Aduatuci, who named the place Nam, after one of their gods. They were attracted by the site's strategic position at the confluence of the rivers Sambre and Meuse plus a topography which encouraged fortification, with the sharp "V" formed by the junction of the rivers enclosing a narrow low-lying area set beneath a steep and craggy hill. In medieval times, a succession of local counts elaborated each other's fortifications and by the fourteenth century the town was protected by four sets of walls, which guarded the riverfront and climbed steeply up the hill behind. By the early sixteenth century, it was clear that improved artillery had rendered stone walls obsolete and every major European city set about redesigning its defences. Here in Namur the riverside fortifications were gradually abandoned while the section near the top of the hill – now loosely known as the **Château des Comtes** – was incorporated into a partly buried fortress, the **Médiane**, whose ramifications occupy the eastern portion of today's citadel. This part of the fortress was always the most vulnerable to attack and for the next two hundred years successive generations of military engineers, including Vauban and the Dutchman Coheoorn, tried to figure out the best way to protect it. The present structure reflects this preoccupation, with the lines of defence becoming more complex and extensive the further up you go. To further strengthen the fortress, the Spanish completed the **Terra Nova** bastion at the west end of the citadel in the 1640s, by which time Namur was considered one of the most important strongholds in Europe, attracting the attentions of Louis XIV, who besieged the town in 1692, and of William of Orange just three years later. The Dutch rebuilt the citadel between 1816 and 1825, and most of the remains date to this period.

The citadel is readily accessible by the *téléférique* **cable car** (April–Sept daily 10am–7pm; Oct–March & Sun 10am–6pm; F190 round trip, F160 one-way), a long and exhilarating ride beginning near the **Pont du Musée**. More prosaically, you can drive to the top – follow the signs from near the *Beauregard* hotel, beside the Meuse. When it's too windy for the cable car, the tourist office lays on a minibus service from their information chalet. It takes about five minutes to stroll from the cable car terminal to the citadel's **main entrance**, past the **Ouvrages à Cornes** – earthworks the shape of horns – and on into the Terra Nova bastion, site of the audiovisual show and terminal of the mini-train. From here you can also visit – with a guide – the fortress's underground passages, including the **Galeries Boufflers**, which extend for 300m and include a "War Office" used by Richelieu and Louis XIV. You can see the differences in the tunnels of different periods: the oldest, built in typical Spanish style, are the dryest and best preserved because they were built with two layers of bricks. Also inside the citadel, the **Espace Archéologique Saint-Pierre** (Tues–Fri noon–5pm & Sat–Sun 10am–5pm; free) has temporary displays on local archaeological digs and discoveries, while other exhibition areas focus on military history – artillery, uniforms and so forth.

Eating and drinking

Namur has an excellent selection of **restaurants** and a good supply of lively **bars**, many of them clustered in the quaint, pedestrianized squares just west of rue de l'Ange – on and around place Marché-aux-Legumes and neighbouring place Chanoine Descamps.

Restaurants

La Bonne Fourchette, rue Notre Dame 112. Pint-sized, informal and family-run restaurant down below the citadel on the way to the casino. A little off the beaten track, so the prices are very reasonable and the food is delicious. Closed Wed.

La Fondue, rue St Jean 19. Medium-sized restaurant serving excellent fondues and steaks for around F600 a head. Just off place Marché-aux-Legumes.

Le Grill des Tanneurs, rue des Tanneries 13. Situated upstairs in the *Hôtel Les Tanneurs*, this is an especially good lunch stop if you're visiting the nearby Trésor du Prieuré d'Oignies. It's open in the evening too, but dinner costs a packet. First rate French-style cuisine.

Le Moulin à Poivre, rue Bas de la Place 23. Cosy little restaurant offering tasty French food from premises just off place d'Armes.

La Petite Fugue, pl Chanoine Descamps 5 (☎081/23 13 20). Outstanding restaurant with mouth-watering Franco-Belgian dishes – F1200 for a three-course feast, but worth every centime. Closed Sunday evening and Monday.

Aux Petits Brasseurs, rue des Brasseurs 61. Smart little bistro with flowers on the table and pastel-painted walls. Excellent Franco-Belgian cuisine with prices to match.

Le Temps des Cerises, rue des Brasseurs 22. Pocket-sized, intimate restaurant offering a quality menu of dishes prepared in the French manner.

Bars

Le Chapitre, rue du Séminaire 4. Unassuming, sedate little bar with an extensive beer list. Behind the cathedral.

L'Exterieur Nuit, pl Chanoine Descamps. Bustling brasserie-cum-bar with occasional live music.

Henry's Bar, pl St Aubain 3. Right by the cathedral, this is a big loud brasserie in the best tradition.

Le Monde à L'Envers, rue Lelièvre 28. Lively, fashionable bar just up from the cathedral. A favourite spot for university students.

Piano Bar, pl Marché-aux-Legumes. One of Namur's most popular bars, with live jazz Friday and Saturday evenings from about 10pm.

Around Namur – L'Abbaye de Floreffe and Les Jardins d'Annevoie

Namur is a pleasant place to spend two or three days, which gives you time to visit the area's two main attractions: **L'Abbaye de Floreffe** with its magnificent seventeenth-century choir stalls, to the west of town, and the classically landscaped **Jardins d'Annevoie**, set beside the Meuse about 18km to the south, halfway to Dinant (see p.278). A visit to the gardens is readily incorporated into a longer day-trip (by car or train) along this stretch of the **Meuse**. The river is too wide to be all that dramatic, but it's still an enjoyable journey as it passes through a varied landscape of gentle wooded slopes interrupted by steep escarpments and jagged crags capped by ruined castles. The area draws rock-climbers in their droves and it was around here – a few miles to the northeast of Namur – that King Albert I fell to his death in a climbing accident in 1934. If you're not bothered about the gardens or abbey, you can travel straight from Namur to Dinant by **boat** on Sundays in July and August, leaving at 10am, and returning at 7pm with two hours in the middle to nose around Dinant (F650 round trip; ☎082/22 23 15).

L'Abbaye de Floreffe

A few kilometres west of Namur, towards Charleroi, the attractively sited **L'Abbaye de Floreffe** (one-hour guided tours, April–Sept daily 1.30, 2.30 & 4pm; F80; ☎081/44 53 03) makes a comfortable afternoon excursion. Founded in 1121, little remains of the original complex – the domestic buildings are mainly eighteenth-century – but the **abbey church** is certainly worth the detour, principally for its carved oak **choir stalls**. The work of one man, Pierre Enderlin, who took sixteen years (1632–48) over them, they're a remarkable achievement. In a superb state of preservation and displaying a marvellous inventiveness and intricacy, the choir stalls are carved with an array of figures – biblical characters, eminent and holy persons, and some 220 angels – each one of them different. Many of the faces are obviously portraits, humorous, sometimes satirical in tone, and include a self-portrait of the artist hidden among them. Also in the church is a very graceful wooden Virgin, carved in 1692, with the sculpting of her robes being extremely adept. In the restored Romanesque part of the church there's also a small **museum**, displaying various art objects, and the tour finishes with a video on the history of the abbey and the choir stalls. Tours are conducted in French, but some of the guides speak a little English.

The abbey is also home to the Romanesque **Moulin Brasserie** (all year, Mon–Fri 11am–6pm, Sat & Sun 11am–8pm), restored in 1972 and famous for three beers. The most distinctive, a dark, sweet ale, is sold here, though it's no longer brewed on the premises.

To get to the abbey from Namur by public transport, either catch the Charleroi train to Floreffe (1 hourly; 10min) and walk from the station – it takes about fifteen minutes – or catch bus #28 (9 daily; 30min) from Namur train station.

Les Jardins d'Annevoie

Les Jardins d'Annevoie are a favourite destination south of Namur, created in 1775 by Charles Alexis de Montpellier, and occupying the grounds of an eighteenth-century château (gardens April–Oct daily 9.30am–6.30pm; château July & Aug daily 9.30am–1pm & 1.30–6pm, Easter–June Sat & Sun only 9.30am–1pm & 1.30–6pm; F180, F210 including château). Montpellier mixed formal French and Italian styles to create the gardens, and it is in their use of water, with fountains and tree-lined canals, that the gardens combine these styles. They are a five-minute signposted walk up the hill from the Meuse, or a fifteen-minute walk from **Godinne** train station, which lies on the other side of the bridge. They're also reachable by bus from Namur or Dinant (4 daily; 55min).

Dinant and the Meuse and Lesse valleys

The centre of the Meuse valley tourist industry, **DINANT** has all the makings of a very picturesque town, slung along the river beneath craggy green cliffs. But once here the river and the cliffs hem in the town, making it feel oppressive, particularly at the height of summer when there are far too many visitors for a place of its size. There's also not a huge amount to see here and, although the countryside around is pretty good for walking and canoeing, it's not as wild as you'll find in other parts of the Ardennes.

Apart from the numerous boat trips downriver and on the nearby Lesse (see p.282), transport connections to more interesting places are very limited.

Basically, there are more beautiful destinations deeper in the Ardennes, and unless you're passing there's little reason to stop.

The Town

The **citadel**, on the central place Reine-Astrid but visible from just about anywhere in town (Jan Sat & Sun only 10am–4pm; April–Oct daily 10am–6pm; Nov–Dec & Feb–Mar daily 10am–4pm; F195, including *téléférique*), is the most obvious attraction in town, although it's something of a letdown if you've already visited the fortress at Namur. Reached either by way of the cable car or by a flight of four hundred or so steps, cut way back in 1577, the site was previously occupied by a fortified castle, but this was destroyed by the French in 1703 and the present structure was built by the Dutch from 1818 to 1821. The Germans occupied the place briefly in 1914, leading to a fierce battle during which they torched the town and executed hundreds of civilians. The Germans took the citadel again in 1940, and it was the scene of more bitter fighting in 1944 when the Allies took three days to dislodge them. The view from the top is good, while the inside has been turned into what is essentially a historical museum, with models recreating particular battles and the Dutch occupation, and a military section with weapons from the Napoleonic era to the last war. You can also see the wooden beams which supported the first bridge in Dinant, built nine hundred years ago by monks and found again by accident in 1952, as well as prison cells and the kitchen and bakery of the Dutch stronghold.

Immediately below the citadel, Dinant's most distinctive landmark is the originally Gothic church of **Notre-Dame** (daily 10.30–6pm; free), topped with the bulbous spire that features on all the brochures. There's not a huge amount to see inside – the church has been rebuilt several times since the twelfth century – but it's worth a quick look for the stained glass windows in the south transept and a couple of paintings by Antoine Wiertz, who was born in the town. If you want to see the birthplace of another native of Dinant, **Adolphe Sax**, the inventor of the saxophone, walk down rue A. Sax; the house where he lived, no. 35, is marked by a neat stained glass mural of the great man blowing his horn.

There is another **cable car**, or *télésiège*, in Dinant, made up of rickety two-person contraptions that head up from rue en Rhée (a block back from rue Grande) to the **Tour Mont Fat** (April–Sept daily 10.30am–7pm; F160), with its fine views, restaurants and kids' attractions including a playground and go-carts. Most visitors also take in the **Grotte La Merveilleuse** (daily: June–Aug 10am–6pm; March–May & Sept–Nov 11am–5pm; guided visits on the hour, in French and Flemish only; F180), across the bridge from the church down route de Philippeville 142, about 500m from the railway station. If you're a speleologist the unique feature of these ones is the whiteness of their rock formations, although again there are better caves to explore in the Ardennes proper (principally at Han-sur-Lesse – see p.286).

A couple of museums have recently opened just out of town focusing on *Dinanderie* – products of the town's once-flourishing copper industry. The **Musée Vivant de la Dinanderie** (also known as the Atelier de Dinanderie; March–Dec daily 10am–6pm; F160), at avenue des Combattants 54, is a copper workshop, opened to the public as an experiment in 1996. It's about as exciting as it sounds, with a guided tour in French explaining the working of copper and the former importance of the industry to Dinant. More bizarre, but also more interesting, the

Weathercock Museum (Easter–Sept Tues–Sun 1.30–6pm; F160) at route de Givet 27, has 86 church weathercocks from all over Europe, dating from the seventeenth century to 1990. An alarming number are punctured with bullet holes – presumably a result of target practice rather than wayward shooting. Upstairs, there is a room full of *Dinanderie* – plates, vases, boilers and bedwarmers – and a video in French explains how the design of weathercocks has evolved. To get to the museums, cross the bridge from place Reine-Astrid and turn left down avenue des Combattants; the Musée Vivant is ten minutes' walk away on your right and the Weathercock Museum another five minutes' walk further on.

Practicalities

Dinant's **train station** is on the opposite side of the river and five minutes' walk from the town centre; head right then turn left across the central bridge. The **tourist office** is a five-minute walk from the main place Reine-Astrid at rue Grande 37 (daily: June–Aug 9am–8pm; rest of the year 8.30am–noon & 2–5pm; ☎082/22 28 70), one block up from the river; the post office can be found on the river bank at avenue Winston Churchill 22. Much of the cheapest **accommodation** is near the station – the easy-going *Hôtel de la Gare* (☎082/22 20 56, fax 22 71 03; ③), and the more basic *Derby* a few doors along (☎082/22 41 96; ②) – while *Taverne Le Rouge et Noir* (☎082/22 69 44; ②), at rue Grande 26 near the tourist office, has recently added a few double rooms above the bar/restaurant. In town, the *Hôtel de la Couronne* is about as central as it's possible to get – right by the church at rue A. Sax 1 (☎082/22 24 41, fax 22 70 31; ③); it isn't a lot more expensive, and has a nice bar and restaurant to boot. Along the river, about two kilometres out of the centre, *Hôtel Vachter* (☎082/61 13 14, fax 61 28 58: ⑤) at chaussée de Namur 140, has comfortable, modern doubles for F2700, an excellent restaurant, and is the ideal quiet retreat, though unless you're prepared to hike up from the town, you'll need a car. The tourist office also has details of private **rooms**, although these are few and far between. There is no hostel, but there are plenty of **campsites**, the closest being *Camping de Bouvignes* (☎082/22 40 02; March–Oct), across the main bridge and left along the river for just over a kilometre.

To cater to Dinant's substantial day-tripper trade, there are plenty of cheap places to **eat** like snack bars, but quality restaurants are thinner on the ground. *Villa Casanova*, by the water at avenue Churchill 9, has good pasta and pizza all day from F300 a head, and there are half a dozen cafés nearby offering reasonably priced plats du jour. In the evening, *Duc de Bourgogne* in place Reine-Astrid has a good Belgian menu and great mussels, with meals starting at F450. Other promising options include *Isle de Grand-Mère*, past the tourist office at place St Nicolas 11, with a three-course menu for F800, the lively pasta joint at *Amical Taverne*, rue Grande 20, and across the river, *Villa Mouchenne*, avenue des Combattants 30, which is housed in an impressive château-like building and offers a set four-course menu for F850.

Le Sax, place Astrid 13, is an unpretentious **bar** with a good beer selection – sit outside and watch the floodlit citadel – and the *Bridge Pub* nearby has a small club upstairs where you can hear local trad-jazz bands play their hearts out on a weekend. *Café du Pont*, opposite, is more sedate and very popular, while *Le Charles Quint* across the bridge is another sound choice. To escape the summer crowd, head down rue Grande – the further out you go, the less touristy it feels.

WALKING AND BIKING AROUND DINANT

The Dinant **tourist office** sells the Institut Géographique National's map *Dinant et ses anciennes communes*, which shows fifteen circular walks, five mountain-bike routes and one cycling circuit in the local area. Each of the **walks** has a designated starting point at one of the hotels.

As you'd expect, the best walking is alongside the two rivers. **Walk 6** starts in Anseremme (seven minutes by train from Dinant) and can be combined with **walk 5** to take in the region's highlights. Head down from the train station and straight on to the River Meuse, then turn left along the footpath past the abbey. After the tennis courts you have to turn left onto an unpromising road past a small housing estate (and signs warning against unauthorized climbing) until a path takes you along the riverbank as far as the Château de Freyr on the other side. From here keep a look out for the path that climbs steeply through the woods to the main road, which you follow for half a kilometre before turning left through the Ferme de Haut, with fine views of the valley as you drop down to the Lesse. Turn right by the campsite until you cross the bridge; the path heads left through the car park and climbs up above the river for more magnificent views before turning down through the woods to the village. Expect the combined routes to take around three hours of walking time.

Both 5 and 6 involve some reasonably testing ascents. A gentler walk is to ignore the circular routes and follow **GR route 126** – around two and a half hours of walking – along the Lesse between Houyet and Gendron-Celles. Trains take twenty minutes from Dinant to Houyet – take the timetable along with your picnic and you can plan to arrive at Gendron-Celles in time for the return train to Dinant. Alternatively, if you become enamoured with the scenery, there are a couple of **campsites** at each village.

Walk 8 is not one of the more spectacular routes – much of it is over tarmac road – but it does allow you to visit a couple of places of interest. From Gendron-Celles station the route leads northwest along a small tributary of the Lesse to Veves, whose renovated fifteenth-century **château** (April–Oct daily 10am–6pm; F120) is perched on a ridge overlooking the surrounding countryside, with an armoury and eighteenth-century period rooms. A couple of kilometres further on, **Celles** is one of the prettiest villages in the area, gently filing up the slope of a wooded hill, underneath the huge tower and Lombard arches of the Romanesque **Église St Hadelin**. The church's thirteenth-century stalls are the oldest in the country along with those of Hastière-Par-Delà (see below). If you fancy staying over, Celles has several **hotels**, including *La Clochette*, rue de Veves 1 (☎082/66 65 35; ③), which is actually the designated starting point of the walk, or you can continue back to Gendron-Celles around the Bois de Hubermont.

The five routes for **mountain-bikes** range from five to forty kilometres, though to see the most attractive scenery you need to get out on the longer routes 19 and 20. You can normally rent mountain-bikes from the canoe operators in Anseremme (try Kayaks Ansiaux on ☎082/22 23 25), or ask at the tourist office in Dinant for the best deals.

The Meuse valley

The stretches of the **Meuse** south of Dinant are not the river's most impressive, but the town's wharves are nevertheless lined with leisure boats pushing **cruises**. There are several different companies located on avenue Winston Churchill, each with boats leaving at different times, though the prices are roughly the same whichever you go with. While the river is not especially picturesque, taking a boat is one way of moving south if that's where you're headed. Destinations include the two places most worth visiting on this part of the river: Freyr (F320 round trip) and Hastière (F420); excursions also head out to Anseremme (F180) and Givet (F520), as well as to Heer-Agimont on the French border, although even this far down the scenery is fairly tame, the river wide and gently curving.

If you actually want to have time to look around the following places on a day trip, you're better off getting the **GIVET** bus, #154a from outside Dinant station, which calls at each of them (Mon–Fri 12 daily, Sat 7 daily, Sun 4 daily). **FREYR** itself is home to an eighteenth-century château (July & Aug Sat & Sun 2–6pm; F220), pushed up against the riverbank and edged by a small but well-kept formal French garden. On the opposite side of the river, the sheer cliff face of Rocher Freyr is used for training by climbers of the Club Alpin school. **WAULSOURT**, farther along, is a resort with faded elegance and a yacht club, its riverfront fringed by gracefully ageing mansions. Three kilometres away, **HASTIÈRE** is the most interesting place to stop, due mainly to its Romanesque-Gothic church over the river at **HASTIÈRE-PAR-DELÀ**. The **church** (April–Oct daily 2–5pm; free) was built by Irish monks around 1035 and had a Gothic choir added in the thirteenth century, though as a whole it's now much restored after destruction by Huguenots in 1568, and again by French revolutionaries two centuries later. It's a typical church of the Mosan Romanesque style, with a flat wooden roof, plain square pillars and Lombard arches, similar to the church at Celles (see box on p.281). A faded painting on the triumphal arch dates from the original construction, but the crypt is the oldest surviving part, containing Merovingian sarcophagi. The wooden thirteenth-century choir stalls are among the oldest in Belgium, with original and unique carvings – some allegorical, some satirical and mocking – a number of which were, in 1443, replaced with a plain triangle since they were considered too disrespectful. Hanging above the altar is an unusual German fifteenth-century Calvary, which has Christ, Mary and St John standing on a dragon. Near the baptismal font is a beautiful sixteenth-century statue of the Virgin, whose graceful posture has earned it a place in several national exhibitions.

The Lesse valley

Exploring the valley of the **River Lesse**, which spears off the Meuse a little way south of Dinant, is perhaps the most exciting thing you can do in the area around the town – something most people do in reverse order travelling back downriver from Houyet by **canoe**. There are three companies which run trips, and prices and options are fairly uniform, with the standard itinerary beginning at Anseremme, where you buy a ticket and take a special morning bus to Houyet; trains also leave Dinant for Anseremme and Houyet once hourly. The return leg from Houyet to Anseremme along the river is 21km and takes about five hours. There are boats for one or two, plus large steered "barges" for those who don't feel up to canoeing, and plenty of places to stop for lunch along the way. Groups, by prior arrangement, may leave from Gendron, which reduces the return paddle to 12km or two and a half hours.

The course is wild and winding, with great scenery, though be warned that sometimes it gets so packed there's a veritable log-jam of canoes. Get to Anseremme/Houyet as early as possible if you want to enjoy the river in peace. For prior reservations (a good idea in high summer) and further details call

☎082/22 61 86 or 22 23 25; reckon on paying F600 for a single canoe for a day, doubles F800.

Halfway to Anseremme you pass by the **Parc National de Furfooz** (April–May 10am–5pm; June–Aug 10am–6pm; Sept–Oct 10am–4.30pm; F100), scenically the best part of the trip. Occupying a promontory overlooking the Lesse, it's not a large park and, if you want to explore it, ninety minutes should be time enough to complete the marked circuit of 3.5km. There's not actually a great deal to see, but a scattering of archeological remains and geological formations give purpose to what is a pleasant walk. There are reconstructed Roman baths, from where you can walk up to a high ridge overlooking the river. There are also foundations of a Roman fortress, converted in the Middle Ages and used many times since.

The park can also be reached by **train** from Dinant. Get off at Gendron-Celles (10min), turn left out of the station, make a sharp left before the bridge into the campsite and then a sharp right under the bridge. A path goes alongside the river for about twenty minutes to the park entrance (car drivers should use another marked entrance on the other side of the park, approached via the village of Furfooz).

You can also make a canoe trip on another part of the river, up from Wanlin to Houyet, a distance of 12km. If you're headed for the more southerly reaches of the Ardennes, the train from Dinant through Gendron-Celles and Houyet goes on to Bertrix for connections to Libramont, a main train junction, with regular services to Luxembourg, Arlon and Virton. Bertrix is also the place to pick up a bus to Bouillon, although they're not at all regular – get the times from Dinant's train station or tourist office.

Rochefort and Han

A little distance beyond the source of the River Lesse, to the south, lies one of the Ardennes' most beautiful regions, centring on the tourist resorts of **Han-sur-Lesse** and **Rochefort**. The area also offers sights like the Han-sur-Lesse caves, the most spectacular in the country, as well as the odd castle, and the surrounding countryside, thickly wooded and with good roads and gentle hills, is perfect for cycling.

As for **transport**, access is difficult from Dinant – in fact, it's easier to go back to Namur and take the train to **Jemelle** (direction Luxembourg), the nearest large train junction; trains also go to Jemelle from Libramont, Liège and Arlon. Besides the train, and bikes, there are reasonably frequent **buses** between Jemelle station, Rochefort, Lessive, and Han. Also in July and August a special **tourist train** operates twice a day from Rochefort to Lavaux Ste Anne – a one-hour journey. It stops at Han, but you must begin the journey from Rochefort; details from Rochefort tourist office (see below).

Rochefort

Situated in the midst of some lovely countryside, the small town of **ROCHEFORT** is as good a centre for exploring the Ardennes as you'll find. It's not an especially attractive place in itself, but it does have a good range of cheap accommodation, as well as other facilities like bike rental, and it has none of the crass commercialism of its neighbour, Han.

The Town

Rochefort follows the contours of an irregularly shaped hill, its long and pleasant main street, rue de Behogne, slicing through the centre from north to south, although the only things of tangible interest are actually outside the town centre. The main thing to see in the town itself is the **Grotte de Lorette** (July & Aug daily 10am–4.30pm; April–June & Sept to mid-Nov Thurs–Tues 10am–4.30pm; guided tours every 45min; F190), a ten-minute walk from the central crossroads, place Albert 1er – walk down rue Jacquet and take the first left up the hill, rue de Lorette, bearing right at the top. First discovered in 1865 by a man walking his dog (the dog disappeared suddenly through a hole in the ground), the caves are cold and eerie, their most impressive feature the huge Salle du Sabbat – no less than 85m high. Renovations have recently been made to improve access and lighting – the most spectacular innovation being an underground sound and light show.

Close by the entrance, the small **Lorette Chapel** dates from the 1620s. Built for the countess de Marck, it's a reproduction of the Santa Casa chapel in Loreto, Italy; according to local legend, a monkey stole the countess's child and she promised to build the chapel if the child was returned unharmed.

Back at the bottom of the hill, turn left up rue Jacquet for Rochefort's other main attraction – the ruins of the medieval **Château Comtal** (June–Sept daily 10am–6pm; April–May Sat & Sun only 10am–6pm; F60), which offers fine views from its rocky outcrop. The original castle dates from 1155, although there was almost certainly some sort of fortification here a lot earlier. In the 1740s the local count decided to convert it into a more informal, less forbidding place, demolishing the keep and incorporating the old walls into a new palace. Within a century, though, the owners had run into financial trouble and the château was gradually demolished; some of the massive stones were used in the adjoining Maison Carré (square house), built in 1840, and in the new neo-Gothic castle of 1906 which now houses the ticket office. Other fragments of the old castle were sold off to local builders and the distinctive, irregular limestone stones are now incorporated in buildings all over town. Unsurprisingly, there's not an awful lot left of the old castle now, but it's a pleasant enough place to wander for an hour or so. Alongside the remains of the old walls there are a couple of wells that were dug out of the bare rock while, in the small park just below the entrance, you can see the eighteenth-century arcades added to prop up the fashionable formal gardens. A tiny museum in the castle has objects from down the centuries: old cannonballs, ceramics, oyster shells and wine bottles.

The town's surroundings also reward exploration (see box on p.285 for suggested routes). Thirty minutes' walk through the woods to the north, the **St Remy Abbey** is a Cistercian monastery founded in 1230, best known today for producing the Rochefort Trappist beer. The monastery buildings are closed to the public but you are welcome to attend the daily services in the recently renovated church (times from the tourist office – see below). The church is down the slope to the right and then on your left after you enter the monastery grounds.

Practicalities

Rochefort's friendly and well-organized **tourist office**, rue de Behogne 5 (Mon–Fri 9am–12.30pm & 1–6pm, Sat 9.30am–12.30pm & 1–5pm; ☎084/21 25 37), has information on the town and can make accommodation reservations for no charge, including rooms at a number of bed-and-breakfast places. Of a number of

WALKING, CYCLING AND CANOEING AROUND ROCHEFORT AND HAN

There is some attractive countryside around Rochefort, criss-crossed by several rivers and providing opportunities for good walking, canoeing and mountain-biking. **Walkers** should get hold of the map produced by the Institut Géographique National, *Rochefort et ses villages* (F280 from the tourist offices in Rochefort and Han), which lists 27 walks, as well as eight routes for **mountain-bikers** and three for **cyclists**.

One of the most scenically varied **walks** is no. 12, Resurgence d'Eprave, a twelve-kilometre circular walk **from Rochefort**. Take rue Jacquet out of town past the château and the route is signposted to the right, through Hamerenne, with its tiny Romanesque chapel of St Odile, and across fields full of wildflowers to the River Lhomme. Follow the riverbank to the spot where the River Wamme emerges from underground to join the Lhomme; don't try to cross the river but double back and turn right for the stiff climb uphill past the Eprave Grotto for grand views over the cornfields. Fifteen minutes' walk further on, the village of Eprave has a restored mill with a working waterwheel and, opposite, the *Auberge du Vieux Moulin* (☎084/37 73 18, fax 37 84 60; ③) makes a delightful place to stay or eat. The walk back to Rochefort from here is rather dull, following the road, and you may want to retrace your steps, or join route 4, Grotte d'Eprave, to Han for the bus back to Rochefort (5 daily, 9 on Sat & Sun; 6min).

A couple of good shorter walks around Rochefort include no. 7, Lorette, a thirty-minute climb through the woods above town, taking in the Lorette chapel (see above) and some decent views over the castle. Head up rue de Lorette towards the caves and turn left, keeping to the left, where the track is signposted. The six-kilometre route 10, Abbaye, goes the other way out of town, across the bridge and cutting north off the main road through some thickly wooded scenery as far as St Remy Abbey (see opposite), before looping back to Rochefort.

The **walks around Han** are less interesting, though you can create a very pleasant half-day itinerary by following route 2, Turmont, through the Lesse and Lhomme Nature Reserve to Auffe, where route 20, Les Etouneaux, climbs up through the dense woods of Serivau – good hunting territory in the past and still with a bit of a "Hansel and Gretel" feel to it. Returning past Auffe, take route 24, Les Pics Epeiches, across the fields as far as Lessive, where you can get a decent lunch at *Le Vieux Lessive* (closed Mondays between October and May) before returning to Han.

If you want to mess about on the river, **canoes** can be rented from SPRL Kayak Lesse et Lhomme (☎082/22 43 97) near the bridge in Han. The office has a few kayaks and pedal boats for just splashing around by the town, but it's much more scenic and fun to take their shuttle service to Lessive, 4km away, and then canoe from there to Villers-sur-Lesse (3km; F600 per two-seater kayak), Wanlin (13kms; F1600) or Houyet (23km; F1800). The price for each trip includes the return bus ride to Han or rental of a bike to make your own way back; the office is open from 10am–4pm, but you'll need to get there before 1pm if you're heading to Wanlin and before 11.30am if you're planning the lengthy trip to Houyet. In high summer the water level on the Lesse can drop far enough to make canoeing impossible; call ahead before you make the journey to Han. The kayak office rents out **mountain-bikes** for F800 per day and regular bikes for F400 per day; mountain-bikes can also be rented from the tourist office in Rochefort for F700 per day.

reasonable **hotels** in the centre of Rochefort, the *Central,* at place Albert 1er 30 (☎084/21 10 44, fax 21 22 19; ②), is an economical option, as is *Le Limbourg* down the road at no. 21 (☎084/21 10 36, fax 21 44 23; ③). There are two inexpensive hotels close together on rue Jacquet, just uphill from the centre, the comfortable *Le Vieux Logis*, at no. 71 (☎084/21 10 24; ③), housed in a lovely old building, and *La Fayette*, no. 87 (☎084/21 42 73, fax 22 11 63; ②), which is rather more basic, but correspondingly cheaper. *La Malle Poste*, rue de Behogne 46 (☎084/21 09 86; ④), is a pleasant if spookily old-fashioned place and has an excellent restaurant attached (closed Wed) which serves delicious traditional Belgian food. It also has a convivial bar – *La Coterie* – which dates back to the sixteenth century and is fully stocked with a fine selection of traditional Belgian beers. If you're **camping**, there's a convenient site, *Camping Communal*, a five-minute walk from the centre of Rochefort – simply follow route de Marche out of town from place Albert 1er and take the first left after the river, rue du Hableau. Nearby, on the same road at no. 25, there's also an 86-bed **gîte d'étape** (☎084/21 46 04; ①).

For **eating**, *Bella Italia*, just next door to the *Hôtel La Malle Post*, offers substantial pizzas, pasta dishes, and truly splendid calzone from F300, as well as an extensive menu of good-value and tasty Belgian cuisine. Further down the road, veering left just before the bridge, *Le Must* is the liveliest bar in town, and serves cheap beer and croque-monsieurs; *Le Limbourg*, place Albert 1er 21, serves excellent local specialities, and has set menus from F800. Opposite the tourist office, *La Gourmandise* at rue de Behogne 24 has the best crêpes in town (F250–350), and also serves simple, good-value meals – pasta, salads – for around F250.

Han-sur-Lesse

Just 6km southwest of Rochefort, tiny **HAN-SUR-LESSE** is well known for its caves, which are the most impressive in the Ardennes – with the result that in summer at least the village is packed. There are masses of hotels and eating places to absorb the invasion, most in the immediate vicinity of the centre, but the frantic atmosphere may make you want to curtail your visit.

In fact there's not much to actually see in Han apart from the **Grottes de Han**, located outside the village a little way downriver (May–Aug trips every 30min daily 9.30–11.30am & 1–5pm, 6pm in July & Aug; April, Sept & Oct trips every hour daily 10am–noon & 1.30–4.30pm, 5.30pm on Sat & Sun; March & Nov trips every 2hr daily 10am–4pm; closed Dec–Feb; F350), but in fact accessible from the central ticket office, which dominates the village centre on the corner of rue J. Lamotte – you're taken by special train to the caves' entrance and after the tour are left a little way up the river, five minutes' walk from the village centre. The **Speleotheme** (same hours and ticket as the Grottes), on the first floor of the Dry Hamptay Farm near the exit, is a short audiovisual display about the caves.

The caves were discovered at the beginning of the nineteenth century and measure about 8km in length, a series of limestone galleries carved out of the hills by the River Lesse millions of years ago. Tours only visit a small part of the cave system, taking in the so-called Salle du Trophée, the site of the largest stalagmite, the Salle d'Armes, where the Lesse reappears after travelling underground for 1000m (it enters at the Belveux Gap), and the massive Salle du Dome – 145m long and 20m high – part of which holds a small lake.

For an insight into how the caves were formed, go to the **Musée du Monde Souterrain** (daily July & Aug 10am–7pm; March–June & Sept to mid-Nov

11am–5pm; F120), opposite the caves' ticket office at place Theo Lannoy 3, behind the tourist office. A section of the museum explains the process, while other sections display the findings of archeological digs in the region – most were found where the Lesse surfaces again after travelling through the grottoes – among them flints, tools and bone ornaments from the Neolithic period, as well as weapons and jewellery from the Bronze Age.

Han's other attraction is a **wild-animal reserve** (same hours as the caves; F250) just outside the town, an area of 2.5 square kilometres containing animals which inhabited the Ardennes in prehistoric times – bison and bears – along with deer and wild boar. A special bus trawls around for about an hour and a half, seeking them out; it's certainly worth doing if you're travelling with kids – otherwise you might as well concentrate on the caves.

A combined ticket to the caves, the museum, the Speleotheme and the wildlife reserve costs F550.

Practicalities

The **tourist office**, based in a chalet opposite the caves' ticket office (May–Sept daily 11am–4pm; ☎084/37 75 96), has a list of a dozen private homes that rent **rooms** (②). **Hotels** are quite numerous and relatively cheap in Han. The *Hôtel des Ardennes*, right in the centre of town at rue des Grottes 2 (☎084/37 72 20, fax 37 80 62; ③), has a wide variety of rooms and a fairly decent restaurant; *Hôtel des Ardennes 2*, next door (same phone and fax numbers; ⑤), has eighteen modern rooms and is somewhat smarter, though more expensive. The *Henry IV*, five minutes' walk away on rue des Chasseurs Ardennais 59 (☎084/37 72 21, fax 37 81 78; ④), the road towards Rochefort, is also a pleasant spot, and has the advantage of being a little way removed from Han's summer hubbub. A good, cheap place to stay in Han is the **gîte d'étape**, handily located in the centre of the village, just behind the car park at rue Gîte d'Étape 10 (☎084/37 74 41; ①). There are also two **campsites**, both by the river's edge: *Camping le Pirot* (☎084/37 72 90; open year-round) and *Camping de la Lesse* (☎084/37 72 90; open year-round) – turn right out of the tourist office and walk 100m.

There are lots of places to **eat** reasonably, although standards aren't particularly high and prices tend to be inflated almost everywhere. *La Stradella*, rue d'Hamptay 59, has good Italian food and is one of the few places in town where you can get a meal late in the evening; *Café Luxembourg*, next door, sells cheap snacks and is probably Han's liveliest bar. The more expensive restaurant at the *Hôtel des Ardennes* is also pretty good, and the bar has a great choice of beers. If it's breakfast you're after, check out *Le Marron Glacé*, rue de Grottes 9, a bakers-cum-café which serves the best croissants in town. Further down the road *Bell Vue Café*, at rue Lamotte 1, is well known for its traditional Belgian cuisine and offers good-value three-course lunch menus for F490.

Lessive and Lavaux Ste Anne

Five kilometres northwest of Han, **LESSIVE** is home to the Belgian space and satellite station or **RTT** (April–Oct daily 9.30am–5pm; F220). Topped with three huge antennae, it's something of a local tourist attraction, built here in a sheltered valley, far from wind and phone interference, and because the schist soil is very stable. Here they both broadcast TV programmes and receive and transmit information by satellite. There's an exhibition dedicated to its advanced technology and a museum demonstrating the first telephone and telegraph services. You can also try out a video telephone.

About 5km west of Han, **LAVAUX STE ANNE** is home to what was originally a fourteenth-century **château** (daily: March–June & Sept–Oct 9am–6pm; July & Aug 9am–7pm; Nov–Feb 9am–5pm; F175), surrounded by a moat, with three fifteenth-century towers and one from the fourteenth century. The exterior has a medieval appearance, and Renaissance buildings surround the sturdy interior courtyard. Inside, there's a **Museum of Nature and Hunting** and a **Museum of the Countryside and Folklore** (same hours and ticket as château) – neither exactly vital stops, but reasonable diversions if you're in the area.

St Hubert and around

About 20km southeast of Rochefort, **St Hubert** is another popular Ardennes resort, named after the patron saint of hunters, who is said to have undergone his strange conversion in the woods nearby, afterwards becoming a monk at Stavelot Abbey. According to legend, Count Hubert, a young Frankish nobleman, was hunting in the Ardennes on Good Friday in the year 685 when he caught a stag. He was about to kill it when a vision of Christ on the Cross appeared between the animal's antlers, beseeching him to lead a more religious life – Hubert renounced his title and became a hermit.

Later, in the seventh century, an abbey was founded here, giving its name to the town that grew up around it – these days one of the more peaceful of the Ardennes settlements, deep in the heart of the forest. It's still a popular hunting centre and a great base for some gentle hiking, but its best-known attraction is the **Basilique St Hubert** (Mon–Sat 9am–noon & 1–6pm; free), whose grand facade of 1731 is visible from just about anywhere in town. Most of the rest of the church is sixteenth-century and Gothic in style, although the crypt's Romanesque arches date back another five hundred years. The slender columns of the ambulatory are one of the church's finest features, a curving corridor of grey and yellow stone with a retable of 24 – albeit spoiled – Limoges enamels in one of the chapels. The restored eighteenth-century choir stalls are delightful too, with two meticulously carved strips tracing the stories of St Hubert and St Benedict.

The town's high point is the annual **festival** of Juillet Musical de St Hubert (throughout July; contact tourist office for exact dates) which features a variety of classical music concerts and recitals – including a performance by the Belgian National Orchestra – held in the Basilique and l'Eglise St Gille.

Practicalities

Next door to the church, the abbey's oldest domestic buildings house the **tourist office** (July–Aug daily 10am–noon & 1.30–5.30pm; Sept–June Sat & Sun only 10am–noon & 1.30–5.30pm; ☎061/61 30 10), which sells maps of the area's marked walks, as well as stocking plenty of other Ardennes bumf. The nearest **train station** to St Hubert is 6km away at Poix St Hubert, from where you can either take a bus (Mon–Fri 12 daily, Sat & Sun 4 daily; 15min) or rent a bike to the town.

Of the four **hotels** in the town centre, the *Hôtel du Luxembourg* (☎061/61 10 93, fax 61 32 20; ③), on place du Marché, is a friendly place with a good, family-run restaurant well known for its excellent fish dishes, while *Cor de Chasse* (☎061/61

WALKING AROUND ST HUBERT

The tourist office has produced a functional *Carte des Promenades Pedestre* (F50) with eleven circular walks to get you out into the countryside around St Hubert. The sixteen-kilometre **route 6** heads north to Fourneau St Michel (see below) and is a decent idea for a day-trip, though much of it simply follows the road. A shorter and more interesting option is **route 5** (around two and a half hours' walking time) which takes you through the thickly wooded forest and onto the edge of some open moorland.

16 44, fax 61 35 15; ③), down rue St Gilles and just past the church at avenue Nestor Martin, is a little smarter. *Hôtel de l'Abbaye* (☎061/61 10 23, fax 61 34 22; ②), place du Marché 18, is the cheapest of the lot, and has a good-value restaurant attached, although its rooms are pretty basic; opposite, *Hôtel Borquin* (☎061/61 14 56, fax 61 20 18; ②), on place de la Basilique, is more upmarket, but not that much more expensive.

The nearest **campsite** is *Europacamp* on rue de Martelange (☎061/61 12 69; year-round), 2km southwest of town. For **food**, *L'Entracte* at rue St Gilles 9 is cheap and cheerful and the *Taverne St Gillies* across the road has excellent Belgian dishes and is only slightly dearer. Otherwise, the hotels normally offer reasonably priced set menus.

Around St Hubert

St Hubert is quite a good base for the surrounding area, the highlights of which include excursions to a wild-animal park, **Parc à Gibier**, 2km to the north, and, a few kilometres farther north (though within easy cycling distance of the town), to **Fourneau St Michel** – a centre for ironworking, with an old forge and a museum showing old tools and the like (July–Aug daily 9am–6pm; Sept–Dec & March–June daily 9am–5pm, closed Jan & Feb; F100, F150 including admission to the Musée de la Vie Rurale – see below). Housed in the same building, the **Musée Redouté** (same times and dates; F20) presents the life and work of the artist Pierre-Joseph Redouté who was born in St Hubert in 1759. Part of the same complex, the **Musée de la Vie Rurale en Wallonie** (same times and dates; F100) spreads out over a large area, an open-air museum made up of reconstructions of typical Walloon rural buildings. There are farmhouses and stables, a sawmill and a chapel, along with the usual cafés and restaurants.

Immediately west of St Hubert, right by the A11 autoroute, a few kilometres north of the village of **LIBIN**, the **Euro Space Centre** (April–Sept daily 10am–5pm; F395) is a hugely popular attraction. Easily identified by the space rocket parked outside, its hangar-like premises house a hi-tech museum that tells you everything you ever wanted to know about space travel and the applications of space and satellite technology. There are lots of buttons for kids to press in the many interactive displays, as well as full-scale models of the space shuttles Amicitia and Ariane and of the Mir space station.

A short drive further on, across the other side of the autoroute, **REDU** is a small village that, like its British counterpart, Hay-on-Wye (with which it has been twinned), is full of bookstores selling new and used books, prints and pictures – a pleasant place, bustling with buyers and browsers in season, although obviously most of the books are in French or Flemish. Worth the brief detour if you're a bibliophile.

Bouillon and around

Forty-odd kilometres southwest of St Hubert, close to the French border, **BOUILLON** is a well-known resort centre on the edge of the Ardennes, enclosed in a loop of the River Semois and crowned by an outstanding castle. It's a relaxed and peaceful place, and it gives easy access to some lovely walking in the countryside around, which is wilder than that farther north.

The Town

The most distinctive feature of Bouillon is its **castle** (Jan Sat & Sun 10am–5pm; Feb Mon–Fri 1–5pm, Sat & Sun 10am–5pm; March–June & Sept–Nov daily 10am–5/6pm; July–Aug daily 9.30am–7pm; Dec Wed–Sun 10am–5pm; F170; combined ticket with museum F230), set up on a ridge which runs the length of the town, and with superb views from the top of the Austrian Tower. Access by road is clearly marked via rue du Château; if you're on foot, a set of steep steps climb from rue de Moulin, one street back from the river and halfway between the Pont de Liège and the Pont de France. The castle was originally held by a succession of independent counts who controlled most of the land around Bouillon. There were five of these, all called Godfrey de Bouillon, the fifth and last of whom left on the First Crusade in 1096, selling his dominions (partly to raise the cash for his trip) to the prince-bishop of Liège. Later on, the castle was confiscated by Louis XIV, and Vauban, his military architect, was charged with modifying it – the results of which are by and large what you see now. It's an intriguing old place, and paths wind through most of its courtyards, along the battlements and towers, and through dungeons filled with weaponry and instruments of torture. A brochure in English (F30) describes the various parts of the structure and is well worth the money. The Salle de Godfrey, hewn out of the rock and named after the crusader, contains a statue of the last ruler of Bouillon and an ancient wooden cross in the floor that was only recently discovered. The so-called Salle de Godfrey is a lookout, also cut out of solid rock, and one of the oldest parts of the castle.

Downhill from the castle, the **Musée Ducal** (July–Aug daily 10am–6pm; April–June & Sept–Oct daily Mon–Fri 10am–1pm & 2–6pm, Sat & Sun 10am–6pm; Nov–Dec & mid-Jan to March Sat & Sun noon–5pm; F120) displays various artefacts relating to Godfrey's crusade, most notably a replica of his tomb in Jerusalem, where he died in 1100 after contributing to the success of the First Crusade, plus plundered Islamic ceramics, as well as some beautiful thirteenth-century Limoges enamels. More gruesome paraphernalia includes some medieval weaponry and some vicious, spiked dog collars for wolf-hunting, while another section of the museum concentrates on the folklore and history of the town and region. Downstairs, there is a large-scale model of the town in 1690, various shooting and hunting accessories and a room devoted to the printing activities of local author Pierre Rousseau, who printed the work of some of the authors of the Enlightenment in Bouillon after they were banned in France. Upstairs, a series of period rooms showcase local industries from weaving to clog-making. A tape recording guides you from section to section and talks you through the exhibits, but it's all done at a bit of a gallop, and you may want to revisit some of the rooms.

Practicalities

A regular **bus** service connects Bouillon with the **train station** at Libramont, 30km northeast (Mon–Fri 9 daily, Sat & Sun 3 daily; 50min). There's also an infrequent service from Bertrix station, 23km away. Most buses stop on the quai des Remparts near the Pont de Liège and at the bus station, just above the Pont de France. The town's **tourist office** is based in the castle, and shares its complex opening times (see above; ☎061/46 62 57, fax 46 82 85); there's also an **information chalet** beside the Pont de France (July–Aug daily 10am–1pm & 2–7pm; April–June & Sept–Oct Sat & Sun 10am–1pm & 2–6pm; ☎061/46 62 89).

Details of the few **rooms to let** in private homes can be got from the tourist office, and there's a **youth hostel** at route du Christ 16, on the opposite hill from the castle (☎061/46 81 37; ①); for a short cut, take the steps up from place St Arnould, just across the Pont de Liège, which lead there direct. Around a dozen **hotels** line the river: the grand old *Hôtel de la Poste* (☎061/46 51 51, fax 46 51 65; ⑤), right by the Pont de Liège at place St Arnould 1, is the best place in town and has a cool bar; the more basic *La Tannerie* (☎061/46 62 27; ③) is a stone's throw away at quai de la Tannerie 1, and has five good-value rooms. There's also a small cluster of places on fauborg de France, by the Pont de France, a quiet area of town with fine views of both the river and the castle. These include the charming *Auberge d'Alsace* at no. 3 (☎061/46 65 88, fax 46 83 21; ④), the slightly cheaper *Hôtel de France* (☎061/46 60 68, fax 46 83 21; ④), and *La Porte de France* (☎061/46 62 66, fax 46 89 15; ④). Near the bus station is the *Hostellerie Aux Armes de Bouillon*, rue de la Station 9–15 (☎061/46 60 79, fax 46 60 84; ③), a decent hotel with a swimming pool. The nearest **campsite** is the *Halliru*, next to the river, just south of the town on the route de Corbion (☎061/46 60 09 or 46 74 11; April–Sept) – an easily walkable distance through the tunnel next to the information chalet, and then left. There's a second campsite 1km south of town, *Moulin de la Falize*, at vieille route de France 64 (☎061/46 62 00, fax 46 72 75; Easter–Oct), which is well equipped with a restaurant, swimming pool, tennis courts and cross-country skiing in winter. They also organize canoe trips – Cugnon–Bouillon (30km), Maka–Bouillon (20km), Dohan–Bouillon (15km), and Saty–Bouillon (9km) – down the lovely River Semois. Trips cost F450–900; you're dropped off by minibus at the relevant destination and then you paddle back into town.

There's a string of **restaurants** on the riverside quai des Remparts: the popular *Des Remparts* at no. 24 (closed Thurs) has superb Belgian menus from F500; *Roy de la Moule*, at no. 42–43, is a solid mussels-and-chips restaurant and has an adjoining wooden-bench bar with a wide choice of beers; and *Les 4 Saisons*, at no. 12, serves good-value Belgian fish and meat dishes. *Villa d'Este*, rue de la Maladrerie 17, is a cheap and cheerful Italian place near the Pont de Liège; while *La Vieille Ardenne*, at Grande rue 9, has lots of regional specialities and menus from F500–850, and is also a good place for a drink, with a broad list of different beers. Most restaurants close early (often before 10pm), although there's a good-value Chinese restaurant, *Le Sawadie*, on quai des Remparts, which opens until 11.30pm. For a quiet drink head to *La Porte de France*, which has a lovely terrace overlooking the river. Close by, the Carat **supermarket** is the place to go for picnic food.

Around Bouillon – Exploring the Semois Valley

The valley of the River Semois is ideal for venturing into the great outdoors; it's a quiet area, and a short walk or canoe ride can get you to some genuinely wild spots. **Bouillon** (see p.290) makes the best base – it's more attractive and lively than its neighbours – but there are other hotels and campsites scattered around if you're after somewhere really quiet (see "Accommodation" below).

Walkers should get hold of the map *Cartes des Promenades du Grand Bouillon* (F100 from the tourist office in Bouillon), with nine "grandes promenades" marked and a further ninety circular walks that begin and end in Bouillon or one of the nearby villages. The routes are well marked, but you need to study the map carefully if you want to avoid having to walk on major or minor roads; the map also gives suggested times for completing the walks, though these are pretty generous. Note that the marked river crossings are not bridges and you'll get wet feet!

Around Bouillon **route 11** heads south to the French border, a pretty walk through woods, although the return is mostly along a main road. A better option is to take **route 12** through the arboretum and down to the Halliru campsite by the river, joining **route 13** along the riverbank up to the Rocher du Pendu and as far as Moulin de l'Épine, where you can wade across the river to a superb restaurant-bar – with great local food at around F500 for a main meal – and the minor road that leads back to town above the Semois. More serious walkers can pick up **routes 37** or **72** at Moulin de l'Épine for some fabulous views either side of the river, 72 being particularly glorious as it heads around Le Tombeau du Géant. If you just want a brief walk around Bouillon, **route 16** is a good choice – a 75-minute walk that climbs up out of town, with great views of the castle and surrounding countryside, and back through the outskirts of the Ferme de Buhan.

There are lovely walks, too, around **Poupehan**, a small resort sloping up from the banks of the Semois west of Bouillon and reachable by canoe (see below). **route 70** runs north through the woods from here as far as **Rochehaut**, whose ancient stone houses are surrounded by some heavily forested hills and whose eighteenth-century church is worth a peek for its medieval font and modern murals. As you come out of the village you get spectacular views over the tiny village of **Frahan** and the chance for a decent lunch at *Taverne du Point de Vue* before the path drops down to the river and back to Poupehan.

In the other direction from Bouillon, the Semois twists its way to the resort-village of **Dohan**. The mammoth **route 19** runs direct to Dohan from Bouillon although it's more attractive to follow the river via **route 17** as far as Saty from where you can either canoe back to Bouillon (see below), or join **19** towards Dohan. Finally, for an ambitious and varied day's walking, you can take **route 7** from the Pont de France in Bouillon across the Ferme du Buhan and through Saty and Dohan as far as La Maka. Here you can pick up **route 45**, which incorporates the waterfalls at Saut de Sorcières and the lovely views over the river valley from Mont de Katron. From Les Hayons, **route 6** runs directly back to Bouillon through Moulin Hideux.

If you want to **canoe**, the riverscape is gentle and sleepy, the Semois slow-moving and meandering – and the whole shebang is less oversubscribed than, say, Dinant. Semois Kayaks (☎061/46 72 29) are by the loop in the river north of town and offer trips downriver to Poupehan (15km; F900 for a two-seater) or from Poupehan to Frahan (5km; F600). The former takes around three hours, with time for refreshments at a small café on the river about halfway down near Wardon; the latter about an hour. For an active day out, you can canoe to Poupehan and either pick up routes back to Bouillon or walk one of the circular routes around the village – if you do the latter, check what time the last of the canoe company's buses return to Bouillon. Moulin de la Falize (☎061/46 62 00), in a hut by the Pont de France, offer trips ending in Bouillon and starting from various points upriver including Saty (9km; F450 for a two-seater) and a three-day trip from Chiny (73km; F2400). Some of the scenery around Chiny is majestic but, unless you want to spend all day in a canoe, your best bet is to get on the river below Bouillon.

Mountain-bikes can also be rented from Moulin de la Falize or Semois Kayaks, and they'll provide a map with suggested biking routes; reckon on around F500 for half a day, F800 for a day.

Accommodation

Poupehan has a couple of decent hotels: the best value are *Auberge le Vieux Moulin* (☎061/46 61 29, fax 46 74 66; ④) on the main road through the village at rue du Pont 18, and *Hôtel Chaire à Precher* (☎061/46 61 54; ④) on the same road at no. 1, while the smart *Auberge du Mousty* (☎061/46 77 67; ⑤) is at chemin de la Buchaille 17. There are also five campsites including *d'Houlifontaine* (☎061/46 73 15) by the river on rue des Sneviots. Whether you're staying or just passing through, *La Rochette* up the hill near the church offers good-value food all day though the service can be a bit bad-tempered. There's also a Spar **supermarket** in town if you're after a picnic.

In **Rochehaut**, an affordable if rather bland option is *Les Tonnelles* (☎061/46 40 18, fax 46 40 12; ③) at place Marie Howet 5, although *Auberge de la Ferme* (☎061/46 41 66, fax 46 41 67; ④) at rue de la Cense 21, and its sister hotel the *Auberge de la Fermette* (same ☎ & fax; ⑤) a few doors up at no. 33, are only marginally more expensive, but much more upmarket.

Frahan is a much more attractive place to stay although prices are higher: *Hôtel Beau Séjour*, rue du Tabac 7 (☎061/46 65 21, fax 46 78 80; ④) and *Aux Roches Fleuries*, rue des Crêtes 32 (☎061/46 65 14, fax 46 72 09; ⑤), right beside *Le Tombeau du Géant*, are both good choices. The tourist office in Rochehaut at rue de la Cense 37 (☎061/46 69 70) can also help with finding cheaper accommodation in private houses in both Rochehaut and Frahan (though you're unlikely to find any available in high season), and there are a handful of campsites in the area, including *Ban de Laviot* (☎061/46 62 44; April–Sept) at Laviot 30, Rochehaut 6830.

Florenville and around

Shortly after rejoining the main N83, **FLORENVILLE**, right on the French border, is a good base for the surrounding countryside, an attractive little town set around a large square and a bustling main street, although there is not much to see in the town itself. There's a **tourist office** right on the square (Mon–Sat 9am–noon & 2–6pm, Sun 10am–noon & 2–5pm; ☎061/31 12 29), and the venerable *Hôtel de France* on the main street (☎061/31 10 32, fax 31 47 24; ④) has comfortable rooms, an excellent restaurant, and a lovely garden. If you're camping, head for *La Rosière* (☎061/31 19 37, fax 31 48 73; April–Oct) 500m from the main street, down by the riverbank. There are lots of **bars and restaurants** around the main square: *Brasserie Albert 1er* on the corner is a good spot for a drink while, opposite, *Le Relais* offers decent Belgian food, with *Pizzas Artisanales* a cheaper alternative next door. There's also a small tearoom here, *L'Étoile du Sud*, which sells excellent-value breakfasts – tea or coffee, cheese, bread rolls, preserves and honey – for only F150, and a wide range of tasty snacks and pastries.

If you're staying over, the tourist office sells **walking** maps with circular routes around the local countryside and some lovely walks near Les Epioux in the forests to the north, while *Le Batifol* (☎061/31 41 38) organize **canoeing** trips on a scenic stretch of the River Semois, starting from Chiny, 15km away. Their minibus runs to Chiny from *La Rosière* campsite – a two-seater canoe costs F850 for the day.

Herbeumont

There is more good walking around the pretty village of **HERBEUMONT**, 12km away, and the tourist office at rue des Combattants 7 (☎061/41 24 12) has a small brochure listing fifteen routes along the Semois and through the Forêt d'Herbeumont. Five minutes' walk from the centre of the village is its ruined, originally twelfth-century **castle**, high on a bluff over the river. It's little more than a shell now but worth the scramble up the hill as the views are quite spectacular. There's also a splendid turn-of-the-century **viaduct**, just outside the village off the main road towards Florenville. There are several **campsites**, best of which is the *Champ de Monde* (☎061/41 17 41; year-round), right by the viaduct, and a clutch of **hotels** around Grand-Place, including *La Renaissance* at no. 3 (☎061/41 10 83; ③) and *La Chatelaine* at no. 8 (☎061/41 12 22, fax 41 22 04; ⑤). The best places to eat are also around the main square, with decent local food at *L'Herbeumont* at Grand-Place 4, and there is the small crêperie, *L'Abri*, nearby on rue des Ponts 4.

Orval

South of Florenville, beside the main road, the **Abbaye d'Orval** (daily: April–May & Oct 9.30am–12.30pm & 1.30–6pm; June–Sept 9.30am–12.30pm & 1.30–6.30pm; Nov–Feb 10.30am–12.30pm & 1.30–5.30pm; F100) is a place of legendary beginnings. It was founded, so the story goes, when Countess Mathilda of Tuscany lost a gold ring in a lake and a fish recovered it for her, prompting the countess to donate the surrounding land to God for the construction of a monastery. A fish with a golden ring is still the emblem of the monastery, and can be seen gracing the bottles of beer for which the abbey is these days most famous.

It's worth a visit if you've got your own transport, but is otherwise a difficult pilgrimage. Bus #46 runs from nearby Florenville, the nearest town on the train network, but they're not at all frequent. Bear in mind also that the abbey is by no means as complete or untouched as it might be. Originally a Benedictine foundation, then Cistercian, it has always been first and foremost a working community, making beer, cheese, and bread (samples of which are on sale in the abbey shop), but of the original twelfth- and thirteenth-century buildings, only the ruins of the Romanesque-Gothic church of Notre-Dame are left, with the frame of the original rose window and Romanesque capitals in the nave and transept. The rest was rebuilt in the eighteenth century, but most of this, too, was destroyed in the French Revolution, and the abbey was left abandoned until 1926, when the Trappist order acquired the property and built on the site to the seventeenth-century plans, creating an imposing new complex, complete with a monumental statue of the Virgin. You can wander around the ruins, and they are picturesque enough, but many of the new buildings are closed to the public. The only parts you can visit are the eighteenth-century cellars complete with a small museum and a model of how the abbey looked in 1760. After a visit to the abbey, head back to the main road, where you'll find the *Nouvelle Hostellerie d'Orval* (☎061/31 43 65, fax 32 00 92; closed Mon; ②). It has six simple but comfortable rooms, and a restaurant which serves good-value Belgian fare – three-course lunch menus from F425, as well as bar snacks including large platters of locally produced Orval cheese.

Virton

The hilly and thickly wooded area around Orval is known as the **Gaume**, effectively an extension of the Ardennes. **VIRTON**, the main town, is a lively settlement whose compact centre retains the circular shape of its medieval walls, although there's not much, quite frankly, to hold you here for more than an hour or two beyond its one real attraction, the **Musée Gaumais**, situated on the way out of the centre at rue d'Arlon 38–40 (April–May & Sept–Nov Wed–Mon 9.30am–noon & 2–6pm; June–Aug daily 9.30am–noon & 2–6pm; F100). The museum's collection of period rooms and prehistoric finds is saved from mediocrity by an outstanding array of iron fireplaces, a local speciality dating from as early as the fifteenth century, some of which are superbly decorated, illustrating Biblical themes and the like.

A minor stop on the train line from Libramont and Bertrix, Virton's **train station** is 1km from the centre, straight down avenue Bouvier. The **tourist office** is at rue des Grasses Oies 2b (July & Aug daily 10am–noon & 1.30–5.30pm; Sept–June Mon–Fri 9am–noon & 1.30–5pm, Sat 9am–noon; ☎063/57 89 04), and there's one reasonably priced **hotel**, *Le Cheval Blanc*, at rue du Moulin 1 (☎063/57 89 35, fax 58 13 61; ②). There are a few **restaurants**, the most notable being the pretty *La Maison Verte* close by the church on the square, which serves cheap Belgian specialities, and the larger *Brasserie du Chalet*, rue Dr Jeanty 7, which has a wide menu of inexpensive snacks such as croque-monsieurs, salads, and soups. Strangely enough, one of the region's few nightclubs – *Club Virton* (Fri & Sat midnight–7am; free) – can be found next door.

Arlon

The chief town of Luxembourg province, **ARLON** is one of the oldest towns in Belgium, a trading centre for the Romans as far back as the second century AD. These days it's a comfortable, prosperous place, with a relaxed and genial atmosphere that makes for a pleasant pit-stop – although again there's not a lot to see. The modern centre of the town is **place Léopold**, with the Palais de Justice at one end and a World War II tank in the middle, commemorating the American liberation of Arlon in September 1944. Behind the Palais de Justice, to the left, the

Musée Luxembourgeois, rue des Martyrs 13 (Mon–Sat 9am–noon & 2–5pm; mid-June to mid-Sept also Sun 10am–noon & 2–5pm; F100), has a good collection of Roman finds from the surrounding area, many of which are wonderfully evocative of daily life in Roman times. There are pieces from the Merovingian era, too, as well as a marvellously realistic sixteenth-century retable.

A couple of minutes' walk from place Léopold, up a flight of steps, is Arlon's diminutive **Grand-Place**, where there are more fragments from Roman times, the **Tour Romaine**, in the corner, formerly part of the third-century ramparts. From here, rue des Carmes leads down to the seventeenth-century church of **St Donat**, which gives good views over the surrounding countryside and, a little way beyond down rue des Thermes, a few scattered ruins of a first-century **Roman baths**.

The **train station** is five minutes' walk away from the centre of town and Arlon's **tourist office** (Mon–Fri 8.30am–noon & 1–5pm, May–Aug also Sat same times; ☎063/21 63 60) is just off the main square on rue des Faubourgs, next door to the *Café de Nord*. For **accommodation**, the budget option is *Les Druides* at rue de Neufchâteau 106 (☎063/22 04 89; ③); from the train station turn left up avenue de la Gare to place des Fusilles, then right up rue Leon Castilhon, and rue de Neufchâteau is the second turning on the left. Alternatively, head for *A L'Ecu de Bourgogne*, place Léopold 10 (☎063/22 02 22; ⑤), which is more central and rather more comfortable.

For **food**, the *Maison Knopes* on the Grand-Place serves excellent crêpes as well as more substantial meals, and does a great line in coffee. For a cheaper meal head to place Léopold where *Gathay*, at no. 7, and *Les Arcades*, at no. 5, are both popular local haunts for traditional Belgian food.

Bastogne

Forty kilometres north of Arlon is the important road and rail junction of **BASTOGNE**, best known for its heroic defence by the Americans in December 1944, who held out here against heavy bombardment from the encroaching Germans. A key engagement of the Battle of the Bulge (see box opposite), the American commander in chief's response to the German demand for surrender – "Nuts!" – is one of the more quotable, if apocryphal, of World War II rallying cries. Not surprisingly the town and its environs are full of reminders of the battle.

The main square is known as **place McAuliffe** after the American commander, and is the site of an American tank. Just around the corner from here is the **Musée des Pays d'Ardennes**, on the left a little way down rue de Neufchâteau (daily 9am–4pm; F100), which displays a hotch-potch of odds and ends from the war years, including some touching letters from ex-GIs alongside an array of stuffed Ardennes wildlife.

Halfway between place McAuliffe and the American Memorial on Mardasson Hill there are a handful of places worth a visit. **St Peter's Church** on place St Pierre has a twelfth-century tower, and its Flamboyant Gothic nave has some elaborately decorated vaulting, covered in scenes from the Bible. Just up the road and to the right the fourteenth-century **Porte de Trevi** is the last vestige of the town's medieval walls, while the nearby **Maison Mathelin** (July & Aug Tues–Sun 10am–noon & 1–6pm; F60) has a model of the medieval town and exhibits illustrating Bastogne's history since Roman times. The **Musée en**

THE BATTLE OF THE BULGE

Though there's not a lot to see now beyond parked tanks and the odd war memorial, the Ardennes was the site of some of World War II's fiercest fighting during the **Battle of the Bulge**. The Allied campaign of autumn 1944 had concentrated on striking into Germany from Maastricht in the north and Alsace in the south, leaving a central section of lightly defended front line extending across the Ardennes from Malmédy to Luxembourg. In December 1944, Hitler embarked on a desperate plan to change the course of the war by breaking through this part of the front, seizing Antwerp and forcing the Allies to retreat. In command of the operation was one of his best generals, Von Rundstedt, who hoped to benefit from the wintry weather conditions which would limit Allied aircraft activity. Carefully prepared, Von Rundstedt's offensive began on December 16, 1944, and one week later had created a "bulge" in the Allied line that reached the outskirts of Dinant – though the American 101st Airborne Division held firm around Bastogne. The success of the operation depended on rapid results, however, and Von Rundstedt's inability to reach Antwerp meant failure. Montgomery's forces from the north and Patton's from the south launched a counterattack, and by the end of January the Germans had been forced back to their original position. The loss of life was colossal – 75,000 Americans and over 100,000 Germans died in the battle.

Piconrue opposite (normally Tues–Fri 1.30–6pm, Sat & Sun 10am–6pm; F100), has excellent exhibitions of religious art each summer – details from the tourist office.

The story of the battle is more fully told at the **American Memorial**, situated about 2km outside Bastogne to the northeast, a good fifteen-minute walk from Bastogne-Nord train station. The star-shaped structure, inscribed with the names of all the American states, probably looks a great deal better from the air than it does from the ground, but the panels around the side do an excellent job of recounting different episodes from the battle, and it's possible to climb up onto the roof for a windswept look back at Bastogne and the slag heaps and quarries of the countryside that surrounds it. Down below, the crypt is covered with murals by Fernand Léger. Next door to the memorial, the **Bastogne Historical Centre** (mid-Feb to April & Nov–Dec 10am–4pm; May–June & Sept–Oct daily 9.30am–5.30pm; July & Aug 8.30am–7pm; F295) collects together all manner of war-related artefacts – uniforms, vehicles, etc – in an impressive and imaginative display, and shows a film of the attack and defence.

Although there are few other attractions in Bastogne itself, there are two notable sights nearby. Five kilometres north of Bastogne, in Recogne, is the incongruous **La Ferme des Bisons** (April–June & Sept Mon–Fri, Sun noon–7pm; July & Aug Mon–Fri noon–7pm; exhibition F150; to visit bison F80), a park dedicated to the American Indian, featuring exhibits such as wigwams, tools, hunting equipment, and a herd of 180 bison. Around 10km from Bastogne, in the direction of Houffalize, **L'Église de Ranchamps** is of breathtaking beauty, its interior home to ancient columns and arches, and a glorious muralled ceiling.

Practicalities

There's no real reason to stay over in Bastogne. The **tourist office** in the middle of place McAuliffe (summer Mon–Fri 10am–5pm; rest of year Mon–Fri

8.30am–noon & 1.30–5.30pm,; ☎061/21 27 11) has information on the town and runs regular trips up to the American Memorial for F120 per person. If you do decide to stay, *Hôtel Du Sud* (☎061/21 11 14, fax 21 79 08; ③) is fifty metres from place McAuliffe at rue de Marche 39, or there is the smarter *Le Caprice* (☎061/21 81 40, fax 21 82 01; ⑤) at place McAuliffe 25. The *Hôtel Melba* (☎061/21 77 78, fax 21 55 68 ⑤), close by at avenue Mathieu 49–51, is modern, quiet, and friendly, though a little more expensive. There's a **campsite** at *Camping de Renval*, about ten minutes' walk west of the centre along route de Marché.

For **food**, there are lots of places on and around place McAuliffe. The *Café 1900* does decent light lunches and snacks or there is all-day Italian and French food at *Giorgio's*, place McAuliffe 30. *Restaurant Leo*, housed in an old railway carriage, is excellent and moderately priced, but inevitably very popular. *Le Café des Sports* on rue du Vivier is a lively place for a drink; *Couleur Café*, close to place McAuliffe, is the place to go for dance music and a younger clientele.

La Roche-en-Ardenne and around

The unofficial capital of the Ardennes, around 25km northeast of St Hubert, **LA ROCHE-EN-ARDENNE** is amazingly picturesque, hidden by hills until you're right on top of it and crowned by romantic castle ruins. It's a strange mixture: a hidden place, geographically cut off from the rest of the world and surrounded by some of the wildest scenery in the Ardennes, yet it teems with people during the summer, and – by Ardennes standards – has a relatively animated nightlife, with plenty of bars and late-night restaurants.

The Town

The centre of La Roche squeezes into one bend in the river, its high street winding between the two bridges, an unashamedly exploitative stretch of shops flogging Ardennes ham and camping gear. That, however, is about it as far as development goes, and the streets around are unspoiled and quiet. The only tangible "sight" is the **castle** (July & Aug daily 10am–7pm; April–June & Sept–Oct daily 10am–noon & 2–5pm; Nov–May Mon–Fri 1.30–4.30pm, Sat & Sun 10am–noon & 2–4pm; F100), construction of which began in the ninth century and continued over four hundred years. Destroyed in the late eighteenth century, its ruins still command sweeping views around the area, and you can just about make out fragments of the curtain wall that once enclosed the town. There is also a tiny museum with archeological finds and a pictorial history of La Roche; to get to the castle, take the steps that lead up from the high street.

On the high street itself, the **Musée Bataille des Ardennes** (daily 10am–6pm; F160), a small collection of military artefacts dedicated to the war years in the Ardennes, is pretty missable, especially if you've been to the superior museum at Bastogne. If you've got kids, the tourist train, which departs from the church, takes you around La Roche and then on to the **Wildlife Park** (daily: July & Aug 10am–8pm; Sept–June 10am–5pm; F100), which is situated on the Deister plateau, and is home to various creatures including red deer, pheasants, and wild boar. You can also get there by taking the no. 4 signposted walk.

Practicalities

The **tourist office** on the main street at place du Marché 15 (daily: July & Aug 10am–6pm; Sept–June 10am–noon & 2–5pm; ☎084/41 13 42) has maps and booklets on the town and details of accommodation possibilities, including plenty of private **rooms** (②). Despite the abundance of **hotels**, booking is advisable in season. Across the river, the very pleasant *Luxembourg*, avenue du Hadja 1a (☎084/41 14 15; ②), is one of the town's better-value options, as is the slightly cheaper *Hôtel de Liège*, opposite at rue de la Gare 16 (☎ & fax 084/41 11 64; ②), while for a little more money, the *Hôtel de la Place*, rue de Beausaint 1 (☎084/41 12 52, fax 41 22 52; ③), is a nice old-fashioned hotel, very handily placed, and with a decent restaurant. *La Clairefontaine*, route de Hotton 64 (☎084/41 24 70, fax 41 21 11; ⑥), a kilometre outside town on the edge of the forest, is a lovely hotel set in its own grounds, although the cheaper rooms in the new annex have depressing 1970s decor; the cosy *Les Genêts* (☎ 0 84/41 18 77, fax 41 18 93; ④) has good views over the town from its perch at corniche de Deister 2, ten minutes' walk from the centre – walk towards the bridge by the tourist office, turn left out of town on rue Clerue and left again up rue St Quolin. There are no fewer than nine **campsites** in the vicinity, most packed with trailers. Among the closest is a group along rue de Harzé by the Ourthe, north of the town – the *Benelux* (☎084/41 15 59; Easter–Sept), about an eight-hundred-metre walk down along rue de la Gare, *Camping de l'Ourthe* (☎084/41 14 59; mid-March to mid-Oct), and *Le Grillon* (☎084/41 20 62; Easter–Oct), just beyond. There are also a couple in the opposite direction, towards Houffalize – try *Floréal* (☎084/21 94 67; year-round), about 1.5km from the town centre, also by the river.

There are lots of **restaurants** to choose from, though many along the main street are tourist traps and the main square, place du Bronze, at the southern entrance of the town centre is a better option. *La Sapinière*, just off here at rue Nulay 4, serves good-value Belgian country food, as does *Restaurant L'Apero*, rue Clerue 5, a small, family-run restaurant with fine local cooking. Alternatives include the cheap pizzas of the brash *Mezzogiorno*, place du Bronze 1, while gastronomes can head for the *Hôtel Clairefontaine*, whose superb menus start at F1000. If you just want to **drink**, the *Vénetien* halfway down the main street is a popular local bar.

Most people come to La Roche to get out to the countryside and walk or canoe. **Canoes** can be rented from Zimmer Sports, opposite the church on the main street. **Bikes** are available from M. Hennebert, place du Bronze, or from the *l'Escale* hotel on quai Gravier, but the area's very hilly – and you're probably better off with a **mountain-bike** (also from Zimmer Sports). In winter there's crosscountry skiing at nearby Samrée. You can buy a combined walking and cycling map (*Carte des Promenades Pedestres et Circuits Cyclotouristes*) from the tourist office, which can also give you details of the guided walks that are arranged every Tuesday and Thursday in July and August.

Around La Roche

Nine buses a day on a weekday (4 Sat & Sun) travel the 20km from La Roche to Melreux train station, where you can pick up trains north to Liège and south to Jemelle. Some 10km north of Melreux, tiny **DURBUY** is a very pleasant overgrown village, surrounded by low-lying wooded hills and set around a large main

OUT AND ABOUT IN THE OURTHE VALLEY

The tourist office in La Roche sells a walking map (*Carte des Promenades Pedestres*; F150), with a dozen circular walks marked in the vicinity. The longest and most attractive of the routes is **no. 5**, which starts on rue Bon Dieu du Maka near place du Bronze and rises steeply before levelling out through the woods above town and across fields of wildflowers. The walk follows GR route 57, dropping sharply to the river at **Maboge** where several cafés offer lunch, then rejoining the main road for 500 metres until it turns left alongside a tributary of the Ourthe as far as the farm at Borzee. From here the route is easy to find, again heading through the woods with fabulous views, but when it descends towards the town keep your eyes peeled for a right and then immediate left down an unpromising footpath that drops you onto the main road by the river. From here, take the second right for a final gentle stretch above the road with good views over the town. Allow around three hours' walking time for the 13 kilometres; if you want to extend the route by an hour or so, pick up **no. 12** at Borzee, joining **no. 11** as far as the small town of Samree and returning through the forest to La Roche.

For the ambitious, **GR route 57** provides a full day's walking between La Roche and Houffalize, a distance of around 35km. There is a twice-daily bus between the two towns or you can stop over in **Houffalize**, a shabby little resort occupying a great position on both sides of the river valley. The place was almost entirely destroyed during World War II when it was the site of a key battle to halt a German advance: a German tank bears testimony to this. Numerous **hotels** include *Le Relais*, rue de Bastogne 12 (☎061/28 81 64; ③), and the nearby *Hôtel des Postes et du Luxembourg* (☎061/28 97 00, fax 28 97 02; ③). Almost halfway along the route, the village of **Nadrin** is home to a belvedere – actually a high tower with a restaurant attached – from which you can see the Ourthe at six different points on its meandering course in and out of the tightly packed hills. Nadrin also has a **campsite** and a couple of places to stay, or you can walk up to the main road for the bus back to La Roche (check times with the tourist office before you leave). A couple of kilometres further on towards Houffalize, the **Barrage de Nisramont** is a dam across the River Ourthe, where there are places to eat and a series of well-signposted paths (13km in total) encircling the man-made lake and the various spears of the Ourthe, taking in a number of belvederes and refuges. The area is easily accessible by car and gets busy with day-trippers in the summer.

If you just want a brief walk, follow **no. 4** out of town – from the tourist office head for place du Bronze and before you cross the bridge turn left on rue Clerue and sharp left again up rue St Quolin – and turn left at the top to **St Margaret's Chapel**, built in 1600 and once connected to the castle by an underground passage. Just left of the chapel a steep slope scrambles up to a look-out point with views over La Roche, and continuing up the footpath brings you to the attractive but rather twee and often crowded **Parc Forestier du Deister**. The tourist office has a map of the park (F50), including descriptions of where various types of tree have been planted. If you continue through the park you'll rejoin walk no. 4, looping briefly north and then dropping back to town, all along the roadway.

Renting a **mountain-bike** allows you to see more of the surrounding forests: eight circular routes are set out in the *Carte des Circuits Cyclotouristes* – F150 from the tourist office. Bikes can be rented for F800 per day from Zimmer Loisirs (☎084/41 13 47), rue de l'Église 27, or, in summer, from a chalet below the bridge by avenue du Hadja. Zimmer Loisirs also organize **canoeing** trips on the Ourthe, bussing you (or letting you mountain-bike) to Maboge for the 10km paddle downstream to La Roche (F500 per person/F800 with the bike ride), or to Nisramont for the strenuous 25km trip (F700). They also organize **river rafting** and **cross-country skiing** in the winter.

square, with a tranquil old quarter of narrow cobbled streets and seventeenth-century houses. It's very difficult to reach without your own transport – the nearest station is at **Barvaux**, 4km away – but it's a pretty place, good for canoeing on the river and gentle walking, and it has stacks of hotels and restaurants which makes it a good, if sometimes busy, base for the area. Of the **hotels**, the *L'Esplanade*, on the main street, is good (☎086/21 16 81; ③), or there's the lovely *Les Roches Fleuries* at Grand-Place 2 (☎086/21 28 82, fax 21 11 68; ⑤).

Alternatively, five buses a day (3 Sat & Sun) head west for the busy town of **MARCHE-EN-FAMENNE**, on the main train line between Liège and Jemelle and with one attraction worth stopping for – the tiny **Lace Museum** (April–Oct Tues–Sat 9am–noon & 2–5pm, Sun 10am–noon & 2–5pm; F80), housed in a tower that was once part of the city walls. The museum has a collection of lace from around the world, including some exquisite Chantilly lace, and plenty of pieces from Marche itself, which was once a regional centre for lace-making before mechanization squeezed out the local cottage industries. You are required to take the hourly guided tours, given in French (although the guides normally speak pretty good English), and tickets are sold around the corner at the **tourist office** on rue des Brasseurs (same hours; ☎084/31 21 35). From the train station head up rue du Luxembourg, take the second right on rue des Tanneurs and rue des Brasseurs is the first left. There's little reason to **stay** in Marche but if you get caught, *Hôtel Alfa* (☎084/31 17 93, fax 32 11 75; ②) is between the tourist office and the station at avenue de la Toison d'Or 11, while *Hôtel le Manoir* (☎084/31 38 71, fax 31 52 81; ⑤) is a little more central at rue du Manoir 2.

From Marche station it's possible to rent a bike to visit some caves on the southern outskirts of **HOTTON**, 9km back toward Melreux (April–Oct daily 10am–5pm, until 6pm July & Aug; F200); they're noted for their unusual chalk formations – allow around an hour for a visit.

Huy and around

Midway between Namur and Liège, and easily accessible by train, the bustling little town of **HUY** – aside from Liège, the major centre of the northern Ardennes – spreads across both sides of the Meuse. One of the oldest towns in Belgium and for a long time a flourishing market centre, the place was badly damaged by the armies of Louis XIV in the late seventeenth century. Little remains of the old town, but Huy is certainly worth a brief look, mainly for its splendid church, even if you're only passing through on the way to Liège.

The Town

Most sights are on the opposite side of the river from the train station, principally the **Collégiale Notre-Dame** (Mon–Sat 9am–noon & 2–5pm, Sun 9am–12.30pm & 2–6pm; F50), an imposing Gothic church that occupies a prime site right by the water. Built between 1311 and 1536, it's a superb example of the style, its restored rose window is a dazzling conglomeration of reds and blues, and the choir is a huge structure, occupying a third of the total nave and cut with slender twenty-metre-high stained glass windows. On the right side of the nave as you enter, stairs lead down to a Romanesque crypt of 1066, where the relics of Huy's patron saint, St Domitian, were once venerated. His original twelfth-century shrine stands upstairs in the treasury under the rose window (F50), along with three other large shrines from the twelfth and thirteenth centuries, crafted by the Mosan gold- and silversmiths for which Huy was once famous – they're somewhat faded, but the beauty and skill of their execution still shines – through.

On leaving the church, walk down the alleyway to the side that leads to the **Porte de Bethléem**, above which is a mid-fourteenth-century arch decorated with scenes of the nativity. It's a short walk from here across the busy avenue des Ardennes to the nominal centre of town at the **Grand-Place**, with its bronze fountain of 1406 decorated with a representation of the town walls interspersed with tiny statues of the same saints commemorated in the church. The wrought-iron and stone vats were added in the eighteenth century. The square is flanked on the far side by the solid-looking eighteenth-century **Hôtel de Ville**, behind which place Verte has the small **Juvenal Art Gallery** (Tues–Sun 2.30–6.30pm; free). Place Verte gives way to rue St Mengold which in turn leads to the pedestrianized rue des Frères Mineurs, on the corner of which is the oldest house in Huy, the **Maison de la Tour** – an example of Gothic civil architecture of the late twelfth century.

At the top of rue des Frères Mineurs, the late seventeenth-century cloistered former friary of the same name houses the varied exhibits of the **Musée Communal** (April–Oct daily 2–6pm; F80). There is old wine-making equipment, including a winepress of 1719 – wine was a major business in the area from the seventh until the sixteenth century – alongside items of daily life, reconstructions of period rooms and displays of ceramics, coins and religious paintings. The prize exhibit is an oak carving of Christ on the Cross, called the *Beau Dieu de Huy*, a typical Mosan thirteenth-century sculpture.

The last one of Huy's sights worth taking in is its **citadel** (Easter–Sept Mon–Fri 10am–5pm, Sat & Sun 10am–6pm, until 8pm July & Aug; F120), accessible on foot from the quai de Namur by taking the path up to the left before the bridge, or by cable car (May, June & Sept Sat 1–6pm & Sun 10am–12.30pm & 1–6pm; July & Aug daily 10am–12.30 & 1–7pm; one-way F100, round trip F150) from avenue Batta on the other side of the river – cross over the Pont Roi Baduouin and turn left down the riverside quai du Halage. Huy's present citadel is not actually all that old, although it occupies a vantage point that has been fortified for over a thousand years. Built in the early nineteenth century by the Dutch, it was used as a prison by the Nazis during World War II, and it's now a museum of that period, preserving prisoners' cells and the Gestapo interrogation room. It's a massive complex, and the marked tour of the seemingly endless galleries is eerie and disorientating.

Practicalities

Huy's **train station** is a ten-minute walk from the town centre on place Z. Gramme: walk up rue des Jardins or the parallel avenue Albert 1er until you hit rue St Pierre and chaussée de Liège, the first major intersection; turn right as far as place St Germain and then turn left. The **tourist office** (April–June & Sept Mon–Fri 8am–noon & 2–6pm, Sat & Sun 10am–noon & 2–5pm; July & Aug Mon–Fri 8am–1pm & 2–6pm, Sat & Sun 10am–1pm & 2–6pm; Oct–March Mon–Fri 8am–noon & 1.30–5pm; ☎085/21 29 15, fax 23 29 44) is across the bridge and to the right at quai de Namur 1, by the church.

There are four central **hotels**: *Hôtel du Fort*, chaussée Napoleon 5–6 (☎085/21 24 03, fax 23 18 42; ②), five minutes' walk along the river past the tourist office;

La Reserve, close by at nos. 8–9 (☎085/21 24 03, fax 23 18 42; ④); *La Renaissance*, rue des Soeurs Grises 16–18 (☎085/21 28 45; ②) – from Grand-Place take rue des Brasseurs and it's first on the left; and the *Sirius*, quai de Compiègne 47 (☎085/21 24 00, fax 21 24 01; ⑥), right by the church at rue de la Collégiale 5. However, you might just as well stay in Liège or in a more bucolic location further south.

Huy doesn't have much in the way of **restaurants**. *Le Jupy*, quai de Namur 10, is an affable bar that serves mussels in many guises; *San Martin*, past the tourist office at Chaussée Napoleon 2, does good French/Italian food, *Le Central* in the Grand-Place has reasonably priced plats du jour while nearby, at rue Griange 14, *Les Fleurs des Îles* offers a rare chance to try Caribbean cooking. Most people do their drinking around Grand-Place too – try *Aux Caves d'Artois* or *La Brasserie*; a cheaper and easy-going alternative is the *XIXieme*, by the Porte de Bethléem.

Around Huy – Château de Modave

A rewarding day trip, if you're in Huy for any length of time, is the fourteen-kilometre journey to the mostly seventeenth-century **Château de Modave** (April to mid-Nov daily 9am–6pm; F150), perched on a rock above the River Hoyoux, and with great views over the valley. The château was the home of a string of lesser members of the aristocracy after its completion in 1673 and twenty of the rooms are now open to the public, all crammed with period furniture, Brussels tapestries and some impressive stucco ceilings by Jean-Christian Hansche. An hourly bus, #126a (direction Ciney), runs from Huy's train station past the château.

Liège

Though the effective capital of the Ardennes, and of its own province, **LIÈGE** isn't the most obvious stop on most travellers' itineraries. It's a large, grimy, industrial city, with few notable sights and little immediate appeal. However, if you're heading down this way from Holland it is hard to avoid – trains on both routes to Luxembourg, for example, pass through the city – and once you've got to grips with its size, Liège even has a few surprises up its sleeve. Certainly, if you're overnighting, you'd be well advised to give it at least half a day before moving on.

Liège was actually independent for much of its history; from the tenth century onward it was the seat of a line of prince-bishops, who ruled over bodies as well as souls for around eight hundred years. The last prince-bishop was expelled in 1794 by soldiers of revolutionary France, who also torched the cathedral. It was later incorporated into the Belgian state, rising to prominence as an industrial city. The coal and steel industries here date back to the twelfth century, but it was only with the nineteenth century that real development of the city's position and natural resources took place – not least under one Charles Cockerill, a British entrepreneur whose name you still see around town. However, the heavy industry Cockerill bequeathed has been in decline, and the city is ringed by the decaying remnants of industrial glories long past.

Arrival and information

You'll probably arrive in Liège at **Guillemins Station**, about 2km south of the city centre. At the station there's a small **information** office (April–Sept Mon–Sat

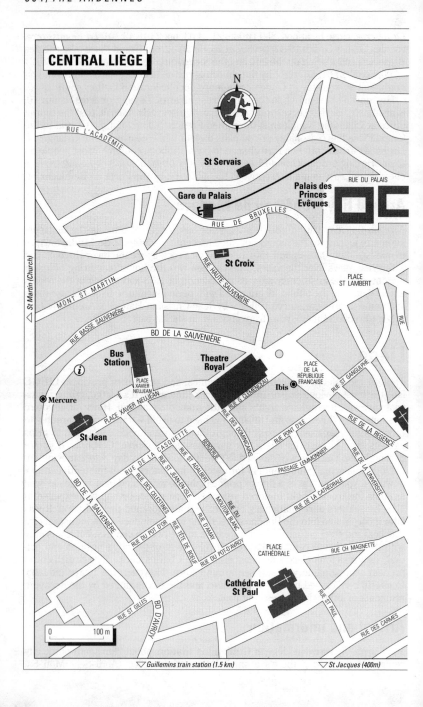

CENTRAL LIÈGE

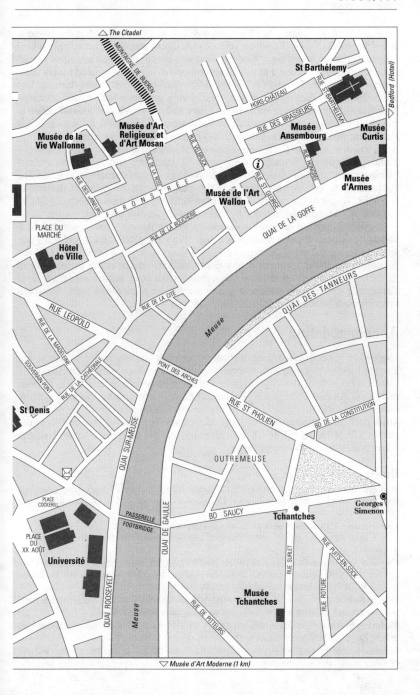

9am–noon & 1.30–5.30pm, Sun 10am–noon & 1–4pm; Oct–March Mon–Sat 10–noon & 1–4pm; ☎041/252 44 19), where you can pick up city maps, hotel lists and walking tours of the town, including a "Georges Simenon Route" through the author's childhood area of Outremeuse. For more comprehensive information, head for the main **tourist office** at Feronstrée 92 (Mon–Fri 9am–6pm, Sat 10am–4pm & Sun 10am–2pm; ☎041/221 92 21), where they're very generous with maps, advice on accommodation and what's on in town. There's also a **provincial tourist office** in the centre of town at boulevard de la Sauvenière 77 (Mon–Fri 8.30am–5pm, Sat 9am–1pm; ☎041/232 65 10), although they're less helpful on city matters.

All trains stop at the Guillemins Station, but Liège also has two other stations – **Palais**, on rue de Bruxelles near place St Lambert, and **Jonfosse**, on rue Stephany, not far from boulevard de la Sauvenière – which handle local trains and connections to Verviers and Eupen in the east, Tournai, Mons and Charleroi in the west. To get to the centre of town from Guillemins Station, take bus #1 or #4 to place St Lambert; the journey by taxi will cost you around F250.

In general, **getting around** is easiest on foot in the city centre, which is reasonably compact. However, Liège is a big, sprawling place, and to get from one side of town to the other, or to make a quick short hop, you'll need to take a **bus**. Tickets cost F40 for a journey of any length, either from the driver or from one of the ticket booths located at major bus terminals like place St Lambert, place de la Cathédrale or the train station. If you're staying for a couple of days, it's worth investing in a book of eight tickets for F210.

Accommodation

Liège's low ranking as a tourist destination means it has relatively few **hotels**, but also means they're rarely full, especially at weekends, when some even close completely. The bulk of the city's visitors are businesspeople, which tends to push prices up. As usual, the most economical choices are around the train station, either on the station square itself or up rue des Guillemins. There are no **campsites** particularly convenient to Liège; the closest is the lovely site at Wegimont (☎041/377 21 78, fax 377 38 00; open all year); bus #69 from place Xavier Neujean (direction Soumagne) stops nearby.

Hotels

Bedford, quai St Léonard 36 (☎041/228 81 11, fax 227 45 75; open all year). Large, comfortable, hotel with full range of facilities – TV, telephone, private bathroom, garage, banquet room – though rather expensive. ⑨.

Comfort Inn L'Univers, rue des Guillemins 116 (☎041/254 55 55, fax 254 55 00). Near the train station and rather more comfortable than its neighbours; breakfast costs an extra F250 per person. ④.

Cygne d'Argent, rue Beeckman 49 (☎041/223 70 01, fax 222 49 66). Small and friendly place ten minutes' walk from the station – cross the road and head left up rue Dartois, turn right on rue du Jardin Botanique and take the first left. ③.

Ibis, pl de la République Française 41 (☎041/230 33 33, fax 223 04 81). Large central hotel offering around a fifteen percent reduction on room rates at weekends. ⑥.

Mercure, bd de la Sauvenière 100 (☎041/221 77 11, fax 221 77 01). Plush establishment geared mainly to business travellers. ⑦.

Metropole, rue des Guillemins 141 (☎041/252 42 93, fax 252 55 52). Cramped rooms but otherwise a reasonably well-maintained place and the best bet if you're after a single room. ③.

Pensions des Nations, rue des Guillemins 139 (☎041/252 44 34). A basic but friendly hotel handily located near to Guillemins Station. ②.

Hostels

Georges Simenon, rue Georges Simenon 2 (☎041/344 56 89, fax 344 56 87). Brand new youth hostel in Outremeuse, near the church of St Nicolas. ①.

The City

Liège is a large city, and you'd be wise to concentrate on the central area. Situated on the west bank of the Meuse, this divides into two parts – the so-called **new town**, girdled by the traffic artery of boulevard de la Sauvenière, which curls around to the nominal centre of town at **place St Lambert**; and the **older section**, north of here, with Feronstrée as its spine, right below the steep heights that ascend to the former citadel. Most other places are lacking interest, though the separate district of **Outremeuse** across the river, on what is in effect an island in the Meuse, harbours a cluster of fine bars and restaurants.

The main squares

The centre of the city is a bit of a mess really, the new and old sections colliding at **place de la République Française**, more of a traffic circle than a square, flanked on one side by the shed-like Neoclassical Théâtre Royale, in front of which stands a statue of the Liège-born composer André Grétry (his heart is contained in the urn just below). The square fades seamlessly into **place St Lambert**, where the city is supposed to have begun – ironic considering its present-day use as car parks and bus stops. The **Palais des Princes Evêques** (palace of the prince-bishops), behind, does its best to provide a stately backdrop to the mayhem of the square, but even its vast frontage, built in the early sixteenth century and rebuilt a century later, can't help looking tawdry by association. You can wander into its main courtyard during office hours, though there's not much to see beyond the carved grotesques on its pillars. Cut through the building and you may be able to get into its second court, a smaller, prettier square, planted with greenery.

Old Liège: north of place St Lambert

East of the palace, the open space of place St Lambert narrows to **place du Marché**, really just another car park, its right side taken up by the eighteenth-century **Hôtel de Ville**. From here, **Feronstrée** leads east, the central spine of the so-called old town, which climbs up the sharp bank from the river to the citadel above. This rather grimy area, as opposed to the more pleasant new town on the southern side of place St Lambert, contains the city's densest concentration of museums, and there's a vigorous Sunday-morning market, **La Batte**, which stretches along the riverfront all the way from the quai de la Goffe to the corner of rue Hongrée.

The first turn off Feronstrée to the left, rue des Mineurs, leads up to the **Musée de la Vie Wallonne** (Tues–Sat 10am–5pm & Sun 10am–4pm; F80), one of several museums in the area devoted to aspects of Walloon culture. Housed in a restored former Franciscan friary, it has lots of photographs of nineteenth-century Walloon village life, a reconstruction of a typical Ardennes kitchen from days gone by and displays of tools of various trades, including those used in traditional

Ardennes industries like glassblowing and "Dinanderie" or copper-working – once practised in Huy and still a craft of Dinant. There's also a guillotine that used to await custom in place de la République Française.

Almost next door, along rue Hors Château, the **Musée d'Art Religieux et d'Art Mosan** (Tues–Sat 11am–6pm & Sun 11am–4pm; F50) is another museum focusing on local themes, with a sensitively displayed, roughly chronological assortment of Christian carvings and paintings from the Middle Ages on from Liège and the surrounding area. In Liège, at least, many of the best pieces remain in the churches themselves, but there are one or two nice exhibits from outside the city, including some sixteenth-century wood carvings of St Lambert and St Hubert – the latter, patron saint of hunting in the Ardennes, pictured with his symbol, a stag. There is also a seated Christ from 1240, and the carved *Virgin of Berselius*, an exquisite sculpture in wood from 1530. Among the paintings is a *Virgin with St Donatrice and Mary Magdalen* by the master of St Gudule, as well as landscapes by the early sixteenth-century Antwerp painter Joachim Patenier – lush canvases that depict unfolding landscapes of hills and villages not unlike the scenes of Bruegel.

Further along the same street, the four hundred or so steps of the very steep **Montagne de Bueren** lead up to the **citadel** – not much more than its ramparts these days, which enclose a modern hospital. The views, however, are superlative, worth what is a genuinely lung-wrenching trek, looking right out over the city and the rolling countryside beyond. Afterwards you can follow an interesting route back into the centre of the city by way of rue du Pery and rue Volière, which brings you out behind Gare de Palais.

On the opposite side of Feronstrée, further down, is the third of the area's Walloon museums, the **Musée de l'Art Wallon**, Feronstreé 86 (Tues–Sat 1–6pm, Sun 11am–4.30pm; F50), housed in a modern building by the river. This is a small collection of some quality, comprising works by French-speaking Belgian artists, and is the best laid-out of all the museums here. The museum is arranged chronologically, starting at the top with the wonderfully varied sixteenth-century paintings of Henri Bles dit Civetta – including his Bosch-like *Temptation of St Anthony* – and leading down in a descending spiral. The nineteenth- and early twentieth-century sections are strongest, including a number of works by Constanin Meunier – the large *La Coulée à Ourgrée* is one – Antoine Wiertz's fleshy (and enormous) *Greeks and Romans in Dispute over the Body of Patrocles*, and the delicate paintings of women by Armand Rassenfosse. Look out, also, for the small group of works by Delvaux and Magritte, notably the former's wacky *L'Homme de la Rue*, as well as more conventional earlier paintings by the same artist.

Further along Feronstrée, a little way past the tourist office, the **Musée d'Ansembourg** (Tues–Sun 1–6pm; F50) hosts a sumptuous collection of eighteenth-century furniture and decorations in an authentic period setting. It's something of a visual treat, with stucco ceilings, leather wallpaper, Delftware and other ceramics, and an army of clocks that includes an extraordinary six-faced piece by Hubert Sarton from 1795. Almost opposite, standing aloof from the street, the church of **St Barthélemy** (daily Mon–Sat 10am–noon & 2–5pm, Sun 2–5pm; F80) is a Romanesque edifice, with a late twelfth-century exterior, that has been pretty much spoiled inside by an insensitive eighteenth-century restoration. Its pride and joy though, a bronze baptismal font of 1118, remains pristinely intact. The work of Renier de Huy, it rests on ten oxen and is decorated with a circular relief depicting various baptisms in progress. The figures are graceful and naturalistic, and the oxen bend their heads and necks as if under the weight of the great bowl.

On the riverfront, two further museums may command your interest before you turn back towards the city centre proper. The **Musée d'Armes** (Mon, Wed–Sat 10am–1pm & 2–5pm; Sun 10am–1pm; closed Tues; F50) has, alongside an Ingres portrait of a young and dashing Napoleon, lots of beautifully engraved ornate pistols and rifles from the eighteenth to twentieth centuries along with examples of military modelling, suits of armour and ancient swords, some dating back to the sixth century.

The next museum along, the **Musée Curtius** (same times and price as Musée d'Armes) is a better bet. Housed in a turreted red-brick mansion from the early seventeenth century, it forms the sister collection to the Ansembourg, displaying archeological finds and decorative arts from the environs of Liège up to the nineteenth century. The rooms downstairs have a rather jumbled collection of artefacts from the Roman and Frankish periods – coins, weapons, ornaments and pottery – and a batch of unexceptional religious statuary. The collection of furniture, silver and tapestries upstairs hints at the enormous wealth of the city in its heyday, and there is also the late tenth-century Gospel Book of Bishop Notger, with a contemporary ivory frontispiece. Even more impressive is the display of glassware, housed in a separate part of the museum – and one of the world's finest collections. The display begins upstairs with a small cabinet of pre-Christian glassware, including Egyptian amphorae and jewellery, remarkably well preserved. The main room showcases work from most of the world's main glass-making centres up to the nineteenth century, from European crystal to gorgeous medieval Islamic artefacts, with local efforts represented by some exquisitely carved flute glasses. Downstairs, a roomful of colourful and sometimes breathtaking exhibits shows the direction in which Art Deco and Art Nouveau have taken the industry over the last century.

New Liège: south and west of place de la République Française

Walking in the opposite direction from place St Lambert takes you into the heart of the **newer part of the city**, bordered roughly by the boulevard de la Sauvenière in the west, and the river and avenue Maurice Destenay to the south. In many ways this area is preferable to the quarter around Feronstrée, partly pedestrianized, livelier and more engaging, with the bulk of the city's shops, bars, restaurants and nightlife. A short walk from rue Léopold, the church of **St Denis** (Mon–Sat 9am–noon & 1.30–5pm, Sun 9–10am), on the square of the same name, is a curious mix of styles, the original, austere pillars of the nave and the brown brick of the base of the tower contrasting markedly with the later ornate stucco topping. At the end of the south aisle, the church's retable is by far its most remarkable feature – an early sixteenth-century work, carved in wood, that stands a good five metres high. The top – and principal – section has six panels showing the Passion of Christ, very Gothic in tone, full of drama, with assertively carved depictions of grieving, leering and abusing humanity. The bottom set of panels is later and gentler in style, with smaller figures, less sensationally observed, telling the story of St Denis from baptism to decapitation.

From St Denis, rue de la Cathédrale leads down to the **Cathédrale St Paul** (daily 8am–noon & 2–5.15pm), the square in front of which is a busy spot to sit and watch the world go by. The church itself was actually only elevated to cathedral status in 1801, the replacement of an earlier, by all accounts more impressive building that was destroyed in 1794 by revolutionary French guards during the final days of the last prince-bishop. A fairly spartan structure, begun in the fourteenth century and not completely finished until the nineteenth, it has a couple of notable features, not least the swirling roof paintings of 1570 and a late thirteenth-century polychrome *Madonna and Child* at the base of the choir. But the **treasury** (Tues–Sun 2–5pm, but also often open outside these hours; F150) in the cloisters is of most interest, its small collection including a massive 90-kilogram bust reliquary of St Lambert, the work of a goldsmith from Aachen, and dating from 1508 to 1512. It contains the skull of the saint and depicts scenes from his life – the miracles he performed as a boy, his burial in Maastricht and the translation of his body from Maastricht to Liège by St Hubert, who succeeded him as bishop of the area. There are also some lovely examples of ivory work from the eleventh century, and a similarly dated missal, stained by the waters of a 1920s flood that afflicted the church.

South of the cathedral, just off avenue Maurice Destenay, the church of **St Jacques** (June–Sept Mon–Fri 10am–noon & 2–6pm, Sat 10am–noon & 2–4.15pm, Sun 2–6pm; Oct–May Mon–Fri & Sun 8am–noon & 5–7pm, Sat 8am–noon & 4–6pm) is comparable to the cathedral in size and exhibits a transition of styles that ranges from the Romanesque west front and pillar bases to the frilly, *joyeuse gothique* of the rest of the church – note the lighter-coloured stone used in the upper levels of the building.

There's one other church you should see in the new town, that of **St Jean** (Mon–Wed, Fri 10am–noon & 2–5pm, Thurs 2–5pm, Sat & Sun 2–6pm), on place Xavier Neujean, just off boulevard de la Sauvenière. This was originally a tenth-century church, modelled on Charlemagne's chapel in Aachen – hence the unusual shape – though only the tower remains from the first structure. Inside, behind glass, there's a beautifully carved statue of a Madonna and Child, dating from the thirteenth century but still with its original gilt surface, next door to which are two figures of the Virgin and St John, again exquisitely carved and wonderfully preserved.

Over the river: Outremeuse and more museums

The district across the river from the centre of Liège, **Outremeuse**, is supposedly the city's most characteristic neighbourhood, a working-class quarter that's said to be the home of the true Liègeois – it's sometimes known as the "free republic of Outremeuse", in part due to the traditional radicalism of the city's workers. This is a slightly phoney idea these days but it is epitomized by the figure known as **Tchantchès** (Liège slang for "Francis"), the so-called "Prince of Outremeuse". Tchantchès is a character from Liège folklore, an earthy, independent-minded, brave but drunken figure who is said to have been born between two Outremeuse paving stones on August 25, 760. In later life, legend claims, he was instrumental in the campaigns of Charlemagne, thanks to the use of his enormous nose. Nowadays Tchantchès can be seen in action in traditional Liège puppet shows; he's also represented in a **statue** on place l'Yser, the traditional place of his death, carried as a symbol of freedom by a woman dressed as a coal miner.

There's a **museum** devoted to Tchantchès nearby at rue Surlet 56 (Tues & Thurs 2–4pm, closed in July; F40), which displays various artefacts, costumes and other paraphernalia relating to the figure and his life as a puppet character. It's also worth considering a visit to the **Maison de la Métallurgie** (Mon–Fri 9am–5pm, Sat & Sun 2–6pm; F100), a fifteen-minute walk south at boulevard R. Poincaré 17, where you can see displays of metalwork and a reconstructed forge from the eighteenth century.

Further south, out of Outremeuse proper, the **Musée d'Art Moderne** (Tues–Sat 1–6pm, Sun 11am–4.30pm; F50) is in the southern part of the leafy Parc de Boverie, five minutes' walk from the Palais de Congrès. The museum is something of a curate's egg, giving a whistle-stop tour of art since 1850. Many major artists are represented – Picasso in blue mood with *La Famille Soler*, Gauguin's Tahitian *Le Sorcier d'Hiva-Oa* and Signac's *Le Château de Comblat* – but these are relatively minor works, and it's the lesser-known artists who catch the eye: Alfred Steven's wistful *La Parisienne Japonaise*, Emile Claus's truculent *Le Vieux Jardinier* and the coastal scenes of Eugène Boudin.

Eating, drinking and nightlife

Liège can be an excellent place to eat, and you don't always need to pay through the nose. For **lunch**, at least, there are lots of places in the centre of town, especially around place de la République Française, with low-price plats du jour and menus. You might also consider a trip across the river to **Outremeuse**, where rue Roture, a narrow street which spears right off the main shopping thoroughfare of rue Puits-en-Sock, is thick with restaurants and bars.

Bruit qui Court, boulevard de la Sauvenière. Less than five-minutes' walk from l'Église St Jean, this trendy eatery is decked out safari-style and serves simple, inexpensive meals – crêpes, salads, lasagne – and has a cool bar in an old converted bank-vault downstairs.

Le Canaillou, rue Puits-en-Sock 18. Has an excellent four-course menu for F875.

L'Ecailler du Café Robert, rue des Dominicains 26. Behind the Théâtre Royale, this popular resto is a good place for fish and seafood, with main meals at F600, and set three-course menus from F950.

La Fondue Royale, rue Puits-en-Sock 68. Has tasty cheese, meat and chocolate fondues.

Grand Comptoir Liègeois, place du Marché 19. A traditional place serving the local delicacy called boulettes de Liège – meatballs filled with a sweet black filling made of apples and pears, and known locally as sirop de Liège.

Mame Vi Cou, rue de la Wache 9. Just off the main squares, this is the last word in traditional Liègeoise cooking, where you can sample all manner of local specialities – though at rather hefty prices, with full meals starting at around F1000.

Au Parc de Moules, rue Tête de Boeuf 19. Serves up the usual bowl of mussels for around F500.

La Perle d'Asia, rue du Pot d'Or 49. Has excellent and authentic Vietnamese food, particularly seafood, with set menus for lunch from F280, and for dinner from F400. It also has an excellent-value plat du jour for F190, and a four-course vegetarian meal will only set you back F395. Closed Monday.

Pizzeria da Michele, rue de la Casquettes 25. An established pizzeria with pizzas from F200.

Au Point de Vue, pl de la République Française. Claims to be the oldest tavern in Liège, and its blend of homey bar atmosphere, a local crowd, and cheap lunchtime and evening meals is worth experiencing.

Rivoli, Feronstrée 83 on the corner of rue St Jean Baptiste. Makes a good lunch option in the museum area with daily specials for F180.

Taverne L'Opéra, on the corner of rue des Dominicans. This is a less interesting restaurant than many in the area but has many dishes for under F250.

Le Thème, impasse de la Couronne 9. Near to the main tourist office, the tiny *Thème* serves excellent and quite reasonably priced French cuisine, and, as its name suggests, changes its décor every six months.

Ups and Downs, bd de la Sauvenière 141. Newly established and *the* place for cheap tacos, burgers, or even a full American breakfast.

Bars and nightlife

The grid of streets that runs north from rue Pont d'Avroy up to rue de la Casquette is the city's most popular area for **nightlife**, home to many good bars and clubs, as well as restaurants. Rue Pont d'Avroy itself has lots of **bars**, including the popular *Crocodile*, but most of the best establishments are on the narrower streets behind. Start at rue d'Amay and its continuation rue St Jean en Isle – *Les Trois Frères* at no. 3 is lively and atmospheric, as is *Cour St Jean* at no. 23. Rue Tête de Boeuf has *La Notte* at no. 10, with live jazz on Tuesday (F250 cover charge), while *Les Apéros de Bouldou*, at no. 15, is one of the main student hangouts and has live music at weekends (no cover charge), as well as a nightclub –"En Bas" (Fri–Sat 11pm–8am; free) – downstairs. There are also a couple of good bars on place du Marché opposite the Hôtel de Ville. *A Pilori*, at no. 7, is a tiny historic tavern with wooden beams and a cosy feel, whereas a few steps further down, *Blue-Note*, at no. 29, is a real locals' pub with a transvestite show every other Saturday. Rue Roture in Outremeuse also has a couple of decent bars; *Luigi's* at no. 22 has a piano player most nights.

Being a fairly large student town, Liège has its share of **clubs**, the most popular student hangouts being *Le Cave*, at rue d'Amay 10, which also hosts live rock bands, the cheap and trashy *Le Trimaran*, rue du Pot d'Or 39 or, if you're into dance music, *Le Premier*, next door. Another student haunt is *L'Aquarelle*, on the corner of rue de Pot d'Or and rue Tête de Boeuf, which also plays good music. Less student-oriented is *Le Lion S'Envoile*, in Outremeuse, rue Roture 13, a hip club-cum-venue, well known for its programme of cool live jazz acts.

Listings

Books Pax, pl Cockerill 4, has a small stock of English paperbacks.

Bureaux de change There's a 24-hour office at Guillemins Station.

Buses Timetable information on ☎041/222 05 61.

Car rental Avis, bd d'Avroy 238b (☎041/252 55 00); Europcar, bd de la Sauvenière 37 (☎041/222 40 07); Hertz, bd d'Avroy 60 (☎041/222 42 73).

Laundry Ipsomat, Feronstrée 146 (daily 7am–10pm).

Newspapers English-language newspapers are available from the train station bookstand, or in the centre of town at Bellens, rue de la Régence 6, and at Libro Plus, on Feronstrée just before C&A.

Post office The main central post office is at rue de la Régence 61 (Mon–Fri 8.30am–6pm, Sat 8.30am–noon).

Train enquiries ☎041/229 26 10.

Travel agents Nouvelles Frontières, bd de la Sauvenière 32 (☎041/223 67 67); Wasteels, pl Xavier Neujean 25 (☎041/223 70 26).

East of Liège: Verviers and Eupen

East of Liège, the River Vesdre winds through some lovely wooded countryside, with sharp hills plunging down into deep wooded valleys as soon as you get free of the sprawl of Liège. **VERVIERS** is the main town of the Vesdre valley, a small place of around fifty thousand people that is a good base for the area, though in itself it isn't the sort of place you'd make a beeline for; indeed you're far better off heading south into the Ardennes proper. However, if you're travelling east into

Germany and find yourself here at midday, you may want to stop for lunch, in which case there are a couple of reasonable museums, together worth an hour or so of your time.

The centre of town, five to ten minutes' walk from the train station down past the war memorial, is **place Verte** and – a block away – **place des Martyrs**. Five minutes' walk from the latter, down rue de Collège and left onto rue Renier, is the **Musée des Beaux Arts** (Mon, Wed & Sat 2–5pm, Sun 3–6pm; free), with a small, quality collection of paintings, which includes a number of canvases by Dutch artists. Notable among these are a small landscape by Jan van Goyen, a fine crowded *Adoration of the Magi* by Gerrit Dou, a portrait of a child by Cornelis de Vos, as well as later nineteenth-century works by Johan Barthold Jongkind, such as *The Skaters*. You should also look out for Jan Weenix's portrait of Admiral van Heemskerk, and a room entirely decorated with murals depicting views of the valley of the Vesdre (which runs alongside the museum) and parts of Malmédy by an unknown eighteenth-century artist.

Verviers' other museum, the **Musée d'Archéologie** (Tues & Thurs 2–5pm, Sat 9am–noon, Sun 10am–1pm; free), is of less interest, but it is nearby at rue des Raines 42, so you may as well have a look. Expect a handful of rooms furnished in period style, some weaponry, artefacts pertaining to a local nineteenth-century violinist, Henri Vieuxtemps, and a small collection of Roman coins and other local historical finds.

For maps of the town, a walking tour, and other information, the **tourist office** is halfway between place Verte and the station at rue Vieille-Xhavée 61 (Mon–Fri 9am–12.30pm & 1.30–5pm, Sat 9am–12.30pm & 1.30–4pm; ☎087/33 02 13). There are three reasonable **hotels**: *Des Ardennes*, near the station at place de la Victoire 15 (☎087/22 39 25; ③), the more comfortable eighteen-room *Park*, opposite the tourist office at rue Vielle-Xhavée 90 (☎087/33 09 72, fax 31 60 91; ④), and the four-star *Amigo* just south of place du Général Jaques at rue Herla 1 (☎087/22 11 21, fax 23 03 69; ⑥–⑦).

Eupen

Trains continue on to **EUPEN**, as the landscape unfolds into a gentler affair of undulating pastureland. This again is pleasant enough, but has nothing especially to attract you other than its role as capital of the German-speaking part of Belgium. This area has been largely German since the early nineteenth century, when it was part of Prussia and a policy of enforced Germanization was undertaken. The area was ceded to Belgium under the Treaty of Versailles in 1919, but German is the main language here – both spoken on the streets and used on signs, street names and menus. Eupen certainly has a definite Teutonic feel, not least in the curvy twin towers of the eighteenth-century church of **St Nicholas** on the main Marktplatz, ten minutes' walk from the train station (5min from the bus station), which sports some ornate Baroque altarpieces and an extravagant pulpit that could be straight out of provincial Bavaria. Just outside the town, Eupen's main attraction is its **barrage**, a few kilometres to the east (reachable by bus from the bus station), the largest dam in Belgium, with a tower that gives marvellous views over the reservoir below and the area beyond. In the unlikely event that you stay over in Eupen, *Ambassador Hôtel Botsen*, 77–81 Haasstrasse (☎087/74 08 00, fax 74 48 41; ⑤–⑥), is comfortable, if a little pricey; the *Rathaus*, Rathausplatz 13 (☎087/74 28 12, fax 74 46 64; ②), is a much cheaper option.

South of Liège: Remouchamps, Stavelot, Malmédy and the Hautes Fagnes

Midway between Liège and Stavelot, **REMOUCHAMPS**, connected by reasonably frequent buses or trains to the nearby station of Aywaille, is a small resort on the River Amblève, visited mainly for the **Grottes de Remouchamps** in the centre of town (Feb–Nov daily 9am–6pm; Dec & Jan Mon–Fri 9.30am–5pm; last departure 1hr before closing; F300). You can see the caves by way of what is claimed to be the longest subterranean boat trip in the world, through beautiful coloured galleries of stalagmites and stalagtites. There's little reason to stay, although if you do, *Royal Hôtel Bonhomme*, rue de la Reffe 26 (☎384 20 06, fax 384 59 46; ④), is reasonably priced and has a good restaurant.

Stavelot and around

A couple of stops further down the train tracks, **Trois Ponts** is the starting point for hourly buses to the busy resort of **STAVELOT**, a ten-minute trip. A small town set on a hill, Stavelot was the scene of fierce fighting during the Ardennes campaign of the last war, and some of the Nazis' worst atrocities in Belgium were committed here. These days Stavelot is a pleasant old place with a former abbey which – with that of nearby Malmédy – was home to a line of powerful abbot-bishops who ran the area as an independent fiefdom from the seventh right up to the end of the eighteenth centuries. Most of the buildings that remain are eighteenth-century, but there's a sixteenth-century archway from the original abbey church and other parts of the abbey are being excavated. Otherwise Stavelot is a nice place just to wander in, and several of its pretty streets are lined by eighteenth-century houses with exposed wooden beams.

The abbey houses a number of different museums, most notably the **Musée Régional d'Art Religieux et de l'Ancienne Abbaye** (daily: April–Oct 10am–12.30pm & 2–5.30pm; Nov–March 10am–12.30pm & 2–4.30pm; F125), which displays religious art of the Ardennes from the fourteenth to the twentieth centuries – sculpture, silver and gold carvings, reliquaries and a lot of liturgical dress. The collection can't compare with the museums in Namur – most of the abbey's treasures were destroyed by the French Revolutionary armies or sold off long ago – but it's worth a brief look. Other adjoining sections are devoted to the history of the town, its folklore and fine arts. In another wing of the abbey, the **Musée du Circuit de Spa-Francorchamps** (same times and ticket) contains a superb array of racing cars and motorcycles from the nearby race track. Just over the courtyard, on the second floor of the Hôtel de Ville, the **Musée Guillaume Apollinaire** (July & Aug daily 10am–12.30pm & 2–5.30pm; outside these months, apply at the nearby library, closed Sun & Mon; F70) was set up to commemorate the eponymous French writer, who spent the summer of 1899 in the town and wrote many poems about Stavelot and the Ardennes. The museum contains newspaper articles, letters, poems, sketches and photos relating to the man who – despite his premature death – was one of the most influential of early twentieth-century writers.

A couple of minutes' walk up the hill from here, **place St Remacle** is the attractive main square. Around the corner, the church of **St Sebastien** (Mon–Sat

10am–12.30pm & 2–5pm; free) has an enormous thirteenth-century shrine of Saint Remacle, founder of Stavelot abbey in the seventh century – you'll see him on the town's coat of arms, building the abbey with the aid of a wolf he supposedly tamed for the purpose. Mosan in style, the shrine is of gilt and enamelled copper with filigree and silver statuettes, though you can normally only view it from a distance. A short walk downhill, the little **chapel of St Laurent** was founded in 1030 by Saint Poppon, Abbot of Stavelot, and contains the sarcophagus that originally held his remains. To get there, turn left out of the abbey tower, walk downhill across the bridge, and take the first left.

Practicalities

If you can manage it, the best time to be in Stavelot is for its **carnival**, first celebrated here in 1502 and since the early 1900s a renowned annual event, held on the third weekend before Easter, from Saturday to Monday evening. The main protagonists are the Blancs Moussis, figures with white hoods and long red noses. There are also festivals of theatre and music in July and August respectively, with performances in the abbey buildings. For more information, consult the **tourist office** in the abbey ticket office (daily: April–Oct 10am–12.30pm & 2–5.30pm; Nov–March 10am–12.30pm & 2–4.30pm; ☎080/86 27 06).

Accommodation can be difficult to find during carnival time, but generally the most reasonable **hotel** is the centrally placed *Mal Aime*, rue Neuve 12 (☎080/86 20 01; ③). Alternatives include the lovely *Hôtel d'Orange*, a couple of minutes east of place St Remacle at rue Devant les Capucins 8 (☎080/86 20 05, fax 86 42 92; ⑤), the equally pleasant *Maison du Crouly*, on place St Remacle 19 (☎080/86 41 65, fax 88 02 75; ⑤), and the plush four-star *Le Val d'Amblève*, route de Malmédy 7 (☎080/86 23 53, fax 86 41 21; ⑤–⑥). The nearest **campsite** is *Camping des Challes*, near the River Amblève, a fifteen-minute walk east of the centre at route de Challes 5 (☎086/86 23 31; April–Nov).

For **food**, the intimate *Restaurant de l'Abbaye* on place St Remacle has good local cuisine, *La Vecchia Romagna* opposite has reasonable Italian food, and the *Hôtel d'Orange* and *Maison du Crouly* both have three-course menus from F500. Elsewhere, *Pizzeria Figaro*, place du Vinâve 4, does tasty and well-priced pastas and pizzas. If you're just after a **drink**, try *Aux Vieilles Caves d'Artois*, overlooking the abbey buildings at avenue Ferd Nicolay 7, or the arty bar at *Hôtel Mal Aime* – Apollinaire once stayed here and his poems are scrawled over the walls.

Around Stavelot

The tourist office has a **walking map** (*Carte des Promenades de Stavelot*) which marks fourteen circular routes starting in Stavelot or one of the nearby villages, with the most attractive walks heading east along the Amblève towards Warche or west through Ster to the waterfalls at **COO**, 7km away. Coo has its own train station and can get quite congested with tourists in the summer, with a riot of amusements just off the main street – restaurants, go-carts, a deer park and a cable car up the mountain (F150 round trip) – but a little walking gets you away from the crowd. Coo is also the starting-point for **canoe trips** on the Amblève (March to mid-Nov), either 9km to Cheneux (F600 for a two-seater kayak) or 23km to Lorce (F800), and in high summer it's worth booking in advance – contact Cookayak in Stavelot (☎080/68 42 65, fax 68 44 43). Finally, Play Bike, at rue Haute 15 in Stavelot, rent out **mountain-bikes** for F600 per day and can suggest biking circuits, and there is an excellent open-air **swimming pool** (July & Aug

10am–1pm & 2–7pm; F70) five minutes' walk from the tourist office at plaine des Bressais.

Malmédy

Eight kilometres away, accessible by bus from Stavelot or direct from Spa, **MALMÉDY** is a less attractive town, though it revels in a pretty riotous carnival, the Cwarmê. A museum on the subject, the **Musée du Cwarmê** (Tues–Sun: July & Aug 3–6pm; rest of the year 2–5pm; F100), is on the third floor of Maisons de Cavens, the big white mansion on the central place de Rome that was once the local orphanage. The same building houses the **Musée National du Papier** (same times and ticket) but, other than the nearby **Cathédrale** (guided visits July & Aug; 10am–noon & 2–5pm), there's not much else to Malmédy, and no reason to stay; all in all, it's a rather characterless place and useful only as a relatively inexpensive base for the Hautes Fagnes.

Practicalities

The **tourist office** is in the town centre at place du Chatelet 10 (Mon–Fri 9am–noon & 1.30–5pm, Sat 10am–noon & 2–4pm; ☎080/33 02 50, fax 77 05 88). Reasonable **accommodation** is available at *Hôtel du Rome*, place de Rome 23 (☎080/33 94 60; ③), at *La Forge*, nearby at rue Devant-les-Religeuses 31 (☎080/33 99 79, fax 33 97 62; ③), and at *Albert 1er*, place Albert 1er 40 (☎080/33 04 52, fax 33 06 16; ④–⑤). Otherwise try the centrally located *Saint-Géreon*, place St Géreon 7–8 (☎080/33 06 77, fax 33 97 46; ③), or *Chambertin*, just down from the tourist office at rue J. Steinbach 17 (☎080/33 03 14, fax 77 03 38; ③–④). The closest campsite is *Mon Repos*, avenue de la Libération 3 (☎080/33 86 21; open all year), about 2km out of town.

The moderately priced *Au Petit Louvain*, rue Chemin 47, is a good choice for an evening **meal**, or there's the snacky *L'Ange Gourmand* at no. 21. *Carthage* on place de Rome serves inexpensive pizzas, and various cafés nearby offer decent lunch menus. Elsewhere, *á Vî Mám'di*, place Albert 1er 41, serves good regional food, and *Chalet de la Truite Argentée*, rue Bellevue 3, is a pleasant and well-priced fish restaurant.

Robertville, Reinhardstein Castle and the Hautes Fagnes

The high plateau that stretches north of Malmédy up as far as Eupen is known as the **Hautes Fagnes** (also known as the Hohes Venn, or High Fens), nowadays protected as a national park. This area marks the end of the Ardennes proper, sandwiched between the Eifel hills which stretch into Germany, but is in fact home to Belgium's highest peak, the Signal de Botrange. The rest of the area is boggy heath and woods, windswept and rather wild – excellent hiking country.

ROBERTVILLE, a few kilometres north of Malmédy, is a bland resort that has grown up around the lake created by the **barrage** of the same name. There's little to do in the town itself, but it makes an excellent base for the surrounding area. There's a couple of good hotels on rue du Barrage, most notably the pretty *Chaumière du Lac*, at no. 23 (☎080/44 63 39, fax 44 46 01; ⑥), and, close by at no. 5, the cheaper *Résidence du Lac* (☎080/44 46 94, fax 44 77 52; ⑤). Alternatively head for the three-star *La Frequence*, rue Centrale 32 (080/44 54 80, fax 44 48 58;

WALKING AROUND THE HAUTES FAGNES

Large parts of the Hautes Fagnes are protected zones and are only open to walkers with a registered guide. Three- to six-hour walks in these areas are arranged by the **Centre Nature Botrange** at weekends and by other groups during the week (F120–160; ☎080/44 57 81 for details), with each walk organized around a feature of the local ecology, from medicinal plants to the endangered tetras lyre bird. In summer the walks can feel a bit crowded, and the guide's patter is normally in French or German, but they're a good way to see some genuinely wild country that would otherwise be off-limits.

If you want to see some of the moorland on your own, you can follow a two-hour circular walk from the Centre that takes in the **Fagne de la Poleur** to the north. Head out through the car park and take the signposted right turn after about a kilometre; the route is shown on the Centre's less-than-helpful map *Promenades dans les Hautes Fagnes* and can get pretty busy.

Dozens more local routes are marked on the map *Promenades Malmédy*, also available from the Centre or from any of the local tourist offices, though most are south of the Hautes Fagnes around Robertville, Xhoffraix and Malmédy. The varied 11km route **M6** can be picked up in Botrange, crossing the heath as far as the main road before dropping down through the woods and along the river to Bayhon, returning through some attractive, almost Alpine scenery. From M6 you can take a detour north to incorporate the Fagne de la Poleur into the walk, or cross the main road and join route **M9**, which winds through the woods to Baraque Michel and then cuts south across the moors on the edge of the protected Grande Fagne.

④). Of the cheaper places to stay, *Auberge du Lac*, rue de Lac 24 (☎080/44 41 59, fax 44 58 20; ③), is the cheapest option, and is a friendly old place, if a tad basic. The **tourist office** is at rue Centrale 53 (Mon–Sat 9am–noon & 1–6pm, Sun 11am–noon & 1–3pm; ☎080/44 64 75).

The lake itself is the start of a lovely one-kilometre walk to **Reinhardstein Castle** (mid-June to mid-Sept Sun tours every hour from 2.15 to 5.15pm; July & Aug also Tues, Thurs & Sat at 3.30pm; F150) – which is also reachable by road from the village of Orvifat, though you still have to leave your vehicle half a kilometre from the castle and walk the rest of the way. A squat stone structure nestled in the valley, and still privately owned, the castle was originally built in the fourteenth century and restored earlier this century; it now houses the usual array of weaponry and old paintings – an intriguing insight into the life of your average Belgian aristocrat.

North of Robertville, the **Centre Nature Botrange** (Mon 1–6pm, Tues–Sun 10am–6pm; closed two weeks mid-Nov; F150) provides a focus for explorations of the Hautes Fagnes park, though it's difficult to get to without a car. A bus does run to Botrange from Verviers and Eupen, but if you're coming from Stavelot or Malmédy you have to change at Waimes and connecting buses are not at all frequent. Multilingual headphones guide you around a permanent exhibition that describes the flora and fauna of the area and explains how the *fagnes* were created and how they've been exploited. There's a coffee shop, a bookstore and, most importantly, a roaring log fire when the weather turns cold. The centre also has bikes for rent for F600 a day and runs organized hikes (see box).

A kilometre or so further up the main road, the **Signal de Botrange** is, at 694m, Belgium's highest peak, although the high-plateau nature of the Hautes

Fagnes means it actually doesn't feel very high at all. A tower marks the spot, offering a good panorama over the *fagnes*, and there's a restaurant that's ultra-popular with coach parties and walkers.

Spa

SPA was the world's first health resort, established way back in the sixteenth century: Pliny the Elder knew of the healing properties of the waters here, and Henry VIII was an early visitor. Since then it's given its name to thermal resorts worldwide, reaching a height of popularity in the eighteenth and nineteenth centuries, when it was graced by monarchs, statesmen, intellectuals and aristocrats from all over Europe. Later the town went into slow decline – when Matthew Arnold visited in 1860 he claimed it "astonished us by its insignificance". The years since have been no kinder, with moneyed flashiness replacing glamour – fast cars and big, pedigree dogs are the order of the day. A waft of sophistication comes from the casino in the centre of town, but that's about it, and you'd do better to visit Spa for its ease of access to the surrounding countryside and its small towns, notably Stavelot (see above).

The town

There is little to see or do in Spa. The main thermal baths, **Les Thermes de Spa** (Mon–Fri 7.30am–noon & 1.30–4.30pm, Sat & Sun 7.30am–noon; prices start from F2350 per day; ☎087/77 25 60), are right in the centre on the main place Royale 41, next door to the casino, and provide a very grand setting for the arthritis- and hypertension-curing mud and water treatments – which, if you're feeling flush, you'll need to book a couple of weeks in advance. A little further along down rue Royale, to the left, is the **Pouhan-Pierre-le-Grand**, the town's main mineral spring, named after Peter the Great, who appreciated the therapeutic effects of its waters and visited often (daily: April–Oct 10am–noon & 1.30–5pm; Nov–March 1.30–5pm); for just F7 you can get yourself a glass of the water – it tastes disgusting. Spa's waters contain iron and bicarbonate of soda, allegedly beneficial for lung and heart ailments, as well as rheumatism. There are **four other springs** around Spa: Tonnelet, Barisart, Géronstère and Sauvenière. A little tram-bus (called a *baladeuse*) plies between them, but they don't normally let you get off to take the waters and there's precious little to see. The buses are stationed around the main square, and trips (there's a variety of itineraries) cost about F140.

In the town you can also visit the **Musée de la Ville d'Eau**, back toward the station, opposite rue de la Gare at avenue Reine Astrid 77b (mid-June to mid-Sept daily 2.30–5.30pm; mid-Sept to Dec & mid-March to mid-June Sat & Sun only 2.30–5.30pm; F80), which displays posters and objects relating to the resort and its waters. The museum is situated in the former mansion of Queen Marie-Henriette, and the stables next door have been turned into a **Musée du Cheval** (same times; F40; combined ticket F100), exhibiting all things equine. The town's only other museum is the almost frighteningly surreal **Musée de la Lessive**, a ten-minute walk south of the tourist office on route de la Géronstère 10 (July & Aug daily 2–5pm; F50), which is the last resting place of dozens of antiquated washing machines.

If you're around in the winter, check out the skiing at Thier des Rexhons (contact Ski Club de Spa ☎087/77 37 22), 5km out of the town and 500 metres from the Géronstère spring. They open as soon as there's enough snow to practise skiing, and although the slopes are small (575m), it's pretty cheap.

Practicalities

The **train station** is five minutes' walk from the town centre; go straight down rue de la Gare and turn right. The **tourist office**, in a pavilion opposite the baths at place Royale 41 (July & Aug daily 10am–6pm; rest of year Mon–Fri 9am–12.30pm & 2–6pm, Sat & Sun 10am–12.30pm & 2–6pm; ☎087/79 53 53, fax 79 53 54), is extremely well stocked with books, walking routes, cycle circuits and maps. Free guided walks in the area are organized three or four times a week in July and August, with a few during Easter holidays.

Spa's cheapest **rooms** are above the café at *Le Relais de la Poste*, rue de la Poste 17 (☎087/77 47 55; ②), just beside the baths. A nicer alternative is *Le Relais*, place du Monument 22 (☎087/77 11 08; fax 77 25 93; ③), which is handily placed and reasonably priced, or there's the peaceful *Les Sorbiers*, at avenue de Barisart 215 (☎087/77 41 66, fax 77 08 25; ⑤), ten minutes' walk from *Le Relais* up place Verte and rue de Barisart. The six-roomed *Hostellerie Le Tri Renard*, close to place Salés at boulevard Chapman 5 (☎087/77 26 01, fax 77 22 40; ⑥), is slightly more expensive, but very comfortable. There are several **campsites** outside Spa. The nearest, *Camping Havette*, is southeast of the centre at rue Chelui 21 (☎087/77 37 87; April–Oct); follow rue Royale down to where it runs into rue de la Sauvenière, and rue Chelui is a right turn a few hundred metres along. *Camping du Parc des Sources* is farther along on rue de la Sauvenière itself, at no. 141 (☎087/77 23 11; April–Oct).

Among Spa's many **restaurants**, the hotel restaurant *Le Relais* has good, reasonably priced food served in convivial surroundings; a few doors along at no. 15, *La Belle Époque* also has excellent food, with fish dishes from F500 and three-course menus from F995. *Grand Café des Thermes*, opposite the casino on rue Royale, has several plats du jour for F300, and the nearby *La Cortina* serves good-value spaghetti, pizza and steak on its largely Italian menu – supplemented, in a traditional Belgian way, by a wide selection of mussel dishes. Just along from here, the *Bidule* is a popular bar for evening **drinking**, especially at weekends. Around the corner on place Pierre Le Grand, *Le Sanglier* is a good local bar.

travel details

Trains

Arlon to: Jemelle (6 daily; 50min); Libramont (6 daily; 30min); Luxembourg (hourly; 20min); Namur (6 daily; 1hr 30min).

Dinant to: Anseremme (every 2hr; 10min); Bertrix (every 2hr; 1hr 20min); Gendron-Celles (every 2hr; 20min); Houyet (every 2hr; 25min); Libramont (every 2hr; 1hr 40min).

Jemelle to: Antwerp (hourly; 2hr); Brussels Midi (hourly; 1hr 30 min); Libramont (hourly; 20 min); Luxembourg (hourly; 1hr 10min); Namur (hourly; 40 mins).

Libramont to: Bastogne (every 2hr; 45min); Bertrix (every 2hr; 10min); Florenville (every 2hr; 30min); Poix St Hubert (every 2hr; 18min); Virton (every 2hr; 50min).

Liège to: Aywaille (every 2hr; 30min); Barvaux (every 2hr; 1hr); Brussels (hourly; 1hr 10min); Cologne (hourly; 1hr 50min); Huy (every 30min; 20min); Jemelle (every 2hr; 1hr 25min); Leuven (hourly; 50min); Marloie (every 2hr; 1hr 20min); Melreux (every 2 hours; 1hr 10min); Namur (every 30min; 45min); Tienen (hourly; 40min); Trois Ponts (every 2hr; 60min); Verviers (hourly; 18min), change at Verviers-Central for Eupen (hourly; 22min) and Spa (hourly; 30min).

Namur to: Arlon (hourly; 1hr 20min); Charleroi (1–2 an hour; 50min); Dinant (every 30min; 30min); Floreffe (1–2 an hour; 10min); Godinne (every 30min; 20min); Huy (every 30min; 25min); Jemelle (hourly; 40min); Libramont (hourly; 1hr); Liège (every 30min; 45min); Luxembourg (hourly; 1hr 40min).

Rochefort to: Lavaux Ste Anne (July & Aug 2 daily; 1hr).

Buses

Bertrix to: Bouillon (Mon–Fri 7 daily, Sat & Sun 4 daily; 30 min); Herbeumont (Mon–Fri 6 daily, no weekend service; 40min).

Dinant to: Givet (France) (6 daily; 45min).

Jemelle to: Han-sur-Lesse (June–Aug Mon–Fri 5 daily, Sat & Sun 10 daily; Sept–May Mon–Fri 4 daily, Sat 3 daily, no Sun service; 16 min); Rochefort (as for Han-sur-Lesse; 7 min).

Libramont to: Bouillon (Mon–Fri 7 daily, Sat & Sun 4 daily; 50min).

Liège: (Guillemins) to: Remouchamps (6 daily; 35min).

Melreux to: Hotton (Mon–Fri 10 daily; Sat & Sun 5 daily; 5min); La Roche-en-Ardenne (Mon–Fri 8 daily, Sat & Sun 4 daily; 30min).

Namur to: Annevoie (every 2hr; 30min); Floreffe (8 daily; 30min).

Poix St Hubert to: St Hubert (Mon–Fri 12 daily, Sat & Sun 4 daily; 15min).

Trois Ponts to: Malmédy (hourly; 10min); Stavelot (hourly; 20min).

Boats

Dinant to: Anseremme (every 20min; 45min round trip); Freyr (1 daily; 1hr 30min round trip); Heer Agimont (1 daily in July & Aug; 5hr round trip); Namur (Sun only; 3hr 30min one-way).

CHAPTER SIX

LUXEMBOURG

cross the border from the Belgian province of Luxembourg (with which it has a closely entwined history), the **Grand Duchy of Luxembourg** is one of Europe's smallest sovereign states, a tiny independent principality with a total population of 400,000, living in an area of just over 2500 square kilometres. As a country it's relatively neglected by travellers, which is surprising considering its varied charms, not least its marvellous scenery: the green hills of the Ardennes bump over the Belgian border to form a glorious heartland of deep wooded valleys spiked with sharp, craggy hills crowned with châteaux. Indeed, Luxembourg boasts no fewer than 130 châteaux – some austere, fortified castles, others lavish country houses.

A visit to the capital, **Luxembourg City**, home to over one-fifth of the population, is a real pleasure too: once the Habsburg's strongest fortress, portions of its massive bastions and zigzag walls have survived in good order, making the city one of the most handsome in Europe. Furthermore, the broken terrain, with its deep winding valleys and steep hills, has restricted development and the city still feels more like a grouping of disparate villages rather than a European city or the leading administrative focus for the EU and world financial centre. The city is not over-endowed with sights but there are lots of first-rate restaurants and a reasonable selection of bars and clubs as well as a constant stream of cultural events. Luxembourg City is also the hub of the country's public transport system and is therefore the best base for day-tripping out into the rest of the Grand Duchy.

The **Minett region**, southwest of Luxembourg City, is carved with autoroutes heading south into France, and is home to most of the country's heavy industry, largely concentrated around the Grand Duchy's second city, **Esch-sur-Alzette** – although the area also boasts attractive walks and cycle rides through the old mining areas, where forest is being encouraged to camouflage the worst industrial ravages. The southeast is more immediately attractive, with tourism focusing on the vineyards of the **River Moselle**, whose left bank forms the border with Germany. These slopes hold some pretty towns and a modest wine industry, which produces some very drinkable (and surprisingly affordable) white and sparkling wines.

The central part of Luxembourg – known as the **"Gutland"** – can be reached by way of the spinal road and rail route through Ettelbruck up to Clervaux. This passes through some of Luxembourg's most spectacular scenery, as it heads north into the Oesling (Éisléck in Luxembourgish), a region of rich green hills and valleys climaxing in the wooded terrain of the **Luxembourg Ardennes**. Without your own transport, visiting many of the attractions hereabouts can be problematic, but it is worth the effort. Possible bases include the tiny and ancient abbey town of **Echternach**, the more mundane little town of **Diekirch**, or **Vianden** to the north, surrounded by high green hills and crowned by a magnificent castle.

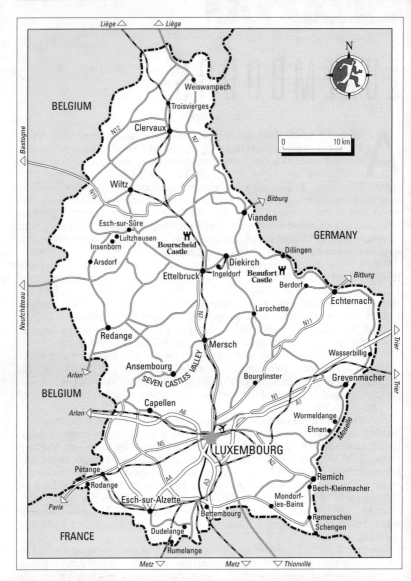

With regard to public **transport**, there's a fairly regular bus service to and between most villages, though buses in the more remote districts are often geared to the needs of commuters and schoolchildren. Much of the country can be seen on day-trips from the capital – nowhere is more than a couple of hours' journey away – although for anywhere north of Ettelbruck you're better off staying overnight. In addition to services centred on the capital, bus routes also

THE LUXEMBOURG CARD

Available in the summertime, the **Luxembourg Card** gives substantial discounts on a variety of attractions across the Grand Duchy and also covers public transport. Cards are valid for one (F300), two (F500) or three days (F700) and there are family cards too (2–5 people; F700, F1100, F1500). They are available from tourist offices, hotels and campsites.

Luxembourg City sells its own card, **La Carte-Musée**, which runs on similar principles but is available all year and is, of course, only of use in the city. It's sold for two-day periods only (F250 per person, F400 for families).

start in Esch-sur-Alzette, Echternach, Diekirch, Vianden and Clervaux. They all serve the local train station where appropriate and, in theory at least, are coordinated; timetables can be bought at newsstands, tourist offices, and train and bus stations.

If you have your own transport, exploring **off the beaten track** can be rewarding – not least for the abundance of wildlife you might encounter: those who tread softly will see storks and cranes fishing in the rivers, and chance upon deer and wild boar in the forests. In isolated villages, you may still come across horses dragging out cut trees in the traditional manner, while some of the semi-fortified or walled farms are quite beautiful.

Some history

Perhaps the most surprising thing about **Luxembourg** is that the **modern state** exists at all. As it's sandwiched between European superpowers France and Germany, you'd think that one or the other would have gobbled it up – which they would have done but for some strange quirks of history. There was a time when Luxembourg was but one of several hundred petty kingdoms in central Europe, its origins dating back to the Romans, who founded a settlement here, and more especially to **Count Siegfried of Lorraine**, who first fortified the place, building a citadel on a rocky spur called the Bock in 963. The city soon became a major staging point on the trade route between German Trier and Paris, its strategic importance enhanced by its defensibility, perched high above the sheer gorges of the Pétrusse and Alzette rivers. Count Siegfried and his successors ruled the area as independent princes and then as (nominal) vassals of the Holy Roman Emperor, but, in the early fourteenth century, dynastic politics united Luxembourg with Bohemia. In 1354 Luxembourg was independent again, this time as a **duchy**, and its first dukes – John the Blind and his son Wenceslas – extended their lands up to Limburg in the north and down to Metz in the south. This state of affairs was short-lived too. In 1443, Luxembourg passed to the dukes of Burgundy and then, forty years later, to the Habsburgs and thereafter its history mirrors that of Belgium, successively becoming part of the Spanish and Austrian Netherlands before occupation by Napoleon.

In 1814, the Congress of Vienna decided to create the **Grand Duchy of Luxembourg**, and though the country remained nominally independent, the throne was given to William I of the House of Orange-Nassau, the monarch of the new united Kingdom of The Netherlands (including Belgium). This arrangement proved deeply unpopular in Luxembourg and when the Belgians rebelled in 1830, the Luxembourgers joined in. It didn't do them much good. The Great Powers

LUXEMBOURG'S LINGUISTIC MIX

Luxembourg has three **official languages**: French, German and **Luxembourgish** or Lëtzebuergesch, which is a Germanic language derived from the Franconian dialect of the Rhineland and Salian Franks who moved into the area in the fourth or fifth century AD. Most education is in **French** and **German**. French is the official language of the government and judiciary, but German is spoken with equal ease by all Luxembourgers. **English** is very widely understood and spoken well, especially by the younger generation, many of whom also speak **Italian** and **Portuguese**, a reflection of several decades of southern European immigration into the Grand Duchy. Portuguese is the dominant language in a few areas, such as the château town of Larochette, while the towns of Esch-sur-Alzette and Dudelange are centres of the Italian community.

Immigrants now represent about thirty percent of the population, but Luxembourgers are keen to maintain their identity and have no intention of changing their national motto, which can be seen engraved or painted on buildings around the country: *Mir Wöelle Bleiwe Wat Mir Sin* (We want to remain what we are). Visitors trying their hand at **Lëtzebuergesch** are well received.

Moien	Good morning/hello
Äddi or *a'voir*	Goodbye
Merci (*villmols*)	Thank you (very much)
Pardon	Sorry
Entschëllegt	Excuse me
Wann-ech-glift (pronounced as one word)	Please
Ech verstin Iech nët	I don't understand you
Ech versti kee Lëtzebuergesch	I don't understand any Luxembourgish

recognized an independent Belgium, and promptly gave them a chunk of Luxembourg's Ardennes – now the *province* of Luxembourg – while the Duchy was forced to keep King William. By these means, however, Luxembourg's survival was assured: neither France nor Germany could bear to let the Duchy pass to its rival and London made sure the Duchy was declared neutral. The city was demilitarized in 1867, when most of its fortifications were torn down, and the Duchy remained the property of the Dutch monarchy until 1890 when the ducal crown passed to another (separate) branch of the Orange-Nassaus.

In the **twentieth century**, Luxembourg was overrun by the Germans in 1914 and 1940, when it was incorporated into Hitler's Third Reich. The royal family and government fled to Britain and the USA via Lisbon. The Luxembourgish language was banned and young Luxembourgish conscripts were sent to fight at the Russian front. Liberation by US forces came in September 1944, when Luxembourg witnessed some of the bitterest fighting of **World War II**. During the freezing winter of 1944–45 the key engagements of the **Battle of the Bulge** were decided here. This is not an episode the country wishes to forget, and there are a number of museums honouring the dead. After the war, Luxembourg was a founder member of the UN, NATO and the EU.

Modern Luxembourg is a constitutional monarchy, ruled at present by Grand Duke Jean, who came to the throne in 1964. The grand duke has a twelve-member cabinet of ministers, selected from a directly elected chamber of deputies that meets in the Parliament building in the capital. Luxembourg politics has a relaxed feel, with a number of green and special interest parties vying with the more established centre-left and conservative parties, and the telephone directory lists direct lines for all ministers.

LUXEMBOURG CITY

LUXEMBOURG CITY is one of the most spectacularly sited capitals in Europe. The valleys of the rivers Alzette and Pétrusse, which meet here, cut a green swathe through the city, their deep canyons once key to the Duchy's defences but now providing it with a beautiful setting. These gorges have curtailed expansion and parcel the city up into clearly defined districts. There are four main sections: the old town on the northern side of the Pétrusse valley, which is where you'll find most of the sights and the best restaurants; the early twentieth-century (and fairly mundane) quarter on the opposite bank (known as Gare); the river valleys down below, a curious mixture of huddles of houses, vegetable plots and parkland; and the Kirchberg plateau, to the northeast, home to several EU institutions.

The **Old Town**, high up on a tiny plateau no more than a few hundred metres across, is not actually very old, its tight grid of streets maintaining much of the medieval layout, but mostly flanked by formal eighteenth- and nineteenth-century buildings. The **Musée National d'Histoire et d'Art** is a key attraction here, though this rambling collection comes second best to the old **fortifications** whose extraordinarily well-preserved bastions and mighty walls are seen to best advantage on the east side along the **chemin de la Corniche** walkway. On the south side of the Pétrusse, connected by two main bridges, the Pont Adolphe and the Pont Viaduc, lies the **more modern part of the city** – home to the city's train station, the majority of its cheap hotels and some rather unsavoury bars and strip joints. Things are much more enjoyable **down in the gorge**. There's a delightful park between these two bridges and, further east, directly below the chemin de la Corniche, lies the cluster of antique houses that constitute the **Grund**, an attractive village-like enclave that once housed the city's working class, but is now partly gentrified. There's more gentrification just to the north, below the jutting outcrop of the Bock bastion, in the tiny hamlets of **Clausen** and neighbouring **Pfaffenthal**, beside the River Alzette. Finally, on the far side of the Alzette valley is the **Kirchberg plateau**, where the **Centre Européen** accommodates – amongst several EU institutions – the European Investment Bank and the Court of Justice. The plateau is joined to the rest of the city by the imposing modern span of the Pont Grand-Duchesse Charlotte, usually known as the "Red Bridge" for reasons that will be immediately apparent.

Arrival, information and transport

Luxembourg's **airport**, Findel, is situated 6km east of the city on the road to Trier. There are a number of ways of getting into town from here. **Bus** #9 runs every thirty minutes from the airport to the bus station in the old town on place E. Hamilius before proceeding on to the train station; the whole journey takes about 25 minutes and costs a flat F40, plus a small extra charge for any large items of luggage. There are also Luxair buses to the same places, which are faster

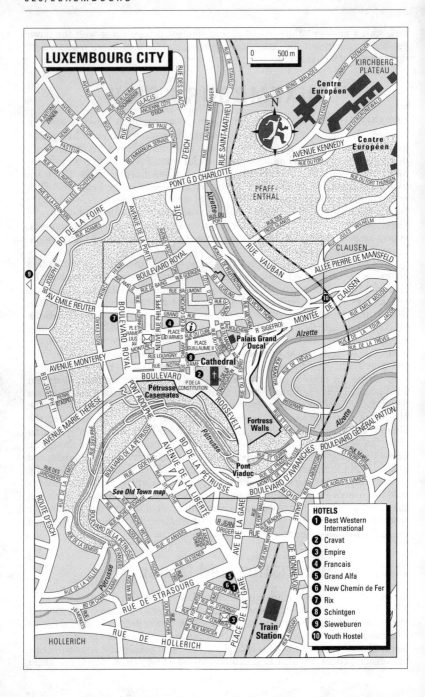

LUXEMBOURG CITY

HOTELS
1. Best Western International
2. Cravat
3. Empire
4. Francais
5. Grand Alfa
6. New Chemin de Fer
7. Rix
8. Schintgen
9. Sieweburen
10. Youth Hostel

(15min) but more irregular – about a dozen services a day connecting with major flight arrivals and departures; it costs F120 a head. Before collapsing into a **taxi**, bear in mind that Luxembourg's are expensive, and even the locals – some of the richest citizens in Europe – think twice before calling a cab. From the airport, expect to pay F500–600 to the station, F600–700 into the city centre.

The **train station** is in the city's modern quarter, a ten- to fifteen-minute walk from the old town. Almost all of the city's buses are routed through the train station and the vast majority go on to (or come from) the bus station on place E. Hamilius. The train station has a left luggage office and coin-operated luggage lockers and many of the city's cheaper hotels are located near by. Most **long-distance buses** stop beside the train station.

Information

There are branches of the **national tourist office** at the airport (April–Oct Mon–Fri 10am–2.30pm & 4–7pm, Sat 10am–1.45pm, Sun 10am–2.30pm & 3.30–6.30pm; Nov–March same times but closed Sun; ☎42 82 82 21) and inside the train station concourse (late Sept to June daily 9am–noon & 2–6.30pm; July to mid-Sept Mon–Sat 9am–7pm, Sun 9am–noon & 2–6.30pm; ☎42 82 82 20). These have city maps, transit maps, all manner of glossy leaflets, details of guided tours and can advise on – and book – accommodation right across the Grand Duchy. There's also a busy **Luxembourg City tourist office**, in the Old Town on place d'Armes (April–Sept Mon–Sat 9am–7pm, Sun 10am–6pm; Oct–March Mon–Sat 9am–6pm; ☎22 28 09; *www.luxembourg-city.lu/touristinfo/*), which offers basically the same facilities though, as its name suggests, it deals only with the city. They also dish out copies of the French-language *Rendez-Vous*, a bi-monthly entertainments magazine.

These services are supplemented by a network of **interactive terminals** available in a variety of locations including the airport and motorway service areas. They give tourist information of a general nature and allow hotel bookings to be made with a credit card.

City transport and tours

Luxembourg City has a good **public bus system**, but it's such a small place, with such a compact centre, that the only time you'll usually need to take a bus is either between the centre and the station (though even this is easily walkable), or out to the airport, campsites or wooded periphery. Most of the main routes have a stop-off outside the train station and on place E. Hamilius in the Old Town. **Tickets** on the city's buses cost a flat F40 and are valid for an hour; a block of ten tickets costs F320. Day tickets for the whole of the Duchy's public transport system cost just F160, F640 for five. They are valid from the time of cancellation (in one of the orange machines on buses and station platforms) up to 8am the following morning. Tickets are available from bus drivers and at bus and train enquiry offices. Incidentally, note that you can reach the Pétrusse and Alzette river valleys from the Old Town by road, steps and elevator. The main elevator (6.30am–3.30am) runs from the underground car park on place St Esprit to the Grund.

To orient yourself, you may want to take a **guided tour**, though the multilingual commentary that accompanies most of them is wearying. There are the usual **bus tours**, run by, among others, Voyages Sales Lentz, off place d'Armes at rue du Curé 26, who will whisk you around the main city and suburban sites in two hours, every afternoon between April and October (F450 per person). These tours leave from place de la Constitution and operate on a "first come, first served" basis. Rather more enjoyably, the tourist office organize an excellent programme of **guided walks**, with the basic two-hour version taking place on most days and costing a reasonable F240. Alternatively, a **miniature train** – the Pétrusse Express – travels along the floor of the Pétrusse valley from Pont Adolphe to Grund and up to the plateau du Rham immediately to the east. This hour-long tour gives a good idea of the full extent of the city's fortifications and takes in some pleasant parkland too. The train (April–Oct daily 10am–6pm) leaves at regular intervals from place de la Constitution, where you buy tickets – F230 per person or F660 per family.

Accommodation

Most of the city's **hotels** are clustered near the railway station, which is disappointing as this is the least interesting part of town – and indeed the sidestreets opposite the station (rue d'Epernay etc) are a little seedy. You're much better off staying in the Old Town and won't necessarily pay much more, though you are limited to just a handful of places. Budget accommodation is available at the **youth hostel** below the Bock fortress. In all cases, advance booking is a good idea during the busy months of July and August.

Hotels

Best Western International, pl de la Gare 20 (☎48 59 11, fax 49 32 27). No points for originality, but this sprightly modern hotel, part of the *Best Western* chain, is reliable and the rooms are comfortable. Near the station. ⑦.

Cravat, bd Roosevelt 29 (☎22 19 75, fax 22 67 11). Medium-sized, four-star hotel in the heart of the Old Town. The exterior of this five-storey block is rather glum, but the interior is suitably plush, and so are the rooms. ⑨.

Empire, pl de la Gare 34 (☎48 52 52, fax 49 19 37). Straightforward modern hotel with 35 rooms opposite the station. Hardly sets the pulse racing, but is perfectly adequate. ⑥.

Francais, pl d'Armes 14 (☎47 45 34, fax 46 42 74). This attractive three-star hotel has smart and spotless rooms furnished in a crisp modern style. Great location too, on the main square in the Old Town. Highly recommended. ⑥.

Grand Hôtel Mercure Alfa, pl de la Gare 16 (☎49 00 11, fax 49 00 09). Occupying an attractive and recently refurbished Art Deco building, this flashy hotel has every convenience. Opposite the train station. ⑨.

ACCOMMODATION PRICE CODES

All the **hotels and hostels** detailed in this chapter have been graded according to the following price categories. Apart from ①, which is a per-person price for a hostel bed, all the codes are based on the rate for the least expensive double room during high season. For more on accommodation, see p.33.

① Up to F1000 per person	④ F2000–2500 per room	⑦ F4000–5000 per room
② F1000–1500 per room	⑤ F2500–3000 per room	⑧ F5000–6000 per room
③ F1500–2000 per room	⑥ F3000–4000 per room	⑨ F6000 and over, per room

New Chemin de Fer, rue Joseph Junck 4 (☎49 35 28, fax 40 30 69). Rather unkempt, bargain basement hotel in what passes for the city's red-light area. ④.

Rix, bd Royal 20 (☎47 16 66, fax 22 75 35). Smart, four-star hotel conveniently situated a couple of minutes' walk west of place d'Armes – but just outside the Old Town: bd Royal is home to most of the city's offshore banking businesses, hence the high-rise office blocks. Just twenty pleasant rooms. ⑦.

Schintgen, rue Notre Dame 6 (☎22 28 44, fax 46 57 19). Bang in the middle of the Old Town, this simple, unassuming hotel is short on accessories, but it is reasonably priced. ⑥.

Sieweburen, rue des Septfontaines 36 (☎44 23 56, fax 44 23 53). Alpine-lodge style accommodation in the countryside just 2km northwest of the Old Town in the district of Rollingergrund. Three-star hotel plus a popular restaurant. Bus #2. ⑥.

Hostel and campsite

Youth hostel, rue du Fort Olisy 2 (☎22 68 89, fax 22 33 60). This barracks-like HI **hostel** is located down below the Bock fortress in the Alzette valley. It's open all year and has a laundry, cooking facilities and cycle rental. It's reachable from the train station by taking bus #9 – ask the driver to point out the stop as the hostel's not on a main road; on foot it takes about thirty minutes to cover the 3km from the train station. Including breakfast, the overnight price for a dorm bed is F500, rising to F650 per person in a double room. ①.

Camping Bon Accueil, rue du Camping 2 (April–Sept; ☎36 70 69). This small campsite is located just 5km south of the city on the banks of the River Alzette in the village of Alzingen. It's the nearest campsite to the city. ①.

The City

Most of the medieval city was destroyed by a gunpowder explosion in 1554 and what you see today dates largely from a late seventeenth-century remodelling with wholesale modifications made a couple of hundred years later. Furthermore, over half of the **ramparts** and bastions were knocked down when the city was demilitarized in 1867 – boulevards Royal and Roosevelt are built on their foundations – though the more easterly fortifications have survived pretty much intact. These give a clear sense of the city's once formidable defensive capabilities, and were sufficient to persuade UNESCO to designate the old city a **World Heritage Site** in 1994. Dating from 1051, the earliest surviving fortifications are the towers and gateway (Hellespuert) on the Montée du Grund, which links the Old Town with Grund below. There's more medieval masonry on the Bock, but for the most part the remaining walls, bastions and subterranean artillery casemates reflect the combined endeavours of generations of military engineers from the seventeenth century to the nineteenth.

Place d'Armes and place Guillaume II

At the centre of the Old Town is **place d'Armes**, a shady oblong fringed with pavement cafés. It's a delightful spot and throughout the summer there are daily free concerts – everything from jazz to brass bands – as well as a small (and expensive) flea market on most Saturday mornings. Near the square are the city's principal shops, concentrated along **Grand Rue** and rue des Capucins to the north, rue du Fossé to the east, and rue Philippe II running south. Just off the southeast corner of the square, on **rue du Curé**, a side entrance into the Palais Municipal accesses the **Maquette de la Forteresse** (July–Sept daily 10am–5pm; F60), a scale model of the old city equipped with a multilingual commentary and

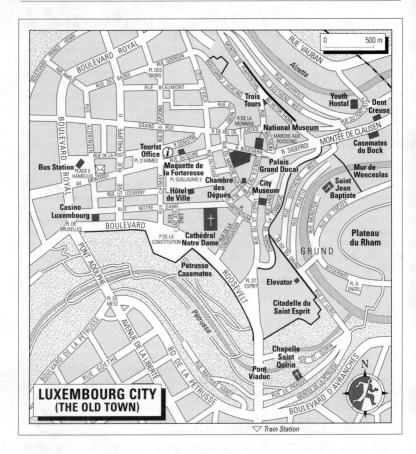

LUXEMBOURG CITY
(THE OLD TOWN)

spotlights illustrating how and when the city developed. It's not a bad introduction, but it's hardly riveting and soon you'll be moving on – take the narrow passage from the southeast corner of place d'Armes through to the expansive **place Guillaume II**, in the middle of which is a jaunty-looking equestrian statue of William II. The square, which is the site of Luxembourg's main fresh food market on Wednesday and Saturday mornings, is flanked by pleasant old townhouses as well as a solid Neoclassical Hôtel de Ville adorned by a pair of stuffy stone lions. There's also a modest stone water fountain bearing a cameo of the nineteenth-century Luxembourg poet Mighel Rodange.

The cathedral, Pétrusse Casemates and the Casino Luxembourg

From place Guillaume II, it's a brief stroll south down the steps beside the Rodange fountain to rue Notre Dame, where an ornate Baroque portico leads into the back of the **Cathédrale Notre Dame**, whose slender black spire dominates the city's puckered skyline. It is, however, a real mess of a building: dating to the 1930s, the transepts and choir are in a clumping Art Deco style and they have been glued onto the (much more appealing) seventeenth-century nave. Items of interest are few and far between, but there is a plaque in the nave honouring those priests killed in World War II and the Baroque gallery at the back of the nave is a likeable affair graced by alabaster angels and garlands of flowers; it was carved by a certain Daniel Muller in 1622. In the apse is the country's most venerated icon, *The Comforter of the Afflicted*, a seventeenth-century lime-wood effigy of the Madonna and Child which is frequently dressed up in all manner of lavish gear with crowns and sceptres, lace frills and gold brocade.

Across from the front of the cathedral, place de la Constitution sits on top of one of the old bastions whose subterranean depths are entered by a stone stairway leading down to the **Casemates de la Pétrusse** (Easter, Whitsun & July–Sept guided visits daily 11am–4pm; F70). These were dug by the Spaniards in the 1640s and make for a dark and dank visit. Place de la Constitution also acts as the starting point for the Pétrusse Express (see above).

A couple of hundred metres away to the west, at rue Notre Dame 41, is the **Casino Luxembourg**: it's not a "Casino" in the sense of gaming at all, but an old bourgeois salon that has been turned into a gallery for contemporary art, featuring often challenging exhibitions (Mon, Wed, Fri–Sun 11am–6pm, Thurs 11am–8pm; closed Tues; F150).

The ducal palace and Marché aux Poissons

Just to the east of place **Guillaume II** on rue du Marché aux Herbes, the **Palais Grand-Ducal** (guided tours mid-July to Aug Mon, Tues, Wed & Thurs pm & Sat am; 1 daily in English; 45min; F200) was built originally as the town hall, but was adopted by the Luxembourg Royal Family as their winter residence in the nineteenth century. Remodelled on several occasions, the exterior with its dinky dormer windows and spiky little spires reveals a Moorish influence – though the end result looks more Ruritanian than anything else. The interior is, as you might expect, lavish in the extreme with dazzling chandeliers, Brussels tapestries, frescoes and acres of richly carved wood panelling. Tours are very popular, so book at least a day or two in advance at the tourist office.

To the right of the palace, an extension of 1859 houses the Luxembourg Parliament, the **Chambre des Députés**, in plainer but similarly opulent surroundings. Walk round the corner, left along **rue de l'Eau**, and you'll soon reach **Marché aux Poissons**, an attractive little plaza flanked by immaculately restored, antique buildings, all turrets and towers, arcaded galleries and stone balconies. This is the heart of the Old Town.

Musée National d'Histoire et d'Art

A group of patrician mansions bordering the **Marché aux Poissons** have been converted into the country's largest museum, the **Musée National d'Histoire et d'Art** (Tues–Sun 10am–5pm; F100). The museum makes a promising start on the ground floor with an extensive collection of Gallo-Roman archeological finds mainly unearthed in the south of the country and including bronzes and terracottas, glassware, various funerary objects, a fine if weathered marble bust of Septimius Severus and a magnificent mosaic from Vichten, southwest Luxembourg. But thereafter things get rather confused: a winding stairway leads to a veritable rabbit warren of tiny rooms which contain everything from military knick-knacks, details of the Luxembourg royal lineage and models of the old fort, through to displays on local folklore. Neither does it help that the labelling is inadequate. That said, look out for the room devoted to black magic – inverted crosses, strange statuettes and such like – an apothecary's shop and a room crammed with folkloric Madonnas.

Moving on, a lift leads to the fine art section, where there's an enjoyable sample of fifteenth- and early sixteenth-century **paintings**, notably a bold and brassy *Actuality* by Lucas Cranach the Younger; an exquisite *Pietà* by Adriaen Isenbrandt; an expressive *Presentation in the Temple* by Quentin Matsys; and a madly romantic *Bacchus, Venus and Love* by Rosso Fiorentino. Later Dutch works include a soft *Young Girl on the Balcony* by Ferdinand Bol, a portrait by Hals, genre scenes by Jan Steen and Adrien van Ostade, Brouwer's *Mussel Eater* and a Turner (he spent a lot of time here, and painted some evocative landscapes incorporating the fortress).

Finally, across an inconspicuous footbridge is a section devoted to industrial archeology: Luxembourg's first car, the development of the steel industry, railways and textiles, plus activities that once sustained the rural economy such as charcoal burning and tanning.

On from Marché aux Poissons

Back outside the museum, on **Marché aux Poissons**, there's a tempting choice of routes: to the **north**, a cobbled lane leads round the side of the museum to a fork where one alley tunnels down to the medieval **Porte des Trois Tours** gateway, while the other, rue du Palais de Justice, weaves uphill through one of the most attractive parts of the Old Town on its way to meet rue du Nord. To the **east** lie the Casemates du Bock and the chemin de la Corniche (see below) and to the **south** rue Large plunges down to Grund (see p.333) via the medieval fortifications on the Montée du Grund. Also to the south, rue du St Esprit offers the **Musée d'Histoire de la Ville de Luxembourg** (Tues, Wed & Fri–Sun 10am–6pm, Thurs 10am–8pm; F200). Converted from four historic houses, this hi-tech museum tells the story of the city, taking full advantage of interactive displays and models to enliven the exhibits, which include wooden models of the city through the ages. Even the glass lift is used to highlight the geology of the area as it moves through various layers of rock.

The Bock and the chemin de la Corniche

In 963 Count Siegfried of Lorraine decided to build a castle on the **Rocher du Bock**, a sandstone outcrop rising high above the Alzette. The city of Luxembourg originated with this fort, but precious little survives of Siegfried's construction: it was incorporated into the much more impressive fortifications that were built round the city from the seventeenth century onwards and the only significant piece of masonry to survive is the so-called **Dent Creuse** (Hollow Tooth) stone tower on the north side of the rue Sigefroi/Montée de Clausen. This same road, linking the Old Town with the suburb of Clausen, makes it doubly difficult to appreciate the layout of the original castle, which was – in medieval times – linked to the Marché aux Poissons by a drawbridge, but the views looking out over the spires, outer fortifications and aqueducts of the Alzette valley are superb.

In 1745, the Spaniards began digging beneath the site of Siegfried's castle. Eventually, they honeycombed the Bock with around 20km of tunnels and galleries and here they placed bakeries, kitchens, stables and all the other amenities necessary to support a garrison. Today a tiny portion of the tunnels can be visited on a guided tour of the **Casemates du Bock** (March–Oct daily 10am–5pm;

F70). It's a rather damp and drafty way to spend half an hour, and there's nothing much to see beyond a few rusty old cannons, but it's good fun all the same.

From just above the Casemates du Bock on rue Sigefroi, you can follow the pedestrian **chemin de la Corniche** along the ramparts marking the eastern perimeter of the main fortress. The views are absolutely spectacular and there's no better way to get a sense of the strength of the city's fortifications which several major European powers struggled to improve, no one more than the French who, after 1684, made Luxembourg into one of the continent's most strongly defended cities – the so-called "Gibraltar of the north". After a few minutes you emerge at place St Esprit and more fortifications in the form of the **Citadelle du St Esprit**, a colossal, brick-faced bastion built in 1685. Its flattened top is where you'll find the main elevator down to Grund (see below) and, beyond in a grassy little park that's also above the bastion, there are views over the Pétrusse Valley and of the Pont Viaduc, which leads south toward the train station.

Out of the Old Town

Outside of the Old Town there's not very much to see. The best option is to stroll down Montée de Clausen from the Bock (see above) for the fifty-minute stroll along the bottom of the **Alzette** and **Pétrusse river valleys**. It's the general setting that appeals – with the walls of the fortress rising steeply to the right and the valley dotted with ancient, pastel-painted houses and the battered remains of the outer fortifications – but there are one or two specific sights and several good bars (see below). At the beginning of the walk, well-heeled **Clausen** musters a cluster of dignified old houses and a bar or two as well as the youth hostel (see p.329). From here, rue de la Tour Jacob tracks along the riverside, passing the ricketty Mousel Brewery before reaching the medieval curtain wall – the **Mur de Wenceslas** – which both spans the Alzette and serves as a fortified footbridge leading back towards the Old Town. Dead ahead, through the gate, is **Grund**, once a thriving working-class quarter but now an uneven mixture of fine old houses and dilapidation that strings along the river for a few hundred metres. The most striking building here is the church of **St Jean Baptiste**, down near the river on rue Munster, an imposing structure with a massive spire, and a black Madonna and Baroque altar inside.

At the centre of Grund, a chunky little bridge spans the Alzette. On the far side, you can regain the Old Town either by taking the elevator up to place St Esprit or by hoofing it up Montée du Grund. Alternatively, a left turn leads along **rue St Ulric**, where the markers at no. 14 show how high the river has risen in flood years – the worst inundation was in 1756. Continuing, rue St Ulric cuts beneath the massive walls of the Citadelle du St Esprit before emerging beside the Pétrusse valley whose wooded parkland holds the mostly fourteenth-century chapel of **St Quirin**. You can wander along the Pétrusse valley for a kilometre or two to emerge to the west of the train station, or exit at any one of several points along the way.

KIRCHBERG

Fans of EU institutions can travel by bus #16 to the plateau of **Kirchberg**, on the northeast outskirts of the city, where a brigade of Eurocrats beaver away in the 22-storey **Centre Européen**, the European Investment Bank and the European Court of Justice. Most of these institutions can be visited by groups only, but the Court of Justice is an exception – individuals can attend lectures on its workings and observe proceedings (contact the Head of the Information Office, Court of Justice of the European Communities, L-2925 Luxembourg).

Eating and drinking

Luxembourg City's Old Town is crowded with **cafés** and **restaurants** from inexpensive places where a filling plat du jour will cost you a reasonable F350 through to lavish establishments with main courses costing twice as much and more. French cuisine is popular here and traditional Luxembourgish dishes are found on many menus too, mostly meaty affairs such as neck of pork with broad beans (*judd mat gaardebounen*), black sausage (*blutwurst*) and chicken in Riesling (*hahnchen im Riesling*), not to mention freshwater fish from the River Moselle. Keep an eye out also for *Gromperenkichelchen* – potato cakes usually served with apple sauce – and in winter, stalls and cafés selling *Glühwein*, hot wine mulled with cloves. One of the great Luxembourg traditions is **coffee and cakes** in a salon or one of the city's numerous patisseries – *Oberweis*, at Grand Rue 19, is as good as any – and here, as in Belgium, pavement cafés are thronged in the summertime, with place d'Armes being the centre of café society. Multilingual menus are the norm.

Most visitors to the city are content to drink where they eat, but there is a lively **bar** and **club** scene spread around the various parts of town – bars in the Old Town, Grund and Clausen, clubs mostly west of the train station in Hollerich. Opening hours are fairly elastic, but bars usually stay open till around 1am, clubs till 3am. While you're out on the tiles, try one of the local pilsener ales – *Mousel* and the tasty *Bofferding* are the most widely available.

Restaurants and cafés

Brasserie Chimay, rue Chimay 15. Small, pleasantly old-fashioned café-restaurant off place d'Armes. Traditional, straightforward dishes at inexpensive prices.

Bredewee, rue Large 9 (☎22 26 96). Excellent little restaurant at the expensive end of the market offering gourmet, mostly French-style cuisine. The (summer) terrace has superb views over the Alzette valley. In the Old Town. Reservations advised. Closed Sun.

Club 5, rue Chimay 5. One of the city centre's trendier hangouts, with an excellent and not overpriced restaurant upstairs and a café-bar down below. At both, the speciality is *carpaccio* – thin slices of air-dried beef served with fries and salad. Off place d'Armes. Closed Sun.

Francais, pl d'Armes 14. The pavement café of the *Hôtel Francais* offers tasty salads and a wide-ranging menu including several Luxembourgish favourites. The daily specials are a real snip.

Giorgio's Pizzeria, rue du Nord 11. A sociable and eminently fashionable place that serves until about 11pm, although pizzas often run out before then. Great pizzas from F350. Tucked away off côte d'Eich in the Old Town. Closed Sun.

Kirin, rue des Bains 17. Decorated like Aladdin's cave, this reasonably priced and popular restaurant serves Chinese, Thai and Vietnamese dishes, with main courses averaging about F450, less for the plat du jour. In the Old Town.

L'Ocean, rue Louvigny 7. Smart and expensive seafood restaurant in the Old Town. One of several restaurants on this little street just south of place d'Armes.

Maison des Brasseurs, Grande Rue 48. On a modern shopping street just to the north of place d'Armes, this long-established and smartly decorated restaurant sells delicious Luxembourgish dishes. Sauerkraut is the house speciality. 11am–11pm; closed Sun.

Um Dierfgen, côte d'Eich 6. A rather staid bar-cum-restaurant that's good for inexpensive light meals and omelettes. In the Old Town.

Via Sud, rue du Curé 22. Intimate, tastefully furnished restaurant serving wonderful food from a Franco-Mediterranean menu. Each dish is thoughtfully prepared. Highly recommended and not too expensive. Off place d'Armes. Closed Sun.

Bars and clubs

Café des Artistes, Montée du Grund 2. Charming café-bar close to the bridge in Grund. Piano accompaniment and traditional songs on most nights.

Chiggeri, rue du Nord 11. Groovy bar in the Old Town which has a great atmosphere, funky decor and a mixed clientèle.

Conquest, rue du Palais de Justice 7. Old Town gay club. House music.

Didjeridoo, rue Bouillon 31, Hollerich. Everything from jungle to techno at this boisterous club in the Hollerich district west of the train station. Open Wed, Fri & Sat.

Melusina, rue de la Tour Jacob 145, Clausen. Varied sounds plus live jazz and folk music nights, as well as occasional theatrical performances. Ex-pat favourite.

Pula Pula, rue Sigefroi 8. Smart and trendy (in the Armani style) bar with Porsches outside and high heels within. Special party nights.

Pulp, bd d'Avranches 36. Established club with house and techno sounds, themed nights and occasional live acts. On the south side of the Pétrusse valley on the way to the train station. Ring for schedule ☎49 69 40.

Pygmalion, rue de la Tour Jacob 19, Clausen. Busy Irish bar down in the depths of Clausen. Open till 1am weekdays and 3am weekends.

Scott's, by the bridge in Grund. Pubby English bar where ex-pats congregate for draught Guinness and bitter.

Sodaz Café Bar, rue de la Boucherie 16. Small and crowded bar featuring cocktails plus soul and rock. Old Town.

Vis à Vis, at the junction of rue des Capucins and rue Beaumont. Laid-back, comfortable brasserie-bar with old posters, fancy drapes and woodwork. Old Town.

Listings

Airlines British Airways, at the airport (☎0800 2000); Luxair, at the airport (☎47 98 42 42); Sabena, at the airport (☎47 98 25 88). Icelandair, the only airline to fly direct from the US to Luxembourg, are at rue Glesener 59 (☎40 27 27 27).

Airport enquiries ☎47 96 29 75.

American Express av de la Porte-Neuve 34 (☎22 85 55).

Bike rental rue Bisserwe 8, Grund (Mon–Fri 1–8pm, Sat–Sun 9am–noon & 1–8pm; ☎47 96 23 83): F100 an hour, F250 for a half-day, F400 a day, and F2000 for a week. Discounts of twenty percent available for groups and under-26s. Advance booking is advised, and a repair service is also available. A cycle trail encircles the city – details here or at the tourist office.

Bookshops Papeterie Ernster, rue du Fossé 21, has a reasonable range of English-language books and newspapers. Footsteps from place Guillaume II.

Bureaux de change You can change money at virtually any bank. Cash machines are dotted round the centre – there's a Caisse d'Epargne cash machine at the east end of pl Guillaume II on rue du Fossé.

Car parks There are four central underground car parks: one off bd Royale near the bus station; another on pl du Théâtre; a third under pl Guillaume; and a fourth on bd Roosevelt. Spaces can still be hard to find. All cost around F40 per hour during the day with cheaper rates in the evening and on the weekend.

Car rental Avis, pl de la Gare 2 (☎48 95 95), and at the airport (☎43 51 71); Europcar, rte de Thionville 84 (☎40 42 28), and at the airport (☎43 45 88); Hertz, at the airport (☎43 46 45); Thrifty, bd Prince Henri (☎22 11 81) and at the airport (☎43 52 43).

Cinemas These show films in their original language, which means that English predominates. On the pl du Théâtre, the Cinémathèque (☎29 12 59) has a varied programme of international classics; Utopia, av de la Faiencerie 16 (☎47 21 09), has five screens; Utopolis, av Kennedy 45 (☎42 95 95), is a big, new multi-screen in Kirchberg.

Doctor ☎112 for medical assistance.

Embassies Belgium, rue des Girondins 4 (☎44 27 46); Ireland, rte d'Arlon 28 (☎45 06 10); Netherlands, rue C.M. Spoo 5 (☎22 75 70); UK, bd Roosevelt 14 (☎22 98 64); USA, bd E. Servais 22 (☎46 01 23).

Emergencies Fire & Ambulance ☎112. Police ☎113.

Festivals The city's main knees-up is the Schueberfouer, three weeks of jollity beginning in late August and with one of the biggest funfairs in Europe.

Laundry Quick-Wash, rue de Strasbourg 31; several dry cleaners around the city – look out for branches of 5 à sec.

Left luggage There are coin-operated lockers and a luggage office at the train station.

Newspapers English-language newspapers are available from most newsagents from about 11am on the day of publication.

Pharmacies Molitor, pl d'Armes 5, and Mortier, av de la Gare 11. Duty rotas are displayed in pharmacy windows.

Police Main station rue Glesener 58–60. Emergencies ☎113.

Post office The main post office is on pl E. Hamilius (Mon–Fri 7am–7pm, Sat 7am–5pm). There's also an office opposite the train station (Mon–Fri 9am–noon & 1–5pm, Sat 9am–noon).

Telephones International calls can be made from all public telephones and booths have multilingual instructions. Buy phone cards from post offices or newsagents.

Train enquiries The CFL office in the station is open daily 7am–8pm (☎49 90 49 90).

Walking tours The city tourist office in pl d'Armes co-ordinates a first-rate programme of guided walking tours. Options include a City Promenade (Easter–Oct 1 daily, Nov–Easter 3 weekly; 2hr; F240); the Vauban Walk (May–Oct 1 weekly; 2hr; F240); and the Wenzel Walk (May–Oct 1 weekly; 2hr; F280) – touted as "a thousand years in a hundred minutes" – which starts from the Casemates du Bock, and takes you right around the fortifications on the east side of the Old Town.

THE GRAND DUCHY

Luxembourg is a city soon exhausted, and it's a good idea to spend some time while you're here seeing something of the **rest of the country**. The minor attractions of the south and centre are best seen on day-trips, but the lovely scenery of the Ardennes region, up north, merits at least an overnight stay. Obviously your own transport gives you more flexibility, but you can do a remarkable amount of travelling by public transport.

The Luxembourg **rail network** reaches up through the centre of the Grand Duchy, connecting the capital with Ettelbruck, Clervaux and Kautenbach in the north (branch lines run from Ettelbruck to Diekirch and from Kautenbach to Wiltz), and extending arms down to Esch-sur-Alzette in the south, and Wasserbillig on the Moselle – from which trains run on to Trier and Koblenz. You're bound at some point to have to take a **bus**, many of which are also run by CFL and supplement the rail system. Without a car, though, you're not going to be able to do much touring in a day. It's better to select a centre and see as much on foot as is practical – no great hardship in the more scenic parts of the country.

In the south of the country, it's the **Moselle** which is of most interest, mainly for the vineyards of the Luxembourg wine industry. To the north, the first major rail junction is **Ettelbruck**, which, although not of interest in itself, provides access by bus to the first taste of the country's finest scenery, for which **Diekirch**, 5km east, is a possible base, home to the country's largest brewery and a decent museum remembering the Battle of the Bulge, much of which was fought in the surrounding area. Further east, **Echternach** is a pretty place built around an ancient abbey and is close to the rolling hiking country of the area known, with some exaggeration, as **Petite Suisse**. To the north, **Vianden,** one of Luxembourg's most popular resorts, lies in the heart of the Ardennes, surrounded by craggy green hills and topped by a glowering, newly restored castle. It's a possible centre for seeing the best of the countryside around – the castle of **Bourscheid** a little way southwest, the tiny settlement of **Esch-sur-Sûre**, clasped in the horseshoe bend of its river, and the village of **Clervaux**, also with its castle – though this last is on the main rail line from Luxembourg and easily seen on a day-trip.

Southern Luxembourg

The **south** of Luxembourg has relatively dull scenery and – southwest of Luxembourg City – much of its industry around the towns of **Esch-sur-Alzette** and **Dudelange**. The western bank of the **River Moselle**, which for 25km or so forms the border between Luxembourg and Germany up as far as Wasserbillig (where it spears off toward Trier), is a highlight, its gentle slopes covered with vineyards which produce the grapes for Luxembourg's **wine industry**. Almost all of the wine produced is white, perked up with a little rosé, and most is good quality, varying from fruity Rieslings to delicate Pinot Blancs and flowery Gewurztraminers, as well as some excellent, underrated *méthode champenoise* sparkling wines. There are a number of producers, and their *caves* are open in season for tours and tasting – and buying if you're keen.

The **southwestern corner** is reasonably easily seen by train and bus – there are regular connections to Esch – but for the Moselle you ideally need a car. Buses and (in summer) boats run up and down the river in a more or less coordinated fashion, but they don't always tie in very conveniently with the sometimes awkward opening hours of the various *caves*.

The Luxembourg Moselle

If you are constrained by timetables, **REMICH** is probably the easiest place to reach from Luxembourg, and is as good a place as any to see something of the wine industry. It's also a major stop for the ferry boats that ply up and down the river during the summer, connecting Remich with Schengen to the south and Grevenmacher, Wormeldange and, eventually, Trier (Trèves) and Bernkastel to the north (see "Travel Details", pp.349–50, for more on schedules).

There's not much to Remich in itself, which is a fairly typical border settlement, full of shops hawking cheap cigarettes and booze to bargain-hunting Germans. But the town is headquarters of the Moselle wine industry, and the **Caves St Martin** (April–Oct daily 9–11.30am & 1.30–5.30pm; F100), a mainly sparkling wine producer, fifteen minutes' walk north from the centre of town on the left of the main road, offers one of the region's most interesting *caves* tours, taking in the minutiae of the *méthode champenoise* process, which at St Martin is still carried out in a fairly traditional way – the bottles, for example, are still turned by hand. The polyglot guides are informative and entertaining, and, as at most of the wineries, there's a free tasting afterwards of the excellent St Martin product.

If you want to **stay** in Remich, there's the *Hôtel Beau-Séjour*, at quai de la Moselle 30 (☎69 81 26, fax 66 94 82; ⑤), and the *Auberge des Cygnes*, rue Esplanade 11 (☎69 88 52, fax 69 75 29; ④) or, heading upmarket, the *Hôtel des Vignes* at route de Mondorf 29 (☎69 91 49, fax 69 84 63; ⑥) and the *St Nicolas* at Esplanade 31 (☎69 88 88, fax 69 88 69; ⑥). Both the *Auberge des Cygnes* and the *St Nicolas* have pleasant and reasonably priced **restaurants**, but on a hot evening the terrace at the *Hôtel d'Esplanade*, rue Esplanade 5, is the place to eat. For a quick snack, head for *Café des Bons Amis*, rue Macher 7, a real locals' bar which serves excellent-value soups, sandwiches and cheap beer.

Walk for twenty minutes in the other direction from the centre of Remich, and you can indulge in more wine-tasting. The village of **BECH-KLEINMACHER** is home to the **Musée A Possen** (May–Oct Tues–Sun 2–7pm, Nov–April Fri–Sun only; F150), a small museum of wine and folklore, housed in the former home of a local grower. Prefaced by a short slide show (in English) giving background on the industry, a number of authentic-looking rooms attempt to re-create life for wine growers in centuries past, with pin-neat bedrooms, a loom and spinning wheel, a kitchen with its walls blackened by cooking, and a facsimile bar as well as the usual displays of wine-making equipment. Exit is through a real wine bar where you can sample (at a price) some of the local wines and *eaux de vie*.

Further up river from Remich, the pretty village of **EHNEN** has yet another museum devoted to the wine industry, the **Musée du Vin** (April–Oct Tues–Sun 9.30–11.30am & 2–5pm; F120), on the main street. Housed in the rather less decrepit mansion of another local wine baron, this is a rather more organized, less nostalgic affair than the Musée A Possen, with informative exhibits in the old fermenting cellar detailing various aspects of the wine-making process, past and present. If you feel like hanging around, the *Bamburg*, route du Vin 131 (☎76 00 22, fax 76 00 56; ⑤–⑥), is a pleasant hotel with a good restaurant. **WORMEL-DANGE**, the next village along, strung out beside the river for a good kilometre, gives the opportunity to visit another working wine producer, the **Caves Cooperatives** (May–Aug daily 9am–5pm; F100), housed in the big pink building on the far side of the village; you can also pick up a free brochure from here, and follow the 4km Promenade Viticole through the vineyards, with the vine-growing process explained along the way. If by this time you're too befuddled to make it back, head for the *Koeppchen Hotel*, Berreggaass 9 (☎76 00 46; ④).

GREVENMACHER, about 10km on from Wormeldange, is the capital of the Luxembourg Moselle and its most pleasant town, with a small but lively pedestrianized centre set above the river. There are more wineries here, the most prominent of which is the **Caves Bernard Massard** (April–Oct daily 9am–5.30pm; F90), on the southern side of the town centre, right next to the main street and river – follow rue de Trèves from the bus stop and turn left as if to go over the bridge. Like the St Martin *caves*, Bernard Massard is known for its sparkling, *méthode champenoise* wine, though it is a much bigger concern, producing around four million bottles a year to St Martin's eight hundred thousand or so. It shows in the production methods, which are far more automated, which makes it a less interesting – and shorter – tour (though it is preceded by a short slide show and a tasting in the slick hospitality suite afterwards).

The Bernard Massard organization is also responsible for Grevenmacher's other attraction, the **Jardin des Papillons**, on the other side of the town at the far end of route de Trèves (April to mid-Oct daily 9.30am–5.30pm; F180), where around forty species of butterfly are viewable in a specially created hothouse (28°C constant). There's a lush array of flowers and plants, and at certain times of year you can watch the butterflies hatching, but it's rather overpriced – although you do get yet another free glass of wine as well.

Grevenmacher is an appealing place to stay, although it's not very easy to get to from Luxembourg City – basically you have to take a train to the next town north, **WASSERBILLIG**, and a bus (5km) from there (12 daily; 10min). There's a **campsite**, the *Route du Vin*, in Grevenmacher on the northern edge of town, next to the butterfly garden, and a **youth hostel**, *Romain Schwachtgen* (☎75 02 22; ①), a short walk up rue de Centenaire from the **bus stop** on route de Trèves. As for **hotels**, there's the *Mosellan*, at rue de Trèves 35 (☎75 01 57; ③).

MONDORF-LES-BAINS, "inland" to the west from Remich, is the country's major spa town, attracting the rich of several countries who come to take the waters, and play the **Casino 2000**, and less wealthy Luxembourgers who can receive a prescription from their doctor to spend time there for free. At the spa, found in an attractive 85-acre park, mineral water emerges at a steady 24°C. Visitors are attracted by Mondorf's reputation as a sports centre, especially for equestrian events, and horses can be hired at the nearby **Elvange**.

Perhaps not surprisingly, Mondorf has **hotels** from the middle to the top end of the price bracket. The cheapest are the *Dolce Vita*, avenue Dr Klein 4 (☎67 61 61, fax 67 68 70; ⑤), and next door, the *Beau-Séjour* (☎66 81 08, fax 66 08 89; ⑤). At the *Mondorf Parc*, avenue Dr E. Feltgen (☎66 12 12, fax 66 10 93; ⑧–⑨), guests have access to all the sports facilities of the spa, including a large park with outdoor pools for adults and children; the casino also has its own hotel, *Casino 2000* (☎661 01 01, fax 66 10 10; ⑦) at rue Flammang.

The southwest

The area immediately southwest of Luxembourg City used to be pretty dire, an iron-ore mining and steel-making region whose heavy industry and urban sprawls were best glimpsed from a train window on the way to somewhere else. However, over the past few years, much of the steel-making has closed down, its vestiges have been ripped out and the towns are being pleasingly gentrified. **ESCH-SUR-ALZETTE** is Luxembourg's second biggest city, with a population of around twenty-five thousand including a large number of Italians, drawn to the steelworks before banking in Luxembourg City replaced steel in Esch as the country's main source of income. Esch in recent years has become an exercise in urban regeneration, whose pedestrianized zone around the main street, rue de l'Alzette, offers varied and reasonable shopping, some good cafés and an aura of well-being that other cities in Europe's rust belts might envy. But there's no reason to get off the train in this area unless you want to visit a couple of worthwhile museums. In Esch itself, the **Musée de Résistance Nationale** in place de la Résistance (Thurs, Sat & Sun, 3–6pm; call to arrange a visit outside these hours, ☎54 73 83; free) is an excellent museum of its type and warrants at least a couple of hours. In the nearby town of **RUMELANGE**, the **Musée National des Mines** is devoted to the mining history of the area (Easter–Oct daily 2–6pm; Nov–Easter second Sat & Sun of each month 2–6pm; F100). Situated in a disused mine shaft, 1000m deep, guided tours of the museum last an hour and a half, and include displays of ancient and modern tools, photos and charts, and assorted machinery from the nineteenth and twentieth centuries. While you're at Rumelange, go to the cemetery and find the plaque commemorating the tomb that was dug out and used as an underground newspaper editorial office during the German occupation.

Northeast of Esch, the **Parc Merveilleux** at nearby **BETTEMBOURG** (April–Oct daily 9.30am–7pm; adults F150, children F120) is a very popular summer destination with Luxembourg families, its large site containing a children's zoo, miniature train rides and lots of Disneylandish attractions. In the other direction, **RODANGE** is home to a contraption known as **Train 1900** (May–Sept Sun only at 3pm & 4.20pm; F150), a steam train that runs around the nearby Titelberg hill – an important Gallo-Roman archeological site; there are some rebuilt walls in the forests around the plateau, with explanatory noticeboards. Rodange is, like Esch, connected with Luxembourg by rail, and the steam train departs from a (marked) point fifteen minutes' walk away from the main train station.

Central Luxembourg

As you head north from the capital, Luxembourg's landscapes grow more spectacular. The main road and rail lines run parallel, shadowing the course of the River Alzette and it is **MERSCH** that is the first town that feels totally free of the sway of the capital, and the first real stop on the train line. It's a rather unexciting place, with little to attract you beyond the rather thin remains of a **Roman villa**, southwest of the centre on rue des Romains. If you have your own transport, you might want to make a detour from here down to one of the country's most beautifully sited **youth hostels**, housed in the old castle of **Hollenfels**, 10km southwest of Mersch (☎30 70 37; ①).

This region is known as the **Seven Castles valley** for reasons that will quickly become apparent. For a glimpse of castles (though none are open to vistors), head south a kilometre or so to the village of **Ansembourg**, where a beautiful country house and the medieval castle compete for your attention. Following the main road back along the valley towards Mersch, you soon come to the old **Convent of Marienthal**. Originally a medieval foundation for the daughters of the nobility, it was adopted during the last century by the White Brothers, a Belgian missionary order of monks, but is now used mostly as a field study centre.

Also worth a stop, just off the main road northeast from the capital to Echternach, is the **Château de Bourglinster**. Set in a wooded valley, the château is kept in excellent condition by the state, and used as a space for art exhibitions and chamber music concerts. The château also has an expensive restaurant – and a much less expensive brasserie next door – but you could save on accommodation by staying in the **BOURGLINSTER** village's **youth hostel** at rue de Gonderange 2 (①).

Ettelbruck

Situated at the meeting point of the Alzette and Sûre river valleys, **ETTELBRUCK** is an important provincial centre, a town of around 6500 people that occupies a central position in the country and is an important road and rail junction. There's not really much to see in the town: Ettelbruck suffered very heavy damage during the fighting of late 1944 and is pretty much without historic interest beyond a few mementos of the war – a **memorial** to Patton in the shape of a US tank out on the Diekirch road, and a **Musée Patton** at the junction of Grande Rue and rue du Canal (July to mid-Sept daily 10am–noon & 1–5pm; mid-Sept to June Sun 2–5pm; F75). A memorial service and parade by US troops is still held each year at the end of May or beginning of June.

There's a **tourist office** in Ettelbruck's train station (Mon–Fri 9am–noon & 1.30–5pm; ☎81 20 68, fax 81 98 39). For **accommodation** you're better off staying in Diekirch (see below) unless you're hostelling. Ettelbruck's **youth hostel** is on rue Grande-Duchesse Josephine-Charlotte (☎81 22 69; ①). There's also a campsite, *Kallesdelt* (April–Sept; ☎81 21 85), at rue du Camping 22.

Diekirch

Five kilometres east, and easily accessible by bus or train from Ettelbruck station, **DIEKIRCH** is a more appealing place, although it too suffered during the 1944 fighting. However, it is a good base for seeing some of the surrounding area (with a couple of good campsites), and it does have one or two interesting museums.

One of these, the **Musée National d'Histoire Militaire**, 200m from the main square of place Guillaume, on the right up Montée de la Seitert (Easter–Oct daily 10am–noon & 2–6pm; Nov–March 2–6pm; F200), provides an excellent historical survey of the Battle of the Bulge, with a special, if rather adulatory, emphasis on the liberating US troops. The photographs on display are the real testament, showing both sets of troops in action and at leisure, some recording the appalling freezing conditions of December 1944, others the horrific state of affairs inside the medics' tent. There's a variety of dioramas, many modelled diligently on actual photographs (which are often displayed alongside), along with a hoard of military paraphernalia – explosives, shells, weapons, and personal effects of both American and German soldiers (prayer books, rations, novellas, etc). There's also a display entitled "Veiner Miliz", detailing the activities of the Luxembourg resistance movement based in Vianden; another room is devoted to Tambow, the camp to which all the Luxembourgers captured by the Russians were sent. Other exhibits recount the history of the Luxembourg army, and pay tribute to World War II casualties and those who spearheaded the resistance. Ask here for the free *Battleground Luxembourg* brochure, which outlines a car tour of the major sites, monuments and remains.

Diekirch's other museum, the **Musée Mosaïques Romaines**, is on the other side of the square (Easter–Oct Fri–Wed 10am–noon & 2–6pm; F50) – essentially two rooms, each featuring a reasonably well-preserved Roman floor mosaic, one from the middle of the first century, the other from around the third century, found on a site in the centre of Diekirch, just off rue Esplanade, together with a handful of other artefacts. The best mosaic is the one in the right-hand room, its design centring on a two-faced depiction of Medusa. Alongside it are a couple of skeletons, one still in its original wooden coffin, which were also found nearby.

For the ghoulish there are more skeletons on the other side of the pedestrianized town centre, in the church of **St Laurent** (Easter–Oct Tues–Sun 10am–noon & 2–6pm; free), 100m east of the other main square, place de la Libération, at the top of the main shopping street of Grande Rue. This turreted church, some parts of which date back to the ninth century, is home to a set of eerie medieval tombs that were discovered under the floor.

Practicalities

Diekirch's **bus** and **train station** are five to ten minutes' walk south of the centre of town on avenue de la Gare, next door to the Diekirch brewery– the country's largest beer producer – although buses also stop outside the *Kremer* hotel in the centre. The **tourist office** is on the corner of place Guillaume (July & Aug daily 9am–noon & 2–7pm; Sept–June Mon–Fri 10am–noon & 2–5pm; ☎80 30 23), and can help with maps and accommodation. Of the town's **hotels**, try the *Au Bon Accueil*, avenue de la Gare 75 (☎80 34 76, fax 80 28 10; ③), and the *Hôtel de la Gare*, avenue de la Gare 73 (☎80 33 05, fax 80 23 52; ⑤), both opposite the bus station. The town's two **campsites** – *de la Sûre* (April–Sept; ☎80 94 25) and *Op de Sauer* (all year round; ☎80 85 90) – are handily placed a few minutes' walk from the centre by the river; follow the road 100m east from the *Hôtel Europe*, cross over the bridge and take the riverside path. There's also another site, the *Gritt* (April–Oct; ☎80 20 18), a few minutes by bus toward Ettelbruck in **INGELDORF**, which has a lovely location, also by the river.

There aren't many **restaurants** in Diekirch: you could try the reasonably priced pizzas and pasta in the *Rialto*, at Grande Rue 15, or the more traditional and the slightly more expensive Luxembourg fare at the excellent *Brasserie du Commerce*, at the top end of Grand Rue on place de la Libération, or stick with the hotel restaurants, all of which serve traditional dishes. If you're feeling wealthy, and want to blow in excess of F4000 per head on a celebration meal, the *Hotel Hiertz* (☎80 35 62), renowned as one of the best restaurants in the region, is the place to go; booking several days in advance is essential. For cheap snacks and simple meals, head for *City Restaurant*, Grand Rue 46, which serves tasty good-value tortellini, soups, and salads. Opposite, *Cafe de Groen* is a popular watering hole come nightfall.

Diekirch makes a good base for **touring** the surrounding area, either by car or by bike. You can rent **bikes** from the *de la Sûre* campsite (F200 per half-day, F300 per day); or from the Outdoor Centre (rue de la Sûre 10, Dillingen; ☎86 91 39), which also has mountain-bikes (F800 per day). It's also possible to **canoe** down the river to **Echternach** from Dillingen, Wallendorf or Diekirch, the start point depending on the time of year; it makes an easy and safe, but exciting trip – reckon on about five or six hours. Again, the Outdoor Centre are the people to talk to, and rates start at F1000 for a double kayak; advance booking is advisable.

Echternach and around

Ten kilometres or so east of Diekirch, the Sûre becomes the border between Luxembourg and Germany, edging the pretty area known as **Petite Suisse** because of its thickly wooded hills and rocky valleys. **ECHTERNACH** is the main centre of this region, a town of around four thousand people that is one of Luxembourg's prime resorts. Echternach grew up around an abbey that was founded here in 698 by a monk called St Willibrord, a Yorkshire missionary who, according to legend, cured epilepsy and cattle, and led the effort to convert much of northern Germany and the low countries to Christianity. He is commemorated by the renowned day-long dancing procession and **festival** around the saint's tomb and town centre, held annually on the Tuesday after Pentecost since 1553. If you want to go to this, either take one of the special buses from Luxembourg City, or get there by about 9.30am and park some distance away – in any case, be prepared for a crush.

The centre of town is the wedge-shaped **place du Marché**, an elegant conglomeration of ancient buildings, most notable among which is the fifteenth-century turreted old **town hall**, with its Gothic loggia of 1520. A short walk east of here there's the **Musée de Préhistoire** on the right-hand side of rue du Pont (April–Oct Tues–Sun 10am–noon & 2–5pm; July & Aug 10am–5pm; F50). But the town's real attraction is the **abbey** itself, just off place du Marché to the north, signalled by the spires of its enormous **basilica**. This has had a long and rather varied history. The original church of St Willibrord was a much smaller affair, but it was destroyed by fire in 1016. A new structure erected later that century was pressed into service as a pottery factory during the French Revolution, and then restored in 1862. It was again rebuilt to the former eleventh-century plan after sustaining heavy bomb damage during the Battle of the Bulge in 1944, and reconsecrated in 1952. It's a simple basilical structure with a Romanesque arched nave, but succesive reconstruction has eradicated much of the original church. The piece of crucifix on the left-hand wall is the only part of the furnishings of the old abbey which survived the war. Downstairs, the crypt is the only major part of St Willibrord's church to have survived. Dating from around 900, its whitewashed walls are home to some unfinished frescoes and the primitive coffin of the saint himself, covered by an ornate canopy made in 1906.

The huge abbey complex spreads out beyond the church to a set of formal gardens by the river, its mainly eighteenth-century buildings used for a variety of secular activities these days – notably a variety of concerts given as part of the annual festival. One of the buildings houses the **Musée de l'Abbaye** (April–Oct daily 10am–noon & 2–6pm; Nov–March Sat & Sun 2–5pm; F50), which contains more fragments of St Willibrord's first monastery and church – foundations mainly, along with some rather macabre eighth-century tombs complete with skeletons. The rest of the museum is well laid out and has some high-quality exhibits. Highlights include a piece of mosaic flooring from the Roman villa just outside Echternach (see below) and various examples of medieval calligraphy and illumination, including the eleventh-century *Codex Aureus* of Echternach, whose superb jewelled cover, from 990, was the work of a Trier craftsman.

Practicalities

There's little in the way of sights to detain you in Echternach, but like Diekirch it is one of Luxembourg's prettiest countryside bases. The **bus station** is five minutes from the centre of town, down the long rue de la Gare, a lively street lined with tourist boutiques, hotels, and restaurants. The **tourist office** opposite the abbey church (Mon–Fri 9am–noon & 2–5pm, also Sat & Sun in high season; ☎72 02 30), has maps of the town and information on accommodation.

Echternach has plenty of **hotels**, many along rue de la Gare, among which there are a number of reasonable options. Both the *Pavillon* at no. 2 (☎72 98 09, fax 72 86 23; ⑤), and the inexpensive *Aigle Noir* at no. 54 (☎72 03 83, fax 72 05 44; ③), are worth checking out, but there's also the *Petite Poète* at place du Marché 13 (☎72 00 72, fax 72 74 83; ③) which is very central and serves hearty meals. There's a **campsite** (☎72 02 72) 300m beyond the bus station following the river out of town, and another at the opposite end of the lake, *Alferweiher* (☎72 02 71). The **youth hostel** is at rue André Deutscher 9 (☎72 01 58; ①) – follow the street that runs south from the corner of place du Marché and rue de la Gare.

On the same corner, the *Benelux* **restaurant** is very reasonably priced, as is the *Hôtel de l'Abbaye* restaurant on rue la Gare, with plats du jour and prix fixe menus, and the *Hôtel du Commerce* on place du Marché, which serves a three-course special. For snacks, or just a drink, use the *Bit Beim Dokter* bar, up by the tourist office, which serves sandwiches and light meals for around F200. *Giorgio's Pizzeria*, 4 rue Duchscher, is more upmarket than its twin in Luxembourg City (same owner), but still very good value.

Around Echternach

About a kilometre south of Echternach, following the road to **Lauterborn**, a large artificial **lake** provides good, if crowded, distraction on hot summer afternoons – and has public barbecues at its far end. Nearby lie the remains of a mainly second-century **Roman villa**, though these are very scant – more or less the foundations only.

Further afield, west into the heart of Petite Suisse, back toward Diekirch, the village of **BERDORF** is a popular climbing centre and a good starting point for gentle hikes into the craggier reaches of the region – paths are marked clearly and take you through some delightful spots. The walk from Echternach to Berdorf up the **Gorge du Loup** is a favourite; at the top of the gorge are an open-air theatre and grottoes which may have been where the Romans cut mill stones.

Another destination might be the castle at **Beaufort**, about 6km west (April–Oct daily 10am–6pm; F50), which enjoys a marvellous location nestled among the surrounding wooded hills. The site was originally a Roman encampment, and the oldest part of the castle dates from the mid-twelfth century; later parts were added in 1380 and 1500. It's no more than a ruin now, but you can wander through the site freely, enjoying the views and poking around the crumbling nooks and corners. There's a **youth hostel** in Beaufort village, a pleasant modern affair at rue de l'Auberge 6 (☎83 60 75; ①), and a couple of reasonable hotels, including the inexpensive *Hostellerie de Beaufort* (☎83 60 46, fax 86 91 74; ③), Grand Rue 59. If you want a destination for moving on to, there's another castle at **LAROCHETTE**, a few kilometres south of Beaufort, poking out of the trees high above what is a very pretty little town. This one is a ruin, too, but the later section has been restored and now has regained its roof and turrets. If you like the place, you could stay at the **youth hostel** at Osterbour 45 (☎83 70 81; ①), or at the more upmarket *Hôtel du Château* (☎83 70 09, fax 87 96 37; ⑤) at rue de Medernach 1. If you stay at the comfortable *Hôtel de la Poste* (☎87 81 78, fax 83 70 07; ⑤), place Bleiche 11, ask to see the parchment signed by a former pope, elevating an ancestor to sainthood. There are also two **campsites** – *Auf Birkelt* (March–Oct; ☎87 90 40) at rue de la Piscine 1, and *Daytona* (March–Oct; ☎87 87 79), rue de Christnach 3. As for **eating**, the restaurant at the *Hôtel de la Poste* is fine, or trawl the bars on the square.

Northern Luxembourg

The **northern** part of Luxembourg, within the narrowing neck of the country's triangle, is its most spectacular region, repeating the scenic highlights of the Belgian Ardennes. Again, transport connections are difficult without a car, and it's far enough from the capital to make day-trips not nearly so feasible or enjoyable.

Vianden

Though it's not centrally placed, the best base for seeing the Luxembourg Ardennes is **VIANDEN**, on the German border. A tiny place, not much more than a village, Vianden is probably the most strikingly sited of all Luxembourg's provincial towns, and it consequently gets very crowded in summer. Confined by a bowl of green wooded hills, it spreads up the slope from the River Our, in part still surrounded by ramparts and totally dominated by the newly restored castle, which towers on the hill immediately above.

The main street curves down to the river, almost entirely lined by hotels and restaurants and finishing up at the bridge, on which a Rodin bust of **Victor Hugo** signals a house that was the part-time home of the French writer between 1862 and 1871. Hugo has since become Vianden's most famous adopted son, and his house has been turned over to a museum (currently closed for renovation but due to re-open in early 2000) commemorating his stay here, with many letters and copies of poems and manuscripts, including his *Discourse on Vianden*, written in 1871. There are also photographs of the town during the nineteenth century, and sketches by the great man of local places of interest – the castles at Beaufort and Larochette, for example. Sadly, though, there's not much left from Hugo's stay, apart from the bedroom furniture, complete with original bed.

There is one other **museum** in Vianden, one of "Rustic Arts", at Grande Rue 96 (Easter–Oct daily 10am–noon & 2–6pm; F100), with rooms devoted to rural furniture and clothes, a sprawling display of toys and, on the top floor, a small room devoted to some fascinating historical documents relating to the town and castle, and photographs of Vianden. But Vianden's major sight is inevitably the **castle** itself (daily: March & Oct 10am–5pm; April–Sept 10am–6pm; Nov–Feb 10am–4pm; F120), open in its entirety following a very thorough restoration, before which much was in ruins. Originally a fifth-century structure, the present building dates mostly from the eleventh century and shows features from the Romanesque style to the Renaissance. It was the home of the counts of Vianden, who ruled the town and much of the area during the twelfth and thirteenth centuries – until they fell under the sway of the House of Luxembourg in 1264. Later, in 1417, the Luxembourg family took over the building, and it remained the property of the grand ducal family until 1977 when it was handed over to the state. It forms a very large complex, and the renovation has been sensitively done, though the crowds trooping through the pristine halls and galleries can't help but dispel the hushed atmosphere. On display are the inevitable suits of armour and such-like, but much has just been left empty, notably the long Byzantine Room, with its high trefoil windows, and the octagonal upper chapel next door, surrounded by a narrow defensive walkway. There are, too, exhibits on the development of the building, detailing its restoration, and on the history of the town. Some rooms have been furnished in period style – the **Banqueting Hall** and the huge **Counts' Hall**, decorated with seventeenth-century tapestries – though the piped music doesn't lend much atmosphere. For more authentic mustiness, peek down the well just off the old kitchen – its murky darkness is lit to reveal profound depths (in which, locals maintain, a former count can be heard frantically playing dice to hold the Devil at bay, his soul at stake) – and leave through the unrestored Gothic dungeon, perhaps the most evocative part of the entire building.

Beyond the castle it's the **countryside** around Vianden which beckons most positively – something you can survey from the hill above by taking the **Télésiège** or cable car to its 450m summit (Easter to mid-Oct daily 9.30am–6.30pm; F160 return). This runs from a station on rue du Sanatorium, just off rue Victor Hugo on the western edge of the town centre. At the top there's a restaurant with a terrace and you can also walk down to the castle by way of a footpath.

There's little else to hold the interest unless you happen to be around on the second Sunday of October (first Sunday in 1999 because of the national elections), when you'll be able to experience the annual **nut festival** – dozens of stalls throng the city selling everything nutty from local walnut wine and spirits to walnut cheese and walnut cake, and local musicians perform throughout the day.

Practicalities

Buses to Vianden stop on the far eastern edge of town on the route de la Frontière, about five minutes' walk from the **tourist office** on rue de Vieux Marché 1, in the centre (daily 9.30am–noon & 1–6pm, outside high season Mon–Fri 9am–noon & 2–6pm; ☎83 42 57, fax 84 90 81), which has copious information and maps.

Accommodation isn't too much of a problem in Vianden – virtually every other building is a hotel – although during the high season you'd be wise to reserve in advance. Among the cheaper alternatives on the castle side of the river is *Hôtel Collette*, Grande Rue 68–70 (☎83 40 04, fax 83 47 05; ④; April–Nov). A few doors down, the venerable *Hôtel Heintz*, Grand Rue 55 (☎83 41 55, fax 83 45 59; ④) is comfortable, friendly, and has an excellent restaurant, as does the *Auberge de l'Our*, over the river on the right at rue de la Gare 35 (☎83 46 75, fax 84 91 94; ③). There are any number of other possibilities on both sides of the road as far as the bus station: for example the *Petry*, rue de la Gare 15 (☎83 41 22; ④; midFeb to Nov). There's also a **youth hostel** nicely placed at the top of Grande Rue, right below the ramparts of the castle at Montée du Château 3 (☎83 41 77; ①). The nearest **campsite** is *Op dem Deich* (☎83 43 75) by the river near the bus station; there are also two other campsites further on down the road to Echternach – *De l'Our* (☎83 45 05) and *Du Moulin* (☎83 45 01) – though all are closed from Oct to April.

Most of the hotels have **restaurants**, and these form the bulk of the town's eating options. The *Auberge de l'Our* hotel by the bridge serves a good array of Luxembourgeois specialities, though its terrace by the river means it gets very crowded; its **bar** is also about the most convivial and cheapest place to drink in Vianden. On the other side of the river, the *Café de la Poste* on Grande Rue offers reasonably priced set menus; the *Hôtel Bingen*, further up, charges a little more. If you're feeling flush, you might try the rather swankier surroundings of the *Auberge de la Château* restaurant further up Grande Rue. At the other extreme, fast food abounds, especially around the bridge and the Télésiège. **Bikes** can be rented from the Pavillon de la Gare (bus station) for F500 per day (9–11am, 1–3pm & 6–8pm; ☎84 92 48).

Bourscheid, Esch and Wiltz

The only way to go from Vianden and remain in Luxembourg is **west**, a route which takes you through the best of the Ardennes scenery, though you'll need a car to do it comfortably. The **castle** at **BOURSCHEID** (April Mon–Fri 11am–5pm; May–June & Sept Mon–Fri 10am–6pm; July & Aug Mon–Fri 10am–7pm; Oct Mon–Fri 11am–4pm; Nov–March Sat–Sun and holidays only 11am–4pm; F80; ☎9 05 70) provides one of the most spectacular stops. Perching high above the surrounding wooded hills, it is without question the most superbly sited of all Luxembourg's castles. The first proper fortifications were erected here around the year 1000, when a stone wall was substituted for a previous wooden structure. Nothing much is left from this period and most of the later buildings you see now went up during the fourteenth century. It's currently being rebuilt, but there's still not much to see beyond the shape of the walls, the odd tower, and some dusty artefacts in the gabled late fourteenth-century **Stolzembourg house**, supplemented by temporary exhibitions of the work of local artists. In its way the castle is more impressive than Vianden, if only because it's less crowded – except during July, when there is a **Schlassfest** (castle festival) with Gregorian masses, jousting, archery, concerts, barbecues and general medieval revelry (contact tourist office in front of the castle; July & Aug daily 11am–6pm; ☎9 05 64). If you want to linger in the area, head for the village of **Lipperscheid** on the opposite bank, where the *Hôtel Leweck* (☎90 02 24; ⑥) has a swimming pool, tennis courts and can arrange horse riding. Alternatively you can arrange it yourself with the *Auberge-Restaurant Ponies Haff* (☎9 00 22; ④).

Below the castle, the River Sûre winds a picturesque route through its valley – a beauty spot you can take most advantage of from a couple of **campsites** situated right by the river in **BOURSCHEID MOULIN** – the *Moulin* (May–Oct; ☎99 03 31, fax 99 06 15) and *Um Gritt* (May–Oct; ☎99 04 49, fax 90 80 46). In the opposite direction, the road continues up towards the village of Bourscheid proper, home to a handful of good hotels, most notably *Auberge de Bourscheid*, rue Principale 5 (☎99 00 08, fax 90 80 17; ③), and *Hôtel St Fiacre*, rue Principale 4 (☎99 00 23, fax 99 06 66; ⑤), both of which have good restaurants.

Esch-sur-Sûre and around

From Bourscheid village, you can follow the Sûre to **ESCH-SUR-SÛRE**, a small village of just three hundred people with a fame out of all proportion to its size, mainly due to its gorgeous situation within an ox-bow loop in the river. Once here, there's nothing to see in particular, and Esch itself is not even especially attractive, but the location is a fine one, surrounded by a high wall of green in its sheltered position at the bottom of the valley. The castle above, perched on two entirely separate crags, each part of which you can wander around, dates from the tenth century and has been lying in ruins for a couple of hundred years. **Accommodation** includes the *Auberge de la Sûre* at rue du Pont 1 (☎83 91 10, fax 89 91 01; ③) and the *Beau-Site* (☎83 91 34, fax 89 90 24; ⑤), rue de Kaundorf 2, on the banks of the river. There's also a large campsite, *Im Ahl* (☎83 95 14) which is open all year round.

For those with a car or bike, the hilly country **west of Esch** is worth visiting. Take the road to the **Barrage de la Haut Sûre**, a dam that has created a stretch of water that meanders through several valleys. It is popular with watersports enthusiasts, who congregate in **LULTZHAUSEN** and **INSENBORN**, the latter just 6km from Esch. Just before Lultzhausen, the headquarters of the **Parc Naturel de la Haute Sûre** (Mon, Tues, Thurs & Fri 10am–noon & 2–6pm, Sat & Sun 2–6pm; free) makes a worthwhile diversion, especially if you're travelling with children. Housed in a converted cloth mill, exhibits explain the ecology of the area, and there are guide and activity booklets. In Lultzhausen itself, there's a **youth hostel** (☎83 94 24; ①) – with canoes for rent (book in advance) – while at Insenborn, the ten-roomed *Hotel Peiffer* (☎83 98 97, fax 89 93 27; ②) is modest, but very reasonably priced. For a grandstand view of the lake above Esch-sur-Sûre, climb the hill to Kaundorf, a small village with an unpretentious restaurant and inn, *Zeimen* (☎95 85 61), where you can while away a few hours. If you're returning to the main Luxembourg road, the back routes via **ARSDORF** offer fine rural views and a hidden gem of a hotel, the *Diligence* (☎64 95 55, fax 64 92 10; ④), with a friendly restaurant.

Wiltz

About 10km north of Esch, **WILTZ** is one of the larger, but not one of the Grand Duchy's most appealing centres; by and large it's a sprawl of unchecked development. However, its upper town holds one or two items of mild interest around its **château**, a largely seventeenth-century building, though built on twelfth-century foundations. High above the wooded valley, the somewhat overzealously restored château is home to the Wiltz **tourist office** (July & Aug Mon–Fri 10am–6pm; Sept–June Mon–Fri 10am–noon & 2–5pm; ☎95 74 44) and **two museums**. One is another tired display devoted to the **Battle of the Bulge** (June to mid-Sept daily 10am–noon & 1–5pm; mid-Sept to May daily 1–5pm; F70) and the other is the **Musée Arts et Métiers** (July & Aug Mon–Fri 10am–6pm; Sept–June Mon–Fri 10am–noon & 2–5pm; F50), with ceramics, agricultural tools, basketwork and a huge still. Part of the château gardens are laid out for performances of the town's open-air **theatre and music festival** in July while **paths** lead down into the wooded grounds below. (Another festive occasion occurs on Ascension Day when the town and surrounds are thronged with Portuguese on their annual pilgrimage to the **Lady of Fatima shrine** on the opposite hill.) The strange lighthouse-like monument near the château is the national **memorial** to the victims of the **National Strike**, which took place from 30 August to 3 September 1942 in protest at the conscription of Luxembourgers into the German Army.

It's not really worth stopping overnight in Wiltz unless the festival is on, as for most of the year it's fairly quiet. While the festival's in progress, several **hotels** in the vicinity offer special packages with dinner, bed and breakfast and tickets included (check with the tourist office), although the *Hôtel Beau Séjour* (☎95 82 50, fax 95 89 47; ③), rue du X Septembre 21, with its rustic charm and lovely flower garden, is good value for money at any time. Oddly, Wiltz also boasts a disproportionate number of **campsites** – there are eight to be exact, the main one being *Camping Kaul* (May–Oct; ☎95 00 79) on the edge of the forest – and in summer the place swarms with outward-bound Scouts. For **food**, the *Zumm Treffpunkt*, on Grande Rue close to the château, is good and reasonably cheap; more expensive restaurants cluster around the castle.

Clervaux and around

About 15km from Wiltz, in the far north of Luxembourg, **CLERVAUX** is another small town topped with a castle and built around a loop in the river. Clervaux's castle dates from the twelfth century, but was rebuilt in the seventeenth century and again after considerable damage in the last war, as is recounted in the **Battle of the Bulge Museum** across the atmospheric, cobblestone courtyard (June Mon–Sat 1–5pm, Sun 10am–5pm; July to mid-Sept daily 10am–5pm; mid-Sept to Dec & March–May, Sun & holidays only 1–5pm; F50). Another part of the castle holds a **museum of models** (same times and price), with dioramas incorporating several of the castles of Luxembourg. The crowning glory of the castle's exhibitions though, is the **Family of Man**, a remarkable collection of photographs compiled by Edward Steichen (March–Dec Tues–Sun 10am–6pm; F150; ☎92 96 57). Elsewhere, the **Toy Museum** on Grand Rue 9 (Jan–Easter Sat & Sun 11am–noon & 2–5pm; Easter–Dec daily 10am–noon & 1.30–6pm; F95) holds a

EUROPE – ON THE GROUND

East of the village of **Weiswampach**, in the northeastern corner of Luxembourg, is the only piece of Europe that exists on the ground, not just in the imagination. Follow signs to Ouren (in Belgium) and a little way to the south of the village you'll find a corner of a foreign field that is forever Europe. In the early 1970s Belgium, Luxembourg and Germany – whose territories meet here – each ceded a piece of land precisely one third the size of this field, so no one owns it (but Belgium mows the lawn). On the road you are in Luxembourg, you have to go through Belgium to get there and Germany is just across the river Our. The stones in the field are tributes to the signatories of the original EU treaties – Spaak, Schuman and Adenauer.

modest but interesting collection of toys from down the ages, including a magnificient dolls' house dating back to the 1880s. The nineteenth-century **Abbaye Bénédictine St Maurice**, a 1km hike from the castle up the hill, has exhibitions on The Monastical Life (daily 9am–7pm) as well as Gregorian masses and vespers (daily 10.30am & 6.30pm).

Clervaux is on the main rail line, but bear in mind that it's a good ten-minute walk into town from the **station**. The **tourist office** can be found in the castle (Mon–Sat; mid-April to June 2–5pm; July–Aug 9.45–11.45am & 2–6pm; Sept 9.45–11.45am & 1.30–5.30pm; Oct 9.45–11.45am & 1–5pm; ☎92 00 72), and has details on accommodation in Clervaux. There are plenty of **hotels** for a place of this size, including the modern and centrally located *Hôtel du Commerce*, rue de Marnach 2 (☎92 91 81, fax 92 91 08; ⑤), and the picturesque *Hôtel du Parc*, rue du Parc 2 (☎92 06 50, fax 92 10 68; ⑤), which clings to a wooded hill overlooking the town. There's also a couple of **campsites**, *Camping Officiel* (April–Nov; ☎92 00 42) at Klatzewé 33, near to the cemetery, and *Camping Reilerweiher* (April–Nov; ☎92 01 60), about 2km out of town on the Vianden road, beside the river. The best place **to eat** in a town of pricey restaurants is the *Splendid*, Grande Rue 32, which has a good selection of seafood, although a cheaper alternative is *Vieux Château*, rue du Château 4, located opposite the tourist office. It's a quiet, rustic place, and serves good-value and tasty fish, beef, and chicken main courses, as well as a wide variety of mussel dishes.

North of Clervaux is the small town of **TROISVIERGES**, which enjoys a certain notoriety as the place where World War I started on 1 August 1914 when a group of German soldiers crossed the border, ripped up a length of railway line (for reasons that never became clear) and then were led off by an irate officer. They came back next day.

travel details

Trains

Luxembourg to: Arlon (hourly; 20min) – all carry on to Namur and Brussels (2hr 30min), with connections to Amsterdam (5hr 30min); Clervaux (hourly; 1hr 5min); Diekirch (change at Ettelbruck) (every 45min; 40min); Ettelbruck (every 30min; 35min); Kautenbach (hourly; 1hr); Koblenz (hourly; 2hr); Liège (for Maastricht) (7 daily; 2hr 30min);

Trier (hourly; 45min); Wasserbillig (every 30min; 30min); Wiltz (change at Kautenbach) (hourly; 1hr 10min).

Buses

Note: *Services vary dramatically depending on the day. Many schoolchildren are free on Tuesday and Thursday afternoons, so buses on those days are often fewer than at other times.*

Diekirch to: Echternach (hourly; 35min); Vianden (hourly; 20min).

Ettelbruck to: Diekirch (every 10min; 10min); Echternach (15 daily; 45min); Esch-sur-Sûre (6 daily; 40min); Vianden (12 daily; 30min).

Grevenmacher to: Echternach (every 30min; 40min).

Luxembourg to: Diekirch (every 2hr; 1hr 20min); Echternach (every 45min; 1hr 10min); Mondorf-les-Bains (hourly; 30min); Remich (hourly; 45min).

Remich to: Grevenmacher (5 daily; 30min); Wormeldange (5 daily; 15min).

Wasserbillig to: Echternach (hourly; 30min).

Wiltz to: Esch-sur-Sûre (4 daily; 25min).

Ferries

Schengen–Remich–Wormeldange–Grevenmacher–Wasserbillig–Trier (mid-April to end-Sept around 6 weekly).

For full timetable details of the Moselle ferry boats, contact Navigation Touristique de l'Entente de la Moselle Luxembourgeoise, route de Thionville 32, Grevenmacher (☎75 82 75), or pick up a brochure from most tourist offices.

PART THREE

THE
CONTEXTS

THE HISTORICAL FRAMEWORK

Jumbled together throughout most of their history, the countries which are now known as Belgium, Luxembourg and the Netherlands didn't reach their present delimitations until 1830. Until then their borders were continually being redrawn following battles, treaties and alliances, and, inevitably, what follows is a brief history of the whole region – commonly called the "Low Countries" – rather than individual accounts of the states concerned. Incidentally, we've termed the language of the northern part of Belgium "Flemish" to save confusion, though "Dutch" or even "Netherlandic" are sometimes the preferred options among Belgians themselves; also note that the term "Holland" refers to the province – not the country – throughout.

BEGINNINGS

Little is known of the prehistoric settlers of the **Low Countries**, their visible remains largely confined to the far north of the Netherlands, where mounds known as *terpen* were built to keep the sea at bay. Clearer details do, however, emerge at the time of Julius Caesar's conquest of Gaul (broadly France) in 57 to 50 BC. He found three tribal groupings of Iron Age

agriculturalists living in the region: the mainly Celtic **Belgae** (hence the nineteenth-century term "Belgium") settled by the rivers Rhine, Maas and Waal to the south; the Germanic **Frisians** living on the marshy coastal strip north of the Scheldt; and the **Batavi**, another Germanic people, inhabiting the swampy river banks of what is now the southern Netherlands. The Belgae were conquered and their lands incorporated into the imperial province of **Gallia Belgica**, but the territory of the Batavi and Frisians was not considered worthy of colonization, and these tribes were granted the status of allies, a source of recruitment for the Roman legions and curiosity for imperial travellers. In 50 AD Pliny observed, "Here a wretched race is found, inhabiting either the more elevated spots or artificial mounds . . .When the waves cover the surrounding area they are like so many mariners on board a ship, and when again the tide recedes their condition is that of so many shipwrecked men."

The **Roman occupation** continued for five hundred years until the legions were pulled back to protect the heartlands of a crumbling empire. But despite the length of their stay, there's a notable lack of material evidence to indicate their presence, an important exception being the odd stretch of city wall in Tongeren, one of the principal Roman settlements. As the empire collapsed in chaos and confusion, the Germanic **Franks**, who had been settling within Gallia Belgica from the third century, filled the power vacuum to the south, and, along with their allies the Belgae, established a **Merovingian** kingdom based around their capital in Tournai. A great swathe of forest extending from the Scheldt to the Ardennes separated this predominantly Frankish kingdom from the more confused situation to the north and east, where other tribes of Franks settled along the Scheldt and Leie – a separation which came to delineate the ethnic and linguistic division that survives in Belgium to this day. North of the Franks of the Scheldt were the Saxons and finally the north coast of the Netherlands was settled by the Frisians.

Towards the end of the fifth century, the Merovingians extended their control over much of what is now north and central France. In 496 their king, Clovis, was converted to Christianity, a faith which slowly filtered north, spread by energetic missionaries like Saint Willibrord, first bishop of Utrecht from about 710, and Saint Boniface, who was killed by the Frisians in 754 in a final act of pagan resistance before they too were converted. Meanwhile, after the death of the last distinguished Merovingian king, Dagobert, in 638, power passed increasingly to the so-called "mayors of the palace", a hereditary position whose most outstanding occupant was Charles Martel (c690–741). Martel dominated a large but all too obviously shambolic kingdom whose military weakness he determined to remedy. Traditionally, the Merovingian (Frankish) army was comprised of a body of infantry led by a small group of cavalry. Martel replaced this with a largely mounted force of highly trained knights, who bore their own military expenses in return for land, the beginnings of the feudal system. Actually, these reforms came just in time to save Christendom: in 711 that extraordinary Arab advance which had begun at the beginning of the seventh century reached the Pyrenees and a massive Moslem army occupied southern France in preparation for further conquests. In the event, Martel defeated the invaders outside Tours in 732, one of Europe's most crucial engagements and one that saved France from Arab conquest for good. Ten years after Martel's death, his son, Pepin the Short, formally usurped the Merovingian throne with the blessing of the pope, becoming the first of the **Carolingian** dynasty, whose most famous member was **Charlemagne**, son of Pepin and king of the west Franks from 768.

In a dazzling series of campaigns, Charlemagne extended his empire south into Italy, west to the Pyrenees, north to Denmark and east to the Oder, his secular authority bolstered by his coronation as the first **Holy Roman Emperor** in 800, a title bestowed on him by the pope to legitimize his claim to be the successor to the emperors of imperial Rome. The strength and stability of Charlemagne's court at Aachen spread to the Low Countries, bringing a flurry of building activity that spawned churches like Maastricht's St Servaas, and a trading boom, utilizing the region's principal rivers. However, unlike his Roman predecessors, Charlemagne was subject to the divisive inheritance laws of the Salian tribe of Franks, and after his death in 814, his kingdom was divided between his grandsons into three roughly parallel strips of territory, the precursors of France, the Low Countries and Germany.

THE GROWTH OF THE TOWNS

The tripartite division of Charlemagne's empire placed the Low Countries between the emergent French- and German-speaking nations, a dangerous location which was subsequently to decide much of its history, though this was not apparent in the cobweb of local alliances that made up early feudal Western Europe in the ninth and tenth centuries. During this period, French kings and German emperors exercised a general authority over the Low Countries, but power was effectively in the hands of local lords who, remote from central control, brought a degree of local stability. From the twelfth century, feudalism slipped into a gradual decline, the intricate pattern of localized allegiances undermined by the increasing strength of certain lords, whose power and wealth often exceeded that of their nominal sovereign. Preoccupied by territorial squabbles, this streamlined nobility was usually willing to assist the growth of towns by granting charters which permitted a certain amount of autonomy in exchange for tax revenues, and military and labour services. The first major cities were the **cloth towns** of Flanders, particularly Ghent, Bruges and Ieper, which grew rich from the manufacture of cloth, their garments exported far and wide and their economies dependent on a continuous supply of good-quality wool from England. Meanwhile, the smaller towns north of the Scheldt concentrated on trade, exploiting their strategic position at the junction of several of the major waterways and trade routes of the day.

Predictably, the economic interests of the urbanized merchants and guildsmen soon conflicted with those of the local lord. This was especially true in Flanders, where the towns were anxious to preserve a good relationship with the king of England, who controlled the wool supply, whereas their count was a vassal of the king of France, whose dynastic aspirations clashed with those of his English rival. As a result, the history of thirteenth- and fourteenth-century Flanders is punctuated by sporadic fighting, as the two kings and the guildsmen slugged it out, the fortunes of war oscillating between the parties but the underlying class conflict never resolved.

BURGUNDIAN RULE

By the late fourteenth century the political situation in the Low Countries was fairly clear: five lords controlled most of the region, paying only nominal homage to their French or German overlords. In 1419 **Philip the Good** of Burgundy succeeded to the countship of Flanders and by a series of adroit political moves gained control over Holland, Zeeland, Brabant and Limburg to the north, and Antwerp, Namur and Luxembourg to the south. He consolidated his power by establishing a strong central administration in Bruges and curtailing the privileges granted in the towns' charters. During his reign **Bruges** became an emporium for the Hanseatic League, a mainly German association of towns which acted as a trading group and protected their interests by an exclusive system of trading tariffs. The wealth of Bruges was legendary, and the Burgundian court patronized the early and seminal Nederlandish painters like Jan van Eyck and Hans Memling, whose works are displayed in Ghent and Bruges today.

Philip died in 1467 to be succeeded by his son, Charles the Bold, who was killed in battle ten years later, plunging his carefully crafted domain into turmoil. The French seized the opportunity to take back Arras and Burgundy and before the people of Flanders would agree to fight the French they kidnapped Charles's successor, his daughter Mary, and forced her to sign a charter that restored the civic privileges removed by her grandfather Philip.

THE HABSBURGS

After her release, Mary married the **Habsburg** Maximilian of Austria, who assumed sole authority when Mary was killed in a riding accident in 1482. Today, her tomb stands beside that of her father in the Onze Lieve Vrouwekerk in Bruges. Maximilian continued to rule until 1494, when he became Holy Roman Emperor and transferred control of the Low Countries to his son, Philip the Handsome, and then – after Philip's early death – to his grandson **Charles V**, who in turn became king of Spain and Holy Roman Emperor in 1516 and 1519 respectively. Charles was suspicious of the turbulent burghers of Flanders and, following in Maximilian's footsteps, favoured Antwerp at their expense. Indeed, the great Flemish towns of Ghent and Bruges were in decline, their economies undermined by England's cloth-manufacturing success and, in the case of Bruges, by the silting of the river Zwin, which – in connecting the town to the North Sea – was its

economic life-line. **Antwerp** became the greatest port in the Habsburg empire, part of a general movement of trade and prosperity away from Flanders to the cities further north.

By sheer might, Charles systematically bent the merchant cities of the Low Countries to his will, but regardless of this display of force, a spiritual trend was emerging that would soon not only question the rights of the emperor but also rock the power of the Catholic Church itself.

STIRRINGS OF THE REFORMATION

An alliance of church and state had dominated the medieval world: pope and bishops, kings and counts were supposedly the representatives of God on earth, and crushed religious dissent wherever it appeared. Much of their authority depended on the ignorance of the population, who were entirely dependent on their priests for the interpretation of the scriptures, their view of the world carefully controlled.

There were many complex reasons for the **Reformation**, the stirring of religious revolt that stood sixteenth-century Europe on its head, but certainly the **development of typography** was a crucial element. For the first time, printers were able to produce relatively cheap Bibles in quantity, and the religious texts were no longer the exclusive property of the priesthood. A welter of debate spread across much of Western Europe, led initially by theologians who wished to cleanse the Catholic church of its corruptions, superstitions and extravagant ceremony; only later did many of these same thinkers decide to support a breakaway church. Humanists like **Erasmus of Rotterdam** (1465–1536) saw man as the crowning of creation rather than the sinful creature of the Fall; and, most importantly, in 1517 **Martin Luther** produced his 95 theses against indulgences, rejecting among other things Christ's presence in the sacrament of the Eucharist, and denying the Church's monopoly on the interpretation of the Bible. His works and Bible translations were printed in the Low Countries and his ideas gained a following in a group known as the Sacramentarians. They, and other reforming groups branded as **Lutheran** by the Church, were persecuted and escaped the towns to form fugitive communes where the doctrines of another reformer, **John Calvin** (1509–64), became popular. Luther stated that the Church's political power was subservient to that of the state; Calvin emphasized the importance of individual conscience and the need for redemption through the grace of Christ rather than the confessional. The seeds of Protestantism fell on fertile ground among the merchants of the cities of the Low Countries, whose wealth and independence could not easily be accommodated within a rigid caste society. Similarly, their employees, the guildsmen and their apprentices, had a long history of opposing arbitrary authority, and many were soon convinced of the need to reform an autocratic, venal church. In 1555, Charles V abdicated, transferring his German lands to his brother Ferdinand, and his Italian, Spanish and Low Countries territories to his son, the fanatically Catholic **Philip II**. In the short term, the scene was set for a massive confrontation, while the dynastic ramifications of the division of the Habsburg empire were to complicate European affairs for centuries.

THE REVOLT OF THE NETHERLANDS

On his father's abdication, Philip decided to teach his heretical subjects a lesson. He garrisoned the towns of the Low Countries with Spanish mercenaries, imported the Inquisition and passed a series of anti-Protestant edicts. The opposition to these measures was, however, so widespread that he was pushed into a tactical withdrawal, recalling his soldiers and transferring control to his sister Margaret of Parma in 1559. Based in Brussels, the equally resolute Margaret implemented the policies of her brother with gusto. In 1561 she reorganized the church and created fourteen new bishoprics, a move that was construed as a wresting of power from civil authority, and an attempt to destroy the local aristocracy's powers of religious patronage. Protestantism and Protestant sympathies spread to the nobility, who now formed the "League of the Nobility" to counter Habsburg policy. The League petitioned Philip for moderation but were dismissed out of hand by one of Margaret's Walloon advisers, who called them "ces geux" (those beggars), an epithet that was to be enthusiastically adopted by the rebels. In 1565 a harvest failure caused a winter famine among the workers, and in many towns, particularly Antwerp, they ran riot in the churches, sacking them of their wealth and destroying their rich decoration in the **Iconoclastic Fury**.

The ferocity of this outbreak shocked the higher classes into renewed support for Spain, and Margaret regained the allegiance of most nobles – with the principal exception of the country's greatest landowner, Prince William of Orange-Nassau, known as **William the Silent**. Of Germanic descent, he was raised a Catholic but the excesses and rigidity of Philip had caused him to side with the Protestant movement. A firm believer in individual freedom and religious tolerance, William became a symbol of liberty; but after the Fury had revitalized the pro-Spanish party, he prudently slipped away to his estates in Germany.

Philip II saw himself as responsible to God for the salvation of his subjects and therefore obliged to protect them from heresy. In 1567, keen to take advantage of the opportunity provided by the increased support for Margaret, he appointed the **Duke of Alva**, with an army of ten thousand men, to enter the Low Countries and suppress his religious opponents absolutely. Alva's arrival prompted Margaret to withdraw in a huff, and the Low Countries came under military rule. Alva's first act was to set up the **Council of Blood**, which tried and condemned twelve thousand of those who had taken part in the rioting of the year before. Initially the repression worked: in 1568, when William attempted an invasion from Germany, the towns, garrisoned by the Spanish, offered no support. William waited and conceived other means of defeating Alva. In April 1572 a band of privateers entered Brielle on the Maas and captured it from the Spanish. This was one of several commando-style attacks by the so-called Waterguezen or sea-beggars, who were at first obliged to operate from England, although it was soon possible for them to secure bases in the Netherlands, whose citizens had grown to loathe Alva and his Spaniards.

After the success at Brielle, the revolt spread rapidly: by June the rebels controlled the province of Holland and William was able to take command of his troops in Delft. Alva and his son Frederick fought back, taking Gelder, Overijssel and the towns of Zutphen and Naarden, and in June 1573 Haarlem, massacring the Calvinist ministers and most of the defenders. But the Protestants retaliated: utilizing their superior naval power they cut the dykes and the Spanish forces, unpaid and threatened with destruction, were forced to withdraw. Frustrated, Philip replaced Alva with Luis de Resquesens, who initially had some success in the south, where the Catholic majority were more willing to compromise with Spanish rule than their northern neighbours.

William's triumphant relief of Leiden in 1574 increased the confidence of the rebel forces, and when de Resquesens died in 1576, his unpaid garrison in Antwerp mutinied and attacked the town, slaughtering some eight thousand of its people in what was known as the **Spanish Fury**. Though Spain still held several towns, the massacre alienated the south and pushed its peoples into the arms of William, whose troops now controlled most of the Low Countries. Momentarily, it seemed possible for the whole region to unite behind William, and the various provinces signed the **Pacification of Ghent** in 1576, an agreement that guaranteed freedom of religious belief. However, differences between Protestant north and Catholic south proved irreconcilable, with many Walloons and Flemings suspicious of both William's ambitions and his Calvinist cronies. Consequently, when another army arrived from Spain, under the command of Alexander Farnese, Duke of Parma, the south was reoccupied without much difficulty, beginning a separation that would lead, after many changes, to the creation of three modern countries.

In 1579 seven provinces (Holland, Zeeland, Utrecht, Groningen, Friesland, Overijssel and Gelderland) signed the **Union of Utrecht**, an alliance against Spain that was to be the first unification of the Netherlands as an identifiable country – the **United Provinces**. The agreement stipulated freedom of belief in the provinces, an important step since the struggle against Spain wasn't simply a religious one: many Catholics disliked the Spanish occupation and William did not wish to alienate this possible source of support. This liberalism did not, however, extend to freedom of worship, although a blind eye was turned to the celebration of Mass if it was done privately and inconspicuously. The assembly of these United Provinces was known as the **States General**, and met at The Hague; it had no domestic legislative authority, and could only carry out foreign policy by unanimous decision, a formula designed to make potential waverers feel more secure. The role of **Stadholder** was the most

important in each province, roughly equivalent to that of governor, though the same person could occupy this position in any number of provinces.

THE SPANISH NETHERLANDS (1579–1713)

In 1579, representatives of the southern provinces of Hainaut, Artois and Douai signed the **Union of Arras**, a Catholic-led agreement that declared loyalty to Philip II and counterbalanced the Union of Utrecht in the north. Subsequently, Alexander Farnese used this area as a base to reconquer the cities of Flanders, recapturing Antwerp after a long and bitter siege in 1585. As Farnese edged north, so the Netherlanders became increasingly nervous, especially without the steadying influence of William the Silent, who had been murdered by a French Catholic, one Balthazar Gerard, in Delft in 1584. In desperation the United Provinces turned first to Henry III of France, who refused help even with the offer of sovereignty, and then to Elizabeth I of England, who offered the Earl of Leicester as governor general. The offer was accepted but Leicester completely mishandled the situation militarily, alienating the Dutch into the bargain. In the event, control of the United Provinces passed into the capable hands of Johan van Oldenbarneveldt, who finally stalled the Habsburg advance, thereby deciding the shape of the **Spanish Netherlands**, broadly equivalent to today's Belgium and Luxembourg.

Although the Spanish were prepared to permit some degree of economic and political autonomy, exercising control through a Habsburg governor in Brussels, they were determined to eradicate Protestantism, and in the last years of the sixteenth century thousands of weavers, apprentices and skilled workers – the bedrock of Calvinism – were obliged to leave, moving north to fuel the economic boom in the province of Holland. It took a while for this migration to take effect, and for several years the Spanish Netherlands had all the trappings – if not, perhaps, the substance – of success, though a complete economic catastrophe was warded off by the fostering of new enterprises to meet the luxury tastes of the Habsburg elite – silk weaving, diamond processing and lacemaking in particular. This commercial restructuring underpinned a brief flourishing of artistic life centred on **Rubens** and his circle of friends, including Anthony Van Dyck and Jacob Jordaens, in Antwerp during the first decades of the seventeenth century.

Meanwhile, months before his death in 1598, Philip II had granted control of the Spanish Netherlands to his daughter and her husband, appointing them the **Archdukes Isabella and Albert**. Failing to learn from experience, the ducal couple continued to prosecute the war against the Protestant north, but with so little success that they were obliged to make peace – the **Twelve-Year Truce** – in 1609. When the truce ended in 1621, Albert was dead and Isabella's independence was curtailed by the new Spanish king Philip IV, who resumed the campaign with vigour, this time as part of a general and even more devastating conflict, the **Thirty Years' War** (1618–48), a largely religious-based conflict between Catholic and Protestant countries that involved most of Western Europe. The Spanish were initially successful, but they were weakened by war with France and by Dutch seapower. From 1625, the Spaniards suffered a series of defeats on land and sea that forced them out of what is today the southern part of the Netherlands, and in 1648 they were compelled to accept the humiliating terms of the **Peace of Westphalia**. This was a general treaty that ended the Thirty Years' War, and its terms recognized the independence of the United Provinces and closed the Scheldt estuary, an action designed to destroy the trade and prosperity of Antwerp. By these means, the commercial pre-eminence of Amsterdam was assured, and the city's Golden Age began, its immense wealth accumulating from its role as an emporium for products from Europe and Asia and from the profits of its enormous merchant fleet. The city's Calvinist bourgeoisie gently indulged themselves in fine canal houses; the arts flourished; religious tolerance stretched even to the traditional scapegoats, the Jews; and migrating Protestants escaping persecution in the Catholic south were welcomed with open arms.

The only major fly in the United Provinces' ointment was the conflict between central authority and provincial autonomy. Although the **House of Orange** had established something like royal credentials, many of Holland's leading citizens were reluctant to accept its right to power. The republicans held the upper hand for most of the seventeenth century until an attack on the country by Louis XIV in 1672 forced the States General to seek the help of **William of Orange**, whose success in dealing with the crisis resulted in his appointment to the office of Stadholder (which had actually been abolished in 1650). It was this same William who was to become the king of England (and his wife Mary the queen) in 1689.

In stark contrast, the Spanish Netherlands paid dearly for its adherence to the Habsburg cause. In the course of the war, it had teetered on the edge of chaos – highwaymen infested the roads, trade had almost disappeared, the population had been halved in Brabant, and acres of fertile farmland lay uncultivated – but the peace was perhaps as bad. Denied access to the sea, Antwerp was ruined and simply withered away, while the southern provinces as a whole spiralled into an economic decline that pauperized its population. Yet the ruling families seemed proud to appear to the world as the defenders and martyrs of the Catholic faith; those who disagreed left.

Politically dependent on a decaying Spain, economically ruined and deprived of most of its more independent-minded citizens, the country turned in on itself, sustained by the fanatical Catholicism of the **Counter-Reformation**. Religious worship became strict and magnificent, medieval carnivals were transformed into exercises in piety, and penitential flagellation became popular, all of which was encouraged by the Jesuits. Indeed, the number of **Jesuits** was extraordinary. The whole of France had only 2000, but the Spanish Netherlands 1600, and it was here they wrote their most important works, exercised their greatest influence and owned vast tracts of land. Supported by draconian laws that barred known Protestants from public appointments, declared their marriages illegal and forbade them municipal assistance, the Catholic priests overwhelmed the religious opposition and in half a century transformed this part of the Low Countries into an introverted world shaped by a mystical faith, where Christians were redeemed by the ecstasy of suffering.

The visible signs of the change were all around, from extravagant Baroque churches to crosses, calvaries and shrines scattered across the countryside. Literature disappeared, the sciences vegetated and religious orders multiplied, all at the time the Dutch were building the greatest fleet in the world. In painting, artists – such as Rubens – were used to confirm the ecclesiastical orthodoxies, their canvases full of muscular saints and angels, reflecting a religious faith of mystery and hierarchy; others, such as David Teniers and the later Bruegels, retreated into minutely observed realism.

The Peace of Westphalia freed the king of France from fear of Germany, and the political and military history of the Spanish Netherlands after 1648 was dominated by the efforts of **Louis XIV** to add the country to his territories. Fearful of an over-powerful France, the United Provinces, England and Sweden, among others, determinedly resisted French designs and, to preserve the balance of power, fought a long series of campaigns beginning with the **War of Devolution** in 1667 and ending in the **War of the Spanish Succession**. The latter was sparked by the death in 1700 of Charles II, the last of the Spanish Habsburgs, who had willed his territories to the grandson of Louis XIV of France. The anti-French countries refused to accept the settlement and there ensued a haphazard series of campaigns that dragged on for eleven years, only distinguished by the spectacular victories of the Duke of Marlborough – Blenheim, Ramillies, Malplaquet. At one time or another, many of the region's major cities were besieged and badly damaged, and only with the **Treaty of Utrecht** in 1713 did the French abandon their attempt to conquer the Spanish Netherlands, which now passed under the control of the Austrian Habsburgs in the figure of the emperor Charles VI.

THE AUSTRIAN NETHERLANDS (1713–1794)

The transfer of the country from Spanish to Austrian control made little appreciable difference: there were more wars and more invasions and a remote central authority continued to operate through Brussels. In particular, the **War of the Austrian Succession**, fought over the right of Maria Theresa to assume the Austrian Habsburg throne, prompted the French to invade and occupy the country in 1744, though the country was returned to imperial control in 1748 by the **Treaty of Aix-la-Chapelle**. These dynastic shenanigans had little effect on the country's agriculture, which survived the various campaigns and actually became more productive,

leading to a marked increase in the rural population especially after the introduction of potato cultivation. But intellectually the country remained vitrified and stagnant – only three percent of the population were literate, workers were forbidden to change towns or jobs without obtaining permission from the municipal authorities, and skills and crafts were tied to particular families.

This sorry state of affairs began to change in the middle of the eighteenth century as the Austrian oligarchy came under the influence of the Enlightenment, that belief in reason and progress – as against authority and tradition – that had first been preached by French philosophers. In 1753, the arrival of a new and progressive governor, the Count of Cobenzl, signified a transformation of Habsburg policy. Determined to shake the country from its torpor, he initiated an ambitious programme of public works, including extensive road and canal construction, organized financial incentives to industry, and took a firm line with his clerical opponents, who tried to encourage the population to thwart him in his aims.

In 1780, emperor **Joseph II** came to the throne, determined to organize further reforms himself. Authoritarian and impulsive, his efforts to "root out silly old prejudices", as he put it, resulted in a deluge of edicts and decrees that managed to offend most of the country's major groups – from peasants to nobility, bureaucrats and clerics to traders. Pandemonium ensued, and opposition crystallized around the Flemish lawyer François Vonck, whose liberal-minded **Vonckists**, with their demands for a radical, republican constitution, were countered by the conservative **Statists**, whose assorted reactionaries, including priests and landowners, were led by Henri van der Noot.

In 1789, the Habsburgs dispatched an army to restore order, but the Vonckists and Statists, inspired by the outbreak of revolution across the border in France, combined to defeat the Austrians outside Turnhout in what became known as the **Brabant Revolution**. In January 1790, the rebels announced the formation of the United States of Belgium, but the uneasy alliance between Vonck and Noot soon broke down and the latter, with the assistance of the priests, raised the peasantry to arms and encouraged them to attack the Vonckists, who were killed in their hundreds. The Statists now had the upper hand, but the country remained in turmoil and when emperor Joseph died in 1790, his successor, Leopold, was quick to withdraw many of the reforming acts and send in his troops to restore imperial authority.

FRENCH OCCUPATION & THE NETHERLANDS (1794–1830)

The new and repressive Habsburg regime was short-lived. French Republican armies brushed the imperial forces aside in 1794, and the Austrian Netherlands were annexed the following year, an annexation that was to last until 1814. The **French** imposed radical reforms: the Catholic Church was stripped of much of its worldly wealth, feudal privileges were abolished, a consistent legal system was formulated and, most unpopular of all, conscription was introduced, provoking a (brutally repressed) Peasants' Revolt in 1798. Napoleon, in control from 1799, rebuilt the docks of Antwerp and forced the Netherlanders, whose country the French had also occupied in 1795, to accept the re-opening of the Scheldt. Unrestricted access to French markets boosted the local economy, kick-starting the mechanization of the textile industry in Ghent and Verviers and encouraging the growth of the coal and metal industries in Hainaut, but, with the exception of a radical minority, the French occupation remained unpopular.

The Republican regime was generally disliked in the Netherlands too. The French had begun by dissolving the United Provinces, setting up the "Batavian Republic" in its stead. In this, they were aided and abetted by a group of local sympathizers, pro-French merchants who called themselves "Patriots" in opposition to their bitter rivals, the "Orangists" (after the House of Orange) – factional squabbling had dogged the country throughout the second half of the eighteenth century. The Netherlanders were, however, unenthusiastic about helping the French in their war against England and paid the price in 1806 when Napoleon appointed his brother Louis as their king. In the event, this didn't satisfy Bonaparte either and just four years later he incorporated the country into the French Empire.

Direct imperial rule didn't last long. In 1812, Napoleon's disastrous retreat from Moscow brought the Orangists out of the woodwork and French control had evaporated long before

Napoleon's final defeat just outside Brussels at the Battle of Waterloo in June 1815. At the **Congress of Vienna**, called to settle Europe at the end of the Napoleonic Wars, the main concern of the great powers was to create a buffer state against any possible future plans the French might have to expand to the north. With scant regard to the feelings of those affected, they therefore decided to establish the **Kingdom of the Netherlands**, which incorporated both the old United Provinces and the Spanish (Austrian) Netherlands, and on the throne they placed Frederick William of Orange, appointed **King William I**. The great powers also decided to give Frederick William's German estates to Prussia and in return presented him with the newly independent **Grand Duchy of Luxembourg**. This was a somewhat confused arrangement, as the duchy, which had previously been part of both the Spanish and Austrian Netherlands, was detached from the rest of the Low Countries constitutionally and pushed into the German Confederation at the same time as it shared the same king with the old United Provinces and Austrian Netherlands.

Given the imperious way the new Kingdom of the Netherlands had been established, it required considerable royal tact and resourcefulness to make things work. William lacked the former and indeed some of his measures seemed designed to inflame his French-speaking subjects, the Walloons. He made Dutch the official language of the country; in a move against the Catholics, he tried to secularize all Church-controlled schools; and the two former countries each had the same number of representatives at the States General despite the fact that the population of the old United Provinces was half that of its neighbour. There were competing economic interests too. The north was reliant on commerce and sought free trade without international tariffs; the industrialized south wanted the opposite as it sought to increase its productivity in relation to its international competitors. William's refusal to impose tariffs along with his measures against Catholic schools united his opponents in the south, where both industrialists and clerics now clamoured for change.

The **revolution** against William began in the Brussels opera house on August 25, 1830, when the singing of a duet, *Amour Sacré de la*

BELGIUM'S KINGS

Leopold I (1830–1865). Foisted on Belgium by the great powers, Leopold, the first king of the Belgians, was imported from Germany, where he was the prince of Saxe-Coburg – and the uncle of Queen Victoria. Despite lacking a popular mandate, Leopold made a fairly good fist of things, keeping the country neutral as the great powers had ordained.

Leopold II (1865–1909). Energetic and forceful, Leopold II encouraged the urbanization of his country and promoted its importance as a major industrial power. He was also the man responsible for landing Brussels with such pompous monuments as the Palais de Justice and for the imposition of a particularly barbaric colonial regime on the peoples of the Belgian Congo (now the Republic of Congo).

Albert I (1909–1934). Easily the most popular of the dynasty, Albert's bravery in World War I, when the Germans occupied almost all of the country, made the king a national hero whose untimely death, in a climbing accident, traumatized the nation.

Leopold III (1934–1951). In contrast to his predecessor, Leopold III had the dubious honour of becoming one of Europe's least popular monarchs. His first wife died in a suspicious car crash; he nearly lost his kingdom by remarrying (anathema in a Catholic country); and he was badly compro-

mised during the German occupation of World War II, when he remained in the country rather than face exile, fuelling rumours that he was a Nazi collaborator – though his supporters maintained that he prevented thousands of Belgians from being deported. After several years of heated postwar debate, the issue of Leopold's return from exile was put to a referendum in 1950. Just over half the population voted in Leopold's favour, but there was a clear French/Flemish divide, with opposition to the king concentrated in Wallonia. Fortunately for Belgium, Leopold abdicated in 1951 in favour of his son,

Baudouin I (1951–1993). A softly spoken family man, Baudouin did much to restore the popularity of the monarchy, not least because he was generally thought to be even-handed in his treatment of the French- and Flemish-speaking communities. He also hit the headlines in April 1990 by standing down for a day so that an abortion bill (which he as a Catholic had refused to sign) could be passed.

Albert II (1993–). The present king will have his work cut out if he wants to become the national figurehead that his father was. The Belgian royal family is one of the few unifying forces in a country divided by French-Flemish antagonisms; one slip off the linguistic tightrope could have untold consequences.

Patrie, hit a nationalist nerve and the audience poured out onto the streets to raise the flag of Brabant in defiance of the king. At first the revolutionaries only demanded a scaling down of royal power and a separate "Belgian" administration, but negotiations soon broke down and in late September the **Kingdom of Belgium** was proclaimed. William prepared for war, but the liberal governments of Great Britain and France intervened to impose the peace, and in January of the following year, at the **Conference of London,** the great powers recognized Belgium's independence, with the caveat that the country be classified a "neutral" state, that is, one outside any other's sphere of influence. To bolster this new nation, they ceded to it the western segments of the Grand Duchy of Luxembourg and dug out the uncle of the future Queen Victoria, Prince Leopold of Saxe-Coburg, to present with the crown. William retained his crown and even received the remainder of Luxembourg as his

personal possession, but he still hated the settlement and there was a further bout of sabre-rattling before he finally caved in and accepted the new arrangements in 1839 .

INDEPENDENT BELGIUM (1830–1914)

Shrewd and capable, **Leopold I** (1830–65) was careful to maintain his country's neutrality and encouraged an industrial boom that saw coal mines developed, iron-making factories established and the rapid expansion of the railway system. One casualty, however, was the traditional linen-making industry of rural Flanders. The cottagers who spun and wove the linen could not compete with the mechanized mills, and their pauperization was compounded by the poor grain harvests and potato blight of 1844–46. But their sufferings were of only limited concern to the country's political representatives, who were elected on a strictly limited franchise which ensured the domination of the middle classes. The latter divided into two loose groups, the one attempting to undermine Catholic influence and control over such areas as education, the other profoundly conservative in its desire to maintain the status quo. Progressive elements within the bourgeoisie coalesced in the **Liberal party**, which was free trade and urban in outlook; wheras their opponents, the **Catholic party**, promised to protect Belgian agriculture with tariffs and, retreating from the industrialized and radicalized cities, began to identify with the plight of rural Dutch-speaking Belgians – as against the French-speaking ruling and managerial classes.

Leopold II's (1865–1909) long reign was dominated by similar themes, and saw the emergence of Belgium as a major industrial power. However, the 1860s and 1870s also witnessed the first significant stirrings of a type of **Flemish nationalism** which felt little enthusiasm for the unitary status of Belgium, divided as it was between a French-speaking majority in the south of the country – the Walloons – and the minority Dutch-speakers of Flanders, Antwerp and Limburg in the north. There was also industrial unrest towards the end of the century, the end results being a body of legislation improving and controlling working conditions and, in 1893, the extension of the franchise to all men over the age of 25. The Catholic party also ensured that, under the Equality Law of 1898, Dutch was ratified as an official language, equal in status to French. Another matter of concern was the Belgian Congo, which Leopold had developed as his personal fiefdom. In the early 1900s, the level of exploitation, slavery and atrocity became too great to ignore and the Belgian state was ultimately shamed into taking over its administration in 1908.

BELGIUM IN THE TWENTIETH CENTURY

King Leopold died in 1909, to be succeeded by his nephew **Albert I** (1909–34), whose enormous popularity was founded on his actions during **World War I**. Indifferent to Belgium's proclaimed neutrality, the German invasion of 1914 extended over almost all of the country, the exception being a narrow strip of territory around De Panne, where Albert was forced to move to continue his administration. For four years, the Belgian army manned the northern part of the Allied line, successfully keeping the

Germans at bay from their trenches running from the outskirts of Ieper along the Yserkanaal and the River Yser through Diksmuide to Nieuwpoort and the North Sea. The Belgians' spirited resistance, the bravery of their king, and the violation of the country's neutrality attracted worldwide sympathy and admiration, though this was to have few tangible results after the war. From the Belgian sector, the Allied trenches, which cut south all the way to Switzerland, bulged in the vicinity of Ieper and it was here that the principal engagements on Belgian soil took place, with the British and the Germans engaged in a series of futile, bloody battles which came to epitomize the pointlessness of the war and the tactical stupidity of its generals.

After the war, under the terms of the **Treaty of Versailles**, Belgium was granted extensive reparations from Germany as well as some German territory – the slice of land around Eupen and Malmédy and, in Africa, Rwanda and Burundi. The treaty also cancelled the country's neutrality and by 1920 Belgium had signed a military agreement with France, though this was cancelled and neutrality restored in 1936. The Belgian government also extended the franchise to all men over the age of 21, a measure which, in the event, ended several decades of political control by the Catholic party, who were now only able to keep power in coalition with the Liberals – usually with the Socialists, the third major party, forming the backbone of the opposition. The political lines were, however, increasingly fudged as the Catholic party moved towards the left, becoming a Christian Democrat movement that was keen to co-operate with the Socialists on such matters as social legislation. The political parties may have been partly reconciled, but the economy staggered from crisis to crisis even before the effects of the Great Depression hit Belgium in 1929. The political class also failed to placate those Flemings who felt discriminated against. There had been a widespread feeling among the Flemish soldiers of World War I that they had borne the brunt of the war and now an increasing number of Flemings came to believe the Belgian government to be overly Walloon in its sympathies – and not without justification. Only reluctantly did the government give in to pressure and make Flanders and Wallonia legally unilingual regions in 1930, and even then the linguistic boundary was left unspecified in the hope that French-speakers would come to dominate central Belgium. Furthermore, these communal tensions were fuelled by changing expectations. The Flemings had accepted the domination of the French-speakers without much protest for several centuries, but as their region became more prosperous and as their numbers increased in relation to the Walloons, so they grew in self-confidence, becoming increasingly unhappy with their social and political subordination. Inevitably, some of this discontent was sucked into **Fascist** movements, which drew some ten percent of the vote in both the Walloon and Flemish communities, though for very different reasons: the former for its appeal to a nationalist bourgeoisie, the latter for its assertion of "racial" pride among an oppressed group.

In May 1940, the **Germans** launched their sudden, surprise attack on the Netherlands, Belgium and Luxembourg. This time there was no heroic resistance by the Belgian king, now Leopold III (1934–51), who ignored the advice of his government and surrendered both unconditionally and in such haste that the British and French armies were, as their Commander-in-Chief put it "suddenly faced with an open gap of twenty miles between Ypres and the sea through which enemy forces might reach the beaches". It is true that the Belgian army had been badly mauled and that a German victory seemed inevitable, but the manner of the surrender infuriated many Belgians, as did the king's refusal to form a government in exile. It took time for the Belgians to adjust to the new situation, but by 1941 a resistance movement was organizing acts of sabotage against the occupying forces. The **liberation** came in the autumn of 1944, and, with the exception of the Battle of the Ardennes (aka the Battle of the Bulge) and extensive damage to the port of Antwerp by Hitler's V1 and V2 rockets, it went relatively smoothly.

After the liberation, the Belgians set about the task of economic reconstruction, helped by aid from the United States, but hindered by a divisive controversy over the **wartime activities of King Leopold**. Many felt his surrender to the Germans was cowardly and his subsequent willingness to work with them treacherous; others pointed out his efforts to increase the country's food rations and his negotiations to secure the release of Belgian prisoners. Inevitably, the complex shadings of collaboration and forced co-operation were hard to disentangle, and the debate continued until 1950 when a referendum narrowly recommended his return from exile as king. Leopold's return was, however, marked by rioting across Wallonia, where the king's opponents were concentrated, and Leopold abdicated in favour of his son, **Baudouin** (1951–1993).

The development of the postwar Belgian economy follows the pattern of most of Western Europe – reconstruction in the 1950s; boom in the 1960s; recession in the 1970s; and retrenchment in the 1980s and 1990s. Significant events have included the belated extension of the franchise to women in 1948; an ugly, disorganized and hasty evacuation of the Belgian Congo in 1960 and of Rwanda and Burundi in 1962; the transformation of Brussels from one of the more insignificant European capitals into the home of the EU and NATO; acute labour unrest in the Limburg coalfield in the early 1980s, following plans to close most of the remaining pits; and the legalization of abortion in 1990. But, above all, the postwar period has been dominated by the increasing **tension between the Walloon and Flemish communities**. Every national institution is now dogged by the prerequisites of bilingualism – speeches in parliament have to be delivered in both languages – and in Brussels, the country's one and only bilingual region, every instance of the written word, from road signs to the yellow pages, has to be bilingual as well. Politically, the parties reflect three broad shades of opinion – conservative, liberal and socialist – but they are also divided into Flemish- and French-speaking sections, further complicating the structure of national administrations from an already complex system of proportional representation. In 1962 the Linguistic Divide (or Language Frontier) was formally delineated, and in 1980 central government was partially regionalized, with major areas of administration transferred to regional councils. In many ways, therefore, Belgium is a divided society, the two linguistic groups viewing each other with suspicion punctuated by hostility – a situation which began to take on the dimensions of a crisis in the early 1990s as it became increasingly impossible to govern and at the same time appease the country's various factions.

THE BELGIAN LANGUAGE DIVIDE

Belgium is sandwiched between France and Germany, and the tensions between the two nations have long been a threat to the prosperity and welfare of the Belgian people. What's more, the Belgians are themselves divided between two main groups, the **Walloons**, French-speakers who account for around forty percent of the population, and the **Flemings**, Dutch- or Flemish-speakers, who form about sixty percent, out of a total population of some ten million. There are even, in the far east of the country, a few pockets of German-speakers around the towns of Eupen and Malmédy, while more recent immigrant groups, speaking a variety of other first languages, are clustered in the cities.

The Flemish-French **language divide** has troubled the country for decades, its historical significance rooted in deep class and economic divisions. Prosperity has shifted back and forth between the two communities over the centuries: in medieval times Flanders grew rich on its textile trade; later Wallonia developed mining and steel industries. However, Francophones have always dominated the aristocracy, and, since the Middle Ages, the middle classes as well. The setting-up of the Belgian state in 1830 crystallized this antagonism, with the final arrangements favouring the French-speakers. French became the official language, Flemish was banned in schools (the Belgian Civil Code was only translated into Flemish in 1961), and the industries of Wallonia were regarded as pre-eminent. Nowadays, however, Flanders is the industrial powerhouse of Belgium, and the heavy industries of Wallonia are in decline, an economic change of fortunes which has made the Flemish-speakers more assertive in their demands for linguistic and cultural parity. However, Flemish "parity" is often perceived as "domination" by Walloons.

The line between the two cultures – officially called the "language divide" and effectively cutting the country in half, west to east – was drawn in 1962, but this did little to ease underlying tensions and, in response to increasing acrimony between the two communities, the constitution was redrawn (in 1980) on a federal basis, with three separate **communities** – the Flemish North, the Walloon South and the German-speaking east – responsible for their own cultural and social affairs and education. At the same time, Belgium was simultaneously divided into three **regions** — the Flemish North, the Walloon South and Brussels (which is officially bilingual, although its population is eighty percent French-

speaking), with each regional authority dealing with matters like economic development, the environment and employment.

Although the niceties of this partition have calmed troubled waters, in bilingual Brussels and at national government level the division between Flemish and French speakers still influences many aspects of working and social life. Schools, political parties, literature and culture are all segregated along linguistic lines, and mutual stereotypes are deeply ingrained, leading to a set of complex, face-saving rules and regulations which can verge on the absurd. Governmental press conferences, for example, must have questions and answers repeated in both languages, one after the other. Across Belgium as a whole, bitterness about the economy, unemployment and the government smoulders within (or seeks an outlet through) the framework of this linguistic division, and individual neighbourhoods can be paralysed by language disputes. The communities of Fourons/Voeren, for instance, a largely French-speaking collection of villages in Flemish Limburg, almost brought down the government in the mid-Eighties when the Francophone mayor, Jose Happart, refused to take the Flemish language exam required of all Limburg officials. Barred from office, he stood again and was re-elected, prompting the prime minister at the time, Wilfred Martens, to offer his own resignation. The Fourons affair was symptomatic of the obstinacy that besets the country to this day. Jose Happart could probably pass the Flemish exam easily – indeed rumour has it that he is fluent in the language – but he simply chose not to submit, fuelling the confict and giving succour to the political extremists on both sides – namely the Vlaams Blok on the Flemish side, and, for the French-speakers, the Front des Francophones (FDF).

All this said, it would be wrong to assume that Belgium's language differences have gone beyond the level of personal animosity and institutionalized mutual suspicion. Belgian language extremists have been imprisoned over the years, but very few, if any, have died in the fight for supremacy. Indeed, some might see a bilingual nation as a positive thing in a Europe where trading – and national – barriers are being increasingly broken down. Suggesting this to a Belgian, however, is normally useless, but there again the casual visitor will rarely get a sniff of these tensions. It's probably better to speak English rather than Flemish or French in the "wrong" part of Belgium, but if you make a mistake, the worst you'll get is a look of glazed indifference.

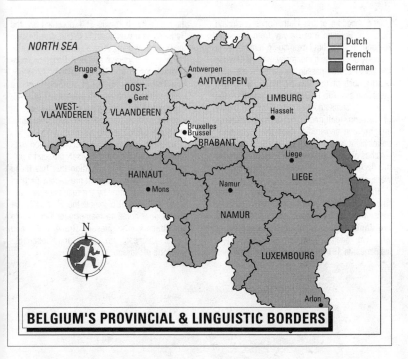

BELGIUM'S PROVINCIAL & LINGUISTIC BORDERS

In essence, the Walloons fear that the wealthier and more numerous Flemings will come to dominate the state, and indeed they may make this a self-fulfilling prophecy with their reluctance to learn Flemish – bilingualism being a prerequisite for any national job. The Flemings, on the other hand, want political and cultural recognition, and many bristle at what they perceive as Wallonian cultural and linguistic arrogance. Such nebulous but pervasive fears are hard to combat, and it's difficult to see what will hold the country together. On the other hand, it seems that the majority of Belgians want to remain as one nation, and, up until now, coalitions of right- and left-wing politicians have always managed, with some energetic horse-trading, to keep the national government going. In this regard, the example of Antwerp is also instructive: in local elections, the right-wing, nationalist Fleming Vlaams Blok poll about 25 percent of the vote, making them the largest municipal party, but they have been excluded from power by all sorts of unlikely alliances – with Greens and Christian Democrats, for instance, working together to shut them out.

Finally, although it's doubtful if it will have much long-term effect on the country's political structures, the whole of Belgium has been shocked and disturbed by the activities of a **child sex ring** led by Marc Dutroux. In August 1996, the police discovered two of his dead victims and other grisly discoveries followed. This was dreadful enough, but in the ensuing months the police investigation verged on farce – so much so that many Belgians became convinced that the whole investigation was a cover-up designed to protect the police and maybe some big-shot politicians too. Some of the heat has gone out of the issue now, but it's left a bitter after-taste.

THE GRAND DUCHY OF LUXEMBOURG FROM 1830

At the Congress of Vienna in 1815, Luxembourg had been designated a **Grand Duchy** by the great powers and given (as personal property) to King William I of Orange-Nassau, the ruler of the

United Kingdom of the Netherlands (including Belgium). Belgium broke away from William's kingdom in 1830, but Luxembourg remained the property of the Dutch monarchy until 1890 when the ducal crown passed to another (independent) branch of the Nassau family, who have ruled ever since. In 1867, the great powers made further decisions about Luxembourg: the **Treaty of London** reaffirmed the duchy's territorial integrity and declared it neutral in perpetuity, thereby – it was hoped – protecting it from the clutches of both Germany and France. Following this declaration, Luxembourg City's fortifications were largely destroyed.

The second half of the nineteenth century saw Luxembourg's poor, agricultural economy transformed by the discovery and mining of **iron ore deposits**, which led to the foundation of what was soon one of Europe's largest steel industries. In 1914, the Grand Duchy confirmed its neutrality, but was still occupied by the Germans as it was again in World War II when the Luxembourgers put up a stubborn resistance, leading to many brave acts of defiance and considerable loss of life. The Battle of the Ardennes (also know as the "Battle of the Bulge") was a major disaster and, as the war ended in 1945, one third of the country's farmland lay uncultivated, the public transportation system in ruins, and some 60,000 people homeless.

In the **postwar years**, reconstruction was rapid and the government wisely pursued a policy of industrial diversification that has made the country one of the most prosperous parts of Europe. Disappointed by the results of neutrality, Luxembourg also joined the EC and NATO and is now home to many major Community departments. The present Grand Duke and Grand Duchess are Jean and Josephine Charlotte of Nassau.

AN INTRODUCTION TO BELGIAN ART

The following outline is the very briefest of introductions to a subject that has rightly filled volumes and is designed to serve only as a quick reference on your way round the major galleries. Inevitably, it covers artists that lived and worked in both Holland and Belgium as these two countries have both been, for most of their history, bound together as the so-called Low Countries. For more in-depth and academic studies, see the recommendations in the "Books" listings on p.380. For a few ideas as to where to find the paintings themselves, turn to the "hit list" on p.371.

THE EARLY FLEMISH MASTERS

Throughout the medieval period, Flanders was one of the most artistically productive parts of Europe with each of the prosperous cloth towns – especially Bruges (see p.148) and Ghent (see p.168) – trying to out-do its rivals with the quality of its religious art. Today the works of these early Flemish painters, known as the **Flemish Primitives**, are highly prized and an excellent sample is displayed in both these towns as well as in Brussels. **Jan van Eyck** (1385–1441) is generally regarded as the first of the Flemish Primitives, and has even been credited with the invention of oil painting itself – though it seems more likely that he simply perfected a new technique by thinning his paint with the recently discovered turpentine, thus making it more flexible. His fame partially stems from the fact that he was one of the first artists to sign his work – an indication of how highly his talent was regarded by his contemporaries. Van Eyck's most celebrated work is the *Adoration of the Mystic Lamb*, a stunningly beautiful altarpiece displayed in St Baafskathedraal in Ghent (see p.174). The painting was revolutionary in its realism, for the first time using elements of native landscape in depicting Biblical themes, and was underpinned by a complex symbolism which has generated analysis and discussion ever since. Van Eyck's style and technique were to influence several generations of Low Countries artists.

Firmly in the Eyckian tradition were the **Master of Flemalle** (1387–1444) and **Rogier van der Weyden** (1400–64). The Flemalle master is a shadowy figure: some believe he was the teacher of van der Weyden, others that the two artists were in fact the same person. There are differences between the two, however. The Flemalle master's paintings are close to van Eyck's, whereas van der Weyden shows a greater degree of emotional and religious intensity. Van der Weyden influenced such painters as **Dieric Bouts** (1415–75), who was born in Haarlem but was active in Leuven (see p.230) and is recognizable by his stiff, rather elongated figures and horrific subject matter, all set against carefully drawn landscapes. **Petrus Christus** (d.1472), a contemporary of Bouts, was also influenced by van der Weyden and van Eyck, whose pupil he may have been. His portraits have a directness and simple clarity, but with the exception of a *Lamentation* in Brussels' Musée d'Art Ancien, most of his masterpieces are now on display in foreign galleries. **Hugo van der Goes** (d.1482) was the next Ghent master after van Eyck, most famous for the Portinari Altarpiece in Florence's Uffizi. After a short painting career, he died insane, and his late works have strong hints of his impending madness in their subversive use of space and implicit acceptance of the viewer's presence. Few doubt that **Hans Memling** (1440–94) was a pupil of van der Weyden. Active in Bruges throughout his life, he is best remembered for the pastoral charm of his landscapes and the quality of his portraiture, much of which survives on the rescued side panels of triptychs. The museum named after him in Bruges (see p.161) has an excellent survey of his work and the Musée d'Art Ancien holds several of his paintings too. **Gerard David** (1460–1523) moved to Bruges in 1484, and was the last of the great painters to work in that city, before it was overtaken in prosperity by Antwerp – which itself became the focus of a more Italianate school of art in the sixteenth century.

Hieronymus Bosch (1450–1516) lived for most of his life in Holland, though his style is linked to that of the Flanders painters (see below). His frequently reprinted religious allegories are filled with macabre visions of tortured people and grotesque beasts, and appear at first faintly unhinged, though it's now thought that these are visual representations of contemporary sayings, idioms and parables. While their interpretation is far from resolved, Bosch's paintings draw strongly on subconscious fears and archetypes, giving them a lasting, haunting fascination.

THE SIXTEENTH CENTURY

At the end of the fifteenth century, the Flemish cloth towns were in decline and the leading artists of the day were drawn instead to the booming port of Antwerp. The artists who worked here soon began to integrate the finely observed detail that characterized the Flemish tradition with the style of the Italian painters of the Renaissance. **Quentin Matsys** (1464–1530) introduced florid classical architectural details and intricate landscapes to his works, influenced perhaps by the work of Leonardo da Vinci. As well as religious works, he painted portraits and genre scenes, all of which have recognizably Italian facets, and paved the way for the Dutch genre painters of later years. **Jan Gossart** (1478–1532) made the pilgrimage to Italy, and his dynamic works are packed with detail, especially finely drawn classical architectural backdrops. He was the first Low Countries artist to introduce the subjects of classical mythology into his works, part of a steady trend through the period towards secular subject matter, which can also be seen in the work of **Joachim Patinir** (d.1524), who painted small landscapes of fantastic scenery.

The latter part of the sixteenth century was dominated by the work of **Pieter Bruegel the**

Elder (c.1525–69), whose gruesome allegories and innovative interpretations of religious subjects are firmly placed in Low Countries settings. Pieter also painted finely observed peasant scenes, though he himself was well connected in court circles in Antwerp and, later, Brussels. **Pieter Aertsen** (1508–75) also worked in the peasant genre, adding aspects of the still life: his paintings often show a detailed kitchen scene in the foreground, with a religious episode going on behind. Bruegel's two sons, **Pieter Bruegel the Younger** and **Jan Bruegel**, were lesser painters: the former produced fairly insipid copies of his father's work, while Jan developed a style of his own – delicately rendered flower paintings and genre pieces that earned him the nickname "Velvet". Towards the latter half of the sixteenth century the stylized Italianate portrait became the fashion, its chief exponent being **Frans Pourbus**.

RUBENS AND HIS FOLLOWERS

Belgian painting of the seventeenth century is dominated by **Pieter Paul Rubens** (1577–1640), who was the most influential Low Countries artist of the early seventeenth century and the most important exponent of Baroque painting in northern Europe. Born in Siegen, Westphalia, he returned with his parents to their native Antwerp when Rubens was a child. He entered the Antwerp Guild in 1598, became court painter to the Duke of Mantua in 1600, and until 1608 travelled extensively in Italy, absorbing the art of the High Renaissance and classical architecture. By the time of his return to Antwerp in 1608 he had acquired an enormous artistic vocabulary: the paintings of Caravaggio in particular were to influence his work strongly. His first major success was *The Raising of the Cross*, painted in 1610 and displayed today in Antwerp cathedral. A large, dynamic work, it caused a sensation at the time, establishing Rubens' reputation and leading to a string of commissions that enabled him to set up his own studio. *The Descent from the Cross*, his next major work (also in the cathedral), consolidated this success: equally Baroque, it is nevertheless quieter and more restrained.

The division of labour in Rubens' studio, and the talent of the artists working there (who included Antony van Dyck and Jacob Jordaens) ensured a high output of excellent work. The degree to which Rubens personally worked on a canvas would vary – and would determine its price. From the early 1620s onwards he turned his hand to a plethora of themes and subjects – religious works, portraits, tapestry designs, landscapes, mythological scenes, ceiling paintings (including that of the Banqueting Hall in Whitehall, London – a commission for Charles I, by whom he was knighted) – each of which was handled with supreme vitality and virtuosity. From his Flemish antecedents he inherited an acute sense of light, and used it not to dramatize his subjects (a technique favoured by Caravaggio and other Italian artists), but in association with colour and form. The drama in his works comes from the tremendous animation of his characters. His large-scale allegorical works, especially, are packed with heaving, writhing figures that appear to tumble out from the canvas.

The energy of Rubens' paintings was reflected in his private life. In addition to his career as an artist, he also undertook diplomatic missions to Spain and England, and used these opportunities to study the works of other artists and – as in the case of Velázquez – to meet them personally. In the 1630s, gout began to hamper his activities, and from this time his painting became more domestic and meditative. Hélène Fourment, his second wife, was the subject of many portraits and served as a model for characters in his allegorical paintings, her figure epitomizing the buxom, well-rounded women found throughout his work.

Rubens' influence on the artists of the period was enormous. The huge output of his studio meant that his works were universally seen, and widely disseminated by the engravers he employed to copy his work. Chief among his followers was the portraitist **Anthony van Dyck** (1599–1641), who worked in Rubens' studio from 1618, often taking on the depiction of religious figures in his master's works that required particular sensitivity and pathos. Like Rubens, he was born in Antwerp and travelled widely in Italy, though his initial work was influenced less by the Italian artists than by Rubens himself. Eventually van Dyck developed his own distinct style and technique, establishing himself as court painter to Charles I in England, and creating portraits of a nervous elegance that would influence the genre there for the next hundred and fifty years. Most of his great portraiture remains in England, but his best religious works

– such as the *Crucifixion* in Mechelen cathedral and a *Lamentation* in Antwerp's Museum voor Schone Kunsten – can be found in Belgium. **Jacob Jordaens** (1593–1678) was also an Antwerp native who studied under Rubens. Although he was commissioned to complete several works left unfinished by Rubens at the time of his death, his robustly naturalistic works have an earthy – and sensuous – realism that's quite distinct in style and technique.

Other artists working in the Low Countries during the early seventeenth century were also, understandably enough, greatly influenced by the output of Rubens' studio. **Gerhard Seghers** (1591–1651) specialized in painting flowers, usually around portraits or devotional figures painted by other artists, including Rubens himself. **Theodor Rombouts** (1579–1637) was strongly influenced by Caravaggio following a trip to Italy, but changed his style to fall in line with that of Rubens when he returned to Antwerp from Holland, and although **Frans Snijders** (1579–1657) took up still-life painting where Aertsen left off, amplifying his subject – food and drink – to even larger, more sumptuous canvases, he too was part of the Rubens art machine, painting animals and still-life sections for the master's works.

As well as the Baroque creations of Rubens and his acolytes, another style emerged in the seventeenth century, that of **genre painting**, a term which was at first applied to everything from animal paintings and still lifes through to historical works and landscapes, but later came to be applied only to scenes of everyday life. In the southern Netherlands the most skilful practitioner was **Adriaen Brouwer** (1605–38), whose peasant figures rivalled those of the painters Jan Steen and Adriaen van Ostade to the north. Brouwer's output was unsurprisingly small given his short life, but his riotous tavern scenes and tableaux of everyday life are deftly done, and were well received in their day, collected by, among others, Rubens and Rembrandt. Brouwer studied in Haarlem for a while under Frans Hals (and may have picked up much of his painterly technique from him), before returning to his native Flanders to influence **David Teniers the Younger** (1610–1690), who worked in Antwerp, and later in Brussels. Teniers' early paintings are Brouwer-like peasant scenes, although his later work is more delicate and diverse, including *kortegaardje* – guardroom scenes that show soldiers carousing.

THE EIGHTEENTH CENTURY

By the end of the seventeenth century, French influences had overwhelmed Belgium's native artistic tradition with painters like **Jan Joseph Horemans I** and **Balthasar van den Bossche** modifying the Flemish genre painting of the previous century to suit Parisian tastes. Towards the end of the century Neoclassicism came into vogue, a French-led movement whose leading light was **Jacques Louis David**, the creator of the *Death of Marat*, an iconic work displayed in Brussels' Musée des Beaux Arts. **Laurent Delvaux** (1696–1778) was also an important figure during this period, a Flemish sculptor who produced a large number of works for Belgian churches, including the pulpit of Ghent's cathedral and other pieces in Brussels.

THE NINETEENTH CENTURY

French artistic fashions ruled the Belgian roost well into the nineteenth century, and amongst them Neoclassicism remained the most popular. Of the followers of Jacques Louis David, **François Joseph Navez** (1787–1869) was the most important to work in Belgium, furthering the influence of the movement via his position as director of the Brussels academy. With Belgian independence (from Holland) in 1830, came, as might be expected, a new interest in nationalism, and artists such as **Louis Galliat** (1810–87) spearheaded a romantic interpretation of historical events, idealizing Belgium's recent and medieval history.

Antoine Wiertz (1806–65) – see p.91 – was celebrated for his grandiose amalgamation of romantic and Neoclassical themes in his sculptures and paintings, whilst **Henri de Braekeleer** (1840–88) was highly regarded for his Dutch-inspired interiors and landscapes. Indeed landscape painting underwent a resurgence of popularity throughout Europe in the mid-nineteenth century, and Belgian artists once again reflected the tastes and movements of France, with artists like **Théodor Fourmois** and **Eugène Huberti** involved with the Barbizon group, and **Émile Claus** (1849–1924) adapting French Impressionist ideas into an individual style known as Luminism. **Théo Rysselberghe** (1862–1926) also took his lead

from the Impressionists, but retained a distinctive local approach, while the talented **Fernand Khnopff** (1858–1921) was inspired by the English Pre-Raphaelites.

One artist who stands out during this period is **Constantin Meunier** (1831–1905), a painter and sculptor whose naturalistic work depicting brawny workers and mining scenes was the perfect mirror of a fast-industrializing Europe – and Belgium. Much of Meunier's work shows life in the industrial parts of Hainaut, notably the Borinage, and in Brussels his old house and studio have been turned into a museum (see p.97). But the most original Belgian artist of the late nineteenth century was **James Ensor** (1860–1949). Ensor, who lived in Ostend for most of his life, painted macabre, disturbing works, whose haunted style can be traced back to Bosch and Bruegel and which was itself a precursor of Expressionism. He was active in a group known as **Les XX** (Les Vingt), which organized exhibitions of new styles of art from abroad, and greatly influenced contemporary Belgian painters.

THE TWENTIETH CENTURY

Each of the major modern art movements had its followers in Belgium, and each was diluted or altered according to local taste. **Expressionism** was manifest in a local group of artists established in a village near Ghent, with the most eye-catching paintings produced by **Constant Permeke** (1886–1952), whose bold, deeply coloured canvases can be found in many Belgian galleries. **Surrealism** also caught on in a big way, perhaps because of the Belgian penchant for the bizarre and grotesque. **René Magritte**, one of the leading lights of the movement, was born and trained in Belgium and returned there after being involved in the movement's birth in 1927. His Surrealism is gentle compared to the work of Dalí or de Chirico: ordinary images are used in a dreamlike way, often playing on the distinction between a word and its meaning. His most famous motif was the man in the bowler hat, whose face was always hidden from view. **Paul Delvaux** (1897–1994) adopted his own rather salacious interpretation of the movement – a sort of "What-the-butler-saw" Surrealism.

Most of the interwar artists were influenced by van Doesburg and de Stijl in Holland, though none figured highly in the movement. The

THE GALLERIES OF BELGIUM AND LUXEMBOURG: A HIT LIST

Brussels' Musées Royaux des Beaux Arts together comprise an excellent survey of Low Countries painting: the Flemish Primitives, Bruegel and Rubens in the Musée d'Art Ancien, Ensor, Magritte and Delvaux in the Musée d'Art Moderne. **Antwerp's** Museum voor Schone Kunsten has everything from Flemish Primitives to nineteenth-century masters, with all the great names – van Eyck, van der Weyden, Rubens, van Dyck, Jordaens, Brouwer, Teniers, Ensor and Delvaux – getting a look in. The Mayer van den Burgh museum has work by Quentin Matsys and Bruegel, and the cathedral two of Rubens' seminal works. The Memling Museum in **Bruges** has some of the artist's best works, housed in a magnificent medieval hospice; the Groeninge Museum has a wonderful sample of the work of the Flemish Primitives: van der Weyden, van der Goes, Gerard David and an important van Eyck. Van Eyck's greatest work, *The Adoration of the Mystic Lamb*, is housed in St Baafskathedraal in **Ghent**.

Luxembourg is poorly served in terms of great collections, although the Musée National d'Histoire et d'Art in Luxembourg City musters a reasonable selection of fifteenth- and sixteenth-century Flemish paintings.

abstract geometrical works of **Victor Severanckx** (1897–1965) owed much to de Stijl, and he in turn inspired the postwar group known as **La Jeune Peinture**, which gathered together some of the most notable artists working in Belgium, the antecedents of the Abstract Expressionists of the 1950s. A similar collective function was served by **CoBrA**, founded in 1948 and taking its name from the first letters of Copenhagen, Brussels and Amsterdam. While none of the Belgian participants in CoBrA achieved the fame of one of its Dutch members, Karel Appel, the name of **Pierre Alechinsky** (1927–) is certainly well known in his hometown, Brussels. Probably the most famous recent Belgian artist is **Marcel Broodthaers** (1924–76). He initially worked in the Surrealist manner, but soon branched out, quickly graduating from cut-paper geometric shapes into both the plastic arts and most famously, sharp and brightly coloured paintings of everyday artefacts.

BELGIUM'S GREAT BEERS

Belgian beers have recently become fashionable, yet the pleasures they offer have been truly explored by only a discerning minority of drinkers. The rule "Never ask for 'a beer'" applies especially in Belgium. Such a request will bring forth a perfectly acceptable lager, but of a type that could just as easily be found in many other countries. The great beers of Belgium are not its lagers. Its native brews are in other styles, and they offer an extraordinary variety, some so different from more conventional brews that at the initial encounter they are scarcely recognizable as beers. Yet they represent some of the oldest traditions of brewing in the Western world. No other country (even those with far more breweries) has among its native styles of beer such diversity, individuality, idiosyncrasy and colour. Nor does any other country present beers so beautifully. Belgian brewers often use wired and corked champagne bottles, and serve each beer in its own shape of glass, ranging from flutes to snifters and chalices. It is something of a Belgian speciality to bottle beers with a sediment of live yeast, so that they can be laid down to mature. This technique is usually indicated on the label by the phrase "re-fermented in the bottle" (*refermentée en bouteille /hergist in de fles*).

The following introduction includes all the major types of Belgium beers: from winey-tasting Lambics, some with whole fruit added; "white" wheat beers in the vein of the popular Hoegaarden; sour-ish red and brown beers; strong ales from Trappist monasteries; powerful golden brews like the famous Duvel; plus endless local and seasonal specialities.

THE LAMBIC FAMILY OF BEERS

The winiest of all the world's beers, and specific to the Brussels area. There are several possible explanations for the odd name (which is spelled in a variety of ways), but its most likely origin is the small town of Lembeek ("Lime Creek"), to the immediate southwest of Brussels, in the heart of the producing area. A handful of breweries around Lembeek, Beersel and Schepdaal, all in the valley of the River Zenne, have persisted with techniques that predate the culturing of yeasts. Their brews are of the type seen in Bruegel's paintings, and represent the oldest style of beer readily found in the developed world. Lambic beers gain their tartness from a content of at least thirty percent raw wheat in addition to the more usual malted barley, but their defining characteristic is the use of wild yeast. This "wild", or "spontaneous", fermentation imparts the distinctive acidity. The yeasts of the atmosphere descend into open vessels in the attics of the breweries, and the fermentation and maturation continue in wooden casks, some more than one hundred years old, many previously used to transport wine. The casks, and the walls of the breweries, play host to a menagerie of wild yeasts. Elsewhere in the world of brewing, wood is today scarcely used in fermentation or maturation. While conventional ales ferment and mature for a week or two, and lagers for a month or two, Lambics may have two or three years of fermentation. Most of these beers have a conventional alcohol content, in the range of 4.0 to 6.0 percent alcohol by volume (or abv).

STRAIGHT LAMBIC

In its most natural form a draught beer, almost still, unsweetened and unblended, straight Lambic can seem less like a beer than some hybrid of hard cider and fino sherry. Some of the yeasts that develop during its fermentation are, indeed, very similar to those at work in sherry bodegas. Straight Lambic is hard to find. It is served in only one or two cafés in Brussels and a handful in the area of production. Typically, it is tapped directly from the cask, and decanted from a pitcher into tumblers. In much the way that fino sherry is served in Andalusia with tapas, so Lambic is sometimes offered with snacks of sharp, soft cheeses like the fresh-curd Plattekaas and the acidic Pottekaas, with silverskin onions, radishes, brown bread, and sometimes sausages similar to English saveloys or black pudding.

The most central Lambic café, albeit offering sweetened interpretations, is just behind the lower end of Brussels' Grand-Place. Facing downhill on the square, turn right into rue Tabora, and look for a sign announcing *A la Bécasse* (The Woodcock). (This café is actually down an alley.) It has "Dutch" tiled walls and scrubbed tables, and serves the beer with snacks. *Le Vieux Château d'Or*, rue Ste Catherine 26, in the market area, can, on occassion, also have straight Lambic.

A rare bottled version, very dry and lemony, is sometimes available to visitors at the renowned small brewery Cantillon, a working museum of Lambic, rue Gheude 56 (☎02/521 49 28), in the Anderlecht neighbourhood. The brewery, near Brussels Midi railway station, is an essential visit for anyone with even the slightest interest in beer. Cantillon is one of the most traditional Lambic producers, along with the brewery of Frank Boon (pronounced as in "bone" – or "Beaune"), in Lembeek itself (☎02/356 66 44). Boon has tours (July–Sept Wed 3pm) starting at *Café Kring*, next to the main church. A third traditionalist is Girardin, a brewery that grows its own wheat, but unfortunately does not have tours. Other well-known Lambic breweries include Timmermans, Lindemans, De Troch, Mort Subite and Belle-Vue. The last two are genuine Lambic brewers owned by national groups, respectively better known for Kronenbourg and Stella Artois lagers.

Belle-Vue has a tasting room at its brewery in the Brussels neighbourhood Molenbeek, Quai du Hainaut 43 (☎02/412 44 11). It offers a sweetened blend of Lambics on draught. The Mort Subite beer was originally brewed for a classic Brussels café of the same name. *Café Mort Subite* is at rue Montagnes aux Herbes Potagères 7, not far from the Grand-Place (☎02/513 13 18). It was founded in about 1880, refitted in 1926, and was the inspiration for a ballet by Maurice Béjart. Straight Lambic is not usually served, though Gueuze and Kriek (see below) are.

FARO

Faro is also hard to find, but is sometimes available at Lambic cafés. This is a version of Lambic sweetened with rummy-tasting dark candy sugar, and occasionally spices. Some cafés serve a do-it-yourself version, with a pestle or cocktail barman's muddler to crush the sugar. Faro was once the restorative for the working man in Brussels.

GUEUZE

A bottled, sparkling style, Gueuze is much easier to find than its fellow Lambics. It often has the toasty and Chardonnay-like notes found in champagne. The word Gueuze (hard "g", and rhymes with "firs") may have the same etymological origins as the English words *gas* and *ghost*, and the Flemish *gist* (yeast), referring to carbonation and rising bubbles. The carbonation is achieved by blending young Lambic (typically six months old) with more mature vintages (two to three years). The residual sugars in the young Lambic and the yeasts that have developed in the old cause a new fermentation. The most traditional examples may bear on the label the endorsement of the consumerist organization De Objectieve Bierproevers. References to "old" (*oud, vieux, vieille*) on the label indicate a minimum of six months and a genuine Lambic process. Without these legends, a Lambic may have been "diluted" with a more conventional beer. Apart from the producers mentioned above, blenders like Drie Fonteinen and, Hanssens produce outstanding examples andthe equally outstanding Cam can be found in the village of Gooik, 10km west of Brussels, adjoining a café (next door to the police station).

The following café-restaurants in the producing region often need reservations. In Schepdaal, *Café In De Rare Vos*, Markt Plaats 22, serves aged Gueuze with dishes including mussels, pigeon and horse (closed Tues & Wed). In Beersel, in addition to Drie Fonteinen, Herman Teirlinck Plein 3 (☎02/331 06 52), which also blends beers, there is *Oud Beersel*, a café with its own brewery on Laarheide Straat 232. In the same town, *Drie Bronnen*, Hoog Straat 13 (☎02/331 07 20), and *Oude Pruim*, Ukkelse Steenweg 87 (☎02/331 05 59), are also well worth visiting. All of these Beersel café-restaurants close on Tuesday.

FRUIT LAMBIC

The acidity of Lambic provides a particularly good base for fruit beers. Because these begin with a fermentation of grain, and are primed with fruit later, they are beers and not wines. The use of fruit (like that of spices) almost certainly pre-dates the hop as a flavour-modifier in beer. In the traditional method, the fruit is added during the maturation of the beer, causing a further fermentation. The happiest results are arguably with fruits that have stones, which can impart a balancing, almondy dryness. The best of Belgian fruit beers have the dryness of a pink champagne, rather than the sweetness of a soda-pop. Like champagnes, they are often served in flute-style glasses. In the Brussels area, the home of Lambic, a typical local fruit is a small, dark, variety of cherry, known in Flemish as the *kriek*. Lambic-based Kriek beers are the most traditional fruit brews. Raspberries, known in Flemish as *frambozen*, and French as *framboises,* are also widely used. The Cantillon brewery has in recent years experimented to interesting effect with Muscat grapes, which are grown under glass in Belgium as dessert fruit. More exotic fruits, added as syrups, are used in novelty beers by the more commercially minded breweries. The term Lambic is used only when that style of beer is used as the base. Contrary to misunderstandings in some other countries, there is no connection between the term Lambic and the use of fruit. Equally, many good fruit beers in Belgium are not based on Lambic. For example, several of the brown brews made in Oudenaarde are used as the base for Kriek or Frambozen beers.

WHITE BEERS

The best-known Belgian *witbier* or *bière blanche* is the principal product from Hoegaarden, a small town in a wheat-growing region east of Brussels. The Hoegaarden beer, which in the 1960s revived the traditional style of the region, has inspired many other examples throughout Belgium. This style is usually made from equal portions of raw wheat and malted barley, spiced with ground coriander seeds and dried Curaçao orange peels, and fermented with a fairly conventional yeast. The fruitiness imparted by the wheat, sometimes with suggestions of plum, apple or banana, melds well with the orange and coriander. Beers in this style, usually with a conventional alcohol content, are regarded especially as a summertime refresher, though they also make a good accompaniment to fruity desserts. They are typically served in chunky tumblers. Wheat beers are identified as being "white" in several brewing nations. The designation may refer to the pale head formed during fermentation, or to the fact that these beers are often unfiltered, and therefore hazy. Wheat beers can be filtered, but less easily than those made from barley malt.

For good examples of the beer look no further than Hoegaarden itself or the creamy Limburgse Witte, the honeyish-tasting Brugs Tarwebier, the cinnamon-spiced Steendonk, the Lambic-based

Witte (two t's), from Timmermans, and Wittekerke Wit, smoothened with oats. The last is named after a Flemish soap-opera.

Hoegaarden produces a slightly stronger (5.6abv), less wheaty, winter companion called Speciale. It also has several non-wheat beers with the same spicing, including: an amber ale with an older spelling, Hougaerdse DAS (the mysterious initials are a revival of an old beer name in Belgium); the strong (8.7abv), golden, Hoegaarden Grand Cru; and the strong (9.0abv), dark "Forbidden Fruit", labelled as Le Fruit Defendu in French and De Verboden Vrucht in Flemish. The last two beers are Belgian classics.

The Hoegaarden brewery has its own public restaurant, *Het Kouterhof*, Stoopken Straat 24, Hoegaarden (☎016/76 74 33), offering the full range of its beers, and dishes prepared with them.

BROWN BEERS

Many distinctive variations of dark brown ales are made in Belgium, especially in Flanders. The classic style, with an interplay of caramel-like malty sweetness and a sourness gained in several months of maturation (usually in metal tanks), is sometimes identified as *oud* (old) *bruin* (the pronunciation is almost the same as the English word "brown"). The most complex examples have a secondary fermentation in the bottle. The flavour and acidity render these the perfect base for the Flemish beef stew *carbonnade flamande*. The most famous producing town is Oudenaarde (also known for Gothic architecture and Gobelin tapestries), not far from Ghent, in East Flanders. Oudenaarde's water, low in calcium and high in sodium carbonate, gives a particularly textured character to the beers. Its small Felix brewery, owned by a family named Clarysse, the weekend-only brewery of the Cnudde family and the larger brewery of the Roman family all make examples of the style. Roman, which dates from 1545, has magnificent 1930s buildings, and a brewhouse from the same period. It makes a "single" version at 5.5abv and a "double" at 8.0abv. These are labelled Special Roman and Dobbelen Bruinen respectively. The most typical example of browns, in three ages and strengths, are fermented and matured at Liefmans, in Oudenaarde, from brews made by Riva of Dentergem, in West Flanders. The classic example, Goudenband (Golden Band), at 8.0-plus, is also the basis for an excellent cherry beer, Liefmans' Kriek.

Liefmans offers tours, a small museum and an art gallery. Their bar-restaurant *Zaal de Baudelot*, Aalst Straat 200, Oudenaarde, (Mon–Fri 8am–5pm;☎055/31 13 91), is open for breakfast and serves Flemish dishes for lunch. Weekends by arrangement only.

RED BEERS

The world-classic beers of the Rodenbach brewery, and several similar products from competitors, mainly in West Flanders, are a distinct style without a name but might be described as "red" beers. They are more sharply acidic, leaner, more reddish, half-brothers to the brown beers of East Flanders, with the additional difference that they are often filtered and pasteurized. Their sharpness makes them perhaps the most quenching beers in the world, and their acidity renders them very food-friendly. The sharp acidity, and some of the colour, derives from ageing in large, fixed, wooden tuns. Rodenbach, in Roeselare, has ten or eleven halls full of these tuns. There is nothing comparable in any brewery elsewhere in the world, and the whole establishment is a museum of industrial archaeology. The brewery's Rodenbach Grand Cru (5.2–5.6abv) is aged for between eighteen months and two years or more. The regular Rodenbach Bier (4.6–5.0abv) is a blend containing some younger beer. The slightly stronger Rodenbach Alexander (5.2–5.6abv) is sweetened with cherry essence but generally Rodenbach beers have a distinct passion-fruit character. Rivals include the more chocolatey Petrus Oud Bruin; the tart Bellegems Bruin; the smoother Bourgogne des Flandres; the slightly lactic Bios Vlaamse Bourgogne; the fruity Vichtenaar; and the rich Duchesse de Bourgogne.

In Roeselare, *Den Haselt*, Diksmuidse Steenweg 53 (☎051/22 52 40), is a *haute cuisine* restaurant, using the Rodenbach range as both an accompaniment and an ingredient.

BRITISH-STYLE ALES

During the two world wars, the beers brought by British troops to Belgium inspired similar brews locally. Several Belgian brewers still produce "Le Pale Ale" and "Le Scotch". The first is usually stronger, hoppier and fruitier than an English pale ale or bitter, and is served as sociable beer. The second is typically more potent, maltier and richer, than a strong dark ale in Scotland, and is served as a digestif or winter warmer, often in a thistle glass. John Martin's is a well-known example of a Belgian-brewed "English Pale Ale". Other British brews include Gordon's Highland Scotch Ale (8.0abv) and a fractionally stronger Christmas version both brewed in Scotland for the Belgian market.

(AMBER) BELGIAN ALES

Beers similar to an English pale ale or bitter, but with no direct allusion to Britain, are often made by Belgian brewers. Some are labelled with the English word "Ale", others as "Special" (various spellings), as a simple distinction from standard lager beers. Some of these are spiced (eg Petrus Speciale, with coriander), and others simply derive a spicy taste from the yeasts used. Typical examples, all at around 5.0abv, include the fruity Palm Special; the spicy Horse Ale; the hoppy Op-Ale; dry Ginder Ale (named after a brewer named van Ginderachter); and the sherbety Vieux Temps. The most famous example of all is made by the De Koninck brewery of Antwerp. This is identified as neither ale nor special, but simply as De Koninck. In the Antwerp area, where it is very much the local brew, it is colloquially ordered in a Bolleke, a reference to its curved goblet. The beer has a dense head, a toasty palate, and a spicy, delicate hop in the finish. Its subtlety is much more evident on draught than in the bottle.

The *Pelgrim*, opposite the De Koninck brewery, at Boomgaard Straat 8, Antwerp, is a traditional café. Locals ask for a shot-glass of the brewery yeast with their first or last Bolleke of the evening. De Koninck is widely available and outlets include *Den Engel*, on the Grote Markt, one of Antwerp's main squares; and *Quinten Matsijs*, Moriaan Straat 17, the city's oldest pub, dating from 1565.

SAISONS

Saisons are nominally seasonal beers for the summer but are available all year round. Only in a country with so many strong beers would brews of 5.0 to 6.5 percent be regarded as "light" summer specialities. Despite their typical strengths, saisons usually have a citric, peppery, quenching quality, due variously to hard water, heavy hopping, spicing or deliberate souring. They are usually amber to orange in colour, and often quite dry. Saisons are largely local to the French-speaking part of the country, especially the western part of the province of Hainaut, in old, small, farm-like breweries close to the Borinage coalfield. Examples include the crisp Saison 1900, from the brewery Lefèbvre, in Quenast, south of Brussels; the tart Saison Silly (named after its home village); and the spiced Saison de Pipaix. The last is made by a steam-powered brewery dating from the 1780s. The brewery Brasserie a Vapeur, rue de Maréchal 1, Pipaix (☎069/66 20 47), works only on the last Saturday of the month, starting at 9am, but it runs tours on Sundays at 11am with an opportunity to buy the produce from a shop open in the second half of the week. The hugely lively Saison Dupont is made at a farm brewery, Basse 5, in the village of Tourpes, near Pipaix, that uses its spent grain in bread and also produces a hop-flavoured cheese. There is a café opposite the brewery in which to sample the produce. The perfumy Saison D'Epeautre (made with spelt grain) is produced commercially at a private house in the village of Blaugies, near Dour, south of Mons, rue de La Frontière 435 (☎065/65 06 30). The aromatic Saison Régal is from a larger independent brewery, in Purnode, in the province of Namur. A variety of beers for different seasons are made by the Fantôme brewery, rue Préal 8, which opens its own café at weekends and school holidays, in the village of Soy, province of Luxembourg (☎086/47 70 44). Many small breweries in the French-speaking part of Belgium make similar beers, not necessarily identified as saisons.

The saison style does not exist in the Flemish-speaking part of the country, but a paler, wonderfully flowery, hoppy, beer called Sezoens, made by the Martens brewery, of Bocholt, in Belgian Limburg, is something of a counterpart. This is a house speciality at a café called *De Ultieme Hallucinatie*, rue Royale 316, Brussels (☎02/217 06 14).

TRAPPIST BEERS

This term is properly applied only to a brewery in a monastery of the Trappists, one of the most severe orders of monks. This order, established at La Trappe, in Normandy, has a stricter observance of the Cistercian rule (from Cîteaux, in Burgundy), itself a breakaway from the Benedictines. Among the dozen or so surviving abbey breweries in Europe, seven are Trappist, six in Belgium and one just across the Dutch border, all established in their present form by Trappists who left France after the turbulence of the Napoleonic period. The Trappists have the only monastic breweries in Belgium, all making strong ales with re-fermentation in the bottle. Some gain a distinctive rummy character from the use of candy sugar in the brew-kettle. They do not represent a style, but they are very much a family of beers. The three in the French-speaking part of the country are all in the forest region of the Ardennes, where hermitages burned charcoal to fuel early craft industries. It is not usually possible to visit the abbeys without prior arrangement by letter and it can be difficult even then. Most offer their beers in a nearby café or *auberge*.

ORVAL

Orval is the most singular of the Trappist brewing abbeys, in both its architecture and its beer. It can be found on the French frontier, at Villers-devant-Orval in the Belgian province of Luxembourg, not far from Florenville. The name derives from Vallée d'Or (Golden Valley). Legend has it that Countess Matilda of Tuscany (c1046–1115) lost a gold ring in the lake and when it was brought to the surface by a trout, she thanked God by endowing a monastery. The monastery, originally Benedictine, later Cistercian, was certainly brewing before the French Revolution when it was sacked and it was only rebuilt in the 1930s. The finest craftsmen of the period worked on this abbey, which was specially refurbished to crown the centenary of the modern kingdom of Belgium. The present abbey, officially called Notre Dame d'Orval, stands alongside the ruins of the old.

Bread and cheese are made for sale, as well as a startlingly dry, hoppy, ale of approximately 6.2abv, with a dark orange colour. This world-classic brew gains some of its astonishing complexity from a secondary fermentation with multiple strains of yeast, including "semi-wild" brettanomyces yeast which imparts a "hop-sack" or "horse-blanket" character. Devotees like to bottle-age this beer for between six months and three years. It is a powerful aperitif. There is a shop at the abbey, and a bar-restaurant nearby at *A l'Ange Gardien*, rue d'Orval 3 (☎061/31 18 86).

CHIMAY

The best known of the Trappist brewing monasteries. This abbey, also called Notre Dame, stands on a small hill called Scourmont, near the hamlet of Forges, not far from the town of Chimay. Originally a glass-smelting town, Chimay is now a centre for tourism in the Ardennes. The abbey, in the Romanesque style, was built in 1850. While the early abbeys brewed for their own communities, Chimay was the first to sell its beer commercially. Between the two world wars, it coined the appellation "Trappist Beer". After the Second World War, Chimay's great brewer, Father Théodore, worked with a famous Belgian brewing scientist, Jean De Clerck, to isolate the yeasts that identified Chimay's beers as classic Trappist brews. These yeasts, which work at very high temperatures (up to 30°C/86°F), impart a character reminiscent of Zinfandel or port wine, especially to Chimay's 7.0abv and 9.0abv beers, which have a colour to match. Between the two is a drier, paler, hoppier version at 8.0abv. In ascending order of strength, the standard bottlings are identified by red, white and blue crown tops. There are also larger, corked bottles as Première, Cinq Cents and Grande Réserve. The strongest will mature in the bottle for at least five years. It makes an excellent accompaniment to Chimay's Trappist cheese (similar to a Port Salut) and is even better with Roquefort. The beers are widely available, and can be found near the abbey at the *Ferme des Quatre Saisons* restaurant, rue de Scourmont 8b, Forges.

ROCHEFORT

The least well known of the established Trappist breweries. Rochefort is brewed in Notre Dame de St Rémy near the small town of Rochefort, in the province of Namur, where the valley of the River Meuse rises into the Ardennes. The settlement dates from at least 1230, when it was a convent, and brewing started at least as early as 1595. The oldest parts of the buildings date from the 1600s but restoration was required after the Napoleonic period. The beers, tawny to brown in colour, have an earthy honesty, perhaps deriving from a quite simple formulation, in which dark candy sugar is a significant ingredient. They have flavours reminiscent of figs, bananas and chocolate. The range is divided, according to an old Belgian measure of density, into beers of 6.0, 8.0 and 10.0 degrees. These have 7.5, 9.2 and 11.3 percent alcohol by volume respectively. The brewery has always quietly gone about its business, but in recent years its 10.0 degree beer has won a growing appreciation. The abbey does not have its own inn, but the beers can be tasted locally at two hotels: *Limbourg*, place Albert 2 (☎084/21 10 36), which also serves good charcuterie and game, and the slightly more expensive *Malle Post* (which also has jazz weekends), rue de Behogne 46 (☎084/21 09 87).

WESTVLETEREN

The smallest of the Trappist breweries. The abbey of St Sixtus, at Westvleteren, near Ieper and Poperinge, dates from the 1830s. Its beers are not filtered or centrifuged at any stage of production, and emerge with firm, long, big, fresh, malty flavours and suggestions of plum brandy. The Belgian degree system is again used to identify the beers. The figures 4.0°, 6.0°, 8.0° and 12.0° on the crown cork roughly reflect the alcohol content in this instance (though that cannot be precise in a strong, bottle-conditioned ale). The strongest might be closer to 11.5 but has on occasion been rated the most potent beer in Belgium. The beers are available next door at the café *In De Vrede*. Otherwise, trade and public alike have to go to a serving hatch at the abbey. A recorded phone message (☎057/40 10 57) tells callers which beer will be available, and when. If the 12° is on sale, cars will begin queuing long before the 10am opening time. Each car is rationed to ten cases and the monks are inflexible on this point, even toward a café-owner who makes a 1500-mile round-trip from Odense, on the Danish island of Fynen. "We make as much beer as we need to support the abbey – and no more," say the monks.

WESTMALLE

Westmalle is famous for one beer in particular, a world classic, though it also makes two others. The abbey of Our Lady of the Sacred Heart is in flat countryside at Westmalle, between the city of Antwerp and the Dutch border. The monastery was established in 1794, and has brewed since 1836. It is thus the oldest of Belgium's post-Napoleonic Trappist breweries. Its renown, though, derives from the introduction of golden

Trappist ales to meet competition from fashionable Pilseners after the Second World War. Its beers include a marvellously subtle, golden "Single" (curiously called Extra), brewed at 4.0 percent for the monks' own consumption, but sometimes also found outside the abbey; a dark-brown, fruity Dubbel (the Flemish spelling), at 6.5 percent; and its most famous beer, its golden-to-bronze, aromatic, orangey-tasting, complex Tripel, at 9.0 percent. These Trappist classics have popularized the notion that an "abbey-style Double" should be strong and dark and a "Triple" yet more potent but pale. The beers are available in the village at the café *Trappisten*, Antwerpse Steenweg 478.

ABBEY BEERS

This term is applied to ranges of strong ales in a similar vein to some of the famous Trappist brews, but not made in monasteries. Some have names indicating a business relationship between an abbey (which may have brewed on its own in the past) and a commercial brewery. The Norbertine abbeys of Leffe and Grimbergen, for example, have royalty agreements with Interbrew and Alken-Maes respectively. So does the Benedictine monastery of Maredsous, with the brewery that also makes Duvel. Another Benedictine monastery, Affligem, played a significant role in the history of hop-growing and brewing, and made beer until the First World War. Its excellent beers are now made by the De Smedt brewery. There are several other religious institutions that license breweries, and other beers that are simply named after an abbey ruin or local saint. An excellent newcomer is Karmeliet. This beer owes something to a style made by the Carmelite monks of Dendermonde, in East Flanders, in the 1600s. It contains barley, wheat and oats, in both raw and malted forms, and is very heavily spiced. It is made by the Bosteels Brewery, which also produces a pleasant dark ale called Kwak, famously served in a stirrup cup.

GOLDEN ALES

In seeking to compete with Pilsener lagers by using very pale malts and Czech, Slovenian or German hops, while retaining ale yeasts, Belgium has created a wide range of aromatic, fruity-tasting, golden specialities. Some of these are at a conventional alcohol content, like the Special made by Anne De Ryck at her brewery in Herzele, near the hop-growing town of Aalst, in East Flanders. Others are stronger, like the 6.0 percent Straffe Hendrik Blonde, which has its own brewery-restaurant, in Bruges (Wal Plein 26). The most famous are the very strong ones like the deceptively drinkable classic Duvel, at 8.5 percent. This has a very complex regime of four temperature stages in its fermentation and maturation. The name (pronounced Doov'l) is a corruption of the Flemish for Devil. This beer has many competitors, usually with devilish names. A good example is Hapkin, named after an axe-wielding count of Flanders.

LOCAL SPECIALITIES

Many breweries in Belgium produce characterful beers that defy categorization. Van Honsebrouck's very strong (11.0 percent) Château/Kasteel Beer, aged in a castle or mansion house at Ingelmunster, East Flanders, is perhaps comparable to a strong old ale or dark-brown barley wine in the English-speaking world. A wide range of strong specialities is made by De Dolle Brouwers, at Esen, near Diksmuide, not far from Ostend. These "Mad Brewers" are a family of professional people (an architect, a doctor...). They stepped in when their local brewer retired due to ill-health. They operate the brewery at weekends, and open a sample room and shop (Sat 9am–7pm, Sun 2–7pm). It is a fine example of a country brewery – and its beers are well worth tasting. So is Grottenbier Bruin, partly aged (for one to two months) in limestone caves, and turned weekly like champagne. This project has been a long-term dream of the ever-inventive Belgian brewer Pierre Celis. The beer is made by the De Smedt brewery, noted for its Affligem range. The "Grotto Beer" is a strongish (6.5abv) dark ale, in which small quantities of "exotic" spices are added to create a gentle, balancing dryness and crispness. A lover of pale barley wines would enjoy the powerful but beautifully balanced Bush Beer, at 12 percent, a Belgian classic from Dubuisson, of Pipaix, in Hainaut. In the same province, the town of Binche, famous for its pre-Lenten Carnival, also has a brewery, La Binchoise, which makes a range of honeyish, spicy-tasting beers. North of Bastogne, near the small town of Houffalize, the Ardennes hamlet of Achouffe has a well-known speciality brewery. Its emblem is La Chouffe, a bearded gnome wearing a red hood. The brewery La Chouffe has a tavern and dining room serving dishes prepared with its beers (☎061/28 81 47) and a shop selling its products. The principal beer, made with soft (piney?) spring water and coriander, has great complexity and delicacy, and can be laid down to mature.

GOLDEN LAGERS

The world's first golden lager was made in the town of Pilsen, in Bohemia, in what is now the Czech Republic. The best of the Czech and German Pilsener-style beers still have more malt and hop character than most derivatives elsewhere in the world, including Belgium. The Belgian examples, and some of those from just across the Dutch border, are in general slightly more characterful than the better-known labels from the Netherlands and Denmark. In the rest of the world, the best-known Belgian Pilsener is the lightly hoppy, grassy Stella Artois. Within Belgium, the slightly maltier Jupiler is a bigger

seller. Both are made by Interbrew. The rival national grouping produces the flowery Maes and the beautifully clean, dry Cristal-Alken. Among the national brews, Cristal-Alken is the truest to the description Pilsener. It is made in the province of Limburg, bordering on Germany. Other good examples of Pilsener are Pax and Martens' Pils, perhaps the two best from independent brewers.

THE BEERS OF LUXEMBOURG

The Grand Duchy (as opposed to the Belgian province) has no specific brewing tradition. Its five breweries produce standard Pilsener derivatives, plus the odd unfiltered, dark or strong lager. The most characterful are those from the smallest brewery, Battin, of Esch-sur-Alzette, in the old coal and steel area. In Luxembourg City, the Mousel brewery has its own "tap": *Mousel's Cantine*, Montée de Clausen 46. Closed Sunday.

©. Michael Jackson

BOOKS

Most of the following books should be readily available in the UK, US or Canada. We have given publishers for each title in the form UK/US publisher, unless the book is published in one country only; o/p means out of print.

HISTORY

William Allison & John Fairley, *The Monocled Mutineer* (Quartet). An antidote to all those tales of soldiers dying for their country in World War I, this little book recounts the story of one Percy Toplis, a Nottinghamshire lad turned soldier, mutineer, racketeer and conman who was finally shot by the police in 1920. Intriguing account of the large-scale mutiny that broke out along the British line in 1917.

Galbert of Bruges, *The Murder of Charles the Good* (University of Toronto). Something of a specialist book, this is a contemporary chronicle of the tempestuous events that rattled early twelfth-century Bruges. A detailed yarn giving all sorts of insights into medieval Flanders.

Niall Ferguson, *The Pity of War* (Penguin). A controversial account of World War I which challenges many of the beliefs concerning the start and continuation of the war. An immensely readable and well-researched history.

Pieter Geyl, *The Revolt of The Netherlands 1555–1609* (Cassell o/p). Geyl's authoritative history presents a concise account of the Netherlands during its formative years, chronicling the uprising against the Spanish and the formation of the United Provinces. Without doubt the definitive book on the period.

Martin Gilbert, *First World War* (HarperCollins/Henry Holt). Highly regarded account of the war published in 1995.

Michael Glover, *A New Guide to the Battlefields of Northern France and the Low Countries* (Michael Joseph o/p). Battlefields guide that is not entirely devoted to the Low Countries but has substantial sections on the conflicts at Bastogne, Arnhem, Ypres and Waterloo. Deliberately readable, well illustrated, and an essential handbook if you're exploring the region.

E. H. Kossmann, *The Low Countries 1780–1940* (OUP). Gritty, technically detailed but ultimately rather turgid narrative of the Low Countries from the Austrian era to World War II. Concentrates on the narrow arena of party politics. Oxford History of Modern Europe series.

Lyn MacDonald, *Voices and Images of the Great War* (Penguin). Personal recollections from those who fought in World War I.

Geoffrey Parker, *The Dutch Revolt* (Penguin). Compelling account of the struggle between the Netherlands and Spain. Certainly one of the best works of its kind. Also *The Army of Flanders and the Spanish Road 1567–1659* (CUP). The title may sound academic, but this book gives a fascinating insight into the Habsburg army which occupied "Belgium" for well over a hundred years – how it functioned, was fed and moved from Spain to the Low Countries along the so-called Spanish Road. Also by the same author, there is the similarly enjoyable *Philip II* (Court) and *The Thirty Years' War* (Routledge & Kegan Paul).

Simon Schama, *The Embarrassment of Riches: An Interpretation of Dutch Culture in the Golden Age* (Fontana/Vintage). Schama is a specialist in Dutch history and this chunky volume draws on a huge variety of archive sources. It remains the biggest-selling book on Dutch history ever written. Also by Schama, *Patriots and Liberators: Revolution in the Netherlands 1780–1813* (Fontana/Vintage) focuses on one of the less familiar periods of Dutch history and is particularly good on the Batavian Republic set up in the Netherlands under French auspices.

A.J.P. Taylor, *The First World War: An Illustrated History* (Penguin/Perigee). First published in 1963, this superbly written and pertinently illustrated history offers a penetrating analysis of how the war started and why it went on for so long. Many of Taylor's deductions were controversial at the time, but such was the power of his arguments that much of what he said is now mainstream history.

ART AND ARCHITECTURE

Eugene Fromentin, *The Masters of Past Time: Dutch and Flemish Painting from Van Eyck to Rembrandt* (Phaidon). Entertaining essays on the major Dutch and Flemish painters.

Rudolf Herman Fuchs, *Dutch Painting* (Thames & Hudson). Thoughtful and well-researched title which tracks through the history of its subject from the fifteenth century onwards. Each of the book's seven chapters tackles its period thematically – for instance "Virtue explained: Genre painting in the seventeenth century". Extensively illustrated.

Walter S. Gibson, *Bosch* (Thames & Hudson). Everything you wanted to know about Bosch, his paintings and his late fifteenth-century milieu. Superbly illustrated. By the same author, and also beautifully illustrated, is *Bruegel* (Thames & Hudson), which takes a detailed look at the artist with nine well-argued chapters investigating the components of Pieter Bruegel's art.

Paul Haesaerts, *James Ensor* (o/p). It may weigh a ton, but this excellent volume is an outstanding exploration of the work of this often neglected Ostend-born painter. The illustrations and photos are excellent.

Melissa McQuillan, *Van Gogh* (Thames & Hudson). Extensive, in-depth look at van Gogh's paintings as well as his life and times.

Alastair Smart, *The Renaissance and Mannerism outside Italy* (o/p). A very readable survey that includes lengthy chapters on van Eyck and his contemporaries, their successors, Bosch and Bruegel, and the later, more Mannerist-inclined painters of the Low Countries. A fine introduction to an extraordinary period.

Mariet Westerman, *The Art of the Dutch Republic 1585–1718* (Everyman). Most of Belgium's better art musums have a good healthy sample of Dutch painting. This fascinating and excellently written, and well-illustrated, book tackles its subject by theme and is enthralling.

Christopher White, *Rembrandt* (Thames & Hudson). White knows his paintings and his knowledge is distilled in this detailed text exploring Rembrandt's life and work. He has also written *Pieter Paul Rubens: Man and Artist* (Yale), but this is currently out of print.

TRAVEL AND SPECIFIC GUIDES

Charlotte and Emily Bronte; ed. Sue Lonoff, *The Belgian Essays* (Yale). The Bronte sisters left their native Yorkshire for the first time in 1842 to make a trip to Brussels. Charlotte returned to Brussels the following year. This handsome volume reproduces the 28 essays they penned (in French) during their journey and provides the English translation opposite. It makes a delightful read; particular highlights are "The Butterfly", "The Caterpillar" and "The Death of Napoleon".

Alan Castle, *Walking in the Ardennes* (Cicerone). The best available general guide to hiking in Belgium's most scenic landscapes.

Chris Craggs, *Selected Rock Climbs in Belgium and Luxembourg* (Cicerone). All you could ever wish to know about climbing in these two countries. Scores of route descriptions and loads of helpful advice. In Belgium, most of the climbs are in the Namur-Dinant area and in Luxembourg the focus is around Berdorf.

S. A. Delta inc, *Guide Delta Bruxelles* (Delta in Belgium). Over five hundred pages of detailed and perceptive hotel and restaurant reviews covering every nook and cranny of the capital. New edition every year. Ideal if you're moving to Brussels. In French only.

Ernest Gilliat-Smith, *The Story of Brussels* (J.M. Dent o/p). Quirky, good-humoured account of Brussels written in 1906. Pick it up at the library or a second-hand bookshop.

Michael Jackson, *The Great Beers of Belgium* (Prion). Belgium produces the best beer in the world. Michael Jackson is the best beer writer in the world. The result is cheeky, palatable and sinewy with just a hint of fruitiness. Other more general guides include the indispensable *Beer Companion* (Mitchell Beazley/Running Press 2nd edn), outlining a beer tour of world proportions, and the simply-named *Beer* (Dorling Kindersley), which graphically illustrates the best brews in all their glory.

Tim Webb, *Good Beer Guide to Belgium and Holland* (CAMRA/Storey Book). Detailed and enthusiastic guide to the regions' bars and breweries. A good read, and well informed to boot.

LITERATURE

Hugo Claus, *The Sorrow of Belgium* (Penguin). Born in Bruges in 1929 and now resident in Antwerp, Claus is generally regarded as Belgium's foremost Flemish-language novelist, and this is widely acclaimed as his most compelling novel. It charts the growing maturity of a young boy living in Flanders under the Nazi occupation. Claus's style is somewhat dense, to say the least, but the book gets to grips well with the guilt, bigotry and mistrust of the period, and caused a minor uproar when it was first published in the early 1980s. By the same author is *Swordfish* (Dufour), a novella dealing with the same general themes, and – newly published by Penguin (US) – Claus's *Desire*, a bizarre tale of a couple of Flemings on the loose in Las Vegas. It's a fascinating novel, witty and disturbing at the same time.

Robert Graves, *Goodbye To All That* (Penguin/Anchor). Written in 1929, this is the classic story of life in the trenches. Bleak and painful memories of First World War army service written by Graves, a wounded survivor.

Alan Hollinghurst, *The Folding Star* (Vintage). Not a Belgian novel, but the British writer Hollinghurst's evocation of a thinly disguised Bruges, in this novel of sex, mystery and obsession, is enthralling. The enthusiastic descriptions of gay male sexual encounters make this a climactic book in more ways than one.

Barbara Kingsolver, *The Poisonwood Bible: A Novel* (Faber/HarperCollins). In 1959, an American Baptist missionary and his family set out to convert souls in the jungly depths of the Belgian Congo. They are unprepared for the multiple disasters that befall them – from great, stinging ants to irregular Congolese soldiers.

Jean Ray, *Malpertuis* (Atlas). This hackle-raising, spine-chilling Gothic novel was written by a Belgian in 1943. It's set in Belgium, where the suffocating Catholicism of the Inquisition provides a perfect backdrop.

Georges Rodenbach, *Bruges la Morte* (Atlas). First published in 1892, this slim and subtly evocative novel is all about love and obsession – or rather a highly stylized, Decadent view of it. It's credited with starting the craze for visiting Bruges, the "dead city" where the action unfolds.

Siegfried Sassoon, *The Memoirs of an Infantry Officer* (Faber & Faber). Sassoon's moving and painfully honest account of his experiences in the trenches of the First World War. A classic and infinitely readable. Also Siegfried Sassoon's *Diaries 1915–1918* (Faber & Faber o/p).

Emile Zola, *Germinal* (OUP). Written in 1885, this powerful novel is set in the coalfields of northeast France. It exposes the barbarous conditions under which the miners toiled and describes the organization of a strike. An immensely influential book in both France and Belgium, and Zola's grasp of the technicalities of deep-shaft mining is remarkable. Conditions just across the border in the Borinage coalfield near Mons (see p.250) were identical – and equally as appalling.

LANGUAGE

Throughout the northern part of Belgium, in the provinces of East and West Flanders, Antwerp, Limburg and Flemish Brabant, the principal language is Dutch, which is spoken in a variety of distinctive dialects commonly (if inaccurately) lumped together as Flemish. Most Flemish-speakers, particularly in the main towns and in the tourist industry, speak English to varying degrees of excellence. Indeed, Flemish-speakers have a seemingly natural talent for languages, and your attempts at speaking theirs may be met with bewilderment – though this can have as much to do with your pronunciation (Dutch is very difficult to get right) as surprise you're making an effort.

Flemish-speakers have equal language rights in the capital, Brussels, where the majority of Belgians speak a dialect of **French** known as **Walloon**, as they do in the country's southern provinces, known logically enough as Wallonia. Walloon is almost identical to French, and if you've any knowlege of the language, you'll be readily understood. French is also the most widely spoken language in **Luxembourg**, along with German – although most Luxembourgers also speak a local and distinctive German dialect, **Lëtzebuergesch**.

FLEMISH

Flemish, or Dutch, is a Germanic language – the word "Dutch" itself is a corruption of Deutsche, a label inaccurately given by English sailors in the seventeenth century. Though the Dutch are at pains to stress the differences between the two languages, if you know any German you'll spot many similarities. As noted above, English is very widely spoken, but in smaller towns and in the countryside, where things aren't quite as cosmopolitan, the notes that follow will prove handy; they can be supplemented with the detailed "Food Glossary" on p.40.

The most widely available **dictionary** is the *Teach Yourself Dutch Dictionary* (Hodder & Stoughton), which has a perfectly adequate dictionary section and also provides a useful introduction to grammar and pronunciation.

PRONUNCIATION

Dutch is pronounced much the same as English. However, there are a few Dutch sounds that don't exist in English, which can be difficult to pronounce without practice.

Consonants

v is like the English f in **f**ar

w like the v in **v**at

j like the initial sound of **y**ellow

ch and g are considerably harder than in English, enunciated much further back in the throat; in Antwerp at least, where the pronunciation is particularly coarse, there's no real English equivalent. They become softer the further south you go, where they're more like the Scottish lo**ch**.

ng is as in bri**ng**

nj as in o**ni**on

Otherwise double consonants keep their separate sounds – kn, for example, is never like the English "knight".

Vowels and diphthongs

Doubling the letter lengthens the vowel sound:

a is like the English **a**pple

aa like c**ar**t

e like l**e**t

ee like l**a**te

o as in p**o**p

oo in p**o**pe

u is like the French t**u** if preceded but not followed by a consonant (eg nu); it's like w**oo**d if followed by a consonant (eg bus).

uu the French t**u**

au and ou like h**o**w

FLEMISH WORDS AND PHRASES

Basics and greetings

yes	*ja*	do you speak English?	*spreekt u Engels?*
no	*nee*	I don't understand	*ik begrijp het niet*
please	*alstublieft*	women/men	*vrouwen/mannen*
(no) thank you	*[nee] dank u or bedankt*	children	*kinderen*
hello	*hallo or dag*	when?	*wanneer?*
good morning	*goedemorgen*	I want	*ik wil*
good afternoon	*goedemiddag*	I don't want	*ik wil niet. . . (+verb)*
good evening	*goedenavond*		*ik wil geen. . .(+noun)*
goodbye	*tot ziens*	how much is. . .?	*wat kost. . .?*
see you later	*tot straks*		

Finding the way

how do I get to. . .?	*hoe kom ik in. . .?*	left/right	*links/rechts*
where is. . .?	*waar is. . .?*	straight ahead	*recht uit gaan*
how far is it to. . .?	*hoe ver is het naar. . .?*	platform	*spoor*
far/near	*ver/dichtbij*	through traffic only	*doorgand verkeer*

Money

post office	*postkantoor*	cashier	*kassa*
stamp(s)	*postzegel(s)*	ticket office	*loket*
money exchange	*wisselkantoor*		

Useful words

good/bad	*goed/slecht*	cheap/expensive	*goedkoop/duur*
big/small	*groot/klein*	hot/cold	*heet/koud*
open/shut	*open/gesloten*	with/without	*met/zonder*
push/pull	*duwen/trekken*	here/there	*hier/daar*
new/old	*nieuw/oud*	men's/women's toilets	*heren/dames*

Days and times

Sunday	*Zondag*	Saturday	*Zaterdag*	minute	*minuut*
Monday	*Maandag*	yesterday	*gisteren*	hour	*uur*
Tuesday	*Dinsdag*	today	*vandaag*	day	*dag*
Wednesday	*Woensdag*	tomorrow	*morgen*	week	*week*
Thursday	*Donderdag*	tomorrow	*morgenocht-*	month	*maand*
Friday	*Vrijdag*	morning	*end*	year	*jaar*

Numbers

When saying a number, the Dutch generally transpose
the last two digits: eg, *vijf en twintig* is 25.

0	*nul*	9	*negen*	18	*achttien*	80	*tachtig*
1	*een*	10	*tien*	19	*negentien*	90	*negentig*
2	*twee*	11	*elf*	20	*twintig*	100	*honderd*
3	*drie*	12	*twaalf*	21	*een en twintig*	101	*honderd een*
4	*vier*	13	*dertien*	30	*dertig*	200	*twee honderd*
5	*vijf*	14	*veertien*	40	*veertig*	201	*twee honderd*
6	*zes*	15	*vijftien*	50	*vijftig*		*een*
7	*zeven*	16	*zestien*	60	*zestig*	500	*vijf honderd*
8	*acht*	17	*zeventien*	70	*zeventig*	1000	*duizend*

FRENCH WORDS AND PHRASES

Basics and greetings

now	*maintenant*	big	*grand*
later	*plus tard*	small	*petit*
man	*un homme*	a lot	*beaucoup*
woman	*une femme*	good	*bon*
here	*ici*	bad	*mauvais*
there	*là*	hot	*chaud*
open	*ouvert*	cold	*froid*
closed	*fermé*		

Finding the way

how do I get to . . .?	*Comment est-ce que je peux arriver à . . .?*	look out	*attention*
where is . . .?	*Où est . . .?*	roadworks	*travaux*
how far is it to . . .?	*Combien y a-t-il jusqu'à . . .?*	far	*loin*
		left	*à gauche*
		right	*à droite*
near/not far	*près/pas loin*	straight on	*tout droit*
through traffic only	*voie de traversée*	behind	*derrière*

Useful words

excuse me	*pardon*	good morning /afternoon	*bonjour*
do you speak English?	*vous parlez anglais?*		
yes	*oui*	good evening	*bonsoir*
no	*non*	good night	*bonne nuit*
I understand	*je comprends*	how are you?	*comment allez-vous?/ Ça va?*
I don't understand	*je ne comprends pas*		
OK/agreed	*d'accord*	sorry	*pardon, Madame, Monsieur/je m'excuse*
please	*s'il vous plaît*		
thank you	*merci*	leave me alone (aggressive)	*fichez-moi la paix!*
hello	*bonjour*		
goodbye	*au revoir*	please help me	*aidez-moi, s'il vous plaît*

Days and dates

Sunday	*dimanche*	Friday	*vendredi*	hour	*heure*
Monday	*lundi*	Saturday	*samedi*	day	*jour*
Tuesday	*mardi*	today	*aujourd'hui*	week	*semaine*
Wednesday	*mercredi*	yesterday	*hier*	month	*mois*
Thursday	*jeudi*	tomorrow	*demain*		

Numbers

1	*un*	12	*douze*	30	*trente*	95	*quatre-vingt-quinze*
2	*deux*	13	*treize*	40	*quarante*		
3	*trois*	14	*quatorze*	50	*cinquante*	100	*cent*
4	*quatre*	15	*quinze*	60	*soixante*	101	*cent-et-un*
5	*cinq*	16	*seize*	70	*soixante-dix*	200	*deux cents*
6	*six*	17	*dix-sept*		*(local usage*	300	*trois cents*
7	*sept*	18	*dix-huit*		*is septante)*	500	*cinq cents*
8	*huit*	19	*dix-neuf*	75	*soixante-quinze*	1000	*mille*
9	*neuf*	20	*vingt*	80	*quatre-vingts*	1,000,000	*un million*
10	*dix*	21	*vingt-et-un*	90	*quatre-vingt-dix (local usage is nonante)*		
11	*onze*	22	*vingt-deux*				

ei and ij as in fine, though this varies strongly from region to region; sometimes it can sound more like lane.

oe as in soon

eu is like the diphthong in the French leur

ui is the hardest Dutch diphthong of all, pronounced like how but much further forward in the mouth, with lips pursed (as if to say "oo").

FRENCH

French – which will get you by in Wallonia and Brussels – isn't a particularly easy language, despite the number of words shared with English, but learning the bare essentials is not difficult and makes all the difference. Even just saying "Bonjour, Madame/Monsieur" when you go into a shop and then pointing will usually get you a smile and helpful service. People working in hotels, restaurants, etc, almost always speak some English and tend to use it if you're struggling – be grateful, not amused.

Differentiating words is the initial problem in understanding spoken French – it's very hard to get people to slow down. If, as a last resort, you get them to write it down, you'll probably find you know half the words anyway. Hopefully, the "Words and Phrases" box printed here will be useful and see also the French "Food Glossary" on p.40.

Of the available **dictionaries**, our own *French Phrasebook* should sort you out better than most.

Consonants

Much as in English, except that: ch is always sh, c is s, h is silent, th is the same as t, ll is like the y in yes, w is v, and r is growled (or rolled).

Vowels

These are the hardest sounds to get right. Roughly:

a as in hat

e as in get

é between get and gate

è between get and gut

eu like the **u** in hurt

i as in machine

o as in hot

o, au as in over

ou as in food

u as in a pursed-lip version of **u**se

More awkward are the **combinations** in/im, en/em, an/am, on/om, un/um at the ends of words, or followed by consonants other than n or m. Again, roughly:

in/im like the **an** in **an**xious

an/am, en/em like the d**on** in D**on**caster when said with a nasal accent

on/om like the d**on** in D**on**caster said by someone with a heavy cold

un/um like the **u** in **u**nderstand.

GLOSSARIES

FLEMISH TERMS

ABDIJ Abbey or group of monastic buildings.

BEIAARD Carillon (ie a set of tuned church bells, either operated by an automatic mechanism or played by a keyboard).

BEGIJNHOF Convent occupied by beguines (begijns), ie members of a sisterhood living as nuns but without vows and with the right of return to the secular world.

BELFORT Belfry.

BEURS Stock exchange.

BOTERMARKT Butter market.

BRUG Bridge.

BURGHER Member of the upper or mercantile classes of a town, usually with certain civic powers.

FIETSPAD Bicycle path, and **fiets** — bicycle.

GASTHOF Inn

GASTHUIS Hospital.

GEMEENTE Municipal: eg Gemeentehuis – town hall.

GERECHTSHOF Law Courts.

GILDE Guild.

GRACHT Urban canal.

GROENTENMARKT Vegetable market.

GROTE MARKT Central town square and the heart of most north Belgian communities, normally still the site of weekly markets.

HAL Hall.

HOF Court(yard).

HUIS House.

INGANG Entrance.

JEUGDHERBERG Youth hostel.

KAAI Quai.

KAPEL Chapel.

KASTEEL Castle.

KERK Church; eg Grote Kerk – the principal church of the town; Onze Lieve Vrouwekerk – church dedicated to the Virgin Mary.

KONING King

KONINGIN Queen

KONINKLIJK Royal.

KORENMARKT Corn market.

KUNST Art.

KURSAAL Casino.

LAKENHALLE Cloth hall. The building in medieval weaving towns where cloth would be weighed, graded, stored and sold.

LUCHTHAVEN Airport.

MARKT Market-place.

MOLEN Windmill.

MUSEUM Museum.

OMMEGANG Procession.

PALEIS Palace.

POORT Gate.

POSTBUS Post office box.

PLAATS A square or open space.

PLEIN A square or open space.

RIJK State.

SCHEPENZAAL Aldermean's Hall.

SCHOUWBURG Theatre.

SCHONE KUNSTEN Fine arts.

SIERKUNST Decorative arts.

SPOOR Track (as in railway) – trains arrive and depart on track (as distinct from platform) numbers.

STADHUIS The most common word for a town hall.

STATION (Railway or bus) station.

STEDELIJK Civic, municipal.

STEEN Fortress.

STITCHING Institute or foundation.

TOREN Tower.

TUIN Garden.

UITGANG Exit.

VLEESHUIS Meat market.

VOLKSKUNDE Folklore.

FRENCH TERMS

ABBAYE Abbey or group of monastic buildings.

AÉROPORT Airport.

AUBERGE DE LA JEUNESSE Youth hostel.

BEAUX ARTS Fine arts.

BEFFROI Belfry.

BÉGUINAGE Convent occupied by beguines, ie members of a sisterhood living as nuns but without vows and with the right of return to the secular world.

BICYCLETTE Bicycle.

BOURSE Stock exchange.

CASINO Casino.

CHAPELLE Chapel.

CHÂTEAU Mansion, country house, or castle.

COUR Court(yard).

COUVENT Convent, monastery.

DÉGUSTATION Tasting (wine or food).

DONJON Castle keep.

ÉGLISE Church.

ENTRÉE Entrance.

ÉTAGE Floor (of a museum etc).

FERMETURE Closing period.

FOUILLES Archeological excavations.

GARE Railway station.

GÎTE D'ÉTAPE Dormitory-style lodgings situated in relatively remote parts of the country which can house anywhere between ten and one hundred people per establishment.

GRAND-PLACE Central town square and the heart of most French communities, normally still the site of weekly markets.

HALLE AUX DRAPS Cloth hall. The building in medieval weaving towns where cloth would be weighed, graded, stored and sold.

HALLE AUX VIANDES Meat market.

HALLES Covered, central food market.

HÔPITAL Hospital.

HÔTEL Hotel or mansion.

HÔTEL DE VILLE Town hall.

JARDIN Garden.

JOURS FERIÉS Public holidays.

MAISON House.

MARCHÉ Market.

MOULIN Windmill.

MUNICIPAL Civic, municipal.

MUSÉE Museum.

NOTRE DAME Our Lady.

PALAIS Palace.

PLACE Square, market-place.

PONT Bridge.

PORTE Gateway.

QUAI Quay, or station platform.

QUARTIER District of a town.

SORTIE Exit.

SYNDICAT D'INITIATIVE Tourist office.

TOUR Tower.

TRÉSOR Treasury.

ART AND ARCHITECTURAL TERMS

AMBULATORY Covered passage around the outer edge of the choir in the chancel (see entry) of a church.

APSE Semicircular protrusion at (usually) the east end of a church.

ART DECO Geometrical style of art and architecture popular in the 1930s.

ART NOUVEAU Style of art, architecture and design based on highly stylized vegetal forms. Popular in the early part of the twentieth century.

BAROQUE The art and architecture of the Counter-Reformation, dating from around 1600 onwards, and distinguished by extreme ornateness, exuberance and complex but harmonious spatial arrangement of interiors.

BASILICA Catholic church with honorific privileges.

CARILLON A set of tuned church bells, either operated by an automatic mechanism or played by a keyboard.

CAROLINGIAN Dynasty founded by Charlemagne; mid-eighth to early tenth century. Also refers to art, etc, of the time.

CARYATID A sculptured female figure used as a column.

CHANCEL The eastern part of a church, often separated from the nave by a screen (see "rood screen" below). Contains the choir and ambulatory.

CLASSICAL Architectural style incorporating Greek and Roman elements – pillars, domes, colonnades etc – at its height in the seventeenth century and revived, as **Neoclassical**, in the nineteenth century.

CLERESTORY Upper story of a church, incorporating the windows.

FLAMBOYANT Florid form of Gothic (see "Gothic" below).

FRESCO Wall painting – durable through application to wet plaster.

GABLE The triangular upper portion of a wall – decorative or supporting a roof.

GALLO-ROMAN Period of Roman occupation of Gaul, from the first to the fourth century AD.

GENRE painting. In the seventeenth century the term "genre painting" applied to everything from animal paintings and still lifes through to historical works and landscapes. In the eighteenth century, the term came only to be applied to scenes of everyday life.

GOBELINS A rich French tapestry, named after the most famous of all tapestry manufacturers, based in Paris, whose most renowned period was in the reign of Louis XIV. Also loosely applied to tapestries of similar style.

GOTHIC Architectural style of the thirteenth to sixteenth centuries, characterized by pointed arches, rib vaulting, flying buttresses and a general emphasis on verticality.

MEROVINGIAN Dynasty ruling France and parts of Germany from sixth to mid-eighth centuries. Refers also to art, etc, of the period.

MISERICORD Ledge on choir stall on which occupant can be supported while standing; often carved with secular subjects (bottoms were not thought worthy of religious ones).

NAVE Main body of a church.

NEOCLASSICAL Architectural style derived from Greek and Roman elements – pillars, domes, colonnades, etc – popular in the Low Countries during and after French rule in the early nineteenth century.

RENAISSANCE Movement in art and architecture developed in fifteenth-century Italy.

RETABLE Altarpiece.

ROCOCO Highly florid, light and graceful eighteenth-century style of architecture, painting and interior design, forming the last phase of Baroque.

ROOD SCREEN Decorative screen separating the nave from the chancel. A **rood loft** is the gallery (or space) on top of it.

ROMANESQUE Early medieval architecture distinguished by squat forms, rounded arches and naive sculpture.

STUCCO Marble-based plaster used to embellish ceilings, etc.

TRANSEPT Arms of a cross-shaped church, placed at ninety degrees to nave and chancel.

TRIPTYCH Carved or painted work on three panels. Often used as an altarpiece.

TYMPANUM Sculpted, usually recessed, panel above a door.

VAUBAN Seventeenth-century military architect – his fortresses still stand all over Europe and the Low Countries.

VAULT An arched ceiling or roof.

Stay in touch with us!

ROUGH*NEWS* is Rough Guides' free newsletter. In three issues a year we give you news, travel issues, music reviews, readers' letters and the latest dispatches from authors on the road.

I would like to receive ROUGH*NEWS*: please put me on your free mailing list.

NAME . . . .

ADDRESS . . . .

Please clip or photocopy and send to: Rough Guides, 62–70 Shorts Gardens, London WC2H 9AB, England or Rough Guides, 375 Hudson Street, New York, NY 10014, USA.

HOSTELLING
INTERNATIONAL

The last word in accommodation

Safe reliable accommodation
from $8 a night at over 4500 centres
in 60 countries worldwide

http://www.iyhf.org

the perfect getaway vehicle

low-price holiday car rental.

rent a car from holiday autos and you'll give yourself real freedom to explore your holiday destination. with great-value, fully-inclusive rates in over 4,000 locations worldwide, wherever you're escaping to, we're there to make sure you get excellent prices and superb service.

what's more, you can book now with complete confidence. our £5 undercut* ensures that you are guaranteed the best value for money in holiday destinations right around the globe.

drive away with a great deal, call holiday autos now on **0990 300 400** and quote ref RG.

holiday autos miles ahead

*in the unlikely event that you should see a cheaper like for like pre-paid rental rate offered by any other independent uk car rental company before or after booking but prior to departure, holiday autos will undercut that price by a full £5. we truly believe we cannot be beaten on price.